THE PENGUIN BOOK OF
WOMEN'S LIVES

Edited by PHYLLIS ROSE

VIKING

VIKING

Published by the Penguin Group
Penguin Books Ltd, 27 Wrights Lane, London w8 5TZ, England
Penguin Books USA Inc., 375 Hudson Street, New York, New York 100014, USA
Penguin Books Australia Ltd, Ringwood, Victoria, Australia
Penguin Books Canada Ltd, 10 Alcorn Avenue, Toronto, Ontario, Canada M4V 3B2
Penguin Books (NZ) Ltd, 182–190 Wairau Road, Auckland 10, New Zealand

Penguin Books Ltd, Registered Offices: Harmondsworth, Middlesex, England

First published in the USA as *The Norton Book of Women's Lives*
by W. W. Norton and Company Inc. 1993
First published in Great Britain by Viking 1994
1 3 5 7 9 10 8 6 4 2

Printed in England by Clays Ltd, St Ives plc

A CIP catalogue record for this book is available from the British Library

ISBN 0–670–85430–1

To my mother
Minnie P. Davidoff
best critic

CONTENTS

Contents

INTRODUCTION

This anthology of excerpts from twentieth-century memoirs, journals, and autobiographies by women draws on a body of work that's exceptionally rich, perhaps the richest vein of women's literature. It aims dually to suggest that richness and the richness of female experience on which it is based. On my part, the book is the product of a lifelong and personal interest in women's autobiographical writing, an interest which had little material to feed on in my childhood but now is treated to a rich harvest.

No sooner did I realize I was likely to grow up to be a woman than I wanted to know what the possibilities were for women's lives. I turned to biographies and autobiographies of contemporary women, but in the years just after World War II the only women represented in our little local library in a white middle-class suburb of New York were Helen Keller, Eleanor Roosevelt, and the Duchess of Windsor. None of these women's paths seemed relevant to me when I was a girl. For good or ill, I had no handicaps to overcome, like Helen Keller. I say "for good or ill," because I so much admired Helen Keller's book that I sometimes wished I did have handicaps so I could overcome them as stalwartly and stylishly as Helen Keller did, in the process acquiring what I fervently wanted and feared I would never have—a life story. As for the other two, I wasn't greatly interested in women who, no matter how admirable, were known in the final analysis because of whom they had married, and the Duchess of Windsor, as my mother informed me, wasn't even all that admirable. "What did she do to deserve a biography," Mother somewhat rhetorically asked, "except to marry someone she shouldn't?"

I myself was ambitious. I wanted to be a cowgirl. I was seeking something no term then existed for—a role model. I sensed it would be hard to find biographies or autobiographies of cowgirls, but the story of almost any woman who had achieved something (besides marriage) would have served, although "woman" in the 1940s and 1950s meant "white woman" to such an extent that I doubt I could have projected myself into the heroism of a Harriet Tubman or Sojourner Truth. I was down on marriage, as I recall, because my mother was married. I wanted to do something different. My personal imagery for "something different" came from the westerns I loved so much: "Bobby Benson and the B-Bar-B Riders" on radio and movies starring the likes of John Wayne, Audie Murphy, and James Stewart—with a slight transposition of gender, cowgirls, and my image of independence and accomplishment for longer than I'd like to say.

Whatever my reservations, I read Eleanor Roosevelt's autobiography, *This Is My Story*, with almost sinful excitement because for me then (as now) an autobiography held out the promise of dark truths that only friends confess to one another but are the knowledge you need to live. Some of this I found in Eleanor Roosevelt's book. She, too, was shy! She, too, had weak ankles! She, too, was a physical coward! She, too, was nuts about her father! This was the knowledge I needed to live! But soon she was sent to England to school, an enlargement I needed never fear, however appropriate for an American girl of a patrician family being raised to do her duty.

I didn't want to do my duty. Nor did I want models, like Mrs. Roosevelt, of noble self-sacrifice and altruism. I wanted wild women, women who broke loose, women who lived life to the full, whatever that meant. What *did* it mean to live life to the full? How fully could a woman live? These were the questions I wanted biography and autobiography to answer.

A girl encaged in a hidden set of rooms, who has not felt sun or open air for years, may seem like a strange exemplar of the full life, but for many of us growing up in postwar America, Anne Frank was a heroine— and not just for her courage and optimism. She saw so much in those rooms behind the bookcase. She expressed so much of her own feelings, which turned out to be the feelings of many adolescents. And she accomplished so much by the very writing of her diary.

The teenaged Jewish girl, whose family's self-imposed captivity was a futile attempt to save themselves from the Nazis, began the diary out of loneliness and a frustrated desire to talk over her daily life with friends. She was thirteen when they went into hiding, fifteen when she died. She called the diary Kitty and wrote her entries in the form of letters to this friend.

Part of the tremendous impact of this book comes from dramatic irony: We know that Anne will not survive the war, but she does not. "I think Cissy van Marxveldt is a first-rate writer. I shall definitely let my children read her books." The heartrending power of that line is, in a sense, accidental, inadvertent. But little of the rest of the book is inadvertent, and the level of talent is so remarkable that you can almost understand some people's reluctance to believe it was written by a fifteen-year-old. There are the brilliant vignettes of her fellow inmates, like Mrs. Van Daan, pushy and vulgar, thinking herself "modest and unassuming," and the fussy dentist, Dussel, with whom Anne is forced to share a room. There are adolescent agonies dramatically presented, her preference for her father over her mother and the guilty pain that causes her, her jealousy of her sister, her sense that everyone wants her to be different from what she is.

Long after she started keeping the diary, a radio program made her realize its potential importance as a historical document. The Dutch minister of education, broadcasting from London in 1944, urged that people keep diaries and letters "if our descendants are to understand fully what we as a nation have had to endure and overcome during these years." History, he said, cannot be written on the basis of documents and decisions alone. Anne looked forward to publishing her diary and thereby contributing to people's knowledge of what Jews had endured. She also had plans to use it in establishing herself as a writer.

Rescued after the war, Anne Frank's diary was published in Dutch in 1947 and in English in 1952. The book had a tremendous readership in the 1950s, especially after the stage version opened on Broadway in 1955. Anne Frank stood for all the Jews who were murdered in the Holocaust, but she also stood for adolescent girls, trying to assert their individuality in the complicated context of family life. If Holden Caulfield was the quintessential male literary adolescent of the fifties, Anne Frank was, for all the extraordinary nature of her circumstances, the representative female adolescent. And although Holden Caulfield may have resonated with young girls as much as with boys, Anne Frank had a special meaning to girls. For she was real, not a fictional creation. And she had written herself into being. Many girls picked up their pens. With the publication of her diary I would say that the golden age of women's autobiographical writing began.

From the point of view of an American growing up in the 1950s, the next landmark in the literature of women's lives was Simone de Beauvoir's *Memoirs of a Dutiful Daughter,* which came out in English in 1959, the year after its publication in French. Its very title was a revelation. One knew that Simone de Beauvoir was a brilliant and iconoclastic thinker. *The Second Sex* had burst upon the world ten years before, articulating and documenting what many women had vaguely sensed: that women throughout history had systematically gotten a raw deal.

Merely to learn that this rebellious woman had once been a "dutiful daughter," like many of the rest of us, was an inspiration. The title implied—and the book bore out—that it was possible to grow up in a bourgeois family (in Beauvoir's case, a very conservative Catholic family) and to escape from it. The theme of the book was female freedom, a theme picked up in the opening of Beauvoir's next volume of autobiography, *The Prime of Life,* where she describes (the excerpt in this volume) her exhilarated postgraduate life in Paris and her unconventional relationship with Jean-Paul Sartre. Her autobiography was both a sequel to and an extension of *The Second Sex* and a luminous example that the historic oppression of women need not be one's personal fate.

That Beauvoir traced in such detail a girl's coming of age was also new and exciting. In those years, if you wanted to read a narrative of a feisty, unconventional girl emerging into young womanhood, you had to turn to fiction, and hardly contemporary fiction at that: George Eliot's Gwendolen Harleth in *Daniel Deronda* or perhaps Henry James's Isabel Archer in *The Portrait of a Lady.* And look how they ended up! *Memoirs of a Dutiful Daughter* had the denseness of fiction, providing a month-by-month account of Beauvoir's coming into adulthood, which she portrayed not as a dead end but as an enlargement. Continued in *The Prime of Life, Force of Circumstance,* and *All Said and Done,* her autobiography was distinguished by its sheer scale, in addition to the power of the mind that she brought to bear on her own experience.

When I was a teenager in my New York suburb in the late 1950s, reading *The New Yorker* was considered a mark of advanced intellect and savoir faire, and as it happened, the magazine in those years encouraged women's memoirs. From 1946 to 1957 it ran many of the pieces that later were collected to form Mary McCarthy's *Memories of a Catholic Girlhood,* another of my personal landmarks in the literature of women's lives. The impression of Mary McCarthy's work, both as it appeared serially and with the publication of the completed book, was stunning. Here was a woman, as someone said at the time, who wrote better than anyone else, writing better than herself—about the material of her own life. It was not lost upon those of us growing up in America that albeit she was a woman, McCarthy had both formidable intelligence and prodigious ego. She wrote about herself in a way that suggested she expected to be feared and respected. In my own radically flattened field of possible female exemplars, she seemed like the answer to Eleanor Roosevelt. Hers was not the path of cuddliness and lovability—or of altruism and self-sacrifice. In no way did she hold herself up as a moral paragon. My favorite chapter, the one included in this collection, tells how, at a Catholic girls' school, she pretended to lose her faith as a way of getting attention and making herself popular with the other girls, then to her own dismay lost her faith.

It is a shock now to realize how much autobiographical work by women *The New Yorker* published in the fifties. Indian writer Santha Rama Rau's memoirs ran in almost yearly installments throughout the decade. Emily Hahn, Sylvia Townsend Warner, and Rumer Godden were other writers whose memoiristic work appeared regularly. It seems ungrateful to suggest that the context to some extent "emasculated" its women writers. Yet in that era when the magazine had no table of contents and little broke the suave uniformity of its graphic presentation, these women (and their male colleagues) became *New Yorker* writers, an ungendered group of scribblers clothed in elegant unisex wit and sophistication. To remove the women's works from their original context is like stripping the varnish off a piece of furniture to reveal the power of the wood. What seemed like charming stories, wispy pieces of nostalgia in the fifties now read differently. The bite is there, for example, in Santha Rama Rau's work—in the excerpt in this collection, about the resentment of a young Indian girl at an English school who eats the wrong food at lunch and has the wrong kind of name. Pioneer spirit, as well as a certain exoticism, permeates the life and work of Emily Hahn, who lived with Pygmies in Africa and got addicted to opium in China, as described in the selection in this book.

Memoirs didn't change, but the times did. In the late sixties the civil rights movement and the war in Vietnam politicized literature, not only making literary work about current events seem important but also attuning us to the ideological content in works we had thought of as neutral. Women's memoirs took on a new edge as people began to realize that the publication of life stories by Americans outside the mainstream constituted political statement, even when there was nothing overtly political about the books. Merely to publish the life story of someone not famous challenged the accepted order, saying, with radical democracy, "This person counts, too." Diane Johnson's biography of the wife of Victorian novelist George Meredith, *Lesser Lives* (1972), was a manifesto for this position, critiquing biography's usual focus on the Famous Person at the expense of all the others around him, seen as lesser characters in his life, although their consciousness was as intense as his and they did not see themselves as lesser. Memoirs and autobiographies, which previously had required celebrity to justify them, now could be justified by their reportorial value or by their art. A favorite of mine from this period is Frank Conroy's *Stop-Time,* which follows its author through a difficult childhood in the Northeast and Florida up to his freshman year at Swarthmore, a nothing-special child moving to a nothing-special fate. According to the old rule of thumb "If you aren't known, use it for a novel," this was not the stuff of autobiography. In the new order, however, the spotlight of truth could rest on the lives of the obscure.

Some of the greatest works in the new literature of obscurity were written by African-Americans, and when they started appearing in the later 1960s, it seemed to many of us white children of privilege like an opening up of our experience of our own generation. Anne Moody's *Coming of Age in Mississippi* (1968), which describes how the author put herself through a small black college in the South and then participated in sit-ins and other civil rights protests, was a life story one would not have heard in other times. Moody was not even thirty when her book appeared; she had no claim to fame. Yet her dense account of her own life is riveting.

Rooted in the slave narratives of the nineteenth century, reinforced by a religious sense of the value of confession and by a historically determined need to find refuge in the privacy and dignity of the self, black autobiography was the glory of the literary movement that accompanied the political activism of the late sixties and early seventies. In addition to *Coming of Age in Mississippi,* there was Claude Brown's *Manchild in the Promised Land,* Eldridge Cleaver's *Soul on Ice,* and *The Autobiography of Malcolm X,* written by Alex Haley. Perhaps the greatest in this group is Maya Angelou's autobiography *I Know Why the Caged Bird Sings,* published in 1970 and instantly recognized as a classic.

Born in 1928, Angelou went to her grandmother in Stamps, Arkansas, at the age of three and was raised by her in the Depression-era segregated Deep South. She rejoined her mother in St. Louis at the age of eight and not long thereafter was raped by her mother's boyfriend. The autobiography follows its subject to the age of sixteen, when, after a single sexual encounter, she got pregnant and had a child.

The life Angelou portrays is hard and sometimes violent, but her character is dreamy, romantic, and literary. As a girl she reads and re-reads *Jane Eyre.* What makes Angelou's book great is her visual sense and the feel for detail deployed throughout the narrative. When writing is this good, we generally say it is novelistic. But it seems wrong to praise Angelou that way when the challenge of nonfiction is to marry art and truth. There are moments when Angelou cannot contain her rage and produces passages of fine political rhetoric, but even more effective are the pages in which the rage is subsumed into narrative, producing scenes such as the one excerpted here in which her grandmother, singing a hymn, faces down the "powhitetrash" girls out to humiliate her.

I Know Why the Caged Bird Sings may be the first masterpiece of American women's autobiography after the war. The date of its publication is certainly a kind of watershed, for after 1970 first-rate autobiographies and memoirs started coming at an ever-increasing pace—to name one, *The Woman Warrior* by Maxine Hong Kingston, published in 1976. I don't think it's accidental that the literature of obscurity has produced so many masterpieces: There is hardly a more powerful motive for writing your life story than to feel that in doing so you are telling the story of a group, a family, a class. Tied in complicated ways to political movements—the women's movement, the civil rights movement, the growing desire that unheard Americans be given a voice—autobiography flourished, not just a vehicle of information but an art form.

There was a sense, in the late sixties and early seventies, that we were finding out things about women's actual experience we hadn't known before. In the realm of books there was an excitement that came with the opening up of new territory. The publication of the first installment of Anaïs Nin's diary in 1966 was a milestone.

Nin, the daughter of a Spanish pianist and composer, had been keeping a diary from the age of eleven, when her father abandoned the family and her mother brought them to the States. As a young woman Nin earned a living as an artist's model and a Spanish dancer. After returning to Paris, she married a banker, Hugo Guiler, and, from 1929, lived with him in Louveciennes, a suburb of Paris. There she wrote experimental fiction and cultivated artistic people. She was analyzed by René Allendy, founder of the French Psychoanalytic Society, and later worked with Otto Rank, the renegade from Freud who specialized in artists. He trained her as an analyst, and for a while, in New York, she practiced, but felt she had to choose between analysis and art and chose art, returning again to Paris.

Nin's diary, which she wrote daily throughout her life, goes beyond monumental, running to some thirty-five thousand pages. She wrote so much that sometimes you wonder how she had time to live. The manuscript was the object of a certain fetishism on her part. She took it with her everywhere, writing on trains, in cafés, in bed. Later she kept the completed volumes in a bank vault. Not only were her friends aware of it, but she allowed them to read parts, and long before the diary was ever published, it had quite a reputation. Henry Miller went on record in the *Criterion* that Nin's diary would "take its place beside the revelations of St. Augustine, Petronius, Abélard, Rousseau, Proust." Everyone realized that her diary, not her elliptical, precious novels, was the major work of her life.

The subjective realm has rarely been documented as fully as by Anaïs Nin. What she feels, what she thinks, what she dreams, what she fantasizes all are articulated. Her first book was a critical study of D. H. Lawrence, and her interest in that prophet of the unconscious shows in the diary, as does her interest in Freudian and Jungian psychology. Relentlessly inner, psychological, poetic, fluid, abjuring boundaries, her diary seemed to many readers to embody a quintessentially feminine sensibility, although to others it seemed repellingly narcissistic and self-congratulatory. However one responded, Nin established a kind of norm for femininity in the later sixties that had to be reckoned with, even by people like me, who did not aspire to her fluidity of consciousness.

Trying perhaps to match Henry Miller, an early lover and a powerful influence, Nin focused on sexual experience, determined not only to have it but to write about it frankly. This led to some quandaries in regard to publication. What she did was to edit the voluminous manuscript ruthlessly, carving from it a story that hung together and had impact, even though it omitted a lot. The first published volume of her diary, drawing on the years between 1931 and 1934, represents about half of the material she wrote. What it omitted was her sexual behavior. Her husband was cut, at his request, and so were her lovers—as lovers, although their presence is felt as friends and mentors. The result is to make her seem to exist in a Jungian void, awash in the tides of the elemental and primal, bouncing between soul mate and soul mate with no physical contact. And since so many of the important people in her life are erased, the effect of narcissism is exaggerated. For example, in a passage describing the birth of a stillborn child in the expurgated Volume 2, the impression that she is the only one involved is heightened by her inability to name the father. In fact, the unexpurgated version of this harrowing episode reveals that what she first presented as a stillbirth was really an abortion.

Her diary made Anaïs Nin a cult figure in America. She succeeded beyond her dreams in speaking not just for herself but for many women. Volumes of her diary continued to appear at regular intervals through the sixties and seventies, and when she lay dying in Los Angeles in 1977, a crowd of adoring fans stood beneath her hospital window, praying for her health.

The complete manuscript of the diary found its way to the UCLA Library, and after the deaths of all the principal players in the erotic games of the 1930s—Nin, her husband, Henry Miller, and his wife, June—the rest of the diary could be published. Now, with all the sexy parts jammed together in one volume, she seems to spend an inordinate amount of time in bed, but physicality tempers to a great extent the narcissistic vapors of the earlier volumes, and the emphasis on inwardness remains. Our selection is from the unexpurgated version of her diary.

Not all the excitement about the literature of women's lives in the early 1970s came through the publication of diaries and autobiographies.

Biographies figured, too. Quentin Bell's biography of Virginia Woolf, perhaps the fullest and most candid biography of a woman writer up to its time, revealed astonishing details about Woolf's asexual marriage, affairs with other women, and insanity. It enabled us to feel a rare intimacy with her, the information about her life answering to a very personal and in some cases almost visceral need of our own to hear the real truth about other women's lives.

Kennedy Fraser has written eloquently about a painful time in her life when reading about the lives of other women writers was the only thing that helped. I would bet that the Woolf biography was one of the books she read. In the course of a review of a later biographical study of Virginia Woolf she wrote:

> I was unhappy, and ashamed of it. I was baffled by my life. For several years in my early thirties, I would sit in my armchair reading books about these other lives. Sometimes when I came to the end, I would sit down and read the book through from the beginning again. I remember an incredible intensity about all this, and also a kind of furtiveness—as if I were afraid that someone might look through the window and find me out. Even now, I feel I should pretend that I was reading only these women's fiction or their poetry—their lives as they chose to present them, alchemized as art. But that would be a lie. It was the private messages I really liked—the journals and letters, and autobiographies and biographies whenever they seemed to be telling the truth. I felt very lonely then, self-absorbed, shut off. I needed all this murmured chorus, this continuum of true-life stories, to pull me through. They were like mothers and sisters to me, these literary women, many of them already dead; more than my own family, they seemed to stretch out a hand.

Fraser drew encouragement from these writers' successes, but was especially grateful to hear about their failures, "the secret, shameful things about these women—the pain: the abortions and misalliances, the pills they took, the amount they drank. And what had made them live as lesbians, or fall in love with homosexual men, or men with wives?"*

What Kennedy Fraser thought she did alone—the insatiable turning to books for information about women's lives—I think many other women were doing simultaneously, if not perhaps in so desperate a spirit. Many of us felt exhilarated that at last there were books to turn to. Bell's biography of Virginia Woolf, which fed the growing fascination with Woolf and supported her position as patron saint of the women's movement, was the first in what seemed like a flood of publication about Bloomsbury which focused on private life. We all profited from Blooms-

*"Ornament and Silence," *The New Yorker* (November 6, 1989).

bury's belief that revelation was revolutionary and specifically that candor about sex and other taboo subjects could set them free from the long-lasting Victorian proprieties that had stifled their childhoods. Many of the members of this loose circle of friends were skilled diary keepers and memoirists, and some of them met in a group called the Memoir Club to read each other the stories of their lives.

One of the most striking of the Bloomsbury publications was Nigel Nicolson's account of the marriage of his parents, the diplomat and memoirist Harold Nicolson and the novelist V. Sackville-West. *Portrait of a Marriage,* which appeared in 1973, revealed that the Nicolsons' marriage, after producing two sons, became sexually inactive, each of them turning to homosexual affairs. Vita's lovers included Virginia Woolf and, as recounted in Nigel Nicolson's book, Violet Keppel Trefusis. *Portrait of a Marriage* included the previously unpublished journal which Vita kept at the time of the affair and which we have excerpted. She had always intended to make it public, in the hope that it would help people understand bisexuality. She felt that she herself had suffered from a lack of information about these matters, and she wanted to offer her own experience so that people like her in the future might suffer less, feeling less abnormal and alone.

Virginia Woolf's own diary had been available in highly edited form since 1953. Leonard Woolf's compilation, *A Writer's Diary,* had omitted all personal detail, focusing, as the title implies, on her professional life. Beginning in 1977, Woolf's complete diary started appearing, along with her letters and her autobiographical sketches. It was another revelation. Here, finally, was the full model of daily life so many of us had been wanting. Responsive, imaginative, observant, Woolf wrote about her creative process, described the difficulties of running a house, catted about her friends, and recorded their conversation in the longest-running chronicle of daily life we had ever known. Anaïs Nin's diary seemed like a hothouse tomato by contrast. Moreover, Woolf's daily account was curiously selfless. Reading it was akin to one's daily telephone chat with friends, staying abreast of their doings. For some of us, Woolf's diary was an even more treasured literary property than her novels.

Alongside the literature of revelation, another tradition had been developing which we might call the literature of meditation. Anne Morrow Lindbergh's *Gift from the Sea,* published in 1955, became another of the books that many women growing up in America in the 1950s and 1960s were likely to be told to read at some point. Lindbergh presents herself as a seeker after equanimity, a woman trying to find her own center and align her life around it. Besieged by the complex demands of a modern woman's life, she turns to the beach as a place for emptying

her mind and letting it fill up again. The essays are based on her responses to shells—the gift from the sea—which teach her various lessons
about living. In prose that's crystalline, stripped down, unpretentious,
and calming as waves on the shore, she uses her writing to explore her
circumstances and regain a grip on what's important. She sees herself as
speaking not for herself alone but for a large group of people, primarily
women, "trying, like me, to evolve another rhythm with more creative
pauses in it, more adjustment to their individual needs, and new and
more alive relationships to themselves as well as others."

Anyone looking in *Gift from the Sea* for details of Lindbergh's vari-
ously glamorous, tragic, and productive life would be disappointed, although she later produced more conventionally autobiographical
volumes, based on diaries and letters, in *Bring Me a Unicorn* (1971) and
Hour of Gold, Hour of Lead (1973). The meditative tradition is not at
all journalistic or reportorial in style, locating itself rather far from the
details of the author's daily life. The quests it recounts are spiritual.
Nature tends to figure prominently, as the locus of the quest, the object,
or the guide. In this sense, Annie Dillard's *Pilgrim at Tinker Creek*
(1974) is the descendant of *Gift from the Sea*, although Dillard's later
volume of memoirs, *An American Childhood* (1987), which we have
excerpted for its dazzling descriptions of childhood perception, is not.

Whatever their authors' intentions, these books feed, as Anaïs Nin's
diaries also did, the American hunger for self-help, serving as how-to
books for the inner life. Hence their immense popularity. They teach
their readers how to be alive—sensitive, centered, creative. To those in
quest of specific information on how to live, diaries are particularly satisfying, and diaries of creative women found a large audience among
women taught by consciousness-raising sessions both to turn to other
women for help and to train their self-confidence and creative powers as
assiduously as their bodies. Alice Koller's *An Unknown Woman* ("A
Journey to Self-Discovery") chronicles a winter Koller spent alone on
Nantucket. Anne Truitt's *Daybook*, excerpted here, records the sculptor's daily struggles to be true to her art and to live life fully. Poet and
novelist May Sarton's diaries, beginning in 1973 with the publication of
Journal of a Solitude, have won her an enormous readership which has
followed her life narrative into old age and sickness, with her recent
volumes *At Seventy, After the Stroke*, and *Endgame*.

The personal began to enter areas in which it had previously been
unwelcome, like so-called objective reporting. In dazzling essays which
started appearing in the latter 1960s, Joan Didion insisted on juxtapos-
ing her personal fragility with the plastic resilience of American culture.
"Because I had been tired too long and quarrelsome too much and too

often frightened of migraine and failure and the days getting shorter, I was sent, a recalcitrant thirty-one-year-old child, to Hawaii, where winter does not come and no one fails and the median age is twenty-three." So begins a characteristic piece from *Slouching towards Bethlehem* (1968), whose new and distinctive mixture of the personal and the observed made a tremendous impact on readers at the time and since.

Joan Didion's work is unique in the way she teases us with glimpses of herself, then withdraws in Garbo-like privacy. It isn't her purpose to lay herself bare. But in putting herself into her work at all, she reflected a growing preoccupation with the autobiographical self. To be trusted, a writer needed at least to hint who she was. The impersonal, disembodied, ungendered, objective observer was no longer credible.

Great books have many lives. As the women's movement validated the literature of women's lives and that literature in turn fueled the women's movement, we took up earlier works in delighted acts of rediscovery. *Out of Africa,* first published in 1937, was reprinted in 1970 for a generation newly interested in women writers and, after the release of the film *Out of Africa* in 1985, began a whole other life. In its third incarnation, however, it read rather differently. With Ralph Lauren safari clothes in the stores and courses on postcolonial literature in the universities, colonial life in Africa had become both a fad and a phobia, and Karen Blixen's efforts to run a coffee farm in Africa and to appreciate the Africans around her no longer seemed entirely praiseworthy to some. Also, another woman's African memoir had been rediscovered. Beryl Markham's *West with the Night,* which was published in 1942 and lost because of the war, became a tremendous best seller when it was reissued by a small California press in 1983. Adventurous Beryl Markham, raised with Masai boys, a horse breeder and an aviator, in posthumous competition with her fellow colonial, seemed perhaps the more authentically heroic figure.

Just as Zora Neale Hurston's novel *Their Eyes Were Watching God* has been reinstated in the history of American literature, so have her autobiographical works, *Dust Tracks on the Road* and the personal chapters of *Mules and Men.* Hurston, the black anthropologist and writer who was famous at the time of the Second World War, then fell into eclipse, was rediscovered at least in part thanks to Alice Walker, who wrote an account, called "Looking for Zora" (1975), of finding Hurston's neglected grave in the Eatonville, Florida, cemetery and ordering her a tombstone. This act of acknowledgment, restitution, and cross-generational bonding has been typical of the recent stages of the women's movement.

The tradition of women's autobiography is now long enough to be nurturing itself. Women writing their memoirs today can find inspiration in women's memoirs from earlier in the century. Judith Ortiz Cofer, beginning her charming reminiscence of a Puerto Rican childhood, acknowledges Virginia Woolf's memoir "A Sketch of the Past," which guided her efforts. Her epigraph, too, is from Woolf: "A woman writing thinks back through her mother." It could stand as the motto for the whole postmodern moment in the literature of women's lives. Cofer's savoring of the community of women in which she grew up is also typical of this moment, informed by recent feminist thought which glorifies women's separateness.

Autobiographers in tune with the Zeitgeist are more likely these days to focus on their mothers than their fathers. This seems fair, since mothers were forgotten for so many years in the Freud-driven obsession with fathers. Vivian Gornick's marvelous *Fierce Attachments* (1987), excerpted here, has become a favorite gift for mothers and daughters to exchange, capturing as it does the frustration and exasperation that are so much a part of love between mothers and daughters. Le Anne Schreiber's *Midstream* (1990) combines an account of her mother's death with the story of her own renewal by a move to the country, the literature of matriarchy meeting the literature of meditation in a very beautiful way. Carolyn Kay Steedman's *Landscape for a Good Woman* (1986), from which a selection is included, exemplifies another trend in contemporary memoirs: the use of memoir to make a point, blurring the traditional line between academic scholarship and personal narrative. Steedman's aim is not only to memorialize her mother but to show that working-class life does not correspond in many ways to theoretical descriptions of it by Marxist scholars.

It would be a mistake, I think, to see the tradition of women's autobiographical writing as emerging *only* out of itself and existing only in relation to itself. Women who eagerly read Anne Moody's *Coming of Age in Mississippi* may also have read James Simon Kunen's account of the student protest at Columbia, *The Strawberry Statement.* Women who read Maya Angelou's *I Know Why the Caged Bird Sings* in 1970 may also have read *The Autobiography of Malcolm X.* While wanting to pay tribute to the encouragement women writers have offered one another in the past, we should not segregate them in the process. Colette's graceful and provocative moves from autobiography to fiction and back again should be compared not only with the autobiographical enthusiasm of Gertrude Stein and the dedicated diary keeping of Virginia Woolf but also with male modernists who treasured fact and worked it delightedly into their fictions, as James Joyce did in *Ulysses.* Annie Dillard might not be pleased to see her line of descent traced to Anne Morrow Lindbergh if she thought herself, with some justification, the heir of Thoreau. And it's hard to imagine Joan Didion "thinking back through her mother" in her tough-minded, risky pursuit of a style that reflected both her strong grasp of current events and her high-strung sensitivity. It makes more sense to see her in a group of innovators working between history and fiction who also include Norman Mailer and Tom Wolfe. Plus she constitutes a group of one. We should never forget that writers confront their own thoughts usually in their own homes, in rooms by themselves, struggling, whether alone or in collaboration, to bring their own vision of their lives into being for other people. Their experience of creation is not that of being part of the groups— whether "women writers" or "New Journalists"—which we critics are so eager, for some reason of ordering and coping, to put them in.

Women writers earlier in the century thought of themselves as alone and unique. Being a woman did not present itself to them as the communal, bonding experience which has been emphasized by feminist thinking since the 1970s but as a radically individual and rather lonely state, however much they hoped, as most writers do, that they spoke for more than themselves. The mothers of the literature of women's lives—Simone de Beauvoir, Mary McCarthy, Virginia Woolf, Anaïs Nin—felt their singularity as women and projected the pioneer's dual sense of exhilaration and terror at being the first to express what it was like to live and feel as they did, showing that womanhood did not limit them or weaken their wills and imaginations, whatever they may have accomplished in their lives.

I realize that it's possible not to applaud the literature of women's lives. It's possible to accuse the whole tradition of narcissism and self-absorption. It's possible to be undemocratically disgruntled with the assumption that everyone has a story and that everyone's story is as good as everyone else's. Some books are better than others, the grumpy elitist mutters. It's invidious, says the grumpy elitist, to put the formation of self at the center of the literary enterprise. It's possible to feel that Americans have been trained—who knows how?—to be too quick on the draw with the story of their lives. Athletes are able instantly to analyze their behavior, relatives of victims to offer coherent narratives to waiting media mikes, applicants to our prestigious colleges to produce in two pages the stories of their lives, with tensions, dramatic highlights, misfortunes, and lessons. Politicians offer, instead of positions, narratives of trauma and recovery. Maybe personal narrative has too much of a sway in our culture. Where has abstract, discursive writing gone?

I take the grumpy elitist seriously because she is *ma semblable, ma soeur.* But I say to her, "Read these selections. The literature of women's lives is not what you think." With some exceptions, there's no narcissism here. For narratives of self, there's remarkably little "self." If you expect these pieces to be concerned with the inner life exclusively, you'll be surprised at the extent to which women portray themselves confronting history, directed outward. We do not live a separate reality, so the literature of our lives is not separate, however refreshing it may be to see it, as in this book, separated out, freestanding, impressive in its mass and quality.

As with so many other maps of literary terrain, the one of autobiography has changed a lot since the fifties, when women constituted a group whose voices had not been heard. The tradition of autobiography used to be male. A respected mid-century theorist of autobiography named Georges Gusdorf put it this way: "The concern, which seems so natural to us, to turn back on one's own past, to recollect one's life in order to narrate it, is not at all universal. It asserts itself only in recent centuries and only on a small part of the map of the world. The man who takes delight in thus drawing his own image believes himself worthy of special interest." The word "man" catches us up and is not incidental. The great autobiographers were St. Augustine and Rousseau. Autobiography was tied to individualism, not to say a certain arrogance—believing oneself "worthy of special interest." In the classic view, autobiography did not exist in large parts of the world not because those people were too illiterate and desperate and otherwise occupied struggling for survival to sit down and write the story of their lives but because they lacked "the concern, which seems so natural to us, to turn back on one's own past and to recollect one's life in order to narrate it."

As we discover more autobiographies and memoirs, however, the empire of self seems to expand—into the Middle Ages, into the desert, into the slums. The more we look, the more we find: Buddhist nuns in ninth-century Japan writing diaries; Glückel of Hameln, a German woman in the Middle Ages, writing an account of her life; women in the Kalahari eager, with a little prodding, to "recollect their life in order to narrate it." If Émilie Carles hadn't written her autobiography, one could go on imagining peasants in the Haute Savoie who had no sense of individual lives but whose lives were tied to the cycle of crops—or some such nonsense. Published third world autobiographies are rare, but every now and then there comes along someone like Carolina Maria de Jesus of Brazil who, despite her poverty and the wretchedness of her life, uses her skill as a writer to record her daily life and inhibit generalization about who has a sense of self and who doesn't.

As this anthology abundantly proves, women *do* write memoirs and autobiography. Some manifestly think themselves worthy of special interest, but many do not, women, as a group, having a lot of humility. So it's probably time to revise the image of the autobiographer. In classic theory, which held that autobiography was connected with individualism, the buried model of the typical autobiographer was a boastful man, vaunting his achievements. But perhaps autobiography also results from the social side of human nature, and the buried model of the autobiographer can change from the boastful man to the confiding woman. Sharing her experience with friends, she may be gossipy, artful, tutorial, cool, forthcoming, evasive, maternal, childish, stoic, narcissistic, boastful, or modest, depending on her nature, but at some level she always feels the autobiographer's characteristic urge: the urge to preserve herself by giving herself away.

To assemble a collection that presumes to speak for all female experience is so humbling a task that I decided not to conceive of my project in that way at all. I have chosen to collect some pieces of twentieth-century autobiographical writing which I especially like or think important. Many I admired had to be left out for lack of room. I could sit down tomorrow and put together another volume of selections equally as good as this one, so rich is this field.

One of the joys of working on this book was that so many people had ideas about it. I found suggestions for reading wherever I went, explaining my project to whomever I spoke to. Parties were especially fertile ground. I pursued the possible anthologee as fervidly as once I pursued the possible mate. Almost always I caught one. Had I read the memoir by the Cambodian woman with the Polish last name? Did I know there was a Japanese TV personality who had written her autobiography? Had I read Peig Sayers? Madeleine L'Engle? Ingrid Bergman? Ethel Waters? Elspeth Huxley? Joan Colebrook? Lucille Clifton? Shusha Guppy? Gayle Pemberton? Emily Carr? Rosario Ferré? Elena Poniatowska? Calamity Jane? And people very often followed up. At a dinner party a woman asked if I'd read the autobiography by "that woman from a French peasant family, the kind of woman you'd never imagine would write an autobiography." Two days later a postcard came, "Émilie Carles, *A Life of Her Own*. You'll like it!"

Some of the works suggested to me were pre-twentieth century or biographies rather than autobiographies or presented themselves as fiction rather than memoir. Then I could rule them out them on blessedly objective grounds. Other calls were harder. I found two memoirs by Russian women who suffered in Stalin's purges: Nadezhda Mandelstam's *Hope against Hope* and Eugenia Ginzburg's *Journey into the Whirlwind*. Stylistic factors came into play. Ginzburg's account was, I felt, more direct and hard-hitting. But primarily the choice was practical: Mandelstam referred to too many people whose names would not be familiar outside Russia; her account needed more explanation than Ginzburg's. Similar practical considerations worked against May Sarton's various journals of her old age and in favor of Florida Scott-Maxwell in the same category. There were too many names to explain in Sarton—no problem when you read the book, but a big problem when you're reading an excerpt.

When I started putting this collection together, my goal was to include as broad a range of experience as possible and especially not to fill the book with selections from autobiographies and memoirs by middle-class literary women, as I could easily have done. To this end I intended to give more weight in my choices to experience and less to literary quality. I wanted to include selections by women from all over the world, all races, religions, and economic classes, and even—in my original and wildly ambitious dreams—all times. I had intended to begin, chronologically, with Lady Nijo's confessions, written in ninth-century Japan by an imperial concubine who became a Buddhist nun. But to keep the possible choices within reasonable bounds, I soon had to limit myself to the twentieth century.

My guiding principles changed in other ways, too. The more I thought about what I read, the more I realized that the opposition I had set up between experience and literature was false. No experience was so interesting in itself that it carried the narrative. Merely naming events, merely citing possibilities were not enough for literature, whether autobiography or fiction. Literature compels us to share experiences, not just admit them as abstract possibilities. A false or inept account gets in the way of the experience, so that all the reader notices is the falsity and ineptness. If a writer tries to describe, for a simple example, the pain of having a thumb bent backward, she is better off saying simply, "He bent my thumb backward," relying upon the reader to know how much that hurts. The moment she tries to embellish and fails—as in "He bent my thumb backward, and it hurt like hell"—our attention is drawn from the event to the expression, in this case, to its banality. In general, bad writing solicits emotional reactions from readers more insistently than does good writing. It is always asking for our emotional assent before proceeding, like an insecure friend who ends every sentence, "Am I right? Do you see what I mean?"

On the other hand, literary talent exists in more forms than I at first, parochially, thought. Even illiterate people may have literary talent. The oral storyteller, like any writer, selects and chooses among experiences those that become part of a coherent narrative line. She chooses, too, the details that make episodes vivid. She has to have sufficient distance from her own experience to sculpt events out of it. Even to collaborate on a good autobiography, she *must* have literary talent.

Marjorie Shostak, the anthropologist who gathered the life story of Nisa, a !Kung woman of the Kalahari, worked with many other women before finding one who, for various reasons, was able to tell a good story about her own life. Some were too overwhelmed by their miseries or absorbed in their pleasures. Some were hopelessly abstract. Some persisted in giving their conclusions about life rather than relating the specifics. Some couldn't concentrate. Others spoke in a language too complicated for Shostak to understand. Shostak gives as an example of a woman who didn't work out one who, asked to tell some of the things her father and mother did to her, replied, "They brought me up, gave me food, and I grew and grew and then I was an adult. That's what they did."

Ida Pruitt, an American woman who found herself in China before the Second World War with nothing much to do and a lot of curiosity, decided to inform herself about local customs. She found an old woman, the mother of one of her husband's employees, who was willing to come and talk to her several days a week. Ida Pruitt was lucky, because her informant was Ning Lao T'ai-t'ai, who, although illiterate, had as much literary instinct as Nisa. Especially in her later years, Ning spent a lot of time at fairs, listening to storytellers, so in her case the instinct had been honed by a tradition of oral raconteurs. She used her own life as an example to illustrate Chinese customs for Ida Pruitt, and Pruitt soon realized that the life of her friend was laid out before her, ready for transcription.

I have included several coauthored or collaborative works, in order to broaden the range of experience represented in this book and because collaborative authorship is typical of much contemporary autobiography, for men as well as women. The collaborations are of various kinds, depending on the subject's degree of ease with the written word. *Nisa* is an account gathered by a professional anthropologist; *Daughter of Han*, an account gathered by an amateur anthropologist. Katherine Clark, the woman who cowrote *Motherwit*, Onnie Lee Logan's account of her work as a lay midwife in Alabama, is an English professor at the University of Alabama. In this case the project originated with Logan, who, like many autobiographers, felt an almost painful need to get out her story before she died. "I got so much experience in here that I just want to explode," she told Clark. "I want to show that I knew what I knew—I want somebody to realize what I am."

Logan, bursting to tell her story, needed a coauthor, whose job is a complicated one of sorting and placing, making breaks and locating continuities as well as merely transcribing what the source has told her. Sometimes an autobiographer needs even more complex—and less acknowledged—help than that. Emma Mashinini, for example, the South

African labor union official and activist, was urged to write her story by Betty Wolpert, a filmmaker based in London who was making a documentary on South African women. Wolpert interviewed Mashinini and taped her story on several occasions. She sent the tapes to a collaborator in London who transcribed them and sent them back to Mashinini as a rough draft. As Mashinini worked over these transcripts, she gradually gained the confidence to write chapters herself. Wolpert then took the completed manuscript to a publisher in London, and it was at Wolpert's house that Mashinini finished the book and worked on it with the editor. What Wolpert did for Mashinini is both less and more than coauthorship. It is birthing.

I want to bring the role of collaboration into the open and celebrate it because sometimes it is regarded as a weakness. Rarely held against men (the assumption seeming to be that the man is too busy to write the book himself), coauthorship is sometimes held against a woman, as though proving that she was too inept to have written the book herself. Even in the cases of women with extraordinary literary talent, you will sometimes hear it said that someone else really wrote the book. For example, Beryl Markham's memoir was rumored to have been written by her husband, screenwriter Raoul Schumacher, and there have been persistent rumors that Anne Frank's diary was written either by her father or by novelist Meyer Levin.

Carles's and Hayslip's are other coauthored texts, cases respectively of women uncomfortable with writing and with an adoptive language. The most problematic coauthored work I've included is Billie Holiday's *Lady Sings the Blues,* which was written by journalist William Dufty. Holiday agreed to pose for author photos, held the copyright, and collected royalties, but she refused to cooperate with Dufty in any way. He wrote the book on the basis of interviews Holiday had given to other journalists, which had already appeared in print. This is an extreme example of a reluctant autobiographer and an active collaborator, which I've felt justified in including because the stories it tells—in many cases false—are the stories Billie Holiday told about her own life.

Everyone agrees that falsity is death to a memoir or autobiography. If a reader has the feeling that the author is a poseur, she will throw the book across the room or quietly switch to a novel. Autobiography depends on truth. But one of the paradoxes of the genre is that someone may seem false while telling the literal truth or seem to be wrenchingly confessional while telling lies. The truth of autobiography is a product of art.

The successful autobiographer, whether working alone or with someone else, must think in scenes. She must be willing to build up a narrative out of dramatic units. She must have patience. She can't rush to conclusions. She can't confuse rhetoric with experience. And she can't confuse facts with experience.

This last is a great temptation because it is easier to record the facts of one's life than it is to come to terms with its meaning. It's as though there are two parts to truth, an inner structure and an outer core of circumstance. Sometimes autobiographers overvalue the mere recapture of the outer husk and lack the energy or the desire or the ability to do the work of finding the essential truth.

Jean Rhys's *Smile, Please,* published in 1980, was a disappointing autobiography by a wonderful writer. Rhys had told the story of her early life in four autobiographical novels written between 1928 and 1939—unforgettable narratives about women alone who can't keep jobs, have no regular income, depend on men for handouts, drink too much, worry about aging, and regard the world with suspicion and distrust. In the past of these women is sometimes a freer, more flamboyant life, such as Rhys herself lived in the Caribbean when she was young.

Rhys was over eighty when she decided to write her autobiography, and the instinct for form which made her novels masterpieces was undermined by alcohol as well as age. She presents facts as talismanic, unconnected by a deeper narrative: The family cook on Dominica was good with fish but not with puddings; one day Rhys botched a piano accompaniment by forgetting to play da capo and earned the enmity of the violinist. *Smile, Please* is filled with memory scraps like that. We learn that Rhys was married three times, and we learn the names of her husbands. But which is truer: that she was married three times or the loneliness that pervades her novels? Which is—or ought to be—the autobiographical "fact"?

Mary McCarthy offers another example of what happens when you cease to work for the inner truth of the experience and get caught up instead remembering the facts or recording the memory pictures. "It may have been that day," she wrote in her last autobiography, *Intellectual Memories,* "that I first saw Martha Gellhorn—blond and pretty, talking of Spain. Or was it Martha Dodd, daughter of our former ambassador to Germany?" The deepest fear of any autobiographer must be to produce the response "Who cares?" Who cares if it was Martha Gellhorn or Martha Dodd? Who cares whether the 1911 *Britannica* went to Philip Rahv when they split up their household or whether it had been lost to an earlier mate? Who cares at what exact moment McCarthy lost her feeling for her second husband, so long as she lost it? To fondle the facts in this way makes the writer seem self-important and self-satisfied, and that impression prevails over everything else. In McCarthy's early autobiography, *Memories of a Catholic Girlhood,* where she admits to taking liberties with minor facts, there is a greater impression of truth.

I am sure that my selections, as much as I have tried to make them diverse and unpredictable, reveal my own biases, preferences, and interests. The women in this book tend not to be homebodies; with the exception of Sophia Tolstoy, their lives are not focused on a husband. Beryl Markham flies a plane around Africa, delivering packages and rescuing safari guides, then flies across the Atlantic alone. Anne Moody fights to get herself educated and then engages in the civil rights battle of the 1960s. Marjorie Kinnan Rawlings wants to raise oranges and live in dynamic peace with her neighbors in backwoods Florida. Anaïs Nin wants to get everything she can out of sexual experience. These women don't so much turn their backs on family life—many of them are married—as simply choose not to focus on it in telling the story of their lives. In their books the deep satisfactions of marriage and maternity are often signaled only by dedications to spouses and children.

If one story dominates, it's the liberation narrative and its dark underside, the captivity narrative. There are a number of accounts of actual imprisonment—Nien Cheng in China, during the Cultural Revolution; Eugenia Ginzburg in Siberia, during the Stalinist purges; Anne Frank in Amsterdam, in World War II; Le Ly Hayslip, in a jail on the border between North and South Vietnam. Anyone who thinks that women are exempt from history is wrong. I was positively scared to realize how little exempt they are. There are close calls: Kate Millett struggling to keep out of a mental institution, Janet Frame released from one only by the providential publication of her first book. And there are many narratives of metaphorical imprisonment: Carolina Maria de Jesus trapped by poverty in a Brazilian slum; Jessica Mitford trapped by privilege in an aristocratic English family; various women trapped by bourgeois convention and domesticity, including Simone de Beauvoir, the dutiful daughter who broke away, and Nina Berberova, a member of the czarist gentry who hated what she called the patriarchal nest.

The classic captivity narrative was the story of a white woman captured by Indians and eventually released. In seventeenth-century America these popular narratives were used as religious tracts, testifying to the power of God who had seen the women through their trials and helped them escape from the demonic. Some powerful and popular accounts still base themselves on the plight of the woman cut off from her kind and forced to live with the powers of darkness, often in a literal, racial sense as well as a metaphorical, moral sense. Patty Hearst's account of her kidnapping by the Symbionese Liberation Army would belong in this category, as would, more recently, Betty Mahmoody's account of being an American woman trapped by her Iranian husband in fundamentalist Iran on what was supposed to have been just a visit to his family. In other accounts the bourgeois family and a traditionally narrow conception of woman's life constitute the powers of darkness from which the autobiographer escapes.

As I see it, the literature of women's lives is a tradition of escapees, women who have lived to tell the tale. By and large, they seem determined to prove that womanhood is no handicap, that women can live as freely as men. They are remarkably inventive about their lives. They resist captivity. They get up and go. They seek better worlds. Jill Ker Conway left Australia, Santha Rama Rau left India, Eva Hoffman left the country her parents took her to, Canada. Joyce Johnson moved out of her parents' apartment and into her own. Émilie Carles broke with the tradition of old-fashioned peasant France to marry a workingman. Mary McCarthy broke with her Catholic faith. Colette left her betraying husband, Willy, and Jessica Mitford left the class she was born into as well as her country. The title of Mitford's memoirs, *Daughters and Rebels,* might stand for much of this collection.

I was so reluctant to categorize these women's experience in any way that I have not organized the following selections, as is common in anthologies, into thematic units of any sort. The units I wanted above all to avoid would have been on the order of "Work," "Family," "Love," "Power." I think we need to rid our minds of these false divisions in women's experience, and this seemed to me as good a place to start as any.

Other possible organizations seemed equally spurious, if not equally pernicious. Time of life? Most autobiographies focus on the early years, for whatever reason. Janet Frame gave a poetic one: "The future accumulates like a weight upon the past. The weight upon the earliest years is easier to remove to let that time spring up like grass that has been crushed. The years following childhood become welded to their future, massed like stone, and often the time beneath cannot spring back into growth like new grass." As writers try to define who they are, they look to who they have been, how they were formed. The past seems another country, romantic or hellish, equally attractive to explore. So there is much about childhood here and much about the middle years, as well, but old age is so radically unrepresented in autobiographical writing that any system of organization based on stages of life would be meaningless. For better or worse, we do not apportion our interest democratically throughout the life cycle.

Geographic? So many of these women live international lives. Does Jill Ker Conway belong in Australia or America? Is Jessica Mitford English or American? Is Sara Suleri from Pakistan, where she was born, or Connecticut, where she now lives? Does it make any sense to present

Suleri, Santha Rama Rau, and Nien Cheng as third world writers, when, by class and education, they are hardly representative of the third world? "There are," says Suleri, "no women in the Third World," by which she means precisely that we do not hear the voices of third world women. Should a book like this create the illusion that we do?

Chronological? There are selections from early in the century. Helen Keller and Ning Lao T'ai-t'ai, in fact, look back to the nineteenth century, as does Colette. Sophia Tolstoy and Nina Berberova write about prerevolutionary Russia, V. Sackville-West about pre-World War I Britain, and Gertrude Stein about pre-World War I France. Vera Brittain writes about the war in Europe, and Isak Dinesen about the outer ripples of that same war in Africa. Kate Simon, Margaret Mead, Virginia Woolf, Billie Holiday, Jessica Mitford, and Simone de Beauvoir write about the 1920s, Zora Neale Hurston, Beryl Markham, Anaïs Nin, M. F. K. Fisher, Marjorie Kinnan Rawlings, Eugenia Ginzburg, Natalia Ginzburg, Mary McCarthy, and Emily Hahn about the 1930s, and Marie Vassiltchikov, Anne Frank, and Marguerite Duras about the Second World War. So a wide range of the events of our century is "covered." But to organize the book chronologically would be to imply what is not the case: that the primary purpose of the volume is to document the twentieth century.

My Borgesian decision was to take refuge in a bibliographic reality— to organize the selections alphabetically. I enjoy the serendipitous juxtapositions which this unorganized organization produces. For example, Beauvoir and Berberova are natural partners, both consciously identifying with the intelligentsia, both savoring freedom and existential choice. Markham and Mashinini offer contrasting glimpses of Africa, the privileged colonial's versus the black factory worker's, yet they share an unromantic, practical temperament. The accidents of alphabet have brought together Nisa, the woman of the Kalahari, and Ning Lao T'ai-t'ai of China, the two storytellers, sitting together in these pages as they might have liked to do in life. The alphabet has also thrown together my two literary wives, Sophia Tolstoy, her husband about to die but still driving her crazy, and Caitlin Thomas, seeking distraction from her widow's grief in an exotic place and with a younger man. The book ends, by chance, with a run of four diarists, Tolstoy, Anne Truitt, Marie Vassiltchikov, and Virginia Woolf, enabling a reader to compare very different uses of the daily form, for complaint, for psychic centering, for historical record, for creative warm-up.

There are benefits, then, for people who read straight through, from start to finish, and for their sake I have also made adjustments for pace and variety. Like a manager with a batting order to produce, I've had to think about strength and position. I confess, for example, that I wanted so much to open with Maya Angelou that it was harder than it might have been for Shirley Abbott and Lou Andreas-Salomé to make the final cut had the organization been other than alphabetical.

However, I expect that many, if not most, people will read this book by the dipping method, moving from one selection to another according to what piques their interest. To facilitate and enrich this sort of reading, I make suggestions of where to go next at the end of many of the headnotes. The headnote explains who the author is in the broadest terms and seeks to provide any information you might need to make the selection understandable. I then mention other selections in this book that could be compared with the one at hand in what seem to me interesting ways. Such connections might be chronological (other selections dealing with World War II, for example), or they might be geographical (other Russian writers, other writers from the British Commonwealth, other Africans), formal (other diaries), ethnic (other Jewish writers, other African-Americans), or thematic (other accounts of marriage, of childhood, of paradise lost, of spiritual quests, etc.). Since the book is alphabetically organized, it should be easy to follow these cross references without resorting to the index, but the index will serve, in effect, as a guide to the cross-references. In the case of some selections, I make suggestions for further reading which is not included in this anthology. For example, in introducing Vera Brittain's *Testament of Youth*, I recommend also Enid Bagnold's account of nursing during World War I, *A Diary without Dates*. I cue these references to works not in the anthology by the use of the word "see," whereas, in suggesting other readings within the anthology, I say "compare."

Diaries, unless titled by the author herself, are given the generic title "Diary." Readers interested in the titles supplied by editors and publishers will find that information on the copyright pages. I have not wanted to perpetuate titles that I find condescending (*The Diary of a Young Girl* for Anne Frank and *Child of the Dark* for Carolina Maria de Jesus) or that I suspect would have made the author writhe (*A Moment's Liberty* for Virginia Woolf).

Except at the start and the end of selections, all my cuts are indicated by marks of elision, three spaced periods after the end of the sentence. If the omission is long, the periods are centered. In general, I've tried to make internal cuts as little as possible, and most such editing has been done to rid the pieces of unnecessary complexities. I use an author's chapter title only when my selection encompasses the whole or almost the whole chapter or when multiple sections are included. Within selections, any untitled new chapters begin with the first paragraph set flush left.

Finally, I should explain the distinction I make between memoir and autobiography. It's a technical point. The distinction is illustrated very nicely by the difference between Simone de Beauvoir's work and Mary McCarthy's. Despite the fact that she used the word "Memoirs" in the title of the first installment, Beauvoir's work (with the exception of *A Very Easy Death*) is autobiography in its aspirations to completeness and its dedication to full chronological development of the narrative. Mary McCarthy's discreet and polished chapters in *Memories of a Catholic Girlhood*, each focusing on one dramatic episode, relationship, or theme, display the cohesiveness and selectivity of the memoir. Memoir, in my sense of it, focuses, is unified by time or theme more than is autobiography. McCarthy's later works, *How I Grew* and *Intellectual Memories*, are, by my definition, autobiographies, not memoirs. *Fierce Attachments*, focusing on the relationship between Vivian Gornick and her mother, is a memoir. *The Loony-Bin Trip*, focusing on Kate Millett's bout with manic depression, is a memoir. Bernadette Devlin's *The Price of My Soul* is an autobiography, as are Margaret Mead's *Blackberry Winter* and Janet Frame's *An Angel at My Table*. The difference between the two is entirely formal in my mind and not a question of merit or quality. Not all students of autobiography and memoir, however, would agree, some using "autobiography" as a praise word and some using "memoir" as one. To me they are neutral, descriptive terms, although, because of my personal preference for the wrought, there are probably more memoirs represented here than autobiographies.

My eightysomething mother recently announced to my wild excitement that she had written her memoirs. She said that she would bring them with her one Sunday afternoon when she came to see me. I couldn't wait. There were so many things I wanted to know. But when she arrived at my apartment, I saw no sheaf of papers. She reached into her handbag and took out a single leaf from a contract bridge score pad, on the back of which she had written the following words:

milk 2
ice
trolley—El
radio
meter
beer
A & P
laundry
Staten Island
movies

She proceeded to weave for me an interesting account of how primitive, technologically, life in New York City had been when she was young. Milk was delivered in horse-drawn carts. Each family sent a child with a bucket into which the milkman ladled what it needed. (The horse-drawn cart and the bucket system constituted two separate things about milk delivery that my mother wanted to tell me, hence her notation "2" next to "milk.") Ice was purveyed in giant blocks, from which the iceman cut off a section which you put in the icebox, to keep food cold, and beer, like milk, came in large barrels, each family ladling out what it needed. My mother could remember her brothers putting together a crystal set, and the excitement of the whole family at first hearing voices over the radio waves. Gas was on a meter, which they had to keep supplied with nickels. Not everyone had a bathtub. For example, she had a cousin who used to go all the way from the Bronx to Staten Island to take a bath. Finally, she could remember the city crisscrossed with trolleys and shadowed by the elevated tracks, while, at the movie theater, a piano player accompanied silent films with improvised music.

Fascinated as I was by my mother's memoirs, I confess I was also disappointed. I wanted the psychological inside scoop on my family: Had my mother felt fulfilled by her years of child rearing in the suburbs? Did she regret giving up her job as a teacher in the New York City school system? Had her marriage with my father been as happy as both of them always claimed? If so, did people of that generation bring different expectations to marriage from those of people of mine? Had she noticed my hostility toward her when I was a teenager, and if so, did she forgive me for it? Did she notice that at some point it had disappeared? When had it disappeared? There were things about my mother I really wanted to know.

But "Milk 2, Ice, Trolley" was a bracing reminder that my mother's Self was not the Self I saw in her, and her life was not her-life-in-relation-to-me or even, it seemed, to my family. And if she saw her life as crucially informed by milk, ice, and beer deliveries, who was I to say it was not? Everyone is entitled to her own autobiography. Every autobiographer gets to choose, select, and otherwise create her own past, her own "Self." (We won't go into the poststructuralist theories that hold there is no self and no referential language to describe it in anyway.)

When you realize how hard it is to know the truth about yourself, you understand that even the most exhaustive and well-meaning autobiography, determined to tell the truth, represents, at best, a guess. There have been times in my life when I felt incredibly happy. Life was full. I seemed productive. Then I thought, "Am I really happy or am I merely masking a deep depression with frantic activity?" If I don't know such basic things about myself, who does?

It is fashionable now to quote Roland Barthes to the effect that biography (autobiography presumably is included) is a counterfeit integration of the subject. But it is equally true and less depressing to say that any integration of the subject—any narrative you choose to make of your own life—represents a creative act, a hypothesis in the face of chaos which is just as much true as it is not true. "Milk 2, Ice, Trolley" is such a hypothesis. Although all autobiography may be, in the final analysis, merely a list compared with the multilayered denseness of reality, even a list has its gallantry.

This book is dedicated to my mother, who gave me an uncharacteristically backhanded compliment but a characteristically accurate assessment when she said, after reading all the following selections from start to finish, "This is the best thing you've ever written, dear."

THE PENGUIN BOOK OF
WOMEN'S LIVES

MAYA ANGELOU
(1928–)

An actress and singer before she was a writer, Maya Angelou began writing books at the encouragement of friends, including James Baldwin, who had heard her tell stories of her childhood. Growing up in the 1930s, she spent much of her childhood with her grandmother in Stamps, Arkansas, a rural town where segregation was so complete that many black children, according to Angelou, "didn't really, absolutely know what whites looked like." Angelou's grandmother, Annie Henderson (called "Momma" by the author and her brother, Bailey), owned and ran a general store in Stamps and was a formidable member of the community. These selections show the author's grandmother in a moment of strength and the author and her brother in a moment of hilarity. *I Know Why the Caged Bird Sings* (1970) tells the story of the author's life to her mid-teens. Several volumes of autobiography by Maya Angelou have followed, one of which, *All God's Children Need Traveling Shoes* (1986), describes a four-year stay she made in Ghana.

For another account of growing up black in the American South, compare Anne Moody, *Coming of Age in Mississippi,* and, in South Africa, Emma Mashinini, *Strikes Have Followed Me All My Life.* For another caged bird's song, compare Anne Frank, *Diary.*

FROM *I Know Why the Caged Bird Sings*

"Thou shall not be dirty" and "Thou shall not be impudent" were the two commandments of Grandmother Henderson upon which hung our total salvation.

Each night in the bitterest winter we were forced to wash faces, arms, necks, legs and feet before going to bed. She used to add, with a smirk that unprofane people can't control when venturing into profanity, "and wash as far as possible, then wash possible."

We would go to the well and wash in the ice-cold, clear water, grease our legs with the equally cold stiff Vaseline, then tiptoe into the house. We wiped the dust from our toes and settled down for schoolwork, cornbread, clabbered milk, prayers and bed, always in that order.

Momma was famous for pulling the quilts off after we had fallen asleep to examine our feet. If they weren't clean enough for her, she took the switch (she kept one behind the bedroom door for emergencies) and woke up the offender with a few aptly placed burning reminders.

The area around the well at night was dark and slick, and boys told about how snakes love water, so that anyone who had to draw water at night and then stand there alone and wash knew that moccasins and rattlers, puff adders and boa constrictors were winding their way to the well and would arrive just as the person washing got soap in her eyes. But Momma convinced us that not only was cleanliness next to Godliness, dirtiness was the inventor of misery.

The impudent child was detested by God and a shame to its parents and could bring destruction to its house and line. All adults had to be addressed as Mister, Missus, Miss, Auntie, Cousin, Unk, Uncle, Bubbah, Sister, Brother and a thousand other appellations indicating familial relationship and the lowliness of the addressor.

Everyone I knew respected these customary laws, except for the powhitetrash children.

Some families of powhitetrash lived on Momma's farm land behind the school. Sometimes a gaggle of them came to the Store, filling the whole room, chasing out the air and even changing the well-known scents. The children crawled over the shelves and into the potato and onion bins, twanging all the time in their sharp voices like cigar-box guitars. They took liberties in my Store that I would never dare. Since Momma told us that the less you say to whitefolks (or even powhitetrash) the better, Bailey and I would stand, solemn, quiet, in the displaced air. But if one of the playful apparitions got close to us, I pinched it. Partly out of angry frustration and partly because I didn't believe in its flesh reality.

They called my uncle by his first name and ordered him around the Store. He, to my crying shame, obeyed them in his limping dip-straight-dip fashion.

My grandmother, too, followed their orders, except that she didn't seem to be servile because she anticipated their needs.

"Here's sugar, Miz Potter, and here's baking powder. You didn't buy soda last month, you'll probably be needing some."

Momma always directed her statements to the adults, but sometimes, Oh painful sometimes, the grimy, snotty-nosed girls would answer her.

"Naw, Annie . . ."—to Momma? Who owned the land they lived on? Who forgot more than they would ever learn? If there was any justice in the world, God should strike them dumb at once!—"Just give us some extry sody crackers, and some more mackerel."

At least they never looked in her face, or I never caught them doing so. Nobody with a smidgen of training, not even the worst roustabout, would look right in a grown person's face. It meant the person was trying to take the words out before they were formed. The dirty little children didn't do that, but they threw their orders around the Store like lashes from a cat-o'-nine-tails.

When I was around ten years old, those scruffy children caused me the most painful and confusing experience I had ever had with my grandmother.

One summer morning, after I had swept the dirt yard of leaves, spear-mint-gum wrappers and Vienna-sausage labels, I raked the yellow-red dirt, and made half-moons carefully, so that the design stood out clearly and mask-like. I put the rake behind the Store and came through the back of the house to find Grandmother on the front porch in her big, wide white apron. The apron was so stiff by virtue of the starch that it could have stood alone. Momma was admiring the yard, so I joined her. It truly looked like a flat redhead that had been raked with a big-toothed comb. Momma didn't say anything but I knew she liked it. She looked over toward the school principal's house and to the right at Mr. McEl-roy's. She was hoping one of those community pillars would see the design before the day's business wiped it out. Then she looked upward to the school. My head had swung with hers, so at just about the same time we saw a troop of the powhitetrash kids marching over the hill and down by the side of the school.

I looked to Momma for direction. She did an excellent job of sagging from her waist down, but from the waist up she seemed to be pulling for the top of the oak tree across the road. Then she began to moan a hymn. Maybe not to moan, but the tune was so slow and the meter so strange that she could have been moaning. She didn't look at me again. When the children reached halfway down the hill, halfway to the Store, she said without turning, "Sister, go on inside."

I wanted to beg her, "Momma, don't wait for them. Come on inside with me. If they come in the Store, you go to the bedroom and let me wait on them. They only frighten me if you're around. Alone I know how to handle them." But of course I couldn't say anything, so I went in and stood behind the screen door.

Before the girls got to the porch I heard their laughter crackling and popping like pine logs in a cooking stove. I suppose my lifelong paranoia was born in those cold, molasses-slow minutes. They came finally to stand on the ground in front of Momma. At first they pretended serious-ness. Then one of them wrapped her right arm in the crook of her left, pushed out her mouth and started to hum. I realized that she was aping my grandmother. Another said, "Naw, Helen, you ain't standing like her. This here's it." Then she lifted her chest, folded her arms and mocked that strange carriage that was Annie Henderson. Another laughed, "Naw, you can't do it. Your mouth ain't pooched out enough. It's like this."

I thought about the rifle behind the door, but I knew I'd never be able to hold it straight, and the .410, our sawed-off shotgun, which stayed loaded and was fired every New Year's night, was locked in the trunk and Uncle Willie had the key on his chain. Through the fly-specked screen-door, I could see that the arms of Momma's apron jiggled from the vibrations of her humming. But her knees seemed to have locked as if they would never bend again.

She sang on. No louder than before, but no softer either. No slower or faster.

The dirt of the girls' cotton dresses continued on their legs, feet, arms and faces to make them all of a piece. Their greasy uncolored hair hung down, uncombed, with a grim finality. I knelt to see them better, to remember them for all time. The tears that had slipped down my dress left unsurprising dark spots, and made the front yard blurry and even more unreal. The world had taken a deep breath and was having doubts about continuing to revolve.

The girls had tired of mocking Momma and turned to other means of agitation. One crossed her eyes, stuck her thumbs in both sides of her mouth and said, "Look here, Annie." Grandmother hummed on and the apron strings trembled. I wanted to throw a handful of black pepper in their faces, to throw lye on them, to scream that they were dirty, scummy peckerwoods, but I knew I was as clearly imprisoned behind the scene as the actors outside were confined to their roles.

One of the smaller girls did a kind of puppet dance while her fellow clowns laughed at her. But the tall one, who was almost a woman, said something very quietly, which I couldn't hear. They all moved backward from the porch, still watching Momma. For an awful second I thought they were going to throw a rock at Momma, who seemed (except for the apron strings) to have turned into stone herself. But the big girl turned her back, bent down and put her hands flat on the ground—she didn't pick up anything. She simply shifted her weight and did a hand stand.

Her dirty bare feet and long legs went straight for the sky. Her dress fell down around her shoulders, and she had on no drawers. The slick pubic hair made a brown triangle where her legs came together. She hung in the vacuum of that lifeless morning for only a few seconds, then wavered and tumbled. The other girls clapped her on the back and slapped their hands.

Momma changed her song to "Bread of Heaven, bread of Heaven, feed me till I want no more."

I found that I was praying too. How long could Momma hold out?

What new indignity would they think of to subject her to? Would I be able to stay out of it? What would Momma really like me to do?

Then they were moving out of the yard, on their way to town. They bobbed their heads and shook their slack behinds and turned, one at a time:

" 'Bye, Annie."

" 'Bye, Annie."

" 'Bye, Annie."

Momma never turned her head or unfolded her arms, but she stopped singing and said, " 'Bye, Miz Helen, 'bye, Miz Ruth, 'bye, Miz Eloise."

I burst. A firecracker July-the-Fourth burst. How could Momma call them Miz? The mean nasty things. Why couldn't she have come inside the sweet, cool store when we saw them breasting the hill? What did she prove? And then if they were dirty, mean and impudent, why did Momma have to call them Miz?

She stood another whole song through and then opened the screen door to look down on me crying in rage. She looked until I looked up. Her face was a brown moon that shone on me. She was beautiful. Something had happened out there, which I couldn't completely understand, but I could see that she was happy. Then she bent down and touched me as mothers of the church "lay hands on the sick and afflicted" and I quieted.

"Go wash your face, Sister." And she went behind the candy counter and hummed, "Glory, glory, hallelujah, when I lay my burden down."

I threw the well water on my face and used the weekday handkerchief to blow my nose. Whatever the contest had been out front, I knew Momma had won.

I took the rake back to the front yard. The smudged footprints were easy to erase. I worked for a long time on my new design and laid the rake behind the wash pot. When I came back in the Store, I took Momma's hand and we both walked outside to look at the pattern.

It was a large heart with lots of hearts growing smaller inside, and piercing from the outside rim to the smallest heart was an arrow. Momma said, "Sister, that's right pretty." Then she turned back to the Store and resumed, "Glory, glory, hallelujah, when I lay my burden down."

Reverend Howard Thomas was the presiding elder over a district in Arkansas that included Stamps. Every three months he visited our church, stayed at Momma's over the Saturday night and preached a loud passionate sermon on Sunday. He collected the money that had been taken in over the preceding months, heard reports from all the church groups and shook hands with the adults and kissed all small children. Then he went away. (I used to think that he went west to heaven, but Momma straightened me out. He just went to Texarkana.)

Bailey and I hated him unreservedly. He was ugly, fat, and he laughed like a hog with the colic. We were able to make each other burst with giggling when we did imitations of the thick-skinned preacher. Bailey was especially good at it. He could imitate Reverend Thomas right in front of Uncle Willie and never get caught because he did it soundlessly. He puffed out his cheeks until they looked like wet brown stones, and wobbled his head from side to side. Only he and I knew it, but that was old Reverend Thomas to a tree.

His obesity, while disgusting, was not enough to incur the intense hate that we felt for him. The fact that he never bothered to remember our names was insulting, but neither was that slight, alone, enough to make us despise him. But the crime that tipped the scale and made our hate not only just but imperative was his actions at the dinner table. He ate the biggest, brownest and best parts of the chicken at every Sunday meal.

The only good thing about his visits was the fact that he always arrived late on Saturday nights, after we had had dinner. I often wondered if he tried to catch us at the table. I believe so, for when he reached the front porch his little eyes would glitter toward the empty dining room and his face would fall with disappointment. Then immediately, a thin curtain would fall over his features and he'd laugh a few barks, "Uh, huh, uh, huh, Sister Henderson, just like a penny with a hole in it, I always turns up."

Right on cue every time, Momma would answer, "That's right, Elder Thomas, thank the blessed Jesus, come right in."

He'd step in the front door and put down his Gladstone (that's what he called it) and look around for Bailey and me. Then he opened his awful arms and groaned, "Suffer little children to come unto me, for such is the Kingdom of Heaven."

Bailey went to him each time with his hand stretched out, ready for a manly handshake, but Reverend Thomas would push away the hand and encircle my brother for a few seconds. "You still a boy, buddy. Remember that. They tell me the Good Book say, 'When I was a child I spake as a child, I thought as a child, but when I became a man, I put away childish things.' " Only then would he open his arms and release Bailey.

I never had the nerve to go up to him. I was quite afraid that if I tried to say, "Hello, Reverend Thomas," I would choke on the sin of mocking him. After all, the Bible did say, "God is not mocked," and the man was

God's representative. He used to say to me, "Come on, little sister. Come and get this blessing." But I was so afraid and I also hated him so much that my emotions mixed themselves up and it was enough to start me crying. Momma told him time after time, "Don't pay her no mind, Elder Thomas, you know how tender-hearted she is."

He ate the leftovers from our dinner and he and Uncle Willie discussed the developments of the church programs. They talked about how the present minister was attending to his flock, who got married, who died and how many children had been born since his last visit.

Bailey and I stood like shadows in the rear of the Store near the coal-oil tank, waiting for the juicy parts. But when they were ready to talk about the latest scandal, Momma sent us to her bedroom with warnings to have our Sunday School lesson perfectly memorized or we knew what we could expect.

We had a system that never failed. I would sit in the big rocking chair by the stove and rock occasionally and stamp my feet. I changed voices, now soft and girlish, then a little deeper like Bailey's. Meanwhile, he would creep back into the Store. Many times he came flying back to sit on the bed and to hold the open lesson book just before Momma suddenly filled the doorway.

"You children get your lesson good, now. You know all the other children looks up to you all." Then, as she turned back into the Store Bailey followed right on her footsteps to crouch in the shadows and listen for the forbidden gossip.

Once, he heard how Mr. Coley Washington had a girl from Lewisville staying in his house. I didn't think that was so bad, but Bailey explained that Mr. Washington was probably "doing it" to her. He said that although "it" was bad just about everybody in the world did it to somebody, but no one else was supposed to know that. And once, we found out about a man who had been killed by whitefolks and thrown into the pond. Bailey said the man's things had been cut off and put in his pocket and he had been shot in the head, all because the whitefolks said he did "it" to a white woman.

Because of the kinds of news we filched from those hushed conversations, I was convinced that whenever Reverend Thomas came and Momma sent us to the back room they were going to discuss whitefolks and "doing it." Two subjects about which I was very dim.

On Sunday mornings Momma served a breakfast that was geared to hold us quiet from 9:30 A.M. to 3 P.M. She fried thick pink slabs of home-cured ham and poured the grease over sliced red tomatoes. Eggs over easy, fried potatoes and onions, yellow hominy and crisp perch fried so hard we would pop them in our mouths and chew bones, fins and all. Her cathead biscuits were at least three inches in diameter and two inches thick. The trick to eating catheads was to get the butter on them before they got cold—then they were delicious. When, unluckily, they were allowed to get cold, they tended to a gooeyness, not unlike a wad of tired gum.

We were able to reaffirm our findings on the catheads each Sunday that Reverend Thomas spent with us. Naturally enough, he was asked to bless the table. We would all stand; my uncle, leaning his walking stick against the wall, would lean his weight on the table. Then Reverend Thomas would begin. "Blessed Father, we thank you this morning . . ." and on and on and on. I'd stop listening after a while until Bailey kicked me and then I cracked my lids to see what had promised to be a meal that would make any Sunday proud. But as the Reverend droned on and on and on to a God who I thought must be bored to hear the same things over and over again, I saw that the ham grease had turned white on the tomatoes. The eggs had withdrawn from the edge of the platter to bunch in the center like children left out in the cold. And the catheads had sat down on themselves with the conclusiveness of a fat woman sitting in an easy chair. And still he talked on. When he finally stopped, our appetites were gone, but he feasted on the cold food with a non-talking but still noisy relish.

In the Christian Methodist Episcopal Church the children's section was on the right, cater-cornered from the pew that held those ominous women called the Mothers of the Church. In the young people's section the benches were placed close together, and when a child's legs no longer comfortably fitted in the narrow space, it was an indication to the elders that that person could now move into the intermediate area (center church). Bailey and I were allowed to sit with the other children only when there were informal meetings, church socials or the like. But on the Sundays when Reverend Thomas preached, it was ordained that we occupy the first row, called the mourners' bench. I thought we were placed in front because Momma was proud of us, but Bailey assured me that she just wanted to keep her grandchildren under her thumb and eye.

Reverend Thomas took his text from Deuteronomy. And I was stretched between loathing his voice and wanting to listen to the sermon. Deuteronomy was my favorite book in the Bible. The laws were so absolute, so clearly set down, that I knew if a person truly wanted to avoid hell and brimstone, and being roasted forever in the devil's fire, all she had to do was memorize Deuteronomy and follow its teaching, word for word. I also liked the way the word rolled off the tongue.

Bailey and I sat alone on the front bench, the wooden slats pressing hard on our behinds and the backs of our thighs. I would have wriggled just a bit, but each time I looked over at Momma, she seemed to threaten, "Move and I'll tear you up," so, obedient to the unvoiced command, I sat still. The church ladies were warming up behind me with a few hallelujahs and Praise the Lords and Amens, and the preacher hadn't really moved into the meat of the sermon.

It was going to be a hot service.

On my way into church, I saw Sister Monroe, her open-faced gold crown glinting when she opened her mouth to return a neighborly greeting. She lived in the country and couldn't get to church every Sunday, so she made up for her absences by shouting so hard when she did make it that she shook the whole church. As soon as she took her seat, all the ushers would move to her side of the church because it took three women and sometimes a man or two to hold her.

Once when she hadn't been to church for a few months (she had taken off to have a child), she got the spirit and started shouting, throwing her arms around and jerking her body, so that the ushers went over to hold her down, but she tore herself away from them and ran up to the pulpit. She stood in front of the altar, shaking like a freshly caught trout. She screamed at Reverend Taylor. "Preach it. I say, preach it." Naturally he kept on preaching as if she wasn't standing there telling him what to do. Then she screamed an extremely fierce "I said, preach it" and stepped up on the altar. The Reverend kept on throwing out phrases like home-run balls and Sister Monroe made a quick break and grasped for him. For just a second, everything and everyone in the church except Reverend Taylor and Sister Monroe hung loose like stockings on a washline. Then she caught the minister by the sleeve of his jacket and his coattail, then she rocked him from side to side.

I have to say this for our minister, he never stopped giving us the lesson. The usher board made its way to the pulpit, going up both aisles with a little more haste than is customarily seen in church. Truth to tell, they fairly ran to the minister's aid. Then two of the deacons, in their shiny Sunday suits, joined the ladies in white on the pulpit, and each time they pried Sister Monroe loose from the preacher he took another deep breath and kept on preaching, and Sister Monroe grabbed him in another place, and more firmly. Reverend Taylor was helping his rescuers as much as possible by jumping around when he got a chance. His voice at one point got so low it sounded like a roll of thunder, then Sister Monroe's "Preach it" cut through the roar, and we all wondered (I did, in any case) if it would ever end. Would they go on forever, or get tired out at last like a game of blindman's bluff that lasted too long, with nobody caring who was "it"?

I'll never know what might have happened, because magically the pandemonium spread. The spirit infused Deacon Jackson and Sister Willson, the chairman of the usher board, at the same time. Deacon

Jackson, a tall, thin, quiet man, who was also a part-time Sunday school teacher, gave a scream like a falling tree, leaned back on thin air and punched Reverend Taylor on the arm. It must have hurt as much as it caught the Reverend unawares. There was a moment's break in the rolling sounds and Reverend Taylor jerked around surprised, and hauled off and punched Deacon Jackson. In the same second Sister Willson caught his tie, looped it over her fist a few times, and pressed down on him. There wasn't time to laugh or cry before all three of them were down on the floor behind the altar. Their legs spiked out like kindling wood.

Sister Monroe, who had been the cause of all the excitement, walked off the dais, cool and spent, and raised her flinty voice in the hymn, "I came to Jesus, as I was, worried, wound, and sad, I found in Him a resting place and He has made me glad."

The minister took advantage of already being on the floor and asked in a choky little voice if the church would kneel with him to offer a prayer of thanksgiving. He said we had been visited with a mighty spirit, and let the whole church say Amen.

On the next Sunday, he took his text from the eighteenth chapter of the Gospel according to St. Luke, and talked quietly but seriously about the Pharisees, who prayed in the streets so that the public would be impressed with their religious devotion. I doubt that anyone got the message—certainly not those to whom it was directed. The deacon board, however, did appropriate funds for him to buy a new suit. The other was a total loss.

Our presiding elder had heard the story of Reverend Taylor and Sister Monroe, but I was sure he didn't know her by sight. So my interest in the service's potential and my aversion to Reverend Thomas caused me to turn him off. Turning off or tuning out people was my highly developed art. The custom of letting obedient children be seen but not heard was so agreeable to me that I went one step further: Obedient children should not see or hear if they chose not to do so. I laid a handful of attention on my face and tuned up the sounds in the church.

Sister Monroe's fuse was already lit, and she sizzled somewhere to the right behind me. Elder Thomas jumped into the sermon, determined, I suppose, to give the members what they came for. I saw the ushers from the left side of the church near the big windows begin to move discreetly, like pallbearers, toward Sister Monroe's bench. Bailey jogged my knee. When the incident with Sister Monroe, which we always called simply "the incident," had taken place, we had been too astounded to laugh. But for weeks after, all we needed to send us into violent outbursts of laughter was a whispered "Preach it." Anyway, he pushed my knee, covered his mouth and whispered, "I say, preach it."

I looked toward Momma, across that square of stained boards, over the collection table, hoping that a look from her would root me safely to my sanity. But for the first time in memory Momma was staring behind me at Sister Monroe. I supposed that she was counting on bringing that emotional lady up short with a severe look or two. But Sister Monroe's voice had already reached the danger point. "Preach it!"

There were a few smothered giggles from the children's section, and Bailey nudged me again. "I say, preach it"—in a whisper. Sister Monroe echoed him loudly, "I say, preach it!"

Two deacons wedged themselves around Brother Jackson as a preventive measure and two large determined-looking men walked down the aisle toward Sister Monroe.

While the sounds in the church were increasing, Elder Thomas made the regrettable mistake of increasing his volume too. Then suddenly, like a summer rain, Sister Monroe broke through the cloud of people trying to hem her in, and flooded up to the pulpit. She didn't stop this time but continued immediately to the altar, bound for Elder Thomas, crying "I say, preach it."

Bailey said out loud, "Hot dog" and "Damn" and "She's going to beat his butt."

But Reverend Thomas didn't intend to wait for that eventuality, so as Sister Monroe approached the pulpit from the right he started descending from the left. He was not intimidated by his change of venue. He continued preaching and moving. He finally stopped right in front of the collection table, which put him almost in our laps, and Sister Monroe rounded the altar on his heels, followed by the deacons, ushers, some unofficial members and a few of the bigger children.

Just as the elder opened his mouth, pink tongue waving, and said, "Great God of Mount Nebo," Sister Monroe hit him on the back of his head with her purse. Twice. Before he could bring his lips together, his teeth fell, no, actually his teeth jumped, out of his mouth.

The grinning uppers and lowers lay by my right shoe, looking empty and at the same time appearing to contain all the emptiness in the world. I could have stretched out a foot and kicked them under the bench or behind the collection table.

Sister Monroe was struggling with his coat, and the men had all but picked her up to remove her from the building. Bailey pinched me and said without moving his lips, "I'd like to see him eat dinner now."

I looked at Reverend Thomas desperately. If he appeared just a little sad or embarrassed, I could feel sorry for him and wouldn't be able to laugh. My sympathy for him would keep me from laughing. I dreaded laughing in church. If I lost control, two things were certain to happen. I would surely pee, and just as surely get a whipping. And this time I would probably die because everything was funny—Sister Monroe, and Momma trying to keep her quiet with those threatening looks, and Bailey whispering "Preach it" and Elder Thomas with his lips flapping loose like tired elastic.

But Reverend Thomas shrugged off Sister Monroe's weakening clutch, pulled out an extra-large white handkerchief and spread it over his nasty little teeth. Putting them in his pocket, he gummed, "Naked I came into the world, and naked I shall go out."

Bailey's laugh had worked its way up through his body and was escaping through his nose in short hoarse snorts. I didn't try any longer to hold back the laugh, I just opened my mouth and released sound. I heard the first titter jump up in the air over my head, over the pulpit and out the window. Momma said out loud, "Sister!" but the bench was greasy and I slid off onto the floor. There was more laughter in me trying to get out. I didn't know there was that much in the whole world. It pressed at all my body openings, forcing everything in its path. I cried and hollered, passed gas and urine. I didn't see Bailey descend to the floor, but I rolled over once and he was kicking and screaming too. Each time we looked at each other we howled louder than before, and though he tried to say something, the laughter attacked him and he was only able to get out "I say, preach." And then I rolled over onto Uncle Willie's rubber-tipped cane. My eyes followed the cane up to his good brown hand on the curve and up the long, long white sleeve to his face. The one side pulled down as it usually did when he cried (it also pulled down when he laughed). He stuttered, "I'm gonna whip you this time myself."

I have no memory of how we got out of church and into the parsonage next door, but in that overstuffed parlor, Bailey and I received the whipping of our lives. Uncle Willie ordered us between licks to stop crying. I tried to, but Bailey refused to cooperate. Later he explained that when a person is beating you you should scream as loud as possible; maybe the whipper will become embarrassed or else some sympathetic soul might come to your rescue. Our savior came for neither of these reasons, but because Bailey yelled so loud and disturbed what was left of the service, the minister's wife came out and asked Uncle Willie to quiet us down.

Laughter so easily turns to hysteria for imaginative children. I felt for weeks after that I had been very, very sick, and until I completely recovered my strength I stood on laughter's cliff and any funny thing could hurl me off to my death far below.

Each time Bailey said "Preach it" to me, I hit him as hard as I could and cried.

SIMONE DE BEAUVOIR
(1908–1986)

In the spring of 1929, when she was finishing her studies in philosophy and preparing for her final exams, Simone de Beauvoir met Jean-Paul Sartre. After finishing second in her class in the exams (Sartre was first), Beauvoir went to the country with her family for the summer. Sartre followed her, and they became lovers. In Paris that fall they worked out the beginnings of their lifelong relationship, which aimed at stability while bypassing bourgeois marriage.

Beauvoir came from a conservative family but yearned for freedom and independence. She arranged a compromise between her own needs and her parents' concern for respectability by renting a room from her grandmother—the farthest room possible from the old woman's and one which granted her a certain degree of privacy.

Few serious autobiographies by women were available in the 1950s. When Beauvoir's first volume of autobiography, *Memoirs of a Dutiful Daughter*, appeared in 1958, it constituted in some ways as important a feminist text as *The Second Sex*, her epic account of women's oppression. She went on to write three more exhaustive volumes, *The Prime of Life* (1960), *Force of Circumstance* (1963), and *All Said and Done* (1972), plus a beautiful memoir about her mother, *A Very Easy Death* (1966).

This selection is the opening of *The Prime of Life* and describes the start of her relationship with Sartre, capturing her delight in adult freedom. The volume covers the years from 1929 to 1944.

For another account of the thrill of choice, compare Nina Berberova, *The Italics Are Mine*. For other dutiful daughters, compare Jill Ker Conway, *The Road from Coorain* and Eleanor Munro, *Memoir of a Modernist's Daughter*.

FROM *The Prime of Life*

The most intoxicating aspect of my return to Paris in September, 1929, was the freedom I now possessed. I had dreamed of it since childhood, when I played with my sister at being a "grown-up" girl. I have recorded elsewhere my passionate longing for it as a student. Now, suddenly, it was mine. I was astonished to find an effortless buoyancy in all my movements. From the moment I opened my eyes every morning I

was lost in a transport of delight. When I was about twelve I had suffered
through not having a private retreat of my own at home. Leafing
through *Mon Journal* I had found a story about an English schoolgirl,
and gazed enviously at the colored illustration portraying her room.
There was a desk, and a divan, and shelves filled with books. Here,
within these gaily painted walls, she read and worked and drank tea, with
no one watching her—how envious I felt! For the first time ever I had
glimpsed a more fortunate way of life than my own. And now, at long
last, I too had a room to myself. My grandmother had stripped her
drawing room of all its armchairs, occasional tables, and knickknacks. I
had bought some unpainted furniture, and my sister had helped me to
give it a coat of brown varnish. I had a table, two chairs, a large chest
which served both as a seat and as a hold-all, shelves for my books. I
papered the walls orange, and got a divan to match. From my fifth-floor
balcony I looked out over the Lion of Belfort and the plane trees on the
Rue Denfert-Rochereau. I kept myself warm with an evil-smelling kerosene stove. Somehow its stink seemed to protect my solitude, and I loved
it. It was wonderful to be able to shut my door and keep my daily life free
of other people's inquisitiveness. For a long time I remained indifferent
to the décor of my surroundings. Possibly because of that picture in *Mon
Journal* I preferred rooms that offered me a divan and bookshelves, but I
was prepared to put up with any sort of retreat in a pinch. To have a door
that I could shut was still the height of bliss for me.

I paid rent to my grandmother, and she treated me with the same
unobtrusive respect she showed her other lodgers. I was free to come
and go as I pleased. I could get home with the milk, read in bed all
night, sleep till midday, shut myself up for forty-eight hours at a stretch,
or go out on the spur of the moment. My lunch was a bowl of
borsch at Dominique's, and for supper I took a cup of hot chocolate
at La Coupole. I was fond of hot chocolate, and borsch, and lengthy
siestas and sleepless nights: but my chief delight was in doing as I
pleased. There was practically nothing to stop me. I discovered, to my
great pleasure, that "the serious business of living" on which grownups
had held forth to me so interminably was not, in fact, quite so oppressive
after all. Getting through my examinations, on the other hand, had been
no joke. I had worked desperately hard, always with the fear of possible
failure, always tired, and with various stubborn obstacles to overcome.
Now I encountered no such resistance anywhere: I felt as though I were
on vacation forever. A little private tutoring and a part-time teaching job
at the Lycée Victor-Duruy guaranteed me enough to live on. These
duties did not even prove a burden to me, since I felt that by performing
them I was involved in a new sort of game: I was playing at being a
grownup. Hunting for private pupils, having discussions with senior mis-

tresses or parents, working out my budget, borrowing, paying back, adding up figures—all these activities amused me because I was doing them for the first time. I remember how tickled I was when I got my first salary check. I felt I had played a practical joke on someone.

Clothes and cosmetics had never interested me overmuch, but I nevertheless took some pleasure in dressing as *I* wanted to. I was still in mourning for my grandfather, and had no wish to shock people, so I bought myself a gray coat, with shoes and toque to match. I had two dresses made, one of the same gray, and the other in black and white. All my life I had been dressed in cotton or woolen frocks, so now I reacted by choosing silk-style materials instead—crepe de Chine and a ghastly fabric of embossed velvet called *velours frappé* which was all the rage that winter. Every morning I would make up with more dash than skill, smothering my face in powder, dabbing a patch of rouge on each cheek, and applying lipstick liberally. It struck me as ridiculous that anyone should dress up more elaborately on Sunday than during the week. Henceforth, I decided, every day was to be a holiday as far as I was concerned, and I always wore the same get-up, whatever the circumstances. It did occur to me that crepe de Chine and *velours frappé* were rather out of place in the corridors of a *lycée,* and that my evening shoes might have been less down at the heel if I hadn't tramped the Paris pavements in them from morning till night; but I couldn't have cared less. My personal appearance was one of those things that I refused to take really seriously.

I moved in, bought a new outfit, had friends in to see me, and went visiting myself; but all these were preliminary activities only. My new life really began when Sartre returned to Paris in mid-October.

Sartre had come to see me when we were in Limousin. He stayed at the Hôtel de la Boule d'Or, in Saint-Germain-les-Belles, and in order to avoid gossip we used to meet out in the country, a good way from town. In the old days I had often wandered here, bitterly hugging my loneliness; but now I hurried blithely across the grassy parkland every morning, skipping over hurdles and plunging through dew-wet meadows. We would sit down together in the grass and talk. The first day I never supposed that, away from Paris and our friends, such an occupation would wholly suffice for us. I had suggested that we might bring some books along, and read. Sartre refused indignantly. He also swept aside all my suggestions that we might go for a walk. He was allergic to chlorophyll, he said, and all this lush green pasturage exhausted him. The only way he could put up with it was to forget it. Fair enough. Though I had received little encouragement in that direction, talking did not scare me. We picked up our discussion at the point where we had left off in Paris;

and very soon I realized that even though we went on talking till Judgment Day, I would still find the time all too short. It had been early morning when we came out, and there was the luncheon bell already. I used to go home and eat with my family, while Sartre lunched on cheese or gingerbread, deposited by my cousin Madeleine in an abandoned dovecote that stood "by the house down the road"; Madeleine adored anything romantic. Hardly had the afternoon begun before it was over, and darkness falling; Sartre would then go back to his hotel and eat dinner among the commercial travelers. I had told my parents we were working together on a book, a critical study of Marxism. I hoped to butter them up by pandering to their hatred of Communism, but I cannot have been very convincing. Four days after Sartre arrived, I saw them appear at the edge of the meadow where we were sitting.

They walked toward us. Under his yellowing straw boater, my father wore a resolute but somewhat embarrassed expression. Sartre, who on this particular day happened to be wearing a decidedly aggressive red shirt, sprang to his feet, the light of battle in his eye. My father asked him, quite politely, to leave the district. People were gossiping, he said; besides, it was hoped to get my cousin married, and such apparently scandalous behavior on my part was harmful to her reputation. Sartre replied vigorously enough, but without too much violence, since he had made up his mind not to leave a minute sooner than he intended. We merely arranged somewhat more secret meeting places, in a chestnut grove a little distance away. My father did not return to the attack, and Sartre stayed on another week at the Boule d'Or. Afterward we wrote to each other daily.

By the time I met him again, in October, I had (as I describe in *Memoirs of a Dutiful Daughter*) jettisoned all past attachments, and now threw myself unreservedly into the development of this new relationship. Sartre was soon due for his military service; meanwhile he remained on vacation. He was staying with his grandparents (his mother's family, that is: their name was Schweitzer) on the Rue Saint-Jacques, and we would meet each morning in the Luxembourg Gardens, where carved stone queens gazed blindly down at us amid a dapple of gray and gold: it was late at night before we separated. We walked the streets of Paris, still talking—about ourselves and our relationship, our future life, our yet unwritten books. Today it strikes me that the most important aspect of these conversations was not so much what we said as what we took for granted, and what in fact was not so at all. We were wrong about almost everything. An accurate character sketch must needs take these errors into account, since they expressed one kind of reality—our actual situation.

As I have said elsewhere, Sartre lived for his writing. He felt he had a mission to hold forth on any subject, tackling it as best suited him in the light of circumstance. He had exhorted me to open my eyes to the manifold glories of life; I too must write, in order to snatch that vision from obliteration by time. The self-evident obviousness of our respective vocations seemed to us to guarantee their eventual fulfillment. Though we did not formulate it in such terms, we were approaching a condition of Kantian optimism, where *you should* implies *you can.* Indeed, how could one's resolution falter in doubt at the very moment of choice and affirmation? Upon such an occasion will and belief coincide. So we put our trust in the world, and in ourselves. Society as then constituted we opposed. But there was nothing sour about this enmity: it carried an implication of robust optimism. Man was to be remolded, and the process would be partly our doing. We did not envisage contributing to this change except by way of books: public affairs bored us. We counted on events turning out according to our wishes without any need for us to mix in them personally. In this respect our attitude was characteristic of that general euphoria affecting the French Left during the autumn of 1929. Peace seemed finally assured: the expansion of the German Nazi party was a mere fringe phenomenon, without any serious significance. It would not be long before colonialism folded up: Gandhi's campaign in India and the Communist agitation in French Indo-China were proof enough of that. Moreover the whole capitalist world was, at the time, being shaken by a crisis of the utmost gravity; and this encouraged the assumption that capitalism as such had had its day. We felt that we were already living in that Golden Age which for us constituted the secret truth of History, and the revelation of which remained History's final and exclusive objective.

At every level we failed to face the weight of reality, priding ourselves on what we called our "radical freedom." We clung so long and so desperately to that word "freedom" that it will be as well to make a closer examination of just what we implied by it.

There was a genuine enough field of experience for it to cover. Every activity contains its own freedom, intellectual activity in particular, because it seldom repeats itself. We had worked hard; we had been forced, unremittingly, to rediscover and revaluate; we possessed a practical, unimpeachable, intuitive awareness of the nature of freedom. The mistake we made was in failing to restrict this concept to its proper limits. We clung to the image of Kant's dove, supported rather than hindered in flight by the resistant air. We regarded any existing situation as raw material for our joint efforts, and not as a factor conditioning them: we imagined ourselves to be wholly independent agents. This spiritual pride, like our political blindness, can be explained in the first instance by the violent intensity which characterized all our plans. To be a writer, to create—this was an adventure scarcely to be embarked upon without a conviction of absolute self-mastery, absolute control over ends and means. Our boldness was inseparable from the illusions which sustained it; circumstances had favored them both. No external hazard had ever compelled us to go against our own natural inclinations. We sought knowledge, self-expression; and now we found ourselves up to our necks in just such activities. Our way of life was so exactly what we wanted that it was as though *it* had chosen *us;* we regarded this as an omen of its regular submission to our future plans. The same fate that had served our purpose also shielded us from the world's adversity.

Nor, on the other hand, did we feel any private emotional obligations. I kept on good terms with my parents, but they no longer had any real hold over me. Sartre had never known his father, and neither his mother nor his grandparents had ever represented authority in his eyes. In a sense we both lacked a real family, and we had elevated this contingency into a principle. Here we were encouraged by Cartesian rationalism, which we had picked up from Alain,* and which we welcomed precisely because it happened to suit our convenience. There were no scruples, no feelings of respect or loyal affection that would stop us from making up our minds by the pure light of reason—and of our own desires. We were unaware of any cloudiness or confusion in our mental processes; we believed ourselves to consist of pure reason and pure will. This conviction was fortified by the eagerness with which we staked our all on the future; we were not tied down to any particular interest, since present and past were continually leap-frogging. We never hesitated to disagree with any point, and indeed with each other, whenever occasion demanded; it was easy for us to criticize or condemn the other's views, since every shift of opinion we regarded as a step forward. As our ignorance kept us unaware of most of the problems that might have worried us, we remained quite content with these revisions of doctrine, and indeed thought ourselves very daring.

So we went our way without let or hindrance, unembarrassed and unafraid; yet how was it that we did not at least stumble into one or two roadblocks? After all, our pockets were virtually empty. I scraped a scanty living, while Sartre was going through a small legacy he had from his paternal grandmother. The shops were laden with goods we could not buy, while all luxury resorts were closed to us. We met these prohibitions with indifference, even with active disdain. We were not ascetics, far from it; but now as before (and in this Sartre and I were alike) only those things within my reach, in particular those I could actually touch, had any true weight of reality for me. I gave myself up so completely to

*Émile Chartier, called Alain, was a professor of philosophy—ED.

present desires and pleasures that I had no energy to waste on mere wishful thinking. What was the point in regretting the absence of a car, when there were so many discoveries we could make on foot, on the Bercy *quais* or along the reaches of the Saint-Martin canal? When we ate bread and *foie gras* Marie in my room, or had dinner at the Brasserie Demory (Sartre adored its heavy smell of beer and sauerkraut) we did not feel deprived of anything. In the evening we would look in at the Falstaff or the College Inn and drink our cocktails like connoisseurs—Bronxes, Sidecars, Bacardis, Alexanders, Martinis. I had a particular weakness for two specialties—mead cocktails at the Vikings' Bar, and apricot cocktails at the Bec de Gaz on the Rue Montparnasse: what more could the Ritz Bar have offered us? Occasionally we broke out and enjoyed ourselves: I remember eating chicken and cranberry sauce one evening at the Vikings' Bar while up on the dais the orchestra played a popular hit of the day called "Pagan Love Song." I am sure this celebration would not have made such an impression on me unless it had been something out of the ordinary: indeed, the very modesty of our resources served to increase my pleasure.

In any case, the pleasure to be derived from expensive possessions is not so simple or direct. They are basically a means to an end; the glamour they acquire is shed upon them by some glamorous third party. Our puritanical education and the firmness of our intellectual commitment ensured that we remained immune to dukes, millionaires, owners of Hispanos,* women in mink, and all such denizens of high society. We actually stigmatized this *beau monde* as the very dregs of the earth, on the grounds that it sucked profit from a regime which we condemned. I felt a certain ironical pity for these people. When I passed by the impenetrable portals of Fouquet's or Maxim's, I pictured them, cut off from the masses, helpless prisoners of their own wealth and snobbery—surely it was they who were the real outsiders. For the most part they simply did not exist as far as I was concerned: I no more missed their refined pleasures than the Greeks of the fifth century B.C. missed cinema or radio. Obviously the cash barrier formed a block to our curiosity; but this caused us no annoyance, since we were convinced that the smart set had nothing to teach us: their mannered self-indulgence concealed a howling void.

We had no external limitations, no overriding authority, no imposed pattern of existence. We created our own links with the world, and freedom was the very essence of our existence. In our everyday lives we gave it scope by means of an activity which assumed considerable importance for us—private fantasies. Most young couples tend to enrich their

*Expensive cars—Ed.

normally somewhat bare past with intimate fantasies and myths. We embraced this pursuit all the more zealously since we were both active people by nature, and for the moment living a life of idleness. The comedies, parodies, or fables which we made up had a very specific object: they stopped us from taking ourselves too seriously. Seriousness as such we rejected no less vigorously than Nietzsche did, and for much the same reason: our jokes lightened the world about us by projecting it into the realm of imagination, thus enabling us to keep it at arm's length.

Of the two of us, Sartre was the most inexhaustible. He made up a whole stream of ballads, counting-out rhymes, epigrams, madrigals, thumbnail fables, and occasional poems of every description. Sometimes he would sing them to airs of his own invention. He considered neither puns nor wordplay beneath him, and enjoyed experimenting with alliteration and assonance. This was one way of coming to grips with the language—by both exploring the potential of words and discarding their everyday usage. From J. M. Synge he had borrowed the myth of Baladin, the eternal wanderer who disguises life's mediocrity with glorious lying fantasies; and James Stephens' *The Crock of Gold* had provided us with the idea of the leprechaun, a gnome who crouches under tree roots and keeps misery, boredom, and doubt at bay by cobbling tiny shoes. Both of them, the adventurer and the stay-at-home, taught the same lesson: literature above all else. But in their hands the motto lost its dogmatic weightiness; and we derived a certain backhanded pleasure from referring to our future books, so dear to our hearts, as "our tiny shoes."

We were both as healthy as horses and of a cheerful disposition. But I took any setback very badly; my face changed, I withdrew into myself and became mulish and obstinate. Sartre decided I had a double personality. Normally I was the Beaver; but occasionally this animal would be replaced by a rather irksome young lady called Mademoiselle de Beauvoir. Sartre embroidered this theme with several variations, all of which ended by making fun of me. In his own case, things very frequently got him down—especially in the morning, when his head was still foggy with sleep, or when circumstances reduced him to inactivity: he would hunch himself into a defensive ball, like a hedgehog. On such occasions he resembled a sea elephant we had once seen in the zoo at Vincennes whose misery broke our hearts. A keeper had emptied a bucketful of little fish down the beast's throat, and then jumped on its belly. The sea elephant, swamped by this internal invasion of tiny fish, raised tiny, hopeless eyes heavenward. It looked as though the whole vast bulk of his flesh were endeavoring to transmit a prayer for help through those two small apertures; but even so embryonic an attempt at communication was denied it. The mouth of the great beast gaped, and tears trickled down over its oily skin; it shook its head slowly and collapsed, defeated.

When Sartre's face took on an unhappy expression, we used to pretend that the sea elephant's desolate soul had taken possession of his body. Sartre would then complete the metamorphosis by rolling his eyes up, sighing, and making silent supplication: this pantomime would restore his good spirits. Our various moods we regarded not as a kind of inevitable symptom engendered physically, but as a species of disguise that we assumed in a perverse moment and could discard at will. All through our youth, and even later, whenever we had to face a difficult or disagreeable situation we would work it out first as a private *ad hoc* drama. We turned it upside down, exaggerated it, caricatured it, and explored it in every direction; this helped us a good deal in getting it under control.

We used the same method in defining our domestic status. When we met again in Paris we found a name for our relationship before we had decided just what that relationship was to be. "It's a morganatic marriage," we said. As a couple we possessed a dual identity. In the ordinary way we were Monsieur and Madame M. Organatique, unambitious, easily satisfied, not very well off, the husband a civil servant. But sometimes I dressed up, and we would go to a cinema on the Champs Elysées, or dancing at La Coupole, and then we were an American millionaire and his wife, Mr. and Mrs. Morgan Hattick. This was not a hysterical joke designed to make us feel that, for a few hours, we were enjoying the pleasures of the idle rich; it was, rather, a parody, which confirmed us in our contempt for high society. Our modest celebrations were quite enough for us: there was nothing further fortune could do for us. We were asserting our actual status. But at the same time we feigned release from it. That penurious pair of *petits bourgeois* whom we called Monsieur and Madame M. Organatique had no real identity with us: by wriggling into their skins for a joke we emphasized the difference.

As I have already made clear, I also regarded my day-to-day activities—among others, my job as a teacher—in the light of a masquerade. By releasing the pressure of reality upon our lives, fantasy convinced us that life itself had no hold upon us. We belonged to no place or country, no class, profession, or generation. Our truth lay elsewhere. It was inscribed upon the face of eternity, and the future would reveal it: we were writers. Any other verdict was the merest false illusion. We believed ourselves to be following the precepts of those ancient Stoics who likewise had staked their all upon freedom. Committed body and soul to the work that depended on us, we threw off the yoke of all obligations irrelevant to this central purpose. We did not go so far as to abstain from such things altogether—we were too experience-hungry for that—but we bracketed them off as mere interludes. Circumstances permitted us a certain measure of detachment, free time, and general insouciance; it was tempting to confuse this with sovereign freedom. To explode this fallacy we would have needed to see ourselves from a distance, in perspective; and we had neither the means nor the desire to do so.

Two disciplines might have clarified our thinking, those of Marxism or psychoanalysis. We had only the most rudimentary knowledge of either. I remember a very fierce quarrel which took place at the Balzar between Sartre and Politzer,* who was attempting to show Sartre up as a *petit bourgeois* at heart. Sartre did not reject the label, but maintained that it was inadequate as a complete definition of his attitude. He posed the thorny problem of the intellectual with a bourgeois background who—according to Marx himself—is capable of rising above the characteristic beliefs of his class. In what circumstances could this happen? How? Why? Politzer's shock of red hair glowed flamelike, and words poured out of him; but he failed to convince Sartre. In any case Sartre would have continued to play his part in the fight for freedom: he still believes in it to this day. But a serious analysis of the problem would have modified the ideas we held about it. Our indifference to money was a luxury we could afford only because we had enough of it to avoid real poverty and the need for hard or unpleasant work. Our open-mindedness was bound up with a cultural background and the sort of activities accessible only to people of our social class. It was our conditioning as young *petit bourgeois* intellectuals that led us to believe ourselves free of all conditioning whatsoever.

Why this particular self-indulgence rather than another? Why continual questing alertness rather than a slumberous dogmatic certainty? Psychoanalysis might have suggested some answers if we had consulted it. It was beginning to spread in France, and certain aspects of it interested us. . . . We looked favorably on the notion that psychoses, neuroses, and their various symptoms had a meaning, and that this meaning must be sought in the patient's childhood. But we stopped short at this point; we rejected psychoanalysis as a tool for exploring a normal human being. We had hardly read any Freud apart from his books *The Interpretation of Dreams* and *The Psychopathology of Everyday Life*. We had absorbed the letter rather than the spirit of these works: we were put off by their dogmatic symbolism and the technique of association which vitiated them for us. Freud's pansexualism struck us as having an element of madness about it, besides offending our puritanical instincts. Above all, the importance it attached to the unconscious, and the rigidity of its mechanistic theories, meant that Freudianism, as we conceived it, was bound to eradicate human free will. No one showed us how the two

*Georges Politzer, a philosopher and man of letters, was one of the first French intellectuals to join the Communist party—ED.

might possibly be reconciled, and we were incapable of finding out for ourselves. We remained frozen in our rationalist-voluntarist position: in a clear-minded individual, we thought, freedom would win out over complexes, memories, influences, or any traumatic experience. It was a long time before we realized that our emotional detachment from, and indifference to, our respective childhoods was to be explained by what we had experienced as children.

If Marxism and psychoanalysis had so little influence on us, at a time when many young people were rallying to both, it was not only because our knowledge concerning them was so sketchy, but also because we had no wish to observe ourselves from a distance with the eyes of strangers. Our first need was to prevent any dissociation between mind and personality. Far from setting theoretical limits to our freedom, we were now practically concerned with safeguarding its existence—for it was in danger.

In this respect there was a marked difference between Sartre and me. It struck me as miraculous that I had broken free from my past, and was now self-sufficient and self-determining: I had established my autonomy once and forever, and nothing could now deprive me of it. Sartre, on the other hand, had merely moved on to a stage of his development as a man which he had long foreseen with loathing. He had more or less shed the irresponsibility of adolescence, and was entering the adult world which he so detested. His independence was threatened. First he would be obliged to do eighteen months' military service, and after that a teaching career awaited him. He had found an answer to this: a French lectureship was being advertised in Japan, and he had put in an application for October, 1931. He counted on spending two years out there, with the possibility of further foreign posts afterward. According to him the writer or storyteller should be like Synge's Baladin, and never settle anywhere for good—or with any one person. Sartre was not inclined to be monogamous by nature: he took pleasure in the company of women, finding them less comic than men. He had no intention, at twenty-three, of renouncing their tempting variety.

He explained the matter to me in his favorite terminology. "What *we* have," he said, "is an *essential* love; but it is a good idea for us also to experience *contingent* love affairs." We were two of a kind, and our relationship would endure as long as we did: but it could not make up entirely for the fleeting riches to be had from encounters with different people. How could we deliberately forego that gamut of emotions—astonishment, regret, pleasure, nostalgia—which we were as capable of sustaining as anyone else? We reflected on this problem a good deal during our walks together.

One afternoon we had been with the Nizans* to a cinema on the Champs Elysées to see *Storm Over Asia.* After leaving them we walked down as far as the Carousel Gardens, and sat down on a stone bench beneath one wing of the Louvre. There was a kind of balustrade which served as a backrest, a little way out from the wall; and in the cagelike space behind it a cat was miaowing. The poor thing was too big to get out; how had it ever gotten in? Evening was drawing on; a woman came up to the bench, a paper bag in one hand, and produced some scraps of meat. These she fed to the cat, stroking it tenderly the while. It was at this moment that Sartre said: "Let's sign a two-year lease." I could arrange to live in Paris during these two years, and we would spend them in the closest possible intimacy. Afterward, Sartre suggested, I ought to take a job abroad too. We would live apart for two or three years, and then rejoin one another somewhere—Athens, maybe—where we could, for a longer or shorter period, live more or less together. We would never become strangers to one another, and neither would appeal for the other's help in vain; nothing would prevail against this alliance of ours. But it must not be allowed to degenerate into mere duty or habit; we had at all costs to preserve it from decay of this sort. I agreed. The separation which Sartre envisaged caused me some qualms; but it lay well in the future, and I had made it a rule never to worry about anything prematurely. Despite this I did feel a flicker of fear, though I regarded it as mere weakness and made myself subdue it; I was helped by the knowledge, based on previous experience, that Sartre meant what he said. With him a proposed scheme was not mere vague talk, but a moment of actuality. If he told me one day to meet him exactly twenty-two months later on the Acropolis, at five o'clock in the afternoon, I could be sure of finding him there then, punctual to the minute. In a more general way I knew that no harm could ever come to me from him—unless he were to die before I died.

There was no question of our actually taking advantage, during our two-year "lease," of those "freedoms" which in theory we had the right to enjoy. We intended to give ourselves wholeheartedly and without reservation to this new relationship of ours. We made another pact between us: not only would we never lie to one another, but neither of us would conceal anything from the other. What is known as *la vie intérieure* aroused the greatest disgust among Sartre's circle of friends, *les petits camarades;* the gardens where sensitive, refined souls cultivated their delicate secrets these folk regarded as stinking swamps, the background for constant discreet trafficking in betrayal, or the consummation of filthy narcissistic pleasures.

*Paul Nizan, the philosopher, was one of Sartre's closest friends—Ed.

In order to dissipate this dark miasmic atmosphere, they themselves had acquired the habit of exposing their lives, thoughts, and feelings in broad daylight. The only limit set on these public revelations was due to lack of interest: any of them who went on too much about himself would have bored the rest. But no such restrictions existed between Sartre and me; and we therefore agreed to tell one another everything. I was used to some reserve, and at first this rule of ours embarrassed me. But I soon came to realize its advantages. I no longer needed to worry about myself: all my actions were subjected to a kindly enough scrutiny, but with far greater impartiality than I could have achieved myself. The picture I thus received I regarded as objective; and this system of control protected me against all those fears, false hopes, idle scruples, fantasies, and minor brainstorms which can so easily breed in conditions of solitude. The absence of solitude did not bother me; on the contrary, I was delighted to have gotten away from it.

The thought that Sartre was now an open book to me, as easily read as my own mind, had a most relaxing effect on me. Later I learned better. Since he concealed nothing from me, I thought myself absolved from any necessity to think about his problems. On several occasions afterward I perceived that this was a lazy way out. But though I reproached myself for sluggish obtuseness, I did not blame the rule that we had adopted. We were never to dispense with that rule; no other would have suited us.

This is not to suggest that in my opinion sincerity is either a universal necessity or a universal panacea. . . . Sometimes speech is no more than a device for saying nothing—and a neater one than silence. Even in a case where words *do* convey information, they lack the power to suppress, sidetrack, or neutralize reality; their function is to *confront* it. If two people manage to convince themselves that they possess any power over the events or people which form the subject of their mutual confidences, then they are deceiving themselves: their "honesty" is the merest pretext. There is a certain type of supposed loyalty which I have often observed, and which in fact constitutes the most flagrant hypocrisy: it is limited to the sphere of sexual relations, and its purpose, far from aiming at any intimate understanding between a man and a woman, is to supply one of them—more often the male partner—with a soothing alibi. He nurses the illusion that by confessing his infidelities he somehow redeems them; whereas actually he inflicts a double hurt upon his partner.

There is no timeless formula which guarantees all couples achieving a perfect state of understanding; it is up to the interested parties themselves to decide just what sort of agreement they want to reach. They have no a priori rights or duties. In my youth I took an opposite view; at that period I was too prone to imagine that what suited me must needs suit everybody.

Today, on the other hand, I feel irritated when outsiders praise or criticize the relationship we have built up, yet fail to take into account the peculiar characteristic which both explains and justifies it—the identical sign on both our brows. The comradeship that welded our lives together made a superfluous mockery of any other bond we might have forged for ourselves. What, for instance, was the point of living under the same roof when the whole world was our common property? Why fear to set great distances between us when we could never truly be parted? One single aim fired us, the urge to embrace all experience, and to bear witness concerning it. At times this meant that we had to follow diverse paths—though without concealing even the least of our discoveries from one another. When we were together we bent our wills so firmly to the requirements of this common task that even at the moment of parting we still thought as one. That which bound us freed us; and in this freedom we found ourselves bound as closely as possible. . . .

To achieve basic understanding with someone is a very rare privilege in any circumstances; for me it took on a literally infinite value. At the back of my memory there glowed, with unparalleled sweetness, all those long hours that Zaza* and I had spent hidden in Monsieur Mabille's study, talking. I too had experienced moments of poignant pleasure when my father smiled at me, and I could tell myself that, in a sense, this peerless man was *mine*. My adolescent dreams projected these supreme moments of my childhood into the future: they were not mere insubstantial fancies, but had a real existence for me—which is why their fulfillment never struck me as miraculous. Certainly circumstances were all in my favor: I might never have found anyone with whom I could reach a state of perfect agreement. When my chance was offered me, I took it; the passion and tenacity with which I did so showed how deeply rooted the urge was in me.

Sartre was only three years older than I was—an equal, as Zaza had been—and together we set forth to explore the world. My trust in him was so complete that he supplied me with the sort of absolute unfailing security that I had once had from my parents, or from God. When I threw myself into a world of freedom, I found an unbroken sky above my head. I was free of all shackling restraint, and yet every moment of my existence possessed its own inevitability. All my most remote and deep-felt longings were now fulfilled; there was nothing left for me to wish—except that this state of triumphant bliss might continue unwaveringly forever. Its sheer intensity carried all before it; it even managed to engulf

*Zaza (Elizabeth Mabille) was a childhood friend who died young—Ed.

the fact of Zaza's death. I was shocked enough at the time: I wept and felt my heart would break; but it was only later that grief made its real, insidious inroads upon me. That autumn my past lay dormant; I belonged wholly to the present.

NINA BERBEROVA
(1901–1993)

Nina Berberova's great-grandfather was the four-hundred-pound slow-to-move landowner on whom the Russian novelist Ivan Goncharov based his famous character Oblomov. She grew up in upper-middle-class ease in czarist Russia. That she should be worrying about a profession at the age of ten, as she says she did in this passage from her autobiography, *The Italics Are Mine* (1969), testifies to her mental liveliness and not to a premature need to make a living. Later, in exile after the 1917 Revolution, first in Berlin and then in Paris, she wrote and lived the strange life of an émigrée, suffering appalling poverty during the Second World War. In 1950 she came to the United States, where she taught for many years in the Slavic Department of Princeton University. Berberova said that she had no trouble liberating herself from her bourgeois upbringing, as many of her contemporaries in France did, because she grew up in a place and at a time "when there was no doubt that the old world would in one way or another be destroyed."

She was in her sixties and already considered her life long when she wrote *The Italics Are Mine*. When she was close to ninety, her novels and the autobiography had a sudden, immense success in France.

For other accounts of intellectuals who rebel against bourgeois norms, compare Simone de Beauvoir, *The Prime of Life* and Mary McCarthy, *Memories of a Catholic Girlhood*. For another Russian émigrée, compare Marie Vassiltchikov, *Berlin Diaries*.

FROM *The Italics Are Mine*

I was ten when I got the idea that it was necessary for me to choose a profession quickly. As I mentally return to this period and burrow into the early events of my childhood, I can now explain, though perhaps only partly, this desire to find a "trade" in life for myself. About four years before this I quite accidentally, but with irrefutable force, learned that boys have something girls don't have. This made a stunning impression on me, though it in no way bothered me and produced neither envy nor a feeling of misfortune. Soon I forgot about this discovery and it played no role, at least explicitly, in my later development, though it probably stuck in my subconscious (or wherever such a place is supposed to be). In the strong desire to have a profession "for life," to have something that would grow with me like an arm or a leg and be a part of me, I now see a kind of compensation for what I lacked as a girl. I sought not only the profession itself, but the act of choosing it, that act of conscious decision. Now I know that in the course of sixty years not all my decisive and "irrevocable" actions were the result of *conscious* decision. My departure from Russia in 1922 was not, but my staying in occupied France in 1940 was. In my entire life I have made responsible, existential choices that bore meaning for the structure of my life and personality (in the "global" or "totalitarian" sense) not more than four or five times; but I must admit that each time these conscious choices gave me an awareness of the force of my existence and of my freedom, a sharp sense of the "electric charge," which one can call bliss whether or not this choice has led in fact to happiness or to an evident despair. And the sense of "electric happiness" is not diminished by the fact that my choices were partly conditioned by the two great laws—of biology and sociology—for I do not conceive of myself outside of them.

The realization of my first strong desire to choose, to decide, to find, to move myself consciously in a chosen direction gave me for my whole life, as I now see it, a feeling of victory not over someone else but over myself, not bestowed from on high but personally acquired.

So I wrote a long list of possible professions on a piece of paper, completely disregarding the fact that I was not a boy, which meant that such professions as fireman and mailman had properly to be excluded. Between fireman and mailman, among forty possibilities, there was the profession of poet (I didn't follow alphabetical order). Everything in me boiled up and it seemed to me that I had to decide then and there what I would like to be so that I could begin to live accordingly. I looked at my list as at a counter all laid out with wares. That dark corner of the Russian alphabet, where the *yat* and the hard sign and the soft sign play hide-and-seek with the *yu* and *ya*, was not yet very clear. But the world was wide open before me, and I began to climb over its shelves and chests.

After lengthy reflections in complete solitude and secrecy, I came to my decision. Verses gushed out of me. I choked in them, I couldn't stop. I wrote them at the rate of two or three a day and read them to myself, to Dasha, to Mademoiselle, to my parents, to their friends, to whoever was there. This rigorous sense of vocation has never left me in my life, though in those years it was, it seems to me, rather peculiar. At ten I was an ordinary child, played games, tried to avoid homework, got punished, stood in a corner picking at the wall plaster. In other words, I behaved like everybody else. Yet parallel to this ran a constant thought—I am a poet, I will be a poet. I want to be friends with poets; I want to read poetry; I want to speak about verse. Now as I look back I see that my two strong and enduring childhood friendships were with those who, like me, wrote verse and had chosen a calling for themselves before they had actually entered life. One was shot in the years of Stalin's terror, the other lost two husbands in Stalin's purges.

I well remember that summer and the search for a profession. I had decided to try everything possible and not to lose time, which I already prized highly. At first a question arose: should I not be an acrobat? For several days I did some gymnastics, but I was very quickly bored. Then I turned to botany and for hours looked for algae in a can filled with pond water. But this, too, seemed uninspiring. When I found out that there were people who studied folklore, I took a notebook and pencil and went to a milking in the evening. There young peasant girls sang, "Peas today and peas tomorrow. Milk the cows and come to me." It wasn't hard to write it down. The song was sung over and over about two hundred times until all the cows were milked, and there were many of them because in those years Grandfather lived principally off the sale of butter and Edam; these were manufactured in a barn which we called the "factory." But folklore did not satisfy me either; something like a black storm cloud now hung over me. I feared I would be made fun of. With all this, it was clear that I could not procrastinate about finding myself a profession. I had loafed for entire days in the house, in the garden, in the yard. I had fallen into nettles, I had been bitten by a goose, had sobbed under the hoop skirts in the attic, but a profession would not come to me.

Yet the village priest's seven daughters, the two youngest of whom were my age, knew from their earliest years that they would become village teachers; I liked this very much. The priest was poor and completely uneducated, but his daughters had scholarships and they lived in the town during the winter. The poverty in their house was horrifying. They were ashamed when I found the older ones barefoot, washing the floors of the house, and the younger ones squelching through manure in the yard, running from a pig to a cow all covered with flies. The houses that stood between Grandfather's house and the church were surrounded by dense lilac, jasmin, and honeysuckle. The deacon had a deaf-mute wife, and the poverty was such that the sacristan's children walked about naked until the age of ten. The fourth house belonged to two old women, one of whom had no nose. They would rush out to kiss my shoulders, my hands, my dress when I walked by. The housemaid, Dasha, told me once that they were "former strollers" and that if one strolled a lot, one would end up without a nose. They were sent the remains of our holiday dinners. Who were these women? Why did Grandfather give them a house between the deacon's house and the priest's? They were called dressmakers, and it is possible that this was once so. When I knew them they were disheveled, filthy, terribly thin, and looked like old crows.

I was ashamed that they kissed me, I was ashamed of the bare legs of the priest's daughters, of my own bare legs, even of my bare arms in the summer, not to mention the bathing suit that was put on me even though I did not go in the water or went in only with a howl. As I remember it, until the age of about twelve or thirteen, I was ashamed of my feet, of my own stupidity, of my mother's ball gown in which she showed her beautiful shoulders. Sometimes I was ashamed of the stupidity of others, too, of the mistake of some idol of the moment. (Khodasevich* jokingly called shame for another's stupidity "hypertrophy of the feeling of responsibility.") But, of course, most of all I was ashamed of my bare toes. When I was washed in a wooden tub, I tried to make the soapy foam cover them, dress them in it. What was most terrifying for me was a pair of light, scraping sandals. "They won't sink in water or burn in fire," said the clerk of the shoe store in the Gostiny Dvor, proud of his wit, as he fitted them to me. It goes without saying that I was wearing ribbed black stockings so that I would somehow endure all this without howling. Those nonburning, nonsinking sandals became a symbol of summer horror for several years.

I didn't go to church. At first I was "taken." Then, when I grew up and could no longer be forced to go, I tried to stay away from the Saint-Mary-Appease-My-Grief icon, and other things with which I felt nothing in common. I remember, when I still had to attend, that every Sunday in the chapel there stood a row of small coffins containing the bodies of newborn infants—six, eight, sometimes even more. The infants were all alike, somewhat similar to dolls, somewhat to Easter suckling pigs (in the mouths of which you put a leaf of lettuce). Unchristened infants were buried on one side of the cemetery, christened ones on the other. Grandfather would say with nostalgia, "Yes, my boy," (he said "my boy" to me) "that's how it is. A godforsaken place! This is not Moscow province, or Orel province. Here, my boy, are our roads— seventy miles to the railroad, thirty-five miles to the nearest hospital, twenty-five miles to the doctor's assistant. And so on, my boy, and so on. No roads—that's how it is, my boy, lack of roads. Woods, swamps, mud. There you are in the slush," (he waved his hand) "when the bridges are carried off, and you can't fetch the doctor or anyone else. You hop, but

*Berberova's first husband was Vladimir Khodasevich (1886–1939), a poet.

you can't hop far enough. Filipp Gennadievich left the day before yesterday and has still not returned. So it is, my boy." ("All in good time," said the Tsar with a sad smile.)

I often sat behind the sofa, in a corner in an old armchair, when the staid muzhiks discussed their mortgages in the Farmer's Credit Bank, saying "they" to Grandfather and "we" to themselves in their low-class manner of address. One of them, Savva Kuzmich Karaulov (to get passports, the majority of them would use the name of the nearest landowner), who had a clever face and clean, strong hands, had recently been made a church elder. His son had set out to open a hardware store in the volost. The conversations, which both Karaulovs found interesting, went on for a long time, for Savva and Grandfather had nowhere to rush off to. It started getting dark. Dasha would bring in the freshly filled kerosene lamp, with its frosted lamp shade covered with all kinds of curious designs. A portrait of Uncle Serezha, my mother's brother who had accidentally shot himself while on a hunt at the age of eighteen, glittered on the wall. The armchair in which I sat was upholstered in some kind of ribbed material. I ran my fingers over the ribbing and dreamt that I had suddenly become blind and was learning to read with my fingers. You see, I would say to them, I have become blind, but this means nothing. I can read all that I want with my fingers. Then it dawned on me that it was time to have supper, that Grandmother would be angry at Grandfather and me, and, astonished, I saw that Savva Kuzmich Karaulov no longer sat before Grandfather, but had been replaced by Timofey, who had no surname, wore shabby bast sandals and sat on the edge of his chair, crumpling his cap in his hands. With tear-filled eyes he looked at Grandfather, who said:

"Eh, eh, my boy, I will give you land for a house, but who will build it for you? Anisya? Matrena? You have to marry them to someone first and get sons-in-law. Your older daughter will soon be twenty? Soon she will be a spinster. She has stayed on too long! Nevertheless, my boy, I will think it over. For the moment you take the timber—do you hear, I'm talking to you?—you take the timber. We will arrange some sort of an agreement. But no land. I have to think about it. I can't think that quickly. I am an old man, my boy, a very old Russian man, not some kind of a French fop. And now go to the kitchen. Go, go you will be given what's needed."

He went out to the dining room and I followed. He said, "Give me that ointment that Dr. Wasserkwelle in Kissingen prescribed for me when I ate too many oysters. Timofey keeps scratching himself under his arms." To this his wife, a fastidious and humorless society woman, answered, "He keeps scratching himself because he is full of lice. His foot-cloths have poisoned the whole atmosphere for us. Now we must air the place or we will all be *suffoqué.* "

She had an uncle who was a minister for Alexander III, and a cousin who was a minister for Nicholas II. But it all ended right there: the nephews were good for nothing, and the son had perished on a hunt.

There was a peculiar stillness in the dark Russian night. It lasted and lasted, as if it had had no beginning and would have no end. "And if you sink in it with your dreams and hopes," I said to myself, "it will drag you in, suck you in, swallow you up, this soundlessness, motionlessness, and lifelessness in the garden, the fields, the woods, right on out to the horizon." I sat on the window sill and thought that I might perhaps take up the cure of the sick, or become a village schoolteacher like the priest's daughters, or go till the fields like Tolstoy, or learn to build those splendid izbas with geraniums on the window sills and carved cocks on the eaves, where I would later put Timofey and his relatives. I was still choosing a profession for myself, and could still not decide. There was no one to get advice from, because at that time mankind, for me, was divided into two halves—well-wishers, who in my opinion understood even less than I about these matters, and enemies, who out of sheer meanness would not give good advice.

I knew how to love people and things then, but I also knew how to hate. I chiefly hated everything that had to do with the "nest," with family spirit, with paternalism, with the defense of small ones—that is, me—from something terrible or dangerous or simply risky. To warm myself near someone, to settle in some secure place, to find a shelter—in a way this seemed to me not only repugnant, but humiliating. I remember how I once, almost roughly, cast my mother's hand from my shoulder. This gesture, a pat on the shoulder, suddenly seemed to me not merely a tender hand movement but the symbol of protection and defense, which I could not endure. I cast the hand away and gave a deep sigh, as if I had pulled from my face a pillow that was about to suffocate me. From what—from what horrors and fears, visions and catastrophes, sicknesses and sadnesses—did they want to protect me? I am ready for them, I expect them, I burst out towards them. I am learning to write with both hands so that if someone cuts off my right one I would outwit him. And if I were condemned to the loss of both legs, I would crawl on the stumps, like that beggar on the church porch. It was not for nothing that for two days I had been learning to crawl on the floor when no one was looking, much to the astonishment of two dogs, a Saint Bernard and a dachshund.

Living in the "nest," I still, of course, did not understand the full import of this concept, but as I saw more than a gesture in the hand placed on the shoulder, so in the nest I saw a symbol. Never in the whole course of my life have I been able to free myself of this, and even now I think that an anthill is better than a nest, that there those near you *warm* you less (this warming is particularly repulsive to me), that in the anthill among a hundred thousand or a million you are freer than in a nest, where all sit around and look at one another, waiting until scientists finally discover ways to make us all mind readers. This does not mean that every family is a nest to me. There are exceptions and there will gradually be more of them. But the psychology of the nest is loathsome to me, and I always sympathize with one who flees his nest, even if he flees into an anthill, where though it is crowded one can find solitude— that most natural, most worthy state of man, that precious and intense state of being conscious of the world and of oneself.

The fundamentally romantic idea that the rock or the stone lives alone, while man lives in a collective, in close unison with his equals, is not only wrong, but in its very essence quite the opposite of the truth. The rock lives in the close unison of its molecules. It is a kind of indivisi- ble unity of billions upon billions of parts that make up one whole. But the farther we go from the stone and the closer we get to man, the more clearly the necessary and immutable differentiation appears. How sur- prisingly alive are false ideas! They even have their own evolution. At first they are highfalutin "truths," then humdrum "laws," and finally superstitions. The concept of immortality belongs, too, to the class of superstitions. Who needs immortality? Who, having lost the ability to change himself, wants to prevent others from changing? Indeed, what is immortality? We are told that that which does not die is immortal. But precisely what in nature does not die? Only that which *multiplies by dividing*. The amoeba is immortal because it is halved when it multi- plies, and thus, in a manner of speaking, it lives eternally. But we, who multiply through sex, die and cannot be immortal, because we do not divide.

Fear, and sometimes horror, of solitude belongs to that class of truth- less superstitions: it has become a kind of scarecrow. Nevertheless, before knowing anything of this, from my earliest years I strove to be alone. Nothing could have been more terrible for me than a whole day, from morning till night, spent with someone else rather than with my own thoughts—without giving an account to anyone for my actions, carrying on dialogues with myself, reading all that I came upon. At first, ads in *Speech* by which I was taught to read—"We recommend our experienced cook" or "Flat with firewood up for rent." Then, "Here is the cat. Is that a cat? Where is the rat? There is the bat," from a then modish ABC book (I have forgotten the name of the author); then, *Childhoodandyouth* (I learned much later that this was not one but three words—my eyes raced across them in a hurry to learn "what was next"); and, finally, *Crime and Punishment,* lying on my stomach under a tree, completely immersed, chewing on bits of grass, sometimes swallowing a tasteless spider along with the juices.

I remember an evening: I am lying in bed with fever, the Petersburg winter evening is blue and black outside, while next to me on the night table are a lamp, tea with lemon, and medicine. The clock shows ten minutes to six, a compress squeezes my throat. Mother sits stiffly and severely on a straight chair next to me. Why is she sitting? Why doesn't she go away? I want to be alone, to cover my head with my blanket, so that quietly in the darkness, warmth, and concentration I will overcome my illness; but she is there so that I won't feel lonesome. I am trying to imagine what will happen when she finally leaves and the room will become mine. I will hear the bells of tramways from Liteiny Avenue. I will imagine the sparks that shoot out in the snow from under the tram cars. I will think about the people walking home in their fur coats and hats, people about whom I would like to know everything knowable that I will never know. I will finally pull my book out of its hiding place under the mattress. But she still does not go away. She offers me tea, a cutlet, and, horror of horrors which turns me to ice, she offers to read aloud. "What's this? You have feet like ice!" she screams, though she doesn't go for the hot-water bottle but instead calls Dasha, who brings me a metal hot-water bottle all wrapped up in a towel, curved obviously in anticipation of someone's very round stomach, and from which water continually seeps. A thousand years pass and still she sits, until an odor of cabbage pie escapes from the kitchen. The telephone rings. Freedom! Everything is over somehow instantaneously. There I am alone in the large half-dark room, while on the foggy window the reflection of a lantern floats by. A cabman is conveying someone, for some reason, to some place. I will never, never find out who he was, where he was going, who lives next door, who thinks of me that very minute as I think of him (though we do not know each other). How much of everything there is in me—even more, it would seem, than there is around me. Life is big and beautiful. Life is long and huge, like the universe itself. I won't have time . . . I won't have time . . . to . . . Wait! Wait! Last a little longer, maybe some twenty or thirty years . . . No, that is too short a time. The fortuneteller said sixty. When will this be? It will be in the year 1961. Oh, what joy that this is still so far off, so infinitely far off, like from Kazan to Ryazan, from Ryazan to Erivan, to Lebedyan, to Tmutorokan . . . "You were delirious and reciting a lesson of geography," I am told when I open my eyes. It is time to take my temperature.

To that realm which I detested wholeheartedly belonged the Christmas tree, branches hung with crackers, candles, and foil. To me, it was the symbol of the "nest." I hated paper angels with stupid pink faces. I was bored by crackers. Not one dunce cap fit my head, as later hats would not. Candles flickered with the false assurance that it was more splendid to live by them than by tungsten lamps. It was impossible to accept this. I considered people who affirmed it my personal enemies. What was most important: in the apartment there suddenly appeared a center where I had to be instead of being alone and free, instead of sitting on the window sill behind the curtains admiring the frost patterns on the window glass, or at my desk in my room, or under the dinner table, or in the kitchen where the solitaire "Napoleon's tomb" was being played. In a word, I had to sit and admire the burning candles, look as if I liked angels and expected presents. Yet only unexpected things brought joy. I had to share the affectation of the adults so unpleasant to me, the same state in which I found people when they read bad verse or listened to gypsy songs. On the other hand, what joy I felt when the dead bare fir was finally carried out!

I feared affectation and false melancholy more than fire. It seemed to me that there was too much of it around, that it would somehow reach me and wear me out, and that I would then perish. There was indeed a lot of it around; for before the 1920's, when for the first time man's profound and important inner depths were unlocked and people revealed themselves, his lyric élans blossomed, and because they were universal, they were not only cheap but mediocre. I remember covers of magazines with whiskered men, and the expanded nostrils of Vera Kholodnaya, snake-woman, bird-woman, fairy-woman, lioness-woman, into which some of my classmates dreamt of transforming themselves but which only threw me into a state of panic. As usual, pushed to extremes either by the instinct of self-preservation or by cold reflection on these matters, I came to doubt, along with the affectation of lyricism, lyricism itself, with those awful verses about moonlit nights—and the nights themselves. All the Liebestraums gave me one and the same aftertaste— an aftertaste of something that is touched with finality, that will not survive the first shock, wherever it may come from, and prevents me from being fully armed for a first encounter with fate. Liebestraums rang out everywhere, bringing astounding delight to our mothers, who, then still quite young, felt that the sources of emotionalism and affectation had opened up to them, about them, for them. They no doubt dreamt that we would follow them into all these romances and nuances as into a worn shoe. As for our children, they would happily settle among them. But we refused to profit from these boons, and instead of semolina kasha, from childhood on we gnawed on the devil knows what, breaking our teeth, and very often hearing a rustling reproach somewhere: ungrateful, coarsened souls, insensitive and dry, they like poetry without meter, music without melody, painting without mood. I must confess that at about twelve I began to doubt the dialogue of Natasha and Sonya at the window, the night that Prince Andrey spent at Otradnoe, the charm of Kitty. To me, all this seemed to be a smoke screen, a camouflage for real life; all these lovely girls were in the very center of their Liebestraums, in the midst of their nest, and farther from me than a Polynesian savage.

No smoke screen over life, no emotional overtones of religion (twilight, icon-lamp, candles, chants for the dead). I developed a profound aversion to false comfort and cosyness. I wanted a hundred-watt light shining on a book in which everything was expressed, everything was said, a clear day, a black night, no ambiguous meanings, no sad improvisations that were covered by a veil of glances, sighs, and hints. These Fata Morganas seemed to me more terrible than cannon fire. Behind them lay my very own life, which I foresaw with the actual cannon fire that thundered over me thrice, my own struggle in which no one dared replace me, where I would not cede my place under fire. Life was gradually becoming a reality from which I had no intention of hiding behind anyone's back.

VERA BRITTAIN
(1893–1970)

Vera Brittain grew up in a comfortable middle-class household in the north of England and was a student at Somerville College, Oxford, where she was part of a brilliant group of women that included Dorothy Sayers, the mystery writer, and Winifred Holtby, the critic and novelist. After her first year at Somerville, less than a year after Britain declared war on Germany, Brittain left the university to serve as a VAD nurse—that is, a volunteer aide who had no training but served under trained, fully qualified nurses. She worked throughout the war in London, in Malta, and at the front in France. *Testament of Youth* (1933), based on diaries and letters written at the time, tells the story of her life from 1900 to 1925 and records with special poignancy the loss of virtually a generation of men, including her fiancé, Roland Leighton, and her brother, Edward Brittain. "Only, I felt, by some such attempt to write history in terms of personal life could I rescue something that might be of value, some element of truth and hope and usefulness, from the smashing up of my own youth by the War."

For another account by an English writer who served as a nurse during World War I, see Enid Bagnold's *A Diary without Dates,* and for an account of a woman trying to cope with a later war's devastation, compare Marguerite Duras, *The War.*

FROM *Testament of Youth*

On Sunday morning, June 16th,* I opened the *Observer,* which appeared to be chiefly concerned with the new offensive—for the moment at a standstill—in the Noyon-Montdidier sector of the Western Front, and instantly saw at the head of a column the paragraph for which I had looked so long and so fearfully:

ITALIAN FRONT ABLAZE

GUN DUELS FROM MOUNTAIN TO SEA

BAD OPENING OF AN OFFENSIVE

*The year is 1918—Ed.

The following Italian official *communiqué* was issued yesterday:

From dawn this morning the fire of the enemy's artillery, strongly countered by our own, was intensified from the Lagerina Valley to the sea. On the Asiago Plateau, to the east of the Brenta and on the middle Piave, the artillery struggle has assumed and maintains a character of extreme violence.

There followed a quotation from the correspondent of the *Corriere della Sera,* who described "the Austrian attack on the Italian positions in the neighbourhood of the Tonale Pass." "Possibly," he suggested,

this is the prelude of the great attack which the Austrian Army has been preparing for so long a time . . . The employment of heavy forces proves that this is not a merely isolated and local action, but the first move in a great offensive plan. The Austrian infantry and the *Feldjäger* have not passed. The Italian defenders met them in their first onslaught and immediately retook the few small positions that had been lost in the first moments of the fighting. This success on the part of the Italian defence is a good augury for the future.

"I'm afraid," I thought, feeling suddenly cold in spite of the warm June sunlight that streamed through the dining-room window. True, the *communiqué* didn't specifically mention the British, but then there was always a polite pretence on the part of the Press that the Italians were defending the heights above Vicenza entirely on their own. The loss of a "few small positions," however quickly recaptured, meant—as it always did in dispatches—that the defenders were taken by surprise and the enemy offensive had temporarily succeeded. Could I hope that Edward had missed it through being still in hospital? I hardly thought so; he had said as long ago as June 3rd that he expected to be "back again in a few days."

However, there was nothing to do in the midst of one's family but practise that concealment of fear which the long years of war had instilled, thrusting it inward until one's subconscious became a regular prison-house of apprehensions and inhibitions which were later to take their revenge. My mother had arranged to stay with my grandmother at Purley that week in order to get a few days' change from the flat; it was the first time that she had felt well enough since her breakdown to think of going away, and I did not want the news from Italy to make her change her plans. At length, though with instinctive reluctance, she allowed herself to be prevailed upon to go, but a profound depression hung over our parting at Charing Cross.

A day or two later, more details were published of the fighting in Italy, and I learnt that the Sherwood Foresters had been involved in the "show" on the Plateau. After that I made no pretence at doing anything but wander restlessly round Kensington or up and down the flat, and, though my father retired glumly to bed every evening at nine o'clock, I gave up writing the semi-fictitious record which I had begun of my life in France. Somehow I couldn't bring myself even to wrap up the *Spectator* and *Saturday Review* that I sent every week to Italy, and they remained in my bedroom, silent yet eloquent witnesses to the dread which my father and I, determinedly conversing on commonplace topics, each refused to put into words.

By the following Saturday we had still heard nothing of Edward. The interval usually allowed for news of casualties after a battle was seldom so long as this, and I began, with an artificial sense of lightness unaccompanied by real conviction, to think that there was perhaps, after all, no news to come. I had just announced to my father, as we sat over tea in the dining-room, that I really must do up Edward's papers and take them to the post office before it closed for the week-end, when there came the sudden loud clattering at the front-door knocker that always meant a telegram.

For a moment I thought that my legs would not carry me, but they behaved quite normally as I got up and went to the door. I knew what was in the telegram—I had known for a week—but because the persistent hopefulness of the human heart refuses to allow intuitive certainty to persuade the reason of that which it knows, I opened and read it in a tearing anguish of suspense.

"Regret to inform you Captain E. H. Brittain M.C. killed in action Italy June 15th."

"No answer," I told the boy mechanically, and handed the telegram to my father, who had followed me into the hall. As we went back into the dining-room I saw, as though I had never seen them before, the bowl of blue delphiniums on the table; their intense colour, vivid, ethereal, seemed too radiant for earthly flowers.

Then I remembered that we should have to go down to Purley and tell the news to my mother.

Late that evening, my uncle brought us all back to an empty flat. Edward's death and our sudden departure had offered the maid—at that time the amateur prostitute—an agreeable opportunity for a few hours' freedom of which she had taken immediate advantage. She had not even finished the household handkerchiefs, which I had washed that morning and intended to iron after tea; when I went into the kitchen I found them still hanging, stiff as boards, over the clothes-horse near the fire where I had left them to dry.

Long after the family had gone to bed and the world had grown silent,

I crept into the dining-room to be alone with Edward's portrait. Carefully closing the door, I turned on the light and looked at the pale, pictured face, so dignified, so steadfast, so tragically mature. He had been through so much—far, far more than those beloved friends who had died at an earlier stage of the interminable War, leaving him alone to mourn their loss. Fate might have allowed him the little, sorry compensation of survival, the chance to make his lovely music in honour of their memory. It seemed indeed the last irony that he should have been killed by the countrymen of Fritz Kreisler, the violinist whom of all others he had most greatly admired.

And suddenly, as I remembered all the dear afternoons and evenings when I had followed him on the piano as he played his violin, the sad, searching eyes of the portrait were more than I could bear, and falling on my knees before it I began to cry "Edward! Oh, Edward!" in dazed repetition, as though my persistent crying and calling would somehow bring him back.

After Edward was killed no wealth of affectionate detail flowed in to Kensington, such as had at least provided occupation for Roland's family at the end of 1915. Roland had been one of the first of his regimental mess to suffer wounds and death, but the many fellow-officers who would have written of Edward with knowledge and admiration had "gone west" before him in previous offensives—the Somme, Arras, the Scarpe, Messines, Passchendaele—that he had either missed or survived. Of the men with whom he had lived and worked in Italy before the Asiago Battle, I hardly knew even the names.

As time went on, however, we did get three letters—from the officer who was second in command of his company, from his servant, and from a non-combatant acquaintance working with the Red Cross—which told us that Edward's part in withstanding the Austrian offensive had been just what we might have expected from his record of coolness and fortitude on the Somme and throughout the 1917 Battles of Ypres. Of these letters, that from the private was the most direct and vivid.

"I was out on Trench Duty with Capt. Brittain about 3 A.M. on the morning of the 15th June when we were caught in a terrific Barrage; we managed to get back to our Headquarters safely. About 8 A.M. the enemy launched a very heavy attack and penetrated the left flank of our Company and began to consolidate. Seeing that the position was getting critical Captain Brittain with a little help from the French led a party of men over driving the enemy out again. Shortly after the trench was regained Capt. Brittain who was keeping a sharp look out on the enemy was shot through the Head by an enemy sniper, he only lived a few minutes. He has been buried in a British Cemetery behind our lines.

. . . Allow me to express my deepest sympathy. Captain Brittain was a very gallant officer and feared nothing."

The cemetery, so the Red Cross friend told us, was in the mountains, 5,000 feet up; he hadn't seen it himself, but Edward's burial the day after the battle was attended by his second in command and the quarter-master of the 11th, who described it to him; they were the only officers out of the line.

" 'Brit.,' " said the quartermaster, "was buried in his blanket with 4 other officers. He was placed lying at the head of the grave upon which a cross 'In loving memory' with the names, etc., was placed."

This seemed to be as much as any of our correspondents, who had not themselves taken part in the battle, were likely to tell us, but long before we received their brief information, I saw by the casualty list which contained Edward's name that his twenty-six-year-old colonel had been wounded, obviously in the same action. Knowing that he, the only sur-viving officer who had been in the battalion with Edward since 1914, could tell me, if he chose, more than anybody else, I visited Harrington House—then the headquarters for information about the wounded and missing—until I tracked him down to a luxurious officers' hospital in the region of Park Lane.

I had heard, from time to time, a good deal from Edward about his youthful C.O., for whom he seemed to have great respect without much affection. Ambitious and intrepid, the son of a Regular Army officer who could not afford to equip him for a peacetime commission, the young man had found in the War the fulfilment of his baffled longing for military distinction. Since 1914 he had been the regiment's "profes-sional survivor," fighting unscathed through every action from the Somme to Asiago, and picking up out of each battle another "pip" and a new decoration. When the 11th Sherwood Foresters were ordered to Italy he went there in command of the battalion; at the time of the Austrian offensive he had already been awarded the D.S.O., M.C., Croix de Guerre and several minor decorations, and from Asiago—which dis-abled him just sufficiently to keep him in England until almost the end of the War—he gathered the crowning laurels of the V.C.

I did not, of course, know that he was destined for this superlative glory when in stoical desperation I went straight from Harrington House to his hospital. My mother, who had not yet received the letters from Italy, had said emphatically that she did not want to hear any details, but though I dreaded more than death whatever I might be self-condemned to learn, I was driven and impelled by a remorseless determination to find out as much as I could. All the same, I did wish that I had someone other than the colonel from whom to demand it, and half hoped, half feared, that he might be too ill to be interviewed by a stranger. But when

I heard that he was severely but not dangerously wounded in the leg, I sent a message by a nurse to ask if Captain Brittain's sister might see him for a moment. She returned almost immediately to fetch me, and, feeling half suffocated, I followed her up the stairs.

I found the colonel propped up in bed, with a large "cradle" over his leg; his features looked pale and drawn, and his dark eyes burned intently from their sunken sockets as I came into the room. Quite obviously he did not want to see me, but this I understood; no wounded man ever did want to see the female relatives of a friend who had been killed; he always expected them to break down, or make a scene, or ask awkward questions. It was a hard young face, I decided; the luminous, vulnerable eyes were probably some accident of heredity. I resolved to be as brusque and brief as possible, and found in the colonel's sister—a girl somewhat older than himself, with gentler features and the same surprisingly tender expression, who sat beside his bed—an unexpected ally in both the asking and the answering of questions.

"I should have known you were Brittain's sister—you've got the same eyes," he began abruptly, and then gave me a brief, matter-of-fact account of the battle without saying very much about Edward's part in it. But the moment for describing his death had to come; he was "sniped," the colonel said, by an Austrian officer just after the counter-attack which he had organised and led had regained the lost positions.

"Where was he shot?" I inquired, as steadily as I could.

Again the young man cast over me his keen, searching glance, as though I were a subaltern whose ability to go calmly "over the top" he was trying to estimate; then he answered curtly: "Through the head."

I looked at him in silent reproach, for I frankly did not believe him. At that late stage of the War—as I had realised only too well from the agitated efforts of Army Sisters to mitigate truth with compassion in letters describing the last moments of men who had died in hospital— the colonels and company commanders on the various fronts were so weary of writing gruesome details to sorrowing relatives, that the number of officers who were instantaneously and painlessly shot through the head or the heart passed far beyond the bounds of probability. But when, a few days later, the quite independent letters from Italy confirmed the colonel's statement, I realised that he had not been trying to spare my feelings, and that Edward had escaped Victor's fate only by the sudden death which he himself had repeatedly said that he would prefer to blindness.

Throughout his protracted convalescence I haunted the colonel quite shamelessly, for I still felt convinced that he knew far more than he chose to reveal. Later in the year an acquaintance of mine reported a conversation which she had heard in a railway carriage between a group of Sherwood Foresters who had been in the battle of 15th June. One of them remarked that he had had "a real good officer, a slim dark chap . . . and a regular *nut*. You'd have thought that he hadn't an ounce of ginger in him, but Lord! miss, he didn't know what fear was." This officer's name, the man said, was "Brittain," and he'd deserved the V.C. for pushing back the enemy "by sheer force" in that "do" on the Plateau.

This type of appreciative judgment from a private who admired his officer was, of course, common enough, but an inward certainty possessed me that it was not unfounded; I could bear, I felt, the colonel's superior claim to the V.C. if only I knew why the men had thought that Edward deserved it too. So, still passionately determined to learn whatever of the truth remained undisclosed, I accepted the colonel's occasional polite but reluctant invitations to luncheon or tea, tried to make him talk though I always felt embarrassed in his presence, and even forced myself to go to Buckingham Palace to watch him receive his Victoria Cross.

But it was all quite useless. Since adding the V.C. to his collection of decorations, the colonel appeared to have become nervously afraid that every young woman he met might want to marry him, and his fears were not altogether unnatural, for with his long row of ribbons, his premature seniority, his painful limp, and his pale, dark-eyed air of a weary Crusader, the tall young man was an attractive and conspicuous figure wherever he went. In those weeks when he sat so securely upon the pinnacle of his martial ambitions, he could hardly have been expected to realise that no decoration could make him appear to me other than a stiff young disciplinarian, impregnated with all the military virtues but limited in imagination and benevolence, or to believe that I was not fascinated by his medals, but merely anxious for information.

The more assiduously I pursued him in the hope of learning the details that I sought, the more resolutely he faded out of my existence until, after the Armistice, I lost sight of him altogether.

Before he went back to the front just in time for the ending of the War, the 11th Sherwood Foresters and several other British regiments had left the demoralised Austrians to the mercy of the now jubilant Italians and returned to France, where the surviving officers from Edward's company had been killed in the last great push. So whether Edward's part in the vital counter-attack on the Plateau really involved some special act of heroism, I shall now never know.

Even if I had found out, it would have made little difference at the time, for as the sudden closing-down of silence upon our four years' correspondence gradually forced on my stunned consciousness the bare fact that Edward was dead, I became progressively unable to take in other facts, or to estimate their value.

So incredible was our final separation that it made life itself seem unreal. I had never believed that I could actually go on living without that lovely companionship which had been at my service since childhood, that perfect relation which had involved no jealousy and no agitation, but only the profoundest confidence, the most devoted understanding, on either side. Yet here I was, in a world emptied of that unfailing consolation, most persistently, most unwillingly alive. I was even alive enough to unpack his possessions when they were returned to us from Italy, and to find amongst them *The Muse in Arms,* which had arrived just after the battle, with my poem inside, unopened and unread. I knew then that he had died without even being aware of my last endeavour to show him how deeply I loved and admired him.

The return of the poem began a period of isolation more bleak, more complete and far more prolonged than the desperate months in 1916 which had followed the death of Roland. My early diaries had been full of the importance of "standing alone," "being sufficient unto one's self," and I sometimes re-read them with sombre cynicism during the time that, for nearly two years after Edward's death, I had to be "sufficient unto myself" whether I liked it or not. However deep our devotion may be to parents, or to children, it is our contemporaries alone with whom understanding is instinctive and entire, and from June 1918 until about April 1920, I knew no one in the world to whom I could speak spontaneously, or utter one sentence completely expressive of what I really thought or felt. I "stood alone" in very truth—and I hope profoundly that I may never repeat the experience. It lasted so long, perhaps, because I decided in the first few weeks after his loss that nothing would ever really console me for Edward's death or make his memory less poignant; and in this I was quite correct, for nothing ever has.

During this period, one or two sympathetic friends wrote earnestly to me of the experimental compensations of Spiritualism. As always in wartime, the long casualty lists had created throughout England a terrible interest in the idea of personal survival, and many wives and mothers and sisters had turned to *séances* and mediums in the hope of finding some indication, however elusive, of a future reunion "beyond the sun."

But I knew that this short cut to convictions which I longed to feel held no comfort for me. I remember walking down the shimmering Sunday emptiness of Kensington High Street on the hot summer morning after the telegram came, intoxicated, strangely *exaltée,* lifted into incongruous ecstasy by a sense that Edward's invisible presence was walking there beside me. After that, everything relapsed into paralysis. I did not want to speak or even to think much about him, and I could find no relief, as after Roland's death, by translating my grief into long replies to letters of sympathy. There was no rush to poems now, no black quotation book, no little library of consecrated volumes; we never had a late meal, nor changed one item of our dull routine. I felt enormously, interminably tired; that was all. One had to go on living because it was less trouble than finding a way out, but the early ideals of the War were all shattered, trampled into the mud which covered the bodies of those with whom I had shared them. What was the use of hypocritically seeking out exalted consolations for death, when I knew so well that there were none?

One day I remembered how Edward had told me that Geoffrey's last letter, written two days before he was killed at Monchy-le-Preux, had ended with the words: "Till we meet again, Here or in the Hereafter." Had they met now in the hereafter, I wondered? On the whole I could not believe that they had. Edward, like Roland, had promised me that if a life existed beyond the grave, he would somehow come back and make me know of it. I had thought that, of the two, Roland, with his reckless determination, would be the more likely to trespass from the infinite across the boundaries of the tangible, and incur any penalties that might be imposed. But he had sent no sign and Edward sent none; nor did I expect one. I knew now that death was the end and that I was quite alone. There was no hereafter, no Easter morning, no meeting again; I walked in a darkness, a dumbness, a silence, which no beloved voice would penetrate, no fond hope illumine. Only, as I went mechanically about my daily occupations, three lines from Sir Walter Raleigh's farewell verses kept beating through my brain:

> Even such is Time, that takes in trust
> Our youth, our joys, our all we have,
> And pays us but with earth and dust.

ÉMILIE CARLES
(1900–1979)

From a peasant family with land in a remote valley in the French Alps, Émilie Allais grew up doing the hard work of the fields and stables. With the brief exception of some months in Paris at the end of World War I, working and studying, she spent all her life in the Clarée Valley and the mountains nearby. She became a schoolteacher who tried to get her students to read and think for themselves, but she always understood how shocking this effort was to the narrow, suspicious people she lived among. She married Jean Carles, a self-educated, freethinking workingman, whom she met on a train, and for a while in the 1930s, as described in this selection, they ran their house as a hotel for workers. In her old age Émilie Carles led her neighbors in a successful fight to save their valley from a proposed superhighway. Her autobiography, published in France in 1977, originally had a more flavorful title than the one it has been given in English, *A Life of Her Own.* In French it was called *Une soupe aux herbes sauvages* (A Wild Herb Soup).

For an account by a woman from a peasant family on the other side of the world, in formerly French Indochina, compare Le Ly Hayslip, *When Heaven and Earth Changed Places.* For other accounts of life in France, compare Simone de Beauvoir, *The Prime of Life,* Colette, *My Apprenticeships,* Marguerite Duras, *The War,* M. F. K. Fisher, *As They Were,* and Anaïs Nin, *Diary.*

FROM *A Life of Her Own*

AGAINST ALL COMERS

Jean Carles took advantage of the July 14 holiday to visit my father and ask for my hand in marriage. We were in the meadow at Fourches that day, turning the hay. I saw a young man coming toward us on a bicycle, wearing a straw hat and white trousers. I didn't recognize him, from a distance you'd have thought it was Maurice Chevalier, he really looked wonderful. I watched him stop to ask each group where to find me, and people point to our meadow. It was right in the middle of the haying season. Peasants run around like crazy when the hay is ripe, never pausing until it's all reaped and stored. That is exactly what we were doing, not losing a moment because although the day was beautiful, possible storms are always a worry.

My mother had been struck by lightning twenty-four years earlier in the very field we were working.

I said: "Look, he's here."

My father immediately stopped turning the hay to watch him approach. He knew I was seeing Jean Carles and I'd mentioned his visit, but I couldn't help feeling a little apprehensive. I had often thought about the two men meeting, and of course I wanted things to go as smoothly as possible, that's to be expected. They were so different I had reason to fear the worst. But everything went well. Jean greeted my father, introduced himself, and seeing we were in the middle of work, pulled off his jacket, rolled up his sleeves and set to work, turning hay right along with us.

That evening when we were back at the house, he asked permission to take a hand at the cooking. I said: "Go right ahead." I had no idea he knew how to cook, and he started off with his characteristic good humor.

"Fine. I'm going to make you tomatoes provençale." He talked as he worked, telling us about his life, his travels, what he'd seen. My father couldn't get over it, and neither could I. Things went so well that it was agreed Jean Carles would spend three days with us.

The next day he asked if he could do the kitchen over. It hadn't been painted in fourteen years and was sadly in need of a new coat. He didn't only scrape, scour, and whitewash the walls, he decorated them as well. He fashioned a stencil simulating ceramic tiles and with that he drew a colored fresco all around. With white walls the kitchen was transformed beyond recognition. Instantly the gray, dark kitchen I'd seen for years welcomed light with the sunbeams bouncing off the wall. I think my father couldn't get over the way Jean transformed the kitchen in such a short space of time.

But that was not the main point. When Jean asked for my hand, my father did not give a straight answer. He certainly didn't say no, he merely assumed a somewhat distant patriarchal manner, and said:

"I will let you know."

Still, "I will let you know" was closer to yes than no. Let's say that on principle, my father wanted to be coaxed. I did not have the slightest doubt that we would marry. I was twenty-eight and I was determined to take full responsibility for myself, but for many reasons my father's consent was important to me.

And so Jean left with an "almost yes," and in the days that followed I was sure I had successfully convinced my father. I was happy. But shortly afterward, things began to go wrong; my father wanted me to reconsider my choice: he explained that on thinking it over, he did not approve of the marriage. It bothered him that Jean Carles was a workingman with no property under the sun. In his eyes it was unthinkable for me to marry a man who didn't own anything, and he asked me to think it over too.

Coming from him, from my father, and on that subject, it was virtually an order. In a word, the suitor didn't amount to much; he had to be sent packing because he was nothing but a tramp. I saw the old antagonism between peasants and workers rising up once more. They all work like dogs, they all sweat blood and water to survive, to eat, to clothe and lodge themselves, but they despise each other nonetheless. My father was one of those people who cannot imagine a convergence of two worlds, his own and the other unknown world he scorned without knowing why.

I fought right back, no one would tell me what to do; father or not, I would not go along.

"I don't know what you want,' I told him. "When you're a workingman you've got your fortune in your two hands. *You* saw what he did, how he cleaned up the kitchen in no time at all; besides, he's nice—there isn't any reason for me to change my mind."

I defended myself with all the passion I could summon, I was ready to do anything except give in: my happiness and my life were at stake. The idea of anyone else making my decisions for me was revolting, and I was not at a loss for arguments.

"Maybe you want an incompetent, alcoholic son-in-law like the one at Draille; well, I don't. There aren't any men around here, all we've got are louts. You won't ever make me back down; I'll never find such a fine man again; therefore, the answer is *yes* and if you don't like it, you can do what you please."

"All right," he said, "If there's nothing to be done, you do what you like."

Things would have been easier if my father had been alone. But there was the family; my father wasn't the worst of the lot because he loved me; I think he truly wanted me to be happy, and he sensed that what I wanted was not wrong. But one of my uncles stepped in as well, a tough man who had no reason to put on kid gloves with me. It all came down to family property; that was the fundamental question, but no one dared talk about it openly. I remember a conversation with my uncle. He said bluntly:

"You are not to marry that harem-chaser!"

In his haste to discredit Jean Carles at any cost, he had unconsciously mixed up "harum-scarum" and "skirt-chaser."

"And why not? What do you know about him?" I said.

"You're letting your feelings run away with you; the man's a good-for-nothing. We've had inquiries made, and if you are unable to keep a level head, with all your education, we will do it for you."

I was beside myself at such maneuvers and I got tough.

"What?" I said. "You have negative information? If you do, you must show it to me."

"We have no information to give you, all we have is advice, and it's advice that you are going to follow."

The more he added, the more transparent the scheme became. They didn't have any information; if they'd had the slightest knowledge, they surely would have used it. It was unworthy of my father; in a sense, he too had allowed his brother to use him. I stood fast, and once more I said no.

Jean did not have the same family problems, but he did have a mother who was a phenomenon in her own way.

Jean Carles invited me to visit him in Tarascon where he was painting a moviehouse. His mother was with him. It was an opportunity to meet her, so I went. They were both waiting for me when I reached the station. From the start, Jean's mother was as unpleasant as she could be. She was a very tall woman, much taller than I, and she wanted to impress me with her manners. The first thing she said was:

"So this is *it*!" looking at me as if I were a worm. Those words hurt, and I remembered them for a long time.

Jean did everything he could to smooth things over, but his mother had set the tone. Every time we were alone, she did not miss a chance to humiliate me:

"When I think of the beautiful girls who were after him; there was a schoolteacher too, but not like you—she was elegant and rich. What's gotten into Jean? What's the matter with him?"

It was unbearable. I think Jean did not realize what his mother was putting me through with her sarcasm. Of course, he told me to overlook all that, grit my teeth, and wait till we were married, but that was hardly satisfactory. Nevertheless, we loved each other enough for me to accept a great many things, and I did even more: at his request, I took his mother with me when I went home to Val-des-Prés.

"You'll take my mother up to Val-des-Prés; it'll be good for her, and I'll join you when I finish my job here."

I agreed. I don't know why I agreed, but I did it in full knowledge of the risks implied for us. She too longed to see our marriage plans quashed; that was so in line with my own family's plans that during her visit in Val-des-Prés, she managed to strike up a friendship with one of her own kind, my bitch of an aunt, and they both tried to break our engagement.

When Jean arrived, I went to meet him. His mother had put me through hell with her slander, and I was determined to put an end to all that. I blurted out:

"If you want to do me a favor, pack your bag—not tonight, it's too late, but first thing in the morning—take your mother and go, don't let me see your face again!"

"But what's going on? What is so terrible?"

"Look here, it's been unbearable, I've spent every night biting my pillow in bed so they wouldn't hear me crying. Your mother is impossible."

"Are you marrying me or my mother?"

"You, of course, but . . ."

"But what? What have *I* done to you?"

"Nothing, but . . ."

"So?"

"Look Jean, this past week I've heard the same sentences all day long; your mother can't stand me and she talks about it to anyone who'll listen, even when I'm right there: 'Jean could have done better; if he were a minor, I'd prevent such foolishness; there's still time, and I'll try to change his mind about marrying Émilie.' I've had it. I've been hearing that for ten days and it's enough already. Besides, she and my aunt, they've been saying the most awful things about me; my aunt said I go off on my bicycle for rendezvous in the woods; I've already been called a whore, but at least by a drunken woman who's not from around here, while those two. . . ! To say that about me when you know very well what I use that bike for, I ride to Le Lauzet."

It's true. At that point, I was seething with exasperation and resolved for the worst, including breaking off. Fortunately Jean took matters in hand, starting with his mother. He had it out with her, apparently crossing the t's and dotting the i's because tongues stopped wagging and everything was back in order. There was no perfect harmony, but it was bearable. Up to the wedding. That day Jean's mother launched a new attack; following Jean around, she'd poke him in the back and say:

"Come on, don't be in such a hurry to say yes."

That day my sister Rose who'd come from Lyons for the wedding chipped in her two cents. She ran after me to say: "There's still time," and after Jean with: "You should have married me. Émilie's too young for you, you'll never get much good out of her, while I'm an experienced woman."

All the same, we were married. It wasn't a big wedding, everything was limited to a strict minimum with the customary family, witnesses, and mayor in attendance.

We ate at home, and Jean catered the lunch himself as we had decided so that we could save money. Jean didn't have a cent coming in, in fact he had debts, and that was one of the reasons that had led him to postpone the wedding. "I have debts, I have debts," he'd say. It wasn't really bad; they were not even his debts but his brother's, and I told him: "At our age, it's time to live together, we'll work off the debts together just as we'll work out the rest."

My father didn't know. If he had, I think it would have been a dreadful blow for him. Furthermore, Jean and I were married without a contract, and that, I am convinced, made it a red letter day as they had never been done in those parts. By custom contracts were drawn up for every marriage, absurd documents, listing what each party brought to the union. I was against it for loads of reasons, and it took a quarrel with my father and my uncle to get my point of view across. I told them:

"It's not worth it, neither Jean nor I want one; if there are children, everything will go to them by law, and if there aren't, we'll see later on."

I wouldn't hear of it. In my eyes, a contract humiliates the person who has nothing. You go to the notary and you draw up the list. We would have written: "Mlle Allais: one house, situated at such and such a place, with so many rooms, and so many outbuildings, covering such and such an area, land worth so much, furniture, linens, livestock, and all the rest," whereas Jean would have listed what? Nothing. I knew that if our positions had been reversed, Jean would have acted the same way, but the others did not understand, all they thought about was material interests. We could not come to an understanding. They talked to me about property and full coffers, and I spoke to them about another kind of wealth. To me, the coffers are empty if the owner has neither love nor human warmth; however, a person with nothing can fulfill a kindred soul—but how could I have made them understand?

Jean was authentic wealth, the only kind I had always wanted and never had. A head full of dreams, a smile laden with promises, a heart heavy with all the goodness on earth, such was the wealth offered and given me. Material wealth cannot compare. That is why I was opposed to marriage contracts. When you love someone, you share everything, and if you part, the contract will not cure the pain. It is nothing but a matter of sous, and for me there is not a shadow of doubt that money soils whatever it touches.

My new life was totally different from the one I had led up to then. I'd been resigned to my life, telling myself I would never know anything but work and devotion to my family. It was not despair, but rather acceptance of my lot, and at twenty-six, twenty-seven, I told myself it was all over and I'd stay an old maid. Yet it occurred to me from time to time that I could have a child. It was the time when a number of women were seeking emancipation, it was the postwar Roaring Twenties with their bachelor girls and the reemergence of suffragette ideas. I would have liked to have had a child, but it wasn't easy. In public education, for example, an unwed mother was automatically dismissed and that's not all, there were other problems, too, like the difficulty of raising a child without a father. By chance, I came across a book on the subject, the story of a young postal worker who decided to have a baby without getting married; it was called *Madame 60 bis*. The subject was indeed the suffering of her fatherless child; she told how there was always some imbecile to call him "bastard" or "love child" at school or anywhere he went. The story gave me food for thought.

Meeting Jean Carles changed all that. Henceforth I could be a maman just as I longed to be. Jean and I agreed on that. My only fear was a bad pregnancy like my sister Catherine's, so I went to see a doctor to find out where things stood.

"No," the fellow told me, "you're completely normal; there is nothing to worry about and you can have as many children as you want."

"Once bitten twice shy," they say, but it doesn't help to watch out or take every precaution; when calamity is on the way, nothing can stop it. My first child was a boy, but he did not survive his difficult delivery. The infant presented so badly that forceps were necessary; the doctor made a false move, injuring the head with his instruments, and the baby was already dead when the doctor pulled him out. I did not even see him; I was so worn out that I was conscious of nothing but pain and tears. But the ultimate absurdity was that while I thrashed about in torment and Jean was like a madman, incapable of tending to anything, the mayor had the infant's body buried in the far end of the cemetery, in the common grave reserved for people who've been drowned or hanged. That is what happened. I know we could have demanded compensation, but neither Jean nor I had the heart to take the necessary steps; we both thought it was better not to look back, and so life went on, life was stronger than all the rest. One year later I gave birth to my son Jojo, and two years after that I had a little girl we named Janny. Jean and I were fulfilled.

Those were happy years. Jean was an extraordinarily considerate and attentive companion, always seeking to please me, and from him I received all of earth's gifts. I always had the privilege of the first violets he had gathered under the dry leaves, the first strawberries from the garden, the first cherries. For my bedside table, he brought the first roses, and to my plate the first March trout. And so, the man who owned nothing under the sun shone on the people around him. Through the warmth he radiated, the gifts he lavished on everyone, Jean Carles dealt out happiness.

He was head over heels in love with liberty. For him there was nothing higher. He stood up for his ideas and was well informed. I had never seen anyone read so much. Right after work, he'd settle down in a corner to read. He subscribed to all the progressive periodicals of the day: *Le Canard enchaîné, The Human Homeland, On the Outside,* and contemporary literature. It was through him that I discovered Panaït Istrati, Céline, Albert Londres, and many others, as well as Henri Poulaille's *New Age in Literature.*

Jean was an idealist, authentic, uncompromising; he was like my father in that respect, he too lived his ideas and would never have tolerated the slightest gap between what he said and what he did. That was not easy, because it's all very well to preach generosity and fraternity, but then you need the wherewithal. It didn't matter. Jean was also a dreamer and a poet; he loathed bureaucratic pettiness, and he couldn't count—or he didn't want to. I am the one who kept our accounts and he called me "the ant,"* telling the children:

"Your mother is unique in this world, there's not another like her."

He might well say that because I don't know how he would have managed without me. Money slipped through his fingers like water; he gave away what he had without counting, and when there was nothing left and his purse was empty, he'd say: "But that's impossible!" and I would reply: "Of course it is, there's nothing left." He counted on the ant so much that the ant had to save up. It was a matter of temperament. At times, I would fly into a rage, and then Jean would put his arms around me and recite one of those poems he had a knack for composing:

> Oh the sweet joy of the lips of a friend,
> To light each day's life with fond words of love,
> And on your lip lighting for yearning caress
> Pour into your soul, that trinity fine
> Of Love and Goodness and Madness divine.

Thus sang Jean Carles, the man who owned nothing under the sun.

---

*In La Fontaine's fable "The Grasshopper and the Ant," the ant spends the summer gathering food for the winter while the improvident grasshopper just sings, enjoying life, but putting nothing aside for the future—ED.

My Four Wards

One day, Carles said to me: "Look, if we're going to stay here, in a house like this, we might as well try to do something with it. It's a big house, most of the space is unused, I know how to cook—we could turn it into a hotel."

I liked the idea. For one thing, Jean had had it with knocking around as a painter, working for other people, and even more important, there was nobody to keep up the farm. Together with my father, we talked it over and finally decided to go ahead. We had some money set aside but everything had to be done, and since we didn't have a cent coming in, hiring a contractor was out of the question. We did every bit of it ourselves, first of all fitting out rooms, installing running water and putting up partitions.

Jean had also said: "First we'll do the rooms and then we'll set up the hotel when we can"; it's true that we couldn't be in a hurry with our methods and our means, and it took us several years to create something more or less finished. The idea was not enough in itself; we needed money to buy bricks, cement, washstands, and pipes. Jean was our mason, and he asked his brother to come give us a hand. He also took care of the bedding, managing pretty well with the springs and mattresses, and my father combed out wool from his sheep that we used to stuff the mattresses and chairs, and we had our blankets made with it. This was indeed a family enterprise.

There wasn't much of a tourist business then, it was still in its infancy. We started out by placing classified ads in the papers we subscribed to, *The Human Homeland, On the Outside,* and the first year, we had five guests, then it went up to fifteen, and each year there were a few more. We started out serving meals family style, but eventually we had to give it up because family-style eating is very special. In the first place, you can't have too many people, then the guests who happen to be there have to like each other; if they don't the slightest squabble will throw things off completely. All it takes is one uncomfortable person to do in the whole table.

Jean found a name for the hotel: Les Arcades. From the very beginning we threw ourselves into the business body and soul, and for me it was a major change. Besides plastering and painting, I looked after the hotel from the time it opened. After school, I did the rooms and washed the linens, waited table in the evening and cleaned the kitchen, not to mention the hours I spent keeping the books, making up orders, and paying bills. All that was unimportant to me, we had created the hotel together and it was our life. This is what I said to Jean:

"Instead of going away on vacation, we have our hotel."

His answer was: "Wait till you see our happy old age; for now we have to work our tails off, but one day we'll live like kings; we'll put money aside from your pension when you retire, and every year we'll take a trip."

We never did take a trip. We thought the hotel would be a good investment, but it never earned much profit. The seasons are too short here, and people did not usually take time off in the thirties before paid vacations were required by law.

No matter, we were happy. The house had recovered its past life and liveliness; besides Jean and me, there were our two children, my father and my mother-in-law who lived with us, and more and more often Marie-Rose's children coming to us for refuge.

For in the meantime Marie-Rose had come back from the psychiatric hospital. The doctor told us she was cured, but the fact is that her health depended on the kind of life she would lead, and the moment she came back, her husband started beating and harassing her again. They were both crazy, in their own ways, and when they were together, they couldn't help falling back into their old wild life. Neither one of them was able to make decisions or assume responsibility; having children was the only thing they agreed on. Marie-Rose gave birth eight times while she lived with Jacques Mercier; only four children survived.

It was pitiful. When a more serious crisis erupted, they would all go their separate ways, my sister would hide somewhere or other without bothering about anything, and the youngsters managed as best they could. Marie would come to us for shelter with her brother and sisters. She was about ten at the time I'm talking about, as mature and serious as an adult. She was like all children forced to protect themselves: she made her own decisions. When her parents had a fight, she would flee from La Draille with the smallest child in her arms, pulling along the two others who were hanging onto her smock, one on each side. Marie had a sixth sense when she came, she would say to herself: I mustn't go to my godmother's house as long as there's a guest up, or they'll wonder what we're doing at our aunt's at this hour of night.

Meanwhile, she hid with the others in the shed across the road, waiting in the dark—and frequently the cold—until I was alone in the kitchen. I made it a practice to give the kitchen a thorough going over every day when the last guest left and I was by myself. I would clean the tables, benches, and floor with caustic soda and a scrubbing brush, and the girl always waited for that time to come in. You should have seen those four youngsters walk in. I'd say:

"So, you're back. Have you had anything to eat at least?"

"Yes, Aunt Émilie, we had a little soup before we left."

"And where's your mother?"

"I don't have any idea."

"And your father?"

"Oh, like always, he grabbed the axe and wanted to cut our mother with it, so we left because we were too scared."

It was happening more often than usual, and that Jacques Mercier gave us all kinds of trouble because he could not stand his kids coming to us at Les Arcades. He kept them away whenever he could, using threats to dissuade them. As a result, our relations were on the strained side. The man was eaten alive with hate; he was jealous and mean and he'd tell his kids:

"I forbid you to go to the moneybag's 'château,' I forbid you to take what they give you."

My sister had done everything possible to push him over the edge so she was to blame too; anyway I think she should have had the sense not to provoke him with her remarks. In their earliest quarrels, she had told him:

"What the hell are you doing here? You don't have a thing of your own; the house is mine, the land is mine, my father paid for the donkey and the cow, so what are you doing here?"

People should never speak that way. It is a shameful trick to use your possessions to reproach the person who has nothing, but my sister was not wise enough to understand; she made him feel the weight of her power and strength and as a result she made him ten times more malicious and violent. I wonder, if I'd done something like that with Jean, if I'd said: "Nothing here is yours." He would have left on the spot and I would never have seen him again. That's natural, a man has his dignity. Besides, with four youngsters there to hear every word, a man won't put up with harassment like that. One day, Jacques Mercier told my sister: "What's the difference? Some day you won't have anything either, you'll lose it all and you won't have any more than me," and that is precisely what happened.

Thanks to Marie-Rose, that man with a grudge against the world from the start became ten times more vicious. The dissension between them was endemic, with scant respite, and unfortunately, the tragedy assumed increasingly frightful proportions with each passing day. They had a fifth child, a boy, Jean-Baptiste, who lived only three weeks. The infant virtually died of starvation; they had reached such a degree of penury and disorder that there was not enough milk, no money to buy any, and one out of two bottles was made with water. Who could have suspected the drama that was brewing? Jacques Mercier went around telling people everywhere that his fifth kid entitled him to the Cognac Prize. What a disgrace! To have children for the money! The Cognac law itself was disgraceful, a temptation designed for the poor. In those days, the state awarded a bonus of 25,000 francs to couples under thirty with five children, and 25,000 francs was a lot of money since you could buy a house for 2000 or 3000 francs; and little Jean-Baptiste was their Cognac Prize and nothing else. They weren't even capable of feeding him properly.

The night the child died, Jacques Mercier was drunk as usual; he'd taken refuge in some bistro or other in the commune, and my sister was so afraid of him that she went and hid too, which meant the baby was alone. It was already too late when Marie-Rose came for me at Les Arcades. She was fretting and fuming, repeating over and over: "Come, I can't go back there alone, we have to dress the little one." She had nothing to dress him decently, even to bury him in, and I had to look through my things to find something, and when we reached La Draille, Jacques Mercier was there with his mother. The first thing he said to us was: "Just look what she did to my Cognac Prize!" It was monstrous to make a remark like that with the body still warm; it was so monstrous that even his mother would not put up with it, and she said: "Shush, she's not the only one to blame, it's your fault too." Jacques Mercier stared at his mother. "What!" he told her. "You, lady, you get twigs ready for your straw fire, you strike the match, and then you don't want it to burn?" Decoded, that meant: "You've always talked against Marie-Rose and now you blame me." I heard it all, I was there trying to clean the little body and dress it for burial.

I wonder, what if the youngster had lived, what if they'd received those 25,000 francs? I cannot say whether things would have worked out. I don't think so; there might have been a respite, but once they ran through the money, it would have been the same old story. As it was, things didn't drag on; a few months later, Jacques Mercier set La Draille on fire, convinced when he did it that he was roasting them all alive. He lit three fires in three different places, one in the hay, one in the woodpile, and a third I don't remember where. Luckily, my sister had left with the kids—as if she had had a premonition—and they all fled to the communal baking oven to escape him. He went off to sit on a hilltop to watch the fire. Everything burned up; the firemen arrived too late and nothing was left but the walls and a few odds and ends of frame. Such was the accomplishment of Jacques Mercier. He was tried and served time in prison. But what was that in comparison with the damage he had done? The four children were traumatized by that night and Marie-Rose was not much better off; she sank back into her madness and we kept her at home with us. It was not long before she had an especially violent fit; I remember she came to Les Arcades and went straight up to my father's room. She began to scream and break everything, hurling everything that came to hand against the wall. She was like a fury; I had to call my husband to bring her under control. He managed to calm her down, but we could not keep her with us any longer and she went back to the psychiatric hospital.

When Jacques Mercier was released from prison, we asked him what he planned to do with the children while his wife was in the hospital.

"Come on," he said, "I can't take care of the four of them."

"But in your family, do they want one or two?"

"Of course not. Put them on Public Assistance."

My husband wouldn't hear of it, he insisted we take in Marie-Rose's children:

"We must not allow Public Assistance to take the children, they'll be scattered all over the département and they'll never know they're brother and sisters."

He was right, there's nothing worse for youngsters, but four more children—that was a burden and a responsibility of no small proportions, and I hesitated. I was willing to take one or two, I was willing to take on Marie, the eldest, since I had raised her from the time she was a baby, but the four of them together were too much.

Jean could be very persuasive when he wanted.

"Look here, Émilie, we don't have the right to let them go off like that; it's worse than sending them off to die. Here, we'll always find some way to work things out; we'll eat what's around, raw dandelions or cooked dandelions if we have to, but they won't go to Public Assistance."

He spoke so well that we were finally won over, my father and I, but it was no simple matter since the courts had to decide. The youngsters had already made their choice; they wouldn't hear of anything but Les Arcades, but the court had to rule.

My older brother François agreed to take the boy Auguste, but only because he was old enough to work and help him out. François exploited him the whole time they spent together in Briançon. He never sent him to school, he made him watch his flock with no thought for his education, and the schoolteacher came to see me at regular intervals:

"Madame Carles, you must tell your brother to send me the little boy. At the rate things are going, he's turning him into an illiterate, the youngster is going on ten and he doesn't know how to read or write."

I went to see François to put him on the right track. I told him: "You must send Auguste to school, or the gendarmes will take him away from you," and he sent him to school for a week and then it started all over again.

Things went on like that for several months. What was intolerable is that an alcoholic pyromaniac, Jacques Mercier, sentenced to prison for setting his own house on fire, was still his children's legal guardian. Even though he was far from being responsible in any sense of the word, the law held that to reach the point of forfeiting his paternal rights, he had to do something more. Jacques Mercier was always after money; when I say money, I mean a little change for the bistro, and he'd have done anything to obtain it. He was known in Briançon for playing the buffoon, and for a few francs, the local jokers would get him to do anything they wanted. With those sous, he'd go straight off to buy cigarettes and drink wine. During one of his drinking bouts, he dropped his trousers and showed everyone his wee-wee. It created a scandal and he was brought to trial for the second time for obscene acts on the public thoroughfare, and for that reason alone the court stripped him of his paternal rights. That is what they call justice! Here's a man who for years did not ever look after his children, who let one of them die of starvation, who tried to burn his whole brood alive along with his wife, and not for an instant did the judges even consider stripping him of his paternal rights. But the moment he exposed his backside in front of the post office in Briançon, he had it. Shoddy justice, taking offense at a harmless indecent act when they had no qualms about abandoning children to the authority of a criminal. After the award was made, the social worker came to see me to find out what we planned to do. I told her:

"What we plan to do? But that's obvious, we'll keep the little girls, besides they don't want to go anywhere else."

"But you must take the boy too," that woman replied. "If you don't, I will be obliged to remove the three girls."

"You think I don't have enough already?"

"Do as you please, but by law they must stay together, otherwise I have to turn them over to Public Assistance."

Jean and I decided to take him too. That made four wards to raise, plus our own two, plus my father, plus my mother-in-law. It was 1936. The hotel frequently brought in less than it cost, and all we had to live on was my monthly salary. At the time, I was earning 700 francs. It came by money order from the prefecture, and when the postman brought it, I signed it but never saw any money. Instead I filled out three pink forms: two 300-franc money orders covering foster care for Catherine, the youngest, and Louisette, and a third for Marie's board at the orphanage. It was a closed circle; there wasn't one cent of my pay left over.

One of my cousins said: "Now really, Émilie, that's crazy, you're not being fair to your children, you're giving away everything you have," because with my father's help, we'd kept a few animals, sheep, rabbits, a little livestock, and we lived on them and on the little the restaurant brought in during the summer. Like many people, my cousin thought we were squandering these assets, and she could not refrain from telling me: "You're not being fair to your children."

I was beside myself: "What! I'm not being fair to my children? How can you say a thing like that? They have everything they need, they aren't naked, they've got shoes and clothes, they're not hungry and they're not cold, and I don't see how I'm being unfair to them. I couldn't bear—not ever—for my children to have everything and then leave the others to Public Assistance."

Jean was the one who had said: "We'll eat dandelions raw and dandelions cooked, but they will not go on Assistance," and that is what we did: we kept them and raised them like our own children. It was hard, but what did that matter? Once Jean convinced me, I was the more tenacious of the two. I had to be, or I don't know how we would have managed. Whenever things got tight, the "ant" was there, and sometimes Jean felt bad about it:

"I was the one who forced your hand, and you're the one who has the most worries with those kids."

That was most certainly true; I had the hardest job, washing, mending, getting them registered in schools, applying for scholarships, and Jean was well aware of it. I'd say:

"When there are children, no matter what you do, it's always the woman who knocks herself out."

There are no two ways about it, when something went wrong, it all fell on me, up to and including borrowing money from neighbors when we didn't have any left. It was a hell of a struggle to raise those four kids, but we did it, and I have never been sorry.

Like a Bird Fallen from the Nest

Who could have foreseen the tragedy? When you're happy, it's absurd to think of tragedy. If someone predicts it or simply talks about it, you call him a bird of ill omen, and you turn away. In 1938, after those few years of happiness, clouds began to gather over our heads. The Popular Front* was fluttering its wings like a wounded bird, civil war was raging in Spain and we were helping the refugees as best we could. We collected old clothes for the Loyalist children already flocking to southern France. The war craze had overtaken all Europe; in Germany Hitler

*The name given to the coalition of parties of the left under the leadership of Léon Blum which came to power in France in June 1936. Having instituted major social reforms, including paid vacations, higher wages, and the forty-hour week, Blum's government fell in 1938—Ed.

and his triumphant Nazis became more threatening with each passing day, and in Italy the Fascist order knew no limits. For pacifists like us, it was hard.

They talked about nothing but war all around us, and the most pessimistic had the feeling that it was inevitable and imminent. But what kind of war? I could not help thinking back to the dreadful years after 1914. I told myself that if they started in again, with modern weapons and technology, the slaughter would be universal. In those circumstances, it is easy to become selfish, and I reassured myself with the thought that Jean was too old to go off and fight and my children were too young to be hurt. My son Jojo was eight, my daughter Nini was six. On that score, I felt secure. How ridiculous! It was directly through the family that tragedy lashed us right in the face.

For years, the soldiers in Briançon had been nothing more than nice young fellows doing their military service, but now they were on the move. Every day they were more in evidence, assuming the importance of people everything depends on. They crisscrossed the countryside in whole convoys. The Italian border is not far, a few kilometers as the crow flies, and the commotion turned into a nightmare at the time of the Munich business. They went by in strings of trucks, traversing villages without slowing down, supposedly transporting war material to the Echelle Pass. I wonder what they could possibly try to defend up there, as if the Italians would attack in a spot like that. . . . But there was nothing to be done, the army was in full steam, nothing could stand in its path.

The absurd thing is that at the age I fell from a height of two stories onto the threshing floor, my little girl fell under the wheels of those trucks. Nini was six, she was riding her little bicycle, she loved it. We had bought her one so that she could come to school with me in Alberts. Every day—morning, evening, and for lunch at noon—we'd travel together. Usually, she rode ahead of me. I often saw her slow down as if she planned to stop. I'd say:

"What's the matter, Nini, that you're slowing down?"

"Maman, didn't you see the little bird? I didn't want to scare him, so I waited till he flew away by himself without me scaring him."

Poor little girl, she was the one who died. She used to play in the road on her bike while I did the rooms of Les Arcades. When the trucks came along, Nini got out of the way, standing beside the road to let them pass. They were carrying enormous posts, projecting several meters over the back of the trucks, and when one of them swerved, the posts teetered and we never knew why. My little girl was caught and blown away like a butterfly. My husband rushed over, he knew as soon as he picked her up that nothing could be done; she was still breathing but her brains were leaking out through her nose. He came back with her in his arms, but he didn't say anything; he acted as if we might still save her. He laid her on the bed while I phoned all the doctors in Briançon. They all said:

"Bring her in right away, we'll give her a transfusion with her father's blood."

Jean agreed to go. He took the car and left with the little one. I stayed home, I did not have the heart to go with them. When he returned two or three hours later, my little girl was dead. Her life ended on the way home. Of course they had not tried anything: the moment they examined her, the doctors saw that her little skull was empty, it was all out there on the road. They did not even try a transfusion, it would have been pointless.

I almost went out of my mind. I think there are no words to describe what I went through at that time. Losing a child, it's . . . How can I put it? I became another person. Nothing was real to me anymore; there was only pain and the terrible longing to disappear, myself. For days on end I did not emerge from that state of combined prostration and aggression. I was like a tigress; I could not tolerate anyone and no one could come near me, not even my husband or my son. I was like an animal broken loose, unable to endure the sight of life. Everything hurt, their voices, their gestures. And my nieces . . . it wasn't just that I could not bear to see them or hear them, worse still I wished I'd never see them again, all I could think of was my little Nini playing with them. I became nastier by the day, I didn't like anyone anymore, or anything. My husband hovered over me like a soul in torment; he had always been a fatalist, and often tried to make me see life the same way. But now, when he tried to reason with me, I could not listen to him.

"I beg you, Émilie," he repeated, "accept the fate meted out to us. That child is like a bird fallen from the nest. On the day of her birth, the day of her death was already written, there was nothing we could do, not you, not me, not anyone."

And my father . . . he was unbearable. For all the love I owe him, I still maintain he was atrocious at the time. He refused to understand why I would weep and be sick because my little girl had died, or else he simply could not bear it. He said:

"Now, you stop crying, it's getting ridiculous. Nobody needs that little girl."

Words like that were unbearable, and I did not understand how my father could say such things.

Guilt followed on pain. I told myself that if my little girl was dead, it was because I hadn't looked after her properly. I found every reason to make myself responsible for her death. It was because of the hotel, because of my nieces, because I worked too hard. All day long, I turned those ideas over and over in my poor head. It was wrong, as wrong as can be, and it served no useful purpose. In the country like here, it's not the same as in the city, no one ever keeps an eye on children, they come and go freely; but the feeling was too strong for me. I blamed myself, I tortured myself, I suffered, and I was destroying myself as time went on.

Her death was so unjust. All the deaths I had seen were unjust—my mother's Catherine, Joseph's*—but this one was far beyond what I could bear. Once and for all, I lost my faith and I broke with the church. It was impossible for me to accept the idea of such an unjust God. If I had abandoned my nieces to Public Assistance, Nini's death might have been a kind of punishment from heaven. Imagining a God of vengeance is harsh; but even so my case was the opposite, I'd kept all four with me, raising them like my own and there was never any question of reward or duty, and when I saw my little girl dead, right away I said: But there is no God of goodness, and if there is, where is He? What is He doing? It's not true, it can't be true, that God is a monster.

From 1918 on, I had kept my distance from the church, but now I broke completely and I never went back.

I was in such bad shape that something had to be done. One day I asked a doctor friend if I was going crazy.

"I'm not alive anymore, I don't let the people around me live either; she's the only thing that matters, the rest doesn't exist for me. Do you think I'll end up like that?"

"No," he said. "Your reactions are human, they are the reactions of a mother who has just lost her child; the passage of time will take care of it. My only advice for you is not to stay here; get away from this place where everything reminds you of your child. You'll see, leaving for a while will do you good."

Jean and I decided to take his advice. We closed the hotel, buckled on our knapsacks and left on foot, straight south. I remember we walked like animals, without saying a word, climbing up and down across the mountains until we couldn't go on, exhausted, breathless, our heads intoxicated with air and altitude. To eat and sleep, we stopped wherever we were, sometimes a climbers' hut, sometimes an inn, mostly out in the open. That hike was like a purification. I don't remember anymore how far we went; we set out for the sea, but we didn't get that far.

Fatalist or not, Jean was right: that death had to be accepted. The passing of my little girl was one more injustice in a family positively singled out by fate. It began with my mother, killed by lightning at the

---

*Her sister Catherine had died in childbirth because she was too modest to let the midwife attend her properly. Her brother Joseph had starved to death in a German prison camp during World War I—Ed.

age of thirty-six; next it was Catherine's turn, dying in childbirth at twenty-two, followed to the tomb by her husband the cheesemaker a few months later; then Joseph, also twenty-two, dead of starvation on the day the armistice was signed. My other brothers and sisters were to meet quick dramatic deaths. Marie-Rose and Rose-Marie both died on the operating table, and as for François, he had the most absurd death of all.

François was one of the "Living Dead" Panaït Istrati describes in *Kyra Kyralina*, people who are dead inside and prevent others from living. He never had any individuality to speak of, he had followed after his priests and they made him a sexton. He was so crafty and unctuous that the job fit him like a glove. Relations between the two of us were never more than cool. From the time we were children, he exasperated every one of us with the constant assertion of his rights as our senior; he was insufferable. When I married, the gap only widened. He never accented the fact that I married a man who was not from around here and a worker to boot, and he never accepted our being atheists. From that time on, he never spoke to us, neither to Jean, the children, nor me. When I happened to meet him in Briançon, it turned my stomach to see him cross the street to avoid me; and when he came upon my children, he would tell people:

"Just look at those little pagans; my own sister had them with her anarchist."

He died a nonsensical death one night during a local fair. It was late afternoon when he realized that one of his lambs was missing, and since he had probably drunk a little more than usual as happens at fairs, and since he insisted on getting his lamb back right away, he set off to look for it. He did try to find a few fellows to keep him company, asking everyone he met:

"Will you help me look for my lamb?"

But no one agreed so he left by himself. He went up to the Fort des Têtes, one of the isolated forts above Briançon, and in the process of looking for his lamb, he leaned a little too far over a well and fell in. They spent two or three days searching for him until they found his swollen body at the bottom of the well.

On my mother's side too, almost all of them died in accidents. One of my aunts was killed by her mule; an uncle, who was an orderly to an army officer in Nice, fell down an elevator shaft—he'd just taken off his shoes and socks, and thought he was going into his room. My mother had two other brothers, and they both cut their throats with a razor.

You could say that every region has its own traditions for suicide. In one spot, they all jump into wells; in another, they drown themselves in the river; somewhere else they use buckshot. Every region has its customs, and you could say their suicides show a family resemblance. In our valley, most men who wanted to end it all would hang themselves in the hayloft, while a few others would drown themselves in the Clarée's icy waters. So it's no surprise that when my uncle killed himself with a razor, people had the impression he was eccentric. Why did he choose that way to die? We never knew. He was a customs man, rather good-looking, and he married well. He had every reason to be happy. Unfortunately, he was the devil's own for gambling; he played like a man possessed, and the more he played the more money he lost. His debts piled up so high that he didn't know which saint to turn to, and gradually he reached the point where extreme measures seemed the only alternative.

He'd married a woman with money and property, but she was impossible to live with. She was an orphan whose guardians did not bring her up properly. She had grown up with the idea that money and property were the be-all and end-all. Her wealth had gone to her head and she had an inflated sense of her own worth. My uncle was miserable with her, beset with complexes over his problems with money. When they married, he gave his solemn promise that he would keep his hands off her dowry and her property. Why had he made such a stupid promise? I think it was pride; in any case, it cost him his life, because instead of talking over his gambling problems with his wife, and working out a solution with her, he chose to keep silent and find his own solution. One evening at suppertime, he said he was going to the cellar for wine, and he did not come back up. When she went down to see what was the matter, she found him stretched out in a pool of blood; he had slit his throat with a thrust of his razor.

They buried him in the potter's field as custom decreed in such cases, and my aunt couldn't think of anything better to do with the razor than give it to her husband's young brother. A rather ghoulish gift, but the boob accepted it and carried it around. That uncle was singled out by fate as well. As a handsome youth of fifteen, he contracted a bad case of scarlet fever that left him deaf and dumb for the rest of his life. He didn't completely lose his voice, but what was left wasn't worth much; he could just about say sentences like "me wit yuh," which in plain language meant "I want to go with you." His disability brought him suffering. Besides, he was a sentimental and supersensitive man, reacting to the misfortunes of his loved ones as if they were his own. In '14, during four years of war, he saw all his friends and close relatives die while his disability kept him home in the village. One after the other, his nephews disappeared in the trenches; he watched his sister waste away bit by bit as each of them was reported missing. She was my Aunt Colombe. When her last son died at Cassino in Italy, she said to me:

"Your mother, well, she's lucky she died."

I was sixteen at the time; it was hard to hear a sentence like that from the mouth of my mother's own sister. I thought to myself: What kind of reasoning is that? and to her I said:

"I don't understand you, Aunt Colombe."

"What do you mean, you don't understand? Émilie, I know what I'm talking about; she didn't see her children die and I have seen every one of my little ones die."

My uncle suffered more than anyone else from those recurring tragedies. He could not bear his nephews dying or his sister's anguish, and he went around saying:

"I can't take it anymore, I'm going to do like Alfred, I'm going to use that thing of his."

He meant the razor that idiot widow gave him to remember his brother. But nobody believed him when he talked like that; instead they made fun of him, and his pals would say: "You talk about it too much to do it," and he would answer: "I'm telling you I will, just like Alfred."

Every time we met, he'd say:

"Jules is dead, Clément is dead, Alfred is dead, my sister Colombe is going to die too."

He looked so sad and desperate that I did not know what to say or do to lift his spirits.

"No indeed," I'd say, "Colombe is not going to die," and I would try to make him see that as it was, enough people were dying from the war already.

One morning they found him dead. He had slit his throat with the razor. They say that it's hard to escape the special attraction those objects hold. In any case, he finally used it. When he was buried the mayor—still the same one—could not think of anything better to tell the gravediggers than:

"Better bury him with the razor."

I don't know, he could have gotten rid of it, thrown it away somewhere or other, but not there, not in the grave. Still, that is what he did, he even threw it in himself.

Seeing my family so markedly singled out led me to reflect, and I came to understand how right my husband was when he talked about fate. "It's not that you should be resigned," he'd say, "but when death comes, you have to accept it; that does not mean that man must accept everything; on the contrary, he must fight all forms of human inequality, he must revolt against exploitation, poverty, and drudgery." That is what he called being alive, and he would add: "The dead must not prevent those who are alive from living." That is how he put me back on track, and when we returned to Val-des-Prés, I was fit to take my place once more in the bosom of the family. We kept what was best of our little girl, the memory of a sweet, innocent child who had not known either evil or sorrow.

NIEN CHENG
(1915–)

Born in Peking, educated at the London School of Economics, Nien Cheng and her husband stayed in China after the Communists defeated Chiang Kai-shek in 1949. Her husband worked for Shell Oil, and after his death from cancer, so did she. Shell left China in 1966, when Mao Zedong launched the Cultural Revolution—an internal class war against intellectuals, officials, and people with foreign connections—but Nien Cheng stayed and soon became a target of the Red Guards. In September 1966 she was imprisoned in the No. 1 Detention House in Shanghai, where she remained in solitary confinement for almost seven years, refusing to admit she was guilty of any crime. Rehabilitated after Mao's death, she was allowed to leave China in 1980; she moved first to Ottawa and then to Washington, D.C.

For other accounts by women of the Cultural Revolution, see *Six Episodes in My Life Underground* by Yang Chiang, *Wild Swans* by Jung Chang, and *To the Storm: The Odyssey of a Revolutionary Chinese Woman* by Yue Daiyun, with Carolyn Wakeman. For other accounts of women imprisoned and tortured, compare Le Ly Hayslip, *When Heaven and Earth Changed Places* and Eugenia Ginzburg, *Journey into the Whirlwind*.

FROM *Life and Death in Shanghai*

One afternoon in January 1971, I was summoned to the interrogation room. The call was so unexpected that my heart was pounding with excitement as I followed the guard through the courtyard; I hardly noticed that a blizzard was beginning. At the door of the interrogation room, the guard suddenly gave me a hard shove, so that I staggered into the room rather unceremoniously. I found five guards in the room. As soon as I entered, they crowded around me, shouting abuse at me.

"You are the running dog of the imperialists," said one. "You are a dirty exploiter of workers and peasants," shouted another. "You are a counterrevolutionary," yelled a third.

Their voices mingled, and their faces became masks of hatred as they joined in the litany of abuse with which I had become so familiar during the Cultural Revolution. While they were shouting, they pushed me to show their impatience. I was passed around from one guard to another like a ball in a game. Trying to maintain my balance, I became dizzy and breathless. Before I could gather my wits together, a young male guard suddenly grabbed the lapels of my padded jacket and pulled me towards him. His face was only inches from mine, and I could see his eyes glistening with sadistic pleasure. Then he bit his lower lip to show his determination and gave me a hard push. I staggered backwards and hit the wall. But before I collapsed onto the floor like a sack, he grabbed my lapels again and pulled me forward, and again he bounced me against the wall. He did this several times with lightning speed, in a very expert manner. All the time, the other guards continued to shout at me. I became completely disoriented. My ears were ringing, my head was splitting, and my body was trembling. Suddenly my stomach heaved, and I vomited. Water from my mouth got on the guard's hands and cuffs. He became furious. Pushing me into the prisoner's chair, the guard swore under his breath.

My heart pounded as if it were going to jump out of my throat. My breath came in gasps. I collapsed into the chair and, trying to recover my equilibrium, closed my eyes. Suddenly a stinging blow landed on my cheek. The voice of a female guard shouted, "Are you going to confess?"

Another sharp blow landed on my other cheek as several voices joined in to shout, "Are you going to confess?"

I remained in the chair with my eyes closed and ignored them. That was my only way to defend myself.

Someone grabbed my hair from behind and jerked my head up. I was forced to look up and found all five of them staring at me expectantly. It seemed that they really thought I would change my mind simply because they had beaten me up. But then, people who resort to brutality must believe in the power of brutality. It seemed to me that these guards at the detention house were rather stupid not to know me better after watching me day and night for so many years. I knew, however, that they were merely carrying out someone else's orders.

One of the female guards was the militant young woman who had made trouble for me on many previous occasions. Now she said, "Are you going to confess, or do you want more punishment?"

When she saw that I remained silent, she gave my cheek another smart slap, took my arms, and draped them around the back of the chair on which I was seated. The young male guard who had pushed me against the wall grabbed my wrists and clamped a pair of handcuffs on them.

"These handcuffs are to punish you for your intransigence. You will wear them until you are ready to confess. Only then will we take them off. If you confess now, we will take them off now. If you confess tomorrow, we will take them off tomorrow. If you do not confess for a year, you will have to wear them for a year. If you never confess, you will have to wear them to your grave," said the militant female guard.

"Think about it! Think about the situation you are in!" a male guard shouted.

"If you decide to confess now, we will take off the handcuffs right away and you can return to your cell," another female guard said.

"What about it? Are you ready to confess? Just say yes, and we will take the handcuffs off," another male guard said.

"Speak! Speak!" several of them shouted.

I looked at them all and said in a feeble voice, "I've done nothing wrong. I have nothing to confess."

"Louder! Louder! Speak louder!" they yelled.

Though I spoke in a low voice, each one of them inside the room had heard what I said. Someone must be listening outside in the corridor. They wanted this person to hear my answer. From where I sat I could not see whether the small window behind the prisoner's chair was open. But I did notice the guards glancing in that direction when they were pushing me around.

I pulled myself together with an effort and stated in a clear and loud voice, "I'm innocent. You have made a mistake. I have nothing to confess."

I heard the small window behind the prisoner's chair close with a loud bang. My tormentors waited a little while before opening the door to usher me out, perhaps to make sure the person outside had time to get out of sight. When I stood up, the militant female guard came behind me and put her hands around the handcuffs to tighten them a few notches so that they fitted snugly around my wrists.

The blizzard was now in full force. Whirling snowflakes were falling from the darkened sky, and the strong wind nearly knocked me over when I stepped out of the interrogation building. The guard said, "Follow me!"

He did not return me to the women's prison but led me in another direction into a small building in a corner of the prison compound. When he opened the door and flipped the switch to put on the dim light, I saw that the place was in an even worse state of neglect than the rest of the prison compound. A thick layer of dust covered the floor and the walls. When we moved down the corridor, cobwebs floated down from the ceiling. The guard unlocked a small door and said, "Get in!"

The room was very dark. I waited for him to switch on the light, but he just closed the door after me. Standing outside, he asked, "Are you going to confess?" When I did not reply, he snapped the lock and went away.

I stood just inside the door in total darkness, trying to make out where I was. An unpleasant odor of staleness and decay assailed my nostrils. Gradually I realized that the tiny room in which I was locked had no windows. However, the door fitted badly; a thin thread of light seeped through the gap. When my eyes became accustomed to the darkness, I saw vaguely that there was a wooden board on the dusty floor and a cement toilet in the corner. Actually I was standing in the only space left, for the room was no more than about five feet square. Something soft dropped on my forehead. I was so startled that I experienced a moment of panic. With my hands tied at my back, I could do nothing to brush it away. I shook my head hard, and it slid down my face to my jacket. Perhaps not many insects could live in this dark room, I thought. It must have been a cobweb from the ceiling.

My heart was still beating very fast. In spite of the unpleasant smell in the room, I breathed in and out deeply and slowly to try to calm down and slow my heartbeat. When I felt better I sat down on the wooden board and tried to look around in the dark. I was relieved not to see anything that suggested blood, excrement, or vomited food left by previous prisoners. I was so tired that I put my head on my drawn-up knees and closed my eyes to rest. The only compensation for being locked in a cement box, I thought, was that without the window to admit the cold air and wind, the place was decidedly warmer than my cell.

The handcuffs felt different from the others I had worn before. I examined them with my fingers. Indeed, they were different, much heavier and thicker, with a square edge, not rounded like the others. My hands felt hot, and my fingers were stiff. I tried to exercise my hands by moving them as much as the handcuffs allowed.

"Are you going to confess?"

The sudden sound of a voice startled me. Had the guard been outside all the while, or had he just come into the building? How was it that I had not heard him?

There was really no point in exhausting what little strength I had, so I did not answer him but remained where I was with my head resting on my knees. I tried to take my mind off the present by recalling beautiful scenes and pleasant experiences of the past. But it was very difficult. The ugly reality was all too real and overpowering.

Other guards came at intervals to ask me the same question. I listened for their footsteps. Some came quite stealthily, others did not bother to soften their tread. When they opened the door of the building to come inside, I could hear the howling wind and the sound of the guards stamping their feet to get rid of the snow. I supposed they were told to come and see if I had succumbed to their new form of pressure. Some of them lingered for a moment after asking their question; others did not wait for my answer but left almost immediately.

Apart from the guards, there was no sound whatsoever. I must have been the sole occupant of that building on that day. If there were other prisoners, surely I would have heard a sigh or a moan long ago.

I did not know how long I sat there. In a dark room, in complete isolation, time assumed a different meaning or had no meaning at all. I only knew that my legs felt stiff and my head ached. But I refrained from moving as long as the guards continued to come. When a guard switched off the light in the corridor on his departure, I thought they might have decided to retire for the night. But I still waited for a while before standing up. It was not possible to walk because there was simply no space and I was afraid to bump into the dirty wall in the dark. So I shuffled my feet to try to restore circulation to my legs. My arms ached from being held at my back in the same position for so long, and my hands felt very hot. I tried to get some relief by moving my shoulders up and down.

After standing for a while, I sat down again. With my head on my knees, I rested. Perhaps I had snatches of real sleep, or perhaps I just dozed while murmuring prayers. Then I would stand up again to repeat my newly devised exercise. I felt very weak. My natural inclination was to move as little as possible, but I compelled myself to do the simple exercise, for I knew that was the best way to keep going. In the past I had not suffered from claustrophobia, but there were moments during the night when I felt myself getting tense. My breathing became difficult, and I had the sensation that the walls were falling on me. To prevent myself from getting into a panic, I would stand up quickly and move my body as much as possible in that confined space. And I would breathe very slowly and deeply until I felt calm again.

The best way for me to snap out of fear was always to take the initiative in doing something positive. Even the simple act of moving my body around made me feel better immediately. If I had just sat there feeling dejected and let my imagination run wild, I could easily have become terribly confused and unable to cope with the guards. Of course I was hungry and my throat was parched. But when I thought of the cement toilet coated with dust and grime, I was reconciled to not having any food or water that might force me to use it.

The night dragged on very slowly. More and more I felt that I was buried in a cement box deep underground. My hands became very hot and uncomfortable. When I found it difficult to curl my fingers into a fist, I knew they were swollen. My hands became my sole preoccupation.

I feared that the brutal and ignorant guards, intent on getting what they wanted from me, might inadvertently cripple me. I knew that when a Communist Party official tried to achieve an objective during a political campaign, he went to excess to carry out his orders and ignored all possible complications. Trained to obey promptly by such slogans as "Wherever Chairman Mao points, there I will run," and fearful of the consequences of appearing hesitant or reluctant, he exaggerated everything he had to do. If the victim suffered more than was intended or was left a cripple, that was just too bad. I had seen this happen again and again. Hands are so important. If my hands were crippled, how would I be able to carry on with my daily life when the Cultural Revolution was over?

I pressed my fingers in turn. At least they were not numb. But I could tell they were badly swollen. I wondered how long I would remain manacled like this and how long I could live without food or water. Vaguely I remembered reading in an article that a human being could live for seven days without sustenance. In my present weakened state, perhaps five days, I thought. In any case, hardly twenty-four hours had passed. At that moment I did not need to think of the threat to my life, only the threat to my hands. What could I do to lessen possible damage to them? It seemed to me the swelling was caused by the tight handcuffs fitted firmly around my wrists, preventing proper circulation. When the militant female guard put her hands around the cuffs to tighten them, she knew exactly what she was doing. If she had not tightened them but had left them as they were, perhaps the state of my hands would not have been so bad now. The guard who first put the handcuffs on had not tightened them, so they had probably not been instructed to do so. In that case, a mild guard might be persuaded to loosen them a little. I decided to show my hands to the guard who came in the morning and request that the handcuffs be loosened.

When finally I heard the sound of a guard coming through the outside door and saw the thin line of light appear again around the cell door, I stood up.

"Are you going to confess? Have you thought over the matter?" It was the voice of a male guard.

"I would like to speak to you for a moment," I said.

"Good! So, you have decided to confess at last."

"No, no, it's not about confession. It's about my hands."

"What about your hands?"

"They are badly swollen. The handcuffs are very tight. Could you loosen them a bit?" I asked.

"You are feeling uncomfortable now, are you? That's good! Why don't you confess? If you confess, the handcuffs will be taken off."

"Can't you loosen them a bit now?"

"Why don't you just confess like the other prisoners? You have brought this on yourself. It's not the fault of the handcuffs."

"Please look at my hands. They are badly swollen."

"I can't do anything about that. If you decide to confess, I will unlock this door and take you out. That's all I can do," the guard said.

"Could you not report to your superior that my hands are very badly swollen?"

"No. If you decide to confess, I will take you out."

It seemed useless to go on. I sat down on the wooden board again.

"Are you going to confess?" he asked me once again. I did not answer. He remained there for a moment longer before going away.

The fact that my hands were badly swollen was no surprise to the guard. Of course he knew the effect of the handcuffs. I could not have been the first person they had done this to. He was probably telling his superior at that moment that I was getting worried and agitated about my hands. From that his superior would think I was nearer to doing what he wanted. They would never loosen the handcuffs to prolong what they regarded as the period of waiting for me to confess. I decided it was useless to ask the guards to loosen the handcuffs. I must just trust God to preserve my hands.

"Come here!" the voice of a female guard said.

I stood up. I was already right by the door. She had turned up rather quickly, I thought.

"I've come to give you some advice," she said in a normal voice, as if she were talking to another guard, not in the harsh tone the guards habitually used to address the prisoners. "You are not a stupid woman. Why don't you do the intelligent thing and confess? Why punish yourself by being stubborn?"

I didn't say anything.

"You are worried about your hands. That's quite right. Hands are very important to everybody, but especially to an intellectual who must write. You should try to protect your hands and not let them be hurt. You can do that easily by just agreeing to confess."

I still did not say anything.

"You know, when they said they would never take the handcuffs off until you agreed to confess, they really meant it. They will do it too. The Dictatorship of the Proletariat is not something to be trifled with, you know."

I continued to remain silent.

She waited for quite a long time. Then she said, "Well, you think carefully about what I have just said. It's good advice I have given you. I'm sorry for you. Think about what I said."

When I heard her footsteps going away from the door, I sat down again.

I was angry with myself for being so stupid. How could I have thought for one moment that they would loosen the handcuffs? Now that I had shown them my weakness, they would be glad and think I might indeed succumb to their pressure out of concern for my hands. I said to myself, "I'll forget about my hands. If I have to be crippled, then I'll accept being crippled. In this world there are many worthy people with crippled hands or no hands at all." I remembered that when my late husband and I were in Holland in 1957, we had bought a painting by a veteran of the Second World War who had lost both his hands. He used his toes to hold the paintbrush, I was told. I used to treasure this painting as a symbol of human courage and resourcefulness. It was slashed by the Red Guards when they looted my home. But the thought of this artist whom I had never met inspired me with courage and helped me to become reconciled to the possibility of losing the use of my hands after this ordeal.

The female guard was followed by others. All of them lectured me on the advantage of obeying the Dictatorship of the Proletariat and confessing. Now that they knew I was suffering discomfort and worrying about my hands, they did not dash away but lingered hopefully outside the door waiting for my answer. After being so long without food and water and not having had much sleep at all, I felt very weak and faint. My intestines were grinding in protest, and I had spasms of pain in the abdomen. But I just continued sitting on the board with my head on my knees waiting for the guards to go away.

The day seemed interminable. Patiently I waited for their next move. At last the door was unlocked. A female voice called, "Come out!"

The icy-cold fresh air in the courtyard miraculously cleared my head, and I felt a surge of life to support my wobbly legs. The guard led me back to the same interrogation room in which they had beaten me up the day before.

The militant female guard and the young male guard who had put the handcuffs on me sat in the place of the interrogator behind the counter. After I had entered the room and bowed to the portrait of Mao, the female guard told me to recite a quotation from memory.

" 'First, do not fear hardship. Second, do not fear death,' " I said. It was the first quotation of Mao that came into my head and, under the circumstances, certainly appropriate.

"That quotation is not for the likes of you! Chairman Mao said that to the revolutionary soldiers," the female guard said indignantly.

But they let it pass. They did not ask me to recite another quotation, although I had one about overcoming ten thousand difficulties to strive for final victory ready to recite if they gave me the opportunity to do so.

"What are you thinking about now?" asked the male guard.

"Nothing very much," I answered.

"Don't pretend to be nonchalant. You are worried about your hands. You would like the handcuffs to be loosened," he said.

I did not say anything.

"What you should think about is why you have to wear them in the first place. It is entirely your own fault. Do we put handcuffs on all the prisoners kept here? Of course not. If you find the handcuffs uncomfortable, you should think why you have to wear them. They can be taken off if you decide to confess. It's up to you entirely," he said.

"Are you going to confess?" asked the female guard.

When she saw that I said nothing, she got angry and shouted, "You deserve all you are getting. You are tired of living, I am sure. I have never seen a prisoner as stubborn and stupid as you!"

"Have you lost all reason? Have you lost the wish to protect yourself? You are being extremely stupid. You are like an egg hitting a rock. You will get smashed," declared the male guard.

A year or two ago, I would have shouted back at them and taken pleasure from it. Now I was too ill and too tired. I no longer cared.

They looked at each other, and they looked past my shoulder at the small window behind the prisoner's chair. Then they stood up.

"Take her out! Take her out! Let her go to see God with her granite head!" the male guard shouted.

It might seem surprising that a guard in a Communist prison should have spoken of God, but what he said was in fact a quotation from Mao Zedong. Referring to political indoctrination and hard labor as a means to change the thinking of intellectuals allegedly opposed to the Communist Party, Mao had declared that the Party's purpose was reform of the enemy rather than annihilation. Then he added, "If some still want to go to see God with their granite heads, it will make no difference." Since the publication of his remark, "to go to see God with his granite head" was generally used to denote a man refusing to change his mind or accept the point of view of the Party.

A guard flung the door open. Although I felt dizzy, I made an effort to walk steadily and followed him out of the room. The icy air outside was like a knife cutting through my clothes. I shivered violently. The guard led me back to the women's prison and my cell. When I passed the small room used by the female guards, I saw from their clock that I had been locked in the cement box in the other building for almost twenty-four hours.

The guard unlocked the door of my cell and said to me, "Now you will continue your punishment in here."

When I was called to the interrogation room the day before, drinking water had just been issued to the prisoners. The water was still in the green enameled mug on the edge of the table where I had hastily placed it. Now I bent over the mug, removed the lid by gripping the knob on top of it with my teeth, and placed it on the table. Then I caught the edge of the mug with my teeth, gradually lowered my body to a squatting position, and tipped the water into my mouth. By this method, I succeeded in drinking quite a bit of water. After that, I moved over to the cement toilet, stood with my back to it, lowered my body, and removed the lid with my imprisoned hands. I strained my hands to unzip my slacks. I was able to sit on the seat I had made with two towels joined together and to relieve myself. But to strain my hands to one side to unfasten the zipper made the handcuffs cut severely into my flesh. It was very painful.

I sat down on the edge of the bed. The cell was very cold and seemed to get progressively colder. But the familiar cell was not as dirty and stuffy as the cement box where I had spent the previous twenty-four hours. When the second meal of the day was delivered to the prisoners, the woman from the kitchen pushed the aluminum container through the small window in the usual manner. Even though I was famished, I had to refuse it, for I simply did not know how I could eat with my hands tightly tied behind my back.

No one came to ask me if I was going to confess. But I knew I was under observation, for I could hear the guards come to the peephole to look into the cell. At bedtime, the guard called at each cell for prisoners to go to bed. She came to my cell as if nothing unusual had happened and said, "Go to sleep!"

With my back to the wooden bed, I unrolled my quilt and blanket and spread them over it. It was slow work and strenuous for one who had not eaten any food for so long. But I managed it. Then I lay down on the bed. First, I lay on one side with my body weight pressing down on one shoulder and arm. It was extremely uncomfortable; my arm ached. Then I tried to lie on my stomach with my face turned to one side. I found this position impossible on the hard wooden bed because my body weight was on my breasts. After lying like this for a little while I had to give up. In any case, I could not cover myself with the blanket. While I was performing these acrobatics with my hands in handcuffs behind my back, I never stopped shivering. The room was bitterly cold. Finally I decided lying down to sleep was out of the question. I should try to get some sleep sitting up. I sat across the bed with my legs up and my back leaning on the toilet-paper-covered wall. Then I closed my eyes, hoping to doze off.

It was such a cold night that there was ice on the windowpanes, and the snow piled against the window did not melt. Inside the cell, the feeble light shone through a haze of cold air. Every breath I took was a puff of white vapor. My body shook with spasms of shivering. My legs and feet were frozen numb. I simply had to get up from time to time and walk around the cell to restore circulation to my limbs. The weight of the handcuffs dragged my hands down, and I tried to hold the cuffs up with my fingers while walking slowly in the cell. They seemed to get tighter and tighter, and my hands seemed to be on fire. I tired so easily that after walking around for only a little while I had to sit down again. Then I got so cold that I had to walk some more. Perhaps I managed a little sleep from time to time when I sat against the wall with my feet up, but the long night was a night of misery and suffering.

However, it came to an end, as everything in life must do, no matter how wonderful or unpleasant. I saw the light of dawn creeping into the room and heard the guard calling outside each cell, "Get up! Get up!"

Soon afterwards the Labor Reform girl pushed the spout of the watering can through the small window to offer me cold water for washing. When she did not see my washbasin, she peered into the cell and looked at me inquiringly. I turned my body a little so that she could see my handcuffs. Quickly she closed the small window and went away.

Under the circumstances, being unwashed was the least of my worries. I could receive water in the empty mug with my back to the window and drink by gradually squatting with the mug in my teeth, but my empty stomach protested with spasms of gripping pain that refused to be assuaged by water. My hands were so hot that I was in a constant state of restless agitation.

On the third day, the pain in my abdomen miraculously stopped. But I felt very weak. My eyes could no longer focus, and the usual sound of prison activities seemed to grow fainter and fainter.

That night, I again sat on the bed, leaning against the wall with my hands crossed to hold the handcuffs with my fingers in an effort to reduce their weight. Though I shivered with cold, I no longer had the strength to get up and walk around the room.

After the prisoners had settled down to sleep, the small window was pushed open gently. I did not hear any sound until a voice that was almost a whisper said through the opening, "Come over!"

I wondered whether it was just another guard urging me to confess. But she had spoken softly, almost stealthily, as if she did not want others in the building to hear her.

With an effort I moved to the small window and saw the face of one of the older guards there. She was bending down to watch my faltering steps through the opening.

From the beginning of my imprisonment I had found this guard the most humane. At first she attracted my attention because she walked in that peculiar way of women whose feet had been crippled with foot-binding, an old custom that lingered into the 1930s in some remote rural areas of China. When the feet of these women were unbound, they were already permanently damaged. This guard was not a native of Shanghai, because she spoke with the accent of North China peasants. I thought she must be one of those country women who had been liberated by the Communist troops as they swept down the plains of North China and had joined their ranks and become a Party member. I observed that she carried out her duty in a matter-of-fact manner and did not seem to enjoy shouting at the prisoners as the other guards did. When the weather got cold, if she was on night duty, I often heard her offering to lend bedding from the prison stock to prisoners who did not have suffi-cient covering. The last time I fainted because of lack of food, it was this guard who took me to the hospital and got the doctor to sign a paper ordering more rice to be given to me. Since it was the Maoists who had reduced my ration to pressure me on that occasion, I thought she couldn't be one of them.

"Why aren't you eating your meals?" she asked me.

I thought, "What a silly question! Doesn't she know I have got the handcuffs on?"

"They will not remove the handcuffs simply because you won't eat, you know. And if you should starve to death, you will be declared a counterrevolutionary. That's the customary procedure for prisoners who die before their cases are clarified," she added.

"I don't know how to eat without using my hands," I said.

"It's not impossible. Think hard. There is a way. You have a spoon."

She sounded sympathetic and concerned. I decided to ask her to loosen the handcuffs a little, as my tightly imprisoned hands were tor-menting me. I was in a constant state of tension because of them. They occupied my mind to the exclusion of all else.

"My hands are swollen and very hot. My whole body feels tormented because of them. Could you please loosen the handcuffs a little bit?" I asked her.

"I haven't got the key to unlock the handcuffs. It is being kept by someone higher up. Just try to eat something tomorrow. You will feel better when you have some food inside you," she said.

A gust of cold wind from the other end of the corridor indicated that the door of the building was being opened and another guard had just entered. She slid the shutter quietly into place and went away.

I returned to the bed and sat there thinking. The guard was right. I should try to eat. To die was nothing to be frightened of. What really frightened me was the possibility that my mind might get so confused that I might sign something without realizing its significance. But how could I handle the food without my hands? The guard said there was a way and told me to think hard. She also mentioned that I had a spoon. My eyes strayed towards the table. First I saw the plastic spoon, and then I saw my clean towels neatly folded in a pile. A plan formulated in my mind, and I decided to try it when food was offered to me again.

The guard had said that the key to unlock the handcuffs was not kept by the guards but by "someone higher up." There was no hope the handcuffs could be loosened. I must think of some way to reduce the heavy weight of the handcuffs, which were not only dragging my hands down but also pulling my shoulders out of their sockets. With difficulty and very slowly, with my back to the bed, I managed to roll up the quilt. Then I pushed the rolled quilt to the wall. When I sat down against the wall, I placed my hands on the soft quilt. The weight was lifted, and I felt a surge of relief.

To have made plans and thought of some way to overcome difficulty gave me a new lease on life. Although I continued to be cold, hungry, and miserable, the long night seemed to pass more quickly.

At daybreak, when the guard called the prisoners to get up, I stood up to stretch my legs. I tried to hold the handcuffs with my fingers and to my horror, felt something sticky and wet. Turning to the quilt on which I had rested my hands throughout the night, I saw stains of blood mixed with pus. It seemed the handcuffs had already broken my skin and were cutting into my flesh. I shuddered with a real fear of losing the use of my hands, for I realized I was powerless to prevent disaster.

When the woman from the kitchen offered me the aluminum container of rice through the small window, I went to accept it. I turned my back to the opening, and she placed the container in my hands. I took it to the table. With my back to it, I picked up a clean face towel from the pile and spread it on the table. Then I picked up the plastic spoon and tried to loosen the rice with it. Shanghai rice was glutinous. When it was cooked in the container, it stuck to it. I had to dig hard with the plastic spoon to push the rice and cabbage onto the face towel on the table. With each movement of my hands, the handcuffs dug deeper into my flesh. My whole body was racked with pain, and tears came into my eyes. I had to rest and take a deep breath. Nevertheless, I persisted in my effort to get the rice out of the container. When I succeeded in getting quite a bit out, I turned around, bent over the towel, and ate the rice like an animal.

I repeated this several times. When the woman came to collect the container, she did not immediately open the small window to demand it back but stood outside watching me struggling to get the rice out. Because of the pain and my fear of infection, I stopped after each scoop to take a deep breath. I was very slow. Still the woman said nothing, though normally she was always in a great hurry. As I blinked back tears of pain, I wondered if eating was really worth the effort. But I continued to try, simply because I had decided to stay alive. When I could not carry on any longer and had got nearly half of the rice onto the towel, I carried the container behind me and pushed it through to her with my wounded hands.

In the afternoon, when rice was given to me again, I found that the woman from the kitchen had already loosened it for me. I had only to tip the container and most of the rice fell out onto the towel and bare table.

My being able to consume food seemed to have infuriated the Maoists, for the guards came to the small window again to threaten me. They never mentioned the word "handcuffs," probably because they did not want the other prisoners within hearing to know what they were doing to me. But they continued to urge me to confess. Although the rice I managed to eat each day did in fact make me feel stronger, I was having difficulty walking. For some reason I could not explain, the handcuffs were affecting my feet. Like my hands, they felt hot and painful. My shoes became so tight and unbearable that I had to kick them off. Fortunately they were soft cloth shoes, so that I was able to press down the backs and wear them as slippers. Now I just staggered about, for my feet could not bear even the reduced weight of my emaciated body. The stains of blood and pus on the quilt became larger and more numerous as the handcuffs cut through more skin on my wrists and bit more deeply into the wounds. Either the weather suddenly got a lot warmer, or I was feverish; I no longer felt the cold but shivered from pain whenever I had to move my hands or stagger across the room.

One day when I was at the small window getting drinking water, my imprisoned hands holding the mug trembled so much that half of the water spilled down the back of my padded jacket and slacks.

"Your hands are very bad. The higher-ups don't know it. Why don't you wail? As long as you don't cry out, they will not know how bad your hands are," the woman from the kitchen whispered through the opening before hastily closing the shutter.

Though the Chinese people were normally restrained about showing emotion, they did wail to show deep grief at funerals or as a protest against injustice that involved death. The sight of someone wailing had always embarrassed me. It was like seeing someone strip himself naked. From childhood I had been disciplined never to show emotion. The memory of trying for many years to fight back tears lingered; gradually I came to regard crying as a sign of weakness. Should I wail now just to call attention to the fact that my hands were being crippled? I decided against it. For one thing, I did not think I knew how to emit that prolonged, inarticulate cry that was so primitive and animallike. For another, I did not want to do anything that might be interpreted as asking for mercy. "The man higher up" had ordered the handcuffs put on my wrists so that I would be tormented by them. He believed my suffering would eventually lead me to give a false confession to save myself. The best way to counterattack was certainly not to show that I could no longer endure suffering. So I ignored the kind advice of the woman from the kitchen.

Several more days passed. The handcuffs were now beginning to affect my mind, probably through their effect on my nervous system. I got muddled periodically and forgot where I was. I no longer remembered how many days ago I was first manacled. Life was just an unending road of acute pain and suffering on which I must trudge along as best I could.

During moments of lucidity, I tried to discipline my mind by doing simple arithmetic. I would repeat to myself, "Two and two makes four, four and four equals eight, eight and eight equals sixteen, sixteen and sixteen equals thirty-two . . ." But after only a little while my ability to concentrate would evaporate, and I would get confused again. The guards still came to the locked door. But what they said was just a jumble of words that made no sense to me.

After several more days, I became so weak that I no longer had the strength to stagger to the small window for rice or water. I tried to refuse when they were offered to me, but whether words came out of my mouth or not I did not know. Perhaps the woman from the kitchen was urging me to take the rice or the drinking water; I did not hear her voice, only sensed that she stood there waiting for something. Most of the time I was so far away that I did not know what was happening around me. After drifting in and out of consciousness like that for some time, I passed out altogether.

When I opened my eyes again, I found myself lying on the dusty floor.

"Get up! Get up!" a man's voice was shouting very near me. "You are feigning death! You won't be allowed to get away with it."

My arms were still bent to my back, but they were no longer held together by the handcuffs.

"Get up! Get up!" a female voice joined in.

I pulled myself together and looked up to find the militant female guard and the young man who had put the handcuffs on me standing over me. The cell door was wide open. Dangling in the hands of the female guard was the pair of heavy brass handcuffs they had removed from my wrists. The handcuffs were covered with congealed blood and pus. Probably the guard considered them repulsive, as she was holding them gingerly by the chain with just two fingers.

"Don't think we are finished with you! There are other ways to bring you to your senses. Those who dare to oppose the Dictatorship of the Proletariat will not be allowed to get away with it," said the man.

The female guard gave my prostrate form a hard kick as they left the cell and locked the door behind them.

I remained on the floor, too exhausted to move. Although the handcuffs were gone, my whole body was aching and hot. Slowly I brought my left arm forward and looked at my hand. Quickly I closed my eyes again. My hand was too horrible to contemplate. After a moment, I sat up and looked at both hands. They were swollen to enormous size. The swelling extended to my elbows. Around my wrists where the handcuffs had cut into my flesh, blood and pus continued to ooze out of the wounds. My nails were purple in color and felt as if they were going to fall off. I touched the back of each hand, only to find the skin and flesh numb. I tried to curl up my fingers but could not because they were the size of carrots. I prayed to God to help me recover the use of my hands.

After a while, I tried to get up. But I had to stifle a cry of pain, for my feet could not support my body. As I was very near the bed, I managed to haul myself up to it. The woolen socks were stuck to my feet with dried pus. When I succeeded in peeling the socks off with my numb and swollen fingers, I saw that my feet were also swollen to enormous size. Under each toe was a large blister. I could not take the socks completely off because some of the blisters had broken and the pus had dried, gluing the socks to my feet. What was making it impossible for me to walk was the fact that some of the blisters had not broken. Obviously I needed a sterile sharp instrument such as a needle to break the blisters and let the fluid out. Also, to prevent infection, I needed bandages and some antiseptic medicine for the wounds on my wrists. I stood up. I almost sat down again immediately because the burning pain in my feet was unbearable. However, I resisted the impulse to sit down and, shuddering, remained standing. I thought that since I had to move about in the cell, the sooner I practiced walking on my swollen feet, the better. I moved one foot forward a couple of inches, shifted my weight onto that foot, and moved the other foot a couple of inches. Eventually I arrived at the door. Leaning against it for support, I called the guard on duty.

"Report!" My voice sounded feeble. But almost immediately the shutter on the small window slid open. The guard had been right outside the door, watching me through the peephole all the time without my knowledge.

"What do you want?"

"May I see the doctor, please."

"What for?"

"My wrists and feet are wounded. I need some medicine and bandages," I explained.

"The doctor does not give treatment when the prisoner has been punished," declared the guard.

"In that case, perhaps you could just give me some disinfectant ointment or Mercurochrome for the wounds?" I knew the guards kept a supply of these in their little room.

"No, not allowed."

"The wounds may become infected."

"That's your business."

"May I just have a roll of bandages to tie the wounds up?"

I lifted my swollen hands to the window to show her the wounds on my wrists, but she turned her head the other way and refused to look at them.

"May I have some bandages?" I asked her again.

"No."

I got angry. "So, you do not practice revolutionary humanitarianism in accordance with Chairman Mao's teaching," I said.

"Revolutionary humanitarianism is not for you," she said. "Look at you! As argumentative and unrepentant as you were before. You learned nothing from the handcuffs. Perhaps you did not have them on long enough. If you argue any more, I am going to put them on you again." With that threat she retreated to the guards' room and remained there. I knew she had no authority to put the handcuffs back on my wrists again. It was just bluff. She knew I knew it too.

It seemed there was no alternative to relying on myself to deal with the wounds on my wrists and feet. With the help of God, I thought, I would find some way to prevent infection. Very slowly I shuffled to the table and drank up the water in the mug. I heard the woman from the kitchen entering the building with her heavy trolley, on which were two huge buckets of boiled hot drinking water for the prisoners. I waited for her at the small window. When she came to me, she gave me a generous portion, filling the large mug almost three-quarters full. I poured this water into the washbasin and with a clean towel carefully washed the wounds on my wrists and wiped away the dried blood and pus. Then I washed my feet in the same bloodstained water. The feel of hot water on my skin was good. I longed to drink some, but I thought it more important to clean the wounds.

While I sat on the bed drying my feet, I wondered what I could tear up and use as bandages. After so many years, my meager stock of clothing had become even more depleted because I often had to tear up a worn garment to patch those that were just beginning to develop holes. As I was searching my mind for an idea, I saw the pillowcase hanging on the clothesline. I had washed it the morning I was called to the interrogation room. It looked dry. It was the only pillowcase I had left, but I thought I could dispense with it; I could put the pillow under the sheet at night. I raised my arm to take it off the clothesline. To my dismay, I found I could not reach the pillowcase because my arm refused to be raised higher than the level of my shoulders. I supposed that after such long restraint the tendons were paralyzed. I resolved to restore the function of my arms by exercise. But that would take some time. For the moment, at any rate, I would have to leave the wounds on my wrists uncovered.

The Labor Reform girl came with cold water. She poured the water slowly into the washbasin as I held it up to the small window. As soon as she saw my hands shaking because they could no longer bear the weight, she stopped. The washbasin was barely half full. I poured some of the water into one of the mugs for drinking. With the rest, I washed my face. Then I tried to comb my hair. Since my right arm holding the comb could not reach the top of my head, I used my left hand to hold up the elbow of my right arm. With my head bent forward, turning first this way and then that way, I managed to smooth out my hair. I wanted very much to give myself a sponge bath and change my underclothes. But I was afraid I would catch cold in the icy room. In any case, I was already exhausted, and there was no more clean water.

The woman from the kitchen was again at the small window. She handed me the afternoon meal through the opening. The aluminum container was filled to the brim with rice and boiled cabbage. When I pushed the food into my mug, I discovered two hard-boiled eggs buried at the bottom of the container.

To forestall, I am sure, any possibility of my thanking her for the eggs, the woman did not open the window to collect the container as was her habit but shouted through the door as if she were angry, "You are always so slow! Hand the container over to the guard on night duty when you have finished! I can't stand here all night waiting for you!"

I sat down on the edge of the bed to eat. With each mouthful I swallowed, I felt a little strength flowing back to me. When I had finished, I washed the mug and stood up to exercise my arms. I was most anxious that I should be able to reach the pillowcase on the line as soon as possible so that I could make bandages to cover up the wounds on my wrists. I swung my arms up and down many times, each time raising them a little higher in the air to stretch the tendons. My feet were very painful, but I remained standing until I was exhausted. After a short rest, I resumed the exercise.

The guard on night duty came to the small window, handed me the day's newspaper, and took away the aluminum container. I looked at the date on the newspaper and discovered that only eleven days had elapsed since I had been called to the interrogation room and manacled. It seemed much longer. The guard came to tell the prisoners to go to bed.

This was the first time in eleven days that I had the chance of a full night's sleep. But it took me a long time to drop off. Somehow, the tight handcuffs had affected my nervous system. My whole body was aching and hot. No matter on which side I lay, it was painful and uncomfortable. The weight of the blanket and quilt seemed unbearable. Since I did not feel the cold, being feverish, I pulled the blanket off. I tried to arrange my feet and arms in such a way that the blood and pus would not stain the quilt. I soon found this impossible.

To put those special handcuffs tightly on the wrists of a prisoner was a form of torture widely used in Maoist China's prison system. Sometimes additional chains were put around the prisoner's ankles. At other times, a prisoner might be manacled and then have his handcuffs tied to a bar on the window so that he could not move away from the window to eat, drink, or go to the toilet. The purpose was to degrade a man in order to destroy his morale. Before my own imprisonment, victims and their families had simply not told me about such practices. But after my imprisonment, I became a member of that special group, so they did not hesitate to tell me of their experiences. However, since the People's Government claimed to have abolished all forms of torture, the officials simply called such methods "punishment" or "persuasion."

It took me many months of intense effort to be able to raise my arms above my head; it was a full year before I could stretch them straight above me. The minor wounds left no scar after healing, but the deeper wounds where the metal of the handcuffs cut through my flesh almost to the bone left ugly scars that remain with me to this day: a legacy of Mao Zedong and his Revolutionaries. The swelling of my hands and fingers subsided eventually, but the backs of both my hands had no sensation for more than two years. The nerves were so damaged that when I experimentally pricked the back of my hand with a needle to draw blood, I felt nothing whatever. Even now, after more than thirteen years, my hands ache on cold, wet days. In winter, even in a warm room, I have to wear gloves in bed. If I use my hands a little too much in cleaning, typing, or carrying heavy parcels, sometimes I find my right hand suddenly going limp and useless, unable to grip anything. My right hand sustained a greater degree of damage than my left hand, mainly because the zipper on my slacks was on the left side. Since I strained to the left of my body to unzip my slacks whenever I had to use the toilet, the handcuffs cut deeper into the flesh of my right wrist. The irony of the situation was that normally women's slacks in the clothes stores in China had the zipper on the right side. Since my slacks had been specially tailored, I had the zipper on the left, because I had worn it that way long before the Communist regime came into being. I suppose the interrogator would have said that this was another instance of my stubborn reluctance to change my old way of life.

Some of my friends exclaimed, "Why did you bother to zip up your slacks at all when you had your handcuffs on!" I suppose I could have left my slacks unzipped, but I would have felt terribly demoralized. That wouldn't have been good for my fighting spirit. Looking back on those years, I believe the main reason I was able to survive my ordeal was that the Maoist Revolutionaries failed to break my fighting spirit.

JUDITH ORTIZ COFER
(1952–)

Judith Ortiz Cofer's childhood was divided between Puerto Rico, where she was born and where she lived in her maternal grandmother's matriarchal household, and Paterson, New Jersey, where her father's work brought her family for many months every year. In addition to *Silent Dancing* (1990), which was inspired by Virginia Woolf's memoir *Moments of Being,* she has written poetry and a novel.

This selection evokes the sensuousness of her time in Puerto Rico and the charm and wisdom of the women she grew up among. For another version of matriarchy, compare Vivian Gornick, *Fierce Attachments.*

FROM *Silent Dancing*

CASA

At three or four o'clock in the afternoon, the hour of *café con leche,* the women of my family gathered in Mamá's living room to speak of important things and to tell stories for the hundredth time, as if to each other, meant to be overheard by us young girls, their daughters. In Mamá's house (everyone called my grandmother Mamá) was a large parlor built by my grandfather to his wife's exact specifications so that it was always cool, facing away from the sun. The doorway was on the side of the house so no one could walk directly into her living room. First they had to take a little stroll through and around her beautiful garden where prize-winning orchids grew in the trunk of an ancient tree she had hollowed out for that purpose. This room was furnished with several mahogany rocking chairs, acquired at the births of her children, and one intricately carved rocker that had passed down to Mamá at the death of her own mother. It was on these rockers that my mother, her sisters and my grandmother sat on these afternoons of my childhood to tell their stories, teaching each other and my cousin and me what it was like to be a woman, more specifically, a Puerto Rican woman. They talked about life on the island, and life in *Los Nueva Yores,* their way of referring to the U.S., from New York City to California: the other place, not home, all the same. They told real-life stories, though as I later learned, always embellishing them with a little or a lot of dramatic detail, and they told *cuentos,* the morality and cautionary tales told by the women in our family for generations: stories that became a part of my subconscious as I grew up in two worlds, the tropical island and the cold city, and which would later surface in my dreams and in my poetry.

One of these tales was about the woman who was left at the altar. Mamá liked to tell that one with histrionic intensity. I remember the rise and fall of her voice, the sighs, and her constantly gesturing hands, like two birds swooping through her words. This particular story would usually come up in a conversation as a result of someone mentioning a forthcoming engagement or wedding. The first time I remember hearing it, I was sitting on the floor at Mamá's feet, pretending to read a comic book. I may have been eleven or twelve years old: at that difficult age when a girl is no longer a child who can be ordered to leave the room if the women wanted freedom to take their talk into forbidden zones, or really old enough to be considered a part of their conclave. I could only sit quietly, pretending to be in another world, while absorbing it all in a sort of unspoken agreement of my status as silent auditor. On this day, Mamá had taken my long, tangled mane of hair into her ever busy hands. Without looking down at me or interrupting her flow of words, she began braiding my hair, working at it with the quickness and determination which characterized all her actions. My mother was watching us impassively from her rocker across the room. On her lips played a little ironic smile. I would never sit still for *her* ministrations, but even then, I instinctively knew that she did not possess Mamá's matriarchal power to command and keep everyone's attention. This was particularly evident in the spell she cast when telling a story.

"It is not like it used to be when I was a girl." Mamá announced, "Then, a man could leave a girl standing at the church altar with a bouquet of fresh flowers in her hands and disappear off the face of the earth. No way to track him down if he was from another town. He could be a married man, with maybe even two or three families all over the island. There was no way to know. And there were men who did this. Hombres with the devil in their flesh who would come to a pueblo, like this one, take a job at one of the haciendas, never meaning to stay, only to have a good time and to seduce the women."

The whole time she was speaking, Mamá was weaving my hair into a flat plait which required pulling apart the two sections of hair with little jerks that made my eyes water; but knowing how grandmother detested whining and *boba* (sissy) tears, as she called them, I just sat up as straight and stiff as I did at La Escuela San José, where the nuns enforced good posture with a flexible plastic ruler they bounced off slumped shoulders and heads. As Mamá's story progressed, I noticed how my young aunt Laura had lowered her eyes, refusing to meet Mamá's meaningful gaze. Laura was seventeen, in her last year of high school, and already engaged to a boy from another town who had staked his claim with a tiny diamond ring, then left for Los Nueva Yores to make his fortune. They were planning to get married in a year; but Mamá had expressed serious doubts that the wedding would ever take place. In Mamá's eyes, a man set free without a legal contract was a man lost. She believed that marriage was not something men desired, but simply the price they had to pay for the privilege of children, and of course, for what no decent (synonymous with "smart") woman would give away for free. "María la Loca was only seventeen when *it* happened to her." I listened closely at the mention of this name. María was a town "character," a fat middle-aged woman who lived with her old mother on the outskirts of town. She was to be seen around the pueblo delivering the meat pies the two women made for a living. The most peculiar thing about María, in my eyes, was that she walked and moved like a little girl, though she had the thick body and wrinkled face of an old woman. She would swing her hips in an exaggerated, clownish way, and sometimes even hop and skip up to someone's house. She spoke to no one. Even if you asked her a question, she would just look at you and smile, showing her yellow teeth. But I had heard that if you got close enough, you could hear her humming a tune without words. The kids yelled out nasty things at her, calling her *la Loca,* and the men who hung out at the bodega playing dominoes sometimes whistled mockingly as she passed by with her funny, outlandish walk. But María seemed impervious to it all, carrying her basket of *pasteles* like a grotesque Little Red Riding Hood through the forest.

María la Loca interested me, as did all the eccentrics and "crazies" of our pueblo. Their weirdness was a measuring stick I used in my serious quest for a definition of "normal." As a Navy brat, shuttling between New Jersey and the pueblo, I was constantly made to feel like an oddball by my peers, who made fun of my two-way accent: a Spanish accent when I spoke English; and, when I spoke Spanish, I was told that I sounded like a "Gringa." Being the outsiders had already turned my brother and me into cultural chameleons, developing early the ability to blend into a crowd, to sit and read quietly in a fifth story apartment building for days and days when it was too bitterly cold to play outside; or, set free, to run wild in Mamá's realm, where she took charge of our lives, releasing mother for a while from the intense fear for our safety that our father's absences instilled in her. In order to keep us from harm when father was away, mother kept us under strict surveillance. She even walked us to and from Public School No. 11, which we attended during the months we lived in Paterson, New Jersey, our home base in the States. Mamá freed the three of us like pigeons from a cage. I saw her as my liberator and my model. Her stories were parables from which to glean the *Truth*.

"María la Loca was once a beautiful girl. Everyone thought she would marry the Méndez boy." As everyone knew, Rogelio Méndez was no other than the richest man in town. "But," Mamá continued, knitting my hair with the same intensity she was putting into her story, "this *macho* made a fool out of her and ruined her life." She paused for the effect of her use of the word "macho," which at that time had not yet become a popular epithet for an unliberated man. This word had for us the crude and comical connotation of "male of the species," stud; a *macho* was what you put in a pen to increase your stock.

I peeked over my comic book at my mother. She too was under Mamá's spell, smiling conspiratorially at this little swipe at men. She was safe from Mamá's contempt in this area. Married at an early age, an unspotted lamb, she had been accepted by a good family of strict Spaniards whose name was old and respected, though their fortune had been lost long before my birth. In a rocker Papá had painted sky blue sat Mamá's oldest child, Aunt Nena. Mother of three children, stepmother of two more, she was a quiet woman who liked books but had married an ignorant and abusive widower whose main interest in life was accumulating wealth. He too was in the mainland working on his dream of returning home rich and triumphant to buy the *finca* of his dreams. She was waiting for him to send for her. She would leave her children with Mamá for several years while the two of them slaved away in factories. He would one day be a rich man, and she a sadder woman. Even now her life-light was dimming. She spoke little, an aberration in Mamá's house, and she read avidly, as if storing up spiritual food for the long winters that awaited her in Los Nueva Yores without her family. But even Aunt Nena came alive to Mamá's words, rocking gently, her hands over a thick book in her lap. Her daughter, my cousin Sara, played jacks by herself on the tile porch outside the room where we sat. She was a year older than I. We shared a bed and all our family's secrets. Collaborators in search of answers, Sara and I discussed everything we heard the women say, trying to fit it all together like a puzzle that once assembled would reveal life's mysteries to us. Though she and I still enjoyed taking part in boy's games—chase, volleyball and even *vaqueros*, the island version of cowboys and Indians involving cap-gun battles and violent shootouts under the mango tree in Mamá's backyard—we loved best the quiet hours in the afternoon when the men were still at work and the boys had gone to play serious baseball at the park. Then Mamá's house belonged only to us women. The aroma of coffee perking in the kitchen, the mesmerizing creaks and groans of the rockers, and the women telling their lives in *cuentos* are forever woven into the fabric of my imagination, braided like my hair that day I felt my grandmother's hands teaching me about strength, her voice convincing me of the power of storytelling.

That day Mamá told of how the beautiful María had fallen prey to a man whose name was never the same in subsequent versions of the story; it was Juan one time, José, Rafael, Diego, another. We understood that the name, and really any of the facts, were not important, only that a woman had allowed love to defeat her. Mamá put each of us in María's place by describing her wedding dress in loving detail: how she looked like a princess in her lace as she waited at the altar. Then, as Mamá approached the tragic denouement of her story, I was distracted by the sound of my Aunt Laura's violent rocking. She seemed on the verge of tears. She knew the fable was intended for her. That week she was going to have her wedding gown fitted, though no firm date had been set for the marriage. Mamá ignored Laura's obvious discomfort, digging out a ribbon from the sewing basket she kept by her rocker while describing María's long illness, "a fever that would not break for days." She spoke of a mother's despair: "that woman climbed the church steps on her knees every morning, wore only black as a *promesa* to the Holy Virgin in exchange for her daughter's health." By the time María returned from her honeymoon with death, she was ravished, no longer young or sane. "As you can see she is almost as old as her mother already," Mamá lamented while tying the ribbon to the ends of my hair, pulling it back with such force that I just knew that I would never be able to close my eyes completely again.

"That María is getting crazier every day." Mamá's voice would take a lighter tone now, expressing satisfaction, either for the perfection of my braid, or for a story well-told; it was hard to tell. "You know that tune she is always humming?" Carried away by her enthusiasm, I tried to nod, but Mamá would still have me pinned between her knees.

"Well, that's the wedding march." Surprising us all, Mamá sang out, *"Da, da, dará . . . da, da, dará."* Then lifting me off the floor by my skinny shoulders, she led me around the room in an impromptu waltz— another session ending with the laughter of women, all of us caught up in the infectious joke of our lives.

.   .   .

Tales Told under the Mango Tree

María Sabida

Once upon a time there lived a girl who was so smart that she was known throughout Puerto Rico as María Sabida.* María Sabida came into the world with her eyes open. They say that at the moment of her birth she spoke to the attending midwife and told her what herbs to use to make a special *guarapo,* a tea that would put her mother back on her feet immediately. They say that the two women would have thought the infant was possessed if María Sabida had not convinced them with her descriptions of life in heaven that she was touched by God and not spawned by the Devil.

María Sabida grew up in the days when the King of Spain owned Puerto Rico, but had forgotten to send law and justice to this little island lost on the map of the world. And so thieves and murderers roamed the land terrorizing the poor people. By the time María Sabida was of marriageable age, one such *ladrón* had taken over the district where she lived.

For years people had been subjected to abuse from this evil man and his henchmen. He robbed them of their cattle and then made them buy their own cows back from him. He would take their best chickens and produce when he came into town on Saturday afternoons riding with his men through the stalls set up by farmers. Overturning their tables, he would yell, "Put it on my account." But of course he never paid for anything he took. One year several little children disappeared while walking to the river, and although the townspeople searched and searched, no trace of them was ever found. That is when María Sabida entered the picture. She was fifteen then, and a beautiful girl with the courage of a man, they say.

She watched the chief *ladrón* the next time he rampaged through the pueblo. She saw that he was a young man: red-skinned, and tough as leather. *Cuero y sangre, nada más,* she said to herself, a man of flesh and blood. And so she prepared herself to either conquer or to kill this man.

María Sabida followed the horses' trail deep into the woods. Though she left the town far behind she never felt afraid or lost. María Sabida could read the sun, the moon, and the stars for direction. When she got hungry, she knew which fruits were good to eat, which roots and leaves

---

*"Sabida" is from the verb *saber,* "to know how." María Sabida could be translated as Maria the Savvy.—Ed.

were poisonous, and how to follow the footprints of animals to a water-hole. At nightfall, María Sabida came to the edge of a clearing where a large house, almost like a fortress, stood in the forest.

"No woman has ever set foot in that house," she thought, "no *casa* is this, but a man-place." It was a house built for violence, with no windows on the ground level, but there were turrets on the roof where men could stand guard with guns. She waited until it was nearly dark and approached the house through the kitchen side. She found it by smell.

In the kitchen which she knew would have to have a door or window for ventilation, she saw an old man stirring a huge pot. Out of the pot stuck little arms and legs. Angered by the sight, María Sabida entered the kitchen, pushed the old man aside, and picking up the pot threw its horrible contents out of the window.

"Witch, witch, what have you done with my master's stew!" yelled the old man. "He will kill us both when he gets home and finds his dinner spoiled."

"Get, you filthy *viejo.*" María Sabida grabbed the old man's beard and pulled him to his feet. "Your master will have the best dinner of his life if you follow my instructions."

María Sabida then proceeded to make the most delicious *asopao* the old man had ever tasted, but she would answer no questions about herself, except to say that she was his master's fiancée.

When the meal was done, María Sabida stretched and yawned and said that she would go upstairs and rest until her *prometido* came home. Then she went upstairs and waited.

The men came home and ate ravenously of the food María Sabida had cooked. When the chief *ladrón* had praised the old man for a fine meal, the cook admitted that it had been *la prometida* who had made the tasty chicken stew.

"My what?" the leader roared. "I have no *prometida.*" And he and his men ran upstairs. But there were many floors, and by the time they were halfway to the room where María Sabida waited, many of the men had dropped down unconscious and the others had slowed down to a crawl until they too were overcome with irresistible sleepiness. Only the chief *ladrón* made it to where María Sabida awaited him holding a paddle that she had found among his weapons. Fighting to keep his eyes open, he asked her, "Who are you, and why have you poisoned me?"

"I am your future wife, María Sabida, and you are not poisoned, I added a special sleeping powder that tastes like oregano to your *asopao.* You will not die."

"Witch!" yelled the chief *ladrón.* "I will kill you. Don't you know who I am?" And reaching for her, he fell on his knees, whereupon María Sabida beat him with the paddle until he lay curled like a child on the floor. Each time he tried to attack her, she beat him some more. When she was satisfied that he was vanquished, María Sabida left the house and went back to town.

A week later, the chief *ladrón* rode into town with his men again. By then everyone knew what María Sabida had done and they were afraid of what these evil men would do in retribution. "Why did you not just kill him when you had a chance, *muchacha?*" many of the townswomen had asked María Sabida. But she had just answered mysteriously, "It is better to conquer than to kill." The townspeople then barricaded themselves behind closed doors when they heard the pounding of the thieves' horses approaching. But the gang did not stop until they arrived at María Sabida's house. There the men, instead of guns, brought out musical instruments: a *cuatro*, a *güiro*, *maracas*, and a harmonica. Then they played a lovely melody.

"María Sabida, María Sabida, my strong and wise María," called out the leader, sitting tall on his horse under María Sabida's window, "come out and listen to a song I've written for you—I call it *The Ballad of María Sabida.*"

María Sabida then appeared on her balcony wearing a wedding dress. The chief *ladrón* sang his song to her: a lively tune about a woman who had the courage of a man and the wisdom of a judge, who had conquered the heart of the best *bandido* on the island of Puerto Rico. He had a strong voice and all the people cowering in their locked houses heard his tribute to María Sabida and crossed themselves at the miracle she had wrought.

One by one they all came out and soon María Sabida's front yard was full of people singing and dancing. The *ladrones* had come prepared with casks of wine, bottles of rum, and a wedding cake made by the old cook from the tender meat of coconuts. The leader of the thieves and María Sabida were married on that day. But all had not yet been settled between them. That evening, as she rode behind him on his horse, she felt the dagger concealed beneath his clothes. She knew then that she had not fully won the battle for this man's heart.

On her wedding night María Sabida suspected that her husband wanted to kill her. After their dinner, which the man had insisted on cooking himself, they went upstairs. María Sabida asked for a little time alone to prepare herself. He said he would take a walk but would return very soon. When she heard him leave the house, María Sabida went down to the kitchen and took several gallons of honey from the pantry. She went back to the bedroom and there she fashioned a life-sized doll out of her clothes and poured the honey into it. She then blew out the candle, covered the figure with a sheet and hid herself under the bed. After a short time, she heard her husband climbing the stairs. He tip-toed into the dark room thinking her asleep in their marriage bed. Peeking out from under the bed, María Sabida saw the glint of the knife her husband pulled out from inside his shirt. Like a fierce panther he leapt onto the bed and stabbed the doll's body over and over with his dagger. Honey splattered his face and fell on his lips. Shocked, the man jumped off the bed and licked his lips.

"How sweet is my wife's blood. How sweet is María Sabida in death—how sour in life and how sweet in death. If I had known she was so sweet, I would not have murdered her." And so declaring, he kneeled down on the floor beside the bed and prayed to María Sabida's soul for forgiveness.

At that moment María Sabida came out of her hiding place. "Husband, I have tricked you once more, I am not dead." In his joy, the man threw down his knife and embraced María Sabida, swearing that he would never kill or steal again. And he kept his word, becoming in later years an honest farmer. Many years later he was elected mayor of the same town he had once terrorized with his gang of *ladrones*.

María Sabida made a real *casa* out of his thieves' den, and they had many children together, all of whom could speak at birth. But, they say, María Sabida always slept with one eye open, and that is why she lived to be one hundred years old and wiser than any other woman on the Island of Puerto Rico, and her name was known even in Spain.

"Colorín, colorado este cuento se ha acabado." Mamá would slap her knees with open palms and say this little rhyme to indicate to the children sitting around her under the giant mango tree that the story was finished. It was time for us to go play and leave the women alone to embroider in the shade of the tree and to talk about serious things.

I remember that tree as a natural wonder. It was large, with a trunk that took four or five children holding hands to reach across. Its leaves were so thick that the shade it cast made a cool room where we took refuge from the hot sun. When an unexpected shower caught us there, the women had time to gather their embroidery materials before drops came through the leaves. But the most amazing thing about that tree was the throne it had made for Mamá. On the trunk there was a smooth seat-like projection. It was perfect for a storyteller. She would take her place on the throne and lean back. The other women—my mother and her sisters—would bring towels to sit on; the children sat anywhere. Sometimes we would climb to a thick branch we called "the ship," to the right of the throne, and listen there. "The ship" was a thick limb that hung all the way down to the ground. Up to three small children could straddle this branch while the others bounced on the end that sat near the ground making it sway like a ship. When Mamá told her stories, we sat quietly on our crow's nest because if anyone interrupted her narrative she should stop talking and no amount of begging would persuade her to finish the story that day.

The first time my mother took my brother and me back to Puerto Rico, we were stunned by the heat and confused by a houseful of relatives. Mamá's *casa* was filled to capacity with grandchildren, because two of the married daughters had come to stay there until their husbands sent for them: my mother and the two of us and her oldest sister with her five children. Mamá still had three of her own children at home, ranging in age from a teenage daughter to my favorite uncle who was six months older than me.

Our solitary life in New Jersey, where we spent our days inside a small dark apartment watching television and waiting for our father to come home on leave from the navy, had not prepared us for life in Mamá's house or for the multitude of cousins, aunts and uncles pulling us into their loud conversations and rough games. For the first few days my little brother kept his head firmly buried in my mother's neck, while I stayed relatively close to her; but being nearly six, and able to speak as loudly as anyone, I soon joined Mamá's tribe.

In the last few weeks before the beginning of school, when it was too hot for cooking until it was almost dark and when mothers would not even let their boys go to the playgrounds and parks for fear of sunstroke, Mamá would lead us to the mango tree, there to spin the web of our *cuentos* over us, making us forget the heat, the mosquitoes, our past in a foreign country, and even the threat of the first day of school looming just ahead.

It was under that mango tree that I first began to feel the power of words. I cannot claim to have always understood the point of the stories I heard there. Some of these tales were based on ancient folklore brought to the colonies by Spaniards from their own versions of even older myths of Greek and Roman origins—which, as I later discovered through my insatiable reading, had been modified in clever ways to fit changing times. María Sabida became the model Mamá used for the "prevailing woman"—the woman who "slept with one eye open"—whose wisdom was gleaned through the senses: from the natural world and from ordinary experiences. Her main virtue was that she was always alert and never a victim. She was by implication contrasted to María la Loca, that poor girl who gave it all up for love, becoming a victim of her own foolish heart.

The mango tree was located at the top of a hill, on land that belonged to "The American," or at least to the sugar refinery that he managed. *La Central,* as it was called, employed the majority of the pueblo's men. Its tall chimney stacks loomed over the town like sentinels, spewing plumes of grey smoke that filled the air during cane season with the syrupy thick aroma of burnt sugar.

In my childhood the sugarcane fields bordered both sides of the main road, which was like a part on a head of spiky, green hair. As we approached the pueblo on our way coming home, I remember how my mother sat up in the back seat of the *carro público*, the taxi, we had taken from the airport in San Juan. Although she was pointing out the bell tower of the famous church of La Monserrate, I was distracted by the hypnotizing motion of men swinging machetes in the fields. They were shirtless, and sweat poured in streams down their backs. Bathed in light reflected by their blades, these laborers moved as on a ballet stage. I wondered whether they practiced like dancers to perfect their synchronicity. It did not occur to me that theirs was "survival choreography"—merely a safety measure—for wild swinging could lead to lost fingers and limbs. Or, as I heard one of the women say once, "there are enough body parts in the cane fields to put one whole man together." . . .

We sucked on little pieces of sugarcane Mamá had cut for us under the mango tree. Below us a pasture rolled down to the road and the cane fields could be seen at a distance; the men in their perpetual motion were tiny black ants to our eyes. You looked up to see the red roof of the American's house. It was a big white house with a large porch completely enclosed by mosquito screens (on the Island at that time this was such a rarity that all houses designed in that way were known as "American"). At Mamá's house we slept cozily under mosquito nets, but during the day we fought the stinging, buzzing insects with bare hands and, when we lost a battle, we soothed our scratched raw skin with calamine lotion.

During the first few weeks of our visits both my brother and I, because we were fresh, tender meat, had skin like a pink target, dotted with red spots where the insects had scored bulls-eyes. Amazingly, either we built up a natural resistance, or the mosquitoes gave up, but it happened every time: a period of embarrassment as pink "turistas," followed by brown skin and immunity. Living behind screens, the American couple would never develop the tough skin needed for Island survival.

When Mamá told stories about kings and queens and castles, she would point to the big house on the hill. We were not supposed to go near the place. In fact, we were trespassing when we went to the mango tree. Mamá's backyard ended at the barbed-wire fence that led to the American's pasture. The tree stood just on the other side. She had, at some point before my time, placed a strong stick under the barbed wire to make an entrance; but it could only be pulled up so much, so that even the children had to crawl through. Mamá seemed to relish the difficulty of getting to our special place. For us children it was fun to watch our mothers get their hair and clothes caught on the wire and to listen to them curse.

The pasture was a magical realm of treasures and secret places to discover. It even had a forbidden castle we could look at from a distance.

While the women embroidered, my girl-cousins and I would gather leaves and thorns off a lemon tree and do some imaginative stitch work of our own. The boys would be in the "jungle" gathering banana leaves they built tepees with. Imitating the grownups who were never without a cigarette hanging from their mouths, we would pick the tightly wrapped buds of the hibiscus flowers, which, with their red tips, looked to us like lighted cigarettes. We glued wild flower petals to our fingernails and, although they did not stay on for long, for a little while our hands, busy puncturing the leaves into patterns with lemon tree thorns, looked like our mother's with their red nail polish, pushing needle and thread through white linen, creating improbable landscapes of trailing vines and flowers, decorating the sheets and pillowcases we would sleep on.

We picked ripe guavas in their season and dumped them on Mamá's capacious lap for her to inspect for worms before we ate them. The sweetness of a ripe guava cannot be compared to anything else: its pink, gooey inside can be held on the tongue and savored like a caramel.

During mango season we threw rocks at the branches of our tree, hanging low with fruit. Later in the season, a boy would climb to the highest branches for the best fruit—something I always yearned to do, but was not allowed to: too dangerous.

On days when Mamá felt truly festive she would send us to the store with three dollars for ten bottles of Old Colony pop and the change in assorted candies: Mary Janes, Bazooka gum, lollypops, tiny two-piece boxes of Chiclets, coconut candy wrapped in wax paper, and more—all kept in big glass jars and sold two for one penny. We would have our reckless feast under the mango tree and then listen to a story. Afterwards, we would take turns on the swing that touched the sky.

My grandfather had made a strong swing from a plank of heavy wood and a thick length of rope. Under Mamá's supervision he had hung it from a sturdy lower branch of the mango tree that reached over the swell of the hill. In other words, you boarded the swing on level ground, but since the tree rose out of the summit, one push and you took off for the sky. It was almost like flying. From the highest point I ever reached, I could see the big house, as a bird would see it, to my left; the church tower from above the trees to my right; and far in the distance, below me, my family in a circle under the tree, receding, growing smaller; then, as I came back down to earth, looming larger, my mother's eyes glued on me, reflecting the fear for my safety that she would not voice in her mother's presence and thus risk overriding the other's authority. My mother's greatest fear was that my brother or I would hurt ourselves while at Mamá's, and that she would be held accountable by my excessively protective father when he returned from his tour of duty in Europe. And one day, because fear invites accident, I did fall from a ride up to the clouds.

I had been catapulting myself higher and higher, when out of the corner of my eye I saw my big cousin, Javier, running at top speed after his little brother, swinging a stick in front as if to strike the younger boy. This happened fast. The little boy, Roberto, ran towards Mamá, who at that moment, was leaning towards my mother in conversation. Trying to get to his brother before he reached safe haven, Javier struck, accidentally hitting my mother square on the face. I saw it happening. I saw it as if in slow motion. I saw my mother's broken glasses fly off her face, and the blood begin to flow. Dazed, I let go of the swing ropes and flew down from the clouds and the treetops and onto the soft cushion of pasture grass and just rolled and rolled. Then I lay there stunned, tasting grass and dirt until Mamá's strong arms lifted me up. She carried me through the fence and down to her house where my mother was calling hysterically for me. Her glasses had protected her from serious injury. The bump on her forehead was minor. The nosebleed had already been contained by the age-old method of placing a copper penny on the bridge, between the eyes. Her tears upset me, but not as much as the way she made me stand before her, in front of everyone, while she examined my entire body for bruises, scratches, and broken bones. "What will your father say," she kept repeating, until Mamá pulled me away. "Nothing," she said to my mother, "if you don't tell him." And, leaving her grown daughters to comfort each other, she called the children out to the yard where she had me organize a game of hide-and-seek that she supervised, catching cheaters right and left.

When it rained, the children were made to take naps or play quietly in the bedroom. I asked for Mamá's monumental poster bed, and, when my turn came, I got it. There I lay four or five feet above ground inhaling her particular smells of coconut oil (which she used to condition her thick black hair) and Palmolive soap. I would luxuriate in her soft pillows and her mattress which was covered with gorgeously embroidered bed linens. I would get sleepy listening to the drone of the women's conversation out of the parlor.

Beyond the double doors of her peacock blue bedroom, I could hear Mamá and her older daughters talking about things that, at my age, would not have interested me: They read letters received from my father traveling with the navy in Europe, or letters from any of the many relatives making their way in the barrios of New York and New Jersey, working in factories and dreaming of returning "in style" to Puerto Rico.

The women would discuss the new school year, and plan a shopping trip to the nearest city, Mayagüez, for materials to make school uniforms for the children, who by September had to be outfitted in brown and white and marched off to the public school looking like Mussolini's troops in our dull uniforms. Their talk would take on more meaning for me as I got older, but that first year back on the Island I was under María Sabida's spell. To entertain myself, I would make up stories about the smartest girl in all of Puerto Rico.

When María Sabida was only six years old, I began, she saved her little brother's life. He was dying of a broken heart, you see, for he desperately wanted some sweet guavas that grew at the top of a steep, rocky hill near the lair of a fierce dragon. No one had ever dared to climb that hill, though everyone could see the huge guava tree and the fruit, as big as pears, hanging from its branches. María Sabida's little brother had stared at the tree until he had made himself sick from yearning for the forbidden fruit.

Everyone knew that the only way to save the boy was to give him one of the guavas. María Sabida's parents were frantic with worry. The little boy was fading fast. The father tried climbing the treacherous hill to the guava tree, but the rocks were loose and for every step forward he took, he slipped back three. He returned home. The mother spent her days cooking delicious meals with which to tempt her little son to eat, but he just turned his sad eyes to the window in his room from where he could see the guava tree loaded with the only food he wanted. The doctor came to examine the boy and pronounced him as good as gone. The priest came and told the women they should start making their black dresses. All hope seemed lost when María Sabida, whose existence everyone seemed to have forgotten, came up with an idea to save her brother one day while she was washing her hair in the special way her grandmother had taught her.

Her mamá had shown her how to collect rainwater—water from the sky—into a barrel, and then, when it was time to wash her hair, how to take a fresh coconut and draw the oil from its white insides. You then took a bowl of clear rainwater and added the coconut oil, using the mixture to rinse your hair. Her mamá had shown her how the rainwater, coming as it did from the sky, had little bits of starshine in it. This starstuff was what made your hair glossy, the oil was to make it stick.

It was while María Sabida was mixing the starshine that she had the brilliant idea which saved her brother. She ran to her father who was in the stable feeding the mule and asked if she could borrow the animal that night. The man, startled by his daughter's wild look (her hair was streaming wet and she still held the coconut scraps in her hands) at first just ordered his daughter into the house, thinking that she had gone crazy with grief over her brother's imminent death. But María Sabida could be stubborn, and she refused to move until her parents heard what she had to say. The man called his wife to the stable, and when María Sabida had finished telling them her plan, he still thought she had lost her mind. He agreed with his desperate wife that at this point anything was worth trying. They let María Sabida have the mule to use that night.

María Sabida then waited until it was pitch black. She knew there would be no moon that night. Then she drew water from her rainbarrel and mixed it with plenty of coconut oil and plastered her mule's hoofs with it. She led the animal to the bottom of the rocky hill where the thick, sweet smell of ripe guavas was irresistible. María Sabida felt herself caught in the spell. Her mouth watered and she felt drawn to the guava tree. The mule must have felt the same thing because it started walking ahead of the girl with quick, sure steps. Though rocks came tumbling down, the animal found footing, and in so doing, left a shiny path with the bits of starshine that María Sabida had glued to its hoofs. María Sabida kept her eyes on the bright trail because it was a dark, dark night.

As she approached the guava tree, the sweet aroma was like a liquid that she drank through her nose. She could see the fruit within arms-reach when the old mule stretched her neck to eat one and a horrible scaly arm reached out and yanked the animal off the path. María Sabida quickly grabbed three guavas and ran down the golden trail all the way back to her house.

When she came into her little brother's room, the women had already gathered around the bed with their flowers and their rosaries, and because María Sabida was a little girl herself and could not see past the crowd, she thought for one terrible minute that she was too late. Luckily, her brother smelled the guavas from just this side of death and he sat up in bed. María Sabida pushed her way through the crowd and gave him one to eat. Within minutes the color returned to his cheeks. Everyone rejoiced remembering other wonderful things that she had done, and why her middle name was "Sabida."

And, yes, María Sabida ate one of the enchanted guavas herself and was never sick a day in her long life. The third guava was made into a jelly that could cure every childhood illness imaginable, from a toothache to the chicken pox.

"Colorín, colorado . . ." I must have said to myself, "Colorín colorado . . ." as I embroidered my own fable, listening all the while to that inner voice which, when I was very young, sounded just like Mamá's when she told her stories in the parlor or under the mango tree. And later, as I gained more confidence in my own ability, the voice telling the story became my own.

COLETTE
(1873–1954)

Sidonie Gabrielle Colette was twenty when she married Henri Gauthier-Villars, a literary entrepreneur known as Willy who was considerably older than she was. He set her to writing novels featuring a schoolgirl heroine, Claudine, which he published under his own name. He had been betraying her sexually almost from the moment he brought her to Paris from her native Burgundy. In *My Apprenticeships* (1936) she describes the early years of their marriage. When the marriage ended, Colette, who was then thirty-two, supported herself on the music hall stage, an experience which formed the basis of her novel *The Vagabond*. Much of Colette's writing features a character like herself whom she calls Colette and rather systematically blurs the line between fiction and autobiography. It is typical of many aggressively pursued ambiguities in her life, not excluding her sexual identification, that the name she chose to be known by was her father's family name but could just as well be a Frenchwoman's first name.

For accounts of marriages and para-marriages, compare Simone de Beauvoir, *The Prime of Life*, Émilie Carles, *A Life of Her Own*, Eleanor Coppola, *Notes*, Lillian Hellman, *Pentimento*, *Nisa: The Life and Words of a !Kung Woman*, and Sophia Tolstoy, *Diary*.

FROM *My Apprenticeships*

A third floor in the Rue Jacob, between two courtyards. One of the courtyards faced the north and the Rue Visconti, so that I had, at least, a glimpse of old tiled roofs to remind me of the tiles of Burgundy.

No sun. Three living rooms, a small, dark study, a kitchen on the other side of the landing—all this for fourteen hundred francs a year. In the square drawing-room was a salamander stove, and in the recess where I had set out my tub, my basins and my ewers, a gas fire. It was almost a poor man's flat, yet its white doors were early nineteenth century and still had their little carved wreaths and garlands, now half clogged with paint. I had not chosen it. On the day I saw it first it was empty, and I felt that I was only half awake. The last tenant had lived there for fifty years, long enough to complete a most singular form of decoration. The doors, the ornaments on the doors, the cornices, the skirtings, the niche for the porcelain stove in the dining-room, the sham wood panels, the shelves of the cupboards, the window frames and a large surface of the walls themselves, were covered with tiny diamond-shaped confetti of many colours, cut out and glued on by hand, one by one.

"I understood from the gentleman himself," the concierge confided to me in a low, reverent voice, "that there were more than two hundred and seventy-five thousand pieces. I call that work."

Work such as you do in nightmares. The thought of living in these rooms, in the presence of walls that had witnessed so secret a madness, so evil a joy, appalled me. And then I forgot about it. I was only a young bride.

No light, no air, the dark enchantment that sometimes lingers in places that have crushed and stifled many souls. The little flat must, I think, have been profoundly melancholy. And yet, to me, it seemed agreeable. What it is to have known worse! I had gone to it from another lodging, M. Willy's bachelor establishment, a quaking, echoing garret, at the top of one of the houses on the quays, that shivered at every passing bus and lorry. I have never been able to forget that attic and its murky, rattling double windows. Painted in bottle green and chocolate brown, filled with unspeakably sordid cardboard files, soaked in a sort of horrible office gloom, it looked uninhabited, utterly forsaken. The draughts crept over the creaking boards; their slightest breath brought forth, out of the black shadows, from under the sagging springs of the bed, a grey snow, a drift of flakes born, as some frail nests are born, of a thread, a hair, woven with dust as light and soft as down. Heaps of yellowing newspapers occupied the chairs; German postcards were strewn more or less everywhere, celebrating the attractions of under-clothes, socks, ribboned drawers and buttocks. The master of the house would have strongly objected to any attempt on my part to remedy the disorder.

It was a relief to get away, every morning, from these indecent sur-roundings. The place had been adapted solely to the use, the careless convenience of a dissolute bachelor, and I welcomed the daylight that took me from it. I welcomed the daylight also for its own sake, because it drew me out of bed and into the open air. And because I was hungry. By half-past eight or thereabouts, M. Willy and I were crossing the bridge. Ten minutes' walk took us to the humble milkshop where the blue-smocked packers from *La Belle Jardinière* kept up their strength, as we did, on rolls dipped in pale mauve chocolate.

Judging from various incidents that stand out sharply in a haze of unhappy memories, it would appear that M. Willy and I lived very poorly. It is quite possible, I may say probable. I remember that "Sido,"

my mother, came to Paris for a few days in the winter of 1894, or
1895—she always stayed at the Hôtel du Palais Royal—and found that I
had no outdoor coat of any kind against the bitter weather. She said
nothing. She gave her son-in-law a look out of her keen, wide eyes, and
took me off to the *Magasins du Louvre* to buy a black top-coat, trimmed
with "Mongolian" fur that cost a hundred and twenty-five francs and
seemed to me sumptuous. The very young are not deeply affected by
certain forms of hardship. The incongruous, too, often scarcely touches
them. The picture comes back to me suddenly of a heap of gold shining
on the black-painted deal writing-table and its red baize cover—a mass
of gold louis that M. Willy had spilt there out of his pockets.

"Take as much of it," he said, "as you can hold in both hands. You'll
count up afterwards."

I counted eight hundred and twenty francs. Coined gold is a pretty
metal; it has a fine, clear ring, and warms pleasantly to the touch.

"I hope," said M. Willy, "that you won't want any more housekeeping money now for at least two months."

It seemed quite natural to go about with an empty purse, as I had done
before my marriage; it never occurred to me, either, that I might have
lived more comfortably. After the morning's cup of lilac chocolate, I
would hurry back to my dark quarters. I did not realise that in their
strange gloom I was gradually losing strength, that the life was ebbing
from a vigorous country girl, brought up on the wealth that the countryside granted in those days to the poor; milk at twopence a quart, fruit
and vegetables, butter at sevenpence a pound, eggs at sevenpence ha'-
penny the dozen, chestnuts, walnuts . . . In Paris I was never hungry. I
hid in my corner, chiefly because I did not wish to know Paris. The town
filled me with dread, and after ten months of marriage I already had
most excellent reasons for fearing it. A book, hundreds of books, low,
airless rooms, sweets instead of meat, an oil lamp instead of sunshine—
and always the persistent, absurd hope to which I clung: this great evil,
this city life, could not last; it would be cured miraculously, by my death
and resurrection, by a shock that would restore me to my mother's
house, to the garden, and wipe out everything that marriage had taught
me.

Is it hard to understand how to have gone from a village home to the
life I led after 1894 was an adventure so serious that it could bring a child
of twenty to despair? Despair or a wild intoxication. It is true that, at
first, ridden by youth and ignorance, I had known intoxication—a guilty
rapture, an atrocious, impure, adolescent impulse. There are many
scarcely nubile girls who dream of becoming the show, the plaything, the
licentious masterpiece of some middle-aged man. It is an ugly dream
that is punished by its fulfilment, a morbid thing, akin to the neuroses of

puberty, the habit of eating chalk and coal, of drinking mouthwash, of reading dirty books and sticking pins into the palm of the hand.

So I was punished, quickly and thoroughly. One day, dressed in my handsome, hundred-and-twenty-five franc coat, my serpent of hair bound with a new ribbon, I took a cab to the Rue Bochard-de-Saron and rang the bell of a minute, mezzanine-floor flat. Anonymous letters often tell the truth. There, in fact, were M. Willy and Mlle. Charlotte Kinceler, not in bed but sitting in front of—yes!—an open account book. M. Willy was holding the pencil. I listened to the pulse beating in my tonsils, and the two lovers stared, astounded, at the pale young provincial with the long hair, her plait coiled round her neck, her fringe curling on her forehead. What could I say? A dark little woman—four foot ten, to be exact—was watching me, a pair of scissors grasped tightly in her hand; a word, a movement, and she would have flown at my face. Was I afraid? No, I wasn't afraid. Violence, catastrophe, the hope of disaster, blood, a sudden shriek—at twenty, if you look into yourself, you can see tragic landscapes any day that are far finer than that. I should say that neither Mlle. Kinceler nor I seemed in the least put out, whereas M. Willy sat mopping his brow, which was vast, powerful and pink.

"You've come to fetch me?" he said.

I glanced uncertainly at Mlle. Kinceler and my husband, at my husband and Mlle. Kinceler, and found nothing better than to say, in my politest drawing-room manner:

"Why yes. Don't you think . . . ?"

He rose, pushed me in front of him, hustled me out of the front door with almost magical celerity. In the street I felt a little proud of having shown no fear, uttered no threats. But I was sorry I had not heard Mlle. Kinceler's voice. And above all I was taken up, bitterly absorbed, by what I had seen: the neat, tidy little flat, a sunny window, a general air of ease and familiarity, the half-folded table with its American-cloth cover, a cage of canaries, the corner of a large bed just showing in the next room, the shining brasses and enamels of a tiny kitchen, the rather corpulent man seated sideways on a caned chair, the little firebrand of a woman grasping her scissors—and the intruder, the girl with the long plait, silent and slender in her ready-made coat.

I could hear my husband's short, agitated breathing. From time to time he removed his flat-brimmed top hat and wiped his forehead. He could not make out what it all meant, my arrival, my silence, my oddly restrained behaviour. Nor could I. Later, I understood that through the strangeness and the shock, the depths of my amazement and indeed of my despair, I had been able to think quickly, to make up my mind at once that whatever happened I must hide the truth from "Sido." I kept my word.

I was not able to deceive her completely; she had eyes that could see through walls. But for thirteen years I did my best to make her think me altogether happy. It was not easy, especially at first. When I went to stay with her at Châtillon-Coligny, there was always one moment that I looked forward to with dread. The early hours of my visit were simple enough. Although the house was small and poor, very different from the big house at Saint-Sauveur where I was born, merely to be in it, to live a country life again, gave me back my fondness for laughter, for chattering and asking questions, for driving in the wheezy De Dion with my doctor brother and waiting for him by the farmhouse gates. On the evening of my arrival I used to tell my mother of the new people I had met, describe Catulle Mendès and Gustave Charpentier, Judith Gautier's black cat and her green lizard, Courteline. . . . But soon the moment would come, I could feel it drawing near, when my brother's weariness, the exhaustion of fifteen hours' ceaseless rounds, must take his white face and tired limbs to rest, the moment when my father must enjoy the sleep that comes so swiftly to aging men, the moment, the beloved hour when I would be alone with my mother. Stretched out, the hot water bottle at my feet, I had to watch her sit down in the dilapidated armchair beside my bed, her cheeks flushed with pleasure at the sight of me and exasperation at her own fatigue: "Oh, that back . . . that left leg . . . that neck of mine!"

She would have nothing of her ills. Her way of speaking of them was a rejection, a denial of their existence. She had a gesture, too, that seemed to cast them off, as though she were flinging back a cloak that was too hot, or a mane of long thick hair.

"Now tell me, tell me . . ."

Her questions, her eyes searched me with alarming penetration. But I was her daughter and already proficient at the game. So I chattered on of Paris, told her a hundred more tales of the hateful town I knew so little. I talked about plays and concerts, I kept a harsh grip on myself, in terror of that last, that greatest danger: "If she tucks me in, if, before tucking me in, she takes me in her arms, if I smell her soft hair and feel it on my cheek, if she chooses to call me her 'lovely sunshine,' then all is lost."

An hour later she called me her "lovely sunshine," pressed her thin, silky hair against my cheek and tucked the bedclothes under the mattress. I lay stiff and attentive, making no movement, saying no word, allowing nothing, nothing to escape me except a mumble of feigned drowsiness, a pretence of half-sleep. At the cost of such self-denial I got safely to the time when "Sido" would cry: "Eleven o'clock!" take the cat under her arm, pick up the oil lamp with her free hand and leave me until the morrow.

I have never been able to cry with ease, decency and fitting emotion.

Tears are as grievous to me as vomiting; they swell my nostrils and distort my mouth into an ugly square shape; they leave me with stiffened, aching ribs and hideously puffed eyelids. I cry as badly, as painfully as a man. But you can do away with tears if you put your mind to it; after I had been through a thorough training, I scarcely ever indulged in them. I have friends of thirty years standing who have never seen my eyes damp. "What? *You* cry?" they exclaim and stare at me under or over their spectacles, scanning my face, trying to imagine the traces of weeping, there beside the nose, there by the corner of the mouth. "*You* cry! Why how absurd!" They burst out laughing, and so do I, for after all to cry in public is a sort of incontinence that does not give you time, if it comes upon you suddenly, to run away and hide behind the nearest wall. I detest tears—perhaps because I have found them so very hard to conquer.

I saw Charlotte Kinceler again, later on. So did you, if you ever went to Brieux's *Les Hannetons.* "Lotte of Montmartre," daughter of a drink-sodden Communard, tempted Brieux, who wrote this play round her and chose Polaire for the chief part. Lotte seduced Lucien Guitry, dazzled Jules Lemaître and many others of the famous or prominent men who watched and listened to her shyly. Sometimes they slept with her, ritually as it were, hierophants of the new cult of which she was the first young priestess, of the new-born convention that was Montmartre. She was fresh-looking and tainted and could already—even to my inexperienced eyes—be suspected of directing and controlling the natural outflow of her talents, of turning their deep, spontaneous, lusty streams into artificial channels. But she had a long way to go before her dwarf's conceit could become tedious, her crippled urchin's wit irksome. To Jules Lemaître, dining with her and M. Willy at the austere "Foyot's," her prattle was like a chattering of Polynesian natives. He bent over her hands, her extraordinarily small feet, and marvelled. His guest spread her little claws out over the table.

"Five and a quarter I take," she said proudly, "and kids' size in shoes. My sister's the same. It's in the family."

"So you have a sister?"

"I should say so. Madame Ducroquet. She's a *demimondaine.*"

"Oh!" exclaimed Lemaître, "you should have brought her!"

She shook her head loftily.

"Can't be done. She swipes the silver."

"She—what?" Lemaître enquired, wondering. "Wipes the silver? I don't see anything so very strange in that. Of course it depends where you are dining . . ."

"No!" cried Lotte. "She snaffles it, I tell you!"

Lemaître flushed under the reproof.

"She —? I'm sorry, but I really don't understand."

Disheartened, Lotte appealed to M. Willy, whom she commonly addressed as "Kiki." With a sideway glance at the ingenuous Lemaître:

"Kiki!" she protested. "You told me he was clever!"

At this the gentle playwright beamed. His shrewd, kind eyes dwelt, enchanted, upon Lotte.

"What a joy she is! If only one could get her on the stage. . . ."

The native of Montmartre gave him her renewed esteem in a glowing, black and white look, veiled in dense, Oriental lashes.

"Oh! but I want to! Besides, I've got an idea for a play—a real play, none of your rotten funny pieces; they're all my eye; sloppy nonsense I call them—a *real* play. I'd act in it. Shall I tell it you? It's like this . . . I'd be a young married woman. My husband's a soaker, same as father. He drinks half the time and the rest of the time of course he cats. . . . I'm ever so unhappy. A bloke comes along who's rich and handsome and everything. He makes up to me. 'You get a divorce,' he says, 'and your life will be one long, sweet dream.' That looks a bit different to me, naturally! So one evening when I get back from work—"

"What work?" asked Lemaître.

"What work! What work!" Lotte repeated irritably. "What's he interrupting me for with his 'What work!'? I train fleas or I take in sewing. . . . So one evening when I get back from work I begin to cry. 'Ah!' I say to myself, 'the die is cast! I'll chuck the stinker and find true happiness.' But what do I see when I open the door? My husband's come home drunk and vomited everywhere! Vomited over the counterpane, vomited over the rug. Vomited over the curtains and the fern and the china flower-pot. So I kneel down and fold my hands and say—" She put her hands together and raised her eyes until only their whites were visible: "I say: 'This is where my duty lies. . . .' Well? What do you think of that?"

"I—er—of course—" stammered Lemaître. "To tell you the truth I had pictured you rather in comic parts."

"Comic!!!"

Standing up, and scarcely taller than he was sitting in his chair, she blazed at him. She turned to M. Willy, who was finding the party far from dull.

"*My good man,* you'll be kind enough in future not to invite me with flats like this. Stupid I wouldn't mind so much, but heartless—that I *can't* forgive. I'd sooner go home. And d'you want to know what I think? If you pay the bill, I'll say you're as big a bloody fool as he is!"

Lotte and I became, not friendly, but curious of one another, courteous, like duellists after a fight. She confessed to M. Willy that she had been much struck by my composure. "She looks a bit English, your wife, and she wears her hat too far back on her head. And those little curls on her forehead—they make you think of village weddings. All the same, when she came in that day she looked as if the place belonged to her. . . ." For my part I admired in Lotte qualities that I could never achieve as long as I lived: glibness of tongue, a miraculously nimble body, and complete omniscience. When she opened her herbalist's shop in the Rue Pauquet and I went there to buy my boracic vaseline, my handful of camomile tea, we faced each other again, and I did my best, a little over-sweetly, to win her favour. I was meek, I listened with extreme attention, making it plain that, from her, I had everything to learn. She expanded under the flattery. Sometimes, not to be behindhand in good manners, she would call on me, very much the lady in a short astrakhan coat, a great bunch of Parma violets tucked in at her waist, and a chenille-spotted veil stretched over her Peke's nose. One day, on arrival, she opened her fur coat, scented with Corylopsis, and drew from her bodice the edge of a chemise in finest handkerchief lawn, encrusted with Mechlin lace butterflies. M. Willy whistled admiringly.

"My word! Where did you get that?"

"A chap," said Lotte. "Three days. But I've done with him. What with the mug he had and a name like a bad joke—I slung him out."

"What name?"

"Oh! a name—what was it? Richard Lenoir. No, wait a minute, that's wrong. Edmond Blanc."*

There is nothing strange, I think, in my lingering over memories of Lotte Kinceler. She, who lived such a little while, taught me a great deal. With her came my first doubts of the man I had given myself to so trustfully, and the end of my girlhood, that uncompromising, exalted, absurd estate. From her I got my first notions of tolerance and conceal-ment and the possibility of coming to terms with an enemy. Concentra-tion, humility—it was an instructive time. Lotte sold me her zinc oint-ment as though it were worth its weight in gold, but I was still the gainer. In her parlour, behind the shop, I drank lime-flower tea, served on a fringed table-cloth, and lost my foolish belief that because she had de-ceived me with my husband, Lotte had no object in life but to deceive me. The shop-bell tinkled. She would run forward to greet her custom-ers, to recommend this or that type of preservative, to enquire into the condition of a captious bowel, to weigh dried wormwood for a "panic-stricken" mother. To all of them, men and women alike, she spoke the same admirable language, the language of the fortune-teller and the ancient oracles and the old wives who gather and brew simples in the villages. Black as hell, delicately slim, her waist laced to strangulation-

*_Translator's Note:_ Edmond Blanc was a well-known racing man, immensely rich.

point, she would draw herself up with the vigour and the majesty of a serpent and lift a childish forefinger to admonish and to soothe the angry parent.

"When Nature has spoken, Madame, there is nothing to be said. The sharpest of us have only to bow down. Nature has spoken in your daughter, Madame. So she's in trouble—that's Fate. But now," she added, "we shall have to do something about it, shan't we? Nature does not seek the death of the sinner. . . ."

Reaching up towards the crimson ear of a young male customer, she would whisper with precision and authority, the perfect saleswoman, smiling in a manner that allowed of no misunderstanding. The small parcels fetched and spread out on the counter, she would end with these convincing words: "This, my dear Sir, cannot be called a measure of precaution. It is an ornament, a real ornament."

Evening came, and she threw off her white overall, put on a hat, a coat that was invariably in the best taste, and I would leave her, full of envy for the four-foot-ten princess with the button nose, the dazzling teeth and eyes, who was going out to dine in literary Bohemia.

A short time before her death, she got the idea of confession and Communion into her head, she who had never thought of baptism. She went to the confessional as she would have swallowed a drink in a public-house on a very thirsty day. She had to do with a priest no doubt of the very highest genius, a ponderous, rough man whom she saw three or four times and to whom she succumbed instantly. His face was scarcely visible to her through the wooden grating, but she could hear his voice and his heavy gasping, smell his sour breath. She seemed aware of who knows what eagerness, what urge to die, and wrote "Kiki" confused letters, darkly foreboding, slashed with light: "I've been to *that place* again, to see that priest chap. Oh! Kiki! I can't help it—it's the most extraordinary thing—it's sending me potty. He sweats, he stinks, he belches—and he is bringing me to God!"

M. Willy kept the letters carefully, filing them with all his other letters in a box-file of the sort that has a punching apparatus at the side and makes three holes in the margins. But Lotte could not wait for the miracle that was drawing near and disturbing her so much. One afternoon of stifling summer rain she went into her backshop parlour and shot herself through the mouth. She was twenty-six years old and had saved money.

JILL KER CONWAY
(1934–)

Conway moved to the United States in 1960 from Australia, where her parents had pioneered a sheep farm in the outback. Her autobiography, *The Road from Coorain* (1989), describes her life from her isolated childhood in New South Wales through her education in Sydney to her emigration, which was prompted in part by the lack of opportunity for women scholars in Australia and in part by the difficulties of her relationship with her mother. She received her Ph.D. in history from Harvard in 1969 and served as the president of Smith College (its first woman president) from 1975 to 1985.

For another memoir of Australian childhood, see Joan Colebrook, *A House of Trees*. For the autobiography of another feminist scholar and college president, see M. Carey Thomas, *The Making of a Feminist*. For another account of a paradise lost, compare Isak Dinesen, *Out of Africa*.

FROM *The Road from Coorain*

DROUGHT

After the great rain of 1939, the rainfall declined noticeably in each successive year. In 1940, the slight fall was of no consequence because our major worry was that the accumulation of growth on the land would produce serious bushfires. These did occur on land quite close to us, but my father's foresight in getting cattle to eat down the high grass preserved Coorain from that danger.

In 1941, the only rain of the year was a damp cold rain with high wind which came during the lambing season in May and June and carried off many ewes and their newborn lambs. After that there were no significant rainfalls for five years. The unfolding of a drought of these dimensions has a slow and inexorable quality. The weather perpetually holds out hope. Storm clouds gather. Thunder rolls by. But nothing happens. Each year as the season for rain approaches, people begin to look hopefully up at the sky. It mocks them with a few showers, barely enough to lay the dust. That is all.

It takes a long time for a carefully managed grazing property to decline, but three years without rain will do it. Once the disaster begins it unfolds swiftly. So it was with us.

My parents, buoyed up by the good year of 1939, the results of that good year returned in the 1940 wool sales, the new water supply, and the new woolshed, remained hopeful for a long time. By 1942, it was apparent that the drought could be serious and their levels of anxiety began to climb. I was conscious of those anxieties in a variety of ways. That year, 1942, my eighth, was my first one of correspondence school. There was no governess, nor was there any pretense that I would keep a daily school schedule. On Friday afternoons, from 2:00 P.M. until I finished (usually around 4:30 P.M.), I did my week's school. My mother made it a pleasant occasion for me by saying, "Today, you don't have to work out of doors. You can sit in the shade [or if it was winter, in the sun] on the veranda, have your own pot of tea, and do your schoolwork." Thus I was introduced to study as a leisure activity, a gift beyond price. When I was close to finishing, my mother would arrive to glance quickly over the work. Then she questioned me closely about the state of each paddock, what my father had said about it when we were there last, and then, ever so discreetly, she would lead me to talk about how he had seemed as we worked together that week. I needed no instruction not to mention these conversations. I knew why she was anxious.

My father and I would set out to work on horseback as usual, but instead of our customary cheerful and wide-ranging conversations he would be silent. As we looked at sheep, or tried to assess the pasture left in a particular paddock, he would swear softly, looking over the fence to a neighbor's property, already eaten out and beginning to blow sand. Each time he said, "If it doesn't rain, it will bury this feed in a few weeks." It was true and I could think of nothing consoling to say.

His usual high spirits declined with the state of the land, until the terrible day when many of our own sheep were lost because of a sudden cold rain and wind when they had too little food in their stomachs. Although my mother produced her usual ample meals, he began to lose weight his bony frame could ill afford. He lost his wonderful calm, and deliberation in planning, and would be excited by the slightest sign of trouble. A few years ago, a bore losing water flow would have meant there was a problem with the pump, requiring some days' labor to repair it. Now he would instantly worry about whether the water supply was running dry. We would fall to work on raising the pump and assessing the problem as though disaster were at hand.

My mother was impatient with this excitability and in my father's presence, would try to deflate it. But I knew from her questions that she too was worried. When the work to be done on the run didn't need two people, my father would say, "Stay home and help your mother, she needs help in the house." My mother would let him set out for the stables or the garage and then say to me, "I don't need help. Run quickly and go with your father. See if you can make him laugh." So I would set out, and begin to play the child I no longer was. I would think up nonsense rhymes, ask crazy questions, demand to be told stories, invent some of my own to recount. Sometimes it would have the desired effect, but it was hard to distract a man from the daily deterioration of our land and flocks. Every time we stopped to look at the carcass of a dead sheep and dismounted to find out why it had died, it became more difficult to play my role.

My brothers would return home from boarding school to a household consumed with anxiety. Coming, as they did, from the totally enclosed world of a school, with its boyish high spirits, it was hard for them to change emotional gear and set immediately to work on whatever projects had been saved for a time when there were several extra pairs of strong hands available. Mealtimes were particularly difficult because inevitably their world contained many points of reference beyond Coorain. Much of what they reported seemed frivolous to parents who had never attended a fashionable school and had struggled for the considerable learning they possessed. In better times they might have entered enthusiastically into this new world of their sons, but my father in particular jumped to the conclusion that his sons were not working hard at school. In fact they were, but they now lived in a culture in which it was a serious *faux pas* to indicate that one worked hard at study. The two worlds were not easy to mesh. As a result, the boys tended to work together; or we three made our recreations as unobtrusively as possible away from the adult world. Bob's passion was electronics. We spent hours together winding coils and puzzling our way through the diagrams which guided the construction of his first shortwave radio. He instructed me patiently in the characteristics of radio waves, and explained elementary concepts in physics by duplicating many of the demonstrations in his school textbooks. Barry took me with him on his early morning trips to collect the rabbits and foxes he trapped to help control these populations, which were hazards to our sheep. The skins provided him pocket money for investment in a wide variety of projects. While he was home from school, guides on writing short stories, books on muscle building, magazines about automobiles lent the mail bag an excitement lacking at other times.

There was not much room in the household routine for the mood swings and questioning of adolescence. Discipline was strict, and departures from it earned immediate punishment. The cloud of parental disapproval could be heavy when there was no escaping to other society. At sixteen, Bob let slip his religious doubts during a lunchtime conversation. Though these were a logical consequence of his heavily scientific school program, my parents were outraged. They had expected that by sending him to a high Anglican school, his religious education was ensured. Religious belief was a touchy subject in the family because my father adhered to his Catholicism while my mother was outspoken in her criticism of Catholic ideas on sexuality and the subordination of women. There was little occasion for the expression of these differences because there was no place of worship in either faith within seventy to a hundred miles of Coorain. Still, the differences slumbered under the surface. Poor Bob was treated as an unnatural being for his doubts and accused of being ungrateful for the sacrifices made to send him to a religious school. I was glad when the boys returned safely to school a week later without more explosions of discord. I was puzzled about the whole question of religion myself, since my parents both seemed highly moral people to me. As both faiths seemed to produce excellent results, I did not know what to make of the difference. When we made one of our rare visits to Sydney, and my parents separated for the day, my mother to shop, my father to visit banks and wool merchants, I usually went with him, since I got tired and vexed my mother by complaining while she rushed to do a year's shopping in a matter of days. At the end of the day, before setting out for our hotel or flat, my father would stop at St. Mary's Cathedral for vespers. I liked the ritual and the Latin chant. I also understood when he said it would be better not to mention these visits to my mother.

The routine of the academic year required that the boys return to school at the end of the summer vacation before the periods of most intense activity on the property: crutching time in February (when only the withers of the sheep were shorn to limit fly infestation in hot weather) and shearing in early June. Crutching time in 1943 was particularly worrisome. It was a fearfully hot summer. The sheep were poorly nourished and the last season's lambs weak. They needed to be moved slowly, held in paddocks close to the sheepyards, crutched quickly, and returned to their sparse pastures before heat exhaustion took its toll. In addition, to speed the whole process, someone needed to be at the woolshed, counting each shearer's tally of sheep, and pushing the supply of animals into the shed, so that not a moment was lost. It was always an exhausting business, because speed required constant running about in the 100 degree weather. This year, it was clear that my father found it hard to bear the pace.

At home in the evening, I found my mother feeling his pulse, administering brandy, and urging him to lie down. The heat and anxiety had combined to revive the irregular heartbeat that had been one of the factors occasioning his discharge from the army in 1917. My mother was at her best caring for the sick. She radiated calm. The errant pulse was checked regularly and diagnosed as palpitations, but not a serious arrhythmia.

The next day, we went a little more slowly at the work in the yards, advised by my mother that we could still afford to keep the team an extra day or two, or lose a few sheep, provided that my father was in sound health. I now found myself volunteering for jobs I was not quite sure I could do, in order to be sure that he had more time to rest. The next afternoon, after the close of work at the shed, there was a lot of riding still to be done. "These sheep need to go to Rigby's, that mob to Denny's," my father began, about to give me an assignment to return sheep to their paddocks. "I can do both," I said rashly, having never moved so many sheep on my own. "Mind you, move them slowly, and don't let them mix with the rams. Take the dogs, and don't open the gate until you have the dogs holding them at the fence." He had forgotten that I couldn't remount easily, and that the dogs didn't work very well for me. I was half pleased at completing the two assignments, half astonished that anyone had left me to handle them alone. Too much is being asked of me, I thought privately, forgetting that it was I who had volunteered. There was no getting around that the work was there and had to be done, and so I fell early into a role it took me many years to escape, the person in the family who would rise to the occasion, no matter the size of the task.

Shortly afterwards, the first terrible dust storm arrived boiling out of the central Australian desert. One sweltering late afternoon in March, I walked out to collect wood for the stove. Glancing toward the west, I saw a terrifying sight. A vast boiling cloud was mounting in the sky, black and sulfurous yellow at the heart, varying shades of ocher red at the edges. Where I stood, the air was utterly still, but the writhing cloud was approaching silently and with great speed. Suddenly I noticed that there were no birds to be seen or heard. All had taken shelter. I called my mother. We watched helplessly. Always one for action, she turned swiftly, went indoors, and began to close windows. Outside, I collected the buckets, rakes, shovels, and other implements that could blow away or smash a window if hurled against one by the boiling wind. Within the hour, my father arrived home. He and my mother sat on the back step, not in their usual restful contemplation, but silenced instead by dread.

A dust storm usually lasts days, blotting out the sun, launching banshee winds day and night. It is dangerous to stray far from shelter, because the sand and grit lodge in one's eyes, and a visibility often reduced to a few feet can make one completely disoriented. Animals which become exhausted and lie down are often sanded over and smothered. There is nothing anyone can do but stay inside, waiting for the calm after the storm. Inside, it is stifling. Every window must be closed against the dust, which seeps relentlessly through the slightest crack. Meals are gritty and sleep elusive. Rising in the morning, one sees a perfect outline of one's body, an afterimage of white where the dust has not collected on the sheets.

As the winds seared our land, they took away the dry herbage, piled it against the fences, and then slowly began to silt over the debris. It was three days before we could venture out, days of almost unendurable tension. The crashing of the boughs of trees against our roof and the sharp roar as a nearly empty rainwater tank blew off its stand and rolled away triggered my father's recurring nightmares of France, so that when he could fall into a fitful slumber it would be to awake screaming.

It was usually I who woke him from his nightmares. My mother was hard to awaken. She had, in her stoic way, endured over the years two bad cases of ear infection, treated only with our available remedies, hot packs and aspirin. One ear was totally deaf as a result of a ruptured eardrum, and her hearing in the other ear was much reduced. Now her deafness led to a striking reversal of roles, as I, the child in the family, would waken and attempt to soothe a frantic adult.

When we emerged, there were several feet of sand piled up against the windbreak to my mother's garden, the contours of new sandhills were beginning to form in places where the dust eddied and collected. There was no question that there were also many more bare patches where the remains of dry grass and herbage had lifted and blown away.

It was always a miracle to me that animals could endure so much. As we checked the property, there were dead sheep in every paddock to be sure, but fewer than I'd feared. My spirits began to rise and I kept telling my father the damage was not too bad. "That was only the first storm," he said bleakly. He had seen it all before and knew what was to come.

In June, at shearing time, we hired one of the district's great eccentrics to help in the yards. I could not manage mustering and yard work at the same time, and my father could not manage both either without too frenetic a pace. Our helper, known as Pommy Goodman, was a middle-aged Englishman with a perfect Mayfair accent, one of the foulest mouths I ever heard, and the bearing of one to the manner born. He was an example of the wonderful variety of types thrown up like human driftwood on the farther shores of settlement in Australia. One moment he would be swearing menacingly at a sheep that had kicked him, the next minute addressing me as though he were my nanny and about to order nursery tea. I resented being called "child," and noticed that Pommy did more leaning on the fence and offering advice than hard work. But it was good to have a third person on hand, and especially someone who could drive a car, something I could not do, my legs not yet being long enough to disengage a clutch. Pommy could drive ahead and open a gate, making the return of sheep to a paddock a simple task. He could shuttle between the house and woolshed on the endless errands that materialized during the day, and he could count out the sheep from the shearers' pens, something I was not good at because my mathematical labors by correspondence were always done slowly and deliberately. The sheep raced for freedom at a furious pace, leaping through the gate in twos and threes, so that my counts were often jumbled. The shearers, by now old friends, knowing that my father was not well, tolerated my efforts and secretly kept their own tally, so the records were straight at the end of the day.

. . .

As we entered the late summer of 1944, we had about half our usual stock of sheep, now seriously affected by inadequate nourishment. It was clear that they would not make it through the summer unless it rained, or we began to feed them hay or grain to supplement their diet. The question which tormented my parents was whether to let them die, or invest more in maintaining them. If they died, fifteen years of careful attention to the bloodlines was lost. Yet even if fed supplements they might die anyway, for the dry feed would not supply the basic nutrients in fresh grass and herbage.

Now the nighttime conversations were anguished. Both of them had grown up fearing debt like the plague. It hurt their pride to mortgage the land, just like more feckless managers. Furthermore, the feeding would require more labor than my father and I could manage. In the end, it was resolved to borrow the money, buy the wheat, and hire the help. But these actions were taken with a heavy heart. My father was plagued by doubts about the wisdom of the decision. My mother, once settled on a course of action, was imperturbable. Their basic difference of temperament was that she lacked imagination and could not conceive of failure, while my father's imagination now tormented him with ever darker visions of disaster. She regarded this fevered imagination dourly and thought it should be controllable. He tried to keep his worst fears to himself.

Our help came in the wonderful form of two brothers, half aboriginal, half Chinese. The elder brother, Ron, in his early twenties, was light-skinned and slightly slant-eyed; the younger, Jack, looked like a full-blooded aboriginal. They came from the mission station in Menindee, one hundred and seventy miles away. They were as fine a pair of station hands as one could ever hope for. Ron could fix engines and manage all things mechanical. He was quiet, efficient, and totally dependable. Jack could talk to animals, soothe a frightened horse, persuade half-starving sheep to get up and keep walking. Jack could pick up a stone and toss it casually to knock down out of the sky the crows gathering around a foundered animal. He could track anything: snakes, sheep, kangaroos, lizards. Jack's only defect so far as station management was concerned was that at any time he might feel the aboriginal need to go "on walk-about." He was utterly reliable and would always reappear to complete the abandoned task he'd been at work on when the urge came. But he could be gone for days, or weeks, or months.

Feeding the sheep was hard work. Feed troughs made of metal could not be considered because the drifting sand would quickly cover them. If the weaker sheep were to get their nourishment, the expanse of feeding troughs must be large so that every animal would have its chance at the grain. So we settled on burlap troughs hung on wire—light enough for the wind to blow beneath when empty, cheap enough to produce in hundred-foot lengths. Replacement lengths became available each time we emptied a hundredweight bag of wheat. With a bag needle and a hank of twine at hand anyone could mend the troughs, or with a little wire and some wooden pegs, create new ones.

When we began our feeding program in the troughs placed by major watering places, the sheep seemed only slowly to discover the grain. Within a few weeks the hungry animals would stampede at the sight of anyone carrying bags of wheat, and someone had to be sent as a decoy to draw them off in search of a small supply of grain while the major ration was being poured into the troughs. Since I could carry only twenty pounds at a fast run, I was the decoy while the men carried forty- and fifty-pound bags on their shoulders to empty into the feeding troughs. At first the sheep were ravenous but measured in following the decoy. Soon they would race so hard toward the grain that they would send the decoy flying unless he or she outraced them. Then they would pause, wheel on catching the scent of the ration in the troughs, and stampede back toward the food.

Our principal enemies as we carried out this daily process were the pink cockatoos and crows, which tore the burlap to pieces in search of the grains of wheat left behind. Soon the mending of the troughs was a daily task, a task made miserable by the blowflies, the blistering sun, the blowing sand, and the stench of the bodies of the sheep for whom the wheat had arrived too late.

For my father each death was a personal blow, and he took himself to task for the suffering of the animals. Our conversations as we rode about the place took on a grimmer tone. "When I'm gone, Jill, sell this place. Take care of your mother. Make sure she goes to the city. There's nothing but heartbreak in fighting the seasons." Or, "If anything happens to me, promise me you'll take care of your mother. Make her sell this place. Don't let her stay here." I would promise anything to change his mood and get the conversation on another topic. But I rarely succeeded. Usually he would go on to talk about my future, a future in which he clearly did not expect to share. "Work hard, Jill," he'd say. "Don't just waste time. *Make something of yourself.*" Reverting to his idée fixe that my brothers did not try hard enough at their schoolwork, he would continue, "Don't be like your brothers. Don't waste your time in school. Get a real education and get away from this damn country for good." I would promise, choking back tears at the thought of his death and a future away from Coorain. But even I could see that he was right about the battle with the seasons. Without discussing the subject with anyone, I concluded that the God who was supposed to heed the fall of the sparrow had a lesser morality than humans. Each clap of dry thunder and each vista of starving animals made the notion of a loving God a mockery. I kept my father's words about impending death to myself. I was used to being the listener to fears and worries my parents needed to express, but did not want to worry one another about. It seemed too monstrous a possibility to speak about, and in a primitive way I feared that naming it might make it happen.

One troublesome aspect of the frustration of my parents' dreams was the extent to which they transferred their ambitions to their children. My brothers, being five hundred miles away, were not readily available as vehicles for ambition. Being at hand, I became the focus of all the aspiration for achievement that had fueled both parents' prodigious energies. My correspondence school required little of my time and less energy. My teacher's reports were always positive and my work praised. Naturally, it should have been, for I had heard the same lessons discussed in the schoolroom by my brothers and their governess.

I read omnivorously, everything that came to hand, and through reading my mother's books I asked questions about politics and history which both parents took for signs of high intelligence. Lacking playmates, I would retreat from the adult world to my swing, set away in the eucalyptus trees a hundred yards or so from the house. There I would converse at length with imaginary companions, usually characters from some recently read novel or war correspondent's report, which I only dimly understood. I would kick furiously in order to rise up higher and see a little farther beyond the horizon. In the midst of my dreams of glory drawn from highly glamorized accounts of war and feats of heroism, I would sometimes stop crestfallen and wonder if I would ever get away from Coorain. Sometimes, needing to be alone, I would walk for hours, scanning the ground for aboriginal ovens, collecting quartz fragments, observing the insect life—anything to be away from the house and its overwhelming mood of worry.

The nighttime conversations now made me nervous because they frequently settled on what a remarkable child I was, and how gratifying it would be for parents to observe my progress. I had no way of assessing their judgments, but I was certainly uncomfortably aware that I and my performance in life had become the focus of formidable emotional energies.

Like all children, I was occasionally mischievous and misbehaved. In more carefree times my pranks, like my brothers', met with swift punishment from parents who believed that sparing the rod was certain to spoil the child. The occasional token chastisement was easy to resist psychologically. One had only to refuse to apologize and express contrition for enough hours to gain the upper hand on parents who were tired in the evening and wanted to go to bed. Now, however, I encountered more subtle, and to me more terrifying, punishments. If I misbehaved, my parents simply acted as though I were not their child but a stranger. They would inquire civilly as to who I was and what I was doing on Coorain, but no hint of recognition escaped them. This treatment never failed to reduce me to abject contrition. In later life my recurring nightmares were always about my inability to prove to people I knew quite well who I was. I became an unnaturally good child, and accepted uncritically that goodness was required of me if my parents' disappointments in life were ever to be compensated for.

That June most of our older sheep were too weak to be shorn. My father took the few whose wool was worth shearing and who could stand the journey to a neighboring station, since the numbers were too small to warrant bringing a shearing team to Coorain. On the first day of his absence, my mother also left in the afternoon to pick up the mail and carry out some other errands. I had time to fulfill an often neglected promise to my brother Bob that I would listen on his shortwave radio every afternoon and record the stations and countries I heard. That day, the sixth of June, I turned the dial to the point where we had discovered that we could hear the uncensored news being dictated to General MacArthur's headquarters. To my astonishment, I heard the impassive announcer's voice report the news of the Allied landing in Normandy, and the establishment of beachheads beyond Utah and Omaha beaches literally only a few hours earlier. By the time my mother returned in the late afternoon, I was gibbering with excitement and almost incoherent with my news. She listened carefully, sorted out the story, and promised to tell my father when he telephoned that evening. This she did, although the evening Australian news contained no report of the landing. I was not vindicated until the six o'clock news the following night, when the Australian censors decided to release the news of the successful landings. Thereafter, no matter what the circumstances on Coorain, I could always distract my father by reading him reports of the campaign on the various fronts in Europe as we jolted about Coorain in our sulky, traveling to clean watering troughs or mend our feeding troughs. I could supplement the newspaper accounts by the more accurate reporting which I heard on my brother's radio, where the actual figures of casualties were reported rather than the bland announcements made for civilian consumption. Reading about the invasion in Europe was reassuring because our own situation in Australia had grown more precarious as the war in the Pacific unfolded.

We had been jolted out of complacency by the fall of Singapore, the supposedly impregnable British naval base, fortified with guns which pointed only out to sea. My mother and I had been on a brief trip to Sydney when Singapore fell. The newspaper headlines covered the whole front page of the afternoon dailies. So great was the shock that Australians, the most taciturn of people, had actually been moved to speak about the news to total strangers. Handfuls of refugees began to arrive from Hong Kong, but there were none from Singapore, except the Australian commander, Major-General Gordon Bennett, who we were ashamed to learn had deserted his men. Many of our friends and sons of friends had been in the Australian contingent at Singapore, including our fondly remembered Jimmie Walker. We had his smiling picture in his A.I.F. uniform sent just before his departure. The news of Japanese treatment of prisoners and the atrocities committed upon the civilian population of the Philippines made the increasing likelihood of the invasion of Australia seem more threatening.

My parents' conversations on this possibility were chilling but practical. Australia was drained of able-bodied men, away fighting in Europe and the Middle East. These two proudly loyal subjects of the British crown had thrilled to the sound of Churchill's speeches hurling defiance at Hitler, invoking the glory of the British Empire to inspire the defense of England. They were correspondingly shaken to realize that Australia was expendable in Britain's war strategy, and that the Australian government had had great difficulty in securing the return of the battle-scarred

Ninth Division from Tobruk to take part in the defense of Australia. Once this was clear they turned soberly to consideration of what to do in the event of an invasion. They calculated correctly that the continent was too vast to be easily overrun, that the Japanese would concentrate on the ports and the food supplies. We, who were hardy backcountry people, could disappear if need be into the great outback desert and live off the land like aborigines. There were various plans for getting the boys home, and discussions about how that might be achieved in a time of likely national panic. When the call came for civilians to turn over all their hunting rifles to the government to help arm the militia, a pitifully small group of men who had refused to serve overseas when drafted, my father kept back one of his rifles and hid it with a supply of ammunition. If we were ever in danger of capture, he and my mother had calmly agreed that he would shoot his wife and children first and then himself. In preparation for such dire possibilities, we hid supplies in a remote part of Coorain. The gasoline was described as a cache to be reserved for emergencies, and we never spoke about the need for a weapon.

We had very realistic expectations about the defense of Australia, because it was patently apparent that there was a failure of leadership in the country, symbolized by Major-General Gordon Bennett's ignominious flight, the flustered performance of the first wartime leader, the United Australian Party Prime Minister Robert Menzies, and the short-lived Country Party government which followed. The task of defending the country was impossible for Australians alone, and the old empire mentalities of our leaders left them, without the protection of Great Britain, as paralyzed as the defenders of Singapore. My parents were rugged individualists who scorned socialism and the Labor Party as the political recourse of those who lacked initiative. Nonetheless, their spirits soared when the Labor Prime Minister, John Curtin, took office, candidly acknowledged our situation, and called for American assistance. They recognized an Australian patriot, and I learned for the first time that loyalty to Great Britain and love for Australia were not synonymous. It was an important lesson.

After the June shearing of 1944, we knew that if it did not rain in the spring our gamble was lost. The sheep would not live through until another rainy season. There were so few to feed by September 1944 that our friends and helpers, Ron and Jack Kelly, left for another job. We on Coorain waited for the rain which never came. The dust storms swept over us every two or three weeks, and there was no pretending about the state of the sheep when we traveled around the property. The smells of death and the carrion birds were everywhere. The starving animals which came to our feed troughs were now demented with hunger.

When I ran off as decoy to spread out a thin trail of grain while the troughs were filled, they knocked me over and trampled me, desperate to tear the grain from the bag. Their skeletal bodies were pitiful. I found I could no longer bear to look into their eyes, because the usually tranquil ruminant animals looked half crazed.

We lost our appetite for meat because the flesh of the starving animals already tasted putrid. I was never conscious of when the smell of rotting animals drowned out the perfumes from my mother's garden, but by early December, although it still bloomed, our nostrils registered only decaying flesh. By then the sand accumulating on the other side of the windbreak was beginning to bend the cane walls inward by its weight, and we knew it was only a matter of time before it too was engulfed.

My mother, as always, was unconquerable. "It has to rain some day," she told my father. "Our children are healthy. We can grow our food. What does it matter if we lose everything else?" She did not understand that it mattered deeply to him. Other memories of loss from his childhood were overwhelming him. He could not set out in mid-life to be once more the orphan without patrimony. As he sank into deeper depression, they understood one another less. She, always able to rouse herself to action, could not understand how to deal with crippling depression, except by a brisk call to count one's blessings. This was just what my father was unable to do.

My brothers were summoned home two weeks early from school, though to help with what was not clear. There was pitifully little to do on Coorain. There were the same burlap troughs to mend, the same desperate animals to feed, but the size of the task was shrinking daily. The December heat set in, each day over 100 degrees. Now so much of our land was without vegetation that the slightest breeze set the soil blowing. Even without the dust storms, our daily life seemed lived in an inferno.

My mother's efforts to rouse my father were indefatigable. One Saturday in early December was to be a meeting of the Pastures Protection Board in Hillston. Early in the week before, she set about persuading him to drive the seventy-five miles with his close friend Angus Waugh. Reluctantly, he agreed. The Friday before, a minor dust storm set in, and he decided against the drive. It was fearfully hot, over 108 degrees, and we passed a fitful evening barricaded in against the blowing sand.

The next morning I awoke, conscious that it was very early, to find my father gazing intently at me. He bent down to embrace me and said good-bye. Half asleep, I bid him good-bye and saw his departing back. Suddenly, I snapped awake. *Why is he saying good-bye? He isn't going anywhere.* I leapt out of bed, flung on the first clothes to hand, and ran dry-mouthed after him. I was only seconds too late. I ran shouting after his car, "I want to come. Take me with you." I thought he saw me, but, the car gathering speed, he drove away.

Back in the house, my mother found me pacing about and asked why I was up so early in the morning. I said I'd wanted to go with my father, and wasn't sure where he went. He was worried about the heat and the adequacy of the water for the sheep in Brooklins (a distant paddock), she said, and had gone to check on it. It was a hot oppressive day, with the wind gaining strength by noon. I felt a leaden fear in my stomach, but was speechless. To speak of my fears seemed to admit that my father had lost his mental balance. It was something I could not say.

His journey should not have taken more than two hours, but then again he could have decided to visit other watering places on the property. When he was not home by two, my mother and Bob set out after him. Neither Barry nor I, left behind, was inclined to talk about what might have happened. Like a pair of automatons, we washed the dishes left from lunch and settled in to wait. When no one returned by four, the hour when my mother stoked the stove and began her preparations for dinner, we went through the motions of her routine. The potatoes were peeled, peas shelled, the roast prepared, the table laid.

Eventually, Bob arrived home alone. There had been an accident, he said. He must make some phone calls and hurry back. We neither of us believed him. We knew my father was dead. Finally, at six o'clock, the old grey utility my father drove hove into sight driven by my brother Bob; my mother's car followed, with several others in its wake. She took the time to thank us for preparing dinner before saying she had something to tell us alone. We went numbly to our parents' bedroom, the place of all confidential conversations. "I want you to help me," she said. "Your father's dead. He was working on extending the piping into the Brooklins dam. We found him there in the water." My eyes began to fill with tears. She looked at me accusingly. "Your father wouldn't want you to cry," she said.

We watched woodenly as my father's body was brought to rest in that same bedroom. We were dismissed while she prepared it for the funeral which would take place in two days. In the hot summer months, burials had to be speedy and there was no need for anyone to explain why to us children. We had been dealing with decaying bodies for years. Because of the wartime restrictions on travel and the need for haste, there was little time to summon family and friends. Telegrams were dispatched but only my mother's brother and sister-in-law, close to us in Sydney, were actually expected. Eventually, we sat down to dinner and choked over our food, trying desperately to make conversation with the kindly manager from a neighboring station who had come to help. The meal seemed surreal. The food on the plate seemed unconnected to the unreal world without my father in it in which I now lived. I was haunted by the consciousness of his body lying close by in the bedroom, which my mother had sternly forbidden me to enter.

After we went sleeplessly to bed, we heard a sound never heard before, the sound of my mother weeping hopelessly and inconsolably. It was a terrible and unforgettable sound. To moderate the heat we slept on a screened veranda exposed to any southern breeze which might stir. My brother Barry's bed was next to mine. After listening to this terrible new sound, we both agreed that we wished we were older so that we could go to work and take care of her. We tossed until the sun rose and crept out of bed too shocked to do more than converse in whispers.

My mother soon appeared, tight-lipped and pale, somehow a ghost of herself. Dispensing with all possibility of discussion, she announced that Barry and I were to stay with friends for a few days. She did not want us to see our father buried, believing that this would be too distressing for us. Though we complied without questioning the plan, I felt betrayed that I would not see him to his last rest. She, for her part, wanted to preserve us from signs of the body's decay. As we set out, . . . we passed the hearse making its way toward Coorain. Its black shape drove home what had happened.

How my father's death had actually come about we would never know. He was a poor swimmer, and had attempted to dive down in muddy water to connect a fresh length of pipe so that the pump for watering the sheep could draw from the lowered water level of the dam. It was a difficult exercise for a strong swimmer, and not one to undertake alone. Why he had chosen to do it alone when my two brothers, both excellent swimmers, were at home, we could not understand. I did not tell anyone of his early morning visit to me. I realized that we would never know the answer to the question it raised.

Everyone expected that my mother would sell Coorain, move to the city, and allow a bank or trust company to manage our finances. In our part of the world this was what widows did. Our circle of friends and advisers did not bargain for my mother's business sense and her strong will. She would not sell the property when it was worth next to nothing. She planned instead to run it herself, wait for the rains which must come, and manage our one asset for our maximum benefit. The boys were to return to school according to the usual schedule. She would hire some help, and she and I would remain at Coorain. Presented with this plan and a request to finance it, her startled woolbrokers remonstrated with her about the hazards of a woman taking charge of her own affairs.

Seeing her resolve, they acquiesced, and offered her a loan secured by our now virtually nonexistent sheep. So she returned resolute to preserve and enhance the enterprise she and my father had built.

He had not been a man to give much thought to transferring property to wife or children, and so my mother, as his sole heir, became liable for sizable death duties. Some of my first lessons in feminism came from her outraged conversations with the hapless valuation agent sent to inventory and value the assets of the estate for probate. She was incensed to discover that her original investment in furniture, linen, silver, and household equipment was now merged in my father's estate. No value was attributed either to the contributions she had made to the enterprise through the investment of her capital fifteen years before, or to the proceeds of her fifteen years of twelve- and fourteen-hour days of labor. Her outspoken anger cowed the man into some concessions, but her rumblings about this economic injustice continued for years, and instructed me greatly.

Heroic as she was, we would not have fared so well in her defiance of the fates had we not been given the affection, support, and physical presence of my mother's younger brother and his wife. Both worked in essential wartime occupations in Sydney, my uncle as an engineer and my aunt as the senior nurse in a munitions factory. Informed of my father's death, both requested leave to attend his funeral and to help his widow cope with her loss, and both were refused any more than forty-eight hours' absence. In characteristic Australian fashion, they defied the manpower authorities, talked their way onto the train for the west despite the restrictions on civilian travel, and arrived to stay shortly before my father's funeral.

Once they took in the situation my mother faced, they decided to defy the orders they promptly received to return to their respective jobs. Instead, they elected to see her through the harsh first months of bereavement. Their warm hearts, wonderful common sense, and comforting physical presence reassured us children, as my mother grew suddenly thinner, her abundant hair grey almost overnight, and her moods, normally equable, swung to every point of the compass. We struggled through Christmas, trying to celebrate, but at every point in the day we met memories of my father's presence the previous year. At the end of January, the boys left for school, and in late February, my uncle finally obeyed the accumulating pile of telegrams and official letters requiring him to return at once to his wartime post. My aunt remained another month, a calming presence, full of life force, cheerfully sustaining our spirits by her questions about our way of life in a remote part of the country she had never visited. Before my uncle left, our former helper

Ron Kelly returned, leaving a much better job to take care of Coorain and us once again.

By the time he arrived, we were feeding only seven or eight hundred sheep in two paddocks, and working to preserve the various improvements, bores, wells, sheepyards, and fences from the encroaching sand. Each day, the three of us went out with our loads of wheat, and to work on the now hated burlap troughs. They were hateful because they had become tattered with much use, and required daily attention with patches, twine, and bag needle. There was no way to make the repairs except to sit down in the dust, thread one's needle, and go at it. With the sun beating down, no hands free to drive away the flies, and the sounds of the ever-hungry and opportunistic cockatoos waiting to tear apart our handiwork, we could not escape awareness of the repetitious and futile nature of our labors.

Each afternoon, Ron set out for another tour of fences: to dig out those sanding up, to treat posts being attacked by white ants under the sand, and to oil and care for all the working parts of the windmills and pumping equipment. At night after the lamps were lit, the silence in the house was palpable. My mother and I read after dinner, but as the time approached for going to bed she would become unaccustomedly nervous and edgy. She found sleeping alone a nightmare, and after a few weeks of sleepless nights she said she needed my company in her bed. After that it was I who had trouble resting, for she clung to me like a drowning person. Alone, without my father, all her fears of the wilderness returned, and she found the silence as alienating as when she first arrived on the plains. She would often pace the verandas much of the night. Both of us would be grateful for the dawn.

Once a week our friend and neighbor Angus Waugh drove the fifty miles to visit us. He would talk over the state of the sheep and the land with my mother, offer sound advice, and try to make her laugh. I longed for his visits so that for even a few hours the care of this silent and grieving person would not rest only on my shoulders. He could always make me laugh by telling wild nonsense stories, or wickedly funny accounts of the life and affairs of distant residents in the district. My mother, in fact, knew in great detail every aspect of the management of a sheep station. Angus knew this very well, but his weekly presence gave her some adult company, and enabled him to keep a watchful and sensitive eye on how we both were faring.

In February, although my mother was uncertain whether she could afford it, the shearing contractor and his team arrived to crutch our sheep. They followed the bush code of helping those in trouble, and told my mother to pay them when she could, or never if it wasn't possible.

Help appeared from all quarters at crutching time, and our few poor sheep were back in their paddocks before we knew it. My friends on the team never spoke of our bereavement, but they were even more than usually kind about my efforts to keep on top of everything that was happening at the shed.

By the time the boys came home for their holidays in May it was clear that very few of the animals would survive even if it rained within a few weeks. My brothers shot the few remaining large animals we could not feed—the Black Angus bull, formerly the rippling black embodiment of sexual power and energy, now a wraith; the few poor cows; some starving horses. And then in the next weeks the last sheep began to die by the hundreds. We would pile up the carcasses of those that died near the house, douse them with kerosene, and set them alight, to reduce the pervasive odor of rotting flesh. The crows and hawks were fat, and the cockatoos full-breasted on their diet of wheat, but one by one all other forms of life began to fade away.

After the boys went back to school in June, there was little to do on the place. No amount of digging could prevent the silting-up of fences, and the maintenance of equipment did not require much oversight. Once we were alone again, I was more than usually worried about my mother, because she ate next to nothing, fell to weeping unexpectedly, and seemed much of the time in a trance. The effort expended in getting up and carrying on each day exhausted her. This was combined with the effort expended in refusing to accept the possibility that our enterprise at Coorain might go under. Because this fear was repressed, she was fearful of lesser things. Once when I went riding without telling her, her fury startled me. Once when I went to work on a bore with Ron, an individual who would have died to secure our safety, she gave me a tongue-lashing about never again working alone with him.

Shortly after these explosions, Angus arrived for one of his visits. He took a walk with me and asked how we were doing. As I shook my head, uncertain about how to say what was on my mind, he supplied the words for me. "You're worried about your mother, aren't you," he said. I nodded. "She doesn't eat?" "That's right," I said. "She's depressed?" I nodded. "You ought to leave here," he said. "There's not a bloody thing you two can do here now. The pair of you look like something out of Changi and it's to no purpose. Would you like to leave, live like a normal child and go to school?" I felt a great wave of relief. "Yes," I said.

That night Angus talked to my mother as they took a walk around the house and grounds. I heard snatches, and realized that he was playing the other side of the argument skillfully. "You can't keep Jill here forever. It's not right. She should be in school. Neither of you can do anything here. Look at her. She's so skinny she could come from a concentration camp. It's time to leave and go to Sydney, and let her get on with her life. You can hire a manager to take care of this place, and I'll watch over it for you."

The next morning my mother eyed me as though I were a stranger. I was certainly a sight. I was in my eleventh year, so underweight my clothes for an eight- or nine-year-old hung on me, and as Angus said, I looked worried enough to be an old woman. Once she noticed my appearance the matter was settled for my mother. She began to make plans for us to leave.

.   .   .

Departures for Sydney by train took place at the small railroad station at Ivanhoe, some forty miles north of Coorain. There was little to the town but a cluster of railroad maintenance workers' huts, some shunting yards, and a set of stockyards for loading sheep and cattle. A store, a garage, a road haulage company, and a few more ample houses lined the dusty main street. The train itself was the most impressive part of the landscape. The passenger train we rode on for half the journey to Sydney was one of our few chances to encounter modernity. It was diesel-powered, streamlined, air-conditioned, painted a dazzling silver to evoke the site of its origin, Broken Hill, an inland silver mining center. When the boys rode it to school, my father had always tipped the porter so that the boredom of their journey could be broken by an exciting ride in the engine cabin, actually watching the needle of the speedometer climb past eighty miles an hour. When the diesel engine had built up speed, it purred along effortlessly while the countryside outside raced by at a bewildering rate. The Diesel, as we called it, announced itself twenty or more minutes before its arrival by the huge column of red dust it churned up as it tore across the plains. We spent the twenty minutes in careful good-byes, and then piled quickly into the train which stopped only a merciful three minutes in the station. We both now wanted this ordeal over.

As the train pulled out and gathered speed, my mother and I stood at the door waving. We both choked with tears a little as we passed the system of points just outside the station where the train always slowed a little. Once my father, too preoccupied with giving advice to his sons to notice the time, had been obliged to jump from the moving train at that point.

Yet in counterpoint to my grief was overwhelming relief. It was true that we had been cast out from our paradise. But that paradise had become literally purgatorial for us. My mother had seen the product of fifteen years of unremitting labor disappear. She had lost a partnership of work and love which had made her utterly fulfilled. Without it she was at sea. I felt that my heart was permanently frozen with grief by what had happened to both my parents. I feared even greater disasters were we to remain at Coorain. I had lost my sense of trust in a benign providence, and feared the fates. My brother Bob had taken to reading me his favorite Shakespeare plays while home on his last vacation, and I had been transfixed by the line from *King Lear:* "As flies to wanton boys are we to the gods,/ They kill us for their sport." I did not understand the nature of the ecological disaster which had transformed my world, or that we ourselves had been agents as well as participants in our own catastrophe. I just knew that we had been defeated by the fury of the elements, a fury that I could not see we had earned. In the life that lay ahead, I knew I must serve as my father's agent in the family and muster the energy to deal with such further disasters as might befall us. For the moment, we were down on our luck and had to begin all over again.

ELEANOR COPPOLA
(1936–)

In the spring of 1976 Eleanor Coppola, along with her husband, the director Francis Ford Coppola, and their three children, Gio, Roman, and Sophia, moved to the Philippines for the filming of an epic adventure, *Apocalypse Now*. The film was based on Joseph Conrad's *Heart of Darkness*, with the action shifted from Africa in the nineteenth century to Vietnam during the war of the 1960s and 1970s. A Green Beret named Willard, played by Martin Sheen, is sent by river patrol boat (called, in this selection, PBR) to kill an out-of-control operative named Kurtz, played by Marlon Brando. Eleanor Coppola was asked by her husband to make a documentary of the production, and in support of that project she began keeping a journal. The making of *Apocalypse Now* became an epic in itself, a source of great emotional and physical strain to everyone involved. Eleanor Coppola's diary, published in 1979 as *Notes*, records the daily professional crises as well as a crisis in her marriage that occurred during the production. Along the way it manages to capture the surreal splendor of film-making.

The French plantation scene which Eleanor Coppola discusses in these excerpts did not make it into the final version of the film.

For another view of movie illusion, compare Kate Simon, *Bronx Primitive*. For another view of the Vietnam war, compare Le Ly Hayslip, *When Heaven and Earth Changed Places*. For another journal by a keeper of the flame, compare Sophia Tolstoy, *Diary*.

FROM *Notes*

August 8 [1976], Pagsanjan

Last evening was the first night shooting. It was at the Do Long Bridge set. We had all been there several times during the day, but something happened at night. Maybe it was the fires that special effects started, and the arc lights illuminating the hundreds of extras in costume in the trenches. Maybe it was knowing that after all the rehearsing and preparing, this was it. There was a kind of electricity in the air. Parts seemed like a circus. There were so many trucks and strings of lights and cables and people going in and out of the darkness as if the show were about to begin. The main event. The set looked extraordinary. It was better than anyone had imagined. Most things seemed to fall short of expectations, but this was somehow more than anyone had anticipated. It was very hot and humid. I could see the sweat running down people's faces when they passed in front of a light. Both channels of the radio were going as the first shot was being set up. I could hear, "We need ten Vietnamese extras to be dead in the water. Light the downstream burners. Makeup check for GI extras now. Bring in the crane to the upstream position on the tropical side. Bring the generator barge to the camera first position," on and on. A light rain began to fall. I was under some coconut palms by a wall of sandbags on the ridge. I couldn't feel the rain, but I could see it in the paths of light. There were millions of insects around the big lights in the towers. The electricians had wrapped T-shirts around their heads. Only Luciano was just in his bathing suit with a tool belt and gloves. He shouted over the megaphone in Italian to the other light towers and across the river to the generator operator and electricians on that side. I could smell the exhaust from the generator truck near us.

A coconut fell into the trench just in front of me. A GI extra leaped up and grabbed for his helmet. There was a lot of laughing about how he almost got killed, on his way to stardom, by a falling coconut. Several guys tossed it around like a football. The waiting went on. All the extras had live blanks in their machine guns and rifles, and they were excited about firing them. Several swimmers were in the river rehearsing laying mines and dragging dead Vietnamese out of the water. People were drinking sodas or smoking, sitting quietly in the dark, waiting for the camera barge and the PBR to get into position upstream for the first rehearsal of all the action. Occasionally special effects would fire a test rocket or a flare and the whole set would be illuminated. I could see all the extras silhouetted in the trenches and the cables and technicians and trucks in the background. Giant fingers of lightning flashed in the sky above the bridge. It was a kind of tropical lightning that none of us had seen before. I could hear the special effects men laughing over the radio, saying, "Gee, that one was great, Joe, what did you use to do that?"

Finally there was a dinner break and everyone moved toward the road and back to where the caterers had set up. There was a palm frond roof over a large area and rows and rows of tables with lines of crews and cast snaking past the buffet tables. The people who lived in the nipa huts along the road stood around the edge of the eating area, watching the technicians and GIs and everyone having dinner. Little kids called out,

"Hi, Joe," choruses of little voices. The site of the set was where a bridge had been blown up by the Japanese in World War II, and never rebuilt. The concrete footings, sticking up from the riverbed, formed the base for the bridge our crew built. The set bridge is scheduled to be blown up, too.

Gio was an extra. He had a full pack GI outfit on and was carrying an M-16 automatic rifle. He had black makeup on his face. He is twelve. He was as tall as some of the shorter men. After the meal break, everyone got into position and the rehearsals began. The first shot got off about 11:00 P.M., with the PBR coming downriver and the camera boat trying to maintain a position behind and to the side. Flares, rockets and several big flame balls were set off. It looked great from where I was shooting. While they set up for the second take, it started to rain again. Roman had fallen asleep on some sandbags, and the company nurse told me I should take him home, he would get sick. I woke him up, but he didn't want to go until after the next take. One of the extras gave him a flak jacket to put on the ground next to the wall where it was relatively dry and he went back to sleep. The second shot didn't go until about 12:30 A.M. I woke Roman up, but he kept closing his eyes and missed most of the main effects. I gave the camera to Doug to see if he could get some shots of the effects men during the next take, and I started home with Roman. As we walked along the road toward the car, I could see in the windows of the nipa huts, lit by the production lights. People were sleeping on the floor under mosquito netting or wrapped in a cloth. Francis and Gio came home at around 3:00 A.M.

August 12, Pagsanjan

Catholicism seems decorative here. There are Madonnas and crucifixes, and the jeepneys have religious pictures on their dashboards, but there isn't a heavy Catholic overtone to everything like in Mexico. The Pagsanjan Family Planning Clinic is right across the street from the main church. Sofia is very interested in the story of Jesus. When we got out of the shower the other morning, she wrapped up in her towel and told me she was Baby Jesus. She wanted me to put my towel over my head and play Mother Mary.

August 13, Pagsanjan

It gets dark between six thirty and seven. The evening here is one of my favorite times of the day. People put on their one electric light or kerosene lantern, and as you walk by an open window or door, it is like a framed painting of a little scene. People don't seem to use curtains, or when they do, they are tied in a knot to let in any little current of air. In the daytime, the interiors of the houses are dark, as everyone seeks the cool shadows, but at night, the windows are like illuminated tableaus.

We have all our windows open, too, although we have the luxury of screens. Often, in the evening we look up from the dinner table and there are people chatting at our corner and looking in at us. We are like the local television for our block.

August 14, Pagsanjan

I am at Vittorio's house. Francesca is making zeppole in the kitchen, trying to teach the Filipina maid how to cook them in the hot oil. The maid is getting splattered and wants Francesca to make the globs of dough smaller. Neither can understand the other's few words of English. At the table in the dining room, Tonia, Luciano and his wife are talking loudly, animatedly in Italian. I just get an occasional word like *bambino*. I think they are arguing about the care of Luciano's adopted baby. On the screened porch, Francis and Vittorio are discussing what to do about the scene in the trench that shoots in a few hours. I have taken a couple of stills in the kitchen of the sink and the dish drainer, backlit from the windows that look into the garden. But, essentially, I am stuck. I don't want to sit down with Francis and Vittorio in the middle of their conversation. It's too hot in the kitchen. I don't want to make Tonia and Luciano feel uncomfortable by sitting down near them. She has already said "Excuse me" several times. I am sort of leaning against the wall here, trying to look comfortably occupied, writing in my notebook.

Last night the mood on the set was different. It was the sixth consecutive night of shooting at Do Long Bridge. The circus mood was gone. The set-up was down in a trench. It had been raining and the bottom of the trench was full of water. The shot called for a dolly track. I watched Alfredo work. His men shoveled in a lot of sand and stomped and packed it until the water disappeared into a mass of mud. They laid a layer of sandbags and placed two-by-twelves on top of that. The wood was wet from the rain, and really heavy. I could see the sweat spraying off the men as they moved in front of the lights. When the bottom of the trench was solid, Alfredo laid the track and leveled it with wooden wedges. The dolly was lifted onto the track, the mount and the camera were set. One man had a pole with a chamois attached to the end, and he leaned into the trench and cleaned the mud off the track each time the dolly passed.

Francis began to rehearse the shot with the actors and the camera. On about the third rehearsal, a large section of the trench wall caved in, covering the track with a couple of tons of dirt and sandbags. It was a long time before it was cleared and they were ready to shoot. The shot called for smoke. The special effects man turned on his spray canister, and laid in a blanket of gray mist. It smelled like oily insect repellent. The wind kept changing, and for each take they put in a new batch. Marty, Sam and the camera crew were coughing and rubbing their eyes. I got back a ways. From where I was, it looked beautiful, with the smoke all backlit, the strings of lights on the bridge and the rockets.

Later in the evening, they needed a flare up in the air at a certain height. A Filipino shimmied up a coconut palm. He went up about eighty feet and attached a pulley so the effects man could hoist a flare up and get it down to reload between takes. The night went very slowly with several setups in the trench, each requiring effects. I left around 3:00 A.M. Francis got home about 6:00 this morning.

August 18, Pagsanjan

I was sitting on top of a pile of sandbags on the ridge, watching the evening fall at the Do Long Bridge set. The strings of lights on the bridge came on. They looked like the kind they use at Italian street *festas* in New York City. Luciano's men were up in the lighting towers getting ready to turn on the arcs. I was watching an electrician cut a round yellow gel for a light near me. All the departments were just getting going. The first shot was on the PBR at the river's edge. The camera was already on the boat and Francis was down there talking to Vittorio. The evening looked pretty with the reflections on the water and the special effects fires starting up along the banks. I went down to the boat and got on just as they were pulling out. The first moment reminded me of a night boat ride somewhere, like the Seine, or maybe the Rhine. It was too dark to see the shore. We headed upriver and there was something festive about being on the water in the night with just the running lights. Then the boat swung around, heading downriver toward the set. The radios started blaring. All the lighting instructions were going out on Vittorio's radio and the special effects men were talking over Jerry's. The boat was idling, trying to stay in position while the camera was being set. The shot was a close-up on Albert Hall.

There was a long discussion about whether Albert's look was supposed to be to camera right or camera left. The script supervisor was sure it was camera right, but Vittorio thought it was camera left and wanted to shoot it both ways to be sure. Jerry said there wasn't time to do both. The exhaust smoke from the diesel engines was blowing on us. The evening began to look like just hard work.

August 20, Pagsanjan

It is 3:15 A.M. I have just come home from the set. It was supposed to be the last night of shooting at Do Long Bridge. But it went very slowly. A day of delay means $30,000–$50,000. This set has fallen behind two days. There are many grumbles about why. There are a lot of reasons. Sometimes the camera setup seems slow, sometimes the special effects seem to take a long time to reload. Sometimes an actor needs more rehearsal. Sometimes Francis adds some new dialogue. Tonight Francis laid out a shot early in the evening and came home for about forty minutes to have a cup of soup while the lighting and dolly track were being set. It rained all the time he was home. When he got back to the location, the river had risen nearly six feet. The scene was to be played with the actor walking along the bank through the mud to the boat. Now there was no bank, the scene had to be played with the guy wading waist-deep in the water. Everything was slowed down; by midnight spirits were sagging as it became apparent that the evening's work was going to take another night.

August 23, Pagsanjan

This morning we got up early. I was really tired. I stood at the sink running the cold water on my hand, waiting for it to get warm to wash my face. I stood there a long time before I remembered that there is no hot water. Francis had to be on the set at 7:00 A.M. and it is a fair drive from the house. He was doing a rehearsal with all the actors at the table of the French plantation. Gio and Roman are in the scene, too, so they had to go at the same time. We hadn't eaten breakfast, but we got in the car and I brought some hard-boiled eggs and some tangerines. Roman was leaning on me, putting on his shoes as we drove, and I realized he hadn't brushed his teeth or combed his hair.

I am the mother of these children, the wife of the director of this multimillion-dollar production, and I hadn't given a thought to my family this morning. I had only been thinking about reloading my still camera with some fast film to photograph the interior of the set before the people and lighting equipment were in the way. Riding along in the car I began going through my wife/mother versus artist argument in my head for about the five hundredth time. Both sides have this perfectly reasonable position; neither gives in.

Over the years, Francis has continually been frustrated with me. I have a closet full of equipment at home. He bought me an animation stand when I was making little animated films, a jigsaw when I was making plastic sculpture. I have a sewing machine from my fabric collage period, an airbrush I used for a series of drawings, a Nikon for still photography. I go through each phase arguing with myself the whole way. Saying, "Why am I doing this? I should be focusing on the children and Francis, they are more important than my projects." Yet, I am always compelled by my current interest, wanting to explore it but never getting it to blend comfortably with my family.

When we got to the set I could see that Francis was irritated; there were already people pounding nails and fussing around. He likes to get there before anybody and have that moment of complete stillness to think about the staging before all the other considerations creep in. He asked everyone to leave the room, but that wasn't the same as coming to a perfectly empty, silent set. It makes him feel like he is appearing to be the temperamental director, chasing them out.

I took some shots downstairs and then, as the actors arrived and the rehearsal began, I went upstairs to see if the bedroom was dressed yet. Bob was working on it, just placing the last few things.

I told him the rooms were a work of art. He said, "Thank you," almost before I finished, as if he meant, "Well, of course." He told me about this odd forties dresser he had found by the side of the road and how he had had it painted with scenes from French fairy tales on the cream-colored background. He said that he had really wanted to cover the dresser with leather and trim it with brass but he knew that Francis would get mad if he spent the money to do it.

He was placing some old photos on the bedside table that were supposed to be the actress's relatives. He told me that they were actually photos of his mother and grandmother, and some of the photos of children were he and his brother. The photo stuck in the mirror of the dresser was of his aunt, and downstairs, over the piano, was his mother and father's wedding picture. His life and his art were all mixed together. Why am I always struggling to get them to blend? Francis gets them together, too. He is downstairs right now rehearsing a scene in which Roman plays a child at the dinner table asked to recite a poem by his father. That is right from our own dining room. Francis has asked Roman to recite that French poem at our table, dozens of times.

August 24, Pagsanjan

Today I shot some footage of the construction at the main set, Kurtz Compound. It is supposed to be a decaying Cambodian temple on the river. Dean's department is building a huge temple and a number of outlying buildings out of adobe blocks. I could hear the pumps pumping water from the river up to the area where the adobe was being made. There were crews of men moving the dried blocks. Each block weighed three hundred pounds. Four men would shoulder a bamboo sling and carry a block to one of the building sites. Bamboo hoists, with a long line of men pulling on thick ropes, lifted the blocks into place. Barges ferried men and materials across the river to the work on the other side. I was amazed at how primitive the construction methods were. John La Sandra told me that manpower costs less than machine power here. He said it was more efficient to explain what he wanted built and then let it be done in the local way. He told me that there were nearly seven hundred laborers all together, with all the woodcarvers, mold makers, carpenters, etc.

Coconut palms were being cleared where bamboo huts will be constructed for the Indians who are being recruited to live on the set. In the script, Kurtz's band of renegade soldiers has trained a tribe of local Montagnard Indians to be a fighting team. They live in huts by the temple. Rather than dress up Filipino extras every day, Francis asked Eva, a production assistant, to go to a northern province where the rice terraces are and recruit a real tribe of primitive people to come live on the set and be in the scenes. I hear she is trying to make a contract with a group of 250 Ifugao Indians. The contract includes food, salary, medical care and a number of chickens, pigs and carabao for sacrificial purposes.

August 25, Pagsanjan

Alfredo came at 1:00 P.M. to take us to his house for Sunday dinner. We had just gotten up and were having coffee in our robes. We had gone to bed about four in the morning. Francis had forgotten about the invitation. We dressed quickly and got the kids to comb their hair and we went to the Italian's house. Alfredo's Neapolitan wife was there and his brother, Mario, and his wife, their twenty-two-year-old daughter and a tiny grandchild who looked totally white with blue eyes and yellow-white hair in the arms of a Filipina maid.

We sat down to a meal of pasta with a sauce of olive oil, anchovies, black olives, tomatoes, capers, tuna and garlic. It was super, but I am used to starting the day with a scrambled egg. They kept telling me to eat more. I am apparently too thin for their taste, "too small for such a big husband" was what I could make in translation of their conversation, all in Italian. It was really an effort to eat enough pasta to satisfy them. By the time they took the plates away, I was uncomfortably stuffed. Then they served roast chicken with rosemary and browned potatoes. I had forgotten all about the possibility that there could be more. After the chicken, there was a huge platter of shrimp, then little artichokes in olive oil that had been brought from Italy. Salad was served and then bread and cheese. The whole time they were saying, "What's the matter, you don't like Italian food? You hardly eat. A bird eats more."

When the coffee was served, I took some pictures of everyone at the table. They all turned toward the camera and posed. There was something about the flowered green, plastic tablecloth, the paper napkins in a glass and the women in cotton sundresses, with slip straps showing, that seemed totally Italian, with no overlay of the Philippines at all.

I walked out into the garden and there were several ladies' cotton undershirts on the clothesline. I wondered when they wore those in this heat. The Italian crew on the production are amazing about their personal decorum. Shooting in some muddy trench in the middle of the night, there Vittorio will be with his starched linen shirt, opened halfway to the waist, exposing his tan chest and thick gold Gucci chain. The Americans wear cutoff jeans and stained T-shirts. On one incredibly hot day, in a sweaty patch of jungle, I got a little piece of ice from the soft drink chest to rub on my face and I let the water drip down my shirt. Luciano walked by with a silk scarf tied around his neck, looking really dashing.

When we got back to our house, the French actors were there, waiting to have Sunday dinner with us.

August 26, Pagsanjan

I was talking to Christian Marquand. He said, "Have you seen the big set? It is an incredible construction. It is the best sculpture I have ever seen. It is outside, you can walk all around, there is sky and earth. It is all there for two months and then gone. It is like an exhibition, but somehow better."

Maybe it was his French accent that separated out the information in some new way so I could hear it. All my life I have wanted to be at the center of the really current, pertinent art scene. Be there when it is happening, and know and really be friends with the artists, like when you read about so-and-so, who used to play chess with Duchamp, or drink beer with Jackson Pollock or something. At times I have followed the art world. Met various artists, like Oldenburg, Christo, Andy Warhol, Poons, etc., but they were already famous and established. It was after the fact. I just felt my same shy, uncomfortable self, like with any people I don't know well. I have looked for the center of the art scene. I went to Paris as a student. I lived in Venice, California. When I looked for the art scene around 1970, I thought it was in New York. I saw minimal art end and conceptual art come into the spotlight. I agreed with the conceptual art tenet that pertinent art of the mid-seventies was not the making of a timeless art object, but about creating an event in time and space. But the conceptual art events I went to were mostly dumb and boring. Contemporary dance seemed more alive. I kept thinking the "real" art must be going on somewhere else, maybe Milano or Documenta or some exotic place. I never felt like I was really where it was at. I know Francis has felt that same thing, wanting to be part of where it really was happening. He has always wanted to be in this wonderful community of artists at the moment that people would talk about later as some golden era. He tried to make it happen in San Francisco. He dreamed of this group of poets, filmmakers and writers who would drink espresso in North Beach and talk of their work, and it would be good. They would publish their writing in *City* magazine, do new plays at the Little Fox Theatre, make experimental films at American Zoetrope. There would be this terrific center of exciting art. He spent a lot of money and energy trying to make it happen. When it didn't, he got angry and frustrated and maybe, mostly sad. He threw his Oscars out the window and left for the Philippines.

Well, just this morning, I realized that this is *it*! Right here in Pagsanjan, of all places. I couldn't see it because it isn't some North Beach café or picturesque studio in Paris or a New York City loft. It's right here. Here we both are, right here where we dreamed of being. I started to laugh. When you stop looking for something, you see it right in front of you. This is that community of artists. It's Dean, Bob, Vittorio, Enrico, Joe, Marty and Alfredo. When I think about it, I really believe that this film is about the most pertinent artwork going on today. We call what Dean is doing, sets; that's an old label. He is probably making the most interesting art sculpture event going on anywhere in the world right now. Vittorio is a world-class visual artist. A poet with light. Francis is writing, only he is not in a romantic-looking garret, he is bent over his electric typewriter right here, sweating in Pagsanjan, so he doesn't see it. Francis is actually the conceptual artist, the ultimate conceptual artist I have been wanting to know. The most right-on artist of 1976. This is that moment we've dreamed of being present at. We're swatting mosquitoes, and eating mangos, it doesn't look like it's supposed to, but I'll bet this is that point in time somebody will label as *it*. I am still laughing.

August 27, Pagsanjan

Coming up in the car this morning to the French plantation set, Francis was talking about the scene at the table yesterday and what went wrong. He had the actors do the whole scene in one long piece, over and over, trying to get a sense of the experience of being at that table as a family, arguing with each other. Going through an experience together to produce moments of reality that you don't get when you shoot in pieces, two lines at a time. But it didn't work. Francis was really frustrated, because that technique of creating an experience has always given him some terrific moments and this time it didn't work. He went over and over with himself, why? He decided that maybe it was because they were French, and the English lines were a barrier, or that some of them weren't professional actors. He was angry that the set had gone over budget, and he had tried to save money on casting. He kept saying, "An audience doesn't give a shit about the authentic antiques on the set, they care about the people in the scene." Vittorio wanted to break the scene into little pieces and do just a couple of lines at a time until it worked. That's the way they do it in Europe. Francis said that when Bobby De Niro first worked with Bertolucci, he said it drove him crazy because he never got to develop the character from doing the whole scene, he had to play it line by short line. The European approach is to start with the frame, and get each frame right. Francis works by getting the emotion of the scene going and asking the camera to capture it. This morning, Francis is going to try it in short pieces.

August 27, French Plantation Set

Francis is feeling angry and trapped. The art department has made their art without sparing expense. What they have made is extraordinary, but it is so complete and detailed there is no way Francis can get it all on camera. Vittorio is oriented toward getting the most perfectly beautiful composition of light and dark in each frame. Visual painting that is extraordinary, but it takes a long time to get all the elements just right, and time is money. The shooting goes very slowly when each setup is taken to such perfection. When the shooting goes slowly, the actors wind down and Francis loses the momentum that keeps his creative juices going. Francis works best when he doesn't have much time and relies on his intuitive decisions. He works by shooting the scenes long, using the emotion that develops and then whacking out huge hunks in the editing room. If he shoots the scenes long, with Vittorio's standards of perfection, it will take months longer than it is scheduled and run up the budget by millions. Francis is feeling the pressure of being at the financial limit, having all the chips on the table. His deal is such that, as the film goes over budget, he has to guarantee the overages personally. If the film is a blockbuster it will be okay, but if the film is pretty good but has gone far over budget, he could end up being wiped out financially and owe millions. I think about that sometimes. Perhaps there is a part of me that wants him to fail. Be back in some simple life-style and all that. At one point in the past, it was really strong, as if returning to a "simple" life would take me out of where I was and I would be happier. At least I know now that it doesn't change things that much. You can be rich and unhappy, or poor and unhappy. I guess women have a hard time as the man grows more successful, powerful, and wish for a time when the balance was more equal. It comes from the fact that the relationship changes. The successful man is usually good at what he does, and likes it, and spends a lot of time doing it—and less and less time with his wife and family. When I stopped feeling like a victim, I started having a lot of fun with Francis. We have odd moments of really interesting time to-gether, rather than more usual amounts of time half tuned out.

August 30, French Plantation Set

I am sitting in this fancy chair on the French plantation set. It is 8:00 P.M. The day was supposed to end at 6:00; everyone is tired and on edge. The shot is a master of the dinner table. It has to be finished so that the actors can go home tomorrow. Luciano has burned his hand in a hurry to change a light. There is something exciting about a scene finishing, and maybe some kind of resistance to having it end. I look around at all the things on the set that were never in any shot. Rented for nothing. The last shot just finished. The French actors are being sentimental and kissing good-bye. There is a kind of camaraderie that takes place, like closing night of a play. Every day for the last five days they have been together at the dinner table. They started out eating the French dinner with gusto; after five days of the food served, over and over and over again, under the hot lights, it was all they could do to pick at it.

.   .   .

September 2, Pagsanjan

I went to the French plantation set to see how Francis was doing and how the boys were holding up. The shot was down on the dock, so I walked down there and found Francis in the shade talking to a heavyset man with short gray hair. When I got closer, the man said, "Hi, Ellie." He looked familiar and then I realized that he was Marlon Brando. I was fascinated that he recognized me and knew my name after such brief meetings. He seemed to be looking at me in microscopic detail. As if he noticed my eyebrows move slightly, or could see the irregular stitching on the buttonhole of my shirt pocket. Not in a judgmental way, just in a complete absorption of all the details.

Later, Francis was telling me that is part of what makes him such a great actor. He develops a fix, a vision of a character, down to the most minute detail. Francis has a more conceptual vision. He has the overall idea of how he wants the film to be and he counts on Dean and Vittorio and the actors to fill in many of the details.

September 4

I was talking to Jerry. He said that it seems like almost everyone on the production is going through some personal transition, a "journey" in their life. Everyone who has come out here to the Philippines seems to be going through something that is affecting them profoundly, changing their perspective about the world or themselves, while the same thing is supposedly happening to Willard in the course of the film. Something is definitely happening to me and to Francis.

September 4, Pagsanjan

Marlon is very overweight. Francis and he are struggling with how to change the character in the script. Brando wants to camouflage his weight and Francis wants to play him as a man eating all the time and overindulging.

I heard there are some real cadavers in body bags at the Kurtz Compound set. I asked the propman about it; he said, "The script says 'a pile of burning bodies'; it doesn't say a pile of burning dummies."

This morning Francis was talking about the Kurtz set being so big that there seemed to be no way to get it all in the frame. The only way to get it was perhaps to come in close and look at specific portions to give a sense of the whole. In a way, that is the same problem he is facing in the script. The ideas of what Kurtz represents are so big that when you try to get a handle on them they are almost undefinable. He has to define the specifics to give a sense of the whole. The production reflects the same thing. It is so big it only seems to make sense in specific ways. Today I have been thinking that the only way that I can show the enormity of the making of *Apocalypse Now* is by showing the details and hoping they give a sense of the larger picture.

Francis came home tonight really excited after his long talk with Marlon. He said that Marlon was really incredible. The greatest actor he has ever met, extremely hardworking. Brando had improvised all day. Going one way, then going another, never quitting. They had toughed it out until they came up with a way to go with his character. Brando was going to do something he had never tried before. He was going to play a bigger-than-life character, a mythical figure, a theatrical personage. He is the master of the natural, realistic performance and he was going to go for a different style of acting for the first time in his career. They haven't quite worked out all the details. It will have to be refined over the next few days, but Francis is really excited and he says Marlon is, too.

BERNADETTE DEVLIN
(1947–)

Bernadette Devlin was born and raised in a Catholic family in Cookstown, Northern Ireland. Her early politics were those of the Republican party, which wanted a united Ireland, free of British rule. Sinn Fein (meaning "ourselves alone") is another name for the Republican party, whose military arm is the IRA. As a university student Devlin helped found the Irish civil rights movement, concerned, above all, with the rights of Catholics in Protestant-dominated Northern Ireland. She also worked for a socialist group called People's Democracy, gaining a reputation for her speeches. As a result of complicated infighting, she ended up with the Republican nomination in a by-election in the spring of 1969 and was elected to the British Parliament, the youngest MP and an instant world celebrity. After her term in Parliament she continued active on behalf of civil rights and Irish nationalism. In January 1981 she and her husband, Michael McAliskey, were gravely wounded when gunmen—Protestant extremists—broke into their home in an assassination attempt.

For another account of political activism from the same era, compare Anne Moody's *Coming of Age in Mississippi,* and from an earlier era see Emma Goldman, *Living My Life.* For reports from other outposts of the British Empire, compare Jill Ker Conway, *The Road from Coorain,* Janet Frame, *An Angel at My Table,* and Santha Rama Rau, *Gifts of Passage.*

An Irishwoman's autobiography is required reading for most Irish schoolchildren—often in its original Gaelic. This is *Recollections of an Old Woman* by Peig Sayers, a dweller in the western isles early in the century.

FROM *The Price of My Soul*

I went to a very militantly Republican grammar school and, under its influence, began to revolt against the Establishment, on the simple rule of thumb, highly satisfying to a ten-year-old, that Irish equals good, English equals bad. At the age of twelve I made my first political protest. I decided to enter a talent competition which for some reason or other was being organized in Cookstown. Most of the members of my family are quite talented. My eldest sister, Mary, now a nun, paints a little, but her main gift is for making something out of nothing. When she was a child our house was coming down with Japanese gardens: there would be clay all over the place, and bits of twig, and an old biscuit tin, and suddenly there was a Japanese garden. I'm useless at that sort of thing. She used to write what I, as a younger sister, thought was excellent poetry, but unfortunately she took it all off with her to the convent. Marie is talented in an entirely different way: she does the ordinary things that everyone does, like sewing and knitting and embroidery, but in half the time and twice as well as anyone else, and she cooks brilliantly. Elizabeth is musically talented; she's a very good pianist. Elizabeth, Paddy, and myself all sing, and I'm considered the best singer because I've got the loudest voice. As children we often used to perform either for visitors or at children's concerts, but we were not encouraged to consider ourselves talented children: my mother squashed any tendencies toward conceit.

When I was in my first year at grammar school, I had a long-playing record, "The Rebel," on which the actor Michael MacLiammoir recited the works of Padraig Pearse, one of the martyrs of 1916. I thought it was great stuff, and played it over and over again, and the more I listened to it the more convinced I became that although MacLiammoir had put it over as a work of art, he had failed to convey the true emotion of a patriot saying what he felt. Anyway I learned three pieces from the record for the three heats of the talent competition, and they were all very militant. "The Rebel" ends:

> "I say to the master of my people 'Beware the risen people who will take what you would not give!' "

Another piece I chose was "The Fool," which has this passage:

> "But the fools, the fools! They have left us our Fenian dead! While Ireland holds these graves, Ireland unfree will never be at rest."

And my third and final choice was Robert Emmett's speech from the dock before his execution in 1804.

Well, off I went and recited this fighting stuff at the talent competition, and I recited it well, went through the three heats, and won first prize. Cookstown was outraged. During the three weeks of the competition, the horror grew. "Imagine a daughter of Lizzie Devlin having the cheek to go down there and say a thing like that! That comes from her father's side of the family." I believe I won on merit, but the general townspeople said I had blackmailed the judges, who were local businessmen and so forth, into awarding me first prize because I could have accused them of bigotry if they hadn't. Feeling got very high and on the last day I had to have a police escort home to protect me from the people who would otherwise have given me a cuff on the ear for my impudence. My mother was delighted; she was somewhat embarrassed, but secretly glad and proud that at least I had enough of my father in me to go somewhere I was hated and look people straight in the face. This was a gift both my parents had: they never shied away uncomfortably from company they knew rejected them. As well as showing courage and defiance, I had won £10 and this too was welcome at home. To me it was like £100. I'd got the average weekly wage of a man in Northern Ireland just for standing up and saying a wee bit of prose. A year or two later, from the same feeling of defiance, I wore a tricolor pin in my coat, precisely because the Northern Ireland Flags and Emblems Act forbade it. Only once did a policeman ask me to remove it. "You remove it," I said, but as his hand came out to take the badge, I added: "If you touch me without a warrant, I'll have you in court for assault!" He just laughed and said, "Go on there, you troublemaker!" I trotted on, feeling very proud I had won, but once I'd discovered I could get away with it, I lost interest in the badge.

I went to school from the age of three and a half, to begin with in Miss Murray's nursery school, held in the front parlor of her home in Chapel Street, Cookstown. My primary school was St. Brigid's Convent, Cookstown, a big gray building, with high ceilings and partitioned rooms. A chestnut tree overshadowed the playground, a place I principally remember for having suffered there the torture of organized games. St. Brigid's was run by the Sisters of Mercy and was part primary school, for those going on to grammar school, and part commercial school for the others. The grammar-school potential got special treatment to rush us through examinations, but we were excluded from the music and sewing and cooking classes. As a result we are among the clumsiest, most useless females ever God produced, whereas our non-grammar-school contemporaries from St. Brigid's are some of the handiest.

I went from Miss Murray's into the first grade at St. Brigid's, where I stayed for a year, then straight into the third grade and rapidly into the fourth. There the school inspector found me, not only very small but also very young, and I was kept in the fourth grade another year before I was allowed to take the exam for grammar school. This almost turned out to be the end of my school career. I had always had a bad attendance record, because I was so often ill, and that year, when I was supposed to be absorbing masses of intelligence tests, square roots, and so forth, I was off with asthma every second week. The nuns used to come down to the house: "Get her out of bed! There's an exam to be passed!" I wasn't particularly worried whether I went to grammar school or not, but I passed the examination, to everybody's surprise.

St. Patrick's Academy, Dungannon, where I then went, was a militantly Republican school, and it owed its fiery partisan slant to the vice-principal, Mother Benignus, whom we called Reverend Mother, and who is, among the people who have influenced me, one of those I most respect. To Mother Benignus everything English was bad. She *hated* the English—and with good reason: her entire family had suffered at the hands of the British forces. Everything we did in school was Irish-oriented. She was a fanatic about Irish culture, which was all right for people like me who were also fanatical about it, but which did drive lots of people away from it who couldn't take Irish culture for breakfast, dinner, and tea. She didn't hate Protestants, but her view was that you couldn't very well put up with them, they weren't Irish, and that clinched the argument. When I was a senior, the school produced a netball team that could have beaten any netball team in the North of Ireland, but Mother Benignus wouldn't let it play Protestant schools on the grounds that we might have to stand for the National Anthem and it would be embarrassing. We told her, "Mother, it wouldn't be embarrassing at all: we would stand. Then we'd invite them over here, and play 'The Soldier's Song' and they would stand too. It would be just a matter of politeness." But she wasn't to be persuaded.

We learned Irish history. People who went to Protestant schools learned British history. We were all learning the same things, the same events, the same period of time, but the interpretations we were given were very different. At the state school they teach that the Act of Union was brought about to help strengthen the trade agreements between England and Ireland. We were taught that it was a malicious attempt to bleed Ireland dry of her linen industry, which was affecting English cotton. We learned our Irish history from *Fallon's Irish History Aids,* Fallon's being a publishing firm in Southern Ireland. Now the Ministry of Education had issued a memorandum saying that *Fallon's Irish History Aids* were not to be used in schools, because they were no more than sedition and treason in the name of history. On a point of principle, *all* our books were published by Fallon's. When the Ministry wrote to complain, Mother Benignus wrote back in Irish, just to make another point clear.

We were a very voluntary voluntary school, under the minimum control of the government, and occasionally offers would come of more financial help in exchange for a greater government say in the school. Officers would come from the Ministry of Education, and argue: "Look, if you come under government control, you'll get another 20 per cent grant." And they would be chased off the premises. Immediately a mass movement would start to raise enough money to produce the necessary facility before the Ministry inspector came back. All our days were spent organizing concerts or raffles or draws or competitions to raise the money to get more equipment for the lab, or a new cooker in the kitchen, or for resurfacing the tennis court. This is where it was a good school. It had a good academic reputation, though socially it wasn't a good school: it did not attract the better class of citizen. There was very little discipline and it didn't produce people who took an active part in the community; but at least in our struggle to do without government help and interference, we ended up appreciating things much better than if they had been forced on us.

I knew no Irish when I went to grammar school, but the class I joined was a class of crude political rebels: we knew nothing about politics except what we were for and against, and we were for Ireland and Mother Benignus was our heroine. In addition to our passion for Ireland, we had a very good teacher of Gaelic, with an enthusiastic approach to the subject, so that at the end of my first year the whole class was way above the standard of Irish-speaking expected of eleven-year-olds. Each year the Gael Linn, an organization which exists to preserve the Irish language, sponsors a school competition in Northern Ireland and awards a shield to the school with the best Irish-conversation standard and a scholarship to the best individual pupil. At the end of my first year, our school won the shield and I won the scholarship, and when the shield was presented, special mention was made of my class, which had been partly responsible for the award. Since I was the best of the best who had helped to win the shield, I became the darling of Mother Benignus's life and a protégée to be sent to the stars ever afterwards. I got away with murder in that school on the basis of my heart being in the right place. Each year an Irish drama festival was held in the locality, and other things being equal we were allowed to go to it on Wednesday afternoon. One particular year the program looked very good: it was getting away from the old Irish kitchen-sink drama and presenting plays in translation, such as those of Chekhov. So three of us organized a large-scale truancy and about twenty pupils sat watching plays for three whole days. With twenty of us missing school, Mother Benignus knew perfectly well where we were. She also knew who was responsible. But when the festival was over and we turned up in school once more, she merely said, "I hope you benefited greatly, and that you will keep your enthusiasm in *reasonable* bounds in the future."

When I first joined St. Patrick's Academy, I was a very timid, terrified person. The other girls all seemed to be independent toughies. Their general attitude was: "We know you have to wear your berets coming to school in the morning; that's why we carry them in our pockets." I was so scared of them that I asked to leave the room when the teacher left, so I could get away from them. But my success in Gaelic and the prominence this gave me in the school cured me of that. The combined effect of Mother Benignus and my fellow students turned me into a convinced Republican, and a year of absorbing the lesson, "We are Irish. We are proud of our history, our dead, our culture, and our language," groomed me for the talent competition.

Mother Benignus was a very kind-hearted woman. Financially the school was never what it should have been because when it came to the paying of fees, if you didn't have the money, you didn't pay. It was written off, or held over, and she would just say, "Well, we'll work a bit harder and make up for it." She was a good kind of socialist. She imposed a capital fee to cover the school's expenses on all qualified pupils—the ones getting scholarships from the state, that is; it came to one guinea a term, which of course everybody could afford, and so she collected one guinea a term from all the people who didn't have to pay to make up the deficit of the children who had neither scholarships nor the money for fees. When we got into unreasonable debt, we just held another competition.

But she was narrow-minded. She couldn't bear, for instance, to see women in masculine attire: wearing jeans was disgusting, she said. And knocking around with the scruffy boys in the boys' academy next door was just a total disgrace. This was amusing enough when you were young, but as you got older it became tiresome to feel her eagle eye upon you when you wanted to walk to the bus stop with some reasonably handsome male. She never missed anything, and you would be hauled over the coals next morning: "You were seen eating crisps out of a bag in the street! Have you no self-respect?" Sucking lollipops in the street was considered sinking to the depths of degradation, and the punishment for these things was quite severe; they merited lengthy tellings-off. But if you knocked somebody halfway down the stairs, you wouldn't get a blessing on your work; it was very un-Christian; you had better apologize, and that was that.

When I was a senior pupil our group resented the fact that we didn't have a common room to ourselves, so we took over a small library where we studied and made ourselves at home. We smuggled in a kettle and a jar of instant coffee and some cups and hid them in the library cupboard. When the bell rang for break and everybody was supposed to go outside for fresh air, we locked the library door and made coffee. And talked. We didn't gossip about other girls in the school or make cynical remarks about the teachers; instead, we analyzed the situation in Northern Ireland and discussed why most of us were going to leave it. I was one of the few who didn't plan to leave Northern Ireland. But the only possible future the others could see was either to get a university education and leave Northern Ireland or go to a Catholic training college and become a Catholic teacher in a Catholic school. None of us wanted to be Catholic teachers—and none of us wanted to be nuns. This was a big drama in the school: for something like fifteen years they hadn't produced a nun from the school, until my sister went and broke the record—and was I disgraced! They wanted about six of us to enter the convent, and we had to fight them off tooth and nail.

Anyway, one day when we were dissecting Northern Ireland behind the locked doors of the library, a general assembly was called. I was head girl at that time and should have called it, but when we got to the assembly hall things were already in progress. It was a uniform inspection—one of many—held this time because girls' gym tunics were getting disgracefully shorter with every passing day. So there was a crisis on, and we had missed it. When we made our appearance, Mother Benignus demanded: "Where have you been? And what have you been discussing?"

One of my friends, Bernadette O'Neill, who was about the most militant person I knew at school, roared from the back of the hall: "Politics, Mother. We have been discussing politics!"

"And if," said Mother Benignus, standing up, "the senior girls of this school have nothing better to discuss than politics, I suggest they should be working. Politics is a waste of time." And she the most political person in the school!

I was head girl at that time by popular acclaim, and the next year I was elected head girl by the prefects. Mother Benignus didn't want me to be head girl the second year: she thought it was making me swell-headed and that I was taking over the school from under her feet. In fact there were three of us—Aideen Mallon, Sheila O'Farrell, and myself. For two years we made ourselves responsible for behavior in the school and in that time took it from the brink of chaos and made of it a reasonably civilized society. The nuns weren't prepared to cane anybody: their attitude was we should behave ourselves for the greater honor and glory of God. But delinquent juveniles didn't work on those assumptions, and there was very little discipline or respect for one's betters in the school. Aideen, Sheila, and I created our own detention period. We used to make children stay in after school and anyone who broke the silence merely prolonged the detention period by another three minutes. The extra three minutes were totted up on the blackboard, and sometimes we were there for an hour and a half. Another complaint was that girls didn't change from their heavy outdoor shoes into their indoor shoes, and they were damaging the school floors. We put a guard on the cloakroom: any girl who forgot to bring indoor shoes was made to go in her stocking feet. After about three days of that, people generally discovered that it wasn't hard to remember their indoor shoes. So we built up our little syndicate of Stalinism, which only lasted a few weeks, for all that was necessary was to impose discipline in the first place. We made the school something more than an academic machine by producing a debating society and a netball team, and we widened its interests from exclusively Irish culture to English-speaking drama and debates.

Because it was the kind of school it was, the history teacher, Mrs. Bradley, was Stalin in disguise. Outside the classroom, she was a very friendly, enthusiastic kind of person, but inside the classroom her system of teaching was to thump everything down your throat. "That's it! Learn it! Or out against the wall!" You had to stand up without moving until such time as your brain registered that which it should have registered; or, if you hadn't learned it in the first place, until you gave in and admitted it. But anything she taught you, you never forgot. She came to us in the library one day for help. She had a particularly stupid class, and even her thump-on-the-head-with-a-book, out-against-the-wall, and stand-till-you-drop tactics had failed to get anything into these kids' brains. She decided a bit of the education touch wouldn't do any harm, and so she planned to produce a wall chart and asked us to make it for her. It was to cover the junior history course, which included most of British history from the Stuarts to the Battle of Waterloo.

We got the junior class working to bring us in pictures of all the important British kings and heroes and generals they could find, and we gathered up old encyclopedias and history books, and with all the material we made a good, colorful, lucid chart, showing who was who and what they had done in the fewest words possible. To head it off, we took a page from an educational magazine that showed a picture of Nelson under the caption, "They fought for their country." The chart was put on the wall, Mrs. Bradley was very grateful, the children were most impressed and started reading the facts and learning something.

Mother Benignus walked into the classroom one day and read on the wall at the back of the room: "They fought for their country." Her eyes lit up with their favorite patriotic glow. As she walked down the room, she asked, "Who did this?"

"Oh, Bernadette Devlin and Sheila O'Farrell and the girls in the library did it," said Mrs. Bradley.

"Very good—I'm glad to see the seniors helping the juniors." By which time she had got to the back of the room and old Horatio Nelson caught her eye. In one blinding flash she realized that her patriotic Fenian wall was decorated with British generals and British heroes, and she just tore the chart, from one end to the other, right off the wall. She crumpled it up, stamped on it, and stormed out of the room, threatening to fire Mrs. Bradley on the spot and demanding that Bernadette Devlin be brought to her immediately. A terrified junior came up to the library: "M-m-mother Benignus wants B-b-bernadette Devlin, and she's in an awful temper." So off I trotted to pacify her, and found her back in the classroom. She was white.

"Are you really responsible for this?" she said.

I looked down and saw our weeks of work lying crumpled on the floor, all the kids sitting around shaking, and Mrs. Bradley on the point of exploding in the background. "I'm not responsible, Mother," I said, thinking she wanted to know who had torn it down. "Mrs. Bradley knows we made that chart. I don't know who tore it off the wall."

It was the wrong thing to say.

"*I* tore it off the wall! And I want it in the waste bin immediately!" Whereupon two or three children scuffled down to put it in the waste bin.

"Don't touch that!" roared Mrs. Bradley. "It's going back on the wall the minute it's cleaned up properly."

And a dialogue ensued on the lines of:

"Not on *my* wall!"

"Then I'm not teaching in your school!"

I was called in to referee. Mother Benignus said, "You agree with me, Bernadette, don't you?"

"No, Mother," I said. "I did most of the work on that chart, and it's not my fault, nor Mrs. Bradley's fault that British history is taught in this school. If you don't like it being taught you should take it up with the Ministry of Education. But as long as it is taught, we have to pass exams. And it doesn't do any harm to learn about those people. They did fight, very bravely, for their country, and have as much right to be considered patriots as Pearse or Connolly or anybody else."

That finished it. "They have *no* right to be considered patriots." And she went over the litany of all the British people who had tortured the Irish for five hundred years.

"But, Mother," I said, "those people didn't torture the Irish. They have nothing to do with the Irish Question. They fought mostly on the Continent."

"They are British!"

So I said, "Mother, you are a bigot," and left her, shutting the classroom door behind me.

"Come back here! I'll not be called a bigot by a pupil of mine."

I opened the door again, stuck my head round it, and said, "Mother, you *are* a bigot. I'm very sorry you're a bigot. But you *are* a bigot." I went back up the stairs with Mother Benignus storming up after me. At the top of the stairs we stopped and the argument began again, with Mother Benignus claiming she wasn't a bigot, but a patriot. My favorite habit at that time was waving my finger, so I waved my finger at her and said, "Mother, you are one of the greatest bigots I have ever met!" She had a ruler in her hand and she practically took my finger off with it. She was beaten. She just said, "Don't wave your finger at the principal of this school!"

I had called her a bigot, I had walked out without being dismissed, I had closed the door in her face, I had forced her to walk up the stairs after me. But she knew I was right, and all she said was, "Don't wave your finger at me." The chart went back up. Mrs. Bradley stayed, and there has been a love-hate relationship between Mother Benignus and myself ever since. Although I have outgrown her politics, Mother Benignus will always have my admiration and affection, because she is the most truly charitable person I have known. Her heart is in the right place.

JOAN DIDION
(1934–)

In *Slouching towards Bethlehem* (1968) and *The White Album* (1979), Joan Didion, the Californian novelist and nonfiction writer, gathered some of the most original and influential essays of our time, many of which are autobiographical. She abjured the pose of objectivity, traditional in nonfiction writing and especially in journalism, and insisted instead on placing herself in her reports. Like other American writers in the early 1970s who explored new territory in nonfictional prose, she was said to be practicing something critics called the New Journalism.

For other autobiographical essays, compare Cynthia Ozick, "A Drugstore in Winter" from *Art & Ardor* and Sara Suleri, "Meatless Days" from her book of the same name.

FROM *The White Album*

IN THE ISLANDS

1969: I had better tell you where I am, and why. I am sitting in a high-ceilinged room in the Royal Hawaiian Hotel in Honolulu watching the long translucent curtains billow in the trade wind and trying to put my life back together. My husband is here, and our daughter, age three. She is blonde and barefoot, a child of paradise in a frangipani lei, and she does not understand why she cannot go to the beach. She cannot go to the beach because there has been an earthquake in the Aleutians, 7.5 on the Richter scale, and a tidal wave is expected. In two or three minutes the wave, if there is one, will hit Midway Island, and we are awaiting word from Midway. My husband watches the television screen. I watch the curtains, and imagine the swell of the water.

The bulletin, when it comes, is a distinct anticlimax: Midway reports no unusual wave action. My husband switches off the television set and stares out the window. I avoid his eyes, and brush the baby's hair. In the absence of a natural disaster we are left again to our own uneasy devices.

We are here on this island in the middle of the Pacific in lieu of filing for divorce.

I tell you this not as aimless revelation but because I want you to know, as you read me, precisely who I am and where I am and what is on my mind. I want you to understand exactly what you are getting: you are getting a woman who for some time now has felt radically separated from most of the ideas that seem to interest other people. You are getting a woman who somewhere along the line misplaced whatever slight faith she ever had in the social contract, in the meliorative principle, in the whole grand pattern of human endeavor. Quite often during the past several years I have felt myself a sleepwalker, moving through the world unconscious of the moment's high issues, oblivious to its data, alert only to the stuff of bad dreams, the children burning in the locked car in the supermarket parking lot, the bike boys stripping down stolen cars on the captive cripple's ranch, the freeway sniper who feels "real bad" about picking off the family of five, the hustlers, the insane, the cunning Okie faces that turn up in military investigations, the sullen lurkers in doorways, the lost children, all the ignorant armies jostling in the night. Acquaintances read *The New York Times*, and try to tell me the news of the world. I listen to call-in shows.

You will perceive that such a view of the world presents difficulties. I have trouble making certain connections. I have trouble maintaining the basic notion that keeping promises matters in a world where everything I was taught seems beside the point. The point itself seems increasingly obscure. I came into adult life equipped with an essentially romantic ethic, holding always before me the examples of Axel Heyst in *Victory* and Milly Theale in *The Wings of the Dove* and Charlotte Rittenmayer in *The Wild Palms* and a few dozen others like them, believing as they did that salvation lay in extreme and doomed commitments, promises made and somehow kept outside the range of normal social experience. I still believe that, but I have trouble reconciling salvation with those ignorant armies camped in my mind. I could indulge here in a little idle generalization, could lay off my own state of profound emotional shock on the larger cultural breakdown, could talk fast about convulsions in the society and alienation and anomie and maybe even assassination, but that would be just one more stylish shell game. I am not the society in microcosm. I am a thirty-four-year-old woman with long straight hair and an old bikini bathing suit and bad nerves sitting on an island in the middle of the Pacific waiting for a tidal wave that will not come.

We spend, my husband and I and the baby, a restorative week in paradise. We are each the other's model of consideration, tact, restraint at the very edge of the precipice. He refrains from noticing when I am staring at nothing, and in turn I refrain from dwelling at length upon a newspaper story about a couple who apparently threw their infant and then themselves into the boiling crater of a live volcano on Maui. We also refrain from mentioning any kicked-down doors, hospitalized psychotics, any chronic anxieties or packed suitcases. We lie in the sun, drive out through the cane to Waimea Bay. We breakfast on the terrace, and gray-haired women smile benevolently at us. I smile back. Happy families are all alike on the terrace of the Royal Hawaiian Hotel in Honolulu. My husband comes in from Kalakaua Avenue one morning and tells me that he has seen a six-foot-two drag queen we know in Los Angeles. Our acquaintance was shopping, my husband reports, for a fishnet bikini and did not speak. We both laugh. I am reminded that we laugh at the same things, and read him this complaint from a very old copy of *Honolulu* Magazine I picked up in someone's office: "When President Johnson recently came to Honolulu, the morning paper's banner read something like 'PICKETS TO GREET PRESIDENT.' Would it not have been just as newsworthy to say 'WARM ALOHA TO GREET PRESIDENT'?" At the end of the week I tell my husband that I am going to try harder to make things matter. My husband says that he has heard that before, but the air is warm and the baby has another frangipani lei and there is no rancor in his voice. Maybe it can be all right, I say. Maybe, he says.

1970: Quite early every morning in Honolulu, on that stretch of Waikiki Beach which fronts the Royal Hawaiian Hotel, an employee of the hotel spends fifteen or twenty minutes raking the sand within a roped enclosure reserved for registered guests. Since this "private" beach differs from the "public" beach only by its raked sand, its rope, and its further remove from the water, it is at first difficult to see why anyone would sit there, but people do. They sit there all day long and in great numbers, facing the sea in even rows.

I had been an occasional visitor to Honolulu for several years before I entirely perceived that the roped beach was central to the essence of the Royal Hawaiian, that the point of sitting there was not at all exclusivity, as is commonly supposed on Waikiki, but inclusivity. Anyone behind the rope is presumed to be, by tacit definition, "our kind." Anyone behind the rope will watch over our children as we will watch over theirs, will not palm room keys or smoke dope or listen to Creedence Clearwater on a transistor when we are awaiting word from the Mainland on the prime rate. Anyone behind the rope, should we venture conversation, will "know people we know": the Royal's roped beach is an enclave of apparent strangers ever on the verge of discovering that their nieces roomed in Lagunita at Stanford the same year, or that their best friends lunched together during the last Crosby. The fact that anyone behind the rope would understand the word "Crosby" to signify a golf tournament at Pebble Beach suggests the extent to which the Royal Hawaiian is not merely a hotel but a social idea, one of the few extant clues to a certain kind of American life.

Of course great hotels have always been social ideas, flawless mirrors to the particular societies they service. Had there never been an Empire there would not have been a Raffles. To understand what the Royal is now you must first understand what it was, from 1927 through the Thirties, the distant and mildly exotic "pink palace" of the Pacific, the resort built by the Matson Line to rival and surpass such hotels as the Coronado, the Broadmoor, Del Monte. Standing then almost alone on Waikiki, the Royal made Honolulu a place to go, made all things "Hawaiian"—leis, ukuleles, luaus, coconut-leaf hats and the singing of "I Wanna Learn to Speak Hawaiian"—a decade's craze at country-club dances across the United States. During the fourteen years between the Royal's opening and Pearl Harbor people came in on the Matson Line's *Malolo* and *Lurline* and they brought with them not only steamer trunks but children and grandchildren and valets and nurses and silver Rolls-Royces and ultramarine-blue Packard roadsters. They "wintered" at the Royal, or "summered" there, or "spent several months." They came to the Royal to rest "after hunting in South Africa." They went home "by way of Banff and Lake Louise." In Honolulu there was polo, golf, bowling on the green. Every afternoon the Royal served tea on rattan tables. The maids wove leis for every guest. The chefs constructed, as table decoration, the United States Capitol Building in Hawaiian sugar.

The Royal's scrapbooks for those years survive as an index to America's industrial fortunes, large and small. Mellons and Du Ponts and Gettys and the man who had just patented the world's largest incubator (47,000-egg capacity) seem to differ not at all from one another, photographed at the Royal in 1928. Dorothy Spreckels strums a ukulele on the verandah. Walter P. Chrysler, Jr., arrives with his mother and father for a season at the Royal. A figure on the beach is described as "a Colorado Springs society woman," a young couple as "prominently identified with the young-married set in Akron." At the Royal they met not only one another but a larger world as well: Australian station owners, Ceylonese tea planters, Cuban sugar operators.

In the faded photographs one sees mostly mothers and daughters. The men, when they are present, display in the main an affecting awkwardness, an awareness that they have harsher roles, say as Mayor of Seattle or President of the Overland Motor Company, a resistance to the world of summering and wintering. In 1931 the son of President Hoover spent time at the Royal, was widely entertained, caught thirty-eight fish off the

Kona coast of Hawaii, and had his picture taken on the Royal beach shaking hands with Duke Kahanamoku. This photograph appeared in *Town and Country*, which also reported in 1931 that "the diving boys in Honolulu harbor say that fishing has been good and there are no indications of hard times in the denominations of coins flipped to them as bait from incoming steamers."

Nor did the turnings of the Sixties effect much change at the Royal. What the place reflected in the Thirties it reflects still, in less flamboyant mutations: a kind of life lived always on the streets where the oldest trees grow. It is a life so secure in its traditional concerns that the cataclysms of the larger society disturb it only as surface storms disturb the sea's bottom, a long time later and in oblique ways. It is a life lived by millions of people in this country and largely forgotten by most of us. Sometimes I think I remember it only at the Royal Hawaiian. There in the warm early evenings, the women in turquoise-blue and buttercup-yellow chiffons seem, as they wait for cars under the pink porte-cochere, the natural inheritors of a style later seized upon by Patricia Nixon and her daughters. In the mornings, when the beach is just raked and the air damp and sweet from the dawn rain, I see the same women, now in printed silks and lined cashmere cardigans, eating papaya on the terrace just as they have done every few seasons since they were young girls, in the late Twenties, and came to the Royal with their mothers and sisters. Their husbands scan the San Francisco and Los Angeles papers with the practiced disinterest of men who believe their lives safe in municipal bonds. These papers arrive at the Royal one and sometimes two days late, which lends the events of the day a peculiar and unsettling distance. I recall overhearing a conversation at the Royal's newsstand on the morning after the California primary in June 1968, the morning Robert Kennedy lay dying in Good Samaritan Hospital in Los Angeles. "How'd the primary go?" a man buying cigarettes asked his wife. She studied the day-old headlines. " 'Early Turnout Heavy,' " she said. Later in the morning I overheard this woman discussing the assassination: her husband had heard the news when he dropped by a brokerage office to get the day's New York closings.

To sit by the Royal pool and read *The New York Review of Books* is to feel oneself an asp, disguised in a voile beach robe, in the very bosom of the place. I put *The New York Review of Books* aside and talk to a pretty young woman who has honeymooned at the Royal, because honeymoons at the Royal are a custom in her family, with each of her three husbands. My daughter makes friends at the pool with another four-year-old, Jill, from Fairbanks, Alaska, and it is taken for granted by Jill's mother and aunt that the two children will meet again, year after year, in the immutable pleasant rhythms of a life that used to be, and at the Royal Hawaiian seems still to be. I sit in my voile beach robe and watch the children and wish, against all the evidence I know, that it might be so.

1970: To look down upon Honolulu from the high rain forest that divides windward Oahu from the leeward city is to see, in the center of an extinct volcano named Puowaina, a place so still and private that once seen it is forever in the mind. There are banyan trees in the crater, and rain trees, and 19,500 graves. Yellow primavera blazes on the hills above. Whole slopes seem clouded in mauve jacaranda. This is the place commonly called Punchbowl, the National Memorial Cemetery of the Pacific, and 13,000 of the dead in its crater were killed during World War II. Some of the rest died in Korea. For almost a decade now, in the outer sections just inside the rim of the crater, they have been digging graves for Americans killed in Vietnam, not many, a fraction of the total, one, two, three a week, most of them Island boys but some of them carried here by families who live thousands of miles across the Pacific, a gesture that touches by its very difficulty. Because the Vietnam dead are shipped first to Travis A.F.B. in California and then to the next of kin, those Mainland families burying their sons or husbands in Honolulu must bring the bodies back over the Pacific one last time. The superintendent of Punchbowl, Martin T. Corley, refers to such burials as his "ship-in Vietnams."

"A father or an uncle calls me from the Mainland and he says they're bringing their boy here, I don't ask why," Mr. Corley said when I talked to him not long ago. We were sitting in his office in the crater and on the wall hung the Bronze Star and Silver Star citations he had received in Europe in 1944, Martin T. Corley, a man in an aloha shirt who had gone from South Ozone Park in Queens to the Battle of the Bulge to a course in cemetery management at Fort Sam Houston and finally, twenty-some years later, to an office in an extinct volcano in the Pacific from which he could watch the quick and the dead in still another war.

I watched him leafing through a stack of what he called "transmittals," death forms from Vietnam. There in Martin T. Corley's office Vietnam seemed considerably less chimerical than it had seemed on the Mainland for some months, less last year's war, less successfully consigned to that limbo of benign neglect in which any mention of continuing casualties was made to seem a little counterproductive, a little démodé. There in the crater it seemed less easy to believe that weekly killed-in-action figures under 100 might by some sleight-of-hand add up to zero, a nonexistent war. There in sight of the automatic gravediggers what the figures added up to, for the first twelve weeks of 1970, was 1,078 dead. Martin T. Corley gets a transmittal on each of them. He holds these transmittal forms for fifteen or twenty days before throwing them away, just in case a family wants to bring its dead to Punchbowl. "See, we had a family bring a boy in from Oregon a few days ago," he said. "We've got a California coming in now. We figure they've got their reasons. We pick the plot, open the grave. These ship-in families, we don't see them until the hearse comes through the gate."

On a warm windy afternoon a few days later I stood with Mr. Corley on the soft grass up in Section K of the crater and waited for one such family to come through the gate. They had flown out from the Mainland with the body the night before, six of them, the mother and father and a sister and her husband and a couple of other relatives, and they would bury their boy in the afternoon sun and fly back a few hours later. We waited, and we watched, and then, on the road below, the six Air Force pallbearers snapped to attention. The bugler jumped up from beneath a banyan tree and took his place behind the honor guard. We could see the hearse then, winding up and around the circular road to Section K, the hearse and two cars, their headlights dim in the tropical sun. "Two of us from the office come to all the Vietnams," Mr. Corley said suddenly. "I mean in case the family breaks down or something."

All I can tell you about the next ten minutes is that they seemed a very long time. We watched the coffin being carried to the grave and we watched the pallbearers lift the flag, trying to hold it taut in the warm trade wind. The wind was blowing hard, toppling the vases of gladioli set by the grave, obliterating some of the chaplain's words. "If God is for us then who can be against us," the chaplain said, a red-headed young major in suntans, and then I did not hear any more for a while. I was standing behind the six canvas chairs where the family sat, standing there with Mr. Corley and an Air Force survival assistance officer, and I was looking beyond the chaplain to a scattering of graves so fresh they had no headstones, just plastic markers stuck in the ground. "We tenderly commit this body to the ground," the chaplain said then. The men in the honor guard raised their rifles. Three shots cracked out. The bugler played taps. The pallbearers folded the flag until only the blue field and a few stars showed, and one of them stepped forward to present the flag to the father. For the first time the father looked away from the coffin, looked away from the pallbearers and out across the expanse of graves. A slight man with his face trembling and his eyes wet, he stood facing Mr. Corley and me, and for a moment we looked directly at each other, but he was seeing not me, not Mr. Corley, not anyone.

It was not quite three o'clock. The father, transferring the flag from hand to hand as if it burned, said a few halting words to the pallbearers. I walked away from the grave then, down to my car, and waited for Mr. Corley to talk to the father. He wanted to tell the father that if he and his wife wanted to come back before their plane left, the grave would be covered by four o'clock. "Sometimes it makes them feel better to see it," Mr. Corley said when he caught up with me. "Sometimes they get on the plane and they worry, you know, it didn't get covered." His voice trailed off. "We cover within thirty minutes," he said finally. "Fill, cover, get the marker on. That's one thing I remember from my training." We stood there a moment in the warm wind, then said goodbye. The pallbearers filed onto the Air Force bus. The bugler walked past, whistling "Raindrops Keep Fallin' on My Head." Just after four o'clock the father and mother came back and looked for a long while at the covered grave, then took a night flight back to the Mainland. Their son was one of 101 Americans killed that week in Vietnam.

1975: The 8:45 A.M. Pan American to Honolulu this morning was delayed half an hour before takeoff from Los Angeles. During this delay the stewardesses served orange juice and coffee and two children played tag in the aisles and, somewhere behind me, a man began screaming at a woman who seemed to be his wife. I say that the woman seemed to be his wife only because the tone of his invective sounded practiced, although the only words I heard clearly were these: "You are driving me to murder." After a moment I was aware of the door to the plane being opened a few rows behind me, and of the man rushing off. There were many Pan American employees rushing on and off then, and considerable confusion. I do not know whether the man reboarded the plane before takeoff or whether the woman came on to Honolulu alone, but I thought about it all the way across the Pacific. I thought about it while I was drinking a sherry-on-the-rocks and I thought about it during lunch and I was still thinking about it when the first of the Hawaiian Islands appeared off the left wing tip. It was not until we had passed Diamond Head and were coming in low over the reef for landing at Honolulu, however, that I realized what I most disliked about this incident: I disliked it because it had the aspect of a short story, one of those "little epiphany" stories in which the main character glimpses a crisis in a stranger's life—a woman weeping in a tearoom, often, or an accident seen from the window of a train, "tearooms" and "trains" still being fixtures of short stories although not of real life—and is moved to see his or her own life in a new light. I was not going to Honolulu because I wanted to see life reduced to a short story. I was going to Honolulu because I wanted to see life expanded to a novel, and I still do. I wanted room for flowers, and reef fish, and people who may or may not be driving one another to murder but in any case are not impelled, by the demands of narrative convention, to say so out loud on the 8:45 A.M. Pan American to Honolulu.

1977: I have never seen a postcard of Hawaii that featured Schofield Barracks. Schofield is off the track, off the tour, hard by the shadowy pools of the Wahiawa Reservoir, and to leave Honolulu and drive inland to Schofield is to sense a clouding of the atmosphere, a darkening of the color range. The translucent pastels of the famous coast give way to the opaque greens of interior Oahu. Crushed white coral gives way to red dirt, sugar dirt, deep red laterite soil that crumbles soft in the hand and films over grass and boots and hubcaps. Clouds mass over the Waianae Range. Cane fires smoke on the horizon and rain falls fitfully. BUY SOME COLLARD GREENS, reads a sign on a weathered frame grocery in Wahiawa, just across the two-lane bridge from the Schofield gate. MASSAGE PARLOR, CHECKS CASHED, 50TH STATE POOL-ROOM, HAPPY HOUR, CASH FOR CARS. Schofield Loan. Schofield Pawn. Schofield Sands Motor Lodge. Then, finally, Schofield itself, the Schofield we all know from James Jones's *From Here to Eternity,* the Schofield that is Home of the 25th "Tropic Lightning" Infantry Division, formerly the Hawaii Division, James Jones's own division, Robert E. Lee Prewitt's division, Maggio's and Warden's and Stark's and Dynamite Holmes's division, *Fit to Fight, Trained to Win, Ready to Go. All Wars Are Won in the End by the Infantryman. Through These Portals Pass the Finest Soldiers in the World—25TH INFANTRY DIVISION SOLDIERS. TROPIC LIGHTNING REENLISTMENT.* I have never driven into Schofield and seen those words without hearing the blues that end *From Here to Eternity:*

> Got paid out on Monday
> Not a dog soldier no more
> They gimme all that money
> So much my pockets is sore
> More dough than I can use. Reenlistment Blues.
> Ain't no time to lose. Reenlistment Blues.

Certain places seem to exist mainly because someone has written about them. Kilimanjaro belongs to Ernest Hemingway. Oxford, Mississippi, belongs to William Faulkner, and one hot July week in Oxford I was moved to spend an afternoon walking the graveyard looking for his stone, a kind of courtesy call on the owner of the property. A place belongs forever to whoever claims it hardest, remembers it most obsessively, wrenches it from itself, shapes it, renders it, loves it so radically that he remakes it in his image, and not only Schofield Barracks but a great deal of Honolulu itself has always belonged for me to James Jones. The first time I ever saw Hotel Street in Honolulu was on a Saturday

night in 1966 when all the bars and tattoo parlors were full of military
police and girls looking for a dollar and nineteen-year-olds, on their way
to or from Saigon, looking for a girl. I recall looking that night for the
particular places that had figured in *From Here to Eternity:* the Black
Cat, the Blue Anchor, the whorehouse Jones called the New Congress
Hotel. I remember driving up Wilhemina Rise to look for Alma's house
and I remember walking out of the Royal Hawaiian Hotel and expecting
to see Prewitt and Maggio sitting on the curb and I remember walking
the Waialae Country Club golf course, trying to figure exactly where
Prewitt died. I think it was in the trap near the fifth green.

It is hard to see one of these places claimed by fiction without a
sudden blurring, a slippage, a certain vertiginous occlusion of the imagined and the real, and this slippage was particularly acute the last time I
arrived in Honolulu, on a June day when the author of *From Here to
Eternity* had been dead just a few weeks. In New York the death of
James Jones had been the occasion for many considerations and recon-
siderations. Many mean guilts had been recalled and exorcised. Many
lessons had been divined, in both the death and the life. In Honolulu the
death of James Jones had been marked by the publication, in the
Honolulu Star-Bulletin, of an excerpt from the author's *Viet Journal,*
the epilogue, the part in which he talked about returning to Honolulu in
1973 and looking for the places he had remembered in *From Here to
Eternity* but had last seen in 1942, when he was twenty-one years old and
shipped out for Guadalcanal with the 25th Division. In 1973 the five
pillboxes on Makapuu Head had seemed to James Jones exactly as he
had left them in 1942. In 1973 the Royal Hawaiian Hotel had seemed to
James Jones less formidably rich than he had left it in 1942, and it had
occurred to him with considerable poignance that he was a man in his
fifties who could walk into the Royal Hawaiian and buy whatever he
wanted.

He had bought a beer and gone back to Paris. In June of 1977 he was
dead and it was not possible to buy a copy of his great novel, his living
novel, the novel in which he so loved Honolulu that he remade it in his
image, in any of Honolulu's largest bookstores. "Is it a best-seller?" I was
asked in one, and the golden child in charge of another suggested that I
try the psychic-science shelf. In that instant I thought I grieved for
James Jones, a man I never met, but I think I grieved for all of us: for
Jones, for myself, for the sufferers of mean guilts and for their exorcists,
for Robert E. Lee Prewitt, for the Royal Hawaiian Hotel and for this
golden nitwit who believed eternity to be a psychic science.

I have never been sure whether the extreme gravity of *From Here to
Eternity* is an exact reflection of the light at Schofield Barracks or

whether I see the light as grave because I have read James Jones. "It had rained all morning and then suddenly cleared at noon, and the air, freshly washed today, was like dark crystal in the sharp clarity and sombre focus it gave to every image." It was in this sombre focus that James Jones rendered Schofield, and it was in this sombre focus that I last saw Schofield, one Monday during that June. It had rained in the morning and the smell of eucalyptus was sharp in the air and I had again that familiar sense of having left the bright coast and entered a darker country. The black outline of the Waianae Range seemed obscurely oppressive. A foursome on the post golf course seemed to have been playing since 1940, and to be doomed to continue. A soldier in fatigues appeared to be trimming a bougainvillea hedge, swinging at it with a scythe, but his movements were hypnotically slowed, and the scythe never quite touched the hedge. Around the tropical frame bungalows where the families of Schofield officers have always lived there was an occasional tricycle but no child, no wife, no sign of life but one: a Yorkshire terrier yapping on the lawn of a colonel's bungalow. As it happens I have spent time around Army posts in the role of an officer's child, have even played with lap dogs on the lawns of colonels' quarters, but I saw this Yorkshire with Prewitt's eyes, and I hated it.

I had driven out to Schofield in other seasons, but this trip was different. I was making this trip for the same reason I had walked the Oxford graveyard, a courtesy call on the owner. This trip I made appointments, spoke to people, asked questions and wrote down answers, had lunch with my hosts at the Aloha Lightning NCO Club and was shown the regimental trophies and studied the portraits of commanding officers in every corridor I walked down. Unlike the golden children in the Honolulu bookstores these men I met at Schofield, these men in green fatigues, all knew exactly who James Jones was and what he had written and even where he had slept and eaten and probably gotten drunk during the three years he spent at Schofield. They recalled the incidents and locations of *From Here to Eternity* in minute detail. They anticipated those places that I would of course want to see: D Quad, the old stockade, the stone quarry, Kolekole Pass. Some weeks before, there had been at the post theater a special screening of the movie *From Here to Eternity*, an event arranged by the Friends of the Tropic Lightning Historical Society, and everyone to whom I spoke at Schofield had turned out for this screening. Many of these men were careful to qualify their obvious attachment to James Jones's view of their life by pointing out that the Army had changed. Others did not mention the change. One, a young man who had re-upped once and now wanted out, mentioned that it had not changed at all. We were standing on the lawn in D Quad, Jones's quad, Robert E. Lee Prewitt's quad, and I was watching the idle movement around the square, a couple of soldiers dropping a basketball through a hoop, another cleaning an M-16, a desultory argument at the Dutch door of the supply room—when he volunteered a certain inchoate dissatisfaction with his six years in the 25th Division. "I read this book *From Here to Eternity,*" he said, "and they still got the same little games around here."

I suppose everything had changed and nothing had. A mess hall was now called a "dining facility," but they still served chipped beef on toast and they still called it "S.O.S." A stockade was now called a "confinement facility," and the confinement facility for all military installations on Oahu was now at Pearl Harbor, but the old stockade at Schofield was now the headquarters for the military police, and during the time I was there the M.P.s brought in a handcuffed soldier, bare to the waist and shoeless. Investigators in aloha shirts chatted in the exercise yard. Office supplies were stored in some of the "close confinement" cells, but there were still the plain wooden bunks, "plate beds," beds for those occasions, it was explained to me by a major who had once been in charge of the Schofield stockade, "when a guy is completely berserk and starts ripping up his mattress." On the wall there were still the diagrams detailing the order in which belongings were to be arranged: WHITE TOWEL, SOAP WITH DISH, DEODORANT, TOOTHPASTE, TOOTHBRUSH, COMB, SHAVING CREAM, RAZOR.

In many ways I found it difficult to leave Schofield that day. I had fallen into the narcoleptic movements of the Army day. I had picked up the liquid speech patterns of the Army voice. I took a copy of the *Tropic Lightning News* back into Honolulu with me, and read it that night in my hotel room. During the month of May the Schofield military police had reported 32 arrests for driving under the influence of alcohol, 115 arrests for possession of marijuana, and the theft of a number of items, including one Sansui amplifier, one Sansui pre-amp and tuner, one Kenwood receiver and turntable, two Bose speakers and the tachometer from a 1969 Ford Mustang. One private, two spec fours and one sergeant were asked in the "Troop Talk" column to name their ideal, or favorite, post. One chose Fort Hood. Another chose Fort Sam Houston. None chose Schofield Barracks. In the letters column one correspondent advised a WAC who had objected to the shows at the NCO Club to stay home ("We once had it set up where you girls didn't have to see the entertainment, but the loverly libbers put an end to that"), and another advised "barracks rats" to stop limiting their lives to "erasing Army hatred by indulging in smoke or drink or listening to Peter Frampton at eighty decibels." I thought about barracks rats and I thought about Prewitt and Maggio and I thought about Army hatred and it seemed to me that night in Honolulu that only the details had changed, that James

Jones had known a great simple truth: the Army was nothing more or less than life itself. I wish I could tell you that on the day in May when James Jones died someone had played a taps for him at Schofield Barracks, but I think this is not the way life goes.

ANNIE DILLARD
(1945–)

Annie Dillard was raised in Pittsburgh in comfortable circumstances, which she describes in *An American Childhood* (1987). The book's energy does not come so much from social observation, however, as from the effort to portray the growth of consciousness. In the first of these selections she describes a childhood terror and the effort to figure it out. The second presents adult skin, as perceived by a child—the Brobdingnagian effect. Dillard's temperament may be partly that of a scientist and partly that of a theologian, but she is also part jokester and part athlete. In the third selection she writes about throwing snowballs at cars and running away, an activity which decathlete Dave Johnson has said is the best possible childhood training for sports. Educated at Hollins College in Virginia, Dillard won the Pulitzer Prize for nonfiction in 1975 for *Pilgrim at Tinker Creek*.

For an account of a more communal childhood, compare Judith Ortiz Cofer, *Silent Dancing*. For other selections humorous in various ways, compare Mary McCarthy, *Memories of a Catholic Girlhood*, Jessica Mitford, *Hons and Rebels*, Kate Simon, *Bronx Primitive*, Marjorie Kinnan Rawlings, *Cross Creek*, Natalia Ginzburg, *Family Savings*, and Maya Angelou, *I Know Why the Caged Bird Sings*.

FROM *An American Childhood*

When I was five, growing up in Pittsburgh in 1950, I would not go to bed willingly because something came into my room. This was a private matter between me and it. If I spoke of it, it would kill me.

Who could breathe as this thing searched for me over the very corners of the room? Who could ever breathe freely again? I lay in the dark.

My sister Amy, two years old, was asleep in the other bed. What did she know? She was innocent of evil. Even at two she composed herself attractively for sleep. She folded the top sheet tidily under her prettily outstretched arm; she laid her perfect head lightly on an unwrinkled pillow, where her thick curls spread evenly in rays like petals. All night long she slept smoothly in a series of pleasant and serene, if artificial-looking, positions, a faint smile on her closed lips, as if she were posing for an ad for sheets. There was no messiness in her, no roughness for things to cling to, only a charming and charmed innocence that seemed then to protect her, an innocence I needed but couldn't muster. Since Amy was asleep, furthermore, and since when I needed someone most I was afraid to stir enough to wake her, she was useless.

I lay alone and was almost asleep when the damned thing entered the room by flattening itself against the open door and sliding in. It was a transparent, luminous oblong. I could see the door whiten at its touch; I could see the blue wall turn pale where it raced over it, and see the maple headboard of Amy's bed glow. It was a swift spirit; it was an awareness. It made noise. It had two joined parts, a head and a tail, like a Chinese dragon. It found the door, wall, and headboard; and it swiped them, charging them with its luminous glance. After its fleet, searching passage, things looked the same, but weren't.

I dared not blink or breathe; I tried to hush my whooping blood. If it found another awareness, it would destroy it.

Every night before it got to me it gave up. It hit my wall's corner and couldn't get past. It shrank completely into itself and vanished like a cobra down a hole. I heard the rising roar it made when it died or left. I still couldn't breathe. I knew—it was the worst fact I knew, a very hard fact—that it could return again alive that same night.

Sometimes it came back, sometimes it didn't. Most often, restless, it came back. The light stripe slipped in the door, ran searching over Amy's wall, stopped, stretched lunatic at the first corner, raced wailing toward my wall, and vanished into the second corner with a cry. So I wouldn't go to bed.

It was a passing car whose windshield reflected the corner streetlight outside. I figured it out one night.

Figuring it out was as memorable as the oblong itself. Figuring it out was a long and forced ascent to the very rim of being, to the membrane of skin that both separates and connects the inner life and the outer world. I climbed deliberately from the depths like a diver who releases the monster in his arms and hauls himself hand over hand up an anchor chain till he meets the ocean's sparkling membrane and bursts through it; he sights the sunlit, becalmed hull of his boat, which had bulked so ominously from below.

I recognized the noise it made when it left. That is, the noise it made called to mind, at last, my daytime sensations when a car passed—the sight and noise together. A car came roaring down hushed Edgerton Avenue in front of our house, stopped at the corner stop sign, and passed on shrieking as its engine shifted up the gears. What, precisely, came into the bedroom? A reflection from the car's oblong windshield. Why did it travel in two parts? The window sash split the light and cast a shadow.

Night after night I labored up the same long chain of reasoning, as night after night the thing burst into the room where I lay awake and Amy slept prettily and my loud heart thrashed and I froze.

There was a world outside my window and contiguous to it. If I was so all-fired bright, as my parents, who had patently no basis for comparison, seemed to think, why did I have to keep learning this same thing over and over? For I had learned it a summer ago, when men with jackhammers broke up Edgerton Avenue. I had watched them from the yard; the street came up in jagged slabs like floes. When I lay to nap, I listened. One restless afternoon I connected the new noise in my bedroom with the jackhammer men I had been seeing outside. I understood abruptly that these worlds met, the outside and the inside. I traveled the route in my mind: You walked downstairs from here, and outside from downstairs. "Outside," then, was conceivably just beyond my windows. It was the same world I reached by going out the front or the back door. I forced my imagination yet again over this route.

The world did not have me in mind; it had no mind. It was a coincidental collection of things and people, of items, and I myself was one such item—a child walking up the sidewalk, whom anyone could see or ignore. The things in the world did not necessarily cause my overwhelming feelings; the feelings were inside me, beneath my skin, behind my ribs, within my skull. They were even, to some extent, under my control.

I could be connected to the outer world by reason, if I chose, or I could yield to what amounted to a narrative fiction, to a tale of terror whispered to me by the blood in my ears, a show in light projected on the room's blue walls. As time passed, I learned to amuse myself in bed in the darkened room by entering the fiction deliberately and replacing it by reason deliberately.

When the low roar drew nigh and the oblong slid in the door, I threw my own switches for pleasure. It's coming after me; it's a car outside. It's after me. It's a car. It raced over the wall, lighting it blue wherever it ran; it bumped over Amy's maple headboard in a rush, paused, slithered elongate over the corner, shrank, flew my way, and vanished into itself with a wail. It was a car.

Our parents and grandparents, and all their friends, seemed insensible to their own prominent defect, their limp, coarse skin.

We children had, for instance, proper hands; our fluid, pliant fingers joined their skin. Adults had misshapen, knuckly hands loose in their skin like bones in bags; it was a wonder they could open jars. They were loose in their skins all over, except at the wrists and ankles, like rabbits.

We were whole, we were pleasing to ourselves. Our crystalline eyes shone from firm, smooth sockets; we spoke in pure, piping voices through dark, tidy lips. Adults were coming apart, but they neither noticed nor minded. My revulsion was rude, so I hid it. Besides, we could never rise to the absolute figural splendor they alone could on occasion achieve. Our beauty was a mere absence of decrepitude; their beauty, when they had it, was not passive but earned; it was grandeur; it was a party to power, and to artifice, even, and to knowledge. Our beauty was, in the long run, merely elfin. We could not, finally, discount the fact that in some sense they owned us, and they owned the world.

Mother let me play with one of her hands. She laid it flat on a living-room end table beside her chair. I picked up a transverse pinch of skin over the knuckle of her index finger and let it drop. The pinch didn't snap back; it lay dead across her knuckle in a yellowish ridge. I poked it; it slid over intact. I left it there as an experiment and shifted to another finger. Mother was reading *Time* magazine.

Carefully, lifting it by the tip, I raised her middle finger an inch and released it. It snapped back to the tabletop. Her insides, at least, were alive. I tried all the fingers. They all worked. Some I could lift higher than others.

"That's getting boring."

"Sorry, Mama."

I refashioned the ridge on her index-finger knuckle; I made the ridge as long as I could, using both my hands. Moving quickly, I made parallel ridges on her other fingers—a real mountain chain, the Alleghenies; Indians crept along just below the ridgetops, eyeing the frozen lakes below them through the trees.

Skin was earth; it was soil. I could see, even on my own skin, the joined trapezoids of dust specks God had wetted and stuck with his spit the morning he made Adam from dirt. Now, all these generations later, we people could still see on our skin the inherited prints of the dust specks of Eden.

I loved this thought, and repeated it for myself often. I don't know where I got it; my parents cited Adam and Eve only in jokes. Someday I would count the trapezoids, with the aid of a mirror, and learn precisely how many dust specks Adam comprised—one single handful God wetted, shaped, blew into, and set firmly into motion and left to wander about in the fabulous garden bewildered.

The skin on my mother's face was smooth, fair, and tender; it took impressions readily. She napped on her side on the couch. Her face skin pooled on the low side; it piled up in the low corners of her deep-set eyes and drew down her lips and cheeks. How flexible was it? I pushed at a puddle of it by her nose.

She stirred and opened her eyes. I jumped back.

She reminded me not to touch her face while she was sleeping. Anybody's face.

When she sat up, her cheek and brow bone bore a deep red gash, the mark of a cushion's welting. It was textured inside precisely with the upholstery's weave and brocade.

Another day, after a similar nap, I spoke up about this gash. I told her she had a mark on her face where she'd been sleeping.

"Do I?" she said; she ran her fingers through her hair. Her hair was short, blond, and wavy. She wore it swept back from her high, curved forehead. The skin on her forehead was both tight and soft. It would only barely shift when I tried to move it. She went to the kitchen. She was not interested in the hideous mark on her face. "It'll go away," I said. "What?" she called.

I noticed the hair on my father's arms and legs; each hair sprang from a dark dot on his skin. I lifted a hair and studied the puckered tepee of skin it pulled with it. Those hairs were in there tight. The greater the strain I put on the hair, the more puckered the tepee became, and shrunken within, concave. I could point it every which way.

"Ouch! Enough of that."

"Sorry, Daddy."

At the beach I felt my parent's shinbones. The bones were flat and curved, like the slats in a Venetian blind. The long edges were sharp as swords. But they had unexplained and, I thought, possibly diseased irregularities: nicks, bumps, small hard balls, shallow ridges, and soft spots. I was lying between my parents on an enormous towel through which I could feel the hot sand.

Loose under their shinbones, as in a hammock, hung the relaxed flesh of their calves. You could push and swing this like a baby in a sling. Their heels were dry and hard, sharp at the curved edge. The bottoms of their toes had flattened, holding the imprint of life's smooth floors even when they were lying down. I would not let this happen to me. Under certain conditions, the long bones of their feet showed under their skin. The bones rose up long and miserably thin in skeletal rays on the slopes of their feet. This terrible sight they ignored also.

In fact, they were young. Mother was twenty-two when I was born, and Father twenty-nine; both appeared to other adults much younger than they were. They were a handsome couple. I felt it overwhelmingly when they dressed for occasions. I never lost a wondering awe at the transformation of an everyday, tender, nap-creased mother into an exalted and dazzling beauty who chatted with me as she dressed.

Her blue eyes shone and caught the light, and so did the platinum waves in her hair and the pearls at her ears and throat. She was wearing a black dress. The smooth skin on her breastbone rent my heart, it was so familiar and beloved; the black silk bodice and the simple necklace set off its human fineness. Mother was perhaps a bit vain of her long and perfect legs, but not too vain for me; despite her excited pleasure, she did not share my view of her beauty.

"Look at your father," she said. We were all in the dressing room. I found him in one of the long mirrors, where he waggled his outthrust chin over the last push of his tie knot. For me he made his big ears jiggle on his skull. It was a wonder he could ever hear anything; his head was loose inside him.

Father's enormousness was an everyday, stunning fact; he was taller than everyone else. He was neither thin nor stout; his torso was supple, his long legs nimble. Before the dressing-room mirror he produced an anticipatory soft-shoe, and checked to see that his cuffs stayed down.

Now they were off. I hoped they knocked them dead; I hoped their friends knew how witty they were, and how splendid. Their parties at home did not seem very entertaining, although they laughed loudly and often fetched the one-man percussion band from the basement, or an old trumpet, or a snare drum. We children could have shown them how to have a better time. Kick the Can, for instance, never palled. A private game called Spider Cow, played by the Spencer children, also had possibilities: The spider cow hid and flung a wet washcloth at whoever found it, and erupted from hiding and chased him running all over the house.

But implicitly and emphatically, my parents and their friends were not interested. They never ran. They did not choose to run. It went with being old, apparently, and having their skin half off.

·   ·   ·

On one weekday morning after Christmas, six inches of new snow had just fallen. We were standing up to our boot tops in snow on a front yard on trafficked Reynolds Street, waiting for cars. The cars traveled Reynolds Street slowly and evenly; they were targets all but wrapped in red ribbons, cream puffs. We couldn't miss.

I was seven; the boys were eight, nine, and ten. The oldest two Fahey boys were there—Mikey and Peter—polite blond boys who lived near me on Lloyd Street, and who already had four brothers and sisters. My parents approved of Mikey and Peter Fahey. Chickie McBride was there, a tough kid, and Billy Paul and Mackie Kean too, from across Reynolds, where the boys grew up dark and furious, grew up skinny, knowing, and skilled. We had all drifted from our houses that morning looking for action, and had found it here on Reynolds Street.

It was cloudy but cold. The cars' tires laid behind them on the snowy street a complex trail of beige chunks like crenellated castle walls. I had stepped on some earlier; they squeaked. We could have wished for more traffic. When a car came, we all popped it one. In the intervals between cars we reverted to the natural solitude of children.

I started making an iceball—a perfect iceball, from perfectly white snow, perfectly spherical, and squeezed perfectly translucent so no snow remained all the way through. (The Fahey boys and I considered it unfair actually to throw an iceball at somebody, but it had been known to happen.)

I had just embarked on the iceball project when we heard tire chains come clanking from afar. A black Buick was moving toward us down the street. We all spread out, banged together some regular snowballs, took aim, and, when the Buick drew nigh, fired.

A soft snowball hit the driver's windshield right before the driver's face. It made a smashed star with a hump in the middle.

Often, of course, we hit our target, but this time, the only time in all of life, the car pulled over and stopped. Its wide black door opened; a man got out of it, running. He didn't even close the car door.

He ran after us, and we ran away from him, up the snowy Reynolds sidewalk. At the corner, I looked back; incredibly, he was still after us. He was in city clothes: a suit and tie, street shoes. Any normal adult would have quit, having sprung us into flight and made his point. This man was gaining on us. He was a thin man, all action. All of a sudden, we were running for our lives.

Wordless, we split up. We were on our turf; we could lose ourselves in the neighborhood backyards, everyone for himself. I paused and considered. Everyone had vanished except Mikey Fahey, who was just rounding the corner of a yellow brick house. Poor Mikey, I trailed him. The driver of the Buick sensibly picked the two of us to follow. The man apparently had all day.

He chased Mikey and me around the yellow house and up a backyard path we knew by heart: under a low tree, up a bank, through a hedge, down some snowy steps, and across the grocery store's delivery driveway. We smashed through a gap in another hedge, entered a scruffy backyard and ran around its back porch and tight between houses to Edgerton Avenue; we ran across Edgerton to an alley and up our own sliding woodpile to the Halls' front yard; he kept coming. We ran up Lloyd Street and wound through mazy backyards toward the steep hilltop at Willard and Lang.

He chased us silently, block after block. He chased us silently over picket fences, through thorny hedges, between houses, around garbage cans, and across streets. Every time I glanced back, choking for breath, I expected he would have quit. He must have been as breathless as we were. His jacket strained over his body. It was an immense discovery, pounding into my hot head with every sliding, joyous step, that this ordinary adult evidently knew what I thought only children who trained at football knew: that you have to fling yourself at what you're doing, you have to point yourself, forget yourself, aim, dive.

Mikey and I had nowhere to go, in our own neighborhood or out of it, but away from this man who was chasing us. He impelled us forward; we compelled him to follow our route. The air was cold; every breath tore my throat. We kept running, block after block; we kept improvising, backyard after backyard, running a frantic course and choosing it simultaneously, failing always to find small places or hard places to slow him down, and discovering always, exhilarated, dismayed, that only bare speed could save us—for he would never give up, this man—and we were losing speed.

He chased us through the backyard labyrinths of ten blocks before he caught us by our jackets. He caught us and we all stopped.

We three stood staggering, half blinded, coughing, in an obscure hilltop backyard: a man in his twenties, a boy, a girl. He had released our jackets, our pursuer, our captor, our hero: he knew we weren't going anywhere. We all played by the rules. Mikey and I unzipped our jackets. I pulled off my sopping mittens. Our tracks multiplied in the backyard's new snow. We had been breaking new snow all morning. We didn't look at each other. I was cherishing my excitement. The man's lower pants legs were wet; his cuffs were full of snow, and there was a prow of snow beneath them on his shoes and socks. Some trees bordered the little flat backyard, some messy winter trees. There was no one around: a clearing in a grove, and we the only players.

It was a long time before he could speak. I had some difficulty at first recalling why we were there. My lips felt swollen; I couldn't see out of the sides of my eyes; I kept coughing.

"You stupid kids," he began perfunctorily.

We listened perfunctorily indeed, if we listened at all, for the chewing out was redundant, a mere formality, and beside the point. The point was that he had chased us passionately without giving up, and so he had caught us. Now he came down to earth. I wanted the glory to last forever.

But how could the glory have lasted forever? We could have run through every backyard in North America until we got to Panama. But when he trapped us at the lip of the Panama Canal, what precisely could he have done to prolong the drama of the chase and cap its glory? I brooded about this for the next few years. He could only have fried Mikey Fahey and me in boiling oil, say, or dismembered us piecemeal, or staked us to anthills. None of which I really wanted, and none of which any adult was likely to do, even in the spirit of fun. He could only chew us out there in the Panamanian jungle, after months or years of exalting pursuit. He could only begin, "You stupid kids," and continue in his ordinary Pittsburgh accent with his normal righteous anger and the usual common sense.

If in that snowy backyard the driver of the black Buick had cut off our heads, Mikey's and mine, I would have died happy, for nothing has required so much of me since as being chased all over Pittsburgh in the middle of winter—running terrified, exhausted—by this sainted, skinny, furious redheaded man who wished to have a word with us. I don't know how he found his way back to his car.

ISAK DINESEN
(1885–1962)

Isak Dinesen is the pen name of Karen Blixen, the Danish author of such collections of stories as *Seven Gothic Tales* and *Winter's Tales*. After their marriage in 1914, she and her Swedish husband, Baron Bror Blixen, settled in British East Africa and created a coffee plantation in the hills outside Nairobi. Blixen soon left her to devote himself to the hunting of game and the pursuit of women, and they were divorced in 1921. Karen Blixen kept the farm running for another ten years before a fall in coffee prices forced her to sell the land and return to Denmark. It was then that she turned to literature, including the writing of *Out of Africa* (1937), the memoir of her African life. She wrote all her works in English. In this selection, about adopting a young antelope into her household, Isak Dinesen discusses some of her servants, notably her Kikuyu cook, Kamante, and Farah, a Somali, who headed her household staff.

At the time of Blixen's divorce, in another part of Africa, Nisa, a member of the !Kung tribe, was being weaned, as she described in the autobiography she provided to anthropologist Marjorie Shostak. Compare *Nisa: The Life and Words of a !Kung Woman*. For another memoir of colonial Africa, compare Beryl Markham, *West with the Night,* and see also Elspeth Huxley, *The Flame Trees of Thika.* For other encounters between women and animals, compare the selections from Marjorie Kinnan Rawlings, *Cross Creek* and Lillian Hellman, *Pentimento.*

FROM *Out of Africa*

A GAZELLE

To the East of my farm lay the Ngong Forest Reserve, which then was nearly all Virgin Forest. To my mind it was a sad thing when the old forest was cut down, and Eucalyptus and Grevillea planted in its place; it might have made a unique pleasure-ground and park for Nairobi.

An African Native Forest is a mysterious region. You ride into the depths of an old tapestry, in places faded and in others darkened with age, but marvellously rich in green shades. You cannot see the sky at all in there, but the sunlight plays in many strange ways, falling through the foliage. The grey fungus, like long drooping beards, on the trees, and the creepers hanging down everywhere, give a secretive, recondite air to the Native forest. I used to ride here with Farah on Sundays, when there was nothing to do on the farm, up and down the slopes, and across the little winding forest-streams. The air in the forest was cool like water, and filled with the scent of plants, and in the beginning of the long rains when the creepers flowered, you rode through sphere after sphere of fragrance. One kind of African Daphne of the woods, which flowers with a small cream-coloured sticky blossom, had an overwhelming sweet perfume, like lilac, and wild lily of the valley. Here and there, hollow tree-stems were hung up in ropes of hide on a branch; the Kikuyu hung them there to make the bees build in them, and to get honey. Once as we turned a corner in the forest, we saw a leopard sitting on the road, a tapestry animal.

Here, high above the ground, lived a garrulous restless nation, the little grey monkeys. Where a pack of monkeys had travelled over the road, the smell of them lingered for a long time in the air, a dry and stale, mousy smell. As you rode on you would suddenly hear the rush and whizz over your head, as the colony passed along on its own ways. If you kept still in the same place for some time you might catch sight of one of the monkeys sitting immovable in a tree, and, a little after, discover that the whole forest round you was alive with his family, placed like fruits on the branches, grey or dark figures according to how the sunlight fell on them, all with their long tails hanging down behind them. They gave out a peculiar sound, like a smacking kiss with a little cough to follow it; if from the ground you imitated it, you saw the monkeys turn their heads from one side to the other in an affected manner, but if you made a sudden movement they were all off in a second, and you could follow the decreasing swash as they clove the treetops, and disappeared in the wood like a shoal of fishes in the waves.

In the Ngong Forest I have also seen, on a narrow path through thick growth, in the middle of a very hot day, the Giant Forest Hog, a rare person to meet. He came suddenly past me, with his wife and three young pigs, at a great speed, the whole family looking like uniform, bigger and smaller figures cut out in dark paper, against the sunlit green behind them. It was a glorious sight, like a reflection in a forest pool, like a thing that had happened a thousand years ago.

Lulu was a young antelope of the bushbuck tribe, which is perhaps the prettiest of all the African antelopes. They are a little bigger than the fallow-deer; they live in the woods, or in the bush, and are shy and fugitive, so that they are not seen as often as the antelopes of the plains. But the Ngong Hills, and the surrounding country, were good places for bushbuck, and if you had your camp in the hills, and were out hunting in the early morning, or at sunset, you would see them come out of the bush into the glades, and as the rays of the sun fell upon them their coats shone red as copper. The male has a pair of delicately turned horns.

Lulu became a member of my household in this way:

I drove one morning from the farm to Nairobi. My mill on the farm had burnt down a short time before, and I had had to drive into town many times to get the insurance settled and paid out; in this early morning I had my head filled with figures and estimates. As I came driving along the Ngong Road a little group of Kikuyu children shouted to me from the roadside, and I saw that they were holding a very small bushbuck up for me to see. I knew that they would have found the fawn in the bush, and that now they wanted to sell it to me, but I was late for an appointment in Nairobi, and I had no thought for this sort of thing, so I drove on.

When I was coming back in the evening and was driving past the same place, there was again a great shout from the side of the road and the small party was still there, a little tired and disappointed, for they may have tried to sell the fawn to other people passing by in the course of the day, but keen now to get the deal through before the sun was down, and they held up the fawn high to tempt me. But I had had a long day in town, and some adversity about the insurance, so that I did not care to stop or talk, and I just drove on past them. I did not even think of them when I was back in my house, and dined and went to bed.

The moment that I had fallen asleep I was woken up again by a great feeling of terror. The picture of the boys and the small buck, which had now collected and taken shape, stood out before me, clearly, as if it had been painted, and I sat up in bed as appalled as if someone had been trying to choke me. What, I thought, would become of the fawn in the hands of the captors who had stood with it in the heat of the long day, and had held it up by its joined legs? It was surely too young to eat on its own. I myself had driven past it twice on the same day, like the priest and the Levite in one, and had given no thought to it, and now, at this moment, where was it? I got up in a real panic and woke up all my houseboys. I told them that the fawn must be found and brought me in the morning, or they would all of them get their dismissal from my service. They were immediately up to the idea. Two of my boys had been in the car with me the same day, and had not shown the slightest interest in the children or the fawn; now they came forward, and gave the others a long list of details of the place and the hour and of the family of the boys. It was a moonlight night; my people all took off and spread in the landscape in a lively discussion of the situation; I heard them expatiating on the fact that they were all to be dismissed in case the bushbuck were not found.

Early next morning when Farah brought me in my tea, Juma came in with him and carried the fawn in his arms. It was a female, and we named her Lulu, which I was told was the Swaheli word for a pearl.

Lulu by that time was only as big as a cat, with large quiet purple eyes. She had such delicate legs that you feared they would not bear being folded up and unfolded again, as she lay down and rose up. Her ears were smooth as silk and exceedingly expressive. Her nose was as black as a truffle. Her diminutive hoofs gave her all the air of a young Chinese lady of the old school, with laced feet. It was a rare experience to hold such a perfect thing in your hands.

Lulu soon adapted herself to the house and its inhabitants and behaved as if she were at home. During the first weeks the polished floors in the rooms were a problem in her life, and when she got outside the carpets her legs went away from her to all four sides; it looked catastrophic but she did not let it worry her much and in the end she learnt to walk on the bare floors with a sound like a succession of little angry finger-taps. She was extraordinarily neat in all her habits. She was headstrong already as a child, but when I stopped her from doing the things she wanted to do, she behaved as if she said: Anything rather than a scene.

Kamante brought her up on a sucking-bottle, and he also shut her up at night, for we had to be careful of her as the leopards were up round the house after nightfall. So she held to him and followed him about. From time to time when he did not do what she wanted, she gave his thin legs a hard butt with her young head, and she was so pretty that you could not help, when you looked upon the two together, seeing them as a new paradoxical illustration to the tale of the Beauty and the Beast. On the strength of this great beauty and gracefulness, Lulu obtained for herself a commanding position in the house, and was treated with respect by all.

In Africa I never had dogs of any other breed than the Scotch Deerhound. There is no more noble or gracious kind of dog. They must have lived for many centuries with men to understand and fall in with our life and its conditions the way they do. You will also find them in old paintings and tapestries, and they have in themselves a tendency to change, by their looks and manners, their surroundings into tapestry; they bring with them a feudal atmosphere.

The first of my tribe of deerhounds, who was named Dusk, had been given to me as a wedding-present, and had come out with me when I began my life in Africa, on "The Mayflower," so to say. He was a gallant, generous character. He accompanied me when, during the first months of the war, I did transport for the Government, with ox-waggons in the Masai Reserve. But a couple of years later he was killed by Zebra. By the time that Lulu came to live in my house I had two of his sons there.

The Scotch Deerhound went well with African scenery and the African Native. It may be due to the altitude,—the highland melody in all three,—for he did not look so harmonious at Sea-level in Mombasa. It was as if the great, spare landscape, with the plains, hills and rivers, was not complete until the deerhounds were also in it. All the deerhounds were great hunters and had more nose than the greyhounds, but they hunted by sight and it was a highly wonderful thing to see two of them working together. I took them with me when I was out riding in the Game Reserve, which I was not allowed to do, and there they would spread the herds of Zebra and Wildebeest over the plain, as if it were all the stars of heaven running wild over the sky. But when I was out in the Masai Reserve shooting I never lost a wounded head of game, if I had the deerhounds with me.

They looked well in the Native forests too, dark grey in the sombre green shades. One of them, in here, all by himself, killed a big old male baboon, and in the fight had his nose bitten straight through, which spoilt his noble profile but by everybody on the farm was considered an honourable scar, for the baboons are destructive beasts and the Natives detest them.

The deerhounds were very wise, and knew who amongst my houseboys were Mohammedans, and not allowed to touch dogs.

During my first years in Africa I had a Somali gunbearer named Ismail, who died while I was still out there. He was one of the old time gunbearers and there are no such people now. He had been brought up by the great old big-game hunters of the beginning of the century, when all Africa was a real deer-park. His acquaintance with civilization was entirely of the hunting fields, and he spoke an English of the hunting world, so that he would talk of my big and my young rifle. After Ismail had gone back to Somaliland, I had a letter from him which was addressed to *Lioness Blixen,* and opened: *Honourable Lioness.* Ismail was a strict Mohammedan, and would not for the life of him touch a dog, which caused him much worry in his profession. But he made an exception with Dusk and never minded my taking him with us in mule-trap, he would even let Dusk sleep in his tent. For Dusk, he said, would know a Mohammedan when he saw him, and would never touch him. Indeed, Ismail assured me, Dusk could see at once who was a sincere Mohammedan at heart. He once said to me: "I know now that the Dusk is of the same tribe as you yourself. He laughs at the people."

Now my dogs understood Lulu's power and position in the house. The arrogance of the great hunters was like water with her. She pushed them away from the milk-bowl and from their favourite places in front of the fire. I had tied a small bell on a rein round Lulu's neck, and there came a time when the dogs, when they heard the jingle of it approaching through the rooms, would get up resignedly from their warm beds by the fireplace, and go and lie down in some other part of the room. Still nobody could be of a gentler demeanour than Lulu was when she came and lay down, in the manner of a perfect lady who demurely gathers her skirts about her and will be in no one's way. She drank the milk with a polite, pernickety mien, as if she had been pressed by an overkind host-ess. She insisted on being scratched behind the ears, in a pretty forebear-ing way, like a young wife who pertly permits her husband a caress.

When Lulu grew up and stood in the flower of her young loveliness she was a slim delicately rounded doe, from her nose to her toes unbeliev-ably beautiful. She looked like a minutely painted illustration to Heine's song of the wise and gentle gazelles by the flow of the river Ganges.

But Lulu was not really gentle, she had the so called devil in her. She had, to the highest degree, the feminine trait of appearing to be exclu-sively on the defensive, concentrated on guarding the integrity of her being, when she was really, with every force in her, bent upon the offen-sive. Against whom? Against the whole world. Her moods grew beyond control or computation, and she would go for my horse, if he displeased her. I remembered old Hagenbeck in Hamburg, who had said that of all animal races, the carnivora included, the deer are the least to be relied on, and that you may trust a leopard, but if you trust a young stag, sooner or later he falls upon you in the rear.

Lulu was the pride of the house even when she behaved like a real shameless young coquette; but we did not make her happy. Sometimes she walked away from the house for hours, or for a whole afternoon. Sometimes when the spirit came upon her and her discontent with her surroundings reached a climax, she would perform, for the satisfaction of her own heart, on the lawn in front of the house, a war-dance, which looked like a brief zig-zagged prayer to Satan.

"Oh Lulu," I thought, "I know that you are marvellously strong and that you can leap higher than your own height. You are furious with us now, you wish that we were all dead, and indeed we should be so if you could be bothered to kill us. But the trouble is not as you think now, that we have put up obstacles too high for you to jump, and how could we possibly do that, you great leaper? It is that we have put up no obstacles at all. The great strength is in you, Lulu, and the obstacles are within you as well, and the thing is, that the fullness of time has not yet come."

One evening Lulu did not come home and we looked out for her in vain for a week. This was a hard blow to us all. A clear note had gone out of the house and it seemed no better than other houses. I thought of the leopards by the river and one evening I talked about them to Kamante.

As usual he waited some time before he answered, to digest my lack of insight. It was not till a few days later that he approached me upon the matter. "You believe that Lulu is dead, Msabu," he said.

I did not like to say so straight out, but I told him I was wondering why she did not come back.

"Lulu," said Kamante, "is not dead. But she is married."

This was pleasant, surprising, news, and I asked him how he knew of it.

"Oh yes," he said, "she is married. She lives in the forest with her *bwana*,"—her husband, or master. "But she has not forgotten the people; most mornings she is coming back to the house. I lay out crushed maize to her at the back of the kitchen, then just before the sun comes up, she walks' round there from the woods and eats it. Her husband is with her, but he is afraid of the people because he has never known them. He stands below the big white tree by the other side of the lawn. But up to the houses he dare not come."

I told Kamante to come and fetch me when he next saw Lulu. A few days later before sunrise he came and called me out.

It was a lovely morning. The last stars withdrew while we were waiting, the sky was clear and serene but the world in which we walked was sombre still, and profoundly silent. The grass was wet; down by the trees where the ground sloped it gleamed with the dew like dim silver. The air of the morning was cold, it had that twinge in it which in Northern countries means that the frost is not far away. However often you make the experience,—I thought,—it is still impossible to believe, in this coolness and shade, that the heat of the sun and the glare of the sky, in a few hours' time, will be hard to bear. The grey mist lay upon the hills, strangely taking shape from them; it would be bitterly cold on the Buffalo if they were about there now, grazing on the hillside, as in a cloud.

The great vault over our heads was gradually filled with clarity like a glass with wine. Suddenly, gently, the summits of the hill caught the first sunlight and blushed. And slowly, as the earth leaned towards the sun, the grassy slopes at the foot of the mountain turned a delicate gold, and the Masai woods lower down. And now the tops of the tall trees in the forest, on our side of the river, blushed like copper. This was the hour for the flight of the big, purple wood-pigeons which roosted by the other side of the river and came over to feed on the Cape-chestnuts in my forest. They were here only for a short season in the year. The birds came surprisingly fast, like a cavalry attack of the air. For this reason the morning pigeon-shooting on the farm was popular with my friends in Nairobi; to be out by the house in time, just as the sun rose, they used to come out so early that they rounded my drive with the lamps of their cars still lighted.

Standing like this in the limpid shadow, looking up towards the golden heights and the clear sky, you would get the feeling that you were in reality walking along the bottom of the Sea, with the currents running by you, and were gazing up towards the surface of the Ocean.

A bird began to sing, and then I heard, a little way off in the forest, the tinkling of a bell. Yes, it was a joy, Lulu was back, and about in her old places! It came nearer, I could follow her movements by its rhythm; she was walking, stopping, walking on again. A turning round one of the boys' huts brought her upon us. It suddenly became an unusual and amusing thing to see a bushbuck so close to the house. She stood immovable now, she seemed to be prepared for the sight of Kamante, but not for that of me. But she did not make off, she looked at me without fear and without any remembrance of our skirmishes of the past or of her own ingratitude in running away without warning.

Lulu of the woods was a superior, independent being, a change of heart had come upon her, she was in possession. If I had happened to have known a young princess in exile, and while she was still a pretender to the throne, and had met her again in her full queenly estate after she had come into her rights, our meeting would have had the same character. Lulu showed no more meanness of heart than King Louis Philippe did, when he declared that the King of France did not remember the grudges of the Duke of Orleans. She was now the complete Lulu. The spirit of offensive had gone from her; for whom, and why, should she attack? She was standing quietly on her divine rights. She remembered me enough to feel that I was nothing to be afraid of. For a minute she gazed at me; her purple smoky eyes were absolutely without expression and did not wink, and I remembered that the Gods or Goddesses never wink, and felt that I was face to face with the ox-eyed Hera. She lightly nipped a leaf of grass as she passed me, made one pretty little leap, and walked on to the back of the kitchen, where Kamante had spread maize on the ground.

Kamante touched my arm with one finger and then pointed it towards the woods. As I followed the direction, I saw, under a tall Cape-chestnut-tree, a male bushbuck, a small tawny silhouette at the outskirt of the forest, with a fine pair of horns, immovable like a tree-stem. Kamante observed him for some time, and then laughed.

"Look here now," he said, "Lulu has explained to her husband that there is nothing up by the houses to be afraid of, but all the same he dares not come. Every morning he thinks that to-day he will come all the way, but, when he sees the house and the people, he gets a cold stone in the stomach,"—this is a common thing in the Native world, and often gets in the way of the work on the farm,—"and then he stops by the tree."

For a long time Lulu came to the house in the early mornings. Her clear bell announced that the sun was up on the hills, I used to lie in bed, and wait for it. Sometimes she stayed away for a week or two, and we missed her and began to talk of the people who went to shoot in the hills. But then again my houseboys announced: "Lulu is here," as if it had been the married daughter of the house on a visit. A few times more I also saw the bushbuck's silhouette amongst the trees, but Kamante had been right, and he never collected enough courage to come all the way to the house.

One day, as I came back from Nairobi, Kamante was keeping watch for me outside the kitchen door, and stepped forward, much excited, to tell me that Lulu had been to the farm the same day and had had her Toto,—her baby—with her. Some days after, I myself had the honour to meet her amongst the boys' huts, much on the alert and not to be trifled with, with a very small fawn at her heels, as delicately tardive in his movements as Lulu herself had been when we first knew her. This was just after the long rains, and, during those summer months, Lulu was to be found near the houses, in the afternoon, as well as at daybreak. She would even be round there at midday, keeping in the shadow of the huts.

Lulu's fawn was not afraid of the dogs, and would let them sniff him all over, but he could not get used to the Natives or to me, and if we ever tried to get hold of him, the mother and the child were off.

Lulu herself would never, after her first long absence from the house, come so near to any of us that we could touch her. In other ways she was friendly, she understood that we wanted to look at her fawn, and she would take a piece of sugar-cane from an outstretched hand. She walked up to the open dining-room door, and gazed thoughtfully into the twilight of the rooms, but she never again crossed the threshold. She had by this time lost her bell, and came and went away in silence.

My houseboys suggested that I should let them catch Lulu's fawn, and keep him as we had once kept Lulu. But I thought it would make a boorish return to Lulu's elegant confidence in us.

It also seemed to me that the free union between my house and the antelope was a rare, honourable thing. Lulu came in from the wild world to show that we were on good terms with it, and she made my house one with the African landscape, so that nobody could tell where the one stopped and the other began. Lulu knew the place of the Giant Forest-Hog's lair and had seen the Rhino copulate. In Africa there is a cuckoo which sings in the middle of the hot days in the midst of the forest, like the sonorous heartbeat of the world, I had never had the luck to see her, neither had anyone that I knew, for nobody could tell me how she looked. But Lulu had perhaps walked on a narrow green deerpath just under the branch on which the cuckoo was sitting. I was then reading a book about the old great Empress of China, and of how after the birth of her son, young Yahanola came on a visit to her old home; she set forth from the Forbidden City in her golden, green-hung palanquin. My house, I thought, was now like the house of the young Empress's father and mother.

The two antelopes, the big and the small, were round by my house all that summer; sometimes there was an interval of a fortnight, or three weeks, between their visits, but at other times we saw them every day. In the beginning of the next rainy season my houseboys told me that Lulu had come back with a new fawn. I did not see the fawn myself, for by this time they did not come up quite close to the house, but later I saw three bushbucks together in the forest.

The league between Lulu and her family and my house lasted for many years. The bushbucks were often in the neighbourhood of the house, they came out of the woods and went back again as if my grounds were a province of the wild country. They came mostly just before sun-set, and first moved in amongst the trees like delicate dark silhouettes on the dark green, but when they stepped out to graze on the lawn in the light of the afternoon sun their coats shone like copper. One of them was Lulu, for she came up near to the house, and walked about sedately, pricking her ears when a car arrived, or when we opened a window; and the dogs would know her. She became darker in colour with age. Once I came driving up in front of my house with a friend and found three bushbucks on the terrace there, round the salt that was laid out for my cows.

It was a curious thing that apart from the first big bushbuck, Lulu's bwana, who had stood under the Cape-chestnut with his head up, no male bushbuck was amongst the antelopes that came to my house. It seemed that we had to do with a forest matriarchy.

The hunters and naturalists of the Colony took an interest in my bushbucks, and the Game Warden drove out to the farm to see them, and did see them there. A correspondent wrote about them in the *East African Stàndard*.

The years in which Lulu and her people came round to my house were the happiest of my life in Africa. For that reason, I came to look upon my acquaintance with the forest antelopes as upon a great boon, and a token of friendship from Africa. All the country was in it, good omens, old covenants, a song:

Make haste, my beloved and be thou like to a roe or to a young hart upon the mountain of spices.

During my last years in Africa I saw less and less of Lulu and her family. Within the year before I went away I do not think that they ever came. Things had changed, South of my farm land had been given out to farmers and the forest had been cleared here, and houses built. Tractors were heaving up and down where the glades had been. Many of the new settlers were keen sportsmen and the rifles sang in the landscape. I believe that the game withdrew to the West and went into the woods of the Masai Reserve.

I do not know how long an antelope lives, probably Lulu has died a long time ago.

Often, very often, in the quiet hours of daybreak, I have dreamed that I have heard Lulu's clear bell, and in my sleep my heart has run full of joy, I have woken up expecting something very strange and sweet to happen, just now, in a moment.

When I have then lain and thought of Lulu, I have wondered if in her life in the woods she ever dreamed of the bell. Would there pass in her mind, like shadows upon water, pictures of people and dogs?

If I know a song of Africa,—I thought,—of the Giraffe, and the African new moon lying on her back, of the ploughs in the fields, and the sweaty faces of the coffee-pickers, does Africa know a song of me? Would the air over the plain quiver with a colour that I had had on, or the children invent a game in which my name was, or the full moon throw a shadow over the gravel of the drive that was like me, or would the eagles of Ngong look out for me?

I have not heard from Lulu, since I went away, but from Kamante I have heard, and from my other houseboys in Africa. It is not more than a month since I had the last letter from him. But these communications from Africa come to me in a strange, unreal way, and are more like shadows, or mirages, than like news of a reality.

For Kamante cannot write, and he does not know English. When he, or my other people, take it into their heads to send me their tidings, they go to one of the professional Indian or Native letter-writers who are sitting with their writing desk, paper, pen and ink, outside the Post Offices, and explain to them what shall be in the letter. The professional writers do not know much English either, and can hardly be said to know how to write, but they themselves believe that they can. To show off their skill they enrich the letters with a number of flourishes, which makes them difficult to decipher. They have also a habit of writing the letters in three or four different kinds of ink, and, whatever their motive for this is, it gives the impression that they are short of ink and are squeezing the last drop out of a number of ink-bottles. From all these efforts come the sort of messages that people got from the Oracle of Delphi. There is a depth in the letters that I get, you feel that there is some vital communication which has been heavy on the heart of the sender, which had made him walk in a long way from the Kikuyu Reserve to the Post Office. But it is wrapped up in darkness. The cheap and dirty little sheet of paper that, when it comes to you, has travelled many thousand miles, seems to speak and speak, even to scream to you, but it tells you nothing at all.

Kamante, however, in this as in most other ways was different from other people. As a correspondent he has a manner of his own. He puts three or four letters into the same envelope, and has them marked: *1st Letter, 2nd Letter,* and so on. They all contain the same things, repeated over and over. Perhaps he wants to make a deeper impression upon me by repetition, he had that way in talking when there was anything that he particularly wanted me to understand or remember. Perhaps it is difficult for him to break off when he feels that he has got into contact with a friend at such a great distance.

Kamante writes that he has been out of work for a long time. I was not surprised to hear of it, for he was really caviare to the general. I had educated a Royal Cook and left him in a new Colony. It was with him a case of "Open Sesame." Now the word has been lost, and the stone has closed for good round the mystic treasures that it had in it. Where the great Chef walked in deep thought, full of knowledge, nobody sees anything but a little bandy-legged Kikuyu, a dwarf with a flat, still face.

What has Kamante got to say when he walks in to Nairobi, takes up his stand before the greedy supercilious Indian letter-writer, and expounds to him a message that is to go round half the world? The lines are crooked and there is no order in the phrases of the letter. But Kamante had in him a greatness of soul of which the people who knew him will still hear the note in the cracked disordered music, even as an echo of the harp of the herdboy David.

This is a "2nd letter":

"I was not forget you Memsahib. Honoured Memsahib. Now all your servants they never glad because you was from the country. If we was bird we fly and see you. Then we turn. Then your old farm it was good place for cow small calf black people. Now they had no anything cows goat sheep they has no anything. Now all bad people they enjoy in their heart because your old servant they come poor people now. Now God know in his heart all this to help sometime your servant."

And in a "3rd letter" Kamante gives an example of the way in which the Native can say a handsome thing to you, he writes:

"Write and tell us if you turn. We think you turn. Because why? We think that you shall never can forget us. Because why? We think that you remembered still all our face and our mother names."

A white man who wanted to say a pretty thing to you would write: "I can never forget you." The African says: "We do not think of you, that you can ever forget us."

MARGUERITE DURAS
(1914–)

Born in Vietnam, the daughter of a French mathematics teacher and his wife, Duras emigrated to France at the age of seventeen. From 1935 to 1941 she worked as a secretary in the Ministry of Colonies. During World War II she was part of a resistance unit that was headed by François Mitterrand (code name Morland), now the president of the French Republic. She began to write in 1943 and is well known in France for her novels, plays, and screenplays, especially the dialogue for Alain Resnais's film *Hiroshima, Mon Amour.* In America she first reached a wide audience with *The Lover,* an autobiographical novel about a French girl in Saigon who has an affair with an older Chinese man. After her screenplay for the film version of *The Lover* was rejected, she reworked the material yet again in another and even more autobiographical novel, *The North China Lover.*

The War, which Duras calls a memoir, is based on diaries she kept when she was gathering information about returnees from the concentration camps of Nazi Germany. She was especially looking for her husband, "Robert L.," who had been deported for political activity. Written much later than the events it describes, *The War* was published in France (titled *La Douleur*) in 1985.

For an account by a woman who went to Auschwitz and lived to write about it, see Isabella Leitner, *Fragments of Isabella.* For Simone de Beauvoir's account of what she did during the war, see later sections of *The Prime of Life.* For another account of women's anguish over men in wartime, compare Vera Brittain, *Testament of Youth.*

FROM *The War*

April 20

Today's the day when the first batch of political deportees arrives from Weimar. They phone me from the center in the morning. They say I can come, the deportees won't be there till the afternoon. I go for the morning. I'll stay all day. I don't know where to go to bear myself.

Orsay.* Outside the center, wives of prisoners of war congeal in a solid mass. White barriers separate them from the prisoners. "Do you have any news of so-and-so?" they shout. Every so often the soldiers stop; one or two answer. Some women are there at seven o'clock in the morning. Some stay till three in the morning and then come back again at seven. But there are some who stay right through the night, between three and seven. They're not allowed into the center. Lots of people who are not waiting for anyone come to the Gare d'Orsay, too, just to see the show, the arrival of the prisoners of war and how the women wait for them, and all the rest, to see what it's like; perhaps it will never happen again. You can tell the spectators from the others because they don't shout out, and they stand some way away from the crowds of women so as to see both the arrival of the prisoners and the way the women greet them. The prisoners arrive in an orderly manner. At night they come in big American trucks from which they emerge into the light. The women shriek and clap their hands. The prisoners stop, dazzled and taken aback. During the day the women shout as soon as they see the trucks turning off the Solferino Bridge. At night they shout when they slow down just before the center. They shout the names of German towns: "Noyeswarda?"† "Kassel?" Or Stalag numbers: "VII A?" "III A Kommando?" The prisoners seem astonished. They've come straight from Le Bourget airport and Germany. Sometimes they answer, usually they don't quite understand what's expected of them, they smile, they turn and look at the Frenchwomen, the first they've seen since they got back.

I can't work properly;** of all the names I record none is ever his. Every five minutes I want to give it up, lay down the pencil, stop asking for news, leave the center for the rest of my life. At about two in the afternoon I go to ask what time the convoy from Weimar arrives. I leave the circuit and look for someone to ask. In a corner of the main hall I see about ten women sitting on the floor and being addressed by a colonel. I go over. The colonel is a tall woman in a navy blue suit with the cross of Lorraine in the lapel. Her white hair has been curled with tongs and blue-rinsed. The women look at her. They look harassed, but listen openmouthed to what she says. The floor around them is littered with bundles and cases tied with string. A small child is sleeping on one of the bundles. The women are very dirty and their faces look tired and

*The railroad station, the Gare d'Orsay, was serving as a processing center for prisoners returning to France from Germany—ED.
†The author's note at this point reads: "I haven't been able to find this name in the atlas. I've probably spelled it as it sounded to me."
**Duras has been gathering information from returning prisoners about the location of others. She printed this information in a newsletter for deportees' families—ED.

shocked. Two of them have enormous bellies. Another woman officer stands nearby, watching. I go over and ask her what's going on. She looks at me, lowers her eyes, and says delicately, "STO volunteers."* The colonel tells them to get up and follow her. They rise and follow her. The reason they look so frightened is that they've just been booed by the wives of the prisoners of war waiting outside the center. A few days ago I saw some other STO volunteers arrive. Men, this time. Like the other men they were smiling when they arrived, but gradually they realized and then their faces too looked shocked. The colonel points to the women and asks the young woman in uniform who's just told me who they are, "What are we supposed to do with them?" The other one says, "I don't know." The colonel must have told them they were scum. Some of them are crying. The pregnant ones stare into space. The colonel has told them to sit down again. They sit down. Most of them are factory workers, their hands blackened by the oil of German machinery. Two of them are probably prostitutes, their faces are made up and their hair dyed, but they must also have worked with machinery, they've got the same grimy hands as the others. A repatriation officer comes up. "What's all this?" "STO volunteers." The colonel's voice is shrill, she turns toward the volunteers and threatens, "Sit down and keep quiet . . . Do you hear? Don't think you're just going to be let go . . ." She shakes her fist at them. The repatriation officer goes over to the bunch of volunteers, looks at them, and there, right in front of them, asks the colonel, "Do you have any orders?" The colonel: "No, do you?" "Someone mentioned six months' detention." The colonel nods her beautiful curly head: "Serves them right . . ." The officer blows puffs of smoke— Camels—over the bunch of volunteers, who've been following the conversation with eyes wild with apprehension. "Right!" he says, and goes off, young, elegant, a born horseman, his Camel in his hand. The volunteers watch, looking for some indication of the fate awaiting them. There is none. I stop the colonel as she makes off. "Do you know when the convoy from Weimar arrives?" She gives me a searching look. "Three o'clock," she says. She goes on looking at me, weighing me up, and says with just a touch of irritation, "No point in cluttering up the place waiting. It'll only be generals and prefects. Go home." I wasn't expecting this. I think I insult her. I say, "What about the others?" She bridles. "I can't stand that kind of attitude! Go and complain somewhere else, my dear." She's so indignant she goes and tells a small group of other women in uniform, who listen, are also indignant, and look at

---

*STO: The Service du Travail Obligatoire (Forced Labor Service), introduced in February 1943, was an organized deportation of French workers. Some people actually volunteered to work in Germany—TRANS.

me. I go up to one of them and say, "Isn't *she* waiting for anyone?" The
woman looks at me, scandalized, and tries to calm me down. She says,
"The poor thing's got so much to do, her nerves are in shreds." I go back
to the Tracing Service at the end of the circuit. Soon afterward I go back
to the main hall. D.'s* waiting for me there with a forged pass.

About three o'clock there's a rumor: "They're here." I leave the circuit and station myself at the entrance to a little passage opposite the
main hall. I wait. I know Robert L. won't be there. D. is beside me. His
job is to go and question the deportees to find out if they know Robert L.
He's pale. He doesn't pay any attention to me. There's a great commotion in the main hall. The women in uniform fuss around the volunteers
and make them sit on the floor in a corner. The main hall is empty.
There's a pause in the arrivals of prisoners of war. Repatriation officers
go back and forth. The loudspeaker has stopped too. I hear people saying, "The minister," and see Frenay among the officers. I'm still standing at the entrance to the little corridor. I watch the entrance. I know
Robert L. can't possibly be there. But perhaps D. will manage to find out
something. I don't feel well. I'm trembling, cold. I lean against the wall.
Suddenly, there's a hum of voices: "Here they are!" Outside, the women
haven't shouted. They haven't applauded. Suddenly, two scouts emerge
from the passage carrying a man. He has his arms around their necks.
They've joined hands to support his legs. He's in civilian clothes, shaven,
he appears to be in great pain. He's a strange color. He must be crying.
You couldn't say he's thin, it's something else—there's so little of him
left you wonder if he's really alive. But no, he is alive, his face is convulsed by a terrifying grimace. He doesn't look at anything. Not at the
minister, not at the hall, not at the flags—nothing. The grimace may be
a laugh. He's the first deportee from Weimar to arrive at the center.
Without realizing it I've moved forward, I'm in the middle of the hall
with my back to the loudspeaker. Two more scouts come in carrying
another, an old man. Then another ten or eleven arrive. These appear to
be in better condition, they can walk, with help. They're installed on
garden benches that have been set out in the hall. The minister goes over
to them. The second one to arrive, the old man, is weeping. You can't
tell if he's as old as all that, he may be only twenty, you can't tell his age.
The minister comes over, takes off his hat, goes up to the old man, holds
out his hand. The old man takes it, but doesn't know it's the minister's.
A woman in a blue uniform bawls at him: "It's the minister! He's come
to meet you!" The old man goes on crying, he hasn't even looked up.
Suddenly I see D. sitting down beside him. I'm very cold, my teeth are

---

*"D." is Duras's lover—ED.

chattering. Someone comes up to me: "Don't stay here, there's no point, it's making you ill." I know him, he's a fellow from the center. I stay. D. has started to talk to the old man. I go over it all quickly in my head. There's one chance in ten thousand the old man might have met Robert L. In Paris they're beginning to say the army has lists of survivors from Buchenwald. Apart from the old man crying and the rheumatics, the others don't seem in too bad condition. The minister's sitting with them, as are the senior officers. D. talks to the old man at length. I don't look at anything but D.'s face. I feel this is taking a very long time. I move very slowly toward the bench, into D.'s field of vision. He notices, looks at me, and shakes his head to signify, "No, he doesn't know him." I move away. I'm very tired, I feel like lying down on the ground. Now the women in uniform are bringing the deportees mess tins. They eat, and as they eat they answer questions. What's so remarkable is that they don't seem interested in what's said to them. I'll find out next day from the papers that among these people, these old men, are General Challe; his son Hubert Challe, who had been a cadet at Saint-Cyr and who was to die that night, the night of his arrival; General Audibert; Ferrière, head of the state tobacco industry; Julien Cain, director of the Bibliothèque Nationale; General Heurteaux; Marcel Paul; Professor Suard of the faculty of medicine at Angers; Professor Richet; Claude Bourdet; the brother of Teitgen, the minister of information; Maurice Nègre; and others.

I leave the center at about five in the afternoon and go home along the river. The weather's fine, it's a lovely sunny day. I can't wait to get back, to shut myself up with the telephone, be back again in the black ditch. As soon as I leave the embankment and turn into the rue du Bac, the city is far away again and the Orsay center vanishes. Perhaps he will come back after all. I don't know any more. I'm very tired. I'm very dirty. I've been spending part of the night at the center, too. I must make up my mind to take a bath when I get in, it must be a week since I stopped washing. I feel the cold so badly in the spring, the idea of washing makes me shudder, I have a sort of permanent fever that doesn't seem to want to go away. This evening I think about myself. I've never met a woman more cowardly than I am. I go over in my mind other women who are waiting like me—no, none is as cowardly as that. I know some who are very brave. Extraordinary. My cowardice is such that it can't be described, except by D. My colleagues in the Tracing Service think I'm crazy. D. says, "No one has the right to destroy himself like that, ever." He often tells me, "You're sick. You're a madwoman. Look at yourself— you look like nothing on earth." I can't understand what people are trying to say to me. [Even now, transcribing these things from my youth,

I can't understand the meaning of those expressions.] Not for a second do I see the need to be brave. Perhaps being brave is my form of coward-ice. Suzy is brave for her little boy. The child we had, Robert L. and I, was born dead, he died in the war too: doctors didn't usually go out at night during the war, they hadn't enough gas. So I'm on my own. Why should I husband my strength? There's nothing for me to fight for. No one can know my struggle against visions of the black ditch. Sometimes the vision gets the upper hand and I cry out or leave the house and walk the streets of Paris. D. says, "When you think about it later on you'll be ashamed." People are out in the streets as usual, there are lines outside the shops; there are some cherries already, that's what the women are waiting for. I buy a paper. The Russians are in Strausberg, perhaps even farther, on the outskirts of Berlin. The women standing in line for cher-ries are waiting for the fall of Berlin. I'm waiting for it too. "Then they'll see, then they'll find out what's what," people say. The whole world is waiting for it. All the governments in the world are agreed. When the heart of Germany stops beating, say the papers, it will be all over. Zhu-kov has a ring of guns only a hundred yards apart pounding the city from a range of less than forty miles. Berlin is in flames. It will be burned right down to the roots. German blood will flow among its ruins. Sometimes you think you can smell the blood. See it. A prisoner who's a priest brought a German orphan back to the center. He held him by the hand, was proud of him, showed him off, explained how he'd found him and that it wasn't the poor child's fault. The women looked askance at him. He was arrogating to himself the right to forgive, to absolve, already. He wasn't returning from any suffering, any waiting. He was taking the liberty of exercising the right to forgive and absolve there and then, right away, without any knowledge of the hatred that filled everyone, a hatred terrible yet pleasant, consoling, like a belief in God. So what was he talking about? Never has a priest seemed so incongruous. The women looked away, they spat upon the beaming smile of mercy and light. They ignored the child. A total split, with on the one side the solid, uncompro-mising front of the women, and on the other just the one man, who was right, but in a language the women didn't understand.

·   ·   ·

I can't remember what day it was, whether it was in April, no, it was a day in May when one morning at eleven o'clock the phone rang. It was from Germany, it was François Morland. He doesn't say hello, he's almost rough, but clear as always. "Listen carefully. Robert is alive. Now keep calm. He's in Dachau. Listen very, very carefully. Robert is very weak, so weak you can't imagine. I have to tell you—it's a question of hours. He may live for another three days like that, but no more. D. and

Beauchamp must start out today, this morning, for Dachau. Tell them this: they're to go straight to my office—the people there will be expecting them. They'll be given French officers' uniforms, passports, mission orders, gasoline coupons, maps, and permits. Tell them to go right away. It's the only way. If they tried to do it officially they'd arrive too late."

François Morland and Rodin were part of a mission organized by Father Riquet. They had gone to Dachau, and that was where they'd found Robert L. They had gone into the prohibited area of the camp, where the dead and the hopeless cases were kept. And there, one of the latter had distinctly uttered a name: "François." "François," and then his eyes had closed again. It took Rodin and Morland an hour to recognize Robert L. Rodin finally identified him by his teeth. They wrapped him up in a sheet, as people wrap up a dead body, and took him out of the prohibited part of the camp and laid him down by a hut in the survivors' part of the camp. They were able to do so because there were no American soldiers around. They were all in the guardroom, scared of the typhus.

Beauchamp and D. left Paris the same day, early in the afternoon. It was May 12, the day of the peace. Beauchamp was wearing a colonel's uniform belonging to François Morland. D. was dressed as a lieutenant in the French army and carried his papers as a member of the Resistance, made out in the name of D. Masse. They drove all night and arrived at Dachau the next morning. They spent several hours looking for Robert L.; then, as they were going past a body, they heard someone say D.'s name. It's my opinion they didn't recognize him; but Morland had warned us he was unrecognizable. They took him. And it was only afterward they must have recognized him. Under their clothes they had a third French officer's uniform. They had to hold him upright, he could no longer stand alone, but they managed to dress him. They had to prevent him from saluting outside the SS huts, get him through the guard posts, see that he wasn't given any of the vaccinations that would have killed him. The American soldiers, blacks for the most part, wore gas masks against typhus, the fear was so great. Their orders were such that if they'd suspected the state Robert L. was really in, they'd have put him back immediately in the part of the camp where people were left to die. Once they got Robert L. out, the other two had to get him to walk to the Citroën II. As soon as they'd stretched him out on the back seat, he fainted. They thought it was all over, but no. The journey was very difficult, very slow. They had to stop every half hour because of the dysentery. As soon as they'd left Dachau behind, Robert L. spoke. He said he knew he wouldn't reach Paris alive. So he began to talk, so it should be told before he died. He didn't accuse any person, any race, any people. He accused man. Emerging from the horror, dying, delirious,

Robert L. was still able not to accuse anyone except the governments that come and go in the history of nations. He wanted D. and Beauchamp to tell me after his death what he had said. They reached the French frontier that night, near Wissemburg. D. phoned me: "We've reached France. We've just crossed the frontier. We'll be back tomorrow by the end of the morning. Expect the worst. You won't recognize him." They had dinner in an officers' mess. Robert L. was still talking and telling his story. When he entered the mess all the officers stood up and saluted him. He didn't see. He never had seen that sort of thing. He spoke of the German martyrdom, of the martyrdom common to all men. He told what it was like. That evening he said he'd like to eat a trout before he died. In deserted Wissemburg they found a trout for Robert L. He ate a few mouthfuls. Then he started talking again. He spoke of charity. He'd heard some rhetorical phrases of Father Riquet's, and he started to say these very obscure words: "When anyone talks to me of Christian charity, I shall say Dachau." But he didn't finish. That night they slept somewhere near Bar-sur-Aube. Robert L. slept for a few hours. They reached Paris at the end of the morning. Just before they came to the rue Saint-Benoît, D. stopped to phone me again: "I'm ringing to warn you that it's more terrible than anything we've imagined . . . He's happy."

I heard stifled cries on the stairs, a stir, a clatter of feet. Then doors banging and shouts. It was them. It was them, back from Germany.

I couldn't stop myself—I started to run downstairs, to escape into the street. Beauchamp and D. were supporting him under the arms. They'd stopped on the first-floor landing. He was looking up.

I can't remember exactly what happened. He must have looked at me and recognized me and smiled. I shrieked no, that I didn't want to see. I started to run again, up the stairs this time. I was shrieking, I remember that. The war emerged in my shrieks. Six years without uttering a cry. I found myself in some neighbors' apartment. They forced me to drink some rum, they poured it into my mouth. Into the shrieks.

I can't remember when I found myself back with him again, with him, Robert L. I remember hearing sobs all over the house; that the tenants stayed for a long while out on the stairs; that the doors were left open. I was told later that the concierge had put decorations up in the hall to welcome him, and that as soon as he'd gone by she tore them all down and shut herself up alone in her lodge to weep.

In my memory, at a certain moment, the sounds stop and I see him. Huge. There before me. I don't recognize him. He looks at me. He smiles. Lets himself be looked at. There's a supernatural weariness in his smile, weariness from having managed to live till this moment. It's from this smile that I suddenly recognize him, but from a great distance, as if I were seeing him at the other end of a tunnel. It's a smile of embarrassment. He's apologizing for being here, reduced to such a wreck. And then the smile fades, and he becomes a stranger again. But the knowledge is still there, that this stranger is he, Robert L., totally.

He wanted to see around the apartment again. We supported him, and he toured the rooms. His cheeks creased, but didn't release his lips; it was in his eyes that we'd seen his smile. In the kitchen he saw the clafoutis we'd made for him. He stopped smiling. "What is it?" We told him. What was it made with? Cherries—it was the height of the season. "May I have some?" "We don't know, we'll have to ask the doctor." He came back into the sitting room and lay down on the divan. "So I can't have any?" "Not yet." "Why?" "There have been accidents in Paris already from letting deportees eat too soon after they got back from the camps."
He stopped asking questions about what had happened while he was away. He stopped seeing us. A great, silent pain spread over his face because he was still being refused food, because it was still as it had been in the concentration camp. And, as in the camp, he accepted it in silence. He didn't see that we were weeping. Nor did he see that we could scarcely look at him or respond to what he said.

The doctor came. He stopped short with his hand on the door handle, very pale. He looked at us, and then at the form on the divan. He didn't understand. And then he realized: the form wasn't dead yet, it was hovering between life and death, and he, the doctor, had been called in to try to keep it alive. The doctor came into the room. He went over to the form and the form smiled at him. The doctor was to come several times a day for three weeks, at all hours of the day and night. Whenever we were too afraid we called him and he came. He saved Robert L. He too was caught up in the passionate desire to save Robert L. from death. He succeeded.
We smuggled the clafoutis out of the house while he slept. The next day he was feverish and didn't talk about food any more.

If he had eaten when he got back from the camp his stomach would have been lacerated by the weight of the food, or else the weight would have pressed on the heart, which had grown enormous in the cave of his emaciation. It was beating so fast you couldn't have counted its beats, you couldn't really say it was beating—it was trembling, rather, as if from terror. No, he couldn't eat without dying. But he couldn't go on not eating without dying. That was the problem.

The fight with death started very soon. We had to be careful with it, use care, tact, skill. It surrounded him on all sides. And yet there was still a way of reaching him. It wasn't very big, this opening through which to communicate with him, but there was still life in him, scarcely more than a splinter, but a splinter just the same. Death unleashed its attack. His temperature was 104.5° the first day. Then 105°. Then 106°. Death was doing all it could. 106°: his heart vibrated like a violin string. Still 106°, but vibrating. The heart, we thought—it's going to stop. Still 106°. Death deals cruel knocks, but the heart is deaf. This can't go on, the heart will stop. But no.

Gruel, said the doctor, a teaspoonful at a time. Six or seven times a day we gave him gruel. Just a teaspoonful nearly choked him, he clung to our hands, gasped for air, and fell back on the bed. But he swallowed some. Six or seven times a day, too, he asked to go to the toilet. We lifted him up, supported him under the arms and knees. He must have weighed between eighty-two and eighty-four pounds: bone, skin, liver, intestines, brain, lungs, everything—eighty-four pounds for a body five feet ten inches tall. We sat him on the edge of the sanitary pail, on which we'd put a small cushion: the skin was raw where there was no flesh between it and the joints. . . . Once he was sitting on his pail he excreted in one go, in one enormous, astonishing gurgle. What the heart held back the anus couldn't: it let out all that was in it. Everything, or almost everything, did the same, even the fingers, which no longer kept their nails, but let them go too. But the heart went on holding back what it contained. The heart. And then there was the head. Gaunt but sublime, it emerged alone from that bag of bones, remembering, relating, recognizing, asking for things. And talking. Talking. The head was connected to the body by the neck, as heads usually are, but the neck was so withered and shrunken—you could circle it with one hand—that you wondered how life could pass through it; a spoonful of gruel almost blocked it. At first the neck was at right angles to the shoulders. Higher up, the neck was right inside the skeleton, joined on at the top of the jaws and winding around the ligaments like ivy. You could see the vertebrae through it, the carotid arteries, the nerves, the pharynx, and the blood passing through: the skin had become like cigarette paper. So, he excreted this dark green, slimy, gushing thing, a turd such as no one had ever seen before. When he'd finished we put him back to bed. He lay for a long time with his eyes half shut, prostrated.

For seventeen days the turd looked the same. It was inhuman. It separated him from us more than the fever, the thinness, the nailless fingers, the marks of SS blows. We gave him gruel that was golden yellow, gruel for infants, and it came out of him dark green like slime from a swamp. After the sanitary pail was closed you could hear the bubbles bursting as they rose to the surface inside. Viscous and slimy, it was almost like a great gob of spit. When it emerged the room filled with a smell, not of putrefaction or corpses—did his body still have the where-withal to make a corpse?—but rather of humus, of dead leaves, of dense undergrowth. It was a somber smell, dark reflection of the dark night from which he was emerging and which we would never know. *(I leaned against the shutters, the street went by below, and as they didn't know what was going on in the room I wanted to tell them that here, in this room above them, a man had come back from the German camps, alive.)*

Of course he'd rummaged in trashcans for food, he'd eaten wild plants, drunk water from engines. But that didn't explain it. Faced with this strange phenomenon we tried to find explanations. We thought that perhaps there, under our very eyes, he was consuming his own liver or spleen. How were we to know? How were we to know what strangeness that belly still contained, what pain?

For seventeen whole days that turd still looks the same. For seventeen days it's unlike anything ever known. Every one of the seven times he excretes each day, we smell it, look at it, but can't recognize it. For seventeen days we hide from him that which comes out of him, just as we hide from him his own legs and feet and whole unbelievable body.

We ourselves never got used to seeing them. You couldn't get used to it. The incredible thing was that he was still alive. Whenever anyone came into the room and saw that shape under the sheets, they couldn't bear the sight and averted their eyes. Many went away and never came back. He never noticed our horror, not once. He was happy, he wasn't afraid any more. The fever bore him up. For seventeen days.

One day his temperature drops.

After seventeen days, death grows weary. In the pail his excretion doesn't bubble any more, it becomes liquid. It's still green, but it smells more human, it smells human. And one day his temperature drops—he's been given twelve liters of serum, and one morning his temperature drops. He's lying on his nine cushions, one for the head, two for the forearms, two for the arms, two for the hands, and two for the feet. For no part of his body could bear its own weight; the weight had to be swathed in down and immobilized.

And then, one morning, the fever leaves him. It comes back, but abates again. Comes back again, not quite so high, and falls again. And then one morning he says, "I'm hungry."

Hunger had gone as his temperature rose. It came back when the fever abated. One day the doctor said, "Let's try—let's try giving him something to eat. We can begin with meat extract. If he can take that, keep on giving it, but at the same time give him all kinds of other food, just small amounts at first, increasing the quantity just a little every three days."

I spend the morning going around to all the restaurants in Saint-Germain-des-Prés trying to find a meat-juice extractor. I find one in a fashionable restaurant. They say they can't lend it. I say it's for a political deportee who's very ill, it's a matter of life and death. The woman thinks for a minute and says, "I can't lend it to you, but I can rent it to you for a thousand francs a day." I leave my name and address and a deposit. The Saint-Benoît restaurant sells me the meat at cost price.

He digested the meat extract without any difficulty, so after three days he began to take solid food.

His hunger grew from what it fed on. It grew greater and greater, became insatiable.

It took on terrifying proportions.

We didn't serve him food. We put the dishes in front of him and left him and he ate. Methodically, as if performing a duty, he was doing what he had to do to live. He ate. It was an occupation that took up all his time. He would wait for food for hours. He would swallow without knowing what he was eating. Then we'd take the food away and he'd wait for it to come again.

He has gone and hunger has taken his place. Emptiness has taken his place. He is giving to the void, filling what was emptied: those wasted bowels. That's what he's doing. Obeying, serving, ministering to a mysterious duty. How does he know what to do about hunger? How does he perceive that this is what he has to do? He knows with a knowledge that has no parallel.

He eats a mutton chop. Then he gnaws the bone, eyes lowered, concentrating on not missing a morsel of meat. Then he takes a second chop. Then a third. Without looking up.

He's sitting in the shade in the sitting room near a half-open window, in an armchair, surrounded by his cushions, his stick beside him. His legs look like crutches inside his trousers. When the sun shines you can see through his hands.

Yesterday he made enormous efforts to gather up the breadcrumbs that had fallen on his trousers and on the floor. Today he lets a few lie.

We leave him alone in the room while he's eating. We don't have to help him now. His strength has come back enough for him to hold a spoon or a fork. But we still cut up the meat for him. We leave him alone with the food. We try not to talk in the adjoining rooms. We walk on tiptoe. We watch him from a distance. He's performing a duty. He has no special preference for one dish over another. He cares less and less. He crams everything down. If the dishes don't come fast enough, he sobs and says we don't understand.

Yesterday afternoon he stole some bread out of the refrigerator. He steals. We tell him to be careful, not to eat too much. Then he weeps.

I used to watch him from the sitting-room door. I didn't go in. For two weeks, three, I watched him eat with unremitting pleasure. I couldn't get used to it either. Sometimes his pleasure made me weep too. He didn't see me. He'd forgotten me.

Strength is coming back.

I start to eat again too, and to sleep. I put on some weight. We're going to live. Like him I haven't been able to eat for seventeen days. Like him I haven't slept for seventeen days, or at least that's what I think. In fact, I've slept for two or three hours a day. I fall asleep anywhere. And wake in terror. It's awful, every time I think he's died while I was asleep. I still have that slight fever at night. The doctor who comes to see him is worried about me, too. He prescribes injections. The needle breaks in the muscle in my thigh, my muscles are knotted, as if tetanized. The nurse won't give me any more injections. Lack of sleep gives me eye trouble. I have to hold on to the furniture when I walk, the ground seems to slope away from me, I'm afraid of falling. We eat the meat from which we extracted the juice. It's like paper or cotton wool. I don't cook any more, except coffee. I feel very close to the death I wished for. It's a matter of indifference to me; I don't even think about its being a matter of indifference. My identity has gone. I'm just she who is afraid when she wakes. She who wills in his stead, for him. I exist in that will, that desire, and even when Robert L. is at death's door it's inexpressibly strong because he is still alive. When I lost my younger brother and my baby I lost pain too. It was without an object, so to speak: it was built on the past. But now there is hope, and pain is implanted in hope. Sometimes I'm amazed I don't die; a cold blade plunged deep into the living flesh, night and day, and you survive.

M. F. K. FISHER
(1908–1992)

Mary Frances Kennedy Fisher devoted most of her life to writing about food and the pleasures of eating, beginning with *Serve It Forth* (1937), *Consider the Oyster* (1941), and *How to Cook a Wolf* (1942). In a volume called *The Gastronomical Me* (1943), she collected many of her marvelous food-centered autobiographical pieces. Other memoirs were *Among Friends* and *Maps of Another Town*, in which she described living in Provence with her two daughters. More recently she wrote about the experience of aging in *Sister Age*. This selection, "I Was Really Very Hungry," from the collection *As They Were*, was first published in 1937. M. F. K. Fisher lived, for the most part, in California.

For another close encounter with the culinary, compare Sara Suleri, *Meatless Days*. For another sensuous account of ordinary life, compare Annie Dillard, *An American Childhood*.

FROM *As They Were*

I Was Really Very Hungry

I

Once I met a young servant in northern Burgundy who was almost frighteningly fanatical about food, like a medieval woman possessed by a devil. Her obsession engulfed even my appreciation of the dishes she served, until I grew uncomfortable.

It was the off season at the old mill which a Parisian chef had bought and turned into one of France's most famous restaurants, and my mad waitress was the only servant. In spite of that she was neatly uniformed, and showed no surprise at my unannounced arrival and my hot dusty walking clothes.

She smiled discreetly at me, said, "Oh, but certainly!" when I asked if I could lunch there, and led me without more words to a dark bedroom bulging with First Empire furniture, and a new white bathroom.

When I went into the dining room it was empty of humans—a cheerful ugly room still showing traces of the petit bourgeois parlor it had been. There were aspidistras on the mantel; several small white tables were laid with those imitation "peasant-ware" plates that one sees in Paris china stores, and very good crystal glasses; a cat folded under some ferns by the window ledge hardly looked at me; and the air was softly hurried with the sound of high waters from the stream outside.

I waited for the maid to come back. I knew I should eat well and slowly, and suddenly the idea of dry sherry, unknown in all the village bistros of the last few days, stung my throat smoothly. I tried not to think of it; it would be impossible to realize. Dubonnet would do. But not as well. I longed for sherry.

The little maid came into the silent room. I looked at her stocky young body, and her butter-colored hair, and noticed her odd pale voluptuous mouth before I said, "Mademoiselle, I shall drink an apéritif. Have you by any chance—"

"Let me suggest," she interrupted firmly, "our special dry sherry. It is chosen in Spain for Monsieur Paul."

And before I could agree she was gone, discreet and smooth.

She's a funny one, I thought, and waited in a pleasant warm tiredness for the wine.

It was good. I smiled approval at her, and she lowered her eyes, and then looked searchingly at me again. I realized suddenly that in this land of trained nonchalant waiters I was to be served by a small waitress who took her duties seriously. I felt much amused, and matched her solemn searching gaze.

"Today, Madame, you may eat shoulder of lamb in the English style, with baked potatoes, green beans, and a sweet."

My heart sank. I felt dismal, and hot and weary, and still grateful for the sherry.

But she was almost grinning at me, her lips curved triumphantly, and her eyes less palely blue.

"Oh, in *that* case," she remarked as if I had spoken, "in *that* case a trout, of course—a *truite au bleu* as only Monsieur Paul can prepare it!"

She glanced hurriedly at my face, and hastened on. "With the trout, one or two young potatoes—oh, very delicately boiled," she added before I could protest, "very light."

I felt better. I agreed. "Perhaps a leaf or two of salad after the fish," I suggested. She almost snapped at me. "Of course, of course! And naturally our hors d'oeuvres to commence." She started away.

"No!" I called, feeling that I must assert myself now or be forever lost. "No!"

She turned back, and spoke to me very gently. "But Madame has never tasted our hors d'oeuvres. I am sure that Madame will be pleased.

They are our specialty, made by Monsieur Paul himself. I am sure," and she looked reproachfully at me, her mouth tender and sad, "I am sure that Madame would be very much pleased."

I smiled weakly at her, and she left. A little cloud of hurt gentleness seemed to hang in the air where she had last stood.

I comforted myself with the sherry, feeling increasing irritation with my own feeble self. Hell! I loathed hors d'oeuvres! I conjured disgusting visions of square glass plates of oily fish, of soggy vegetables glued together with cheap mayonnaise, of rank radishes and tasteless butter. No, Monsieur Paul or not, sad young pale-faced waitress or not, I hated hors d'oeuvres.

I glanced victoriously across the room at the cat, whose eyes seemed closed.

II

Several minutes passed. I was really very hungry.

The door banged open, and my girl came in again, less discreet this time. She hurried toward me.

"Madame, the wine! Before Monsieur Paul can go on—" Her eyes watched my face, which I perversely kept rather glum.

"I think," I said ponderously, daring her to interrupt me, "I think that today, since I am in Burgundy and about to eat a trout," and here I hoped she noticed that I did not mention hors d'oeuvres, "I think I shall drink a bottle of Chablis 1929."

For a second her whole face blazed with joy, and then subsided into a trained mask. I knew that I had chosen well, had somehow satisfied her in a secret and incomprehensible way. She nodded politely and scuttled off, only for another second glancing impatiently at me as I called after her, "Well cooled, please, but not iced."

I'm a fool, I thought, to order a whole bottle. I'm a fool, here all alone and with more miles to walk before I reach Avallon and my fresh clothes and a bed. Then I smiled at myself and leaned back in my solid wide-seated chair, looking obliquely at the prints of Gibson girls, English tavern scenes, and hideous countrysides that hung on the papered walls. The room was warm; I could hear my companion cat purring under the ferns.

The girl rushed in, with flat baking dishes piled up her arms like the plates of a Japanese juggler. She slid them off neatly in two rows onto the table, where they lay steaming up at me, darkly and infinitely appetizing.

"*Mon Dieu!* All for me?" I peered at her. She nodded, her discretion quite gone now and a look of ecstatic worry on her pale face and eyes and lips.

There were at least eight dishes. I felt almost embarrassed, and sat for a minute looking weakly at the fork and spoon in my hand.

"Perhaps Madame would care to start with the pickled herring? It is not like any other. Monsieur Paul prepares it himself, in his own vinegar and wines. It is very good."

I dug out two or three brown filets from the dish, and tasted. They were truly unlike any others, truly the best I had ever eaten, mild, pungent, meaty as fresh nuts.

I realized the maid had stopped breathing, and looked up at her. She was watching me, or rather a gastronomic X ray of the herring inside me, with a hypnotized glaze in her eyes.

"Madame is pleased?" she whispered softly.

I said I was. She sighed, and pushed a sizzling plate of broiled endive toward me, and disappeared.

I had put a few dull green lentils on my plate, lentils scattered with minced fresh herbs and probably marinated in tarragon vinegar and walnut oil, when she came into the dining room again with the bottle of Chablis in a wine basket.

"Madame should be eating the little baked onions while they are hot," she remarked over her shoulder as she held the bottle in a napkin and uncorked it. I obeyed meekly, and while I watched her I ate several more than I had meant to. They were delicious, simmered first in strong meat broth, I think, and then drained and broiled with olive oil and new-ground pepper.

I was fascinated by her method of uncorking a vintage wine. Instead of the Burgundian procedure of infinite and often exaggerated precautions against touching or tipping or jarring the bottle, she handled it quite nonchalantly, and seemed to be careful only to keep her hands from the cool bottle itself, holding it sometimes by the basket and sometimes in a napkin. The cork was very tight, and I thought for a minute that she would break it. So did she: her face grew tight, and did not loosen until she had slowly worked out the cork and wiped the lip. Then she poured an inch of wine in a glass, turned her back to me like a priest taking Communion, and drank it down. Finally some was poured for me, and she stood with the bottle in her hand and her full lips drooping until I nodded a satisfied yes. Then she pushed another of the plates toward me, and almost rushed from the room.

I ate slowly, knowing that I should not be as hungry as I ought to be for the trout, but knowing too that I had never tasted such delicate savory morsels. Some were hot, some cold. The wine was light and cool. The room, warm and agreeably empty under the rushing sound of the stream, became smaller as I grew used to it.

My girl hurried in again, with another row of plates up one arm, and a large bucket dragging at the other. She slid the plates deftly onto the table, and drew a deep breath as she let the bucket down against the table leg.

"Your trout, Madame," she said excitedly. I looked down at the gleam of the fish curving through its limited water. "But first a good slice of Monsieur Paul's *pâté*. Oh yes, oh yes, you will be very sorry if you miss this. It is rich, but appetizing, and not at all too heavy. Just this one morsel!"

And willy-nilly I accepted the large gouge she dug from a terrine. I prayed for ten normal appetites and thought with amused nostalgia of my usual lunch of cold milk and fruit as I broke off a crust of bread and patted it smooth with the paste. Then I forgot everything but the exciting faint decadent flavor in my mouth.

I beamed up at the girl. She nodded, but from habit asked if I was satisfied. I beamed again, and asked, simply to please her, "Is there not a faint hint of *marc*, or perhaps cognac?"

"*Marc*, Madame!" And she awarded me the proud look of a teacher whose pupil has showed unexpected intelligence. "Monsieur Paul, after he has taken equal parts of goose breast and the finest pork, and broken a certain number of egg yolks into them, and ground them *very*, very fine, cooks all with seasoning for some three hours. *But,*" she pushed her face nearer, and looked with ferocious gloating at the *pâté* inside me, her eyes like X rays, "he never stops stirring it! Figure to yourself the work of it—stir, stir, never stopping!

"Then he grinds in a suspicion of nutmeg, and then adds, very thoroughly, a glass of *marc* for each hundred grams of *pâté*. And is Madame not pleased?"

Again I agreed, rather timidly, that Madame was much pleased, that Madame had never, indeed, tasted such an unctuous and exciting *pâté*. The girl wet her lips delicately, and then started as if she had been pin-stuck.

"But the trout! My God, the trout!" She grabbed the bucket, and her voice grew higher and more rushed.

"Here is the trout, Madame. You are to eat it *au bleu*, and you should never do so if you had not seen it alive. For if the trout were dead when it was plunged into the *court bouillon* it would not turn blue. So, naturally, it must be living."

I knew all this, more or less, but I was fascinated by her absorption in the momentary problem. I felt quite ignorant, and asked her with sincerity, "What about the trout? Do you take out its guts before or after?"

"Oh, the trout!" She sounded scornful. "Any trout is glad, truly glad, to be prepared by Monsieur Paul. His little gills are pinched, with one flash of the knife he is empty, and then he curls in agony in the *bouillon* and all is over. And it is the curl you must judge, Madame. A false *truite au bleu* cannot curl."

She panted triumph at me, and hurried out with the bucket.

III

She *is* a funny one, I thought, and for not more than two or three minutes I drank wine and mused over her. Then she darted in, with the trout correctly blue and agonizingly curled on a platter, and on her crooked arm a plate of tiny boiled potatoes and a bowl.

When I had been served and had cut off her anxious breathings with an assurance that the fish was the best I had ever tasted, she peered again at me and at the sauce in the bowl. I obediently put some of it on the potatoes: no fool I, to ruin *truite au bleu* with a hot concoction! There was more silence.

"Ah!" she sighed at last. "I knew Madame would feel thus! Is it not the most beautiful sauce in the world with the flesh of a trout?"

I nodded incredulous agreement.

"Would you like to know how it is done?"

I remembered all the legends of chefs who guarded favorite recipes with their very lives, and murmured yes.

She wore the exalted look of a believer describing a miracle at Lourdes as she told me, in a rush, how Monsieur Paul threw chopped chives into hot sweet butter and then poured the butter off, how he added another nut of butter and a tablespoonful of thick cream for each person, stirred the mixture for a few minutes over a slow fire, and then rushed it to the table.

"So simple?" I asked softly, watching her lighted eyes and the tender lustful lines of her strange mouth.

"So simple, Madame! But," she shrugged, "you know, with a master—"

I was relieved to see her go: such avid interest in my eating wore on me. I felt released when the door closed behind her, free for a minute or so from her victimization. What would she have done, I wondered, if I had been ignorant or unconscious of any fine flavors?

She was right, though, about Monsieur Paul. Only a master could live in this isolated mill and preserve his gastronomic dignity through loneliness and the sure financial loss of unused butter and addled eggs. Of course there was the stream for his fish, and I knew his *pâtés* would grow even more edible with age; but how could he manage to have a thing like roasted lamb ready for any chance patron? Was the consuming interest of his one maid enough fuel for his flame?

I tasted the last sweet nugget of trout, the one nearest the blued tail, and poked somnolently at the minute white billiard balls that had been eyes. Fate could not harm me, I remembered winily, for I had indeed dined today, and dined well. Now for a leaf of crisp salad, and I'd be on my way.

The girl slid into the room. She asked me again, in a respectful but gossipy manner, how I had liked this and that and the other things, and then talked on as she mixed dressing for the endive.

"And now," she announced, after I had eaten one green sprig and dutifully pronounced it excellent, "now Madame is going to taste Monsieur Paul's special terrine, one that is not even on the summer menu, when a hundred covers are laid here daily and we have a headwaiter and a wine waiter, and cabinet ministers telegraph for tables! Madame will be pleased."

And heedless of my low moans of the walk still before me, of my appreciation and my unhappily human and limited capacity, she cut a thick heady slice from the terrine of meat and stood over me while I ate it, telling me with almost hysterical pleasure of the wild ducks, the spices, the wines that went into it. Even surfeit could not make me deny that it was a rare dish. I ate it all, knowing my luck, and wishing only that I had red wine to drink with it.

I was beginning, though, to feel almost frightened, realizing myself an accidental victim of these stranded gourmets, Monsieur Paul and his handmaiden. I began to feel that they were using me for a safety valve, much as a thwarted woman relieves herself with tantrums or a fit of weeping. I was serving a purpose, and perhaps a noble one, but I resented it in a way approaching panic.

I protested only to myself when one of Monsieur Paul's special cheeses was cut for me, and ate it doggedly, like a slave. When the girl said that Monsieur Paul himself was preparing a special filter of coffee for me, I smiled servile acceptance: wine and the weight of food and my own character could not force me to argue with maniacs. When, before the coffee came, Monsieur Paul presented me, through his idolater, with the most beautiful apple tart I had ever seen, I allowed it to be cut and served to me. Not a wince or a murmur showed the waitress my distressed fearfulness. With a stuffed careful smile on my face, and a clear nightmare in my head of trussed wanderers prepared for his altar by this hermit-priest of gastronomy, I listened to the girl's passionate plea for fresh pastry dough.

"You cannot, you can not, Madame, serve old pastry!" She seemed ready to beat her breast as she leaned across the table. "Look at that delicate crust! You may feel that you have eaten too much." (I nodded idiotic agreement.) "But this pastry is like feathers—it is like snow. It is in fact good for you, a digestive! And why?" She glared sternly at me.

"Because Monsieur Paul did not even open the flour bin until he saw you coming! He could not, he *could* not have baked you one of his special apple tarts with old dough!"

She laughed, tossing back her head and curling her mouth voluptuously.

IV

Somehow I managed to refuse a second slice, but I trembled under her surmise that I was ready for my special filter.

The wine and its fortitude had fled me, and I drank the hot coffee as a suffering man gulps ether, deeply and gratefully.

I remember, then, chatting with surprising glibness, and sending to Monsieur Paul flowery compliments, all of them sincere and well won, and I remember feeling only amusement when a vast glass of *marc* appeared before me and then gradually disappeared, like the light in the warm room full of water-sounds. I felt surprise to be alive still, and suddenly very grateful to the wild-lipped waitress, as if her presence had sustained me through duress. We discussed food and wine. I wondered bemusedly why I had been frightened.

The *marc* was gone. I went into the crowded bedroom for my jacket. She met me in the darkening hall when I came out, and I paid my bill, a large one. I started to thank her, but she took my hand, drew me into the dining room, and without words poured more spirits into my glass. I drank to Monsieur Paul while she watched me intently, her pale eyes bulging in the dimness and her lips pressed inward as if she too tasted the hot, aged *marc*.

The cat rose from his ferny bed, and walked contemptuously out of the room.

Suddenly the girl began to laugh, in a soft shy breathless way, and came close to me.

"Permit me!" she said, and I thought she was going to kiss me. But instead she pinned a tiny bunch of snowdrops and dark bruised cyclamens against my stiff jacket, very quickly and deftly, and then ran from the room with her head down.

I waited for a minute. No sounds came from anywhere in the old mill, but the endless rushing of the full stream seemed to strengthen, like the timed blare of an orchestra under a falling curtain.

She's a *funny* one, I thought. I touched the cool blossoms on my coat and went out, like a ghost from ruins, across the courtyard toward the dim road to Avallon.

JANET FRAME
(1924–)

Janet Frame, the New Zealand novelist, grew up in a poor, anxious, but close-knit family in Oamaru. She left home to attend Teacher Training College in the city of Dunedin, as described in *An Angel at My Table* (1984). This was her second volume of autobiography, the first being *To the Is-land*. In this excerpt Frame relates how her loneliness and extraordinary shyness led to a suicide attempt which in turn led to commitment to a mental hospital. Diagnosed as schizophrenic, she spent eight years in institutions and was released only because of the publication of her first book. New Zealand man of letters Frank Sargeson gave her his garden shed to live in and encouraged her work until she was able to get away to England.

For another account of a Commonwealth girlhood, compare Jill Ker Conway, *The Road from Coorain*. For accounts of childhood and youth by other novelists, compare Simone de Beauvoir, *The Prime of Life*, Nina Berberova, *The Italics Are Mine*, Natalia Ginzburg, *Family Sayings*, and Cynthia Ozick, *Art & Ardor*.

FROM *An Angel at My Table*

1945: ONE

I arrived with my growing self in Dunedin. This was to be the year of my twenty-first birthday at the end of August. "Twenty-firsts" as they were known, were part of the continuing ritual of growing up, when one became "of age," a legal citizen able to vote, to make a will, or, as the song said,

> I'm twenty-one today.
> I've got the key of the door,
> I've never been twenty-one before.
> I'm twenty-one today.

At the end of the year, also, I hoped I would gain my Certificate as a teacher, after my probationary year at Arthur Street School. I hoped also to add another unit to my arts degree course, and as I felt that English III would prove to be too engulfing of my interest, I decided upon Psychology I, a first year of Psychology.

My secret desire to be a poet, fed by the publication in the College Magazine of my two poems ("Now they'll find out that I'm really a poet!") occupied much of my planning. I was as anxious to impress with my imagination as I had been during my years at school, only here there were so many more people each with so much more imagination, prose writers and poets everywhere, for I was learning to get copies of *Critic* by lingering with apparent casualness around the entrance to the University near the *Critic* "bin" with its enticement, "Take One." Contributions still needed a visit to the office where the poem or story could be placed. I don't know why I didn't post a contribution. I suspect that I was ignorant and innocent in most human activities, including posting letters. I was still not aware of the number of everyday chores dealt with by ordinary people. Based on my life at home, my supposition was that letters were written only to other towns with news of events such as births, deaths, marriages, or past or future travel, while telegrams were mostly a swift form of communicating the fact of death or the time of arrival of a train "passing through" or depositing relations; and parcels meant Christmas. I had scarcely begun to study the primer of adult living. I knew of joy and of love discovered at the point of loss, and I had accepted death. I felt that I could see the feelings of people beneath their faces, in their eyes, their imposed or swift unguarded expressions, and in the words they spoke. The War still haunted and confused me— "the pity of war, the pity war distilled," and it was the poets who continued to illuminate for me the places no-one else seemed to want to talk about or visit. I thought often, with longing, of the prophecy, "Nation shall not lift up sword against nation, neither shall they learn war any more."

I boarded with Mrs. T., a widow with a married daughter, Kathleen, living in the new government housing estate at Wakari, where Mrs. T. spent most of her days, taking the bus after breakfast—"I'm going over to Kathleen's"—and coming home at about the same time I came home from school. Mrs. T.'s only topic of conversation was "Kathleen, Bob and the children," what they did, what they said, how they felt, with much of her thoughts occupied by what she would give them for presents. "I saw something in Arthur Barnetts and I said to myself, 'That will be just right for Kathleen's youngest, Kathleen has been looking everywhere for something like that.' " Bob worked in the Electricity Department, the showroom in Princes Street, and could get heaters at a discount.

For the sake of appearances I sometimes had meals with Mrs. T.

instead of taking them to my room "as I have study to catch up with and lessons to mark and prepare . . ." and then I would sit opposite her and listen, fascinated, while she described the day "over at Kathleen's"— how they'd done the washing together and tidied the house, how Kathleen and Bob were hoping some day to get carpet "edge to edge" in every room. "There are quite a few carpeted now edge to edge." I, the "quiet shy teacher, no trouble, no trouble at all," spent most of my free time in my room marking, preparing lessons, and cutting out paper stars in different colours to reward the children's efforts; and studying my textbook of Psychology; and writing and reading poems. . . .

I delighted in the children at school and in teaching. I was full of ideas for encouraging individual development. I revelled in the children's art and in their poetry, for they wrote poetry and stories almost every day, and these, with the paintings, I pinned around the walls for everyone to enjoy. I took pains, too, in teaching other subjects. My failure was as a member of the staff, for my timidity among people, especially among those who might be asked to judge and comment on my performance as a teacher, led to my spending my free time alone. Too timid to go to morning and afternoon tea with a room full of other teachers, I made excuses about "having work to do in the classroom," aware that I was going against all the instructions about the need to "mix in adult company, take part in social events and discussions with other teachers and parents," and that "morning tea in the teachers' room" was an almost sacred ritual. My fear of being "inspected" by the headmaster or inspector inspired me to devise a means of postponing the day of reckoning, by inventing a serial story which I could continue whenever I heard the steps of authority approaching along the corridor, so that a visit by the headmaster to a class sitting rapt with attention (the content of the story ensured a rapt audience), might "prove" my ability as a teacher with the result that I would "pass" my "C" Certificate at the end of the year.

My escape from teaching was the Psychology class and the Psychology laboratory where we performed a range of interesting experiments and tests supervised by two fresh young lecturers, Peter Prince and John Forrest whom we called Mr. Prince and Mr. Forrest, but whom I nicknamed HRH and Ash (after Ashley, the fair young man in *Gone with the Wind*, played by Leslie Howard). As these two young men—recent graduates, in a world where young men were few—were in a sense for public and student consumption, they became the object of rumour, speculation and fantasy. I preferred HRH because, unlike Ash, he appeared to be an "introvert," and according to the magical fixed classification of people, "introverts" were the artists, the poets. I'd see HRH, his face turned towards the sky, his pipe in his mouth, striding with his long-legged springing gait, down Frederick Street towards the University, and I'd think, "He's in another world." He blushed easily, too, and like my admired G. M. Cameron he had an endearing awkwardness of speech and gesture. Ash, not so tall, was handsome, fairhaired with a lock of hair draped over his forehead, and unlike HRH who wore dark suits, Ash wore a rust-coloured sports coat and tomato-red socks which he actually referred to one day in the laboratory, saying, "How do you like my tomayto socks?" pronouncing tomato the *American* way.

Some of the women swooned over Ash.

It was Ash—Mr. Forrest—who arranged for gramophone recitals to be held regularly in the gramophone room of the Music Department.

"All those records and few people hearing them," he said in his forthright way. (He was becoming known for his "forthrightness" and for his unconventional clothing.)

One day when I decided to go to the recital and I was standing outside the door of the gramophone room trying to pluck up courage to go in, I heard the piano being played. I opened the door and peeped in and there was Mr. Forrest playing the piano. He stopped at once and prepared the records for the recital. But I had heard him playing the piano, up and down the keys in a flourish and swoop like a concert pianist, marshalling the notes together in a travelling force going somewhere, and not simply picking out notes into a "tune," separating them and giving them no say in the whole music. Apart from the loved Schubert songs and the "tunes" of Walt Disney's *Fantasia,* and the new songs we had learned at Training College. . . . I still had little knowledge of classical music, and I had never listened to a long piece of music—a symphony or concerto. That day, Mr. Forrest played a record of Tchaikovsky's *Symphony Pathétique,* and among the handful of students, I listened to the unaccustomed sounds dragging, dragging their awful burden of gloom, on and on, and when the music arrived at the "tune" I knew as

> This is the story of a starry night
> The faded glory of a starry night . . .

I experienced the delight of recognition. I listened to the end, in love with the music and its churning sadness, and Tchaikovsky became (after Schubert) my favourite composer.

"I suppose you all know César Franck," Mr. Forrest said.

The audience looked as if they knew César Franck.

"We'll play César Franck next time," Mr. Forrest said, pronouncing the name with such assurance and familiarity.

The music room became another place where I felt at home and where I learned to listen to music that lasted more than three or five minutes. Why had I not known before that listening to a symphony was like reading a book in all its progressions, with its special shape, and silent and noisy moments? I learned to say, carelessly, "Adagio—did you like the *Adagio*? That *Andante* passage . . ." I began to go to lunch-hour piano recitals in the Town Hall and although at first I clapped in the wrong places, thinking the music was ended, I soon learned the pattern. I talked, too, as people talked who regularly went to music recitals and symphony concerts, "Oh, smell the mothballs in the fur coats! They only listen to music once a year. Just imagine, once a year! And all that coughing, right in the middle of that slow movement, they didn't even cough in the places where they thought it was fair to sneak in a cough or a cleared throat!"

And one day John Forrest startled me into a new perception of him by saying suddenly, in the music room, "But Schubert is my favourite composer."

Schubert! *To Music. Thou holy art in many hours of sadness.*

In spite of the worries about teaching and my future, I found the year mostly pleasurable. At school and University I gave little thought to my home and family, and when I spent one of my few weekends at home, I tried to detach myself from the place and the people. My family appeared like tired ghosts trying to come to life for the occasion; both mother and Dad were still pursued by *toil*, and the extra weariness now lay in the long walk up the hill, Dad with his home-made leather workbag crammed with railway coal, mother, during the day when no-one was home, carrying the groceries which the boy from the Self Help or the Star Stores had delivered to the shed. Coming home for the weekend I'd always find that mother had bought a jar of coffee, that dark sweet liquid with the splurp taste, known as Gregg's Coffee and Chicory where the outside of the bottle became sticky with the spilled syrup. Drinking coffee was a sign of being grown up; therefore I drank coffee. Also, one of the lecturers at University had spoken to me using the name, *Janet*, when I had always been known as *Jean;* therefore I was now officially *Janet*. During the weekend, Dad would bring a pile of Sexton Blake library books for me to read, and I'd race through the exploits of Sexton Blake and Tinker so that I could talk about them with him. The attentive habits of my parents saddened, pleased, and infuriated me, leaving me with a feeling of helplessness—what could I do for them? I could see the pattern of their past lives slowly emerging, like a script written with invisible ink and now being made visible to me, warmed by the fire kindled simply by my growing up. I could see, too, an illumination produced by that same fire, the shadows emerging as recognized shapes of language full of meaning for me: the language of the love and loss and joy and torture of having a place fast within a family when all my awakening longing was directed towards being uprooted, quickly, without leaving behind a cluster of nerve endings, broken threads in danger of being renewed.

The year was half gone. My personal lyric began its silent terrifying progression towards the planets and the stars. At the beginning of the month when I was to celebrate my twenty-first birthday, my coming of age, the War was suddenly over, having pursued me through all the years of my official adolescence, as part of the development of my body and mind, almost as an ingredient of my blood, leaving its trace everywhere, even in my hair and my (picked or bitten) fingernails. There was the usual spring snowfall that year, killing the newborn lambs but letting the early crocuses survive. Everyone rejoiced that the War had ended, and it was enough to rejoice and not notice or think about the fact that the atom bomb had been born, it also given its own life and responsibility. My coming of age was lit by the mushroom fire that made shadows of all those caught in its brightness; a spectacular illumination of the ceremonies of death, "ashes to ashes, dust to dust."

On 28 August I "came of age" without a party but with some special presents given to me by my family—"things" showing that I was a part of the world, after all: I had a new wristlet watch, and a new pair of plaid pompommed slippers with fleecy lining.

That month, as a kind of surface skimming of all the feeling set to boil away until old age, I wrote and published my first story, "University Entrance" for which the *Listener* paid two guineas.

And now the year was passing quickly with the school inspector's crucial final visit soon to be faced. Inevitably, one bright morning of daffodils and flowering currant and a shine on the leaves of the bush along Queen's Drive where I walked to school each morning, of a hint of warm gold in the sharp lemon-coloured sunlight, I arrived at school to find that it was the Day of Inspection, and at midmorning the inspector and the headmaster came to my classroom. I greeted them amiably in my practised teacherly fashion, standing at the side of the room near the display of paintings while the inspector talked to the class before he settled down to watch my performance as a teacher. I waited. Then I said to the inspector, "Will you excuse me a moment please?"

"Certainly, Miss Frame."

I walked out of the room and out of the school, knowing I would never return.

1945: Two

At first, drunk with the sense of freedom, all worry gone, I simply enjoyed the sparkle of the morning. Then, reality, taking over, directed

my route down London Street, the street of doctors, and I chose a
doctor's rooms near the foot of the hill, and walked in to consult a Dr.
William Brown, as harmless and anonymous a name as I could find. I
explained to Dr. Brown that I was very tired and felt I needed a rest of a
few weeks. "I'm in my first year teaching," I said, bursting into tears.

Dr. Brown obligingly gave me a certificate for the headmaster, to
explain my temporary absence.

After posting the certificate in the box at the corner, I began three
weeks of pure freedom. I went to University classes, to music recitals. I
read and wrote. "I have three weeks' leave," I told my landlady who,
absorbed in her family, at once began to talk of when Bob would be
given his annual holiday. Kathleen and the children so much wanted to
go to Queenstown.

"I have so much work to do," I said, "that you probably won't see
much of me, for meals and so on, and I'll leave a note in plenty of time if
I'm not going to be in to dinner."

"You're so thoughtful," Mrs. T. said. "I'm lucky to have such a quiet
student. You wouldn't even know you were in the house, you're so
quiet!"

(A lovely girl, no trouble at all.)

At the end of my third week when school again loomed before me I
was forced to realize that suicide was my only escape. I had woven so
carefully, with such close texture, my visible layer of "no trouble at all, a
quiet student, always ready with a smile (if the decayed teeth could be
hidden), always happy," that even I could not break the thread of the
material of my deceit. I felt completely isolated. I knew no-one to confide in, to get advice from; and there was nowhere I could go. What, *in
all the world*, could I do to earn my living and still live as myself, as I
knew myself to be. Temporary masks, I knew, had their place; everyone
was wearing them, they were the human rage; but not masks cemented
in place until the wearer could not breathe and was eventually suffocated.

On Saturday evening I tidied my room, arranged my possessions, and
swallowing a packet of aspros, I lay down in bed to die, certain that I
would die. My desperation was extreme.

The next morning, near noon, I woke with a roaring in my ears and
my nose bleeding. My first thought was not even a thought, it was a
feeling of wonder and delight and thankfulness that I was alive. I staggered from my bed and looked at myself in the mirror; my face was a
dusky red. I began to vomit, again and again. At last my nose stopped
bleeding but the roaring in my ears continued. I returned to bed and
slept, waking at about ten o'clock that evening. My head still throbbed,
my ears rang. I hurried to the bathroom, turned on the tap, and vomited

again. Mrs. T. who had spent the weekend at Kathleen's and had been home about two hours, came to the door of her bedroom.

"Is everything alright?" she asked.

"Oh yes," I called. "Everything's fine. I've had a busy day." (No trouble, no trouble at all.)

"Kathleen and Bob are in the midst of it all," Mrs. T. said, not explaining but evidently pleased. "In the midst of it all." We said goodnight and I went to my room and slept.

The next morning, the dreaded Monday, I woke with only a slight headache.

"My leave has been extended," I told Mrs. T. "I have research to do." I was now so overjoyed that I was alive when my intention had been to die, that school seemed a minor problem. I explained to the headmaster, possibly over the telephone and later by writing, that I had been advised to give up teaching. I did not say that it was I who was giving myself this advice.

I found a job washing dishes in the student canteen. I tried to turn hopefully towards my future. I felt that I would never again choose to kill myself.

It happened that part of our Psychology course was the writing of a condensed autobiography. When I finished writing mine I wondered whether I should mention my attempt at suicide. I had now recovered; in a way, I was now rather proud for I could not understand how I had been so daring. I wrote at the end of my autobiography, "Perhaps I should mention a recent attempt at suicide . . ." describing what I had done but, to make the attempt more impressive, using the chemical term for aspirin—*acetylsalicylic acid.*

At the end of the class that week, John Forrest said to me, "I enjoyed your autobiography. All the others were so formal and serious but yours was so natural. You have a talent for writing."

I smiled within myself in a superior fashion. Talent for writing, indeed. Writing was going to be my profession!

"Oh I do write," I said. "I had a story in the *Listener* . . ."

He was impressed. Everyone had been impressed, saying, "The *Listener*'s hard to get into."

John Forrest looked at me closely. "You must have had trouble swallowing all those aspros?"

"Oh, I drank them with water," I said calmly.

That evening as I was preparing to go to bed, Mrs. T. answering a knock on the door called to me, "There are three men to see you. From the University."

I went to the door and there were Mr. Forrest, Mr. Prince and the Head of the Department who spoke first.

"Mr. Forrest tells me you haven't been feeling very well. We thought you might like to have a little rest."

"I'm fine thank you." (No trouble, no trouble at all.)

"We thought you might like to come with us down to the hospital—the Dunedin hospital—just for a few days' rest."

I felt suddenly free of all worry, cared for. I could think of nothing more desirable than lying in bed sheltered and warm, away from teaching and trying to earn money, and even away from Mrs. T. and her comfortable home; and away from my family and my worry over them; and from my increasing sense of isolation in a brave bright world of brave bright people; away from the War and being twenty-one and responsible; only not away from my decaying teeth.

"John will come to visit you," the Head of the Department said.

John! The use of first names, common among the young lecturers and their students but still a novelty to me, pleased and alarmed me. "That's kind of you, Mr. Forrest," I said primly.

And so I was admitted to the Dunedin hospital, to Colquhoun Ward which, I was soon shocked to find, was a *psychiatric ward*.

The doctors, Marples and Woodhouse, two young house surgeons, were questioning and kind. The nurse, Maitland Brown, a member of the Evangelical Union training to be a church missionary, talked to me of her hopes and dreams. I remember only one other patient in the bed next to mine, a strange woman who'd had an operation and kept denying it. I, brought up in a film star world of instant judgement on the looks of people, thought her repulsive and ugly with her red face, coarse skin, her small eyes with their ginger lashes and her thinning ginger hair. The dislike of her was general. I wonder now about the treatment of psychiatric and other patients who release, as if it were a chemical, an invitation to be disliked and who therefore have to fight (inducing further dislike and antagonism) for sympathy and fairness. When one day two ambulance men arrived to take the ugly patient to "another hospital," I learned that the "other hospital" was *Seacliff*. Seacliff, up the main trunk line, the hospital of grey stone, built like a castle. Seacliff where the loonies went. "You won't be going there, of course," Maitland said. "There's nothing wrong with you."

And after my three weeks in hospital for observation, that was indeed the verdict. Mother was asked to travel to Dunedin to take me home, and after a holiday at home I'd be good as new, they said.

Faced suddenly with the prospect of going home, I felt all the worries of the world returning, all the sadness of home and the everlasting toil of my parents and the weekly payments on the blankets and the new eiderdown from Calder Mackays, and the payments to the Starr-Bowkett Building Society or we'd be turned out of our house again; and the arguments at home, and mother's eternal peacemaker intervention; and my decaying teeth; and my inability to find a place in the Is-Land that existed by absorbing, faster and faster, each tomorrow. If only I had the world of poetry, openly, unashamedly, without having to hide it in secrecy within myself!

In my state of alarm about my future, when I saw mother standing there at the entrance to the ward, in her pitifully "best" clothes, her navy costume and her navy straw hat with the Bunch of artificial flowers at the brim; with a hint of fear in her eyes (for, after all, I had been in a "mental" ward) and her face transparently trying to adopt the expression *All is well,* I knew that home was the last place I wanted to be. I screamed at mother to go away. She left, murmuring her bewilderment, "But she's such a happy person, she's always been such a happy person."

I supposed, then, that I'd stay in hospital a few more days then be discharged, find a job in Dunedin, continue my University studies, renouncing teaching for ever. I did not realize that the alternative to going home was committal to Seacliff. No one thought to ask me why I had screamed at my mother, no one asked me what my plans were for the future. I became an instant third person, or even personless, as in the official note made about my mother's visit (reported to me many years later), "Refused to leave hospital."

I was taken (third-person people are also thrust into the passive mood) to Seacliff in a car that held two girls from Borstal and the police matron, Miss Churchill. . . .

1945: THREE

Writing an autobiography, usually thought of as a looking back, can just as well be a looking *across* or *through,* with the passing of time giving an X-ray quality to the eye. Also, time past is not time gone, it is time accumulated with the host resembling the character in the fairytale who was joined along the route by more and more characters none of whom could be separated from one another or from the host, with some stuck so fast that their presence caused physical pain. Add to the characters all the events, thoughts, feelings, and there is a mass of time, now a sticky mess, now a jewel bigger than the planets and the stars.

If I look through 1945 I see the skeleton of the year and shadowing it with both the shadow of death and of life, the atom bomb, the homely crocuses surviving in the late spring snow, birthdays and death-days, and two or three other events bringing those dreamed-of planets and stars within the personal world of myself and many others in New Zealand. The events were the publication of *Beyond the Palisade,* poems by a young student at the University, James K. Baxter, *A Book of New Zealand Verse* edited by Allen Curnow, and a collection of stories edited by Frank Sargeson, *Speaking for Ourselves.* As a child I had looked on New Zealand literature as the province of my mother, and when I longed for my surroundings—the hill, the pine plantations, 56 Eden Street, Oamaru, the foreshore and the sea to waken to imaginative life, all I could do was populate them with characters and dreams from the poetic world of another hemisphere and with my own imaginings. There was such a creation as New Zealand literature; I chose to ignore it, and indeed was scarcely aware of it. Few people spoke of it, as if it were a shameful disease. Only in the Modern Bookshop in Moray Place were there shelves of slim New Zealand books from small presses, and I had even bought some, and tried and failed to write poems like those in the books. James Baxter's poems with their worldwide assurance also intimidated me. The anthologies, however, were different: their force and variety gave me hope for my own writing while wakening in me an awareness of New Zealand as a place of writers who understood how I had felt when I imported J. C. Squire to describe my beloved South Island rivers, and though I read the poem again and again I had to be content with the Congo, Nile, Colorado, Niger, Indus, Zambesi: beautiful names but those of another world.

But here, in the anthology of New Zealand verse (they were still not brave enough to call it *poetry*) I could read in Allen Curnow's poems about Canterbury and the plains, about "dust and distance," about our land having its share of time and not having to borrow from a northern Shakespearian wallet. I could read, too, about the past, and absences, and objects which only we could experience, and substances haunting in their unique influence on our lives: the poem "Wild Iron" reads to me like part of a history of New Zealand and its people.

And there was Denis Glover using the names of our own rivers and places, and even writing about the magpies, perfectly recording their cries on a misty autumn morning. Each poet spoke in his and her own way and place, and there was Charles Brasch confiding in the sea as I had confided, without words, in the Clutha, "Speak for us, great sea."

The stories, too, overwhelmed me by the fact of their belonging. It was almost a feeling of having been an orphan who discovers that her parents are alive and living in the most desirable home—pages of prose and poetry.

Time confers privileges of arrangement and rearrangement undreamed of until it becomes Time Past. I have been writing of the memory of publication of stories and poems. In actual memory I am sitting talking to two Borstal girls, on the way to Seacliff Hospital where I shall be a committed patient.

1945: Four

The six weeks I spent at Seacliff Hospital in a world I'd never known among people whose existences I never thought possible, became for me a concentrated course in the horrors of insanity and the dwelling-place of those judged insane, separating me for ever from the former acceptable realities and assurances of everyday life. From my first moment there I knew that I could not turn back to my usual life or forget what I saw at Seacliff. I felt as if my life were overturned by this sudden division of people into "ordinary" people in the street, and these "secret" people whom few had seen or talked to but whom many spoke of with derision, laughter, fear. I saw people with their eyes staring like the eyes of hurricanes surrounded here by whirling unseen and unheard commotion contrasting strangely with the stillness. I grew to know and like my fellow patients. I was impressed and saddened by their—our—capacity to learn and adhere to and often relish the spoken and unspoken rules of institutional life, by the pride in the daily routine, shown by patients who had been in hospital for many years. There was a personal, geographical, even linguistic exclusiveness in this community of the insane who yet had no legal or personal external identity—no clothes of their own to wear, no handbags, purses, no possessions but a temporary bed to sleep in with a locker beside it, and a room to sit in and stare, called the *dayroom.* Many patients confined in other wards of Seacliff had no name, only a nickname, no past, no future, only an imprisoned Now, an eternal Is-Land without its accompanying horizons, foot or handhold, and even without its everchanging sky.

In my book *Faces in the Water* I have described in detail the surroundings and events in the several mental hospitals I experienced during the eight following years. I have also written factually of my own treatment and my thoughts about it. The fiction of the book lies in the portrayal of the central character, based on my life but given largely fictional thoughts and feelings, to create a picture of the sickness I saw around me. When one day a fellow patient, seeing workmen outside digging drains, said to me, "Look, they are digging our graves," I knew she believed this. Her words are an example of the words and behaviour I used to portray Istina Mavet. Even in my six weeks' stay I learned, as if I had entered a foreign land, much of the language and behaviour of the inhabitants of the land. Others also learned fast—the girls from Borstal were adept at livening their day by a "performance" based on example.

My previous community had been my family. In *To the Is-Land* I constantly use the first person plural—we, not I. My time as a student was an I-time. Now, as a Seacliff patient, I was again part of a group, yet more deeply alone, not even a creviced "I." I became "she," one of "them."

When I left Seacliff in December 1945, for a six-month probationary period, to return to a Willowglen summer, the shiningest time at Willowglen, I felt that I carried within me a momentous change brought about by my experience of being in a mental hospital. I looked at my family and I knew that they did not know what I had seen, that in different places throughout the country there were men and women and children locked, hidden away with nothing left but a nickname, with even the word *nick*name hinting at the presence of devils. I noticed that the behaviour of my family had changed in subtle ways related to my having been a patient in Seacliff where the loonies lived. Why do I use once again the metaphor with a spider? It seemed as if, having been in hospital, I had, like a spider, woven about me numerous threads which invisibly reached all those who "knew" and bound them to a paralysis of fixed poses and expressions and feelings that made me unhappy and lonely but gave me also a recognition of the power of having spun the web and the powerlessness of those trapped within it.

When I'd been home a week or two my family grew less apprehensive in my presence—the change showed in the lessening of fear in their eyes; who knows what I might do; I was a loony, wasn't I? Mother, characteristically, began to deny everything. I was a happy person, she said. There must have been some mistake. I found that everyone was pleased when I treated the matter as a joke, talking of amusing incidents at the "country estate," likening it to a hotel. I described the surroundings. "It's like a whole village," I said. "They have their own farm, their own cattle and pigs, and all the waste from the food goes into the pig tin. They have their vegetable garden, and their flowers, too. And the grounds are full of trees, and there's a magnolia tree near where the Superintendent lives."

It was easier to talk as if I were a child describing what I had seen and what adventures I'd had on my holiday.

I didn't tell them how I had peeped through the fence of a building called *Simla*, away upon the hill, where there were strange men in striped shirts and trousers and some without trousers, walking round and round in a paddock with the grass worn away; and how I'd seen a paddock of women, too, wearing the dark blue striped clothes; and how there was a cart, like a rickshaw, that passed every day by the ward, how it was full of coal and two men harnessed to the cart carried the coal, driven by one of the attendants; how, curious as ever, I had peered into a room that stank of urine and was full of children lying in cots, strange children, some of them babies, making strange noises; their faces wet with tears and snot; and I didn't say how there was a special section for the patients with tuberculosis, and how their dishes were boiled in a kerosene tin on the dining room fire, and the nurses spent some time in the small linen cupboard folding the cardboard to make the daily supply of boxes, like strawberry boxes, for the TB patients to spit in.

After Christmas it was suggested that perhaps a holiday would be "good" for me, and so June and I set out for two weeks in Picton, mother's old home town, where we spent the usual summer sandfly-bitten time travelling around the Sounds in launches, meeting relatives, hearing new details of family history, while I, strongly under the influence of my past year of listening to music, composed in my mind what I called my Picton Symphony in Green and Blue. My memory of the holiday is scattered—like seeds, I imagine, a handful eaten by summer-visiting birds migrating from winter memories, or by native birds that feed time-long on the memory, others not surviving, others grown into plants that cannot be recognized or named. I know that I took home the memory of those steep green oppressive hills, their bushclad slopes rising as inescapably close as neighbours.

Asked to describe the holiday, June and I told the family what we knew they wanted to hear, to try to make everyone happy. We had grown up, you see, in a thorough school, in this with our mother as teacher. And once again I began to prepare for another year in Dunedin.

I planned to find a "live-in" job, and to "take" Philosophy II, Logic and Ethics, but sit no examinations. I had been assured that although I sat no end-of-year Psychology examinations I would be granted a pass based on my year's work. Perhaps I neglected to fill in the correct forms: I discovered that I had been marked *Failed.* Failed!

In the meantime, at home, there was the problem of having my life savings of twenty pounds returned from the Public Trust Office who had taken charge of my affairs as I was officially insane. Once again my sisters and my brother and I "banded together" to try to assert our rights, with Isabel composing an earnest letter to the Public Trust Officer who replied that his confiscation of my "property" was in my own interests as I was officially insane and would not have legal rights until my "probation" period of six months had ended, and then only if the doctor declared my sanity.

Perhaps, then, I could be given a sickness benefit until I began working again?

My visit to the Seacliff doctor at the Oamaru hospital brought its own bewilderment, for the medical certificate stated: Nature of Illness; *Schizophrenia.*

At home I announced, half with pride, half with fear, "I've got *Shizzofreenier.*"

I searched through my Psychology book, the chapter on Abnormal Psychology, where I found no reference to *Schizophrenia,* only to a mental illness apparently afflicting only young people like myself—*dementia praecox,* described as a gradual deterioration of mind, with no cure. In the notes at the end of the chapter there was an explanation that *dementia praecox* was now known as *schizophrenia. Shizzophreenier.* A gradual deterioration of mind. Of mind and behaviour. What would happen to me? No cure. Gradual deterioration. I suffered from *shizzophreenier.* It seemed to spell my doom, as if I had emerged from a chrysalis, the natural human state, into another kind of creature, and even if there were parts of me that were familiar to human beings, my gradual deterioration would lead me further and further away, and in the end not even my family would know me.

In the last of the shining Willowglen summer these feelings of doom came only briefly as passing clouds block the sun. I knew that I was shy, inclined to be fearful, and even more so after my six weeks of being in hospital and seeing what I had seen around me, that I was absorbed in the world of imagination, but I also knew that I was totally present in the "real" world and whatever shadow lay over me, lay only in the writing on the medical certificate.

Towards the opening of the University year when I advertised for a live-in job in Dunedin, describing myself as a "research student," I received a reply from Mrs. B. of Playfair Street, Caversham, who kept a boardinghouse and cared for elderly women. I was to be a housemaid-waitress-nurse, with three pounds a week "all found," and afternoons free. Afternoons free. Time to write my stories and poems.

The Boardinghouse and the New World

Once again I travelled south by the slow Sunday train to Dunedin, stopping at every station, looking out from the old-fashioned carriage, tacked on for the few passengers, at the spiralling links of tarpaulin-covered trucks. As usual there were unloadings, loadings, jolts as the trucks were removed, long periods when the carriage at the end seemed to stand alone in the midst of paddocks of gum trees, tussock, manuka scrub, *matagouri,* swamp, sheep, derelict houses, as if it made an excursion into a nowhere that was also a yesterday, filled with peace and sadness. I looked out of the old-fashioned push-up window (as opposed to the newer wind-up windows of the express trains) and I felt a force that could only have been the force of love drawing me towards the land where no-one appeared to be home. I felt a new sense of responsibility to everything and everyone because every moment I carried the memory of the people I had seen in Seacliff, and this knowing even changed the landscape and my feeling towards it.

When the train stopped at Seacliff Station I saw the few *parole* patients waiting on the platform to watch the train go by. I *knew*, you see. Inwardly I kept describing myself in the words that I knew relatives and friends now used, "She's been in Seacliff. They had to take her to Seacliff." And I thought of the horror in mother's voice when, years ago, the doctor had suggested that Bruddie should go there, and mother had replied, "Never. Never. No child of mine will ever go to that place." But I was a child of hers, wasn't I? Wasn't I? And she had signed papers to send me there. I felt uneasy, trying to divide out portions of family love to discover how much was mine.

I looked around the carriage at the "ordinary people." Did they know where I had been? If they knew, would they look at me and then turn away quickly to hide the fear and fascinated curiosity as if they were tasting an experience which—thank God, they thought—they would never know but about which they wondered furiously, fearfully? If they knew about me, would they try to find a sign, as I had done when I, too, used to stare at the "loonies" on Seacliff Station.

Well, I thought, the signs were often secret but I knew them now, I was an experienced observer, I had visited the foreign land.

Also, I remembered with dread, they say I have *shizzofreenier.* A disease without hope.

The wheels of the train, however, which all my railway life had said Kaitangata, Kaitangata, Kaitangata, remained uninfluenced by my strange disease: their iron on iron said, obstinately, *Kaitangata, Kaitangata, Kaitangata.*

The train arrived at Dunedin Station. I felt quite alone, as if I belonged nowhere. All those marvellously belonging days at Training College when we sang "The Deacon went Down," and talked knowledgeably of Party, and crit lessons, and days of control; the English and French lectures, the year of teaching children I had grown to love, had vanished as if they had never been, an impression deepened by the fact that since my disappearance to Seacliff there'd been no word from College or school or University, except a letter from my friend Sheila and a note from John Forrest to invite me to have "little talks" with him during the coming year. I clung to the idea of having someone to talk to, and relished the bonus that the someone was an interesting young man.

I was taking my new status seriously. If the world of the mad were the world where I now officially belonged (lifelong disease, no cure, no hope) then I would use it to survive, I would excel in it. I sensed that it did not exclude my being a poet. It was therefore with a feeling of loneliness but with a new self-possession, unlike my first fearful arrival in the big city of

Dunedin, that I took a taxi to Playfair Street, Caversham, in the heart of the country of the Industrial School.

South Dunedin—Kensington, Caversham, St. Kilda—was a poor community where lives were spent in the eternal "toil" with the low-lying landscape reflecting the lives, as if effort and hope were here washed away in the recurring floods while the dwellers on the hill sub-urbs prospered. I had taught in Caversham school and at Kensington in the school "under the railway bridge," and I had seen the poverty, the rows of decaying houses washed biscuit-colour by time and the rain and the floods; and the pale children lank-haired, damp-looking, as if they emerged each day from the tide.

My memory of the boarders and the landlord and landlady and their child is momentary, like a hastily sketched scene in black and white giving only the outline of each person with the hair growing like grass out of their skull. They still hold, however, an invisible bowl brimful of feeling, and it is their feeling unspoken and spoken, that I remember most vividly. They were unhappy anxious people trying desperately to pretend they were happy, and seizing occasions of joy to recount, each to the others, at mealtimes, as a way of contributing to the possibility of happiness. The men usually were employed at the Railway Workshops, the women in the factories—the chocolate or jam factory—or a branch of the woollen mill. One young man lost his job every few weeks, found another, lost that, and at night, at dinner, the others talked about his success or failure, explaining, excusing, condemning. They criticized each other, poked fun, pounced swiftly on the unconforming. I remem-ber the landlady's husband only as a tall pale stooped man who carried firewood from the shed into the sitting room where everyone gathered in the evening, the women with their knitting, the men with playing cards or their sporting newspapers; and sometimes one of the boarders who was acknowledged to have "failed" in life (as opposed to the others who still had valid excuses and reasons), a thin woman in her middle thirties, without a husband or lover (the basis for her being judged a failure) played the yellowing keys of the piano while the middle-aged bachelor, a salesman, plump, popular ("he's always the same, you know where you are with him") sang the current favourite song,

> Beyond the sunset
> to blissful morning . . .

From the moment of my arrival I explained that I'd be very busy out of working hours and so would prefer at times to have my meals in my room. I was a student, engaged in private research, I said—I with my ready smile (hoping that I concealed my badly decayed teeth), sympathetic voice, no obvious physical deformities; and my upstanding mass of frizzy ginger hair. My duties were to prepare and serve breakfast, to clean the house, and to attend to the four elderly women who lived, bedridden, each in a corner bed, in the large front room. I washed them, helped to turn them or arrange the rubber ring beneath their gaunt bodies where the skin hung in folds like chicken skin with bumps where feathers might once have been. I rubbed methylated spirits on their bedsores, and powdered their bodies. I fed them, sometimes with the aid of a white china feeding-cup. I helped them use the wooden commode or arranged a bedpan beneath their drooping buttocks. . . .

I found that I had gentleness and everlasting patience with the sick and the old. I enjoyed waiting on people, attending to their comfort, doing as they asked, bringing the food they ordered. I had no impatience, irritation, anger, to subdue: I seemed to be a "born" servant. The knowledge frightened me: I was behaving as my mother had done all the years I had known her, and I was enjoying my new role: I could erase myself completely and live only through the feelings of others.

My bedroom, once a linen cupboard, was small with shelves along one wall, and a narrow bed against the other wall. The view from the one small window was "pure Caversham"—dreary grey stone buildings with a glimpse of the tall chimneys of *Parkside*, the home for the aged, resembling my idea of a nineteenth-century English workhouse. When I finished my morning's work I'd go to my room and sit on my bed and write my stories and poems, for just as when I had been a child there was a time for writing and the knowledge that other children were writing their poems, now I was aware of writers in my own country. My inspiration for my stories came partly from my reading of William Saroyan, and my unthinking delight, "I can do that too." And besides the excitement of being in a land that was coming alive with its own writing, *speaking for itself*, with many of the writers returning from the War, bringing their urgency of experience, I felt the inspiration of my own newly acquired treasure—my stay of six weeks in a mental hospital, what I had felt and seen, and what I had become, my official status of schizophrenia. And while I fed the guests at the boardinghouse, they fed me from that invisible bowl of their feelings.

My life away from the boardinghouse consisted of evening lectures on Logic and Ethics, and weekly "talks" with John Forrest in a small room on the top storey of the University building known as the Professors' House. I also spent time in the Dunedin Public Library where I read case histories of patients suffering from schizophrenia, with my alarm and sense of doom increasing as I tried to imagine what would happen to me. That the idea of my suffering from schizophrenia seemed to me so unreal, only increased my confusion when I learned that one of the symptoms was "things seeming unreal." There was no escape.

My consolation was my "talks" with John Forrest as he was my link with the world I had known, and because I wanted these "talks" to continue, I built up a formidable schizophrenic repertoire: I'd lie on the couch, while the young handsome John Forrest, glistening with newly-applied Freud, took note of what I said and did, and suddenly I'd put a glazed look in my eye, as if I were in a dream, and begin to relate a fantasy as if I experienced it as a reality. I'd describe it in detail while John Forrest listened, impressed, serious. Usually I incorporated in the fantasy details of my reading on schizoprenia.

"You are suffering from a loneliness of the inner soul," John said one day. For all his newness and eagerness to practise psychology and his apparent willingness to believe everything I said, his depth of perception about "inner loneliness" was a mark of his special ability. He next made the remark which was to direct my behaviour and reason for many years.

"When I think of you," he said, "I think of Van Gogh, of Hugo Wolf . . ."

I, in my ignorance, knowing little of either Van Gogh or Hugo Wolf, and once again turning to books for my information, discovered that Hugo Wolf "d. insane," and that Van Gogh "shot himself in despair at his condition." I read that Schumann, too, "suffered serious deterioration in mental health." All three were named as *schizophrenic*, with their artistic ability apparently the pearl of their schizophrenia. Great artists, visionaries . . .

My place was set, then, at the terrible feast. I had no illusions about "greatness" but at least I could endow my work and—when necessary—my life with the mark of my schizophrenia.

When John Forrest learned that I was writing poems and stories, he was delighted. He suggested that as I wrote each I should give it to him to keep, and I, therefore, began to bring him my stories and poems. I kept "pure schizophrenia" for the poems where it was most at home, and I looked forward to John Forrest's praise of my efforts; and when I had saved enough money to buy a secondhand Barlock 20 typewriter and type my work using, at first, one or two fingers, I felt that I possessed all in the world that I desired—a place to write, time to write, enough money to live on, someone to talk to or at least someone to try to impress, for most of my thoughts I kept to myself, and a disease interesting enough to be my ally in my artistic efforts and to ensure, provided I maintained the correct symptoms, that I had the continued audience of John Forrest. I was playing a game, half in earnest, to win the attention of a likeable young man whose interest was psychology and art; yet in spite of my pretence at hallucinations and visions I was growing increasingly fearful of the likeness between some of my true feelings and those thought of as belonging to sufferers from schizophrenia. I was very shy, within myself. I preferred to write, to explore the world of imagination, rather than to mix with others. I was never withdrawn from the "real" world, however, although I was convincingly able to "use" this symptom when the occasion required.

I was not yet aware of sexual feelings although I no doubt experienced them, innocently not recognizing them. Then one day when I was exploring a case history of schizophrenia, I read of a woman who was afraid (as I was, although I also was deterred by lack of money) to visit the dentist, and on exploration in the Freudian manner, it was discovered that *fear of the dentist* was common in those suffering from schizophrenia, *fear of the dentist* being interpreted as *guilt over masturbation* which was said to be one of the causes and a continued symptom of schizophrenia!

I pondered this: I was certainly afraid of visiting the dentist as I knew that my teeth were now beyond repair (the general opinion in New Zealand then was that natural teeth were best removed anyway, it was a kind of colonial squandering, like the needless uprooting of forests). As for masturbation, it was a word of which I was ignorant and an act of which I was innocent. This new fact, however, made me curious enough to investigate both meaning and deed, for surely I must know if it were to be thought one of the causes of my disease! It happened that both my sisters and I, feeling we needed further sex education and having no-one to give it to us in its theory, sent for a widely advertised book which arrived in its plain wrapper: *Meeting and Mating.* Everyone who was *educated,* with a wholesome attitude to sex and marriage, was reading *Meeting and Mating,* and recommending it. We found in it details we had searched for in vain in mother's *Ladies' Handbook of Home Treatment* with its chapter "God's Great Out-of-Doors" intended to be read by women about to marry. It referred also to masturbation, describing it in detail, explaining how it was acceptable in both men and women with no need for guilt.

And of course I tried it. And childhood was suddenly long long ago, for I *knew,* and I couldn't return to the state of not knowing, and the remaining curiosity was, How might it be if one never knew? A few weeks later I said to John Forrest, "It's awful, I can't tell you, for years I've been guilty about it. It's . . . it's . . ."

He waited expectantly.

"It's masturbation, worry over masturbation . . ."

"It usually is," he said, and began to explain, as our book had explained, how it was "perfectly alright, everyone did it."

The pattern of that "little talk" was so perfect that I imagine (now) a fleeting triumph passing over John Forrest's Freud-intensive face: here was a textbook schizophrenic.

I continued to fear that I might once again be left with no one to talk to, that is, in a "normal" state of nearness to mental breakdown, for I was on the usual adolescent path of worry and wondering how to "cope" with everyday living; yet, strangely, in order to lessen my anxiety, I found myself forced to choose a more distinctly signposted path where my journey drew more attention and so, I found, drew more practical help. I don't think it occurred to me that people might be willing to help me if I maintained my ordinary timid smiling self. My life so far had trained me to perform, to gain approval by answering questions in examinations, solving problems, exhibiting flashes of "cleverness" and "difference." I was usually ashamed of my clothing. I was baffled by my fuzzy hair and the attention it drew, and the urgency with which people advised that I have it "straightened," as if it posed a threat. I was not fluent in conversation, nor witty, nor brilliant. I was an ordinary grey-feathered bird that spent its life flashing one or two crimson feathers at the world, adapting the feathers to suit the time of life. In my childhood I had displayed number riddles, memorizing long passages of verse and prose, mathematical answers; now, to *suit* the occasion, I wore my schizophrenic fancy dress.

During 1946, when my "probationary" period was over, I was declared sane; I felt a twinge of loss, very slight, for I had written a collection of stories and poems which John Forrest had shown to Denis Glover of the Caxton Press who was interested in publishing the stories in a book, with the poems perhaps following. I felt I had begun my career as a writer.

Then, towards the end of the year, John Forrest announced that he had applied for work as a psychologist in the USA where he hoped to get his Ph.D. He would be leaving New Zealand early in 1947. He suggested that if I needed someone to talk to, he could recommend his friend in Christchurch, Mrs. R., with whom he had spoken about me, he said, adding that she, being of an artistic nature, was interested in my "case."

"I'll find a job in Christchurch and perhaps take a course at the Canterbury University," I said, very calmly as I saw my secure schizophrenic world of "little talks" beginning to fall apart, leaving me alone in an alien city. I wondered why I had ever thought that I belonged in Dunedin or how I would ever belong in Christchurch. The Caxton Press was in Christchurch, and the book they were planning some time to publish—perhaps the book would be like a relation, living near by, and I'd not be isolated?

I wondered where I would go. I knew I could not stay beyond one or two months at home, without being overtaken by unhappiness at the everlasting struggle of everyone there—for money, or love or power or an ocean of peace. There was always a hotel or boardinghouse to give me work, room and board, but why did 1946 need to end?

I stood on the cliff trying to catch at the wings of 1946 as they beat at the salt-strewn earth and grass in preparation for their flight forward into yesterday. In reality, I said goodbye to all at Playfair Street, Caversham—the four old ladies and the boarders with their secret failures and shames and small shared happinesses, and my landlord and landlady and their small child of four who still didn't speak although everyone pretended not to notice; and I left with my brand-new reference should I look for work in Christchurch, "Polite to the guests at all times, industrious, a pleasure . . ." and a tiny black kitten supposedly male but actually female which I named affectionately, Sigmund, changed later to Sigmunde, known as Siggy; and once again, a railway person bound forever to the dock and the wild sweet peas and "the rust on the railway lines," I travelled north on the Express and as the train approached Oamaru, before the Gardens, I caught a quick glimpse, looking left, of Willowglen putting on its gloss for the summer.

ANNE FRANK
(1929–1945)

Anne Frank's mother and father were Jews who left Germany in 1933, when Hitler came to power, and sought refuge in Amsterdam with their two daughters, Anne and her older sister, Margot. Otto Frank reestablished his pharmaceuticals company, and the family settled into its new home. Then the Germans occupied the Netherlands and began interning Jews. In July 1942, rather than leave or allow themselves to be captured, the Franks went into hiding in the building that housed Mr. Frank's offices. They were joined by another family, the Van Daans, who included a teenaged boy named Peter, and later by a dentist named Dussel. Aiding them were Mr. Frank's employees, Miep Van Santen, Elli Vossen, and the men who took over the business, Kraler and Koophuis.

Perhaps the most widely read diary of all time, Anne Frank's account of her two years in that Amsterdam attic hiding from the Nazis is a classic of adolescence as well as a historical document. She was thirteen when they sought out the "secret annexe," not quite sixteen when she died at Bergen-Belsen. Her diary, in the form of letters to "Kitty," captures some typical torments of female adolescence—competition with her sister, disappointment in her mother, frustrated love for her father—and renders the characters of her fellow inmates, with the novelistic skill of a young Jane Austen.

After the annex had been raided and its occupants removed, Elli and Miep found pages of Anne's diary on the floor where they had been thrown by a Gestapo man in search of more obviously valuable stuff. Anne's father, the only member of his family to survive the war, had the diary published in its original Dutch in 1947 under the title *Het Achterhuis* (The House Behind), which is translated in the English text as the "Secret Annexe." The American edition, given the title *The Diary of a Young Girl*, appeared in 1952, followed by Broadway and Hollywood versions, in 1955 and 1959, which made Anne Frank the best-known victim of the Holocaust and arguably the one with the greatest impact on posterity.

For another diary written during the Nazi occupation by a young Jewish woman in the Netherlands, see Etty Hillesum, *An Interrupted Life.* For a memoir by a German Jewish girl who got away, escaping with her family to England and then seeking refuge in the country from the Nazi bombardment of London, see Eva Figes, *Little Eden: A Child at War.*

FROM *Diary*

Dear Kitty,

I had to stop yesterday, long before I'd finished. I just must tell you about another quarrel, but before I start on that, something else.

Why do grownups quarrel so easily, so much, and over the most idiotic things? Up till now I thought that only children squabbled and that that wore off as you grew up. Of course, there is sometimes a real reason for a quarrel, but this is just plain bickering. I suppose I should get used to it. But I can't nor do I think I shall, as long as I am the subject of nearly every discussion (they use the word "discussion" instead of quarrel). Nothing, I repeat, nothing about me is right; my general appearance, my character, my manners are discussed from A to Z. I'm expected (by order) to simply swallow all the harsh words and shouts in silence and I am not used to this. In fact, I can't! I'm not going to take all these insults lying down, I'll show them that Anne Frank wasn't born yesterday. Then they'll be surprised and perhaps they'll keep their mouths shut when I let them see that I am going to start educating them. Shall I take up that attitude? Plain barbarism! I'm simply amazed again and again over their awful manners and especially . . . stupidity (Mrs. Van Daan's), but as soon as I get used to this—and it won't be long—then I'll give them some of their own back, and no half measures. Then they'll change their tune!

Am I really so bad-mannered, conceited, headstrong, pushing, stupid, lazy, etc., etc., as they all say? Oh, of course not. I have my faults, just like everyone else, I know that, but they thoroughly exaggerate everything.

Kitty, if only you knew how I sometimes boil under so many gibes and jeers. And I don't know how long I shall be able to stifle my rage. I shall just blow up one day.

Still, no more of this, I've bored you long enough with all these quarrels. But I simply must tell you of one highly interesting discussion at table. Somehow or other, we got on to the subject of Pim's (Daddy's nickname) extreme modesty. Even the most stupid people have to admit this about Daddy. Suddenly Mrs. Van Daan says, "I too, have an unassuming nature, more so than my husband."

Did you ever! This sentence in itself shows quite clearly how thoroughly forward and pushing she is! Mr. Van Daan thought he ought to give an explanation regarding the reference to himself. "I don't wish to be modest—in my experience it does not pay." Then to me: "Take my advice, Anne, don't be too unassuming, it doesn't get you anywhere."

Mummy agreed with this too. But Mrs. Van Daan had to add, as always, her ideas on the subject. Her next remark was addressed to Mummy and Daddy. "You have a strange outlook on life. Fancy saying such a thing to Anne; it was very different when I was young. And I feel sure that it still is, except in your modern home." This was a direct hit at the way Mummy brings up her daughters.

Mrs. Van Daan was scarlet by this time. Mummy calm and cool as a cucumber. People who blush get so hot and excited, it is quite a handicap in such a situation. Mummy, still entirely unruffled, but anxious to close the conversation as soon as possible, thought for a second and then said: "I find, too, Mrs. Van Daan, that one gets on better in life if one is not over-modest. My husband, now, and Margot, and Peter are exceptionally modest, whereas your husband, Anne, you, and I, though not exactly the opposite, don't allow ourselves to be completely pushed to one side." Mrs. Van Daan: "But, Mrs. Frank, I don't understand you; I'm so very modest and retiring, how can you think of calling me anything else?" Mummy: "I did not say you were exactly forward, but no one could say you had a retiring disposition." Mrs. Van Daan: "Let us get this matter cleared up, once and for all. I'd like to know in what way I am pushing? I know one thing, if I didn't look after myself, I'd soon be starving."

This absurd remark in self-defense just made Mummy rock with laughter. That irritated Mrs. Van Daan, who added a string of German-Dutch, Dutch-German expressions, until she became completely tongue-tied; then she rose from her chair and was about to leave the room.

Suddenly her eye fell on me. You should have seen her. Unfortunately, at the very moment that she turned round, I was shaking my head sorrowfully—not on purpose, but quite involuntarily, for I had been following the whole conversation so closely.

Mrs. Van Daan turned round and began to reel off a lot of harsh German, common, and ill-mannered, just like a coarse, red-faced fishwife—it was a marvelous sight. If I could draw, I'd have liked to catch her like this; it was a scream, such a stupid, foolish little person!

Anyhow, I've learned one thing now. You only really get to know people when you've had a jolly good row with them. Then and then only can you judge their true characters!

Yours, Anne

Tuesday, 29 September, 1942

Dear Kitty,

Extraordinary things can happen to people who go into hiding. Just imagine, as there is no bath, we use a washtub and because there is hot water in the office (by which I always mean the whole of the lower floor) all seven of us take it in turns to make use of this great luxury.

But because we are all so different and some are more modest than others, each member of the family has found his own place for carrying out the performance. Peter uses the kitchen in spite of its glass door. When he is going to have a bath, he goes to each one of us in turn and tells us that we must not walk past the kitchen for half an hour. He seems to think this is sufficient. Mr. Van Daan goes right upstairs; to him it is worth the bother of carrying hot water all that way, so as to have the seclusion of his own room. Mrs. Van Daan simply doesn't bathe at all at present; she is waiting to see which is the best place. Daddy has his bath in the private office, Mummy behind a fire guard in the kitchen; Margot and I have chosen the front office for our scrub. The curtains there are drawn on Saturday afternoons, so we wash ourselves in semi-darkness.

However, I don't like this place any longer, and since last week I've been on the lookout for more comfortable quarters. Peter gave me an idea and that was to try the large office W.C. There I can sit down, have the light on, lock the door, pour my own bath water away, and I'm safe from prying eyes.

I tried my beautiful bathroom on Sunday for the first time and although it sounds mad, I think it is the best place of all. Last week the plumber was at work downstairs to move the drains and water pipes from the office W.C. to the passage. This change is a precaution against frozen pipes, in case we should have a cold winter. The plumber's visit was far from pleasant for us. Not only were we unable to draw water the whole day, but we could not go to the W.C. either. Now it is rather indecent to tell you what we did to overcome this difficulty, however, I'm not such a prude that I can't talk about these things.

The day we arrived here, Daddy and I improvised a pottie for ourselves; not having a better receptacle, we sacrificed a glass preserving jar for this purpose. During the plumber's visit, nature's offerings were deposited in these jars in the sitting room during the day. I don't think this was nearly as bad as having to sit still and not talk the whole day. You can't imagine what a trial that was for "Miss Quack-Quack." I have to whisper on ordinary days; but not being able to speak or move was ten times worse. After being flattened by three days of continuous sitting, my bottom was very stiff and painful. Some exercises at bedtime helped.

Yours, Anne

Thursday, 1 October, 1942

Dear Kitty,

I got a terrible shock yesterday. Suddenly at eight o'clock the bell rang loudly. Of course, I thought that someone had come; you'll guess who I mean. But I calmed down a bit when everyone said it must be some urchins or perhaps the postman.

The days are becoming very quiet here. Lewin, a small Jewish chemist and dispenser, works for Mr. Kraler in the kitchen. He knows the whole building well and therefore we are always afraid that he'll take it into his head to have a peep in the old laboratory. We are as quiet as mice. Who, three months ago, would ever have guessed that quicksilver Anne would have to sit still for hours—and, what's more, could?

The twenty-ninth was Mrs. Van Daan's birthday. Although it could not be celebrated in a big way, we managed a little party in her honor, with a specially nice meal, and she received some small presents and flowers. Red carnations from her husband; that seems to be a family tradition. To pause for a moment on the subject of Mrs. Van Daan, I must tell you that her attempts to flirt with Daddy are a source of continual irritation for me. She strokes his face and hair, pulls her skirt right up, and makes so-called witty remarks, trying in this way to attract Pim's attention. Pim, thank goodness, doesn't find her either attractive or funny, so he doesn't play ball. Mummy doesn't behave like that with Mr. Van Daan, I've said that to Mrs. Van Daan's face.

Now and then Peter comes out of his shell and can be quite funny. We have one thing in common, from which everyone usually gets a lot of amusement: we both love dressing up. He appeared in one of Mrs. Van Daan's very narrow dresses and I put on his suit. He wore a hat and I a cap. The grownups were doubled up with laughter and we enjoyed ourselves as much as they did. Elli has bought new skirts for Margot and me at Bijenkorf's. The material is rotten, just like sacking, and they cost 24.00 florins and 7.50 florins respectively. What a difference compared with before the war!

Another nice thing I've been keeping up my sleeve. Elli has written to some secretarial school or other and ordered a correspondence course in shorthand for Margot, Peter, and me. You wait and see what perfect experts we shall be by next year. In any case it's extremely important to be able to write in a code.

Yours, Anne

Saturday, 3 October, 1942

Dear Kitty,

There was another dust-up yesterday. Mummy kicked up a frightful row and told Daddy just what she thought of me. Then she had an awful fit of tears so, of course, off I went too; and I'd got such an awful headache anyway. Finally I told Daddy that I'm much more fond of him than Mummy, to which he replied that I'd get over that. But I don't believe it. I have to simply force myself to stay calm with her. Daddy wishes that I would sometimes volunteer to help Mummy, when she doesn't feel well or has a headache; but I shan't. I am working hard at my French and am now reading *La Belle Nivernaise*.

Yours, Anne

Friday, 9 October, 1942

Dear Kitty,

I've only got dismal and depressing news for you today. Our many Jewish friends are being taken away by the dozen. These people are treated by the Gestapo without a shred of decency, being loaded into cattle trucks and sent to Westerbork, the big Jewish camp in Drente. Westerbork sounds terrible: only one washing cubicle for a hundred people and not nearly enough lavatories. There is no separate accommodations. Men, women, and children all sleep together. One hears of frightful immorality because of this; and a lot of the women, and even girls, who stay there any length of time are expecting babies.

It is impossible to escape; most of the people in the camp are branded as inmates by their shaven heads and many also by their Jewish appearance.

If it is as bad as this in Holland whatever will it be like in the distant and barbarous regions they are sent to? We assume that most of them are murdered. The English radio speaks of their being gassed.

Perhaps that is the quickest way to die. I feel terribly upset. I couldn't tear myself away while Miep told these dreadful stories; and she herself was equally wound up for that matter. Just recently for instance, a poor old crippled Jewess was sitting on her doorstep; she had been told to wait there by the Gestapo, who had gone to fetch a car to take her away. The poor old thing was terrified by the guns that were shooting at English planes overhead, and by the glaring beams of the searchlights. But Miep did not dare take her in; no one would undergo such a risk. The Germans strike without the slightest mercy. Elli too is very quiet: her boy friend has got to go to Germany. She is afraid that the airmen who fly over her home will drop their bombs, often weighing a million kilos, on Dirk's head. Jokes such as "he's not likely to get a million" and "it only takes one bomb" are in rather bad taste. Dirk is certainly not the only one who has to go: trainloads of boys leave daily. If they stop at a small station en route, sometimes some of them manage to get out unnoticed and escape; perhaps a few manage it. This, however, is not the end of my bad news. Have you ever heard of hostages? That's the latest thing in penalties for sabotage. Can you imagine anything so dreadful?

Prominent citizens—innocent people—are thrown into prison to await their fate. If the saboteur can't be traced, the Gestapo simply puts about five hostages against the wall. Announcements of their deaths appear in the papers frequently. These outrages are described as "fatal accidents." Nice people, the Germans! To think that I was once one of them too! No, Hitler took away our nationality long ago. In fact, Germans and Jews are the greatest enemies in the world.

Yours, Anne

Friday, 16 October, 1942

Dear Kitty,

I'm terribly busy. I've just translated a chapter out of *La Belle Nivernaise* and made notes of new words. Then a perfectly foul math problem and three pages of French grammar. I flatly refuse to do these math problems every day. Daddy agrees that they're vile. I'm almost better at them than he is, though neither of us are much good and we often have to fetch Margot. I'm the furthest on of the three of us in shorthand.

Yesterday I finished *The Assault.* It's quite amusing, but doesn't touch *Joop ter Heul.* As a matter of fact, I think Cissy van Marxveldt is a first-rate writer. I shall definitely let my children read her books. Mummy, Margot, and I are as thick as thieves again. It's really much better. Margot and I got in the same bed together last evening, it was a frightful squash, but that was just the fun of it. She asked if she could read my diary. I said "Yes—at least, bits of it"; and then I asked if I could read hers and she said "Yes." Then we got on to the subject of the future. I asked her what she wanted to be. But she wouldn't say and made a great secret of it. I gathered something about teaching; I'm not sure if I'm right, but I think so. Really, I shouldn't be so curious!

This morning I was lying on Peter's bed, having chased him off at first. He was furious with me, not that I cared very much. He might be a bit more friendly with me for once; after all I did give him an apple yesterday.

I asked Margot if she thought I was very ugly. She said that I was quite attractive and that I had nice eyes. Rather vague, don't you think?

Till next time,

Yours, Anne

Tuesday, 20 October, 1942

Dear Kitty,

My hand still shakes, although it's two hours since we had the shock. I should explain that there are five fire extinguishers in the house. We knew that someone was coming to fill them, but no one had warned us when the carpenter, or whatever you call him, was coming.

The result was that we weren't making any attempt to keep quiet, until I heard hammering outside on the landing opposite our cupboard door. I thought of the carpenter at once and warned Elli, who was having a meal with us, that she shouldn't go downstairs. Daddy and I posted ourselves at the door so as to hear when the man left. After he'd been working for a quarter of an hour, he laid his hammer and tools down on top of our cupboard (as we thought) and knocked at our door. We turned absolutely white. Perhaps he had heard something after all and wanted to investigate our secret den. It seemed like it. The knocking, pulling, pushing, and wrenching went on. I nearly fainted at the thought that this utter stranger might discover our beautiful secret hiding place. And just as I thought my last hour was at hand, I heard Mr. Koophuis say, "Open the door, it's only me." We opened it immediately. The hook that holds the cupboard, which can be undone by people who know the secret, had got jammed. That was why no one had been able to warn us about the carpenter. The man had now gone downstairs and Koophuis wanted to fetch Elli, but couldn't open the cupboard again. It was a great relief to me, I can tell you. In my imagination the man who I thought was trying to get in had been growing and growing in size until in the end he appeared to be a giant and the greatest fascist that ever walked the earth.

Well! Well! Luckily everything was okay this time. Meanwhile we had great fun on Monday. Miep and Henk spent the night here. Margot and I went in Mummy and Daddy's room for the night, so that the Van Santens could have our room. The meal tasted divine. There was one small interruption. Daddy's lamp blew a fuse, and all of a sudden we were sitting in darkness. What was to be done? There was some fuse wire in the house, but the fuse box is right at the very back of the dark storeroom—not such a nice job after dark. Still the men ventured forth and after ten minutes we were able to put the candles away again.

I got up early this morning. Henk had to leave at half past eight. After a cozy breakfast Miep went downstairs. It was pouring and she was glad not to have to cycle to the office. Next week Elli is coming to stay for a night.

Yours, Anne

Thursday, 29 October, 1942

Dear Kitty,

I am awfully worried, Daddy is ill. He has a high temperature and a red rash, it looks like measles. Think of it, we can't even call a doctor! Mummy is letting him have a good sweat. Perhaps that will send his temperature down.

This morning Miep told us that all the furniture has been removed from the Van Daan's home. We haven't told Mrs. Van Daan yet. She's such a bundle of nerves already, and we don't feel like listening to another moan over all the lovely china and beautiful chairs that she left at home. *We* had to leave almost all our nice things behind; so what's the good of grumbling about it now?

I'm allowed to read more grown-up books lately. I'm now reading *Eva's Youth* by Nico van Suchtelen. I can't see much difference between this and the schoolgirl love stories. It is true there are bits about women selling themselves to unknown men in back streets. They ask a packet of money for it. I'd die of shame if anything like that happened to me. Also it says that Eva has a monthly period. Oh, I'm so longing to have it too; it seems so important.

Daddy has brought the plays of Goethe and Schiller from the big cupboard. He is going to read to me every evening. We've started with *Don Carlos.*

Following Daddy's good example, Mummy has pressed her prayer book into my hand. For decency's sake I read some of the prayers in German; they are certainly beautiful but they don't convey much to me. Why does she force me to be pious, just to oblige her?

Tomorrow we are going to light the fire for the first time. I expect we shall be suffocated with smoke. The chimney hasn't been swept for ages, let's hope the thing draws.

Yours, Anne

Saturday, 7 November, 1942

Dear Kitty,

Mummy is frightfully irritable and that always seems to herald unpleasantness for me. Is it just a chance that Daddy and Mummy never rebuke Margot and that they always drop on me for everything? Yesterday evening, for instance: Margot was reading a book with lovely drawings in it; she got up and went upstairs, put the book down ready to go on with it later. I wasn't doing anything, so picked up the book and started looking at the pictures. Margot came back, saw "her" book in my hands, wrinkled her forehead and asked for the book back. Just because I wanted to look a little further on, Margot got more and more angry. Then Mummy joined in: "Give the book to Margot; she was reading it," she said. Daddy came into the room. He didn't even know what it was all about, but saw the injured look on Margot's face and promptly dropped on me: "I'd like to see what you'd say if Margot ever started looking at one of your books!" I gave way at once, laid the book down, and left the room—offended, as they thought. It so happened I was neither offended nor cross, just miserable. It wasn't right of Daddy to judge without knowing what the squabble was about. I would have given Margot the book myself, and much more quickly, if Mummy and Daddy hadn't interfered. They took Margot's part at once, as though she were the victim of some great injustice.

It's obvious that Mummy would stick up for Margot; she and Margot always do back each other up. I'm so used to that that I'm utterly indifferent to both Mummy's jawing and Margot's moods.

I love them; but only because they are Mummy and Margot. With Daddy it's different. If he holds Margot up as an example, approves of what she does, praises and caresses her, then something gnaws at me inside, because I adore Daddy. He is the one I look up to. I don't love anyone in the world but him. He doesn't notice that he treats Margot differently from me. Now Margot is just the prettiest, sweetest, most beautiful girl in the world. But all the same I feel I have some right to be taken seriously too. I have always been the dunce, the ne'er-do-well of the family, I've always had to pay double for my deeds, first with the scolding and then again because of the way my feelings are hurt. Now I'm not satisfied with this apparent favoritism any more. I want something from Daddy that he is not able to give me.

I'm not jealous of Margot, never have been. I don't envy her good looks or her beauty. It is only that I long for Daddy's real love: not only as his child, but for me—Anne, myself.

I cling to Daddy because it is only through him that I am able to retain the remnant of family feeling. Daddy doesn't understand that I need to give vent to my feelings over Mummy sometimes. He doesn't want to talk about it; he simply avoids anything which might lead to remarks about Mummy's failings. Just the same, Mummy and her failings are something I find harder to bear than anything else. I don't know how to keep it all to myself. I can't always be drawing attention to her untidiness, her sarcasm, and her lack of sweetness, neither can I believe that I'm always in the wrong.

We are exact opposites in everything; so naturally we are bound to run up against each other. I don't pronounce judgment on Mummy's character, for that is something I can't judge. I only look at her as a mother, and she just doesn't succeed in being that to me; I have to be my own mother. I've drawn myself apart from them all; I am my own skipper and later on I shall see where I come to land. All this comes about particularly because I have in my mind's eye an image of what a perfect mother and wife should be; and in her whom I must call "Mother" I find no trace of that image.

I am always making resolutions not to notice Mummy's bad example. I want to see only the good side of her and to seek in myself what I cannot find in her. But it doesn't work; and the worst of it is neither Daddy nor Mummy understands this gap in my life, and I blame them for it. I wonder if anyone can ever succeed in making their children absolutely content.

Sometimes I believe that God wants to try me, both now and later on; I must become good through my own efforts, without examples and without good advice. Then later on I shall be all the stronger. Who besides me will ever read these letters? From whom but myself shall I get comfort? As I need comforting often, I frequently feel weak, and dissatisfied with myself; my shortcomings are too great. I know this, and every day I try to improve myself, again and again.

My treatment varies so much. One day Anne is so sensible and is allowed to know everything; and the next day I hear that Anne is just a silly little goat who doesn't know anything at all and imagines that she's learned a wonderful lot from books. I'm not a baby or a spoiled darling any more, to be laughed at, whatever she does. I have my own views, plans, and ideas, though I can't put them into words yet. Oh, so many things bubble up inside me as I lie in bed, having to put up with people I'm fed up with, who always misinterpret my intentions. That's why in the end I always come back to my diary. That is where I start and finish, because Kitty is always patient. I'll promise her that I shall persevere, in spite of everything, and find my own way through it all, and swallow my tears. I only wish I could see the results already or occasionally receive encouragement from someone who loves me.

Don't condemn me; remember rather that sometimes I too can reach the bursting point.

Yours, Anne

Monday, 9 November, 1942

Dear Kitty,

Yesterday was Peter's birthday, he was sixteen. He had some nice presents. Among other things a game of Monopoly, a razor, and a lighter. Not that he smokes much; it's really just for show.

The biggest surprise came from Mr. Van Daan when, at one o'clock, he announced that the British had landed in Tunis, Algiers, Casablanca, and Oran. "This is the beginning of the end," everyone was saying, but Churchill, the British Prime Minister, who had probably heard the same thing in England, said: "This is not the end. It is not even the beginning of the end. But it is, perhaps, the end of the beginning." Do you see the difference? There is certainly reason for optimism. Stalingrad, the Russian town which they've already been defending for three months, still hasn't fallen into German hands.

But to return to affairs in our secret den. I must tell you something about our food supply. As you know, we have some real greedy pigs on the top floor. We get our bread from a nice baker, a friend of Koophuis. We don't get so much as we used to at home, naturally. But it's sufficient. Four ration cards have also been bought illegally. Their price is going up all the time; it has now gone up from twenty-seven florins to thirty-three. And all that for a little slip of printed paper! In order to have something in the house that will keep, apart from our 150 tins of vegetables, we have bought 270 pounds of dried peas and beans. They are not all for us, some are for the office people. They are in sacks which hang on hooks in our little passage (inside the hidden door). Owing to the weight of the contents, a few stitches in the sacks burst open. So we decided it would be better to put our winter store in the attic and Peter was given the job of dragging it all up there.

He had managed to get five of the six sacks upstairs intact, and he was just busy pulling up number six, when the bottom seam of the sack split and a shower—no, a positive hailstorm of brown beans came pouring down and rattled down the stairs. There were about fifty pounds in the sack and the noise was enough to waken the dead. Downstairs they thought the old house with all its contents was coming down on them. (Thank God there were no strangers in the house.) It gave Peter a moment's fright. But he was soon roaring with laughter, especially when he saw me standing at the bottom of the stairs, like a little island in the middle of a sea of beans! I was entirely surrounded up to my ankles in beans. Quickly we started to pick them up. But beans are so slippery and small that they seemed to roll into all the possible and impossible corners and holes. Now, every time anyone goes downstairs they bend down once or twice, in order to be able to present Mrs. Van Daan with a handful of beans.

I'd almost forgotten to mention that Daddy is quite better again.

Yours, Anne

P.S. The news has just come over the radio that Algiers has fallen. Morocco, Casablanca, and Oran have been in British hands for several days. Now we're waiting for Tunis.

Tuesday, 10 November, 1942

Dear Kitty,

Great news—we want to take in an eighth person. Yes, really! We've always thought that there was quite enough room and food for one more. We were only afraid of giving Koophuis and Kraler more trouble. But now that the appalling stories we hear about Jews are getting even worse, Daddy got hold of the two people who had to decide, and they thought it was an excellent plan. "It is just as dangerous for seven as for eight," they said, and quite rightly. When this was settled, we ran through our circle of friends, trying to think of a single person who would fit in well with our "family." It wasn't difficult to hit on someone. After Daddy had refused all members of the Van Daan family, we chose a dentist called Albert Dussel, whose wife was fortunate enough to be out of the country when war broke out. He is known to be quiet, and so far as we and Mr. Van Daan can judge from a superficial acquaintance, both families think he is a congenial person. Miep knows him too, so she will be able to make arrangements for him to join us. If he comes, he will have to sleep in my room instead of Margot, who will use the camp bed.

Yours, Anne

Thursday, 12 November, 1942

Dear Kitty,

Dussel was awfully pleased when Miep told him that she had got a hiding place for him. She urged him to come as soon as possible. Preferably Saturday. He thought that this was rather doubtful, since he had to bring his card index up to date first, see to a couple of patients, and settle his accounts. Miep came to us with this news this morning. We thought it was unwise of him to put it off. All these preparations entail explanations to a number of people, whom we would rather keep out of it. Miep is going to ask if he can't manage to come on Saturday after all.

Dussel said no; now he is coming on Monday. I must say I think it's pretty crazy that he doesn't jump at the proposal—whatever it is. If he were to get picked up outside, would he still be able to do his card index, settle his finances, and see to his patients? Why delay then? I think it's stupid of Daddy to have given in. No other news—

Yours, Anne

Tuesday, 17 November, 1942

Dear Kitty,

Dussel has arrived. All went well. Miep had told him that he must be at a special place in front of the Post Office at eleven o'clock, where a man would meet him. Dussel was standing at the rendezvous dead on time. Mr. Koophuis, who knows Dussel too, went up to him and told him that the said gentleman could not come, but asked whether he would just go to Miep at the office. Koophuis got into a tram and went back to the office, while Dussel walked in the same direction. At twenty past eleven Dussel tapped at the office door. Miep helped him off with his coat, so that the yellow star would not be seen, and took him to the private office, where Koophuis engaged him in conversation until the charwoman had gone. Then Miep went upstairs with Dussel under the pretext that the private office was needed for something, opened the swinging cupboard, and stepped inside before the eyes of the dumfounded Dussel.

We all sat around the table upstairs, waiting with coffee and cognac to greet the newcomer. Miep showed him into our sitting room first. He recognized our furniture at once, and had not the remotest idea that we were there, above his head. When Miep told him he nearly passed out with surprise. But luckily Miep didn't give him much time and took him straight upstairs.

Dussel sank into a chair, speechless, and looked at us all for a while, as if he had to really take it all in first. After a while he stuttered "But . . . *aber, sind* you not in Belgium then? *Ist der Militär nicht* come, *das Auto,* the escape is *sie nicht* successful?"

We explained everything to him, that we had spread the story about the soldiers and the car on purpose to put people, and especially the Germans, on the wrong track, should they try to find us.

Dussel was again struck dumb by such ingenuity and, when he had explored further our superpractical exquisite little "Secret Annexe," he could do nothing but gaze about him in astonishment.

We all had lunch together. Then he had a little nap and joined us for tea, tidied up his things a bit (Miep had brought them beforehand), and began to feel more at home. Especially when he received the following typed "Secret Annexe Rules" (Van Daan product).

Prospectus and Guide to the "Secret Annexe"

Special institution as temporary residence for Jews and suchlike.

Open all the year round. Beautiful, quiet, free from woodland surroundings, in the heart of Amsterdam. Can be reached by trams 13 and 17, also by car or bicycle. In special cases also on foot, if the Germans prevent the use of transport.

Board and lodging: Free.

Special fat-free diet.

Running water in the bathroom (alas, no bath) and down various inside and outside walls.

Ample storage room for all types of goods.

Own radio center, direct communication with London, New York, Tel Aviv, and numerous other stations. This appliance is only for residents' use after six o'clock in the evening. No stations are forbidden, on the understanding that German stations are only listened to in special cases, such as classical music and the like.

Rest hours: 10 o'clock in the evening until 7:30 in the morning. 10:15 on Sundays. Residents may rest during the day, conditions permitting, as the directors indicate. For reasons of public security rest hours must be strictly observed!!

Holidays (outside the home): postponed indefinitely.

Use of language: Speak softly at all times, by order! All civilized languages are permitted, therefore no German!

Lessons: One written shorthand lesson per week. English, French, Mathematics, and History at all times.

Small Pets—Special Department (permit is necessary): Good treatment available (vermin excepted).

Mealtimes: breakfast, every day except Sunday and Bank Holidays, 9 A.M. Sundays and Bank Holidays, 11:30 A.M. approximately.

Lunch: (not very big): 1:15 P.M. to 1:45 P.M.

Dinner: cold and/or hot: no fixed time (depending on the news broadcast).

Duties: Residents must always be ready to help with office work.

Baths: The washtub is available for all residents from 9 A.M. on Sundays. The W.C. kitchen, private office or main office, whichever preferred, are available.

Alcoholic Beverages: only with doctor's prescription.

END

Yours, Anne

Thursday, 19 November, 1942

Dear Kitty,

Dussel is a very nice man, just as we had all imagined. Of course he thought it was all right to share my little room.

Quite honestly I'm not so keen that a stranger should use my things, but one must be prepared to make some sacrifices for a good cause, so I shall make my little offering with a good will. "If we can save someone, then everything else is of secondary importance," says Daddy, and he's absolutely right.

The first day that Dussel was here, he immediately asked me all sorts of questions: When does the charwoman come? When can one use the bathroom? When is one allowed to use the lavatory? You may laugh, but these things are not so simple in a hiding place. During the day we mustn't make any noise that might be heard downstairs; and if there is some stranger—such as the charwoman for example—then we have to be extra careful. I explained all this carefully to Dussel. But one thing amazed me: he is very slow on the uptake. He asks everything twice over and still doesn't seem to remember. Perhaps that will wear off in time, and it's only that he's thoroughly upset by the sudden change.

Apart from that, all goes well. Dussel has told us a lot about the outside world, which we have missed for so long now. He had very sad news. Countless friends and acquaintances have gone to a terrible fate. Evening after evening the green and gray army lorries trundle past. The Germans ring at every front door to inquire if there are any Jews living in the house. If there are, then the whole family has to go at once. If they don't find any, they go on to the next house. No one has a chance of evading them unless one goes into hiding. Often they go around with lists, and only ring when they know they can get a good haul. Sometimes they let them off for cash—so much per head. It seems like the slave hunts of olden times. But it's certainly no joke; it's much too tragic for that. In the evenings when it's dark, I often see rows of good, innocent people accompanied by crying children, walking on and on, in charge of a couple of these chaps, bullied and knocked about until they almost drop. No one is spared—old people, babies, expectant mothers, the sick—each and all join in the march of death.

How fortunate we are here, so well cared for and undisturbed. We wouldn't have to worry about all this misery were it not that we are so anxious about all those dear to us whom we can no longer help.

I feel wicked sleeping in a warm bed, while my dearest friends have been knocked down or have fallen into a gutter somewhere out in the cold night. I get frightened when I think of close friends who have now been delivered into the hands of the cruelest brutes that walk the earth. And all because they are Jews!

Yours, Anne

Friday, 20 November, 1942

Dear Kitty,

None of us really knows how to take it all. The news about the Jews had not really penetrated through to us until now, and we thought it best to remain as cheerful as possible. Every now and then, when Miep lets out something about what has happened to a friend, Mummy and Mrs. Van Daan always begin to cry, so Miep thinks it better not to tell us any more. But Dussel was immediately plied with questions from all sides, and the stories he told us were so gruesome and dreadful that one can't get them out of one's mind.

Yet we shall have our jokes and tease each other, when these horrors have faded a bit in our minds. It won't do us any good, or help those outside, to go on being as gloomy as we are at the moment. And what would be the object of making our "Secret Annexe" into a "Secret Annexe of Gloom"? Must I keep thinking about those other people, whatever I am doing? And if I want to laugh about something, should I stop myself quickly and feel ashamed that I am cheerful? Ought I then to cry the whole day long? No, that I can't do. Besides, in time this gloom will wear off.

Added to this misery there is another, but of a purely personal kind; and it pales into insignificance beside all the wretchedness I've just told you about. Still, I can't refrain from telling you that lately I have begun to feel deserted. I am surrounded by too great a void. I never used to feel like this, my fun and amusements, and my girl friends, completely filled my thoughts. Now I either think about unhappy things, or about myself. And at long last I have made the discovery that Daddy, although he's such a darling, still cannot take the place of my entire little world of bygone days. But why do I bother you with such foolish things? I'm very ungrateful, Kitty; I know that. But it often makes my head swim if I'm jumped upon too much, and then on top of that have to think about all those other miseries!

Yours, Anne

Saturday, 28 November, 1942

Dear Kitty,

We have used too much electricity, more than our ration. Result: the utmost economy and the prospect of having it cut off. No light for a fortnight; a pleasant thought, that, but who knows, perhaps it won't happen after all! It's too dark to read in the afternoons after four or half past. We pass the time in all sorts of crazy ways: asking riddles, physical training in the dark, talking English and French, criticizing books. But it all begins to pall in the end. Yesterday evening I discovered something new: to peer through a powerful pair of field glasses into the lighted rooms of the houses at the back. In the daytime we can't allow even as much as a centimeter's chink to appear between our curtains, but it can't do any harm after dark. I never knew before that neighbors could be such interesting people. At any rate, ours are. I found one couple having a meal, one family was in the act of taking a home movie; and the dentist opposite was just attending to an old lady, who was awfully scared.

It was always said about Mr. Dussel that he could get on wonderfully with children and that he loved them all. Now he shows himself in his true colors; a stodgy, old-fashioned disciplinarian, and preacher of long, drawn-out sermons on manners.

As I have unusual good fortune (!) to share my bedroom—alas, a small one—with His Lordship, and as I'm generally considered to be the most badly behaved of the three young people, I have a lot to put up with and have to pretend to be deaf in order to escape the old, much-repeated tickings-off and warnings. All this wouldn't be too bad, if he wasn't such a frightful sneak and he didn't pick on Mummy of all people to sneak to every time. When I've already just had a dose from him, Mummy goes over it all again, so I get a gale aft as well as fore. Then, if I'm really lucky, I'm called on to give an account of myself to Mrs. Van Daan and then I get a veritable hurricane!

Honestly, you needn't think it's easy to be the "badly brought-up" central figure of a hypercritical family in hiding. When I lie in bed at night and think over the many sins and shortcomings attributed to me, I get so confused by it all that I either laugh or cry: it depends what sort of mood I am in.

Then I fall asleep with a stupid feeling of wishing to be different from what I am or from what I want to be; perhaps to behave differently from the way I want to behave, or do behave. Oh, heavens above, now I'm getting you in a muddle too. Forgive me, but I don't like crossing things out, and in these days of paper shortage we are not allowed to throw paper away. Therefore I can only advise you not to read the last sentence again, and certainly not to try to understand it, because you won't succeed anyhow!

Yours, Anne

.   .   .

Saturday, 12 February, 1944

Dear Kitty,

The sun is shining, the sky is a deep blue, there is a lovely breeze and I'm longing—so longing—for everything. To talk, for freedom, for friends, to be alone. And I do so long . . . to cry! I feel as if I'm going to burst, and I know that it would get better with crying; but I can't, I'm restless, I go from one room to the other, breathe through the crack of a closed window, feel my heart beating, as if it is saying, "Can't you satisfy my longings at last?"

I believe that it's spring within me, I feel that spring is awakening, I feel it in my whole body and soul. It is an effort to behave normally, I feel utterly confused, don't know what to read, what to write, what to do, I only know that I am longing . . . !

Yours, Anne

Sunday, 13 February, 1944

Dear Kitty,

Since Saturday a lot has changed for me. It came about like this. I longed—and am still longing—but . . . now something has happened, which has made it a little, just a little, less.

To my great joy—I will be quite honest about it—already this morning I noticed that Peter kept looking at me all the time. Not in the ordinary way, I don't know how, I just can't explain.

I used to think that Peter was in love with Margot, but yesterday I suddenly had the feeling that it is not so. I made a special effort not to look at him too much, because whenever I did, he kept on looking too and then—yes, then—it gave me a lovely feeling inside, but which I mustn't feel too often.

I desperately want to be alone. Daddy has noticed that I am not quite my usual self, but I really can't tell him everything. "Leave me in peace, leave me alone," that's what I'd like to keep crying out all the time. Who knows, the day may come when I'm left alone more than I would wish!

Yours, Anne

Monday, 14 February, 1944

Dear Kitty,

On Sunday evening everyone except Pim and me was sitting beside the wireless in order to listen to the "Immortal Music of the German Masters." Dussel fiddled with the knobs continually. This annoyed Peter, and the others too. After restraining himself for half an hour, Peter asked somewhat irritably if the twisting and turning might stop. Dussel answered in his most hoity-toity manner, "I'm getting it all right." Peter became angry, was rude, Mr. Van Daan took his side, and Dussel had to give in. That was all.

The reason in itself was very unimportant, but Peter seems to have taken it very much to heart. In any case, when I was rummaging about in the bookcase in the attic, he came up to me and began telling me the whole story. I didn't know anything about it, but Peter soon saw that he had found an attentive ear and got fairly into his stride.

"Yes, and you see," he said, "I don't easily say anything, because I know beforehand that I'll only become tongue-tied. I begin to stutter, blush, and twist around what I want to say, until I have to break off because I simply can't find the words. That's what happened yesterday, I wanted to say something quite different, but once I had started, I got in a hopeless muddle and that's frightful. I used to have a bad habit; I wish I still had it now. If I was angry with anyone, rather than argue it out I would get to work on him with my fists. I quite realize that this method doesn't get me anywhere; and that is why I admire you. You are never at a loss for a word, you say exactly what you want to say to people and are never the least bit shy."

"I can tell you, you're making a big mistake," I answered. "I usually say things quite differently from the way I meant to say them, and then I talk too much and far too long, and that's just as bad."

I couldn't help laughing to myself over this last sentence. However, I wanted to let him go on talking about himself, so I kept my amusement to myself, went and sat on a cushion on the floor, put my arms around my bent knees, and looked at him attentively.

I am very glad that there is someone else in the house who can get into the same fits of rage as I get into. I could see it did Peter good to pull Dussel to pieces to his heart's content, without fear of my telling tales.

And as for me, I was very pleased, because I sensed a real feeling of fellowship, such as I can only remember having had with my girl friends.

Yours, Anne

Dear Kitty,

It's Margot's birthday. Peter came at half past twelve to look at the presents and stayed talking much longer than was strictly necessary—a thing he'd have never done otherwise. In the afternoon I went to get some coffee and, after that, potatoes, because I wanted to spoil Margot for just that one day in the year. I went through Peter's room; he took all his papers off the stairs at once and I asked whether I should close the trap door to the attic. "Yes," he replied, "knock when you come back, then I'll open it for you."

I thanked him, went upstairs, and searched at least ten minutes in the large barrel for the smallest potatoes. Then my back began to ache and I got cold. Naturally I didn't knock, but opened the trap door myself, but still he came to meet me most obligingly, and took the pan from me.

"I've looked for a long time, these are the smallest I could find," I said.

"Did you look in the big barrel?"

"Yes, I've been over them all."

By this time I was standing at the bottom of the stairs and he looked searchingly in the pan which he was still holding. "Oh, but these are first-rate," he said, and added when I took the pan from him, "I congratulate you!" At the same time he gave me such a gentle warm look which made a tender glow within me. I could really see that he wanted to please me, and because he couldn't make a long complimentary speech he spoke with his eyes. I understood him, oh, so well, and was very grateful. It gives me pleasure even now when I recall those words and that look he gave me.

When I went downstairs, Mummy said that I must get some more potatoes, this time for supper. I willingly offered to go upstairs again.

When I came into Peter's room, I apologized at having to disturb him again. When I was already on the stairs he got up, and went and stood between the door and the wall, firmly took hold of my arm, and wanted to hold me back by force.

"I'll go," he said. I replied that it really wasn't necessary and that I didn't have to get particularly small ones this time. Then he was convinced and let my arm go. On the way down, he came and opened the trap door and took the pan again. When I reached the door, I asked,

"What are you doing?" "French," he replied. I asked if I might glance through the exercises, washed my hands, and went and sat on the divan opposite him.

We soon began talking, after I'd explained some of the French to him. He told me that he wanted to go to the Dutch East Indies and live on a plantation later on. He talked about his home life, about the black market, and then he said that he felt so useless. I told him that he certainly had a very strong inferiority complex. He talked about the Jews. He would have found it much easier if he'd been a Christian and if he could be one after the war. I asked if he wanted to be baptized, but that wasn't the case either. Who was to know whether he was a Jew when the war was over? he said.

This gave me rather a pang; it seems such a pity that there's always just a tinge of dishonesty about him. For the rest we chatted very pleasantly about Daddy, and about judging people's characters and all kinds of things, I can't remember exactly what now.

It was half past four by the time I left.

In the evening he said something else that I thought was nice. We were talking about a picture of a film star that I'd given him once, which has now been hanging in his room for at least a year and a half. He liked it very much and I offered to give him a few more sometime. "No," he replied, "I'd rather leave it like this. I look at these every day and they have grown to be my friends."

Now I understand more why he always hugs Mouschi. He needs some affection, too, of course.

I'd forgotten something else that he talked about. He said, "I don't know what fear is, except when I think of my own shortcomings. But I'm getting over that too."

Peter has a terrible inferiority complex. For instance, he always thinks that he is so stupid, and we are so clever. If I help him with his French, he thanks me a thousand times. One day I shall turn around and say: "Oh, shut up, you're much better at English and geography!"

Yours, Anne

Friday, 18 February, 1944

Dear Kitty,

Whenever I go upstairs now I keep on hoping that I shall see "him." Because my life now has an object, and I have something to look forward to, everything has become more pleasant.

At least the object of my feelings is always there, and I needn't be afraid of rivals, except Margot. Don't think I'm in love, because I'm not, but I do have the feeling all the time that something fine can grow up between us, something that gives confidence and friendship. If I get half a chance, I go up to him now. It's not like it used to be when he didn't know how to begin. It's just the opposite—he's still talking when I'm half out of the room.

Mummy doesn't like it much, and always says I'll be a nuisance and that I must leave him in peace. Honestly, doesn't she realize that I've got some intuition? She looks at me so queerly every time I go into Peter's little room. If I come downstairs from there, she asks me where I've been. I simply can't bear it, and think it's horrible.

Yours, Anne

Saturday, 19 February, 1944

Dear Kitty,

It is Saturday again and that really speaks for itself.

The morning was quiet. I helped a bit upstairs, but I didn't have more than a few fleeting words with "him." At half past two, when everyone had gone to their own rooms, either to sleep or to read, I went to the private office, with my blanket and everything, to sit at the desk and read or write. It was not long before it all became too much for me, my head drooped on to my arm, and I sobbed my heart out. The tears streamed down my cheeks and I felt desperately unhappy. Oh, if only "he" had come to comfort me. It was four o'clock by the time I went upstairs again. I went for some potatoes, with fresh hope in my heart of a meeting, but while I was still smartening up my hair in the bathroom he went down to see Boche in the warehouse.

Suddenly I felt the tears coming back and I hurried to the lavatory, quickly grabbing a pocket mirror as I passed. There I sat then, fully dressed, while the tears made dark spots on the red of my apron, and I felt very wretched.

This is what was going through my mind. Oh, I'll never reach Peter like this. Who knows, perhaps he doesn't like me at all and doesn't need anyone to confide in. Perhaps he only thinks about me in a casual sort of way. I shall have to go on alone once more, without friendship and without Peter. Perhaps soon I'll be without hope, without comfort, or anything to look forward to again. Oh, if I could nestle my head against his shoulder and not feel so hopelessly alone and deserted! Who knows, perhaps he doesn't care about me at all and looks at the others in just the same way. Perhaps I only imagined that it was especially for me? Oh, Peter, if only you could see or hear me. If the truth were to prove as bad as that, it would be more than I could bear.

However, a little later fresh hope and anticipation seemed to return, even though the tears were still streaming down my cheeks.

Yours, Anne

Wednesday, 23 February, 1944

Dear Kitty,

It's lovely weather outside and I've quite perked up since yesterday. Nearly every morning I go to the attic where Peter works to blow the stuffy air out of my lungs. From my favorite spot on the floor I look up at the blue sky and the bare chestnut tree, on whose branches little raindrops shine, appearing like silver, and at the seagulls and the other birds as they glide on the wind.

He stood with his head against a thick beam, and I sat down. We breathed the fresh air, looked outside, and both felt that the spell should not be broken by words. We remained like this for a long time, and when he had to go up to the loft to chop wood, I knew that he was a nice fellow. He climbed the ladder, and I followed, then he chopped wood for about a quarter of an hour, during which time we still remained silent. I watched him from where I stood, he was obviously doing his best to show off his strength. But I looked out of the open window too, over a large area of Amsterdam, over all the roofs and on to the horizon, which was such a pale blue that it was hard to see the dividing line. "As long as this exists," I thought, "and I may live to see it, this sunshine, the cloudless skies, while this lasts, I cannot be unhappy."

The best remedy for those who are afraid, lonely, or unhappy is to go outside, somewhere where they can be quite alone with the heavens, nature, and God. Because only then does one feel that all is as it should be and that God wishes to see people happy, amidst the simple beauty of nature. As long as this exists, and it certainly always will, I know that then there will always be comfort for every sorrow, whatever the circumstances may be. And I firmly believe that nature brings solace in all troubles.

Oh, who knows, perhaps it won't be long before I can share this overwhelming feeling of bliss with someone who feels the way I do about it.

Yours, Anne

EUGENIA SEMYONOVA GINZBURG
(1907–1977)

In the Stalinist purges of 1937 Eugenia Ginzburg, a teacher, journalist, and loyal member of the Communist party of the USSR, was arrested and accused of terrorist counterrevolutionary activity. She was then just over thirty, the mother of two young boys, Vaska and Alyosha, and a prominent resident of her native Kazan, capital of the Tartar Republic. Her husband was an important member of the Tartar Committee of the party. After six months in prison in Kazan, she was sent to Moscow for sentencing by military tribunal, as described in this selection. Expecting death, she was overjoyed to receive a sentence of ten years' hard labor. Knowing herself to be innocent of all wrongdoing, she was certain she would be vindicated and released long before the ten years were up. But eighteen years of imprisonment passed before she was allowed to rejoin her family. She spent two years in solitary confinement in a prison northeast of Moscow, an experience she found ennobling compared with the camps of Siberia, which followed.

By the 1960s, when she wrote her autobiography, *Journey into the Whirlwind*, Ginzburg had been rehabilitated and could rejoice that the Stalinist aberration was over. The book was published in Russian in Italy (1967) and in translation throughout the West but never appeared in the Soviet Union.

The literature of women in prison and work camps is large. Compare, in this collection, Nien Cheng, *Life and Death in Shanghai* and Le Ly Hayslip, *When Heaven and Earth Changed Places*. Emma Mashinini's *Strikes Have Followed Me All My Life* has a powerful section about her solitary confinement in a South African prison. For other accounts of Soviet oppression, see Nadezhda Mandelstam, *Hope against Hope* and Irina Ratushinskaya, *Grey Is the Color of Hope*, and for a recent prison diary, from El Salvador, see Nidia Díaz, *I Was Never Alone*.

FROM *Journey into the Whirlwind*

INTRODUCTION TO BUTYRKI

From the moment we arrived in Moscow we could sense the tremendous scale of the operation in which we were involved as victims. The various agencies concerned with carrying it out were inhumanly overworked. People were run off their feet, transport was insufficient, the cells were full to bursting, the courts sat for twenty-four hours a day.

Long after our train reached the station we were kept in the carriage listening to the sound of feet running along the platform, abrupt shouts, mysterious creaking and clanking. . . . At last we were loaded into a Black Maria. From the outside it looked bigger and handsomer than the one in Kazan. It was painted light blue, and passers-by no doubt imagined that it was carrying loaves of bread, milk, or sausages. But the cages inside were even more unendurably stuffy than those at Kazan. They were coated with oil paint and completely airless, so that within minutes on that scorching July day with its smell of melting asphalt, we felt suffocated.

Exhausted and dripping with sweat, our hair matted, we sat gasping in our cages, patiently waiting. It was a long wait—apparently they were short of drivers. Meanwhile the same sounds of running, whispering, knocking, doors slamming. . . . Certainly they were not having an easy time out there.

Guessing by some sixth sense that there was as yet no guard in our van, we began to talk. It turned out that all the occupants were from Kazan but that the only women were the four of us. Among the men were almost the whole of the former government of the Tartar Republic and several members of the regional committee board. Abdullin,* who was soon to be executed, was there too, and we managed to exchange a last farewell with him.

All of a sudden the tramp of boots came closer; the doors banged, the engine roared, and we were off. The drive was a long one. That meant that we were going to the Butyrki prison: the Lubyanka was only a short way from the Kazan station. The air in the van got worse than ever. Someone shouted: "Open the door, I'm going to be sick." "Against orders" was the curt reply. My hands and feet went numb, my brain clouded, strange pictures passed in front of me. I remembered reading

*Bari Abdullin, second secretary of the party regional committee—ED.

that the victims of the French revolution were taken to the guillotine in open tumbrils, and not stifled to death on the way: according to Anatole France, César Birotteau had even read Lucretius, standing up, till the very last moment. In order not to lose consciousness I tried to occupy my mind by picturing the streets we were passing through. Then everything went black before my eyes.

A strong smell of liquid ammonia brought me to myself. The van had stopped, the door of my murder chamber was opened, and someone in a white smock pushed a phial under my nose; then they opened the other doors, one by one, and repeated the process. Evidently the drive had been too much for the male prisoners also.

I must have walked from the van into Butyrki in a semiconscious condition, for I can remember nothing about it. When I came to myself I was sitting on my bundle of clothes in an enormous hall which was not unlike a railway station. Vast and echoing, it was fairly clean, with men and women bustling about in uniforms that were not unlike those of railway employees. There were a lot of doors, and some windowless cabins resembling telephone booths. I learned later that they were the so-called "kennels" into which prisoners were put when they had to wait for any reason. The basic law of prison was strict isolation: none of us was allowed to see anyone except his cellmates. A bell at the door announced the arrival of a new group of prisoners. A wardress came up and said to me quietly: "Over there." In a moment I was in a kennel, locked in and once more by myself. The place was a little larger than a telephone booth, tiled on the inside, with a stool to sit on and a ceiling light. I had hardly had time to look around when the lock clicked again and I was taken out into a large room full of naked or half-dressed women. The wardresses in their black jackets looked like so many jackdaws.

Was this a bath or a medical inspection? No, it was for the purpose of searching the new arrivals.

"Take your clothes off. Let your hair down. Spread your fingers and toes. Open your mouths. Stand with legs apart."

The wardresses, with stony faces and quick, efficient movements, ran their fingers through our hair as if hunting lice, examined our mouths and anuses. Some of the prisoners looked terrified, others disgusted. A great many of them obviously belonged to the educated classes.

The work proceeded swiftly. A pile of confiscated objects soon covered the long table: brooches, rings, watches, earrings, garters, notebooks. These were clearly Moscow women, arrested only today and brought straight from home with all sorts of knickknacks on their persons. They were worse off than I was: I had the advantage of six months' experience behind me, plus the fact that I had nothing left to lose.

"Put your clothes on again!"

A young girl came up to me—almost a child in appearance, with her hair cropped in boyish fashion—and said, "Excuse me, but are you a Party member? You look like one—it seems a funny thing to ask here, but I must know. You are? Well, I belong to the Komsomol, my name's Katya Shirokova, and I'm eighteen years old. I need some advice. You see, that German woman over there has hidden some gold things in her hair and I can't decide whether I ought to tell the wardress. I don't like to give her away, it's disgusting, but on the other hand this is a Soviet prison and for all I know she may be a real class enemy."

"What about you and me, Katya? Are we?"

"Oh, of course it's a mistake about us. You can't make an omelette without breaking eggs. Anyway, they're sure to let us out. But meanwhile it's terribly hard to know what to do, especially about her."

I looked at the woman at whom Katya was pointing, and saw a face of unusually tender beauty and charm. I found out later that she was a well-known German film actress, Carola Heintschke. She had come to the Soviet Union in 1934 with her husband, who was an engineer. The two earrings which she had skillfully concealed from the watchful eyes of the wardresses were a present from her husband, whom she believed to be already dead. With the deft movement of an actress used to playing in adventure films, she had managed to hide them in her luxuriant blonde hair.

Katya's quaint, attractive face was still turned to me in earnest inquiry.

"So you want a directive, Katya, do you?"

"Well, it is difficult, you know, she's a German and . . ."

"Listen to me. Since we're all naked in every sense of the word, I think you should be guided by the instinct which is generally known as conscience. And I imagine yours tells you that it would be a dirty trick to give the woman away."

Thus Carola Heintschke's earrings were saved—like herself, for a short time only. But more of that later.

The formalities went on till late into the night. After the search they took our fingerprints, an equally humiliating procedure. Then we were photographed full-face and in profile, and at last came the long-awaited bath, a joy in itself and an interlude of sanity in this Dantesque Inferno.

There is no place where people become acquainted more quickly than in prison, especially during such "processing," under the influence of a common fear of the immediate future and a shared sense of outraged human dignity. We forty women went through all the stages together, from the morning search onward, awaiting our turn together, telling each other in brief, frightened whispers what we had been arrested for, the names of our children, our griefs and injuries. I already felt that life would be much more bearable if I were not parted from black-haired

Zoya, of Moscow Medical School, about whom I had learned in those few hours as much as one usually learns in ten years of close friendship. She evidently felt the same, and when I came out of the photographing booth she ran up to me with a sigh of relief and said:

"We're still together, Genia. I'm sure they'll put us in the same cell. It would be marvelous!"

But even these small consolations were denied us: we were separated as if at a slave market. Coming out of the shower room, I saw that neither Zoya, nor Katya Shirokova, nor the golden-haired Carola was in the corridor.

"Left!" the warder commanded, and I was led alone through the dark corridors. Then I was handed over to another warder and heard the whisper "To the special block." Here I was taken in charge by a wardress in a dark jacket and with a severe, monastic face.

The doors in my new abode were ordinary ones, locked by a single key, without medieval bolts and padlocks. I stood with my bundle in my hands, gazing around me. The huge cell was crowded with women; the regular noise of breathing was constantly interrupted by shrieks, groans, and muttering. It was clear that the inmates were not only asleep but were having fearful nightmares. Compared to the two prisons I knew, this one was almost luxurious. It had a large window, with a grating of course, but the screen behind it was not of wood but of frosted glass. There were collapsible beds instead of a single plank bed; the enormous slop bucket in the corner had a tightly fitting lid.

All the beds were occupied. After waiting a little I undid my bundle and took out my cotton blanket (a check one, dear to me because Alyosha had used it) and spread it on the floor near the window. I stretched out my legs rapturously. My body was racked with fatigue. I was about to sink into blissful oblivion when the peephole opened and a wardress stuck her head through.

"You mustn't lie on the floor. Get up!"

"But there's no room anywhere else."

"You can sit till morning—it isn't long. Then you'll be taken to another cell."

As soon as her head disappeared, a tousled figure from one of the bunks addressed me in a Caucasian accent:

"Here, comrade, take my place. I can't sleep anyway. Honestly, I'm quite happy to sit up for a while."

She quickly installed me on her bed. What bliss! I had forgotten what it was like to lie on anything except straw. The pillow smelled of something I had forgotten too—cleanliness, a trace of scent.

My new friend understood my thoughts.

"Yes, in Armenia we had a bit of rotten liberalism; I was allowed to bring a pillow and some linen from home. They wanted to take the pillow away here, but the interrogator stuck up for me. He's trying to get around me at the moment, and thinks I'll sign something."

Whether because I was so tired or for some other reason, the voice seemed familiar. I could not see her face: the light had been switched off, and dawn was only just stealing through the opaque glass and grating.

"Are you all right now? Well, that's marvelous!"

This expression too struck a chord. I shook off my sleep and tried hard to remember: that phrase, that tousled head. I took her by the hand and said, "What's your first name?" She replied "Nushik," and I jumped up and threw my arms around her.

"Nushik! Look at me! Don't you recognize me?"

"Genia! How stupid of me! Of course!"

Laughing and crying and interrupting each other, we talked about the past. Eight years before, when we were young postgraduate students, we had slept in the dormitory at a teachers' training college in Leningrad.

"It was nearly as big as this, wasn't it?"

"Yes, but a little different."

It was in fact a big drawing room in the former palace of the Grand Duke Sergey Alexandrovich, close to the Hermitage Museum. One wall was entirely taken up by a plate-glass window which looked out on the embankment. Ten of us slept in the room, which was lit up at night by a ghostly glimmer from the riverside lamps.

"Do you remember the time I woke you up in the middle of the night?"

Of course I did! She had spent the day frantically studying for an exam in dialectical materialism, and she had wakened me to ask: "Tell me, darling—who was it that Marx stood on his head? Hegel? M-arvelous!"

We talked on and on, exchanging pleasant memories, and after a while she said:

"I'm going to give you a bit of information in return. Do you know who's stood everything on its head now?"

I had a pretty good idea, but I let her tell me. She whispered into my ear: "Stalin!"

We went on whispering for a long time, and I could not tell at what moment I fell asleep. When I awoke, it was to feel someone's eyes fixed upon me. A woman aged about fifty-five was sitting beside Nushik at the foot of the bed, an expression of acute suffering on her face. Seeing that I was awake, she moved closer to me and asked, wringing her hands:

"Tell me, have they been tried yet? They've been shot, haven't they?"

"Who? What trial?"

"Are you afraid to talk about them?"

"You needn't be afraid, Genia," Nushik put in. "This is Rykov's wife. She wants to know what's happened to her husband. We've been here for two months, and we don't know anything."

I explained as convincingly as I could that I had been in prison for six months, that I had been brought from another town and knew nothing about Rykov's impending trial. But his wife refused to believe me, partly because I had only just arrived and looked fairly fresh after my bath, but chiefly because people behind bars were no less afraid of betraying themselves than those outside. Although they were already in the spider's web, they felt that they might yet struggle out of it, that their neighbor's offenses might be worse than their own, that they must be careful not to give anything away. I was to meet many such "diplomatic" prisoners, who swore they had not looked at a newspaper for a year before their arrest, and knew nothing whatsoever. There were many, too, who carried on ultra-patriotic conversations at the top of their voice, in the naïve hope that their words would be overheard and reported where they would do most good.

It was humiliating to be mistaken for one of this sort. But there was no time to argue. Again the wardress stuck her head in.

"Get up. Get ready to go to the washroom."

Thirty-eight folding beds creaked. Everybody got up. I looked eagerly into their faces. Who were they? Those four, for instance, in absurd, low-cut evening dresses and high-heeled shoes? All looking bedraggled, of course . . . What could they be?

Nushik came to my assistance:

"They're not tarts, silly. They're Party members, friends of Rudzutak.* They were having supper with him after the theater and were arrested in what they stood up in. That was three months ago, and the poor things haven't been allowed any parcels, so they're still in their evening dresses. I gave the old one a scarf of mine yesterday—clothing the naked, you might say."

All the thirty-eight women dressed as fast as they could, afraid of being late for the washroom. The cell buzzed with low-voiced conversation. Many people were telling their dreams.

"They've nearly all become superstitious," said Nushik. "You see that old girl by the window—she tells her dreams every morning and asks us what they mean, and do you know what she is? She's a professor! . . . Look at that child over there. That's Nina Lugovskaya. She's sixteen. Her father's a Social Revolutionary, he's been in since 1935, and now they've taken his wife and his three girls as well. Nina's the youngest, she's still at school."

*Disgraced Bolshevik leader.

Presently, all of us—thirty-nine including myself, from sixteen-year-old Nina to the seventy-four-year-old veteran Bolshevik Surikova—were milling around in the large and not too dirty washroom which looked like a station cloakroom, and we all hurried as if our train were about to leave.

There was a lot to do, including washing our underclothes. This was strictly forbidden, but people took the risk because most of them got no parcels and had only one set of things.

Everyone made much of Nina—washing her panties, combing her hair, giving her extra lumps of sugar and advice on how to behave during her interrogation.

I felt an almost physical pang of acute pity for the young and the old—Katya Shirokova or little Nina, who was hardly older than our Mayka, and Surikova, nearly twenty years older than my mother.

Yes, I was very lucky—lucky to be over thirty, but not much over it. I had my own teeth and I could see without spectacles. (Everyone who wore glasses had had them taken away, and the near- and far-sighted suffered terribly.) My heart and stomach and all my other organs were in perfect order. At the same time I was old enough to be tough, I wouldn't break, I wasn't a reed like the Ninas and the Katyas.

So I had no business to be sorry for myself. I was luckier than most. There was only one thing. It seemed to me that I suffered more than any of us from the humiliation of all they were doing to us. The worst physical sufferings, it seemed to me, would have been easier to bear than the sense of outrage and degradation.

The only way to overcome it was to tell myself at every hour of the day that those who did these things were not human beings. After all, I would not have felt insulted if a monkey or a pig had scrabbled in my hair, looking for "substantive evidence of my crimes."

THE WHOLE OF THE COMINTERN

The wardress stopped me from going back to the cell with the others. She told me to wait and, having locked the door behind them (I did not even have a chance to say good-by to Nushik), led me along the corridor and pointed to an open door.

"In there!"

It was a cell exactly like the one in which I had spent the night, but empty, as the inmates were in the washroom. The wardress indicated my bed: it was near the door, and therefore near the slop bucket. But in other respects I quite liked the look of things. The sun shone dimly through the frosted glass; there were thirty-five collapsible beds, all tidily made, but the main thing was—did my eyes deceive me? No, there were actually books on each one. I trembled with delight. My beloved, insepa-rable companions whom I had not seen for six months past—six months without leafing through your pages, without smelling the acrid printer's ink! I took up the nearest one—it was Kellermann's *Tunnel* in German. The second one was a volume of Stefan Zweig, also in German; then there was Anatole France in French and Dickens in English. Before long, I discovered that all the books were foreign. The ragged and crum-pled articles of clothing scattered about on the beds also had a foreign look.

The key turned, the door opened again, and in trooped about thirty-five women, chattering in subdued tones in a mixture of foreign lan-guages. They surrounded me and plied me with questions in a friendly manner, talking in German, French, and scraps of Russian. Who was I, when had I been arrested, and what was happening outside? I replied in Russian and, in my turn, asked:

"What about you, comrades? I can see you're foreigners, but where are you from?"

A slim blonde woman of about twenty-nine, who was standing in front of the group, held out her hand and said in broken Russian:

"I introduce myself—Greta Kästner, member of the German Com-munist Party. This is my—how you say—friend Klara. She ran away from Hitler—the Gestapo held her for long time."

Klara was very dark, more like an Italian than a German. She looked at me expectantly and nodded to confirm what Greta had said. Then came another tall blonde, who announced in excellent Russian that she was a member of the Latvian Communist Party. Then a *Communista Italiana*, then a Chinese Party member of uncertain age who put her arms around me and said: "In Russian they call me Genia too—Genia Koverkova. I studied at the Sun Yat-sen University in Moscow, and they gave us all Russian names. But tell us about yourself, comrade."

When they heard that I was a member of the Communist Party of the USSR, they became greatly excited and asked question after question. What were the details of the Red Army plot? Was Wilhelm Pieck* in prison? Had all the Latvian rifle corps† been arrested? When was the trial of Bukharin and Rykov** to begin? Was it true that there had been a July plenum of the Central Committee at which Stalin had demanded that prison regulations be tightened?

I explained that all these matters were new to me, that I had been in prison longer than they and had been brought from a provincial town to

---

*German Communist leader, 1876–1960, first head of the East German State.
†Crack unit known for their fanatical devotion to the Soviet regime.
**Nikolay Bukharin and Aleksey Rykov, Bolshevik leaders executed in 1938.

be tried by a military tribunal. After a while the cluster of women began
to disperse and I was left with the two Germans, Greta and Klara. My
German was as full of mistakes as their Russian, but we talked animatedly to our mutual satisfaction in both languages at once.

"What are you accused of, Greta?"

The "Aryan" blue eyes glistened with unshed tears as she replied:

"Oh, *schrecklich*—espionage."

Then she told me a little about her husband—a true working man.
She herself had belonged to the Communist youth movement since she
was fifteen. But what had happened to her was nothing, it was Klär-
chen . . .

Klara lay down on the bed, turned over on her stomach and pulled up
her skirt. Her calves and buttocks were covered with deep, hideous scars,
as though wild beasts had been clawing at her flesh. Her lips tight in her
swarthy face and her gray eyes flashing pale fire, she said hoarsely:

"This is—Gestapo." Then she quickly sat up again and, stretching
out both her hands, added: "This is NKVD."

The nails of both her hands were deformed, the fingers blue and
swollen. My heart almost stopped beating. What could this mean?

"They have special apparatus to produce—*wie sagt man?*—sincere
confession."

"Torture!" I exclaimed.

Greta nodded sadly. "Night come, you hear."

At that moment I heard a Russian voice say: "May I speak to you for a
moment, comrade?"

Apparently there were a few Soviet citizens in the cell besides myself.
This one was a woman in her late thirties called Julia Annenkova, who
had edited a German newspaper in Moscow. She was not beautiful, but
her face was striking and she looked as though she was of French descent. Her eyes smoldered mournfully. She took my arm, led me to one
side, and whispered confidentially:

"You were quite right not to answer their questions. Who knows
which of them really is an enemy, and which are the victims of a mistake,
like you and me? I advise you to go on being careful, to make sure that
you don't commit a crime against the Party after all. The best way is to
say nothing."

"But it's the truth—I don't know anything. I come from the prov-
inces and I've been in prison for six months. Do *you* know what's going
on in the country?"

"Treason—appalling treason which has worked its way into every
branch of the government and Party organization. Secretaries of territo-
rial committees, secretaries of national minority Communist Parties are
among the traitors—Postyshev, Khatayevich, Eiche, Razumov, Iva-

nov—Antipov, the president of the Soviet Board of Control—lots of army officers . . ."

"But if all these people have betrayed one man, isn't it easier to suppose that he has betrayed them?"

Julia turned pale and, after a moment's silence, said curtly: "I beg your pardon, I was mistaken in you."

She moved away, and I was buttonholed by another Russian, Natasha Stolyarova. She was twenty-two and looked like a schoolgirl with her auburn pigtails and round, freckled face. She had emigrated with her parents at the age of five or six and spent her childhood in Paris, where she became bilingual. A few years earlier she had come back to Moscow as a repatriate. Intoxicated with the Russian atmosphere and the pure Russian speech, she had taken up the career of interpreter. And now she too began to warn me to watch my tongue.

"You're too trusting. Why did you offend Julia like that? You can see how fanatical she is—a person like that can easily be a stool pigeon, and why should you play into the interrogators' hands?"

Natasha assured me that she, with her "fresh eye," could see more than the rest of us.

"Believe me, the Caucasian usurper is even worse than his French predecessors. 'Off with their heads'—that's his answer to everything."

"But can he really be deliberately out to destroy the best elements of the Party? What could he base himself on after that?"

"Just you wait till night comes—you'll hear what he bases himself on."

"But I spent a night in the other cell and I didn't hear anything."

"That's because you didn't arrive till just before dawn. The torturing goes on till three. And the German women, who've been through the hands of the Gestapo, say that the people here must have learned it from them—the style's the same. A spell of foreign training, would you say?"

Natasha's harsh, agonizing words contrasted strangely with her schoolgirl's braids. Specks of sunshine, dimmed by the frosted glass, danced on her reddish hair. In the same way life, light, and human kindness kept breaking through the gloom which surrounded us.

Greta was describing to her friend the ravishing dress which she had worn to the last First of May party at the Bolshoy Theater, and Klara's eyes were sparkling with curiosity. She too was talking about a special dress, drawing its shape in the air, tracing it with her blue fingers with their crushed nails.

As for the Chinese Genia, she was teaching a slim Polish woman named Wanda exercises that were "good for the figure." Looking furtively at the peephole from time to time, the two of them were lying on their backs on the floor and pedaling with their legs in the air, anxious to preserve their figures from the effects of lying about all day, of prison inactivity, of the diet of *kasha* and oatmeal gruel. . . .

Dinner and supper came and went. The evening wash. Inspection. Lights out. We lay in our beds and waited. Soon *it* would begin, inexorable as death.

BUTYRKI NIGHTS

That evening, the general mood was more hectic than usual because of an incident during inspection.

The rule at Butyrki was to count us not by heads but by checking our tin mugs. We were supposed to place these on the table before inspection. The warders and block supervisors would count the mugs and leave us with the usual parting instructions about not talking too loud, going to sleep immediately after "lights out," and so forth.

On this occasion the warder who did the counting was exceptionally, unbelievably stupid. He miscounted several times, arranged the mugs in a tidier pattern, lost count again, and had to start from the beginning, licking his right thumb in a comical manner.

The first to giggle was the Chinese, Genia Koverkova, and this set the rest of us off. When the ceremony was over and the senior warders had gravely withdrawn with their attendants, the cell resounded with peals of crazy laughter such as one sometimes hears in prisons. As if to compensate for their anxiety, grief, and sufferings, prisoners will laugh at the slightest provocation. They explode with a Homeric mirth completely disproportionate to what caused it. Such outbursts are not easy to stop, and on this occasion the warnings of the more cautious among us had no effect.

"Be quiet, all of you!" This shrill command came from Julia Annenkova—her face pale and contorted, her hand lifted in a threatening gesture. "How dare you make fun of him! He is doing his duty as the representative of Soviet power. How dare you, how dare you!"

We stopped laughing abruptly. A tall, earnest, German woman named Erna tried to explain to Julia that our amusement was provoked "by the comic character of the man himself, irrespective of his social functions." We should have laughed at him in the same way if he had not been a warder, but a prisoner like ourselves.

A voice from a group of Poles in the corner said crossly: "Half-wit!" but it was not clear whether this referred to the warder or to Julia.

Julia, deaf to everything, tore off her clothes, lay down, and pulled her blanket over her head, ostentatiously demonstrating her detachment from her neighbors, in every one of whom she, as an orthodox Stalinist, scented the "true enemy."

The rest of us, shaken by this incident, went to bed quickly. Next to me was the Latvian Milda, an elderly woman who had all the marks of an impeccable member of the working class. She looked like a washer-woman, with deep-set eyes, a flat chest and big belly, long thin arms and large hands with prominent veins. The charge against her was that she had lived it up with foreigners in elegant restaurants, seduced Soviet diplomats, and wormed secret information out of them. This was July 1937, when no one cared any longer whether the charges bore the slight-est semblance of probability.

Before lying down, Milda combed her thin yellow hair neatly and drew from under the straw pillow some cotton wool with which she carefully stopped both her ears. She offered me some and, when I looked surprised, explained:

"It was winter when I was arrested, so I have my overcoat, and I pull this out of the lining."

"But what's the idea of stopping your ears?"

She shrugged wearily.

"So as not to hear. So as to get some sleep."

But I did not stop up mine. Rather than play the ostrich, I would see things through to the finish. And I saw them through on that hot July night of the year 1937.

It began all at once, not by degrees or with any sort of prelude. Not one, but a multitude of screams and groans from tortured human beings burst simultaneously through the open windows of our cell. In the Butyrki prison, an entire wing on a certain floor was set aside for night interrogations, and it was doubtless equipped with the latest refinements of the torture chamber. Klara, the ex-victim of the Gestapo, assured us that the implements used here must have been imported from Hitler's Germany.

Over and through the screams of the tortured, we could hear the shouts and curses of the torturers. Added to the cacophony was the noise of chairs being hurled about, fists banging on tables, and some other unidentifiable sound which froze one's blood.

Although these were only sounds, they conjured up such a vivid pic-ture that I felt I could see it in every detail. I imagined all the interroga-tors as looking like Tsarevsky.* As for the victims, I could see them before me with that unmistakable look of theirs—no, I cannot describe it, but to this day I can tell former "guests" of the NKVD by the trace of

---

*State Security Lieutenant Tsarevsky had been Ginzburg's interrogator—ED.

that look which flickers somewhere deep down in their pupils. To this day, in the 1960's, I can startle people I meet in the train or at the seaside by the clairvoyant question: "You were in, weren't you? You've been rehabilitated?"

How long could it go on? Till three o'clock, they had told me. But surely no one could endure this longer than a minute. Yet the noise went on and on, dying down from time to time and then bursting out again. An hour—two, three, and four hours, from eleven till three o'clock every night. I sat up in bed. An old Eastern saying came into my mind: "May I never experience all that it is possible to get used to." Yes, my cellmates had got used even to this. Most of them were asleep or, at all events, were lying quietly, their heads buried under blankets in spite of the stifling heat. Only a few newcomers, like me, were sitting up in their bunks. Some had stuffed their fingers into their ears, some were as if petrified. Every now and then the supervisor would stick her head through the flap-window with the command:

"Lie down! It's against the rules to sit up after lights out."

Suddenly a long-drawn-out shriek of pain was heard, not from a distance but in our cell. A young woman with a long, disheveled braid rushed to the window and, as if demented, beat against it with her head and hands.

"It's him! I know it is, it's his voice! I don't want to go on living, I don't, I can't! Please let them kill me. . . ."

Several women jumped up and surrounded her, dragging her away from the window and trying to convince her that she was mistaken, that it was not her husband's voice. But she was not to be comforted. No, she would know his voice among a thousand—it was he they were torturing and mutilating; and was she to lie here and be silent? If she screamed and made a disturbance they might kill her right away, and that was all she wanted—how could she possibly live after this? . . .

We heard steps in the corridor: the door was flung open and the supervisor came in, accompanied by a senior warder. The latter, with a practiced movement, pinned the woman's arms behind her back and forcibly poured down her throat some liquid from a glass, saying: "Drink this, it's valerian drops."

I doubt, though, that any valerian would have had the effect of making the woman collapse almost instantaneously onto her bunk, close her eyes, and fall into a strange, deathlike sleep.

The cell was quiet again. Milda raised her head, felt under her pillow, and again offered me some cotton wool.

"I don't want it, thanks. Tell me, who is that woman?"

"Oh, she's one of the Poles. There are seven of them in that corner. Her husband's a Russian, a Soviet citizen. They married a short time ago, and there's a baby, three months old. They had to bandage her breast to stop the milk. What she can't stand is the thought that her husband was arrested because of her, for associating with a foreigner."

By now it was nearly three o'clock, and the sounds were dying down. Once more I heard a chair thrown to the ground, once more a man's stifled sob. Then silence.

I could see in my mind's eye the torn, bloody victims as they staggered or were carried out of the torture chamber. I could see the interrogators putting their papers away till the following night.

"Give me some cotton wool now," I begged Milda.

"You won't need it now. It's all over till tomorrow."

"Never mind, please give me some."

She shrugged in bewilderment, but gave me a piece of the gray material. I stopped both my ears, then pulled over my head the prison blanket, smelling of dust and grief, and took a corner of the straw pillow firmly between my teeth. It would be easier like this: I could neither hear nor see. If only I could stop thinking as well! . . .

I knew I should not sleep until I had repeated some poem over to myself ten or a hundred times. I chose Michelangelo's lines:

> Sweet is't to sleep, sweeter to be a stone.
> In this dread age of terror and of shame,
> Thrice blest is he who neither sees nor feels.
> Leave me then here, and trouble not my rest.

In Accordance with the Law of December 1st

In the Butyrki prison, isolation from the outside world was much more absolute than at Kazan. The cells were filled on the principle of grouping together people at the same stage of the interrogation process. Consequently no one joined us direct from outside: any newcomers were either, like me, at the end of their interrogation or at any rate close to it.

We suffered a great deal from our enforced ignorance, but for the rest we managed to achieve some sort of daily routine. The dreadful nights alternated with busy days. Indeed, we had scarcely a moment's free time from reveille to lights out. There were the emptying of the enormous slop bucket, the long queues for the washroom, the distribution of food three times a day from large pails, washing up, mending our frayed stockings and underwear—none of us were allowed to receive parcels— the daily exercise, the taking of orders for the "store" from those who were lucky enough to have a little money, the exchange of books, inspection and roll call—all this filled and even overfilled the daylight hours. By day our cell resembled the hold of a disabled ship, tossing about at the mercy of winds and waves. Just as on a sinking ship, the reactions of individuals varied from the elaborately calm to the exalted and the cowardly. Though of these last there were few.

A day or two after my arrival there was a row over our feeding the birds. It came to the ears of Popov, the prison governor, that we were scattering crumbs out of the window every evening and that the sparrows, having discovered this, would crowd about our window, making a great din; they would even get into the cell and fill it with their twittering, to the delight and entertainment of us prisoners.

Popov, with an escort of warders, burst into the cell at an unscheduled hour and, in a voice choked with fury, made a short but trenchant speech on the theme that this was not a pleasure resort. Every sentence ended with the refrain: "Don't you forget that you're in prison, and in the Butyrki prison at that!" However, we were not put in punishment cells or deprived of our books or exercise. It was said, in fact, that Popov was not such a bad fellow as all that, and that his bark was worse than his bite. In any case, he was soon to have a chance to appreciate his own formula, "the Butyrki prison at that." Before two or three months were out, he had ceased to be the governor of the jail and become one of its inmates.

From time to time one of us was called out of the cell. If we were told to "bring our things," the others would turn pale and whisper with dried lips, "She's to go before the court" or "She's to be told her sentence." We knew, indeed, that some people were sentenced by the courts and others, *in absentia,* by a "special board" of the NKVD; but we had no idea as yet what the sentences were. Much argument raged about this: some spoke chillingly of ten years or even death, but most of us brushed them aside angrily. We relied on the comforting thought: "If Zinovyev and Kamenev, Pyatakov and Radek got only ten years each, then surely we small fry . . ."

If one of us was summoned "without her things," the cell would be thrown into a flutter for a different reason. As soon as the door had shut and the key turned, ominous whispers would be heard in every corner:

"Now I wonder what that's for. Her interrogation was over a long time ago."

"How dare you! She's a decent person."

"I always thought so, but . . ."

"And I, like a fool, talked my head off to her last night."

It was like a psychosis: good and sensible people who had been on friendly terms would suddenly see in their neighbors potential spies and *provocateurs.* Afterward they would often feel ashamed of these fits of distrust and suspicion, this sense of being a wolf among wolves. But a few hours later someone else would be called out "without her things," and the rest would again be petrified with fear. Suppose she were to repeat to the interrogator everything that had been said in the cell the day before?

So when, one bright day that summer, the supervisor put her head through the flap-window and quietly pronounced my name, my first feeling was acute embarrassment. Why without my things? What on earth would my cellmates think of me? . . .

It is curious how a prisoner's traumatic state can affect his reflexes. This was my first call after three weeks in Butyrki, and one would have supposed that my first thought would be of my trial, the sentence that awaited me, whether I was to live or die. But no—I was only worried about whether my cellmates would think I had been called out to inform on them. . . .

I followed the warder's whispered directions almost mechanically through the maze of corridors, till I suddenly found myself back in the central "reception hall" of the prison.

"Over here!" The bolt shot to, and I was again inside one of the "kennels"—a tiled booth with standing room only. Was I to be taken away somewhere?

Leaning against the cold wall, I once more lost track of time. The tiles glittered in the light of a strong bulb. It was still there when I closed my eyes, only less bright. Well, they could not leave me here for ever.

The bolt clicked open. A young officer stood in the doorway and thrust a piece of paper at me.

"Read this." Before I could ask him anything, he had locked me in again.

"This" was my charge sheet, signed by Vyshinsky.* So he had endorsed it. . . . I remembered meeting him once at a summer resort. He wore an embroidered Ukrainian shirt and was accompanied by his ailing, emaciated wife and their daughter Zina, with whom I used to go bathing every day. Had he remembered me when he signed this paper? Or were all names confused in the bloody haze of his mind? He had, after all, not shrunk from sending to execution his old comrade Yevgeni Veger, the secretary of the Odessa regional committee; so why should he spare his daughter's holiday friend?

I ran my eyes over the "preamble" to the act of accusation. There was nothing special here—the usual newspaper claptrap: "A Trotskyist terrorist counter-revolutionary group . . . dedicated to the restoration of capitalism and the physical annihilation of Party and government lead-

---

*Andrey Vyshinsky, 1883–1954, notorious Soviet jurist who acted as prosecutor in the show trials of 1937–38. Later Foreign Minister and Soviet representative at the United Nations.

ers." These formulae, repeated millions of times over, had lost their power to shock and now inspired only a vague nausea: they affected the mind almost like a refrain, or like some oft-repeated fairy tale. People skipped them and would wait with bated breath for the real story to begin, for the ogre to appear. . . .

In my case, after the ritual introduction came a list of "members of the counter-revolutionary Trotskyist terrorist organization among the editorial staff of the newspaper *Red Tartary.*" Again not the slightest attempt at plausibility. Some of the people on the list had never worked on the newspaper; others had long since moved to other towns and were nowhere near at the time of the crime. As I later found out, those who had moved away far enough were never arrested. . . .

I read on. Ah, here was the real story, here came the ogre at last. "On the basis of these facts, the case is referred to the military tribunal . . . in accordance with sections 8 and 11 of Article 58, of the Criminal Code and the law of December 1, 1934."

By now the flutter in my temples had changed to a slow, reverberating throb. What law was this? Its date boded no good. . . .

The young officer opened the door of my kennel again. This time I was able to take in his appearance: he had a sharp little nose and a toothbrush mustache, like the comic policeman in Gorky's play *Enemies.* . . . As if from very far off, I heard him asking for the second time: "Have you acquainted yourself with the indictment? Is it quite clear?"

"No, it isn't. I don't know what the law of December 1, 1934, says."

He looked astonished, as if I had asked him what the sun or the moon were. Then he replied with a shrug:

"It says that the sentence must be carried out within twenty-four hours of its being pronounced."

Twenty-four hours—plus another twenty-four between now and my trial. (They had told me in the cell that people were usually tried on the day after they were shown the indictment.) That made forty-eight hours in all—forty-eight hours to live.

There was once a little girl called Genia. Her mother used to braid her hair, and she grew up and fell in love and tried to discover what life was about. And she lived as a grown-up woman for two whole years, till she was twenty-eight. And she had two sons, Alyosha and Vasya. . . .

The cell was dead silent. It was the first case of its kind known to us. No one from our cell had been before the military tribunal: only before various summary or civil courts. And no one had yet been presented with an indictment and the clause about the sentence being carried out within twenty-four hours. No one had the slightest doubt what was in store for me tomorrow. They stroked my hair, took my shoes off, made me swallow some veronal which had by some miracle been smuggled past the guards: but it had no effect. The organism refuses to waste the last hours of its existence on sleep.

All that night, unreproved by the supervisor, I sat at the table in the middle of the cell. I learned then of what kindness my fellow inmates were capable. It was hard to believe they were the same women who had suspected one another of the blackest treachery. They learned by heart my children's names and my relatives' addresses, so that if they themselves survived they could tell them of my last hours.

One would need to be a Tolstoy to give an account of the thoughts and feelings of a person condemned to death. When I think of that night, I can only remember a curious sharpness in the outlines of objects and a painful dryness in my mouth. As for my thoughts, an exact record of how they ran would read strangely. "Do people have time to feel pain when they are shot? What on earth will Alyosha and Vasya say when they have to fill in forms about their parents? What a shame about that new silk dress that fitted me so well and that I never had a chance to wear. . . ." Such, more or less, were the thoughts that went through my head.

Some books were lying on the table. I opened one. Baransky's *Economic Geography.* Good. I could take another look at a map. There was the world. And there was Moscow, where I had been born, and where now I was about to die. There were Kazan, Sochi, and the Crimea. And there was the rest of the world, which I had not seen and never would.

At dawn some sparrows, who had evidently not heard that this was not a pleasure resort and that Popov, the prison governor, had categorically forbidden all contact between birds and prisoners, perched boldly on the edge of the wooden screen, their tails fluttering comically. With joyful voices they ushered in the grandest month of the year. It was the morning of August 1, 1937.

NATALIA GINZBURG
(1916–1991)

One of Italy's leading postwar novelists, Natalia Ginzburg was the youngest of five children born to Giuseppe Levi, a professor of anatomy at Turin University, and his wife, Lydia. Her father was Jewish and her mother was not, but both were socialists. Although the professor encouraged only their scientific interests, scorning literature and the arts, his three sons—Gino, Mario, and Alberto—and two daughters—Paola and Natalia—did not become scientists. Paola married Adriano Olivetti of the typewriter family, and the Olivetti business gave employment at different times to the Levi sons. Adriano's father, the old industrialist, was one of the few people Professor Levi respected. The author married a Russian émigré writer and anti-Fascist, Leone Ginzburg, in 1938. He died in 1944, after torture, in a Nazi prison in Rome. She later married a professor of English literature at the University of Rome. In 1983 she became a member of the Italian Parliament. She also translated Proust and Flaubert into Italian.

Natalia Ginzburg's memoir *Family Sayings*, published in Italian as *Lessico Famigliare* in 1963, captures the lively confusion of a large family with somewhat eccentric parents. This selection focuses on the turmoil after two of her brothers decided to become "conspirators"—that is, participate in anti-Fascist activity.

For an account of a family similar in some ways despite their very different circumstances, compare Jessica Mitford, *Hons and Rebels*. For an account of a woman's anxiety for a man in prison, compare Marguerite Duras, *The War*.

FROM *Family Sayings*

My grandmother died, and we all went to Florence for the funeral. She was buried there in the family tomb beside grandfather Parente, "poor little Regina" and all the other Margheritas and Reginas.

Henceforth my father always referred to her in a particularly affectionate and commiserating tone as "my poor mother." When she was alive he had always tended to call her stupid, as he did with all of us. But now that she was dead her faults seemed to him innocent and childlike, deserving of pity and sympathy.

She bequeathed her furniture to us. My father said it was of "great value," but my mother did not like it. However, Gino's wife, Piera, also said it was good. My mother was rather shaken. She had confidence in Piera who, she said, knew a great deal about furniture. Still she found it too big and heavy. There were some armchairs which grandfather Parente had brought over from India, made of carved black wood, with elephants' heads on the arm-rests. There were small chairs in black and gold—Chinese I believe—and a quantity of knick-knacks and china; and silver and plates with a crest which had once belonged to our Dormitzer cousins, who had been made barons after lending money to the Austrian Emperor Franz-Joseph.

My mother was afraid that when Alberto came home for the holidays he would take something to the pawnbroker. So she had a small cabinet made with a locking glass front, and there she placed all the smaller pieces of porcelain She maintained, however, that my grandmother's furniture did not suit our house; it got in the way and did not look good. "It is not the sort of furniture," she said every day, "that goes with Via Pallamaglio."

So my father decided that we should move again, and we went to live in the Corso Re Umberto. We had a ground-floor apartment in a low old house overlooking the Corso. My mother was very pleased to be on the ground floor once more because she felt nearer to the street; she could go in and out without going up and down stairs, and without a hat, as she always dreamed of going out without a hat, although her husband had forbidden her to do so.

"But in Palermo," she said, "I always went out without a hat."

"Palermo! Palermo! Palermo! That was fifteen years ago. Look at Frances, she never goes out without a hat."

Alberto left boarding-school and came to Turin for his school-leaving certificate examination. He did very well and had excellent marks. We were all astonished.

"You see what I told you, Beppino!" said my mother. "You see he can work when he wants to."

"And now," said my father, "what shall we do with him now?"

. . . Alberto when he was asked said he was going to read medicine.

He said this with a casual resigned air, shrugging his shoulders. Alberto was now a tall, thin, fair-haired youth with a long nose—a success with the girls. When my mother rummaged in his drawers for pawn-tickets she found a heap of letters from girls, and photographs.

He did not see Pestelli any more now that he was married, nor Pajetta,* who after his time at the approved school had been arrested

*Giancarlo Pajetta, Communist resistance fighter—Ed.

once more, tried by the Political Offences court and sent to prison at Civitavecchia. Albert now had a friend called Vittorio.*

"That Vittorio," said my mother, "is an excellent boy, he works very hard. He comes from a very good family. Alberto is a slacker but he always chooses his friends well." Alberto had not ceased to be, in my mother's parlance, a "tramp" and a "slacker"—though I don't quite know what she meant—even after he had passed his leaving certificate exam.

"Scoundrel! Rascal!" my father shouted when Alberto came home at night. He was so accustomed to shouting that he did so even when Alberto happened to come in early. "But where the devil have you been this late?" "I have just been seeing a friend of mine home," Alberto would reply in a bright breezy voice.

Alberto ran after little milliners, but he chased respectable girls as well. He ran after all the girls, for he liked them all, and because he was so cheerful and kind he even courted the ones he did not like, through sheer kindness of heart. He enrolled for medicine, and when my father found Alberto in his anatomy class he didn't much like it. There was one occasion when the room was dark and my father was showing some slides; he saw the glow of a cigarette in the darkness. "Who is smoking?" he shouted. "What son of a dog has started smoking?" "It's me, papa," said the familiar voice, and everybody laughed.

When Alberto had to sit an examination my father was in a terrible mood from first thing in the morning. "He will show me up badly. He has not done any work at all!" he said to my mother. "Wait, Beppino, wait!" she said. "We don't know yet."

"He got an A," my mother told him. "An A?" he was furious. "An A? They gave him that because he is my son. If he were not my son, they would have failed him." And he was angrier than ever.

Later Alberto became a very good doctor. But my father was never convinced, and when my mother or one of us was not well, and wished to send for Alberto, my father would bellow with laughter, "What! Alberto! What do you expect him to know?"

Alberto and his friend Vittorio used to stroll along the Corso Re Umberto. Vittorio had black hair, square shoulders and a long prominent chin. Alberto had fair hair, a long nose, and a short receding chin. They talked about girls, also about politics, because Vittorio was a political conspirator. Alberto was not at all interested in politics; he did not read the papers, expressed no opinions, and never took any part in the arguments which still erupted between my father and Mario. But he was

---

*Vittorio Foa, prominent socialist politician and trade unionist—ED.

attracted by conspirators. From the time when he and Pajetta were boys in shorts, Alberto had been attracted by conspiracies without, however, taking part in them. He liked to be the friend and confidant of conspirators.

When my father met Alberto and Vittorio on the Corso he nodded to them curtly. It never entered his head that one of them could be a conspirator and the other his confidant. Besides, the people he was used to seeing with Alberto only filled him with suspicion and contempt. He did not think that there were any conspirators left in Italy. He believed that he himself was one of the very few anti-Fascists remaining in the country. The others were the people he used to meet in Paola Carrara's house, my mother's friend who had been, like her, a friend of Kulischov.

"This evening," said my father to my mother, "we are going to the Carraras. Salvatorelli* will be there."

"Oh, lovely! I am really curious to hear what Salvatorelli says."

After spending an evening with Salvatorelli, in Paola Carrara's little sitting-room which was full of dolls which she made for a charity in which she was interested, my father and mother felt reassured. Nothing new had been said really. But many of my parents' friends had become Fascists, or at least were not so openly and avowedly anti-Fascist as they would have liked. So they felt increasingly lonely as the year went by.

Salvatorelli, the Carraras, and old Olivetti were in my father's opinion the few anti-Fascists left in the world. . . . He could not believe there were new conspirators in the rising generation, and if he had suspected that there were any he would have thought them mad. According to him there was nothing, absolutely nothing, to be done against Fascism.

As for my mother, she had an optimistic nature and enjoyed a good piece of drama. She expected someone, someday, somehow, would knock down Mussolini. She would go out in the morning saying, "I am going to see if Fascism is still on its feet. I am going to see if they have knocked Mussolini down." She picked up allusions and views in the shops, and turned them into comforting omens. At dinner she would say, "There is great discontent everywhere. People cannot take any more."

"Who told you that?" shouted my father.

"My greengrocer told me."

My father snorted disdainfully.

Every week Paola Carrara received the *Zurnal de Zenève* (that was the way she pronounced French). She had a sister, Gina, in Geneva, and

*Luigi Salvatorelli, distinguished writer, teacher, and liberal leader—ED.

her brother-in-law, Guglielmo Ferrero.* Both had gone abroad many years before for political reasons. Paola went occasionally to Geneva, but sometimes her passport would be taken away, and then of course she could not go to see Gina. Presently her passport would be returned and then she could go. She came back after a few months full of hope and encouraging news.

"Listen, this is what Guglielmo told me. This is what Gina said."

When my mother wanted to bolster her optimism she went to see Paola Carrara. Sometimes, however, she found her in her little sitting-room, full of pearls and dolls and postcards, in the half dark, and in a frantic state. Either they had taken her passport away or the *Zurnal de Zenève* had not arrived and she suspected that it had been confiscated at the frontier.

Mario left his job at Genoa, came to some understanding with Adriano, and was taken into Olivetti's firm. At heart my father was pleased. But before being pleased about it he was angry because he was afraid that Mario had been taken on because he was Adriano's brother-in-law, and not on his own merits.

Paola now had a house in Milan. She had learned to drive a car and went to and fro between Milan, Turin and Ivrea. My father disapproved of this because he thought she never stayed in one place. But none of the Olivettis ever stayed in one place, they were always in their cars, and my father disapproved.

So Mario went to live at Ivrea; he took a room there, and spent his evenings with Gino discussing problems concerning the factory. His relationship with Gino had always been rather cold, but now they became firm friends. Nevertheless Mario was bored to death at Ivrea. During the summer he had been to Paris. He had gone to see Rosselli,† and had asked to be put in touch with the "Justice and Liberty" group in Turin. He had decided quite suddenly to become a conspirator.

Mario came to Turin on Saturdays. He was the same as ever—mysterious, meticulous about hanging his clothes in the wardrobe, and putting his pyjamas and silk shirts in the drawer. He only stayed a short while in the house, put on his raincoat with a resolute businesslike air, went out, and we saw no more of him.

One day my father met him in the Corso Re Umberto with a man whom he knew by sight, called Ginzburg.

*Guglielmo Ferrero (1871–1942), journalist, historian, and sociologist, signed Croce's anti-Fascist manifesto in 1925—ED.

†Carlo Rosselli (1899–1937). Fled to France in 1925 after the murder by Fascists of the socialist leader of the opposition, Matteoti. Founded the anti-Fascist political movement, Guistizia e Libertà. Assassinated, with his brother, by order of Mussolini—ED.

"What is Mario up to with that man Ginzburg?"

"What has Mario got to do with Ginzburg?" he asked my mother. Some time before she had begun to learn Russian, "so as not to get bored." She and Frances were having lessons from Ginzburg's sister. "He is a very cultivated, intelligent man, who does very fine translations from Russian."

"But he is very ugly," said my father. "We know Jews are all ugly."

"And what about you?" said my mother. "Aren't you a Jew?"

"Well, yes, I am ugly too," said my father.

Relations between Mario and Alberto were still cold. They no longer had bouts of wild and furious quarrelling, but they still never exchanged a word. They took no notice of each other if they met in the passage, and Mario curled his lips in disdain if Alberto was mentioned to him.

Mario, however, knew Alberto's friend Vittorio, and Mario and Alberto happened to meet face to face in the Corso with Ginzburg and Vittorio, who knew each other well, and Mario happened to ask them both, Ginzburg and Vittorio, to the house for tea. The day they came my mother was very happy because she saw Alberto and Mario together and saw that they had the same friends. It was like being back in the days of Via Pastrengo when Gino's friends used to come and the house was always full of people.

In addition to taking Russian lessons my mother also took piano lessons. She had her piano lessons with a teacher who had been recommended to her by someone called Signora Donati, who had also taken up the piano at a mature age. This lady was tall, big and handsome, with white hair. She was also studying painting in Casorati's studio. In fact she liked painting better than the piano. She idolized painting, Casorati, his studio, his wife and his little boy, and also his house where she was occasionally asked to dinner. She was keen to persuade my mother to take lessons from Casorati too. My mother, however, stood out against this. Signora Donati telephoned her every day and described how much fun she had had painting. She would say to my mother, "But you have a sense of colour?"

"Yes," said my mother, "I think I have a sense of colour."

"And volume? Do you have any sense of volume?"

"No, I have no sense of volume," my mother replied.

"You have no sense of volume?"

"No."

"But colour! You have sense of colour!"

Now that there was more money in the house, my mother had some dresses made. This was a constant activity in addition to Russian and the piano, and really a means of "not getting bored," because afterwards she did not know when to wear these dresses as she never felt like visiting

anyone except Frances and Paola Carrara, and to them she could go in
what she was wearing at home. She had her dresses made sometimes "at
Signor Belom's." He was an old tailor who in his younger days had been
my grandmother's suitor in Pisa, when she was looking for a husband and
refused to take "Virginia's leavings." Or she had them made at home by
a dressmaker called Tersilla. Rina no longer came to us, having disappeared into the mists of time, but when my father met Tersilla in
the passage he lost his temper, as he used to do when he saw Rina. Tersilla, however, had more spirit than Rina and used to say hello as she
went past him with her scissors stuck in her belt, and a polite smile on
her small rosy Piedmontese face. My father answered her with a cold
nod.

"Tersilla is here. How come she is here again today?" my father
shouted to my mother.

"She has come to turn an old coat of mine. One of Signor Belom's
coats."

When he heard the name Belom my father was pacified. He had a
high opinion of him because he had been his mother's suitor. He did not
know, however, that Signor Belom was one of the most expensive tailors
in Turin.

My mother swung backwards and forwards between Signor Belom
and Tersilla. When she had a dress made by Belom she would find that it
was not so very well cut, and "fitted badly on the shoulders." Then
afterwards she called in Tersilla, and made her undo it, take it apart, and
start again from scratch. "I shall not go to Signor Belom any more. I shall
have everything made by Tersilla," she declared as she tried on the dress
in front of the looking-glass after one of these remakings. There were,
however, clothes which never fitted and were "never quite right," so she
gave them to Natalina. So Natalina now had a large quantity of clothes
as well. She went out on Sundays in one of Belom's coats which was
black and buttoned all the way down the front so that she looked like a
parish priest.

Paola also had a lot of clothes made. However, she was always at odds
with my mother. She said that my mother's clothes were all wrong and
that she had so many made exactly the same, and that she would get
Tersilla to copy one of Belom's creations a hundred times over, until one
was sick of them. But my mother liked things that way. She said that
when we were little children she always had a number of pinafores made
for us, all exactly the same, and now, like her children, she wished to
have plenty of pinafores for summer and winter. This idea of treating
clothes as pinafores did not convince Paola.

When Paola came from Milan in a new dress my mother embraced
her and said, "I do love to see my children in new dresses." But she

immediately felt like having something new made too; not the same because she always thought Paola's clothes too complicated. She had it made "more pinafore style." The same thing happened with me. When she ordered a new dress for me, she immediatley felt like having one made too. However, she did not admit this to me or to Paola because we used to say that she ordered too many dresses. She would put the material away, neatly folded, in a drawer, until one morning we would see it in Tersilla's hands.

She liked having Tersilla in the house because she enjoyed her company too. "Lydia, Lydia! Where are you?" my father would bellow when he came home. My mother would be in the ironing-room chatting with Natalina and Tersilla.

"You are always with the servants! Tersilla here again today?" he shouted.

"What can Mario be up to with that Russian all the time?" he asked from time to time. "A rising star," he said when he had met his son with Ginzburg on the Corso. However, he saw Ginzburg in a better light and was not over-suspicious of him after he had met him and Salvatorelli on one occasion in Paola Carrara's sitting-room. He still did not understand what Mario had in common with him.

"What can he be up to with that man Ginzburg?" he asked. "What the devil can they say to each other? He is ugly," he said to my mother, meaning Ginzburg, "because he is a Sephardic Jew. I am an Ashkenazy and that is why I am less ugly."

He always spoke rather favourably of the Ashkenazic Jews. Adriano on the other hand always praised people of mixed blood, who were he said the best people. Among these he liked best the children of a Jewish father and a Protestant mother, as he was himself.

In those days we had a game at home which Paola had invented and which she and Mario particularly used to play; sometimes my mother joined in. The game consisted of dividing the people we knew into animal, vegetable and mineral. Adriano was a mineral-vegetable and Paola an animal-vegetable. Gino was a mineral-vegetable. Rasetti, whom anyway we had not seen for many years, was pure mineral, and so was Frances. My father was animal-vegetable and so was my mother.

"Twaddle!" said my father, catching a few words in the passage. "Always that twaddle of yours!"

There were very few vegetables in the world—people of pure imagination; probably only a few great poets had been pure vegetable. Search as we might we could not find a single vegetable among our acquaintances.

Paola said that this game was her own invention. But someone told her later that a classification of this sort had been made by Dante in *De Vulgari Eloquentia.* I do not know whether this is true.

Alberto went to do his military service at Cuneo, and so now Vittorio walked along the Corso alone, since he had already done his service.

One Saturday Mario did not arrive as usual from Ivrea, nor did he appear on Sunday. My mother was not anxious, however, as there had been previous occasions when he had not come. She supposed that he had gone to Switzerland to see his girl friend—the one who was so thin.

On Monday morning Gino and Piera came to tell us that Mario and a friend had been arrested at Ponte Tresa on the Swiss frontier. Nothing else was known. Gino had had this news from someone in the Olivetti office in Lugano.

My father was not in Turin that day. He came home the following morning. My mother had scarcely had time to inform him of what had happened before the house was full of detectives who had come to make a search.

They found nothing. On the previous day, with Gino's help, we had gone through Mario's drawers in case there was anything there that ought to be burnt. We found nothing except all his shirts—"his little wardrobe" as Aunt Drusilla used to say.

The detectives went away taking my father with them to the police station. By the evening my father had not returned and we realized that he had been put in prison.

Gino had been arrested at Ivrea after his return there, and was later transferred to the prison in Turin.

Then Adriano came to tell us that when Mario and his friend were going through Ponte Tresa in the car they had been stopped by customs officers looking for cigarettes. They had searched the car and found some anti-Fascist pamphlets. Mario and his friend were made to get out, and the officers started to escort them along the riverside to the police-post. Suddenly Mario had broken away from his captors. He had plunged into the river fully dressed and had swum towards the Swiss bank. The Swiss guards had then come with a boat to pick him up. So now Mario was in Switzerland, in safety.

Adriano's face wore that expression of mingled happiness and fear in time of danger that it had at the time of Turati's flight.* He put a car and a driver at my mother's disposal, but she did not know what to do, or where to go. She kept putting her hands together, saying with a mixture of happiness, admiration and alarm, "In the water, in his overcoat!"

*Filippo Turati, the founder of Italian socialism, fled to France in 1926 and became the leader in Paris of the Italian anti-Fascist movement—ED.

The friend who had been with Mario at Ponte Tresa and owned the car—for Mario neither owned a car nor could he drive—was called Sion Segre. We had seen him sometimes at home with Alberto and Vittorio. He was a fair-haired youth, rather round-shouldered, with a gentle indolent manner. He was a friend of Alberto and Vittorio but we did not know that he knew Mario too. Paola, however, who drove over from Milan immediately, told us that Mario had confided in her. Mario and Sion Segre had already made a number of trips together between Italy and Switzerland with those pamphlets, and everything had always gone smoothly, so they had become increasingly venturesome and loaded the car with more and more pamphlets and newspapers, neglecting every rule of caution. When he plunged into the river one of the guards had drawn his revolver, but the other one had called to him not to shoot, and so Mario owed his life to that guard. The river was turbulent, but Mario was a good swimmer, and was used to icy water because in fact as my mother remembered, during one of his cruises he had swum in the North Sea with the ship's cook. The other passengers had watched him from the deck and applauded, and when they learned that he was an Italian they began to shout *"Viva Mussolini!"*

Nevertheless, he nearly ran out of strength in the river Tresa, hampered as he was by his clothing, and perhaps because of the tension, but by then the Swiss guards had sent the boat to pick him up.

My mother put her hands together and said, "I wonder if that skinny girl friend of his will give him something to eat."

Sion Segre was now in prison in Turin, and one of his brothers had also been arrested. Ginzburg had been arrested too, and a number of people who had been associated with Mario in Turin. Vittorio had not been arrested. He was quite nonplussed, he told my mother, because he had been constantly with the anti-Fascist conspirators. His long face with its prominent chin was pale, tense and perplexed. He and Alberto, who was home on leave for a few days, walked up and down the Corso Re Umberto.

My mother did not know how to set about providing my father in prison with clean clothing and things to eat. She told me to look in the telephone directory for Segre's family. But Segre was an orphan and had no one but the brother who had also been arrested. But she knew that the Segre boys were cousins of Pitigrilli and she told me to ring him up to find out how he himself was coping and whether he would be taking clothes and books to his cousins in prison. He replied that he would come and see us.

Pitigrilli was a novelist. Alberto was a great reader of his books, and when my father found one in the house, it was as though he had seen a snake. "Lydia, Lydia, hide that book at once!" he shouted. The fact was that he was afraid I might read it, Pitigrilli's novels not being thought at all "suitable" for me. Pitigrilli also edited a review called *Grandi Firme*, and that too was always to be found in Alberto's room in large binders beside his medical books on the shelf.

So Pitigrilli came to see us. He was tall and big. He had long salt and pepper sideburns, and a pale overcoat which he did not take off while he sat solemnly in an armchair and talked to my mother in stern tones with an air of studied concern. He had been in prison once, years ago, and he explained everything to us: the food one could send on certain days of the week to the prisoner, and how one had to shell nuts at home, and peel apples and oranges and cut the bread into thin slices, since knives were not allowed in prison. He explained everything, and then stayed on and talked elegantly to my mother, his legs crossed, his big overcoat unbuttoned, and knitting his bushy eyebrows. My mother told him that I wrote stories and wanted me to show him an exercise-book in which I had made careful fair copies of the three or four stories I had written. Pitigrilli leafed through it for a while with that mysterious, arrogant, sad air of his.

Then Alberto and Vittorio came in and were each introduced to him. And Pitigrilli went out on to the Corso with one of them on either side, walking ponderously, with his arrogant, sad air and his voluminous overcoat over his shoulders.

My father remained in prison for a fortnight or three weeks, I think, and Gino for two months. My mother went to the prison in the morning on the days when one was allowed to send in food, with a bundle of clean clothes and packets of peeled oranges and shelled nuts.

Then she went to the police-station. Sometimes she was received by a man called Finucci, sometimes by a man called Lutri. These two characters seemed to her to be very powerful and to hold the future of our family in their hands. "Today it was Finucci," she would say on her return; she was quite happy because he had reassured her and said that there was no charge against her husband or Gino and that they would shortly be released. "Today it was Lutri," she would say, happy just the same because though his manner was rough, she thought he was perhaps more sincere. She also felt flattered by the fact that both these characters spoke of all of us by name, and seemed to know us all thoroughly. They spoke of "Mario," "Gino," "Piera" and "Paola." They referred to my father as "the professor," and when my mother explained to them that he was a scientist, and had never had anything to do with politics, and only thought about tissue cells, they nodded and told her not to worry. Little by little, however, she began to be frightened because my father did not come home, nor Gino either, and then one day an article appeared in the newspaper, headlined "Group of anti-Fascists discovered in Turin ganging up with Paris exiles." "Ganging up," my mother repeated in distress. This phrase sounded full of dark threats. She wept in the sitting-room with her friends round her—Paola Carrara, Frances, Signora Donati, and all the women younger than herself whom she used to protect and help and comfort when they had no money or their husbands yelled at them. Now it was their turn to help and comfort her. Paola Carrara said that a letter should be sent to the *Zurnal de Zenève.*

"I wrote at once to Gina," she said. "You will see now, there will be a protest in the *Zurnal de Zenève.*"

"It is like the Dreyfus affair," my mother kept on repeating. "It is like the Dreyfus affair."

There was constant coming and going at the house, what with Paola, Adriano, Terni who had come up from Florence specially, and Frances and Paola Carrara. Piera, who was in mourning for her own father and also expecting a baby, had come to live with us. Natalina ran to and from between the kitchen and the sitting-room with cups of coffee. She was excited and happy. She was always happy when there was turmoil— people in the house, noise, days of drama, bells ringing and lots of beds to make.

Then my mother left with Adriano for Rome. Adriano had discovered that there was in Rome someone called Dr. Veratti who was Mussolini's personal doctor. He was an anti-Fascist and prepared to help other anti-Fascists. It was, however, difficult to gain access to him, but Adriano had found two men who knew him, Ambrosini and Silvestri, and through them he hoped to get in touch with the doctor.

Piera and I remained alone with Natalina in the house. One night we were woken up by a ring at the door. We got up, alarmed. Two soldiers had come to look for Alberto who was now an officer cadet at Cuneo. He had not returned to barracks, and it was not known where he was.

He could be court-martialled, Piera said, for desertion. We racked our brains all night as to where he could have got to. Piera thought that he might have taken fright and escaped to France. But the next day Vittorio told us that he had merely gone to meet a girl in the mountains and had spent the time with her, skiing peacefully, forgetting to return to barracks. He had now returned to Cuneo and was under arrest there.

My mother returned from Rome more frightened than ever. Yet she had managed to enjoy herself in Rome because she always enjoyed travelling. She and Adriano had stayed with someone called Signora Bondi, a cousin of my father's, and had tried to get in contact with Margherita as well as with Dr. Veratti. Margherita was one of the many Margheritas and Reginas among my father's relations, and this Margherita was famous because she was a friend of Mussolini. However, my father and mother had not seen her for many years. My mother had not been able to meet her since she was not in Rome at that time, nor had she succeeded in speaking to Dr. Veratti. But Silvestri and Ambrosini had given them some hope, and Adriano had another source—he was always saying "one of my sources"—who had told them that both my father and Gino would very soon be freed. Among the persons arrested the only ones who were really compromised, and they said would be tried, were Sion Segre and Ginzburg. "It's like the Dreyfus affair," my mother kept repeating.

Then one evening my father came home. He had no tie, or laces in his shoes, for they had taken them away in prison. He had a bundle of dirty linen under his arm, wrapped in a sheet of newspaper, and a long beard, and was very pleased with himself for having been in prison.

Gino, however, remained inside for another two months. One day when my mother and Piera's mother were taking some clothes and food to the prison in a taxi, the taxi happened to collide with another car. Neither my mother nor Piera's mother was hurt at all, but there they were, sitting in this smashed up taxi, with their parcels on their knees, with the driver swearing, and a crowd all round them, including some guards, for they were only a few yards from the prison. My mother's only fear was that people would realize that they were taking those parcels to the prison, and would think that they were the relatives of some murderer! When Adriano was told this story, he said there was certainly something bad in my mother's stars and that was why she had so many dangerous adventures at that time.

Finally Gino was released as well, and my mother said: "So now it is back to the ordinary boring life."

My father was furious when he learnt that Alberto was under arrest and in danger of being court-martialled. "That scoundrel! While his family was inside he went off to ski with a girl!"

"I am worried about Alberto," my father said and woke up in the night. "It will be no joke at all if he is court-martialled. I am very worried about Mario. What is he going to do?"

He was, however, happy to have a son who was a conspirator. He had not expected it and had never thought of Mario as an anti-Fascist. When they had arguments Mario would always contradict him, and would disparage the Socialists of former days who were dear to his parents. He used to say that Turati was completely gullible and had piled one mistake upon another. My father used to say as much himself, but when he heard Mario say so he was deeply offended. "He is a Fascist," he would say to my mother at times. "At heart he is a Fascist."

Now he could not say that any more: Mario had become a famous political exile. All the same my father was displeased that his arrest and escape had occurred while he was employed in Olivetti's factory, since he feared that he might have compromised the factory, Adriano and old Olivetti.

"I said that he ought not to go into Olivetti's," he shouted at my mother, "and now he has compromised the factory. How good Adriano is! He has done so much for me. He is very good. All the Olivettis are good."

Through one or other of the Olivetti offices Paola received a letter in Mario's notorious handwriting, which was very small and almost illegible. A note read: "To my vegetable and mineral friends. I am well and not in need of anything."

Sion Segre and Ginzburg were tried before the Political Court Special Tribunal, and were condemned to one year and two years imprisonment respectively. The sentences were halved later, through an amnesty. Ginzburg was sent to the penitentiary at Civitavecchia.

Alberto was not court-marshalled and came home after his military service. He resumed his walks on the Corso with Vittorio. Through force of habit my father shouted once again "Scoundrel" and "Rascal," when he heard him come in, at whatever time of day it might be.

My mother resumed her piano lessons. Her teacher, a man with a little black moustache, was terrified of my father, and crept along the passage on tiptoe with his sheets of music.

"I cannot bear your piano teacher," my father shouted, "he looks very dubious." "Oh no, Beppino, he is a good man. He is very good to his little girl. He is very kind, and teaches her Latin. He is poor."

My mother had given up Russian. She could no longer have lessons from Ginzburg's sister as that would have been compromising.

New phrases had been added to our family vocabulary. "You cannot invite Salvatorelli: it is compromising. You cannot have that book in the house: it could be compromising. There may be a search." Paola said that the main entrance to our building was "under observation," and that there was always a fellow in a raincoat hanging about there, and she thought that whenever she went out she was being followed.

VIVIAN GORNICK
(1935–)

Born and raised in New York City, Vivian Gornick was educated at City College of New York and New York University. From 1969 to 1977 she was a *Village Voice* staff member. She has written on feminism and American communism and has published two memoirs, *In Search of Ali Mahmoud: An American Woman in Egypt* (1973) and *Fierce Attachments* (1987), which focuses on her relationship with her mother both in the past—when the family lived in a largely Jewish tenement in the Bronx—and in the present, when mother and daughter meet occasionally to walk Manhattan's streets, reminiscing and arguing. "My mother is an urban peasant," says Gornick, "and I am her daughter. The city is our element. . . . Walking brings out the best in us." In this selection Nettie is their next-door neighbor in the Bronx, a sexy Ukrainian Christian whose Jewish husband has been killed, leaving her with a baby, named Richie.

For another Bronx Jewish childhood, in an earlier generation, compare Kate Simon, *Bronx Primitive.* For another account of filial exasperation, compare Maxine Hong Kingston, *The Woman Warrior.*

FROM *Fierce Attachments*

My father died at four o'clock in the morning on a day in late November. A telegram was delivered at five-thirty from the hospital where he had lain, terrified, for a week under an oxygen tent they said would save his life but I knew better. He had three heart seizures in five days. The last one killed him. He was fifty-one years old. My mother was forty-six. My brother was nineteen. I was thirteen.

When the doorbell rang my brother was the first one out of bed, Mama right behind him, and me behind her. We all pushed into the tiny foyer. My brother stood in the doorway beneath the light from a sixty-watt bulb staring at a pale-yellow square of paper. My mother dug her nails into his arm. "Papa's dead, isn't he? Isn't he?" My brother slumped to the floor, and the screaming began.

"Oh," my mother screamed.

"Oh, my God," my mother screamed.

"Oh, my God, help me," my mother screamed.

The tears fell and rose and filled the hallway and ran into the kitchen and down across the living room and pushed against the walls of the two bedrooms and washed us all away.

Wailing women and frightened men surrounded my mother all that day and night. She clutched at her hair, and tore at her flesh, and fainted repeatedly. No one dared touch her. She was alone inside a circle of peculiar quarantine. They enclosed her but they did not intrude. She had become magic. She was possessed.

With me they did as they pleased. Passing me among themselves in an ecstasy of ritual pity, they isolated me more thoroughly than actual neglect could have done. They smothered me against their chests, choked me with indigestible food, terrified my ears with a babble of numbing reassurance. My only hope was retreat. I went unresponsive, and I stayed that way.

Periodically, my mother's glazed eye would fasten on me. She would then shriek my name and "An orphan! Oh, God, you're an orphan!" No one had the courage to remind her that according to Jewish custom you were an orphan if your mother died, only half an orphan if your father died. Perhaps it wasn't courage. Perhaps they understood that she didn't really mean me at all. She meant herself. She was consumed by a sense of loss so primeval she had taken all grief into her. Everyone's grief. That of the wife, the mother, and the daughter. Grief had filled her, and emptied her. She had become a vessel, a conduit, a manifestation. A remarkable fluidity, sensual and demanding, was now hers. She'd be lying on the couch a rag doll, her eyes dull, unseeing, tongue edging out of a half-open mouth, arms hanging slack. Suddenly she'd jerk straight up, body tense and alert, eyes sharp, forehead bathed in sweat, a vein pulsing in her neck. Two minutes later she was thrashing about, groveling against the couch, falling to the floor, skin chalky, eyes squeezed shut, mouth tightly compressed. It went on for hours. For days. For weeks, and for years.

I saw myself only as a prop in the extraordinary drama of Mama's bereavement. I didn't mind. I didn't know what I was supposed to be feeling, and I hadn't the time to find out. Actually I was frightened. I didn't object to being frightened. I supposed it as good a response as any other. Only, being frightened imposed certain responsibilities. For one, it demanded I not take my eyes off my mother for an instant. I never cried. Not once. I heard a woman murmur, "Unnatural child." I remember thinking, She doesn't understand. Papa's gone, and Mama obviously is going any minute now. If I cry I won't be able to see her. If I don't see her she's going to disappear. And then I'll be alone. Thus began my conscious obsession with keeping Mama in sight.

It began to snow in the middle of the first night Papa was in the ground. Twisting about on her sodden couch, my mother caught sight of the falling snow. "Oh, woe is me," she cried. "It's snowing on you, my beloved! You're all alone out there in the snow." A new calendar had begun marking time in the apartment: the first time it snowed on Papa's grave, the first time it rained, the first green of summer, the first gold of fall. Each first was announced in a high thin wail that to begin with acted like a needle on my heart, to end with a needle in my brain.

The funeral. Twenty years later when I was living as a journalist in the Middle East, I witnessed Arab funerals almost weekly—hundreds of men and women rushing through the streets, tearing at their clothes, uttering cries of an animal-like nature at a terrifying pitch of noise, people fainting, being trampled, while the crowd whirled screeching on. Westerners who might be standing beside me in the street would shake their heads in amazement at a sight so foreign it confirmed them in their secret conviction that these people were indeed not like themselves. To me, however, it all seemed perfectly familiar, only a bit louder than I remembered, and the insanity parceled out quite a bit more. The way I remembered it, Mama had center stage at all times.

When I woke on the morning of the funeral she was tossing on the couch where she had lain forty-eight hours in clothes she refused to change out of, already crying. The crying was rhythmic, repetitious: it began in a low moan, quickly reached a pitch of shrillness, then receded in a loss of energy that recouped into the original moan. Each cycle was accomplished in a matter of two or three minutes and repeated without variation throughout that interminable morning, while eight or ten people (my brother and I, a few aunts and uncles, the neighbors) wandered aimlessly about the apartment: in and out of the kitchen, in and out of the living room, in and out of the bedrooms.

I remember no conversation; nor do I remember even a wordless embrace. True, explosive behavior was common among us while tender comfort was a difficulty, but it was Mama who had plunged us into muteness. Mama's suffering elevated Papa's death, made us all participants in an event of consequence, told us something had occurred we were not to support, not to live through, or at the very least be permanently stunted by. Still, it was Mama who occupied the dramatic center of the event while the rest of us shuffled about in the background, moving without tears or speech through a sludge of gray misery. It was as though we had all been absorbed into her spectacular abandonment, become witnesses to her loss rather than mourners ourselves. It was Mama who was on our minds as we roamed the gloomy apartment—

who could think of Papa in the midst of such tumult?—Mama who must be watched and attended to, Mama whose mortal agony threatened general breakdown. Disaster seemed imminent rather than already accomplished.

At noon the house was suddenly spilling over with people who instead of going straight to the funeral parlor as they had been asked to showed up at the apartment. These people took us to the edge. As each new face placed itself directly within her view, my mother felt required to deliver up a fresh storm of tears and shrieks. My terror leaped. Now surely she would spin off into a hysteria from which there would be no return.

The time came to lift her from the couch, straighten her clothes, and get her out the door. No sooner were her legs over the side than she became spastic, began to twitch convulsively. Her eyeballs rolled up in her head, her body went limp, her feet refused to touch the floor, and she was dragged out the door like one headed for execution, carried along on a swarm of men and women crying, pleading, screaming, fainting in mimetic sympathy.

At the funeral parlor she tried to climb into the coffin. At the cemetery she tried to fling herself into the open grave. There were other moments at the funeral worthy of permanent record—my brother passed out, I looked so long into the casket I had to be pulled away, a political comrade announced at the grave that my father had been a wage slave in this America—but these moments are without clarity or sharpness of outline. They pall in memory beside the brilliant relentlessness of Mama's derangement.

The day of the funeral seemed to go on for ten days. There were never less than a dozen people wandering around the apartment. My mother lay on the couch weeping and fainting. One by one, each man and each woman in the apartment took a turn at her side, stared helplessly at her for a few minutes, assured her the worst that could happen had indeed happened, and then instructed her: This was *life*. There was nothing anyone could *do*. She had to gather herself to*geth*er. And go *on*. That said, he or she would rise in relief and head for the kitchen, where there were always two to four women waiting to serve a cup of coffee, a bowl of soup, a plate of meat and vegetables. (I remember no cooking. Prepared food appeared magically every day.)

The kitchen was by far the most interesting place to be. Invariably, two of the women were my aunt Sarah and Mrs. Zimmerman, each of whom had less than a loving attachment to her own husband and certainly considered marriage an affliction. Both, however, had been silenced by my mother's awesome performance. Except every now and then irrepressible Mrs. Zimmerman, stirring her own soup at the stove, would mutter, "She lays there crying like a lunatic. If I would come home and find mine dead, it would be a blessing." Sarah would remain silent but someone else in the kitchen, another aunt, a cousin, a friend (why did it always seem to be a woman in a black hat with a dotted veil?), would reprimand Mrs. Zimmerman. "Please, missus!" she'd say. *"She* is not *you*. And a little respect for the dead, if you don't mind." Mrs. Zimmerman would flush deeply and open her mouth wide, but before a sound came out Sarah would lay a hand on her arm and beg that there not be a scene. I'd be at the table, sitting on the wooden bench, often in the crook of Nettie's arm. Animated by the exchange, I'd be disappointed by Sarah's interference. Then Nettie's head would drop, and I'd feel her mouth smiling into my hair. It was as good as if Mrs. Zimmerman had spoken. And shortly, Mrs. Zimmerman did speak. And another tart response cut the air.

I didn't know that not every woman who had lost a husband would be carrying on like Mama, but I did know that the conversation in the kitchen was immensely interesting. One spoke sharply, another speculatively, a third imperiously. The talk was hard and bright, gave the room charge and intensity. Nettie, of course, hardly spoke at all but her body, often in close contact with mine, spoke for her, its speech hidden, restless, amused. I couldn't figure out what was going on in the kitchen, but the responsiveness among the women told me this was a live issue. And the way they dived in! I loved it. Felt nourished and protected, delighted and relieved by it. I remember, especially, the relief.

There was no softness anywhere, not in the kitchen or in the living room, no bland or soothing element on which to heal yourself, or even rub a wound. Still, the difference between the living room and the kitchen was the difference between suffocation and survival. The living room was all monotonous dread, congealed and airless. Here you took a deep breath, held it until you were smothering, then either got out or went under. In the kitchen there was pitch and tone, the atmosphere fell and rose, dwindled away, churned itself up again. There was movement and space, light and air. You could breathe. You could live.

Nettie was around much of the time. Around me, not Mama. She hovered in the doorway or the foyer, sat down shyly in the kitchen, but rarely did she enter the living room. All those respectable Jewish women: she couldn't make her way past them to Mama. Once in a while she'd cross the threshold and stand there like a child, twisting her hands behind her back. My mother would have to spot her, stretch out her arm and wail, "Nettie! I've lost my beloved!" before Nettie felt free (that is, commanded) to rush over, fall to her knees beside the couch, and burst into tears herself.

With me, however, she felt not only free but equal and necessary. She sat with me on the kitchen bench, her arm slung around my neck in an easy embrace, combing my hair with her long fingers. We both knew she had neither the wisdom nor the authority to ease my anxiety (she wasn't even a confidante, she'd always talked more easily to me than I to her), but she could become another orphan, snuggle down companionably with me as she had with Richie, give me the consolation of her warm, helpless body.

Something else began to happen during those funeral-week hours we shared on the kitchen bench. When the women talked about men and marriage, and I felt Nettie's secret smile in my hair and she stifling her laughter against my back, a disturbing excitement ran through me. She knew something no one else in the room knew, and I could feel her wanting to pull me into her knowledge, have me join her there, become her true friend.

The invitation lay in the movement of her body against mine, its freedom and its intimacy. Her motions were rhythmic, her embrace reassuring. She stroked my hair and my shoulder. I felt soothed and sedated. I leaned into her. Her touch began to seem insistent. I felt myself being pulled. Toward what I didn't know. It was as though Nettie stood at the mouth of something dark and soft, drawing me on, her body saying to me: Come. Don't be afraid. I'll pull you through. A dreamy, spreading blur dissolved in my head, my chest. I drowsed against her: open willing aroused.

Suddenly terror prickled on my skin. I felt myself pitching forward, headfirst. The soft dark place was a black void. And she? Who was she? Just a secret-smiling girl-woman, a big kid herself. When we traded fantasies I always felt older. If I went into the dark with her we'd be two kids in there, alone together. How could I trust her? She was no one to trust. My body stiffened in her embrace. She started up, as lost in the hypnotic moment as I, bewildered and alarmed by the suddenness of my withdrawal.

"I want to go see Mama," I said.

Easy as a cat, Nettie's eyes went opaque, her neck grew long, she rearranged her arms and legs. I was free to leave the table.

In the living room I sank to the floor beside my mother, who immediately pressed my head into her breasts. Her strong arms held me, her moans convulsed me. In a matter of seconds the power of Nettie's drowsy allure had been dissipated. I shivered inside myself as though I had made a narrow escape. My anxiety felt cold and scummy. I let Mama crush me against her hot chest. I did not resist. Mama was where I belonged. With Mama the issue was clear: I had trouble breathing but I was safe.

It rained earlier in the day and now, at one in the afternoon, for a minute and a half, New York is washed clean. The streets glitter in the pale spring sunlight. Cars radiate dust-free happiness. Storefront windows sparkle mindlessly. Even people look made anew.

We're walking down Eighth Avenue into the Village. At the corner of Eighth and Greenwich is a White Tower hamburger joint, where a group of derelicts in permanent residence entertain visiting out-of-town-ers from Fourteenth Street, Chelsea, even the Bowery. This afternoon the party on the corner, often raucous, is definitely on the gloomy side, untouched by weather renewal. As we pass the restaurant doors, however, one gentleman detaches from the group, takes two or three uncertain steps, and bars our way. He stands, swaying, before us. He is black, somewhere between twenty-five and sixty. His face is cut and swollen, the eyelids three-quarters shut. His hair is a hundred filthy matted little pigtails, his pants are held up by a piece of rope, his shoes are two sizes too large, the feet inside them bare. So is his chest, visible beneath a grimy tweed coat that swings open whenever he moves. This creature confronts us, puts out his hand palm up, and speaks.

"Can you ladies let me have a thousand dollars for a martini?" he inquires.

My mother looks directly into his face. "I know we're in an inflation," she says, "but a thousand dollars for a martini?"

His mouth drops. It's the first time in God knows how long that a mark has acknowledged his existence. "You're beautiful," he burbles at her. "Beautiful."

"Look on him," she says to me in Yiddish. "Just look on him."

He turns his bleary eyelids in my direction. "Whad-she-say?" he demands. "Whad-she-say?"

"She said you're breaking her heart," I tell him.

"She-say-that?" His eyes nearly open. "She-say-that?"

I nod. He whirls at her. "Take me home and make love to me," he croons, and right there in the street, in the middle of the day, he begins to bay at the moon. "I need you," he howls at my mother and doubles over, his fist in his stomach. "I need you."

She nods at him. "I need too," she says dryly. "Fortunately or unfortu-nately, it is not you I need." And she propels me around the now motion-less derelict. Paralyzed by recognition, he will no longer bar our progress down the street.

We cross Abingdon Square and walk into Bleecker Street. The gentri-fied West Village closes around us, makes us not peaceful but quiet. We walk through block after block of antique stores, gourmet shops, bou-tiques, not speaking. But for how long can my mother and I not speak?

"So I'm reading the biography you gave me," she says. I look at her, puzzled, and then I remember. "Oh!" I smile in wide delight. "Are you enjoying it?"

"Listen," she begins. The smile drops off my face and my stomach contracts. That "listen" means she is about to trash the book I gave her to read. She is going to say, "What. What's here? What's here that I don't already know? I *lived* through it. I know it all. What can this writer tell me that I don't already know? Nothing. To *you* it's interesting, but to me? How can this be interesting to me?"

On and on she'll go, the way she does when she thinks she doesn't understand something and she's scared, and she's taking refuge in scorn and hypercriticality.

The book I gave her to read is a biography of Josephine Herbst, a thirties writer, a stubborn willful raging woman grabbing at politics and love and writing, in there punching until the last minute.

"Listen," my mother says now in the patronizing tone she thinks conciliatory. "Maybe this is interesting to you, but not to me. I lived through all this. I know it all. What can I learn from this? Nothing. To you it's interesting. Not to me."

Invariably, when she speaks so, my head fills with blood and before the sentences have stopped pouring from her mouth I am lashing out at her. "You're an ignoramus, you know nothing, only a know-nothing talks the way you do. The point of having lived through it, as you say, is only that the background is familiar, so the book is made richer, not that you could have written the book. People a thousand times more educated than you have read and learned from this book, but *you* can't learn from it?" On and on I would go, thoroughly ruining the afternoon for both of us.

However, in the past year an odd circumstance has begun to obtain. On occasion, my head fails to fill with blood. I become irritated but remain calm. Not falling into a rage, I do not make a holocaust of the afternoon. Today, it appears, one of those moments is upon us. I turn to my mother, throw my left arm around her still solid back, place my right hand on her upper arm, and say, "Ma, if this book is not interesting to you, that's fine. You can say that." She looks coyly at me, eyes large, head half-turned; *now* she's interested. "But don't say it has nothing to teach you. That there's nothing here. That's unworthy of you, and of the book, and of me. You demean us all when you say that." Listen to me. Such wisdom. And all of it gained ten minutes ago.

Silence. Long silence. We walk another block. Silence. She's looking off into that middle distance. I take my lead from her, matching my steps to hers. I do not speak, do not press her. Another silent block.

"That Josephine Herbst," my mother says. "She certainly carried on, didn't she?"

Relieved and happy, I hug her. "She didn't know what she was doing either, Ma, but yes, she carried on."

"I'm jealous," my mother blurts at me. "I'm jealous she lived her life, I didn't live mine."

Mama went to work five weeks after my father died. He had left us two thousand dollars. To work or not to work was not a debatable question. But it's hard to imagine what would have happened if economic necessity had not forced her out of the house. As it was, it seemed to me that she lay on a couch in a half-darkened room for twenty-five years with her hand across her forehead murmuring, "I can't." Even though she could, and did.

She pulled on her girdle and her old gray suit, stepped into her black suede chunky heels, applied powder and lipstick to her face, and took the subway downtown to an employment agency where she got a job clerking in an office for twenty-eight dollars a week. After that, she rose each morning, got dressed and drank coffee, made out a grocery list for me, left it together with money on the kitchen table, walked four blocks to the subway station, bought the *Times*, read it on the train, got off at Forty-second Street, entered her office building, sat down at her desk, put in a day's work, made the trip home at five o'clock, came in the apartment door, slumped onto the kitchen bench for supper, then onto the couch where she instantly sank into a depression she welcomed like a warm bath. It was as though she had worked all day to earn the despair waiting faithfully for her at the end of her unwilling journey into daily life.

Weekends, of course, the depression was unremitting. A black and wordless pall hung over the apartment all of Saturday and all of Sunday. Mama neither cooked, cleaned, nor shopped. She took no part in idle chatter: the exchange of banalities that fills a room with human presence, declares an interest in being alive. She would not laugh, respond, or participate in any of the compulsive kitchen talk that went on among the rest of us: me, my aunt Sarah, Nettie, my brother. She spoke minimally, and when she did speak her voice was uniformly tight and miserable, always pulling her listener back to a proper recollection of her "condition." If she answered the phone her voice dropped a full octave when she said hello; she could not trust that the caller would otherwise gauge properly the abiding nature of her pain. For five years she did not go to a movie, a concert, a public meeting. She worked, and she suffered.

Widowhood provided Mama with a higher form of being. In refusing to recover from my father's death she had discovered that her life was endowed with a seriousness her years in the kitchen had denied her. She remained devoted to this seriousness for thirty years. She never tired of it, never grew bored or restless in its company, found new ways to keep alive the interest it deserved and had so undeniably earned.

Mourning Papa became her profession, her identity, her persona. Years later, when I was thinking about the piece of politics inside of which we had all lived (Marxism and the Communist Party), and I realized that people who worked as plumbers, bakers, or sewing-machine operators had thought of themselves as thinkers, poets, and scholars because they were members of the Communist Party, I saw that Mama had assumed her widowhood in much the same way. It elevated her in her own eyes, made of her a spiritually significant person, lent richness to her gloom and rhetoric to her speech. Papa's death became a religion that provided ceremony and doctrine. A woman-who-has-lost-the-love-of-her-life was now her orthodoxy: she paid it Talmudic attention.

Papa had never been so real to me in life as he was in death. Always a somewhat shadowy figure, benign and smiling, standing there behind Mama's dramatics about married love, he became and remained what felt like the necessary instrument of her permanent devastation. It was almost as though she had lived with Papa in order that she might arrive at this moment. Her distress was so all-consuming it seemed ordained. For me, surely, it ordered the world anew.

The air I breathed was soaked in her desperation, made thick and heady by it, exciting and dangerous. Her pain became my element, the country in which I lived, the rule beneath which I bowed. It commanded me, made me respond against my will. I longed endlessly to get away from her, but I could not leave the room when she was in it. I dreaded her return from work, but I was never not there when she came home. In her presence anxiety swelled my lungs (I suffered constrictions of the chest and sometimes felt an iron ring clamped across my skull), but I locked myself in the bathroom and wept buckets on her behalf. On Friday I prepared myself for two solid days of weeping and sighing and the mysterious reproof that depression leaks into the air like the steady escape of gas when the pilot light is extinguished. I woke up guilty and went to bed guilty, and on weekends the guilt accumulated into low-grade infection.

She made me sleep with her for a year, and for twenty years afterward I could not bear a woman's hand on me. Afraid to sleep alone, she slung an arm across my stomach, pulled me toward her, fingered my flesh nervously, inattentively. I shrank from her touch: she never noticed. I yearned toward the wall, couldn't get close enough, was always being pulled back. My body became a column of aching stiffness. I must have been excited. Certainly I was repelled.

For two years she dragged me to the cemetery every second or third Sunday morning. The cemetery was in Queens. This meant taking three buses and traveling an hour and fifteen minutes each way. When we climbed onto the third bus she'd begin to cry. Helplessly, I would embrace her. Her cries would grow louder. Inflamed with discomfort, my arm would stiffen around her shoulder and I would stare at the black rubber floor. The bus would arrive at the last stop just as she reached the verge of convulsion.

"We have to get off, Ma," I'd plead in a whisper.

She would shake herself reluctantly (she hated to lose momentum once she'd started on a real wail) and slowly climb down off the bus. As we went through the gates of the cemetery, however, she'd rally to her own cause. She would clutch my arm and pull me across miles of tombstones (neither of us ever seemed to remember the exact location of the grave), stumbling like a drunk, lurching about and shrieking: "Where's Papa? Help me find Papa! They've lost Papa. Beloved! I'm coming. Wait, only wait, I'm coming!" Then we would find the grave and she would fling herself across it, arrived at last in a storm of climactic release. On the way home she was a rag doll. And I? Numb and dumb, only grateful to have survived the terror of the earlier hours.

One night when I was fifteen I dreamed that the entire apartment was empty, stripped of furniture and brilliantly whitewashed, the rooms gleaming with sun and the whiteness of the walls. A long rope extended the length of the apartment, winding at waist-level through all the rooms. I followed the rope from my room to the front door. There in the open doorway stood my dead father, gray-faced, surrounded by mist and darkness, the rope tied around the middle of his body. I laid my hands on the rope and began to pull, but try as I might I could not lift him across the threshold. Suddenly my mother appeared. She laid her hands over mine and began to pull also. I tried to shake her off, enraged at her interference, but she would not desist, and I did so want to pull him in I said to myself, "All right, I'll even let her have him, if we can just get him inside."

For years I thought the dream needed no interpretation, but now I think I longed to get my father across the threshold not out of guilt and sexual competition but so that I could get free of Mama. My skin crawled with her. She was everywhere, all over me, inside and out. Her influence clung, membrane-like, to my nostrils, my eyelids, my open mouth. I drew her into me with every breath I took. I drowsed in her etherizing atmosphere, could not escape the rich and claustrophobic character of her presence, her being, her suffocating suffering femaleness.

I didn't know the half of it.

One afternoon, in the year of the dream, I was sitting with Nettie. She was making lace, and I was drinking tea. She began to dream out loud. "I think you'll meet a really nice boy this year," she said. "Someone older than yourself. Almost out of college. Ready to get a good job. He'll fall in love with you, and soon you'll be married."

"That's ridiculous," I said sharply.

Nettie let her hands, with the lace still in them, fall to her lap. "You sound just like your mother," she said softly.

EMILY HAHN
(1905–)

Prolific nonfiction writer Emily Hahn has lived adventurously and unconventionally since the early 1920s, when she was the first woman to be graduated as a mining engineer from the University of Wisconsin. In 1930 she went to Africa, where she worked at a Red Cross outpost in the Belgian Congo and lived for a year with Pygmies. In 1935, with her sister, Helen, she went to China for a brief visit and ended up staying nine years. She had some celebrated love affairs, including one with the married head of British intelligence in the Far East, Major Charles Boxer, which produced a daughter. Boxer was imprisoned by the Japanese when they took Hong Kong and not released until 1945, at which time he and Hahn married. She discusses these and other adventures in several volumes of memoirs, including *China to Me* and *Times and Places,* from which this selection, "The Big Smoke," was taken. It originally appeared in *The New Yorker* in 1969.

At about the time that Hahn was becoming addicted to opium in Shanghai, Ida Pruitt, an American in Peking, was having Ning Lao T'ai-t'ai to breakfast three times a week and gathering the story of her life. Compare *A Daughter of Han.* For another woman hooked on adventure, compare Beryl Markham, *West with the Night.*

FROM *Times and Places*

THE BIG SMOKE

Though I had always wanted to be an opium addict, I can't claim that as the reason I went to China. The opium ambition dates back to that obscure period of childhood when I wanted to be a lot of other things, too—the greatest expert on ghosts, the world's best ice skater, the champion lion tamer, you know the kind of thing. But by the time I went to China I was grown up, and all those dreams were forgotten.

Helen kept saying that she would go home to California, where her husband was waiting, as soon as she'd seen Japan, but as the time for her departure drew near she grew reluctant and looked around for a good excuse to prolong the tour. As she pointed out to me, China was awfully close by and we knew that an old friend was living in Shanghai. It would be such a waste to let the chance slip. Why shouldn't we go over and take just one look, for a weekend? I was quite amenable, especially as, for my part, I didn't have to go back to America. My intention was to move on south in leisurely fashion, after Helen had gone home, and land someday in the Belgian Congo, where I planned to find a job. All this wasn't going to have to be done with speed, because I still had enough money to live on for a while. My sister accepted these plans as natural, for she knew that a man had thrown me over. Officially, as it were, I was going to the Congo to forget that my heart was broken; it was the proper thing to do in the circumstances. My attitude toward her was equally easygoing. If she didn't want to go home just yet, I felt, it was none of my business. So when she suggested China I said, "Sure, why not?"

We went. We loved Shanghai. Helen shut up her conscience for another two months, staying on and cramming in a tremendous variety of activities—parties, temples, curio shops, having dresses made to order overnight, a trip to Peiping,* embassy receptions, races. I didn't try to keep up with her. It had become clear to me from the first day in China that I was going to stay forever, so I had plenty of time. Without a struggle, I shelved the Congo and hired a language teacher, and before Helen left I had found a job teaching English at a Chinese college. It was quite a while before I recollected that old ambition to be an opium smoker.

As a newcomer, I couldn't have known that a lot of the drug was being used here, there, and everywhere in town. I had no way of recognizing the smell, though it pervaded the poorer districts. I assumed that the odor, something like burning caramel or those herbal cigarettes smoked by asthmatics, was just part of the mysterious effluvia produced in Chinese cookhouses. Walking happily through side streets and alleys, pausing here and there to let a rickshaw or a cart trundle by, I would sniff and move on, unaware that someone close at hand was indulging in what the books called that vile, accursed drug. Naturally I never saw a culprit, since even in permissive Shanghai opium smoking was supposed to be illegal.

It was through a Chinese friend, Pan Heh-ven, that I learned at last what the smell denoted. I had been at a dinner party in a restaurant with him, and had met a number of his friends who were poets and teachers. Parties at restaurants in China used to end when the last dish and the rice were cold and the guests had drunk their farewell cup of tea at a

*Peking (now Beijing) was known as Peiping in the 1930s and 1940s—Ed.

clean table. That night, though, the group still had a lot to say after that—they always did—and we stood around on the pavement outside carrying on a discussion of modern literature that had started at table. We were in that part of town called the Chinese city, across Soochow Creek, outside the boundaries of the foreign concessions. It was hot. A crumpled old paper made a scraping little sound like autumn leaves along the gutter, and the skirts of the men's long gowns stirred in the same wind. During dinner, they had spoken English out of courtesy, but now, in their excitement, they had long since switched to the Chinese language, and I stood there waiting for somebody to remember me and help me find a taxi, until Heh-ven said, "Oh, excuse us for forgetting our foreign guest. We are all going now to my house. Will you come?"

Of course I would. I'd been curious about his domestic life, which he seldom mentioned. So we all moved off and walked to the house—an old one of Victorian style, with more grounds than I was used to seeing around city houses in America. I say Victorian, but that was only from the outside, where gables and a roughcast front made it look like the kind of building I knew. Indoors was very different. It was bare, as one could see at a glance because the doors stood open between rooms—no carpets, no wallpaper, very little furniture. Such chairs and sofas and tables as stood around the bare floor seemed as impersonal as lost articles in a vacant shop. Yet the house wasn't deserted. A few people were there in the rooms—a man who lounged, as if defiantly, on the unyielding curve of a sofa, four or five children scampering and giggling in whispers, an old woman in the blue blouse and trousers of a servant, and a young woman in a plain dark dress.

This last, it appeared, was Heh-ven's wife, and at least some of the children were theirs. I was embarrassed because the whole household gawked at me; one small boy who looked like a miniature Heh-ven said something that made the others giggle louder. Heh-ven spoke briefly to his family and told us to follow him upstairs, where we emerged on a cozier scene. Here the rooms were papered, and though everything still seemed stark to my Western eyes, there was more furniture around. We trooped into a bedroom where two hard, flat couches had been pushed together, heads against a wall and a heap of small pillows on each. In the center of the square expanse of white sheet that covered them was a tray that held several unfamiliar objects—a little silver oil lamp with a shade like an inverted glass tumbler, small boxes, and a number of other small things I didn't recognize. I sat on a stiff, spindly chair, and the men disposed themselves here and there in the room, very much at home as they chattered away, picked up books and riffled through them, and paid no attention to what was going on on the double couch. I found the proceedings there very odd, however, and stared in fascination.

Heh-ven had lain down on his left side, alongside the tray and facing it. He lit the lamp. One of his friends, a plump little man named Hua-ching, lay on his right side on the other side of the tray, facing Heh-ven, each with head and shoulders propped on the pillows. Heh-ven never stopped conversing, but his hands were busy and his eyes were fixed on what he was doing—knitting, I thought at first, wondering why nobody had ever mentioned that this craft was practiced by Chinese men. Then I saw that what I had taken for yarn between the two needles he manipu-lated was actually a kind of gummy stuff, dark and thick. As he rotated the needle ends about each other, the stuff behaved like taffy in the act of setting; it changed color, too, slowly evolving from its earlier dark brown to tan. At a certain moment, just as it seemed about to stiffen, he wrapped the whole wad around one needle end and picked up a pottery object about as big around as a teacup. It looked rather like a cup, except that it was closed across the top, with a rimmed hole in the middle of this fixed lid. Heh-ven plunged the wadded needle into this hole, withdrew it, leaving the wad sticking up from the hole, and modelled the rapidly hardening stuff so that it sat on the cup like a tiny volcano. He then picked up a piece of polished bamboo that had a large hole near one end, edged with a band of chased silver. Into this he fixed the cup, put the opposite end of the bamboo into his mouth, held the cup with the tiny cone suspended above the lamp flame, and inhaled deeply. The stuff bubbled and evaporated as he did so, until nothing of it was left. A blue smoke rose from his mouth, and the air was suddenly full of that smell I had encountered in the streets of Shanghai. Truth lit up in my mind.

"You're smoking opium!" I cried. Everybody jumped, for they had forgotten I was there.

Heh-ven said, "Yes, of course I am. Haven't you ever seen it done before?"

"No. I'm *so* interested."

"Would you like to try it?"

"Oh, yes."

Nobody protested, or acted shocked or anything. In fact, nobody but Hua-ching paid any attention. At Heh-ven's request, he smoked a pipe to demonstrate how it was done, then relaxed against the pillows for a few minutes. "If you get up immediately, you are dizzy," explained Heh-ven. I observed his technique carefully and, by the time I took my place on the couch, had a reasonable notion of how it was done. You sucked in as deeply as possible, and held the smoke there as long as you could before exhaling. Remembering that I'd never been able to inhale cigarette smoke, I was worried that the world of the opium addict might be closed to me. In daydreams, as in night dreams, one doesn't take into account the real self and the failings of the flesh. The romantic is always being confronted by this dilemma, but that night I was spared it. When I breathed in I felt *almost* sick, but my throat didn't close, and after a moment I was fine. I couldn't dispose of the tiny volcano all in one mighty pull, as the others had done, but for a beginner I didn't do badly—not at all. Absorbed in the triumph of not coughing, I failed to take notice of the first effects, and even started to stand up, but Heh-ven told me not to. "Just stay quiet and let's talk," he suggested.

We all talked—about books, and books, and Chinese politics. That I knew nothing about politics didn't put me off in the least. I listened with keen interest to everything the others had to say in English, and when they branched off into Chinese I didn't mind. It left me to my thoughts. I wouldn't have minded anything. The world was fascinating and benevolent as I lay there against the cushions, watching Heh-ven rolling pipes for himself. Pipes—that's what they called the little cones as well as the tube, I suppose because it is easier to say than pipefuls. Anyway, the word "pipeful" is not really accurate, either. Only once, when Hua-ching asked me how I was, did I recollect the full significance of the situation. Good heavens, I was smoking opium! It was hard to believe, especially as I didn't seem to be any different.

"I don't feel a thing," I told him. "I mean, I'm enjoying myself with all of you, of course, but I don't feel any different. Perhaps opium has no effect on me?"

Heh-ven pulled at the tiny beard he wore and smiled slightly. He said, "Look at your watch." I cried out in surprise; it was three o'clock in the morning.

"Well, there it is," Heh-ven said. "And you have stayed in one position for several hours, you know—you haven't moved your arms or your head. That's opium. We call it Ta Yen, the Big Smoke."

"But it was only one pipe I had. And look at you, you've smoked four or five, but you're still all right."

"That's opium, too," said Heh-ven cryptically.

Later that morning, in my own bed, I tried to remember if I'd had drug-sodden dreams, but as far as I could recall there hadn't been dreams at all, which was disappointing. I didn't feel any craving, either. I simply wasn't an addict. I almost decided that the whole thing was just a carefully nurtured myth. Still, I gave it another chance a few days later, and again a third time, and so on. To make a surprisingly long story short, a year of earnest endeavor went by. It's impossible now to pinpoint the moment in time when I could honestly claim to be an addict, but I do remember the evening when Heh-ven's wife, Pei-yu, said I was. I had arrived at their house about six in the evening, when most of the family was in the smoking room. It was a nice domestic scene, the children

playing on the floor, Pei-yu sitting on the edge of the couch really knitting, with wool, and Heh-ven lying on his side in the familiar position,
idly stocking up opium pellets to save time later, now and then rolling a
wad on his second finger to test the texture. A good pellet should be of
just the right color, and not too dry, but not too sticky, either. These
refinements added a lot to one's pleasure. I suppose people who are fussy
about their tea have the same impulse.

I was feeling awful that evening. I had a cold and I'd been up too late
the night before. I was also in a tearing rage with Heh-ven. By this time,
I was publishing a Chinese-English magazine at a press he owned in the
Chinese city—or, rather, I was trying to publish it, and Heh-ven was
maddeningly unbusinesslike about the printing. That day, I'd waited at
home in vain for hours because he had faithfully promised that some
proofs would be delivered before three o'clock. When I marched in on
the peaceful scene in the smoking room, only a fit of sneezing prevented
my delivering him a stinging scolding. At the sound of the sneezes,
Pei-yu looked up at me sharply. Then *she* started scolding Heh-ven. I
hadn't learned any of the Shanghai dialect—it was Mandarin I was
studying—but the spirit of her speech was clear enough.

"Pei-yu says you are an addict and it's my fault," interpreted Heh-ven
cheerfully.

I felt rather flattered, but my feelings about Heh-ven's lack of performance on the press made me sound surly as I replied, "Why should
she say that?" I lay down in the accustomed place as I spoke, and
reached for the pipe.

"Because your eyes and nose are running."

"So? Is that a symptom?" I looked at Pei-yu, who nodded hard. I
inhaled a pipe and continued, "But that isn't why my nose is running.
I've got the most awful cold."

"Oh yes, opium smokers always have colds." Heh-ven prepared another pipe. "When you don't get the Big Smoke, you weep. Still, in your
case, I think my wife is mistaken. You are not yet an addict. Even *I* am
not an addict, really—not very much addicted, though I smoke more
than you. People like us, who have so much to do, are not the type to
become addicted."

No, I reflected, Pei-yu was certainly exaggerating to a ridiculous degree. Of course I could do without it. I liked it, of course—I liked it. I
had learned what was so pleasant about opium. Gone were the old romantic notions of wild drug orgies and heavily flavored dreams, but I
didn't regret them, because the truth was much better. To lie in a quiet
room talking and smoking—or, to put things in their proper order, smoking and talking—was delightfully restful and pleasant. I wasn't addicted,
I told myself, but you had to have a bit of a habit to appreciate the thing.

One used a good deal of time smoking, but, after all, one had a good deal of time. The night clubs, the cocktail and dinner parties beloved of foreign residents in Shanghai would have palled on me even if I'd kept up drink for drink with my companions. Now I hardly ever bothered to go to these gatherings. Opium put me off drinking, and people who didn't smoke seemed more and more remote, whereas smokers always seemed to have tastes and ideas compatible with mine. We would read aloud to each other a good deal—poetry, mostly. Reading and music and painting were enough to keep us happy. We didn't care for eating or drinking or voluptuous pleasures. . . . I seem to fall into a kind of *fin-de-siècle* language when I talk about opium, probably because it was rather a *fin-de-siècle* life I led when I was smoking it, and in a social as well as a literary sense. The modern, Westernized Chinese of Shanghai frowned on smoking—not on moral grounds but because it was considered so lamentably old-fashioned. My friends, in their traditional long gowns, were deliberately, self-consciously reactionary, and opium was a part of this attitude, whereas modern people preferred to stun themselves with whiskey or brandy. Opium was decadent. Opium was for grandfathers.

We used to read Cocteau's book on opium and discuss it. Hua-ching loved the drawings that represent the feelings of a man under cure, in which the pipe grows progressively larger and the man smaller. Then the pipe proliferates—his limbs turn into pipes—until at last he is built up completely of pipes. During such talks, Heh-ven sometimes spoke of himself frankly as an addict but at other times he still said he wasn't. I never knew what sort of statement he was going to make on the subject. "My asthma caused it, you know," he said once. "My father is asthmatic, so he smokes. I, too, am asthmatic, and so is Pei-yu. Now and then, when hers is very bad, she will take a pipe, because it is a good medicine for that disease."

One day, after he had been even more contradictory than was his custom, I drew up a table of the smoker's creed:

1. I will never be an addict.
2. I can't become addicted. I am one of those people who take it or let it alone.
3. I'm not badly addicted.
4. It's a matter of will power, and I can stop any time.

Any time. Time. That was something that had lost its grip on me. It was amazing how watches varied their rate of running, sometimes galloping, at other times standing still. To keep up with my job, I had to look at my watch often; it had a trick of running away when I didn't notice, causing me to forget dates or arrive at appointments incredibly late. I

appeared sleepy. I know this from what outsiders told me about myself—
"You need sleep," they would say—but I never *felt* sleepy, exactly;
inside, my mind was unusually clear, and I could spend a whole night
talking without feeling the need of rest. This was because I was an
addict. I admitted it now, and was pleased that I could feel detached.
We opium smokers, I reflected, *are* detached, and that is one of our
advantages. We aren't troubled with unpleasant emotions. The alcoholic indulges in great bouts of weeping sentiment, but the smoker
doesn't. You never find a smoker blubbering and blabbing his secrets to
the opium seller. We are proud and reserved. Other people might think
us drowsy and dull; we know better. The first reaction to a good long pull
at the pipe is a stimulating one. I would be full of ideas, and as I lay there
I would make plans for all sorts of activity. Drowsiness of a sort came on
later, but even then, inside my head, behind my drooping eyes, my mind
seethed with exciting thoughts.

Still, I couldn't ignore the disadvantages. If I had, I would have been
unworthy of the adjective "detached." Being an addict was awfully in-
convenient. I couldn't stay away from my opium tray, or Heh-ven's,
without beginning to feel homesick. I would think of the lamp in the
shaded room, the coziness, the peace and comfort with great longing.
Then my nose would start to run and I was afraid somebody from outside
would have the sense to understand what was the matter with me.
When I say afraid, that is what I mean—for some reason, there was
dread in the idea of being spotted. This was strange. True, smoking was
against the law in Shanghai, but only mild penalties were likely to have
been visited on me. Still, I was afraid. I think it may have been a physical
symptom, like the running nose.

All of these little points we discussed at great length, lying around the
tray. Hua-ching had a theory that addiction lay not so much in the
smoking itself as in the time pattern one got used to. "If you vary your
smoking every day, you have far less strong a habit," he assured us
earnestly. "The great mistake is to do it at the same hour day after day.
I'm careful to vary my smoking times. You see, it's all in the head."

Jan, a Polish friend who sometimes joined us, disputed this. "It's the
drug itself," he said. "If it's all in the head, why do I feel it in my body?"
The argument tailed off in a welter of definitions. A smoker loves seman-
tics. However, I resolved one day to test myself and see who was master,
opium or me, and I accepted an invitation to spend the weekend on a
houseboat upriver with an English group. In the country, among foreigners, it would be impossible to get opium.

Well, it wasn't as bad as I'd expected. I was bored, and I couldn't keep
my mind on the bridge they insisted that I play, but then I never can. I
had an awful cold, and didn't sleep much. My stomach was upset and my

legs hurt. Still, it wasn't so bad. I didn't want to lie down and scream—it could be borne. On the way home, my cold got rapidly worse—but why not? People do catch cold. The only really bad thing was the terror I felt of being lost, astray, naked, shivering in a world that seemed imminently brutal. . . . Half an hour after I got back, I was at Heh-ven's, the cronies listening to my blow-by-blow report, expressing, according to their characters, admiration, skepticism, or envy. I was glad that none of them failed to understand my impulse to flee the habit. Every one of them, it seemed, had had such moments, but not everyone was as stubborn as I.

"You could have given her pills," said Hua-ching reproachfully to Heh-ven. I asked what he meant, and he said that addicts who had to leave the orbit of the lamp for a while usually took along little pellets of opium to swallow when things got bad. A pellet wasn't the same thing as smoking, but it alleviated some of the discomfort.

Heh-ven said, "I didn't give them on purpose. She wanted to see what it was like, and the pills would have spoiled the full effect. Besides, they are somewhat poisonous. Still, if she wants them, next time she can have them."

Snuggling luxuriously on a pillow, I said, "There won't be a next time."

Some weeks later, I got sick. I must have smoked too much. In a relatively mild case of overindulgence, one merely gets nightmares, but this wasn't mild. I vomited on the way home from Heh-ven's, and went on doing it when I got in, until the houseboy called the doctor. This doctor was an American who had worked for years in the community, but I didn't know him well. Of course, I had no intention of telling him what might be wrong, and I was silent as he felt my pulse and looked at my tongue and took my temperature. Finally, he delivered judgment. "Jaundice. Haven't you noticed that you're yellow?"

"No."

"Well, you are—yellow as an orange," he said. "How many pipes do you smoke in a day?"

I was startled, but if he could play it calm, so could I. "Oh, ten, eleven, something like that," I said airily, and he nodded and wrote out a prescription, and left. No lecture, no phone call to the police, nothing. I ought to have appreciated his forbearance, but I was angry, and said to Heh-ven next day, "He doesn't know as much as he thinks he does. People don't count pipes—one man's pipe might make two of another's." The truth was that I resented the doctor's having stuck his foot in the door of my exclusive domain.

All in all, if I'd been asked how I was faring I would have said I was getting on fine. I had no desire to change the way I was living. Except for the doctor, foreign outsiders didn't seem to guess about me; they must have thought I looked sallow, and certainly they would have put me down as absentminded, but nobody guessed. The Chinese, of course, were different, because they'd seen it all before. I annoyed one or two people, but I managed to pass, especially when the war between China and Japan flared up just outside the foreign-occupied part of the city. Shells fell all around our little island of safety, and sometimes missed their mark and bounced inside it. It is no wonder that the American doctor didn't take any steps about me—he had a lot of other things to occupy his mind. The war didn't bother me too much. I soon got used to the idea of it. Opium went up in price—that was all that mattered.

But the war cut me off definitely from the old world, and so, little by little, I stopped caring who knew or didn't know. People who came calling, even when they weren't smokers, were shown straight into the room where I smoked. I now behaved very much like Heh-ven; there was even an oily smudge on my left forefinger, like the one on his, that wouldn't easily wash off. It came from testing opium pellets as they cooled. Heh-ven, amused by the smudge, used to call the attention of friends to it. "Look," he would say, "have you ever before seen a white girl with that mark on her finger?"

I wasn't the only foreign opium smoker in Shanghai. Apart from Jan, there were several others I knew. One was connected with the French diplomatic service. He and his wife had picked up their habit in Indo-China. It was through them that I met Bobby—a German refugee, a doctor who had built up enough of a practice in Shanghai to live on it. He wasn't an addict—I don't think I ever saw him touch a pipe—but he seemed to spend a lot of time with addicts. Sometimes I wondered why he dropped in at Heh-ven's so often. I rather wished he wouldn't, because he was dull. Still, it didn't matter much whether outsiders were dull or bright, and as he happened to call on me one afternoon when I had received a shattering letter, I confided in him.

"It's about this silly magazine I've been publishing," I said. "They want to expand its circulation—the people who own it, that is—and they say I've got to go to Chungking to talk to them."

"And you can't go, of course," said Bobby.

"I can, too," I lifted myself up on my elbow and spoke indignantly. "Certainly I can go. What do you mean, I can't? Only, it's a bother." I lay down again and started rolling a pellet fast. My mind buzzed with all the things that would have to be done—arranging about my house, getting a permit to travel. And I'd have to go through Hong Kong, taking a boat down there and then flying inland. It was tiring just to think about it, and here was Bobby talking again.

"Listen to me. Listen carefully. You can't do it—*you* can't."

This time he managed to worry me. "Why not?"

"Because of the opium. Your habit," said Bobby.

I laughed. "Oh, that's what it is, is it? No, that'll be all right." The pellet was ready, shaped into a cone, and I smoked it, then said, "I can stop whenever I want to. You don't know me well, but I assure you I can stop any time."

"How recently have you tried?" he demanded, and paused. I didn't reply because I was trying to reckon it. He went on, "It's been some time, I'm sure. I've known you myself for a year, and you've never stopped during that period. I think you'll find you can't do it, young lady."

"You're wrong," I said violently. "I tell you, you're all wrong—you don't know me."

"And in the interior it's not so funny if you're caught using it, you know. If you're caught, you know what happens." He sliced a stiff hand across his throat. He meant that the Kuomintang had put a new law into effect; people they caught smoking were to be decapitated. But surely that couldn't happen to *me*.

I looked at him with new uncertainty and said, "What will I do?"

"You'll be all right, because I can help you," said Bobby, all of a sudden brisk and cheerful. "You can be cured quite easily. Have you heard of hypnosis?"

I said that of course I'd heard of it, and even witnessed it. "There was a medical student at school who put people to sleep—just made them stare at a light bulb and told them they were sleepy."

Bobby made a call on my telephone, talking in German. He hung up and said, "We start tomorrow morning. I have a bed for you at my little hospital—a private ward, no less. Get up early if you can and do what you usually do in the morning—smoke if you like, I have no objections—but be there at nine o'clock. I'll write down the directions for the taxi-driver." He did so. Then, at the door, he added, "Heh-ven will try to talk you out of it, you know. Don't let him."

I said, "Oh no, Bobby, he wouldn't do that. This is my own affair, and he'd never interfere."

"Just don't let him, that's all. Don't forget a suitcase with your night things. You'll probably bring some opium pills, but if you do I'll find them, so save yourself the trouble."

Before I became an addict, I used to think that a confirmed smoker would be frantically afraid of the idea of breaking off. Actually, it isn't like that—or wasn't with me. At a certain stage, a smoker is cheerfully ready to accept almost any suggestion, including the one of breaking off. Stop smoking? Why, of course, he will say—what a good idea! Let's start tomorrow. After a couple of pipes, I was very pleased about it, and rang up Heh-ven to tell him. He, too, was pleased, but couldn't see why I was in such a hurry.

"Oh, wonderful!" he said. "But why tomorrow? If you wait, we can do it together. It's always easier with somebody else. Wait, and I'll ask Bobby to fix me up, too."

"I'd like to, Heh-ven, but he's got everything arranged for me at the hospital, and I can hardly change things around now. And, as he said, I haven't got much time—only a couple of weeks before I have to go to Chungking. It'll be easier when your turn comes."

The high sweetness in his voice when he replied was significant, I knew, of anger. "Of course, since you are so happy to take the advice of a man you hardly know . . ."

It was a struggle, but I hadn't given in by the time I hung up. Full of opium or not, I knew all too well what would happen if I consented to wait for Heh-ven for anything at all—a tea party or a cure. He'd put it off and put it off until it was forgotten. I shrugged, and had another pipe, and next morning I almost overslept, but didn't. The old man who took care of the house carried my bag out to the taxi, talking to himself, and stood there as I climbed in, a worried look on his face. He didn't trust anything about the project. "I come see you soon," he promised.

I had never heard of Bobby's hospital. We drove a long way through the shops and hovels that ringed the foreign town, so that I half expected we would enter the Japanese lines, but before we got that far we found it—a building about as big as most middle-class Shanghai houses and only a little shabbier. Over the entrance hung a dirty white flag and a red cross on it. Bobby was at the door, his teeth gleaming in a relieved smile, his spectacles flashing in the morning sun. Clearly, he hadn't been quite sure I would turn up, and he asked how Heh-ven had taken the news.

"He wants you to fix him up, too—someday," I told him.

"Whenever he's ready. Come in here. The nurse will look after your suitcase."

I followed him to a flimsily walled office filled with, among other things, filing cases, a heavy old desk, and one overstuffed chair, in which he told me to sit. He gave me a pill, and a tin cup of water to help it down. I stared around curiously. There were cardboard boxes piled against the walls, and an instrument cabinet. A patch of sunlight lay on the floor matting. The room was very hot. Sweat rolled down Bobby's face. Though smokers have little sense of smell, I could distinguish a reek of disinfectant. I asked what kind of cases the hospital cared for, and Bobby said it took in everything. He spoke absently, pacing up and down, waiting for the pill to work on me.

I said, "I don't see why you need to use a pill. The medical student just used a light bulb."

"Oh, I could do that, too, but it takes too long," Bobby retorted. "In the future, I want to cure whole roomfuls of addicts all at once, hypnotizing them in groups, and how far do you think I'd get if I tried to put each one under by making him stare at a light? No, barbiturates are quicker. Aren't you sleepy yet?"

"No. Why roomfuls of addicts?"

He explained. There were far too many for one man to cope with unless he employed such methods. In fact, he said, my case was being used to that end. If it worked—and it was going to work, it was bound to work, he assured me—he wanted me to exert all the influence I might have to persuade the authorities involved to hire him as a kind of National Grand Curer-in-Chief of opium addiction. He talked warmly and hopefully of these plans, until, as through a glass brightly, I saw a schoolroom full of white-clad Chinese, row on row, all exactly alike, with their faces lifted toward Bobby on a very high dais. He was saying . . . was . . .

"Will you permit me, while you are under, to make a little psychoanalysis also?" He really was saying it, and to me, not to the white-clad Chinese.

I stirred, and forced my tongue to answer. "Yes, if you'll promise to tell me all about it afterward. Do you promise?"

"Yes, yes." He was pacing again, and said it impatiently, over his shoulder. "You are now getting sleepy. You will sleep. In a few minutes . . ."

It was less than a few minutes, however, before I felt fully awake again, and sat up, saying in triumph, "Your pill didn't work."

Bobby, still pacing, was now rubbing his hands, saying over and over, as if to himself, "Very interesting, ve-ry interesting."

Suddenly the room had become dark again. I said, "It didn't work," and now I felt disappointed. All those preparations had been wasted. Bobby came to a halt in front of me.

"Do you know what time it is?" he asked. Once long ago, I dimly recollected, Heh-ven had asked the same question. But Bobby answered himself. "It's five o'clock in the afternoon, and you went under before ten this morning."

"But what's been going on?" I rubbed my forehead.

"You've been talking almost the whole time. I stopped for lunch."

I was staggered, but Bobby gave me no time to discuss the strangeness of the situation. He looked at me intently and said, "Do you feel any desire to smoke?"

I shook my head. It was true that the picture of the tray and the lighted lamp was no longer there in the middle of my mind. His question, in fact, surprised me. Why *should* I want to smoke?

"You have no wish, no thought of wanting it?" he insisted, and again I shook my head.

Bobby said, "Good. You will go to bed now, and eat something if you like. For tomorrow I've given orders that you're not to have visitors. That will be best for a little, but I'll be coming in later tonight to check up."

I started to stand, but paused as a sneeze overtook me. "I've caught cold," I declared. "Oh, Bobby—the analysis. What did you find out?"

"You are very interesting," he said enthusiastically. "Here is Nurse Wong to take care of you." He walked out.

Nurse Wong led me down the passage as fussily as a tug conveying a liner to its berth. She showed me into a first-floor room with an army cot in it, with whitewashed walls and a French window looking out on a wildly overgrown garden. The bed linen was worn and stained with rust. Nurse Wong had already unpacked my things and hung them on a couple of nails stuck in the wall. Of course, I thought drowsily after I got into bed, Chinese don't hang up their clothes but fold them away in boxes. . . . Later, a supper tray lay on my chest. I had no desire to eat the rice covered with brown goo, and after a while it was taken away. Bobby must have come in that night, but I don't remember him. There was no reason why I should have been so sleepy, I told myself when I woke up in the small hours. I wasn't any longer. I was uncomfortable, though I couldn't say just where the discomfort was. Throat? Arms? Legs? Stomach? It wandered about. The only place it seemed to settle for good was in the conscience. I felt very guilty about everything in the world, but it was not agony. It was supportable. Still, I was glad when the sun rose. Jan had once expressed the feeling of opium very well, I reminded myself; he had a bad leg, and after he'd smoked a pipe or two he'd said. "The pain is still there, but it no longer hurts." Well, I said to myself, that's what's happening. The pain has always been there, and now it hurts again. That is all. It is supportable. It is supportable.

One thing helped a lot. Never through the week that was worst did I have the thought that I would feel a lot better if only I could get to a pipe. That was where the hypnotism came in, I realized. Knowing it, however, didn't spoil the effect. It worked. I wasn't locked in my room, and there was no guard at the front door. If I'd wanted to, I could have dressed and walked out and gone home, or to Heh-ven's, but I didn't want to. Of all my urges, that one was missing. I counted the days after which Bobby said I would feel better. I fidgeted and yawned and sneezed, and my eyes wept torrents, and my watch simply refused to run, but I never tried to get out of the hospital.

For a while, whenever Bobby came and I tried to talk, my voice quivered and I wept. "Just nerves. I can't manage words," I sobbed, but he said I was getting on fine. He added that he realized I really wanted to stop smoking, because I hadn't brought in any pills. He said he knew that because he'd searched my things while I was hypnotized. The night after he said that, I had cramps. Cramps are a well-known withdrawal symptom. They might make themselves felt anywhere in the addict's body, but most people get them in the arms—they feel as if all the bones have broken. I had mine in the legs, all the way up to the hips, and at four in the morning I figured out that this was because I'd had to wear braces on my legs as a baby. I had never been able to remember the braces, but now, I said to myself, my legs were remembering. Then, as if I'd pleased the gods with this decision, I actually fell asleep for a full hour. It was probably the worst night of all.

Bobby let a few friends in to see me after that. I could go out into the overgrown garden with them and walk a little, taking shaky steps to the creek where ducks swam, and then we would drink tea under a tree. They helped the time pass, which was good, because without distraction it dragged terribly. "The mortal boredom of the smoker who is cured!" wrote Cocteau. Most vivid of all, though, was the way I felt about the bed. Night after night, I had to lie on it without sleeping, until I detested it with a bitter, personal spite. I hated the very smell of the mattress. I don't suppose it was really bad, being kapok and nothing else, but for the first time in some years my numbed nose was working, and any scent would have had an unpleasant effect on newly sensitive nerves. To me the mattress stank, and it was lumpy, besides. I knew every lump. I resolved to settle that bed's hash as soon as I was my own master. One morning, I asked Bobby what it would cost to replace it.

"Oh, I don't know. Twenty dollars, I suppose. Why?" he said.

"I want to buy this one when I'm through with it, and burn it in the garden. I hate it."

"If you still want to by then, you may," he said solemnly. "Heh-ven telephoned me today." He paused, looking at me with a cautious expression. "It is not the first time he has tried to reach you," he added, "but I didn't tell you before. Now I think I can trust you to see him. He's coming this afternoon. In fact, he's here now."

"Good." I must have sounded indifferent, because that was the way I felt. I'd almost forgotten Heh-ven. When he walked in, though, I remembered how well I knew him, and how many hours we'd spent smoking together. His eyes looked cloudy, I observed, and his teeth were dirty.

He said, "I'm taking you out."

Bobby said swiftly, "Only for a drive, remember," and looked hard at him.

Heh-ven laughed, and held up his hand reassuringly. "Certainly I'll bring her back. I do not want your patient, Doctor."

"You are not going to smoke," said Bobby, "and you are not taking her anywhere where she can smoke. Is that clear?"

"Perfectly clear," said Heh-ven. We walked out the front door—which I hadn't gone out of for a week—and into his car, and drove away. He was faithful to his promise. We went to a tearoom and sat there and looked at each other, and he said, "You look all right. How are you?"

"I'm all right," I said, "but Cocteau was telling the truth—you know, about the boredom. Still, I'm glad I did it." I was warming up, though Heh-ven still sounded and looked like a stranger.

"I tried, while you were out there," he admitted, "and I couldn't. It didn't last more than about thirty-six hours. I missed the lamp most of all. I find the lamp very nice."

"Well, that's easy," I answered. "Just light it and lie there." We both giggled. It was the first time I'd been able to make a joke about opium. Then he took me back to the hospital. His eyes when he said goodbye were wet, because he needed his tray. I felt smug.

The afternoon I was formally discharged, three days before I was to go to Chungking, Bobby said, "Well, goodbye. You're free. You're all right now. You can go anywhere you like. I don't want any pay, but remember—if you get the chance to convince some higher-up, tell him my method is effective. You'll do that, won't you? I would like to have that job."

I promised, and thanked him, and we shook hands. My bag was packed, and a car waited outside, but I hesitated. "There's one more thing," I said. "The analysis, remember? I've asked you more than once, but you haven't told me what you found out the day you did it."

All Bobby said was "Oh, yes, that. Very interesting."

What's more, I forgot all about burning the mattress.

LE LY HAYSLIP
(1949–)

The sixth child in a peasant family in Quang Nam Province, Le Ly Hayslip came from a family of pious, old-fashioned Buddhists and probably would have lived out her life in the village of her birth had war not intervened. Her father taught her to be a woman warrior, which meant, to him, to stay alive. She managed to do so, although her village, on the border between North and South Vietnam, was engulfed in war all her early life—until 1954 against the French and after that caught between the republican forces of the South, with their American allies, and the Vietcong of the North. Her allegiance was initially to the Vietcong, who showed the peasants more respect and avoided random torture and murder. But in time it became clear that war itself was the enemy. Both sides suspected the villagers of helping the other, and each took reprisals. Eventually Le Ly married an American and went to live in California. Her book *When Heaven and Earth Changed Places* (1989) is a dual account of her past and of a 1986 trip back to Vietnam to see her mother.

For other accounts of women in wars, compare Vera Brittain, *Testament of Youth*, Nien Cheng, *Life and Death in Shanghai*, Marguerite Duras, *The War*, Anne Frank, *Diary*, and Marie Vassiltchikov, *Berlin Diaries*. For an account of the Khmer Rouge horror in Cambodia, see Molyda Szymusiak, *The Stones Cry Out*.

FROM *When Heaven and Earth Changed Places*

On a February morning in 1964, shortly after I had been released from the district jail after my first arrest, I was on sentry duty in Ky La. It was unusually chilly and a heavy mist hung in the valleys on three sides of the village. My shift had started at sunrise—about an hour before—and I knew it would be a long day. The older woman, Sau, who was supposed to be my partner, had not shown up. The Viet Cong were very careful about scheduling the teams of sentries upon whom so much depended. Usually, a team consisted of one mature woman and a girl, or two women—but never two girls, for the temptation to daydream or gossip was too strong and there was always the chance that something unusual would happen—something not foreseen by detailed Viet Cong instructions—which would require quick action and good judgment. Occasionally, Viet Cong inspectors would check us if the area seemed safe—Loi and Mau were the fighters detailed most often to my shift, and we had an easy, friendly relationship. But today, even the birds stayed shivering in their nests.

The fog that morning made everything drippy and caused the world to collapse to my feet. To make matters worse, the white air absorbed all sounds from the village and ever since I arrived I had heard a faint moaning and grinding which my predecessors (the sentries from dusk till dawn) had attributed to mountain spirits.

Consequently, I put my bucket (we always carried a pail or basket to avoid suspicion) on a piece of dry ground beneath the big tree that was our station and made myself a fortress against the ghosts: sitting hunched with my arms over my knees; peeking between them and the brim of my useless sun hat at the watery wall of air.

After what seemed like half the morning, the ground gradually opened around me—ten meters, twenty, finally a hundred and more until the fog touched the dikes at the edge of the field and the trees beyond the road to Phe Binh loomed out of the mist like giants. It was then that I saw the teeming mass of soldiers on the road—Republicans, hundreds of them. The moaning had been their voices, muffled by the fog; the grinding, the soldiers' boots on the rocky road.

Panicked, I jumped up—but saw I had no place to go. The troops were already past my station and almost inside the village. If I ran either way—toward Ky La or away toward the Viet Cong—I would surely be cut down. If I stood still, or attempted to hide among the rocks, I would not only let the Viet Cong walk into a trap, but be caught in the crossfire myself. In the blink of an eye, my situation had gone from nervous boredom to one so desperate that only a desperate act would save me. Despite my terror, I forced myself to walk nonchalantly toward the road, right into the soldiers' teeth. Every few paces, I bent to pick up a sweet potato or low-lying berries that grew around the field, and put them in my bucket. When I got close enough to see out of the corner of my eye the soldiers watching me from the corners of their eyes, I hummed a little tune and paused even longer and more often. *Surely,* they must think, *there is no more loyal Republican than this happy little farm girl out gathering her family's breakfast!*

By good acting or good luck, nobody bothered me and when I was completely past the troops and within a stone's throw of the swamp (the direction from which the Viet Cong usually came), I dropped my bucket and peeled off the top two of the three shirts I always wore. The top shirt—the one I would wear all day if nothing happened—was brown.

Any Viet Cong seeing it would know that conditions were clear in my sector. The second shirt was white, which I would show if anything suspicious had happened—like a helicopter loitering in the area or a reconnaissance team passing through. The bottom shirt, the one I wore now, was all black and meant that a major threat was around—a fully armed patrol or convoy of troops headed in my direction.

As it turned out, a woman I recognized as a Viet Cong scout was coming down the road from the direction of Bai Gian carrying a shoulder pole with two buckets. Her presence meant that the Viet Cong were on the move and probably close behind her. If she was doing her job properly, she would be looking for me in the fields, which were now barely visible through the mist. Sure enough, she scanned the horizon as she walked, then stopped when she saw that I was not at my station. Slowly, she looked around until she saw me in my black shirt pretending to pick berries by the road. Quick as a wink, she unshouldered her pole, pretended to have trouble with one of the ropes that held the buckets, and scuttled back in the opposite direction.

My legs went limp with relief. By giving my signal in time, I had prevented a Viet Cong massacre. But there were still hundreds of enemy troops between me and the village. I had no alternative but to continue playing the innocent schoolgirl.

When my bucket had a respectable load of potatoes and berries, I walked back toward Ky La. The Republicans by now were beginning their sweep through the fields and the quarter-mile of road between me and the village was almost clear. The further I went, the faster I walked until I dashed the last few steps to my house. Inside, my father greeted me with a sigh of relief. He had looked for me on the hillside when the fog lifted and, seeing I wasn't there, became frantic. I told him about the soldiers and the close call with the scout and he told me to change my shirt quickly so that, in case of trouble, the soldiers who saw me couldn't identify me as the girl beside the road.

We then got our tools and went out to watch the situation—but we didn't wait long. The Republican and American soldiers were back within hours, angry because their mission had been spoiled. They sent squads through the village rounding up women who fit my description. Although most girls ran away, I just stood there with my father, trusting my new shirt and loyalty act to get me through. Unfortunately, I had already pushed my luck too far that wintry day. A squad surrounded us at once and I was arrested, along with three other girls, and blindfolded. My hands were tied behind my back and as the soldiers led us to a truck, my father tried to convince the sergeant in charge that I had only been out gathering breakfast, but the soldiers pushed him away and threatened him, too, with arrest if he didn't stop interfering.

The ride to Don Thi Tran prison was unpleasantly familiar. I prayed that my old tormentors would not be on duty when I arrived—especially Sergeant Hoa. I hoped I would be kept in the arrival area instead of the awful cages, and that my sister Ba's policeman husband could be summoned from Danang before I was called for interrogation. To my surprise, all my wishes came true.

The holding room was full of prisoners—mostly girls—and because I had not been charged with anything specific, my priority for interrogation was low. Besides, as I had already learned, the questions and answers were always the same: *Why were you arrested?* "I don't know." *How old are you?* "Fifteen—I'm just a little kid." *Have you seen any Viet Cong?* "Yes." *What do they look like?* "They look like you, but with black clothes," and so on. The problem with their questions was that you could answer most of them honestly, even if you were a cadre leader yourself, and not get into trouble. For most of us, including the district police who inherited us as prisoners, the mass arrests after a raid were little more than a game. The worst part was being held captive while a sweep was going on. The troops would herd us together and make us wait in the hot sun without water or permission to go to the toilet—sometimes for most of the day. We often wondered why heavily armed soldiers worried so much about us women and children, but by this time, experience had taught them never to turn their back on a villager—no matter how skinny, little, or harmless she appeared.

Late the next morning, Ba's husband, Chin, arrived on his bicycle and gave the prison commander an order for my release. When I came out from the cell, both the commandant and my brother-in-law scowled at me.

"The logbook shows you've been here before, Phung Thi Le Ly," the commandant said sourly. "Your brother-in-law vouched for you then, but you can't seem to stay out of trouble. Well, I promise you both that if you're picked up again, even a note from the President won't get you out! Now get out of here! *Di ve*—both of you!"

I could see Chin was even more angered by the commandant's chewing out than by the trouble I had caused him. When we were outside, he pulled me up by the shoulders and gave me a good shaking.

"Look, you little troublemaker," he barked, "I'm finished with you and your whole family! I don't care if we're related or if Ba Xuan cries to high heaven about her poor little sister. You tell your mother and father that I'm finished risking my job for you. One day the soldiers will catch you doing something really bad and then we'll *all* go to prison—this policeman's badge won't mean a thing! Do you understand me?"

I nodded yes and he got onto his bicycle and pedaled away, ringing the bell irritably at some people who blocked his path.

It took me an hour to walk home, and when I got there, the soldiers were gone and the village was buzzing about my exploit.

"You're a hero, Bay Ly!" my mother told me. "The Viet Cong are calling a meeting tonight in your honor!"

It was true. Shortly after sundown, the villagers crept out of their houses and went into the swamp where the cadre leaders were already waiting by a roaring fire. When everyone had gathered, the woman with the shoulder pole testified that I had risked my life by walking right through the enemy column to find a place to give my signal. Next, the cadre leader proclaimed that his small band of fighters would probably have been wiped out by the Republican force, which meant that I was indirectly responsible, too, for saving his own life.

"To honor you, Miss Le Ly," he said, grinning in the firelight, "we will do much more than write your name on the blackboard. We will teach all the children in the village to sing the 'Sister Ly' song in your honor."

The original "Sister Ly" was a Viet Cong fighter who killed many enemies and was very famous, although she was eventually arrested and never seen again. It was Viet Cong practice to dedicate such patriotic songs to a hero's namesake when that person distinguished herself—but it had never before happened in Ky La, and the honor, for such a young girl, was unprecedented. The cadremen passed out papers with the following song printed neatly across it:

Song for Sister Ly

> Sister Ly, who comes from Go Noi,
> Where the Thu Bon washes the trees,
> Has defeated the horse-faced enemy.
> Her daily rice she could not eat
> Without hearing the tortured prisoners.
> Although the moon is covered with clouds,
> Her glory will shine forever.
> One day we heard Sister Ly
> Was in prison—tied up hand and foot.
> Beaten by day—tortured by night
> She sings "Mother don't cry.
> While I live, I still struggle."
> Comrades, please save your tears,
> Sister Ly is still living,
> And her struggle will go on forever.

After the cadreman had led the children through a few choruses of this song, he added: "Miss Le Ly is now assigned the honored task of teaching the young children how to serve the fighters who defend them. She will teach them how to resist their captors in jail—as she has done twice herself—so that they may follow in her glorious footsteps."

The villagers all clapped and the little kids, who were always the most enthusiastic at these meetings, cheered with them. My mother beamed proudly and although my father smiled too, I could see by his eyes that he was worried. He realized that my notoriety might very well put me in more danger over the next few months than any of us had bargained for.

During the next few days, I carried my song sheet around with me constantly, even though I had already memorized the words. I diligently taught our neighbors' children all the Viet Cong songs I knew but told them never to practice them at home, where Republicans might be listening. In the fields, we played the "Viet Cong game" and they all ran and hid and I praised those who were hard to find and made those whom I discovered too easily keep practicing until I had to shout for them to come out. It was just like my old war games at school, except now everyone was on the same side.

One afternoon, at a time that was usually quiet, I was resting in a hammock under the shed that housed our water buffalo, humming "Sister Ly" to myself, when I was completely surprised by a Republican patrol that appeared out of nowhere by the roadside. I could tell from their camouflaged uniforms, red scarves, and painted faces, as well as by the crispness and silence of their movements, that these were not ordinary soldiers, but *linh biet dong quan*—South Vietnamese Rangers. These special forces were seldom seen in our area, and when they were, bad trouble always followed. Where the regular Republican troops feared to go, these tough, clever fighters walked right in. Whenever I saw them, my mind filled with half-forgotten images of *ma duong rach mac*—the "slash face" legionnaires of my most terrifying childhood memories. Now, these ghosts from my past had materialized for real and their weapons were pointed at me.

I rolled out of my hammock and glanced involuntarily at the hillside, wondering why the danger signal had not been given, but it was too late for heroics. One camouflaged trooper stepped up and grabbed me by the collar. The paper with the Viet Cong song on it fluttered to the ground from under my shirttail.

"What's your name?" the soldier demanded.

I stammered an answer and prayed the paper would go unnoticed.

"Hey, look," the soldier beside him said. "She dropped something!"

The first soldier picked up the paper, studied it a moment, then looked me straight in the eye. "Where did you get this, girl?"

"I—I found it—"

"Where?"

I turned and pointed to the swamp.

"You mean somebody gave it to you?"

"No! I found it blowing in the wind. There were lots of them flying around. Just ask the other kids. They all have one too!"

More soldiers crowded around to look at the paper and I could already feel their fists and rifle butts beating me. I chewed my lip and tried to look innocent even though I wanted to cry.

Finally the first soldier shook the paper in my face and said, "You know what we do when we find trash like this?"

I shook my head, wide-eyed with terror.

"We do this!" He took out his lighter, flipped open the top, and in seconds my little song was reduced to ashes. "Wrap her up," he snapped to a subordinate. "We'll take her into the village."

Again, my hands were tied behind my back and I was shoved down the road to Ky La. As we went, more of these camouflaged, fast-moving troopers darted out of the bushes and from behind trees and dikes into the fields. Moments later gunfire broke out but it did not sound like a battle until I arrived with the rest of the villagers at the holding area behind our house. There we were held at gunpoint while Republican helicopters swarmed overhead and landed beyond the trees. Within the hour, thick smoke rose above the distant jungle. "Bai Gian—" the word passed quietly. "The soldiers are attacking Bai Gian!"

Bai Gian was a peaceful forest hamlet tucked in among coconut, orange, and mangrove trees with freshwater pools and waterfalls that were a haven for animals and birds and the many people who used to go there just to enjoy the scenery. It was also a very wealthy place with big houses and people who bore the honorary surname *Cuu,* which meant "village elder." Because it was so quiet and hard to reach, the Viet Cong often used Bai Gian for recreation, and because the Viet Cong were usually lurking nearby, the Republicans avoided it like the plague. That was before the special forces took an interest in the place. When all was said and done, not only Bai Gian, but its poorer, neighboring suburbs and most of its sister village of Tung Lam would be reduced to ashes.

Near sundown the troops came back and, although the battle was continuing, they apparently felt safe enough to let us go back to our homes. My hands were untied and with my parents I went immediately to our bunker where we lived on emergency rations for two days while troops and tanks and airplanes widened the battle zone around Bai Gian.

On the third day we came out. Although the air was hazy from dust and smoke, the sunshine felt good and we were glad to leave the musty bunker, which now smelled of our collective waste and sweat. Rumor had it that the rangers had trapped a few Viet Cong away from their sanctuaries, but the ordinary troops who came in to press the attack had suffered heavy losses. Consequently, the soldiers mopping up after the battle were in a vengeful mood.

While the other troops withdrew, these soldiers stayed behind to question us for clues to the enemy's sanctuaries. When the temporary camp by my school was too full to admit more prisoners, they set up assembly-line interrogation stations in the street and sometimes openly beat the villagers who didn't give satisfactory answers. This caused us to worry even more because such actions showed the soldiers no longer cared about our good opinion. Ominously, they seemed to talk about us the way we talked about our barnyard animals on the day they ceased to be pets and began to look like supper.

Near sundown, when all but a score of Republicans had withdrawn, the last of the soldiers began shooting at random, hitting people and animals that were unlucky enough to be caught in the streets. Others looted houses near the center of town and set them on fire with lighters and gasoline. By the time they had finished, the fire had spread to outlying buildings and over half of Ky La was in flames.

My father and the other village men spent the rest of the night battling the fires as best they could. My mother went from house to house giving food to survivors and consoling several women who had been raped and beaten by departing troops. For my part, I remained in our house and watched over the little children whose parents could no longer care for them. I dressed burns on tiny hands and put bandages on cut legs and bloody heads. The kids' terrified eyes stared back at me in the light of their own burning homes as if they expected the heroic Miss Ly to bind up their breaking hearts as well as their battered bodies. As much as I wanted to raise their spirits, I couldn't think of anything to say.

One little boy with bad burns on his arm saw that I was distressed. In the saddest, smallest voice I ever heard, he began to sing the "Song for Sister Ly." I knelt beside him and, being careful not to disturb his arm, hugged his head and chest so hard that his song turned into sobs. Within moments, all of Ky La's children were wailing as their village and childhood innocence came crashing down around them. Although I could silence Miss Ly's song—which now seemed to me obscene—I could not silence the children's pain. For the pain itself was a voice; a voice that had risen above Ky La as a chorus of deathly smoke.

For several weeks after the three-day battle, the Republicans bombarded the area around my village—attempting to do with aircraft and artillery what ground troops had failed to accomplish: drive the Viet Cong away or slaughter them in their hiding places. Although the aerial attacks didn't occur every day, they happened often enough and with so little warning that we seldom went into the fields, and even then what we found usually did not make the risk worth taking. The paddies would be littered with rubble—upturned trees, shattered rocks, and charred craters where bombs or artillery rounds went astray. Those crops that weren't pulverized were scorched by the blast and lay withering on stalks like embryos cut from the womb. Dead animals lay rotting in the sun— water buffalo with stiff legs and bodies bloated as big as a car; disembow-eled pigs and the remains of jungle animals that had run out of the forest to escape the gunfire only to be ripped apart by the explosions. Every now and then, too, we came across some dead humans—charred like wooden dolls fished from an oven, blackened arms cocked in an eternal embrace with their ancestors.

For the most part, the soldiers ignored civilian and animal casualties and we had to dispose of them as best we could to prevent disease from infecting the living. By the time we cleared our fields of rubble and buried the victims, another attack would usually begin or it would be dark and time to go back to our homes. Like it or not, we had become part of the endless machinery of terror, death, and regeneration.

One afternoon during this long campaign, some families were brought to Ky La from Bai Gian after what was left of that once-beautiful village had been converted to a "strategic hamlet," requiring half of the people to move to a more secure location. Because the bombings and periodic sweeps by Republican and American soldiers had suppressed Viet Cong activity in our area, Ky La was considered a "pacified" village, although government troops seldom spent the night here and when they did, it was always under arms.

Among these refugees reduced to begging was the family of Cuu Loi, the second wealthiest man in Bai Gian and an old friend of my father's. Cuu Loi's number-eight daughter, Thien, was about two years older than I was and a little bit shorter, with the much darker skin typical of people from that area. She was a quiet girl and we always got along well because I loved to talk and, after several years of war, there was a short-age of listeners in the village—the teenagers having gone off with the Viet Cong, the Republicans, or to shallow, premature graves. Thien was also a Viet Cong supporter, but had been arrested more often and (al-though she wouldn't speak of it) had been tortured more intensely and more frequently than I had. When I saw her again after the destruction of Bai Gian, she had the lackluster eyes of one who had seen and suffered too much. She clung to me for security just as I clung to her for compan-ionship—although I could never make her safe any more than she could substitute for my own lost brothers and sisters. Anyway, for the time being, we were all that each other had.

Cuu Loi repaired an abandoned house next to Uncle Huong, who lived at the edge of the village. For several weeks things went well—

Thien's mother set up a garden and tended some hens that we gave her. Her father worked the land next to ours and we girls spent many pleasant hours together helping each other do chores. One night, however, our unaccustomed good luck ran out. Cuu Loi went out after dark to relieve himself and was shot dead outside his door. To make matters worse, no one could claim or examine the body until daybreak—such were the dangers from the government "cat" while Viet Cong "mice" were around our village.

When I went to Thien's house the next morning, it had already been surrounded by troops. After a few minutes' questioning about her father, Thien was arrested once more and taken away in a truck. When she came back two days later, she had been beaten quite badly and could hardly move or speak. I nursed her at our house because she was my friend and because her mother now had to labor in the fields without a husband. Over the next six weeks, Thien was arrested again and again, and each time returned in worse shape than before. Although she was always quiet, she now said nothing at all, and even my mother—who had never particularly liked Thien's family owing to their wealth and high station—began to pity her. As it turned out, she could have saved her pity for us both.

After one evening of particularly intense bombardment, Thien and I were rousted by soldiers from a roadside trench into which we had jumped to escape the shells. As soon as we climbed out, I knew we were in for trouble. The soldier who shone the flashlight in my face was none other than the Republican ranger who had burned my song a while before.

"Didn't we arrest you on the road a few weeks ago?" the ranger said. "Yes—you're the girl with the filthy VC songbook!"

"No, not me—" I protested.

He shone the light at poor Thien, whose face was still raw from a QC (Quan Canh, the Republican military police) beating administered a few days before. "Then maybe, it was you—"

"No—not her either!" I interrupted. "She's from Bai Gian. She's only been in the village a little while!"

"Bai Gian!" the soldier spat. "That shithole is full of VC! Here"—he called to his corporal—*"bat no Di!* [arrest them both!] Two more Charlie for My Thi."

A pair of rangers quickly put us on the ground, frisked us for weapons, and tied our hands; but cold terror at the very mention of My Thi had already paralyzed us like a punch to the stomach. My Thi torture camp—the maximum security POW prison outside Danang—was run by the army, not the district police. It was a place even the toughest Viet Cong couldn't talk about without wincing. While the rangers hustled us back to the village with the day's haul of prisoners, we were all too terrified even to whisper among ourselves.

For about twenty minutes Thien and I rode down the bumpy, darkened road with a half-dozen others, mostly grown-ups I didn't recognize. Although we were in a walled compound when we got out, I recognized the sounds and smells of China Beach immediately. My Thi was a huge camp containing many American-built shacks—some for prisoners, some for guards, some for purposes I did not want to know. As soon as we were off the truck, QCs descended on us like vultures and hustled us off to different places. I was led to a small bare cell where I would spend the rest of the night alone—listening to guards shuffling up and down the hall and, when they went away, to the roaring surf beyond the brightly lit perimeter.

In the morning, I was awakened by human screams. I got off the plywood board that served as a bed and crouched on the cement floor, covering my head to block the sound. Perhaps, if I looked small and pathetic enough, the guards would leave me alone. Such was the state of reasoning even one night in My Thi produced.

Within an hour two guards came to my cell and pulled me into the corridor. They didn't even wait until I was in the interrogation room to brutalize me, but banged me against the walls and punched me with their fists, shouting threats and accusations as we went. Inside the interrogation room, which was at the end of the same long building as my cell, I was shown a number of implements on a table in front of me. There were some electric wires hooked up to a hand-cranked generator, scissors, razor blades, and knives of various shapes (like the kind a surgeon uses), and buckets of soapy water which I knew were not for washing.

Without even asking me a question, the interrogator ordered: "Put your hands on the table!"

As soon as I did, the guards strapped down my wrists and the interrogator clipped a wire to each thumb. He turned the crank casually a few times and flicked a switch the way someone else might turn on a radio. A jolt of electricity knocked my legs out from under me and the entire room went white. A second later I was hanging from the straps, clambering to stand up. My lips were tingly and I could see my fingers twitching in the harness.

"So—you see we're not playing games!" the interrogator said, leaning on the table. "Tell me quickly: Why were you and the other girl hiding in the trench?"

"We jumped in to escape the explosions—"

"*Liar!*" The interrogator slammed the table. "There was a battle going on! You are *phu nu can bo*—VC cadre girl! You were carrying supplies! Where is the ammunition hidden?"

"I don't know anything about ammunition!"

"Then what were you doing on the battlefield? How many battles have you been in, eh? What is your rank?"

"Please! I'm just a little girl! I haven't done anything!" His hand hovered near the crank and I instinctively pulled against the straps. But instead of turning on the electricity, he picked up a short-bladed knife.

"Do you know what these are for?" he asked.

"Yes. I've seen them before."

"Has anyone used them on you?"

I hesitated before answering, "No—"

"Good." He put down the knife and stood up quickly. "Release her."

To my amazement, the guards unbuckled the straps. I backed away from the table like a wary animal and rubbed my wrists.

"Go back to your cell. Think about what these things could do to your body. How would your boyfriend or husband or baby like you without nipples, eh? Or, perhaps, I'll cut some skin off your ass for some sandals, or maybe throw a few of your fingers to the guard dogs. You think well about it, Miss Viet Cong hero—then when you're called again, come prepared to tell me everything you know!"

The guards pushed me to the door and down the hall to my cell. I knew it was as useless to worry about the torture the interrogator described as it was to try and figure out ways to outsmart him. If I was to survive, I must play my own game—not his. Experience had taught me that if you answer one way long enough, it ruins your tormentor's game. After all, for most of them, it's just a job (just like my job now was to be a prisoner). No workman wants to work harder than he has to—especially for no reward. Even a sadistic interrogator has better things to do than terrorize dumb schoolgirls when there is nothing left to learn. With my mind reassured by that plan, I had the luxury of stretching out on my small board and thinking about Thien—wondering where she was, what was happening to her, and what would be left of her should she ever be released. How hopeless it must seem to her—to be in a place like this without a father to grieve for you, work for your release, or greet you when you came back.

The next morning the same two guards took me from my cell, but instead of going back to the interrogation room, I was taken with two other girls whom I did not know to an alley between the buildings where a post was set into the ground. We were ordered to stand against the post, each facing a different direction, while one guard tied us fast with a rope. I had no idea what they intended to do with us—we were too close to the buildings to be set on fire and if they intended to rape us, we would not be left clothed with our legs immobilized by rope. I concluded that, with no interrogator present, we three had, for some reason, been singled out for punishment—and that punishment was to stand under the hot sun, without water or toilet, for the afternoon. Compared with the knives and scissors, there were worse ways we could have spent the day. Besides, feeling the other girls' shoulders against my own was comforting, and after a few moments we found our fingers were locked together in mutual support. Unfortunately, the post held other perils besides the sun.

As soon as we were tied up, one guard brought out a can and began to brush something sticky all over our feet. When I looked down, I saw that the whole area between the buildings was covered with anthills—the small black kind whose bites stung worse than bees. Within minutes, our sticky feet had attracted dozens of them and the girls beside me were screaming and trying to drive them off, but the ropes prevented us from raising our legs. For some reason, I alone had the presence of mind to stand still. *The ants want honey, not me,* I thought, as if it all made perfect sense, *so I will stand still and let them have it.* The more the girls beside me struggled, the more the ants attacked them. The longer I stood still, the higher I could feel the hundreds of little legs on my skin—tickling the fine hair of my body, crawling along my crotch and buttocks and down the backside of my knees—but the fewer times I was bitten. To make matters worse, the guards had gone on about their business and the girls had no one to appeal to with their screams and I had nobody to impress with my self-control. And so we occupied ourselves, shrieking and pulling against the ropes or trying to hold still, while the shadow of the pole crept from one building to the other.

After several hours, our perspiration had carried away most of the honey and we were no more to the ants than what the post had been before. The guards came back and looked us over, smirking at how our legs had become swollen and purple as berries.

"Have our patriotic ants made you girls any smarter?" one of them asked, looking directly at me. "Are you ready to talk now to the interrogator? Huh? Answer me!"

"I'm ready to go *home!*" was the only reply I could think of.

The soldier laughed and went away. A few minutes later he came back with a bucket of water. Gingerly, he rolled up his sleeve, fished around in the bucket, and brought out a glistening water snake about half the length of his arm. This he promptly dropped into my shirt, and repeated the act with two more snakes for the other girls. I knew from their appearance that the little snakes weren't poisonous, but their bite was painful and the awful slithering—as they probed my waist, breasts, armpits, and neck trying to find a way back to the water—was, in its own way, worse than the ants. Besides, whatever patience or self-control I could muster had long ago been exhausted. I screamed at the snake, then screamed at the guards, then screamed at the sky until the noon blue turned black and my voice was reduced to a squeak.

After sundown, the guards untied us and threw water all over us to get rid of the honey and ants and to help them recover their snakes. I was taken again to the interrogator's room where the previous day's encounter was repeated. This time, the interrogator tried to trick me by asking the same question several different ways, banging the table whenever my answer was wrong. "Where do the Viet Cong hide?" he would ask. "I don't know," I would answer. "Okay then, if you don't know where they hide, tell me where they come from!" Then, "If you don't know where they come from, tell me where they go!" and so on. Next he asked if I ever stole weapons and ammunition and went down the list of other commonly pilfered items: first aid kits, clothing, and rations. My only defense was to answer all his questions the same way ("No," "I don't know," and "I don't understand") and avoid playing the interrogator's game: giving measured answers to trick questions which would only whet his suspicions and draw me closer toward the deadly instruments he reserved for his final assault. In the end, he just threw up his hands and had me taken to my cell.

When the door slammed shut I found myself in darkness with a hollow heart, sick stomach, and itchy legs. I lay down on my hard little bed and tried to make sense of what was happening. I truly believed this interrogator was at last convinced I had nothing to hide, but his realization of this was no guarantee of a speedy release—now, or ever. The army had many interrogators and one suspect held in prison would be one less Viet Cong to worry about in the bush. Already, in the few times I had been moved around the camp, I recognized several people from the village—people who had disappeared years before and who, very likely, would call My Thi their home until the end of the war, or death, released them.

The next morning, however, I was taken neither to the interrogation room nor to the torture post, but to the front gate where I was escorted through layers of fences, barbed wire, and curling concertina to the sandy headlands and told simply to "Go home!"

Dumbfounded, I could only stand there and watch the soldiers go back into the compound, wondering why and how I had been so miraculously released. It then occurred to me that perhaps Thien had been released too—maybe ahead of me—so I ran as fast as I could for the road to Danang and my sister Ba's house, where I could get cleaned up and eat a meal before beginning the long walk home.

At Ba's house, however, I was surprised to find my mother waiting for me.

"How did you know I would be released?" I asked her. "Nobody gets out of My Thi in three days!"

"Well, you do, little miss hero—and it cost me more than you can count!" She immediately began inspecting me for damage, her face angry, relieved, and sad all at once.

"Chin got me out?" I didn't believe my policeman brother-in-law could have such clout, let alone such a monumental change of heart—as well as character.

"Chin? Don't be silly! He has no influence in a military camp. He wouldn't even handle the bribe for fear of a corruption charge on his record! No, I had to go to my nephew, Uncle Nhu's son—the Republican lieutenant. He couldn't act directly, but he knew someone I could approach. It cost me half your dowry, but I suppose you're worth it—" She took me by the ear and twisted me around, inspecting my backside for wounds. "Well, I can see you're in one piece. Wash up and I'll take you home before anything else can happen."

As it turned out, there was no more dangerous place we could have gone than Ky La. As soon as we entered the village, I could tell everything had changed. People—even old neighbors—avoided my glance, then stared at me as I passed. That night, the Viet Cong held a rally, but the messenger didn't come to our house. "Just stay at home tonight," my father counseled with a worried look on his face. "It's going to take a while for them to decide what to do."

"Decide about what, Father? Are they angry with me?"

"They're suspicious because nobody gets out of My Thi so quickly—even for a bribe."

"Then why don't we tell them about Uncle Nhu's son?" I asked innocently.

"That would be even worse." My father shook his head. "Then they'd know we had blood ties to the Republicans. Just sit still for a while and let things calm down."

But things didn't calm down—they went from bad to worse. Because the Viet Cong (and because of them, the villagers) didn't trust us, we no longer got warnings about Republican raids or Viet Cong reprisals. When troops appeared, our only defense was to stand still and so we were frequently questioned when Americans and Republicans came to the village—contact that only strengthened the Viet Cong's suspicions. To make things worse, our obvious estrangement from the villagers made us even more trustworthy in Republican eyes, and our house was often spared while the other homes were ransacked. Even my own father, in his attempts to protect me, wound up increasing my danger. He was certain I would not survive another arrest (Thien, in fact, still hadn't come back) and forbade me to go to the fields. Instead, he did all my work himself, even those chores I customarily did for the Viet Cong—delivering rations and making up first aid kits. My absence, however, only convinced them even more that I was cooperating with the Republicans. My father argued that I was sick—first to the Republican soldiers, who remembered me from their patrols, and then to the Viet Cong, when they asked about my absence. Of course, no one believed him, and I could see from his expression each night that the noose around my neck was also tightening around his own. I decided I could not let anything happen to my father because of me.

The next morning, I took my hoe and left the house before my parents, determined to put in a good day's work in front of everyone. On the way, I passed six Republican soldiers, who, having grown more friendly toward me over the last few weeks, only waved. I ignored them, stuck my proud nose higher in the air, and went about my business. Unfortunately, I soon heard their boots on the soil behind me.

The faster I walked, the faster the crunching followed. I forced myself not to look back, but I knew they were behind me. A moment later I heard shouts, followed by the crackle of gunfire, and hit the dirt. But the soldiers weren't firing at me. Instead, they were all shooting furiously into the bushes beside the road. A second later, they charged forward and I heard one yell that they had hit two Viet Cong fighters—killing one and badly wounding the other. Apparently, the Viet Cong were in the process of setting up an ambush and, afraid the soldiers had seen them, tried to run away. Some of them made it, but these two did not.

Now I could hear the Republicans chatter excitedly. They were pleased with their trophies, but wondered if I was a Viet Cong spy sent to lure them to an ambush. One of them started to come after me, then stopped, looked around, and went back to his buddies. Without further delay, they took their prisoner and scuttled down the road the way they came, worried, apparently, that a bigger force of Viet Cong lurked somewhere in the forest.

Now I had no doubt that my days with the Viet Cong were over. Not only had I mysteriously escaped the notorious My Thi prison, but I had just been seen leading a Republican squad toward a Viet Cong position. Nobody would be interested in my side of the story. Nobody would be interested in the truth. The same "facts" were there for everyone to see and truth, in this war, was whatever you wanted to make it. And, as if all this wasn't bad enough, I had brought it on by disobeying my father. I was a disgrace and liability to everyone. I didn't deserve to live.

LILLIAN HELLMAN
(1905–1984)

Lillian Hellman was active as a playwright from the 1930s through the 1950s, the author of *The Little Foxes, Watch on the Rhine, The Children's Hour, The Autumn Garden,* and *Toys in the Attic.* Although she was not a Communist, some of her friends were, and in a celebrated episode in 1952 she refused to supply their names to the House Committee on Un-American Activities, then at the height of its witch-hunting power. "I cannot and will not cut my conscience to fit this year's fashions," she told the committee. She later wrote about these events in a memoir called *Scoundrel Time* (1976).

In 1970 she published her first memoir, *An Unfinished Woman.* It begins as a chronological account but concludes with portraits of people who were important in her life, including poet and wit Dorothy Parker and Dashiell Hammett, the writer of hard-boiled detective novels with whom Hellman lived for some forty years. She continued the portrait method in her next volume of memoirs, *Pentimento* (1973), from which this selection is taken. Among the other portraits in this volume is one of a good friend Hellman called Julia, a wealthy American who daringly helped people escape from Nazi Germany. This section became widely known when a movie was based on it, with Jane Fonda playing Hellman and Vanessa Redgrave as Julia.

In 1980 Mary McCarthy on a television talk show offhandedly named Lillian Hellman as an example of an overrated writer, going on to say that she was a dishonest writer whose every word was a lie, "including 'and' and 'the.' " Hellman sued McCarthy for libel and pursued the case seriously until her death in 1984 made the issue moot. But in the meantime, Hellman's memoirs were subjected to unprecedented scrutiny in attempts by McCarthy and her friends to support the claim that Hellman lied. Much evidence was found. Among other things it was established that Hellman had never met Muriel Gardiner, the American heiress and psychiatrist based in Vienna whose own memoir, *Code Name Mary,* established what many people knew: that she was the model for Hellman's Julia.

For another example of fictionalized memoir, compare Mary McCarthy, *Memories of a Catholic Girlhood.*

FROM *Pentimento*

TURTLE

I had awakened at five and decided to fish for a few hours. I rowed the dinghy out to the boat on that lovely foggy morning and then headed around my side of Martha's Vineyard into the heavy waters of West Chop. Up toward Lake Tashmoo I found the quiet rip where the flounders had been running, put out two lines, and made myself some coffee. I am always child-happy when I am alone in a boat, no other boat to be seen until the light breaks through. In an hour I had caught nine flounders and a couple of tautogs that Helen would like for chowder and decided to swim before going home to work. The boat had drifted out, down toward the heavy chop, but there was nothing new in this, and I was never careless: I tied my two-pound stone to a long rope, carried it down the boat ladder with me, and took it out to where I would swim near it. I don't know how long it took me to know that I wasn't swimming but was moving with incredible swiftness, carried by a tide I had never seen before. The boat had, of course, moved with me, but the high offshore wind was carrying it out of the rip into deep water. There was no decision to make: I could not swim to the boat, I could not force myself against the heavy tide. I have very little knowledge of the next period of time except that I turned on my back and knew that panic was not always as it has been described. For a time I was rigid, my face washed with water; then I wasn't rigid and I tried to see where the tide would take me. But when I turned to raise my head, I went down, and when I came up again I didn't care that I couldn't see the shore, thinking that water had been me, all my life, and this wasn't a bad way to die if only I had sense enough to go quietly and not make myself miserable with struggle. And then—I do not know when—I bumped my head against the pilings of the West Chop pier, threw my arms around a post, and remembered all three of us, and the conversation that took place four days after the turtle died when I said to Hammett, "You understood each other. He was a survivor and so are you. But what about me?"

He hadn't answered and so I repeated the question that night. "I don't know," he said, "maybe you are, maybe not. What good is my opinion?"

Holding to the piling, I was having a conversation with a man who had been dead five years about a turtle who had been dead for twenty-six.

Even in those days, 1940, it was one of the last large places in that part of Westchester County. I had seen it on a Tuesday, bought it on Thursday with royalties from *The Little Foxes,* knowing and not caring that I didn't have enough money left to buy food for a week. It was called an estate, but the house was so disproportionately modest compared to the great formal nineteenth-century gardens that one was immediately interested in the family who had owned it for a hundred and twenty years but who had, according to the agent, disappeared. (This was not true: eight or nine years later a young man of about sixteen or seventeen came by and asked if he could see the house and picnic at the lake. He said he had been born in the house and he took with him a giant branch of the hawthorn tree he said his mother had planted to celebrate his birth.)

In the first weeks, I closed the two guesthouses, decided to forget about the boxwood and rare plants and bridle paths, and as soon as Hammett sold two short stories we painted the house, made a room for me to work in, and fixed up the barn. I wanted to use the land and would not listen to those who warned me against the caked, rock-filled soil. I hired Fred Herrmann, a young German farmer, because I had an immediate instinct that his nature was close to mine, and together, through the years, we drove ourselves to the ends of weariness by work that began at six in the morning and ended at night. Many of our plans failed, but some of them worked fine: we raised and sold poodles, very fashionable then, until we had enough profit to buy chickens; I took the money I got from the movie script of *The Little Foxes* and bought cattle and three thousand plants of asparagus we bleached white and sold at great prices. We crossbred ducks that nobody liked but me, stocked the lake with bass and pickerel, raised good pigs and made good money with them and lost that money on pheasants; made some of it back with the first giant tomatoes, the sale of young lambs and rich unpasteurized milk. But all that was in the good years before the place had to be sold because Hammett went to jail in the McCarthy period and I was banned in Hollywood after I was called before the House Un-American Activities Committee. The time of doing what I liked was over in 1952.

I have a jungle of memories about those days: things learned and forgotten, or half remembered, which is worse than forgetting. It seems to me I once knew a lot about trees, birds, wildflowers, vegetables and some animals; about how to make butter and cheese and sausage; how to get the muddy taste out of large-mouth bass, how to make people sick with the weeds I would dig and boil up according to all those books that say you can. The elegant Gerald and Sara Murphy grew very ill on skunk cabbage I had disguised according to an eighteenth-century recipe.

But the day I remember best was in the first spring I owned the place.

The snow had gone on the bridle paths and, having finished with the morning's work at the barns, I took Salud, the large poodle, and four of his puppies on an early morning walk to the lake. As we reached the heavily wooded small hill opposite the lake, Salud stopped, wheeled sharply, ran into the woods, and then slowly backed down to the road. The puppies and I went past him to the lake and I whistled for him, sure that he had been attracted by a woodchuck. But when I looked back he was immobile on the road, as if he had taken a deep breath and had not let it out. I called to him but he did not move. I called again in a command tone that he had never before disobeyed. He made an obedient movement of his head and front legs, stared at me, and turned back. I had never seen a dog stand paralyzed and, as I went back toward him, I remembered old tales of snakes and the spell they cast. I stopped to pick up a heavy stick and a rock, frightened of seeing the snake. As I heard Salud make a strange bark, I threw the rock over his head and into the woods, yelling at him to follow me. As the rock hit the ground, there was a heavy movement straight in front of the dog. Sure now that it was a snake about to strike, I ran toward Salud, grabbed his collar, and stumbled with the weight of him. He pulled away from me and moved slowly toward the sound. As I picked myself up, I saw a large, possibly three-foot round shell move past him and go slowly toward the water. It was a large turtle.

Salud moved with caution behind the turtle and as I stood, amazed at the picture of the dog and the slowly moving shell, the dog jumped in front of the turtle, threw out a paw, and the jaws of the turtle clamped down on the leg. Salud was silent, then he reared back and a howl of pain came from him that was like nothing I had ever heard before. I don't know how long it took me to act, but I came down hard with my stick on the turtle's tail, and he was gone into the water. Saluda's leg was a mess but he was too big for me to carry, so I ran back to the house for Fred and together we carried him to a vet. A week later, he was well enough to limp for the rest of his life.

Hammett was in California for a few weeks and so I went alone almost every day to the lake in an attempt to see the turtle again, remembering that when I was a child in New Orleans I had gone each Saturday with my aunt to the French market to buy supplies for her boardinghouse. There had been two butchers in the market who had no thumbs, the thumbs having been taken off as they handled snapping turtles.

Hammett came back to the farm upset and angry to find his favorite dog was crippled. He said he had always known there were snappers in the lake, and snakes as well, but now he thought we ought to do something, and so he began his usual thorough research. The next few weeks brought books and government publications on how to trap turtles and

strange packages began to arrive: large wire-mesh cages, meant for something else but stared at for days until Hammett decided how to alter
them; giant fishhooks; extra heavy, finely made rope; and a book on tying
knots. We both read about the origin of snapping turtles, but it didn't
seem to me the accounts said very much: a guess that they were the
oldest living species that had remained unchanged, that their jaws were
powerful and of great danger to an enemy, that they could do nothing if
turned on their backs, and the explanation of why my turtle had come
out of the woods—each spring the female laid eggs on land, sat on them
each day, and took the chance that the hatched babies would find their
way to water.

One day, a month later perhaps—there was never any hurrying Hammett when he had made up his mind to learn about something—we
went to the lake carrying the wire cages, the giant fishhooks, fish heads
and smelly pieces of meat that he had put in the sun a few days before. I
grew bored, as I often did, with the slow precision which was part of
Dash's doing anything, and walked along the banks of the lake as he tied
the bait inside the traps, baited the hooks, and rowed out with them to
find heavy overhanging branches to attach them to.

He had finished with one side of the lake, and had rowed himself
beyond my view to the south side, when I decided on a swim. As I swam
slowly toward the raft, I saw that one limb of a sassafras tree was swinging wildly over the water, some distance from me. Sitting on the raft, I
watched it until I saw that the movement was caused by the guyline that
held one of the hooks Hammett had tied to the branch. I shouted at
Hammett that he had caught a turtle and he called back that couldn't be
true so fast, and I called back that he was to come for me quick because I
was frightened and not to argue.

As he came around the bend of the lake, he grinned at me.

"Drunk this early?"

I pointed to the swinging branch. He forgot about me and rowed over
very fast. I saw him haul at the line, have trouble lifting it, stand up in
the boat, haul again, and then slowly drop the line. He rowed back to the
raft.

"It's a turtle all right. Get in. I need help."

I took the oars as he stood up to take the line from the tree. The line
was so heavy that as he moved to attach it to the stern of the rowboat he
toppled backward. I put an oar into the center of his back.

He stared at me, rubbing his back. "Remind me," he said and tied the
line to the stern. Then he took the oars from me.

"Remind you of what?"

"Never to save me. I've been meaning to tell you for a long time."

When we beached the boat, he detached the rope and began to pull the rope on land. A turtle, larger than the one I had seen with Salud, was hauled up and I jumped back as the head came shooting out. Dash leaned down, grabbed the tail, and threw the turtle on its back.

"The hook is in fine. It'll hold. Go back and get the car for me."

I said, "I don't like to leave you alone, you shouldn't be handling that thing—"

"Go on," he said. "A turtle isn't a woman. I'll be safe."

We took the turtle home tied to the back bumper, dragging it through the dirt of the mile to the house. Dash went to the toolhouse for an axe, came back with it and a long heavy stick. He turned the turtle on its stomach, handed me the stick, and said, "Stand far back, hold the stick out, and wait until he snaps at it."

I did that, the turtle did snap, and the axe came down. But Dash missed because the turtle, seeing his arm, quickly withdrew his head. We tried five or six times. It was a hot day and that's why I thought I was sweating and, anyway, I never was comfortable with Hammett when he was doing something that didn't work.

He said, "Try once more."

I put the stick out, the turtle didn't take it, then did, and as he did, I moved my hand down the stick thinking that I could hold it better. The turtle dropped the stick and made the fastest move I had ever seen for my hand. I jumped back and the stick bruised my leg. Hammett put down the axe, took the stick from me, shook his head and said, "Go lie down."

I said I wasn't going to and he said I was to go somewhere and get out of his way. I said I wasn't going to do that either, that he was in a bad temper with me only because he couldn't kill the turtle with the axe.

"I am going to shoot it. But that's not my reason for bad temper. We've got some talking to do, you and I, it's been a long time."

"Talk now."

"No. I'm busy. I want you out of the way."

He took my arm, moved me to the kitchen steps, pushed me down and went into the house for a rifle. When he came out he put a piece of meat in front of the turtle's head and got behind it. We waited for a long time. Finally, the head did come out to stare at the meat and Hammett's gun went off. The shot was a beauty, just slightly behind the eyes. As I ran toward them the turtle's head convulsed in a forward movement, the feet carried the shell forward in a kind of heavy leap. I leaned down close and Hammett said, "Don't go too near. He isn't dead."

Then he picked up the axe and came down very hard on the neck, severing the head to the skin.

"That's odd," he said. "The shot didn't kill it, and yet it went through the brain. Very odd."

He grabbed the turtle by the tail and carried it up the long flight of steps to the kitchen. We found some newspapers and put the turtle on top of the coal stove that wasn't used much anymore except in the sausage-making season.

I said, "Now we'll have to learn about cutting it for soup."

Dash nodded. "O.K. But it's a long job. Let's wait until tomorrow."

I left a note under Helen's door—it was her day off and she had gone to New York—warning her there was a turtle sitting on the stove and not to be frightened. Then I telephoned my Aunt Jenny in New Orleans to get the recipe for the good soup of my childhood and she said I was to stay away from live turtles and go back to fine embroidery like a nice lady.

The next morning, coming down at six to help Fred milk the cows, I forgot about the turtle until I started down the kitchen steps and saw blood. Then, thinking it was the blood that we had spilled carrying the turtle into the house the evening before, I went on toward the barns. When I came back at eight, Helen asked me what I wanted for break-fast, she had made corn bread, and what had I meant by a turtle on the stove?

Going up to have a bath, I called back, "Just what I said. It's a turtle on the stove and you must know about snappers from your childhood."

After a few minutes she came upstairs to stare at me in the bathtub. "There ain't no turtle. But there's a mess of blood."

"On top of the coal stove," I said. "Just go have a look."

"I had a lot of looks. There ain't no turtle on top a stove in this house."

"Go wake Mr. Hammett," I said, "right away."

"I wouldn't like to do that," she said. "I don't like to wake men."

I went running down to the kitchen, and then fast back upstairs to Hammett's room, and shook him hard.

"Get up right away. The turtle's gone."

He turned over to stare at me. "You drink too much in the morning."

I said, *"The turtle's gone."*

He came down to the kitchen in a few minutes, stared at the stove, and turned to Helen. "Did you clean the floor?"

"Yes," she said, "it was all nasty. Look at the steps."

He stared at the steps that led to the cellar and out to the lawn. Then he moved slowly down the steps, following the path of blood spots, and out into the orchard. Near the orchard, planted many years before I owned the house, was a large rock garden, over half an acre of rare trees and plants, rising steep above the house entrance. Hammett turned toward it, following a path around the orchard. He said, "Once, when I worked for Pinkerton, I found a stolen ferris wheel for a traveling country fair. Then I lost the ferris wheel and, as far as I know, nobody ever found it again."

I said, "A turtle is not a ferris wheel. Somebody took the turtle."

"Who?"

"I don't know. Got a theory?"

"The turtle moved himself."

"I don't like what you're saying. He was dead last night. Stone dead."

"Look," he said.

He was pointing into the rock garden. Salud and three poodle puppies were sitting on a large rock, staring at something in a bush. We ran toward the garden. Hammett told the puppies to go away and parted the branches of the bush. The turtle sidling in an effort at movement, was trying to leave the bush, its head dangling from one piece of neck skin.

"My God," we both said at the same time and stood watching the turtle for the very long time it took to move a foot away from us. Then it stopped and its back legs stiffened. Salud, quiet until now, immediately leaped on it and his two puppies, yapping, leaped after him. Salud licked the blood from the head and the turtle moved his front legs. I grabbed Salud's collar and threw him too hard against a rock.

Hammett said, "The turtle can't bite him now. He's dead."

I said, "How do you know?" He picked up the turtle by the tail. "What are you going to do?"

"Take it back to the kitchen."

I said, "Let's take it to the lake. It's earned its life."

"It's dead. It's been dead since yesterday."

"No. Or maybe it was dead and now it isn't."

"The resurrection? You're a hard woman for an ex-Catholic," he said, moving off.

I was behind him as he came into the kitchen, threw the turtle on a marble slab. I heard Helen say, "My goodness, the good Lord help us all."

Hammett took down one of the butcher knives. He moved his lips as if rehearsing what he had read. Then he separated the leg meat from the shell, cutting expertly around the joints. The other leg moved as the knife went in.

Helen went out of the kitchen and I said, "You know very well that I help with the butchering of the animals here and don't like talk about how distasteful killing is by people who are willing to eat what is killed for them. But this is different. This is something else. We shouldn't touch it. It has earned its life."

He put down the knife. "O.K. Whatever you want."

We both went into the living room and he picked up a book. After an hour I said, "Then how does one define life?"

He said, "Lilly, I'm too old for that stuff."

Toward afternoon I telephoned the New York Zoological Society of which I was a member. I had a hard time being transferred to somebody who knew about turtles. When I finished, the young voice said, "Yes, the *Chelydra serpentina*. A ferocious foe. Where did you meet it?"

"Meet it?"

"Encounter it."

"At a literary cocktail party by a lake."

He coughed. "On land or water? Particularly ferocious when encountered on land. Bites with such speed that the naked human eye often cannot follow the movement. The limbs are powerful and a narrow projection from each side connects them to the carapace—"

"Yes," I said. "You are reading from the same book I read. I want to know how it managed to get down a staircase and up into a garden with its head hanging only by a piece of skin."

"An average snapper weighs between twenty and thirty pounds, but many have weighed twice that amount. The eggs are very interesting, hard of shell, often compared with ping-pong balls—"

"Please tell me what you think of, of, of its *life.*"

After a while he said, "I don't understand."

"Is it, was it, alive when we found it in the garden? Is it alive now?"

"I don't know what you mean," he said.

"I'm asking about life. What is *life*?"

"I guess what comes before death. Please put its heart in a small amount of salted water and be kind enough to send us a note reporting how long the heart beats. Our records show ten hours."

"Then it isn't dead."

There was a pause. "In our sense."

"What is our sense?"

There was talk in the background noise and I heard him whisper to somebody. Then he said, "The snapping turtle is a very low, possibly the lowest, form of life."

I said, "*Is it alive or is it dead?* That's all I want to know, please."

There was more whispering. "You asked me for a scientific opinion, Miss Hellernan. I am not qualified to give you a theological one. Thank you for calling."

Ten or twelve years later, at the end of a dinner party, a large lady crossed the room to sit beside me. She said she was engaged in doing a book on Madame de Staël, and when I had finished with the sounds I have for what I don't know about she said, "My brother used to be a zoologist. You once called him about a snapping turtle." I said to give him my regards and apologies and she said, "Oh, that's not necessary. He practices in Calcutta."

But the day of the phone call I went to tell Hammett about my conversation. He listened, smiled when I came to the theological part, went back to reading an old book called *The Animal Kingdom*. My notation in the front of this book, picked up again on a July afternoon in 1972, is what brought me to this memory of the turtle.

Toward dinnertime, Helen came into the room and said, "That turtle. I can't cook with it sitting around me."

I said to Hammett, "What will we do?"

"Make soup."

"The next time. The next turtle. Let's bury this one."

"*You* bury it."

"You're punishing me," I said. "Why?"

"I'm trying to understand you."

"It's that it moved so far. It's that I've never before thought about *life*, if you know what I mean."

"No, I don't," he said.

"Well, what is life and stuff like that."

"Stuff like that. At your age."

I said, "You are much older than I am."

"That still makes you thirty-four and too old for stuff like that."

"You're making fun of me."

"Cut it out, Lilly. I know all the signs."

"Signs of what?"

He got up and left the room. I carried up a martini an hour later and said, "Just this turtle, the next I'll be O.K."

"Fine with me," he said, "either way."

"No, it isn't fine with you. You're saying something else."

"I'm saying cut it out."

"And *I'm* saying—"

"I don't want any dinner," he said.

I left the room and slammed the door. At dinnertime I sent Helen up to tell him to come down immediately and she came back and said he said he wasn't hungry immediately.

During dinner she said she didn't want the turtle around when she came down for breakfast.

About ten, when Helen had gone to bed, I went upstairs and threw a book against Hammett's door.

"Yes?" he said.

"Please come and help me bury the turtle."

"I don't bury turtles."

"Will you bury me?"

"When the times comes, I'll do my best," he said.

"Open the door."

"No. Get Fred Herrmann to help you bury the turtle. And borrow Helen's prayer book."

But by the time I had had three more drinks, it was too late to wake Fred. I went to look at the turtle and saw that its blood was dripping to the floor. For many years, and for many years to come, I had been frightened of Helen and so, toward midnight, I tied a rope around the turtle's tail, took a flashlight, dragged it down the kitchen steps to the garage, and tied the rope to the bumper of the car. Then I went back to stand under Hammett's window.

I shouted up. "I'm weak. I can't dig a hole big enough. Come help me."

After I had said it twice, he called down, "I wish I could help you, but I'm asleep."

I spent the next hour digging a hole on the high ground above the lake, and by the time I covered the turtle the whiskey in the bottle was gone and I was dizzy and feeling sick. I put a stick over the grave, drove the car back towards the house, and when I was halfway there evidently fell asleep because I woke up at dawn in a heavy rain with the right wheels of the car turned into a tree stump. I walked home to bed and neither Hammett nor I mentioned the turtle for four or five days. That was no accident because we didn't speak to each other for three of those days, eating our meals at separate times.

Then he came back from a late afternoon walk and said, "I've caught two turtles. What would you like to do with them?"

"Kill them. Make soup."

"You're sure?"

"The first of anything is hard," I said. "You know that."

"I didn't know that until I met you," he said.

"I hurt my back digging the grave and I've a cold, but I had to bury that turtle and I don't want to talk about it again."

"You didn't do it very well. Some animal's been at your grave and eaten the turtle, but God will bless you anyway. I gathered the bones, put them back in the hole, and painted a tombstone sign for you."

For all the years we lived on the place, and maybe even now, there was a small wooden sign, neatly painted: "My first turtle is buried here. Miss Religious L.H."

EVA HOFFMAN
(1945–)

Eva Hoffman emigrated with her family from Poland to Canada in 1959 and described the experience in *Lost in Translation* (1989). Her memoir is especially notable for its subtle, sometimes rueful savoring of the complexities of language and the difficulties of exchanging one language for another. A resident of the United States since 1963, she obtained degrees from Rice, Yale, and Harvard and has worked as an editor of the *New York Times Book Review*.

Hoffman's title provides a brilliant metaphor for the experience of being uprooted from one culture and thrust into another. For other memoirs about cultural displacement and other women lost in translation, compare Maxine Hong Kingston, *The Woman Warrior*, Sara Suleri, *Meatless Days*, and Santha Rama Rau, *Gifts of Passage*.

FROM *Lost in Translation*

Every day I learn new words, new expressions. I pick them up from school exercises, from conversations, from the books I take out of Vancouver's well-lit, cheerful public library. There are some turns of phrase to which I develop strange allergies. "You're welcome," for example, strikes me as a gaucherie, and I can hardly bring myself to say it—I suppose because it implies that there's something to be thanked for, which in Polish would be impolite. The very places where language is at its most conventional, where it should be most taken for granted, are the places where I feel the prick of artifice.

Then there are words to which I take an equally irrational liking, for their sound, or just because I'm pleased to have deduced their meaning. Mainly they're words I learn from books, like "enigmatic" or "insolent"—words that have only a literary value, that exist only as signs on the page.

But mostly, the problem is that the signifier has become severed from the signified. The words I learn now don't stand for things in the same unquestioned way they did in my native tongue. "River" in Polish was a vital sound, energized with the essence of riverhood, of my rivers, of my being immersed in rivers. "River" in English is cold—a word without an aura. It has no accumulated associations for me, and it does not give off the radiating haze of connotation. It does not evoke.

The process, alas, works in reverse as well. When I see a river now, it is not shaped, assimilated by the word that accommodates it to the psyche—a word that makes a body of water a river rather than an uncontained element. The river before me remains a thing, absolutely other, absolutely unbending to the grasp of my mind.

When my friend Penny tells me that she's envious, or happy, or disappointed, I try laboriously to translate not from English to Polish but from the word back to its source, to the feeling from which it springs. Already, in that moment of strain, spontaneity of response is lost. And anyway, the translation doesn't work. I don't know how Penny feels when she talks about envy. The word hangs in a Platonic stratosphere, a vague prototype of all envy, so large, so all-encompassing that it might crush me—as might disappointment or happiness.

I am becoming a living avatar of structuralist wisdom; I cannot help knowing that words are just themselves. But it's a terrible knowledge, without any of the consolations that wisdom usually brings. It does not mean that I'm free to play with words at my wont; anyway, words in their naked state are surely among the least satisfactory play objects. No, this radical disjoining between word and thing is a desiccating alchemy, draining the world not only of significance but of its colors, striations, nuances—its very existence. It is the loss of a living connection.

The worst losses come at night. As I lie down in a strange bed in a strange house—my mother is a sort of housekeeper here, to the aging Jewish man who has taken us in in return for her services—I wait for that spontaneous flow of inner language which used to be my nighttime talk with myself, my way of informing the ego where the id had been. Nothing comes. Polish, in a short time, has atrophied, shriveled from sheer uselessness. Its words don't apply to my new experiences; they're not coeval with any of the objects or faces, or the very air I breathe in the daytime. In English, words have not penetrated to those layers of my psyche from which a private conversation could proceed. This interval before sleep used to be the time when my mind became both receptive and alert, when images and words rose up to consciousness, reiterating what had happened during the day, adding the day's experiences to those already stored there, spinning out the thread of my personal story.

Now, this picture-and-word show is gone; the thread has been snapped. I have no interior language, and without it, interior images—those images through which we assimilate the external world, through which we take it in, love it, make it our own—become blurred too. My mother and I met a Canadian family who live down the block today. They were working in their garden and engaged us in a conversation of the "Nice weather we're having, isn't it?" variety, which culminated in their inviting us into their house. They sat stiffly on their couch, smiled in the long pauses between the conversation, and seemed at a loss for what to ask. Now my mind gropes for some description of them, but nothing fits. They're a different species from anyone I've met in Poland, and Polish words slip off of them without sticking. English words don't hook on to anything. I try, deliberately, to come up with a few. Are these people pleasant or dull? Kindly or silly? The words float in an uncertain space. They come up from a part of my brain in which labels may be manufactured but which has no connection to my instincts, quick reactions, knowledge. Even the simplest adjectives sow confusion in my mind; English kindliness has a whole system of morality behind it, a system that makes "kindness" an entirely positive virtue. Polish kindness has the tiniest element of irony. Besides, I'm beginning to feel the tug of prohibition, in English, against uncharitable words. In Polish, you can call someone an idiot without particularly harsh feelings and with the zest of a strong judgment. Yes, in Polish these people might tend toward "silly" and "dull"—but I force myself toward "kindly" and "pleasant." The cultural unconscious is beginning to exercise its subliminal influence.

The verbal blur covers these people's faces, their gestures with a sort of fog. I can't translate them into my mind's eye. The small event, instead of being added to the mosaic of consciousness and memory, falls through some black hole, and I fall with it. What has happened to me in this new world? I don't know. I don't see what I've seen, don't comprehend what's in front of me. I'm not filled with language anymore, and I have only a memory of fullness to anguish me with the knowledge that, in this dark and empty state, I don't really exist.

Mrs. Lieberman, in the bathroom of her house, is shaving my armpits. She has taken me there at the end of her dinner party, and now, with a kind decisiveness, she lifts my arms and performs this foreign ablution on the tufts of hair that have never been objectionable to anyone before. She hasn't asked me whether I would like her to do it; she has simply taken it upon herself to teach me how things are done here.

Mrs. Lieberman is among several Polish ladies who have been in Canada long enough to consider themselves well versed in native ways, and who seem to find me deficient in some quite fundamental respects. Since in Poland I was considered a pretty young girl, this requires a basic revision of my self-image. But there's no doubt about it; after the passage across the Atlantic, I've emerged as less attractive, less graceful, less desirable. In fact, I can see in these women's eyes that I'm a somewhat pitiful specimen—pale, with thick eyebrows, and without any bounce in my hair, dressed in clothes that have nothing to do with the current fashion. And so they energetically set out to rectify these flaws. One of them spends a day with me, plucking my eyebrows and trying various shades of lipstick on my face. "If you were my daughter, you'd soon look like a princess," she says, thus implying an added deficiency in my mother. Another counselor takes me into her house for an evening, to initiate me into the mysteries of using shampoos and hair lotions, and putting my hair up in curlers; yet another outfits me with a crinoline and tells me that actually, I have a perfectly good figure—I just need to bring it out in the right ways. And several of them look at my breasts meaningfully, suggesting to my mother in an undertone that really, it's time I started wearing a bra. My mother obeys.

I obey too, passively, mulishly, but I feel less agile and self-confident with every transformation. I hold my head rigidly, so that my precarious bouffant doesn't fall down, and I smile often, the way I see other girls do, though I'm careful not to open my lips too wide or bite them, so my lipstick won't get smudged. I don't know how to move easily in the high-heeled shoes somebody gave me.

Inside its elaborate packaging, my body is stiff, sulky, wary. When I'm with my peers, who come by crinolines, lipstick, cars, and self-confidence naturally, my gestures show that I'm here provisionally, by their grace, that I don't rightfully belong. My shoulders stoop, I nod frantically to indicate my agreement with others, I smile sweetly at people to show I mean well, and my chest recedes inward so that I don't take up too much space—mannerisms of a marginal, off-centered person who wants both to be taken in and to fend off the threatening others.

About a year after our arrival in Vancouver, someone takes a photograph of my family in their backyard, and looking at it, I reject the image it gives of myself categorically. This clumsy looking creature, with legs oddly turned in their high-heeled pumps, shoulders bent with the strain of resentment and ingratiation, is not myself. Alienation is beginning to be inscribed in my flesh and face.

I'm sitting at the Steiners' kitchen table, surrounded by sounds of family jokes and laughter. I laugh along gamely, though half the time I don't understand what's going on.

Mrs. Steiner, who is Polish, has semiadopted me, and I spend whole days and weekends in her house, where I'm half exiled princess, half Cinderella. Half princess, because I'm musically talented and, who knows, I may become a famous pianist one day. Mrs. Steiner was an aspiring pianist herself in her youth, and she takes pleasure in supervising my musical progress: she has found a piano teacher for me, and often listens to me play. However, the Steiners are fabulously rich, and I am, at this point in my life, quite fabulously poor—and those basic facts condition everything; they are as palpable as a tilted beam that indicates the incline between us, never letting me forget the basic asymmetry of the relationship.

The Steiners' wealth is quite beyond the Rosenbergs', and quite beyond my conception of actual human lives. It exists on some step of the social ladder that jumps clear out of my head, and I can't domesticate its owners to ordinary personhood. Surely, the rich must be different. If I feel like a fairy-tale character near them, it's because they live in the realm of fable. Rosa Steiner is a stepmother with the power to change my destiny for good or evil. Mr. Steiner simply rules over his dominion, quietly, calmly, and remotely. I wouldn't dream of revealing myself to him, of making an imposition on his attention.

This is, of course, only one part of the story, though it is the part of which I am painfully conscious. Stefan Steiner accepts my presence in his domestic life graciously. And as for Rosa, she is, aside from everything else, a friend who understands where I come from—metaphorically and literally—better than anyone else I know in Vancouver. In turn, there is something in her I recognize and trust. She is a vivacious, energetic woman in her forties, beautiful in a high-cheekboned, Eastern European way, with a deep, hoarse voice and with a great certainty of her own opinions, judgments, and preferences. She reminds me of the authoritative women I knew in Poland, who did not seem as inhibited, as insistently "feminine" as the women I meet here. Her views are utterly commonsensical: she believes that people should try to get as much pleasure, approval, money, achievement, and good looks as they can. She has no use for eccentricity, ambivalence, or self-doubt. Her own task and destiny is carrying on the tradition of ordinary life—and she goes about it with great vigor and style. Except for the all-important disparate income, her inner world is not so different, after all, from my parents'. The disparity means that she's the fulfilled bourgeoise, while they've been relegated to aspiration and failure. It is her fulfillment, I suppose—yes, our feelings can be cruel—that reassures me. When I'm near her, I feel that satisfaction and contentment are surely possible—more, that they're everyone's inalienable right—possibly even mine.

Mrs. Steiner's snobberies are as resolute as everything else about her. She too believes there are "better people"—people who are successful, smart, and, most of all, cultured. She envisions her house as a kind of salon, to which she invites groups of Vancouver's elect; sometimes, on these occasions, I'm recruited to raise the tone of the proceedings and perhaps advance my own fortunes by playing some Beethoven or

Chopin. The Steiners' house, which overlooks both the sea and the mountains of Vancouver's harbor, is surrounded by large expanses of grounds and garden; inside, there are contemporary paintings, grand pianos, and enormous pieces of Eskimo sculpture. I don't know whether I like any of this unfamiliar art, but I know that's quite beside the point.

Mrs. Steiner takes me to her house often, and I'm happiest there when I'm with her alone. Then we talk for hours on end, mostly about my problems and my life. I'm a little ashamed to reveal how hard things are for my family—how bitterly my parents quarrel, how much my mother cries, how frightened I am by our helplessness, and by the burden of feeling that it is my duty to take charge, to get us out of this quagmire. But I can't help myself, it's too much of a relief to talk to somebody who is curious and sensitive to my concerns. Although her sensitivity has its limits: she cannot always make the leap of empathy across our differences. My mother's voice on the telephone ("She always sounds as if there's something wrong. Sometimes she speaks so softly I have to tell her to speak up") bothers her. And when my father quits his job at a lumber mill, Rosa is full of disapproval; he has a family to support, she tells me; isn't this a bit irresponsible? Suddenly, I feel the full bitterness of our situation. My father is no longer very young, I tell her; the job was the hardest in the mill. He had to lift heavy logs all day—and he has a bad back, the legacy of the war. He was in pain every day. Rosa is abashed by my sudden eruption, and she retreats. She didn't know all this, she says; of course, I may be right. But there is added irony in this exchange, which isn't lost on either of us: the Steiners own a lumber mill. In the Steiner kitchen, I've heard mention of the problems they've sometimes had with their workers.

Still, I can speak to Rosa frankly; we can hash this sort of thing out. But some of the ease of our exchange vanishes when other members of the family enter the scene. Mrs. Steiner is fiercely devoted to her daughters, and in her eyes they are princesses pure and simple. I believe her; what else can I do? I'm both too shy and too removed from their lives to check out what I think of them for myself. Elisabeth, the older one, has just started going to a small, elite college—a place of which I can only gather that there are extremely interesting young people there, most of them near geniuses, and that Elisabeth has occasionally taken to wearing odd garments, like Mexican skirts and black stockings. Elisabeth talks without fully opening her mouth and swallows the endings of her words—so that I can understand her even less than most people, and I find myself saying "I beg your pardon" so often, that finally it becomes more polite to pretend I know what she's saying than to keep repeating the question.

Laurie is only two years older than myself, and she tries to befriend me. She often comes to our house—I invariably fight embarrassment at its stripped-down bareness—to drive me to the Steiners', and on the way there she talks about herself. Much of the time, it takes an enormous effort on my part to follow her fast chatter and to keep saying yes and no in the right places, to attempt to respond. I try to cover up this virtual idiocy by looking as intelligent as I can. But I do gather from these conversations that Laurie has just been at some international camp in Austria, that she will travel in Europe the following summer, that her parents differ from others in giving her affection and care—she has many friends whose parents try to compensate with money for their basic indifference. Isn't that terrible? I try, at this point, to look properly sympathetic, but the scale of problems she describes is so vastly different from what I know, and our mutual incapacity to penetrate each other's experience is so evident to me, that I harden myself against her. If I were really to enter her world, if I were really to imagine its difficulties, I would be condemned to an envy so burning that it would turn to hate. My only defense against the indignity of such emotion is to avoid rigorously the thought of wanting what she has—to keep her at a long, safe distance.

In the evening, we sit down to a family dinner and its jokey banter—an American ritual meant to sharpen the young women's edges for their encounters with the world and to affirm their superiority in that world. The Steiners, led by Laurie, who is clever and quick, are teasing each other, each bit of witty attack a verbal glove challenging the others to up the ante. I feel miserably out of it, laughing too loud, but knowing that I can't enter the teasing circle. After all, Cinderella can't get snarky with her half sisters, can she? I can only approve; I can't even implicitly criticize—and this seems almost as basic a definition of my position as the lack of money. Razzing can only happen between equals or else it's a deliberate presumption, which brings attention to inferior status. But I'm too proud to engage in this latter kind.

I've had a nice day in the Steiner household; Rosa and I took a long, brisk walk, we ate an excellent lunch, I played the piano for her and she made some comments, and now I'm sitting at their kitchen table, to all appearances almost a family member. When I get home, I'm terribly depressed. There's a yellow light in the downstairs room where my mother is waiting for me; my father, I know, will have fallen asleep in a stupor of disorientation and fatigue. But when my mother asks me about my day with a curiosity that pains me—she almost never gets invited to the Steiners'—I only tell her what a wonderful time I had.

In later years, I'll come to sit at the Steiners' table often, and look back on the polite and rankled girl I was then and flinch a little at the narrowing of sympathies I felt in my narrow straits. I'll come to know that

Laurie might have been jealous of me, might have feared, even, that I would displace her in her mother's affections—but I could not imagine then that I could rouse jealousy in anyone. I'll see how much time and attention and goodwill the Steiners lavished on me, more than in our busy and overfilled lives people can give to each other nowadays. Really, they thought about me more seriously than I thought about myself. Who was I, after all? Eva's ghost, perhaps, a specter that tried not to occupy too much space. They were more generous toward me than I was toward them; but then, a sense of disadvantage and inferiority is not a position from which one can feel the largeheartedness of true generosity.

In *Speak, Memory,* Nabokov makes the poetic, or the playful, speculation that Russian children before the Revolution—and his exile—were blessed with a surfeit of sensual impressions to compensate them for what was to come. Of course, fate doesn't play such premonitory games, but memory can perform retrospective maneuvers to compensate for fate. Loss is a magical preservative. Time stops at the point of severance, and no subsequent impressions muddy the picture you have in mind. The house, the garden, the country you have lost remain forever as you remember them. Nostalgia—that most lyrical of feelings—crystallizes around these images like amber. Arrested within it, the house, the past, is clear, vivid, made more beautiful by the medium in which it is held and by its stillness.

Nostalgia is a source of poetry, and a form of fidelity. It is also a species of melancholia which used to be thought of as an illness. As I walk the streets of Vancouver, I am pregnant with the images of Poland, pregnant and sick. *Tęsknota** throws a film over everything around me, and directs my vision inward. The largest presence within me is the welling up of absence, of what I have lost. This pregnancy is also a phantom pain.

I don't know what to do with this private heaviness, this pregnancy without the possibility of birth. "She's so loyal," Mrs. Steiner says when I tell her that Mrs. Witeszczak was a wonderful piano teacher. There is a hint of criticism in the supposed compliment; the methods of piano teaching are after all more advanced here, Mrs. Steiner suggests, and I should not cling to the ways of the past. That makes me want to defend Mrs. Witeszczak even more. Not everything there is old-fashioned, not everything here better! But everyone encourages me to forget what I left behind. It wasn't any good back there, our Jewish acquaintances say, why would you even want to visit, they didn't want you anyway. I hang my head stubbornly under the lash of this wisdom. Can I really extract

*Nostalgia—Ed.

what I've been from myself so easily? Can I jump continents as if skipping rope?

In our highly ideological times, even nostalgia has its politics. The conservatives of the sentiments believe that recovering their own forgotten history is an antidote to shallowness. The ideologues of the future see attachment to the past as that most awful of all monsters, the agent of reaction. It is to be extracted from the human soul with no quarter or self-pity, for it obstructs the inevitable march of events into the next Utopia. Only certain Eastern European writers, forced to march into the future too often, know the regressive dangers of both forgetfulness and clinging to the past. But then, they are among our world's experts of mourning, having lost not an archaeological but a living history. And so, they praise the virtues of a true memory. Nabokov unashamedly reinvokes and revives his childhood in the glorious colors of *tęsknota*. Milan Kundera knows that a person who forgets easily is a Don Juan of experience, promiscuous and repetitive, suffering from the unbearable lightness of being. Czeslaw Milosz remembers the people and places of his youth with the special tenderness reserved for objects of love that are no longer cherished by others.

"Dear Basia," I write, "I am sitting at a window looking out on a garden in which there is a cherry tree, an apple tree, and bushes of roses now in bloom. The roses are smaller and wilder here, but imagine! All this in the middle of a city. And tomorrow I am going to a party. There are parties here all the time, and my social life is, you might say, blooming." I am repeating a ritual performed by countless immigrants who have sent letters back home meant to impress and convince their friends and relatives—and probably even themselves—that their lives have changed for the better. I am lying. But I am also trying to fend off my nostalgia. I couldn't repudiate the past even if I wanted to, but what can I do with it here, where it doesn't exist? After a while, I begin to push the images of memory down, away from consciousness, below emotion. Relegated to an internal darkness, they increase the area of darkness within me, and they return in the dark, in my dreams. I dream of Cracow perpetually, winding my way through familiar-unfamiliar streets, looking for a way home. I almost get there, repeatedly; almost, but not quite, and I wake up with the city so close that I can breathe it in.

I can't afford to look back, and I can't figure out how to look forward. In both directions, I may see a Medusa, and I already feel the danger of being turned into stone. Betwixt and between, I am stuck and time is stuck within me. Time used to open out, serene, shimmering with promise. If I wanted to hold a moment still, it was because I wanted to expand it, to get its fill. Now, time has no dimension, no extension backward or forward. I arrest the past, and I hold myself stiffly against the future; I want to stop the flow. As a punishment, I exist in the stasis of a perpetual present, that other side of "living in the present," which is not eternity but a prison. I can't throw a bridge between the present and the past, and therefore I can't make time move.

The car is full of my new friends, or at least the crowd that has more or less accepted me as one of their own, the odd "greener" tagalong. They're as lively as a group of puppies, jostling each other with sharp elbows, crawling over each other to change seats, and expressing their well-being and amiability by trying to outshout each other. It's Saturday night, or rather Saturday Night, and party spirits are obligatory. We're on our way to the local White Spot, an early Canadian version of Mc-Donald's, where we'll engage in the barbarous—as far as I'm concerned—rite of the "drive-in." This activity of sitting in your car in a large parking lot, and having sloppy, big hamburgers brought to you on a tray, accompanied by greasy french fries bounding out of their cardboard containers, mustard, spilly catsup, and sickly smelling relish, seems to fill these peers of mine with warm, monkeyish, groupy comfort. It fills me with a finicky distaste. I feel my lips tighten into an unaccustomed thinness—which, in turn, fills me with a small dislike for myself.

"Come on, foreign student, cheer up," one of the boys sporting a flowery Hawaiian shirt and a crew cut tells me, poking me in the ribs good-naturedly. "What's the matter, don't you like it here?" So as the car caroms off, I try to get in the mood. I try to giggle coyly as the girls exchange insinuating glances—though usually my titter comes a telling second too late. I try to join in the general hilarity, as somebody tells the latest elephant joke. Then—it's always a mistake to try too hard—I decide to show my goodwill by telling a joke myself. Finding some interruption in which to insert my uncertain voice, I launch into a translation of some slightly off-color anecdote I'd heard my father tell in Polish, no doubt hoping to get points for being risqué as well as a good sport. But as I hear my choked-up voice straining to assert itself, as I hear myself missing every beat and rhythm that would say "funny" and "punch line," I feel a hot flush of embarrassment. I come to a lame ending. There's a silence. "I suppose that's supposed to be funny," somebody says. I recede into the car seat.

Ah, the humiliation, the misery of failing to amuse! The incident is as rankling to my amour propre as being told I'm graceless or ugly. Telling a joke is like doing a linguistic pirouette. If you fall flat, it means not only that you don't have the wherewithal to do it well but also that you have misjudged your own skill, that you are fool enough to undertake something you can't finish—and that lack of self-control or self-knowledge is a lack of grace.

But these days, it takes all my will to impose any control on the words that emerge from me. I have to form entire sentences before uttering them; otherwise, I too easily get lost in the middle. My speech, I sense, sounds monotonous, deliberate, heavy—an aural mask that doesn't become me or express me at all. This willed self-control is the opposite of real mastery, which comes from a trust in your own verbal powers and allows for a free streaming of speech, for those bursts of spontaneity, the quickness of response that can rise into pleasure and overflow in humor. Laughter is the lightning rod of play, the eroticism of conversation; for now, I've lost the ability to make the sparks fly.

I've never been prim before, but that's how I am seen by my new peers. I don't try to tell jokes too often, I don't know the slang, I have no cool repartee. I love language too much to maul its beats, and my pride is too quick to risk the incomprehension that greets such forays. I become a very serious young person, missing the registers of wit and irony in my speech, though my mind sees ironies everywhere.

If primness is a small recoil of distaste at things that give others simple and hearty pleasure, then prim is what I'm really becoming. Although I'm not brave enough or hermit enough to stay home by myself every night, I'm a pretend teenager among the real stuff. There's too much in this car I don't like; I don't like the blue eye shadow on Cindy's eyelids, or the grease on Chuck's hair, or the way the car zooms off with a screech and then slows down as everyone plays we're-afraid-of-the-policeman. I don't like the way they laugh. I don't care for their "ugly" jokes, or their five-hundred-pound canary jokes, or their pickle jokes, or their elephant jokes either. And most of all, I hate having to pretend.

Perhaps the extra knot that strangles my voice is rage. I am enraged at the false persona I'm being stuffed into, as into some clumsy and over-blown astronaut suit. I'm enraged at my adolescent friends because they can't see through the guise, can't recognize the light-footed dancer I really am. They only see this elephantine creature who too often sounds as if she's making pronouncements.

It will take years before I pick and choose, from the Babel of American language, the style of wit that fits. It will take years of practice before its nuances and patterns snap smartly into the synapses of my brain so they can generate verbal electricity. It will take years of observing the discreet sufferings of the corporate classes before I understand the equally discreet charm of *New Yorker* cartoons.

For now, when I come across a *New Yorker* issue, I stare at the drawings of well-heeled people expressing some dissatisfaction with their condition as yet another demonstration of the weirdness all around me. "What's funny about that?" my mother asks in puzzlement. "I don't know," I answer, and we both shrug and shake our heads. And, as the car veers through Vancouver's neatly shrubberied and sparsely populated streets, I know that, among my other faculties, I've lost my sense of humor. I am not about to convert my adolescent friends to anti-Russian jokes. I swallow my injury, and giggle falsely at the five-hundred-pound canary.

Happy as larks, we lurch toward the White Spot.

If you had stayed there, your hair would have been straight, and you would have worn a barrette on one side.

But maybe by now you would have grown it into a ponytail? Like the ones you saw on those sexy faces in the magazines you used to read?

I don't know. You would have been fifteen by now. Different from thirteen.

You would be going to the movies with Zbyszek, and maybe to a café after, where you would meet a group of friends and talk late into the night.

But maybe you would be having problems with Mother and Father. They wouldn't like your staying out late.

That would have been fun. Normal. Oh God, to be a young person trying to get away from her parents.

But you can't do that. You have to take care of them. Besides, with whom would you go out here? One of these churlish boys who play spin the bottle? You've become more serious than you used to be.

What jokes are your friends in Cracow exchanging? I can't imagine. What's Basia doing? Maybe she's beginning to act. Doing exactly what she wanted. She must be having fun.

But you might have become more serious even there.

Possible.

But you would have been different, very different.

No question.

And you prefer her, the Cracow Ewa.

Yes, I prefer her. But I can't be her. I'm losing track of her. In a few years, I'll have no idea what her hairdo would have been like.

But she's more real, anyway.

Yes, she's the real one.

For my birthday, Penny gives me a diary, complete with a little lock and key to keep what I write from the eyes of all intruders. It is that little lock—the visible symbol of the privacy in which the diary is meant to exist—that creates my dilemma. If I am indeed to write something entirely for myself, in what language do I write? Several times, I open the diary and close it again. I can't decide. Writing in Polish at this point would be a little like resorting to Latin or ancient Greek—an eccentric thing to do in a diary, in which you're supposed to set down your most immediate experiences and unpremeditated thoughts in the most un-mediated language. Polish is becoming a dead language, the language of the untranslatable past. But writing for nobody's eyes in English? That's like doing a school exercise, or performing in front of yourself, a slightly perverse act of self-voyeurism.

Because I have to choose something, I finally choose English. If I'm to write about the present, I have to write in the language of the present, even if it's not the language of the self. As a result, the diary becomes surely one of the more impersonal exercises of that sort produced by an adolescent girl. There are no sentimental effusions of rejected love, erup-tions of familial anger, or consoling broodings about death. English is not the language of such emotions. Instead, I set down my reflections on the ugliness of wrestling; on the elegance of Mozart, and on how Dos-toyevsky puts me in mind of El Greco. I write down Thoughts. I Write.

There is a certain pathos to this naïve snobbery, for the diary is an earnest attempt to create a part of my persona that I imagine I would have grown into in Polish. In the solitude of this most private act, I write, in my public language, in order to update what might have been my other self. The diary is about me and not about me at all. But on one level, it allows me to make the first jump. I learn English through writ-ing, and, in turn, writing gives me a written self. Refracted through the double distance of English and writing, this self—my English self—becomes oddly objective; more than anything, it perceives. It exists more easily in the abstract sphere of thoughts and observations than in the world. For a while, this impersonal self, this cultural negative capability, becomes the truest thing about me. When I write, I have a real existence that is proper to the activity of writing—an existence that takes place midway between me and the sphere of artifice, art, pure language. This language is beginning to invent another me. However, I discover some-thing odd. It seems that when I write (or, for that matter, think) in English, I am unable to use the word "I." I do not go as far as the schizophrenic "she"—but I am driven, as by a compulsion, to the dou-ble, the Siamese-twin "you."

My voice is doing funny things. It does not seem to emerge from the same parts of my body as before. It comes out from somewhere in my throat, tight, thin, and mat—a voice without the modulations, dips, and rises that it had before, when it went from my stomach all the way through my head. There is, of course, the constraint and the self-con-sciousness of an accent that I hear but cannot control. Some of my high school peers accuse me of putting it on in order to appear more "interest-ing." In fact, I'd do anything to get rid of it, and when I'm alone, I practice sounds for which my speech organs have no intuitions, such as "th" (I do this by putting my tongue between my teeth) and "a," which is longer and more open in Polish (by shaping my mouth into a sort of arrested grin). It is simple words like "cat" or "tap" that give me the most trouble, because they have no context of other syllables, and so people often misunderstand them. Whenever I can, I do awkward little swerves to avoid them, or pause and try to say them very clearly. Still, when people—like salesladies—hear me speak without being prepared to listen carefully, they often don't understand me the first time around. "Girls' shoes," I say, and the "girls" comes out as a sort of scramble. "Girls' shoes," I repeat, willing the syllable to form itself properly, and the saleslady usually smiles nicely, and sends my mother and me to the right part of the store. I say, "Thank you" with a sweet smile, feeling as if I'm both claiming an unfair special privilege and being unfairly patronized.

It's as important to me to speak well as to play a piece of music without mistakes. Hearing English distorted grates on me like chalk screeching on a blackboard, like all things botched and badly done, like all forms of gracelessness. The odd thing is that I know what is correct, fluent, good, long before I can execute it. The English spoken by our Polish acquaintances strikes me as jagged and thick, and I know that I shouldn't imitate it. I'm turned off by the intonations I hear on the TV sitcoms—by the expectation of laughter, like a dog's tail wagging in supplication, built into the actors' pauses, and by the curtailed, cutoff rhythms. I like the way Penny speaks, with an easy flow and a pleasure in giving words a fleshly fullness; I like what I hear in some movies; and once the Old Vic comes to Vancouver to perform *Macbeth*, and though I can hardly understand the particular words, I am riveted by the tones of sureness and command that mold the actors' speech into such majestic periods.

Sociolinguists might say that I receive these language messages as class signals, that I associate the sounds of correctness with the social status of the speaker. In part, this is undoubtedly true. The class-linked notion that I transfer wholesale from Poland is that belonging to a "better" class of people is absolutely dependent on speaking a "better" language. And in my situation especially, I know that language will be a crucial instrument, that I can overcome the stigma of my marginality, the weight of presumption against me, only if the reassuringly right sounds come out of my mouth.

Yes, speech is a class signifier. But I think that in hearing these varieties of speech around me, I'm sensitized to something else as well—something that is a matter of aesthetics, and even of psychological health. Apparently, skilled chefs can tell whether a dish from some foreign cuisine is well cooked even if they have never tasted it and don't know the genre of cooking it belongs to. There seem to be some deep-structure qualities—consistency, proportions of ingredients, smoothness of blending—that indicate culinary achievement to these educated eaters' taste buds. So each language has its own distinctive music, and even if one doesn't know its separate components, one can pretty quickly recognize the propriety of the patterns in which the components are put together, their harmonies and discords. Perhaps the crucial element that strikes the ear in listening to living speech is the degree of the speaker's self-assurance and control.

As I listen to people speaking that foreign tongue, English, I can hear when they stumble or repeat the same phrases too many times, when their sentences trail off aimlessly—or, on the contrary, when their phrases have vigor and roundness, when they have the space and the breath to give a flourish at the end of a sentence, or make just the right pause before coming to a dramatic point. I can tell, in other words, the degree of their ease or disease, the extent of authority that shapes the rhythms of their speech. That authority—in whatever dialect, in whatever variant of the mainstream language—seems to me to be something we all desire. It's not that we all want to speak the King's English, but whether we speak Appalachian or Harlem English, or Cockney, or Jamaican Creole, we want to be at home in our tongue. We want to be able to give voice accurately and fully to ourselves and our sense of the world. John Fowles, in one of his stories in *The Ebony Tower,* has a young man cruelly violate an elderly writer and his manuscripts because the legacy of language has not been passed on to the youthful vandal properly. This seems to me an entirely credible premise. Linguistic dispossession is a sufficient motive for violence, for it is close to the dispossession of one's self. Blind rage, helpless rage is rage that has no words—rage that overwhelms one with darkness. And if one is perpetually without words, if one exists in the entropy of inarticulateness, that condition itself is bound to be an enraging frustration. In my New York apartment, I listen almost nightly to fights that erupt like brushfire on the street below—and in their escalating fury of repetitious phrases ("Don't do this to me, man, you fucking bastard, I'll fucking kill you"), I hear not the pleasures of macho toughness but an infuriated beating against wordlessness, against the incapacity to make oneself understood, seen. Anger can be borne—it can even be satisfying—if it can gather into words and explode in a storm, or a rapier-sharp attack. But without this means of ventilation, it only turns back inward, building and swirling like a head of steam—building to an impotent, murderous rage. If all therapy is speaking therapy—a talking cure—then perhaps all neurosis is a speech dis-ease.

BILLIE HOLIDAY
(1915–1959)

"Mom and Pop were just a couple of kids when they got married. He was eighteen, she was sixteen, and I was three." Little in the striking opening of *Lady Sings the Blues* (1956) is factual: Billie Holiday's mother, Sadie Fagan, was nineteen when she was born, and her father, Clarence Holiday, was seventeen. They never *did* marry, never even lived together. Billie Holiday (real name Eleanora Fagan) wasn't born in Baltimore, as she always said, but in Philadelphia. And no one who knew her can imagine Billie Holiday, even young, scrubbing steps—a favorite part of her myth of herself. *Lady Sings the Blues* is a faithful rendition of that myth, but little except what the singer says about music can be taken as fact. Holiday agreed to have *Lady Sings the Blues* published as her autobiography and even posed for author photos at the typewriter, but the book was actually written by newspaperman William Dufty, based largely on interviews with Holiday that had appeared in newspapers. She herself refused to cooperate with him, although her name is on the copyright and she collected royalties.

For other collaborations, compare Onnie Lee Logan, *Motherwit*, Ning Lao T'ai-t'ai, *A Daughter of Han*, Nisa: *The Life and Words of a !Kung Woman*, Émilie Carles, *A Life of Her Own*, and Le Ly Hayslip, *When Heaven and Earth Changed Places*. For other accounts of African-American experience, compare Maya Angelou, *I Know Why the Caged Bird Sings*, Zora Neale Hurston, *Mules and Men*, Audre Lorde, *Zami*, and Anne Moody, *Coming of Age in Mississippi*. For another daughter of Philadelphia, compare Margaret Mead, *Blackberry Winter*.

FROM *Lady Sings the Blues*

By the time Mom and I had got together and found us a place of our own in Harlem the depression was on. At least, so we heard tell. A depression was nothing new to us, we'd always had it. The only thing new about it was the bread lines. And they were about the only thing we missed.

We moved into an apartment on 139th Street, and not long after, for the first time since I could remember, Mom was too sick to make Mass on Sunday. For her, that was really sick. Give her coffee every morning and Mass every Sunday, and she thought she could go on working forever. But she had to quit working out as a maid. She couldn't even walk, her stomach was so shot. She just had to stay put in bed.

What little money we had saved started running out and she was getting panicky. She had worked for most of her life, and it was beginning to tell on her. For almost half of that time she had been grieving over Pop. This didn't help any.

I had decided I was through turning tricks as a call girl. But I had also decided I wasn't going to be anybody's damn maid. The rent always seemed to be due, and it took some scuffling to keep from breaking my vows.

About that time Fletcher Henderson's band was working downtown at the Roseland Ballroom. It was the first Negro band to work there, and Pop Holiday was with them on the guitar. Sick as she was, Mom was too proud to turn to Pop and ask his help with the rent money. But not me.

I used to go right down there and haunt him. Pop was in his early thirties then, but he didn't want anyone to guess it—especially the young chicks who used to hang around the entrance waiting for the musicians.

I was around fifteen then, but I looked plenty old enough to vote. I used to wait for him down in the hallway. I'd try to catch his eye and call out to him, "Hey, Daddy." I soon found out just waving at him would make him feel like forty-five, and he didn't like that. He used to plead with me.

"Please," he'd say, "whatever you do, don't call me Daddy in front of these people."

"I'm going to call you Daddy all night unless you give me some damn money for rent," I'd tell him. That would do it.

I'd take the money home to Mom, proud as all get out. But I couldn't hurt her feelings by telling her where it came from. If she kept worrying me about it, I'd finally tell her I stole it. Then we'd have a fight and she'd tell me I was going to end up in jail again.

One day when the rent was overdue, she got a notice that the law was going to put us out on the street. It was in the dead cold of winter and she couldn't even walk.

I didn't know they did things like that up North. Bad as it was down South, they never put you out on the street. When we were due to get set out on the street the next morning, I told Mom I would steal or murder or do anything before I'd let them pull that. It was cold as all hell that night, and I walked out without any kind of coat.

I walked down Seventh Avenue from 139th Street to 133rd Street, busting in every joint trying to find a job. In those days 133rd Street was the real swing street, like 52nd Street later tried to be. It was jumping with after-hours spots, regular hour joints, restaurants, cafés, a dozen to a block.

Finally, when I got to Pod's and Jerry's, I was desperate. I went in and asked for the boss. I think I talked to Jerry. I told him I was a dancer and I wanted to try out. I knew exactly two steps, the time step and the crossover. I didn't even know the word "audition" existed, but that was what I wanted.

So Jerry sent me over to the piano player and told me to dance. I started, and it was pitiful. I did my two steps over and over until he barked at me and told me to quit wasting his time.

They were going to throw me out on my ear, but I kept begging for the job. Finally the piano player took pity on me. He squashed out his cigarette, looked up at me, and said, "Girl, can you sing?"

I said, "Sure I can sing, what good is that?" I had been singing all my life, but I enjoyed it too much to think I could make any real money at it. Besides, those were the days of the Cotton Club and all those glamour pusses who didn't do nothing but look pretty, shake a little, and take money off tables.

I thought that was the only way to make money, and I needed forty-five bucks by morning to keep Mom from getting set out in the street. Singers were never heard of then, unless it was Paul Robeson, Julian Bledsoe, or someone legit like that.

So I asked him to play "Trav'lin' All Alone." That came closer than anything to the way I felt. And some part of it must have come across. The whole joint quieted down. If someone had dropped a pin, it would have sounded like a bomb. When I finished, everybody in the joint was crying in their beer, and I picked thirty-eight bucks up off the floor. When I left the joint that night I split with the piano player and still took home fifty-seven dollars.

I went out and bought a whole chicken and some baked beans—Mom loved baked beans—and raced up Seventh Avenue to the house. When I showed Mom the money for the rent and told her I had a regular job singing for eighteen dollars a week, she could hardly believe it.

As soon as she could get out of bed she came down to see for herself and became my biggest booster. In those days they had five or six singers in the clubs and they called them "ups." One girl would be "up" and she would go from table to table singing. Then the next one would be "up" and she'd take over. I was an "up" from midnight every night until the tips started thinning out, maybe around three o'clock the next morning.

In those days, too, all the girls took money off the tables, but I broke that up.* With my first loot I got me a pair of fancy drawers with little rhinestones on them. But I didn't like the idea of showing my body. There was nothing wrong with my body, I just didn't like the idea. When the time came to take those bills off the table, I was always messing up.

One night a millionaire came in the joint and put out a twenty-dollar bill on the table. I wanted that twenty-dollar bill so bad. I really tried, but I dropped it so many times he got disgusted and said, "Why, you're nothing but a punk kid. Get the hell away from here."

When I finished my "up" he must have felt sorry for me. Anyway, he asked me to come back and have a drink with him. When I did, he gave me the twenty-dollar bill in my hand. I figured, if a millionaire could give me money that way, everybody could. So from then on I wouldn't take money off tables. When I came to work the other girls used to razz me, call me "Duchess" and say, "Look at her, she thinks she's a lady."

I hadn't got my title Lady Day yet, but that was the beginning of people calling me "Lady."

When Mom came to hear me sing and I started to make the rounds, I would always start at her table. After I'd made five or six bucks in tips I'd split with the piano player and give the rest to Mom to hold. The first night I did this she decided she'd get into the act and do a little shilling. The next time around she made like a big shot and started the ball rolling by handing me a big tip—two or three bucks of my own money. I'd throw it in with the rest, and when I finished the round I'd split with the piano player again. She got me so mixed up, acting like a duchess and handing me my own money, I got into a helluva rassle with the piano player.

When it came time to settle up for the night I tried to get back the money that belonged to me. I had given it to Mom and she had given it back, and this way I was splitting with the piano player three or four times. When I tried to explain this to him and told him my mother had done it, he looked at this young woman sitting at the table and flipped.

"Bitch," he said, "that's not your mother." There was a real hassle before I could convince him Mom was really my mother, and only trying to help. Later on I got Mom a job in the kitchen at the Log Cabin. We had the joint sewed.

*Harlem nightclub singers at the time were expected to pick up tips between their legs—
Ed.

ZORA NEALE HURSTON
(1891–1960)

The author of the novel *Their Eyes Were Watching God* grew up in Eaton-ville, Florida, went to Barnard College, and was trained in anthropology by Franz Boas when few black women pursued that calling. She chose to return to her native town to collect southern black folktales and folk customs. Eventually her passionate curiosity took her to New Orleans, where she studied voodoo. She described her research in an account called *Mules and Men* (1935), from which these excerpts are drawn, one about Eatonville and one about New Orleans. The book reveals more of Hurston's life and temperament than her official autobiog-raphy, *Dust Tracks on a Road* (1942).

For another account of anthropological research, compare Margaret Mead, *Blackberry Winter*. Mead was also a student of Boas. For another memoir of Florida, compare Marjorie Kinnan Rawlings, *Cross Creek*.

FROM *Mules and Men*

As I crossed the Maitland-Eatonville township line I could see a group on the store porch. I was delighted. The town had not changed. Same love of talk and song. So I drove on down there before I stopped. Yes, there was George Thomas, Calvin Daniels, Jack and Charlie Jones, Gene Brazzle, B. Moseley and "Seaboard." Deep in a game of Florida-flip. All of those who were not actually playing were giving advice—"bet straightening" they call it.

"Hello, boys," I hailed them as I went into neutral.

They looked up from the game and for a moment it looked as if they had forgotten me. Then B. Moseley said, "Well, if it ain't Zora Hur-ston!" Then everybody crowded around the car to help greet me.

"You gointer stay awhile, Zora?"

"Yep. Several months."

"Where you gointer stay, Zora?"

"With Mett and Ellis, I reckon."

"Mett" was Mrs. Armetta Jones, an intimate friend of mine since childhood and Ellis was her husband. Their house stands under the huge camphor tree on the front street.

"Hello, heart-string," Mayor Hiram Lester yelled as he hurried up the street. "We heard all about you up North. You back home for good, I hope."

"Nope, Ah come to collect some old stories and tales and Ah know y'all know a plenty of 'em and that's why Ah headed straight for home."

"What you mean, Zora, them big old lies we tell when we're jus' sittin' around here on the store porch doin' nothin'?" asked B. Moseley.

"Yeah, those same ones about Ole Massa, and colored folks in heaven, and—oh, y'all know the kind I mean."

"Aw shucks," exclaimed George Thomas doubtfully. "Zora, don't you come here and tell de biggest lie first thing. Who you reckon want to read all them old-time tales about Brer Rabbit and Brer Bear?"

"Plenty of people, George. They are a lot more valuable than you might think. We want to set them down before it's too late."

"Too late for what?"

"Before everybody forgets all of 'em."

"No danger of that. That's all some people is good for—set 'round and lie and murder groceries."

"Ah know one right now," Calvin Daniels announced cheerfully. "It's a tale 'bout John and de frog."

"Wait till she get out her car, Calvin. Let her get settled at 'Mett's' and cook a pan of ginger bread then we'll all go down and tell lies and eat ginger bread. Dat's de way to do. She's tired now from all dat drivin'.'"

"All right, boys," I agreed. "But Ah'll be rested by night. Be lookin' for everybody."

So I unloaded the car and crowded it into Ellis' garage and got settled. Armetta made me lie down and rest while she cooked a big pan of ginger bread for the company we expected.

Calvin Daniels and James Moseley were the first to show up.

"Calvin, Ah sure am glad that you got here. Ah'm crazy to hear about John and dat frog," I said.

"That's why Ah come so early so Ah could tell it to you and go. Ah got to go over to Wood Bridge a little later on."

"Ah'm glad you remembered me first, Calvin."

"Ah always like to be good as my word, and Ah just heard about a toe-party over to Wood Bridge tonight and Ah decided to make it."

"A toe-party! What on earth is that?"

"Come go with me and James and you'll see!"

"But, everybody will be here lookin' for me. They'll think Ah'm crazy—tellin' them to come and then gettin' out and goin' to Wood Bridge myself. But Ah certainly would like to go to that toe-party."

"Aw, come on. They kin come back another night. You gointer like this party."

"Well, you tell me the story first, and by that time, Ah'll know what to do."

"Ah, come on, Zora," James urged. "Git de car out. Calvin kin tell you dat one while we're on de way. Come on, let's go to de toe-party."

"No, let 'im tell me this one first, then, if Ah go he can tell me some more on de way over."

James motioned to his friend. "Hurry up and tell it, Calvin, so we kin go before somebody else come."

"Aw, most of 'em ain't comin' nohow. They all 'bout goin' to Wood Bridge, too. Lemme tell you 'bout John and dis frog:

It was night and Ole Massa sent John, his favorite slave, down to the spring to get him a cool drink of water. He called John to him.

"John!"

"What you want, Massa?"

"John, I'm thirsty. Ah wants a cool drink of water, and Ah wants you to go down to de spring and dip me up a nice cool pitcher of water."

John didn't like to be sent nowhere at night, but he always tried to do everything Ole Massa told him to do, so he said, "Yessuh, Massa, Ah'll go git you some!"

Ole Massa said: "Hurry up, John. Ah'm mighty thirsty."

John took de pitcher and went on down to de spring. There was a great big ole bull frog settin' right on de edge of de spring, and when John dipped up de water de noise skeered de frog and he hollered and jumped over in de spring.

John dropped de water pitcher and tore out for de big house, hollerin' "Massa! Massa! A big old booger done got after me!"

Ole Massa told him, "Why, John, there's no such thing as a booger."

"Oh, yes it is, Massa. He down at dat Spring."

"Don't tell me, John. Youse just excited. Furthermore, you go git me dat water Ah sent you after."

"No, indeed, Massa, you and nobody else can't send me back there so dat booger kin git me."

Ole Massa begin to figger dat John musta seen somethin' sho nuff because John never had disobeyed him before, so he ast: "John, you say you seen a booger. What did it look like?"

John tole him, "Massa, he had two great big eyes lak balls of fire, and when he was standin' up he was sittin' down and when he moved, he moved by jerks, and he had most no tail."

Long before Calvin had ended his story James had lost his air of impatience.

"Now, Ah'll tell one," he said. "That is, if you so desire."

"Sure, Ah want to hear you tell 'em till daybreak if you will," I said eagerly.

"But where's the ginger bread?" James stopped to ask.

"It's out in the kitchen," I said. "Ah'm waiting for de others to come."

"Aw, naw, give us ours now. Them others may not get here before forty o'clock and Ah'll be done et mine and be in Wood Bridge. Anyhow Ah want a corner piece and some of them others will beat me to it."

So I served them with ginger bread and buttermilk.

"You sure going to Wood Bridge with us after Ah git thru tellin' this one?" James asked.

"Yeah, if the others don't show up by then," I conceded.

So James told the story about the man who went to Heaven from Johnstown.

.   .   .

There was a lot of horn-honking outside and I went to the door. The crowd drew up under the mothering camphor tree in four old cars. Everybody in boisterous spirits.

"Come on, Zora! Le's go to Wood Bridge. Great toe-party goin' on. All kinds of 'freshments. We kin tell you some lies most any ole time. We never run outer lies and lovin'. Tell 'em tomorrow night. Come on if you comin'—le's go if you gwine."

So I loaded up my car with neighbors and we all went to Wood Bridge. It is a Negro community joining Maitland on the north as Eatonville does on the west, but no enterprising souls have ever organized it. They have no schoolhouse, no post office, no mayor. It is lacking in Eatonville's feeling of unity. In fact, a white woman lives there.

While we rolled along Florida No. 3, I asked Armetta where was the shindig going to be in Wood Bridge. "At Edna Pitts' house," she told me. "But she ain't givin' it by herself; it's for the lodge."

"Think it's gointer be lively?"

"Oh, yeah. Ah heard that a lot of folks from Altamonte and Longwood is comin'. Maybe from Winter Park too."

We were the tail end of the line and as we turned off the highway we could hear the boys in the first car doing what Ellis Jones called bookooing* before they even hit the ground. Charlie Jones was woofing† louder than anybody else. "Don't y'all sell off all dem pretty li'l pink toes befo' Ah git dere."

*Loud talking, bullying, woofing. From French *beaucoup*.
†Aimless talking.

Peter Stagg: "Save me de best one!"

Soddy Sewell: "Hey, you mullet heads! Get out de way there and let a real man smoke them toes over."

Gene Brazzle: "Come to my pick, gimme a vaseline brown!"

Big Willie Sewell: "Gimme any kind so long as you gimme more'n one."

Babe Brown, riding a running-board, guitar in hand, said, "Ah want a toe, but if it ain't got a good looking face on to it, don't bring de mess up."

When we got there the party was young. The house was swept and garnished, the refreshments on display, several people sitting around; but the spot needed some social juices to mix the ingredients. In other words, they had the carcass of a party lying around up until the minute Eatonville burst in on it. Then it woke up.

"Y'all done sold off any toes yet?" George Brown wanted to know.

Willie Mae Clarke gave him a certain look and asked him, "What's dat got to do with you, George Brown?" And he shut up. Everybody knows that Willie Mae's got the business with George Brown.

"Nope. We ain't had enough crowd, but I reckon we kin start now," Edna said. Edna and a sort of committee went inside and hung up a sheet across one end of the room. Then she came outside and called all of the young women inside. She had to coax and drag some of the girls.

"Oh, Ah'm shame-face-ted!" some of them said.

"Nobody don't want to buy *mah* old rusty toe." Others fished around for denials from the male side.

I went on in with the rest and was herded behind the curtain.

"Say, what *is* this toe-party business?" I asked one of the girls.

"Good gracious, Zora! Ain't you never been to a toe-party before?"

"Nope. They don't have 'em up North where Ah been and Ah just got back today."

"Well, they hides all de girls behind a curtain and you stick out yo' toe. Some places you take off yo' shoes and some places you keep 'em on, but most all de time you keep 'em on. When all de toes is in a line, sticking out from behind de sheet they let de men folks in and they looks over all de toes and buys de ones they want for a dime. Then they got to treat de lady dat owns dat toe to everything she want. Sometime they play it so's you keep de same partner for de whole thing and sometimes they fix it so they put de girls back every hour or so and sell de toes agin."

Well, my toe went on the line with the rest and it was sold five times during the party. Everytime a toe was sold there was a great flurry before the curtain. Each man eager to see what he had got, and whether the other men would envy him or ridicule him. One or two fellows ungallantly ran out of the door rather than treat the girls whose toe they had bought sight unseen.

Babe Brown got off on his guitar and the dancing was hilarious. There was plenty of chicken perleau and baked chicken and fried chicken and rabbit. Pig feet and chitterlings and hot peanuts and drinkables. Everybody was treating wildly.

"Come on, Zora, and have a treat on me!" Charlie Jones insisted. "You done et chicken-ham and chicken-bosom wid every shag-leg in Orange County *but* me. Come on and spend some of *my* money."

"Thanks, Charlie, but Ah got five helpin's of chicken inside already. Ah either got to get another stomach or quit eatin'."

"Quit eatin' then and go to thinking. Quit thinkin' and start to drinkin'. What you want?"

"Coca-Cola right off de ice, Charlie, and put some salt in it. Ah got a slight headache."

"Aw naw, my money don't buy no sweet slop. Choose some coon dick."

"What is coon dick?"

"Aw, Zora, jus' something to make de drunk come. Made out uh grape fruit juice, corn meal mash, beef bones and a few mo' things. Come on le's git some together. It might make our love come down."

As soon as we started over into the next yard where coon dick was to be had, Charlie yelled to the barkeep, "Hey, Seymore! fix up another quart of dat low wine—here come de boom!"

It was handed to us in a quart fruit jar and we went outside to try it.

The raw likker known locally as coon dick was too much. The minute it touched my lips, the top of my head flew off. I spat it out and "choosed" some peanuts. Big Willie Sewell said, "Come on, heartstring, and have some gospel-bird* on me. My money spends too." His Honor, Hiram Lester, the Mayor, heard him and said, "There's no mo' chicken left, Willie. Why don't you offer her something she can get?"

"Well there *was* some chicken there when Ah passed the table a little while ago."

"Oh, so you offerin' her some chicken *was*. She can't eat that. What she want is some chicken *is.*"

"Aw shut up, Hiram. Come on, Zora, le's go inside and make out we dancin'." We went on inside but it wasn't a party any more. Just some people herded together. The high spirits were simmering down and nobody had a dime left to cry so the toe-business suffered a slump. The heaped-up tables of refreshments had become shambles of chicken

---

*Chicken. Preachers are supposed to be fond of them.

bones and empty platters anyway so that there was no longer any point in getting your toe sold, so when Columbus Montgomery said, "Le's go to Eatonville," Soddy Sewell jumped up and grabbed his hat and said, "I heard you, buddy."

Eatonville began to move back home right then. Nearly everybody was packed in one of the five cars when the delegation from Altamonte arrived. Johnnie Barton and Georgia Burke. Everybody piled out again.

"Got yo' guitar wid you, Johnnie?"

"Man, you know Ah don't go nowhere unless Ah take my box wid me," said Johnnie in his starched blue shirt, collar pin with heart bangles hanging on each end and his cream pants with the black stripe. "And what make it so cool, Ah don't go nowhere unless I play it."

"And when you git to strowin' yo' mess and Georgy gits to singin' her alto, man it's hot as seven hells. Man, play dat 'Palm Beach.' "

Babe Brown took the guitar and Johnnie Barton grabbed the piano stool. He sung. Georgia Burke and George Thomas singing about Polk County where the water taste like wine.

My heart struck sorrow, tears come running down.

At about the thirty-seventh verse, something about:

Ah'd ruther be in Tampa with the Whip-poor-will,
Ruther be in Tampa with the Whip-poor-will
Than to be 'round here—
Honey with a hundred dollar bill,

I staggered sleepily forth to the little Chevrolet for Eatonville. The car was overflowing with passengers but I was so dull from lack of sleep that I didn't know who they were. All I knew is they belonged in Eatonville.

Somebody was woofing in my car about love and I asked him about his buddy—I don't know why now. He said, "Ah ain't got no buddy. They kilt my buddy so they could raise me. Jus' so Ah be yo' man Ah don't want no damn buddy. Ah hope they kill every man dat ever cried, 'titty-mamma' but me. Lemme be yo' kid."

Some voice from somewhere else in the car commented, "You sho' Lawd is gointer have a lot of hindrance."

Then somehow I got home and to bed and Armetta had Georgia syrup and waffles for breakfast.

·   ·   ·

Now I was in New Orleans and I asked. They told me Algiers, the part of
New Orleans that is across the river to the west. I went there and lived
for four months and asked. I found women reading cards and doing mail
order business in names and insinuations of well known factors in conjure. Nothing worth putting on paper. But they all claimed some knowledge and link with Marie Leveau. From so much of hearing the name I
asked everywhere for this Leveau and everybody told me differently. But
from what they said I was eager to know to the end of the talk. It carried
me back across the river into the Vieux Carré. All agreed that she had
lived and died in the French quarter of New Orleans. So I went there to
ask.

I found an oil painting of the queen of conjure on the walls of the
Cabildo, and mention of her in the guide books of New Orleans, but I
did a lot of stumbling and asking before I heard of Luke Turner, himself
a hoodoo doctor, who says that he is her nephew.

When I found out about Turner, I had already studied under five
two-headed doctors and had gone thru an initiation ceremony with each.
So I asked Turner to take me as a pupil. He was very cold. In fact he
showed no eagerness even to talk with me. He feels sure of his powers
and seeks no one. He refused to take me as a pupil and in addition to his
habitual indifference I could see he had no faith in my sincerity. I could
see him searching my face for whatever was behind what I said. The City
of New Orleans has a law against fortune tellers, hoodoo doctors and the
like, and Turner did not know me. He asked me to excuse him as he was
waiting upon someone in the inner room. I let him go but I sat right
there and waited. When he returned, he tried to shoo me away by being
rude. I stayed on. Finally he named an impossible price for tuition. I
stayed and dickered. He all but threw me out, but I stayed and urged
him.

I made three more trips before he would talk to me in any way that I
could feel encouraged. He talked about Marie Leveau because I asked. I
wanted to know if she was really as great as they told me. So he enlightened my ignorance and taught me. We sat before the soft coal fire in his
grate. . . .

"She go to her great Altar and seek until she become the same as the
spirit, then she come out into the room where she listens to them that
come to ask. When they finish she answer them as a god. If a lady have a
bad enemy and come to her she go into her altar room and when she
come out and take her seat, the lady will say to her:

" 'Oh, Good Mother. I come to you with my heart bowed down and
my shoulders drooping, and my spirits broken; for an enemy has sorely
tried me; has caused my loved ones to leave me; has taken from me my

worldly goods and my gold; has spoken meanly of me and caused my friends to lose faith in me. On my knees I pray to you, Good Mother, that you will cause confusion to reign in the house of my enemy and that you will take their power from them and cause them to be unsuccessful.'

"Marie Leveau is not a woman when she answer the one who ask. No. She is a god, yes. Whatever she say, it will come so. She say:

" 'Oh, my daughter, I have heard your woes and your pains and tribulations, and in the depth of the wisdom of the gods I will help you find peace and happiness.

" 'It is written that you will take of the Vinagredes Four Volle* for him, and you will dip into it a sheet of pure parchment paper, and on this sheet you will write the names of your enemies and send it to the house of your enemies, tightly sealed with the wax of the porcupine plant.

" 'Then when the sun shall have risen and gone down three times, you will take of the water of Mars, called War Water, and in front of the house of your enemy you will sprinkle it. This you will do as you pass by. If it be a woman, you will take the egg of a guinea fowl, and put it into the powder of the fruit of cayenne and the dust of Goofer,† and you will set it on the fire in your own house and in clear water from the skies you will boil it until it shall be hard. This you will do so that there shall be no fruit from her womb.

" 'And you shall take of the Damnation Powders, two drachmas, and of the water powders, two drachmas and make a package of it and send it to the home of the one who has spoken badly of you and has treated you mean, so that damnation and trouble shall be on the head of your enemy and not on you.

" 'You will do this so that you will undo your enemies and you will take the power to harm you away from your enemies.

" 'Oh daughter, go you in peace and do the works required of you, so that you will have rest and comfort from your enemies and that they will have not the power to harm you and lower you in the sight of your people and belittle you in the sight of your friends. So be it.' "

By the time that Turner had finished his recitation he wasn't too conscious of me. In fact he gave me the feeling that he was just speaking, but not for my benefit. He was away off somewhere. He made a final dramatic gesture with open hands and hushed for a minute. Then he sank deeper into himself and went on:

"But when she put the last curse on a person, it would be better if that man was dead, yes."

---

*Four Thieves Vinegar, conjure paraphernalia—ED.
†Dirt taken out of a grave.

With an impatient gesture he signalled me not to interrupt him.

"She set the altar for the curse with black candles that have been dressed in vinegar. She would write the name of the person to be cursed on the candle with a needle. Then she place fifteen cents in the lap of Death upon the altar to pay the spirit to obey her orders. Then she place her hands flat upon the table and say the curse-prayer.

" 'To The Man God: O great One, I have been sorely tried by my enemies and have been blasphemed and lied against. My good thoughts and my honest actions have been turned to bad actions and dishonest ideas. My home has been disrespected, my children have been cursed and ill-treated. My dear ones have been backbitten and their virtue questioned. O Man God, I beg that this that I ask for my enemies shall come to pass:

" 'That the South wind shall scorch their bodies and make them wither and shall not be tempered to them. That the North wind shall freeze their blood and numb their muscles and that it shall not be tempered to them. That the West wind shall blow away their life's breath and will not leave their hair grow, and that their finger nails shall fall off and their bones shall crumble. That the East wind shall make their minds grow dark, their sight shall fail and their seed dry up so that they shall not multiply.

" 'I ask that their fathers and mothers from their furtherest generation will not intercede for them before the great throne, and the wombs of their women shall not bear fruit except for strangers, and that they shall become extinct. I pray that the children who may come shall be weak of mind and paralyzed of limb and that they themselves shall curse them in their turn for ever turning the breath of life into their bodies. I pray that disease and death shall be forever with them and that their worldly goods shall not prosper, and that their crops shall not multiply and that their cows, their sheep, and their hogs and all their living beasts shall die of starvation and thirst. I pray that their house shall be unroofed and that the rain, the thunder and lightning shall find the innermost recesses of their home and that the foundation shall crumble and the floods tear it asunder. I pray that the sun shall not shed its rays on them in benevolence, but instead it shall beat down on them and burn them and destroy them. I pray that the moon shall not give them peace, but instead shall deride them and decry them and cause their minds to shrivel. I pray that their friends shall betray them and cause them loss of power, of gold and of silver, and that their enemies shall smite them until they beg for mercy which shall not be given them. I pray that their tongues shall forget how to speak in sweet words, and that it shall be paralyzed and that all about them will be desolation, pestilence and death. O Man God, I ask you for all these things because they have dragged me in the dust and destroyed my good name; broken my heart and caused me to curse the day that I was born. So be it.' "

Turner again made that gesture with his hands that meant the end. Then he sat in a dazed silence. My own spirits had been falling all during the terrible curse and he did not have to tell me to be quiet this time. After a long period of waiting I rose to go. "The Spirit say you come back tomorrow," he breathed as I passed his knees. I nodded that I had heard and went out. The next day he began to prepare me for my initiation ceremony, for rest assured that no one may approach the Altar without the crown, and none may wear the crown of power without preparation. *It must be earned.*

And what is this crown of power? Nothing definite in material. Turner crowned me with a consecrated snake skin. I have been crowned in other places with flowers, with ornamental paper, with cloth, with sycamore bark, with egg-shells. It is the meaning, not the material that counts. The crown without the preparation means no more than a college diploma without the four years' work.

This preparation period is akin to that of all mystics. Clean living, even to clean thoughts. A sort of going to the wilderness in the spirit. The details do not matter. My nine days being up, and possessed of the three snake skins and the new underwear required, I entered Turner's house as an inmate to finish the last three days of my novitiate. Turner had become so sure of my fitness as a hoodoo doctor that he would accept no money from me except what was necessary to defray the actual cost of the ceremony.

So I ate my final meal before six o'clock of the evening before and went to bed for the last time with my right stocking on and my left leg bare.

I entered the old pink stucco house in the Vieux Carré at nine o'clock in the morning with the parcel of needed things. Turner placed the new underwear on the big Altar; prepared the couch with the snake skin cover upon which I was to lie for three days. With the help of other members of the college of hoodoo doctors called together to initiate me, the snake skins I had brought were made into garments for me to wear. One was coiled into a high headpiece—the crown. One had loops attached to slip on my arms so that it could be worn as a shawl, and the other was made into a girdle for my loins. All places have significance. These garments were placed on the small altar in the corner. The throne of the snake. The One* was called upon to enter the garments and dwell there.

*The Spirit.

I was made ready and at three o'clock in the afternoon, naked as I came into the world, I was stretched, face downwards, my navel to the snake skin cover, and began my three day search for the spirit that he might accept me or reject me according to his will. Three days my body must lie silent and fasting while my spirit went wherever spirits must go that seek answers never given to men as men.

I could have no food, but a pitcher of water was placed on a small table at the head of the couch, that my spirit might not waste time in search of water which should be spent in search of the Power-Giver. The spirit must have water, and if none had been provided it would wander in search of it. And evil spirits might attack it as it wandered about dangerous places. If it should be seriously injured, it might never return to me.

For sixty-nine hours I lay there. I had five psychic experiences and awoke at last with no feeling of hunger, only one of exaltation.

I opened my eyes because Turner called me. He stood before the Great Altar dressed ceremoniously. Five others were with him.

"Seeker, come," Turner called.

I made to rise and go to him. Another laid his hand upon me lightly, restraining me from rising.

"How must I come?" he asked in my behalf.

"You must come to the spirit across running water," Turner answered in a sort of chant.

So a tub was placed beside the bed. I was assisted to my feet and led to the tub. Two men poured water into the tub while I stepped into it and out again on the other side.

"She has crossed the dangerous stream in search of the spirit," the one who spoke for me, chanted.

"The spirit does not know her name. What is she called?"

"She has no name but what the spirit gives."

"I see her conquering and accomplishing with the lightning and making her road with thunder. She shall be called the Rain-Bringer."

I was stretched again upon the couch. Turner approached me with two brothers, one on either side of him. One held a small paint brush dipped in yellow, the other bore one dipped in red. With ceremony Turner painted the lightning symbol down my back from my right shoulder to my left hip. This was to be my sign forever. The Great One was to speak to me in storms.

I was now dressed in the new underwear and a white veil was placed over my head, covering my face, and I was seated in a chair.

After I was dressed, a pair of eyes was painted on my cheeks as a sign that I could see in more ways than one. The sun was painted on my forehead. Many came into the room and performed ceremonial acts, but none spoke to me. Nor could I speak to them while the veil covered my face. Turner cut the little finger of my right hand and caught the gushing blood in a wine cup. He added wine and mixed it with the blood. Then he and all the other five leaders let blood from themselves also and mixed it with wine in another glass. I was led to drink from the cup containing their mingled bloods, and each of them in turn beginning with Turner drank mine. At high noon I was seated at the splendid altar. It was dressed in the center with a huge communion candle with my name upon it set in sand, five large iced cakes in different colors, a plate of honeyed St. Joseph's bread, a plate of serpent-shaped breads, spinach and egg cakes fried in olive oil, breaded Chinese okra fried in olive oil, roast veal and wine, two huge yellow bouquets, two red bouquets and two white bouquets and thirty-six yellow tapers and a bottle of holy water.

Turner seated me and stood behind me with his ceremonial hat upon his head, and the crown of power in his hand. "Spirit! I ask you to take her. Do you hear me, Spirit? Will you take her? Spirit, I want you to take her, she is worthy!" He held the crown poised above my head for a full minute. A profound silence held the room. Then he lifted the veil from my face and let it fall behind my head and crowned me with power. He lit my candle for me. But from then on I might be a candle-lighter myself. All the candles were reverently lit. We all sat down and ate the feast. First a glass of blessed oil was handed me by Turner. "Drink this without tasting it." I gulped it down and he took the glass from my hand, took a sip of the little that remained. Then he handed it to the brother at his right who did the same, until it went around the table.

"Eat first the spinach cakes," Turner exhorted, and we did. Then the meal began. It was full of joy and laughter, even though we knew that the final ceremony waited only for the good hour of twelve midnight.

About ten o'clock we all piled into an old Studebaker sedan—all but Turner who led us on a truck. Out Road No. 61 we rattled until a certain spot was reached. The truck was unloaded beside the road and sent back to town. It was a little after eleven. The swamp was dismal and damp, but after some stumbly walking we came to a little glade deep in the wood, near the lake. A candle was burning at each of the four corners of the clearing, representing the four corners of the world and the four winds. I could hear the occasional slap-slap of the water. With a whispered chant some twigs were gathered and tied into a broom. Some pine straw was collected. The sheets of typing paper I had been urged to bring were brought out and nine sheets were blessed and my petition written nine times on each sheet by the light from a shaded lantern. The crate containing the black sheep was opened and the sheep led forward into the center of the circle. He stood there dazedly while the chant of strange syllables rose. I asked Turner the words, but he replied that in good time I would know what to say. It was not to be taught. If nothing came, to be silent. The head and withers of the sheep were stroked as the chanting went on. Turner became more and more voluble. At last he seized the straw and stuffed some into the sheep's nostrils. The animal struggled. A knife flashed and the sheep dropped to its knees, then fell prone with its mouth open in a weak cry. My petition was thrust into its throat that he might cry it to the Great One. The broom was seized and dipped in the blood from the slit throat and the ground swept vigorously—back and forth, back and forth—the length of the dying sheep. It was swept from the four winds toward the center. The sweeping went on as long as the blood gushed. Earth, the mother of the Great One and us all, has been appeased. With a sharp stick Turner traced the outline of the sheep and the digging commenced. The sheep was never touched. The ground was dug from under him so that his body dropped down into the hole. He was covered with nine sheets of paper bearing the petition and the earth heaped upon him. A white candle was set upon the grave and we straggled back to the road and the Studebaker.

I studied under Turner five months and learned all of the Leveau routines; but in this book all of the works of any doctor cannot be given. However, we performed several of Turner's own routines.

Once a woman, an excited, angry woman, wanted something done to keep her husband true. So she came and paid Turner gladly for his services.

Turner took a piece of string that had been "treated" at the altar and gave it to the woman.

"Measure the man where I tell you. But he must never know. Measure him in his sleep then fetch back the string to me."

The next day the woman came at ten o'clock instead of nine as Turner had told her, so he made her wait until twelve o'clock, that being a good hour. Twelve is one of the benign hours of the day while ten is a malignant hour. Then Turner took the string and tied nine knots in it and tied it to a larger piece of string which he tied about her waist. She was completely undressed for the ceremony and Turner cut some hair from under her left armpit and some from the right side of the groin and put it together. Then he cut some from the right armpit and a tuft from the left groin and it was all placed on the altar, and burned in a votive light with the wish for her husband to love her and forget all others. She went away quite happy. She was so satisfied with the work that she returned with a friend a few days later.

Turner, with his toothless mouth, his Berber-looking face, said to the new caller:

"I can see you got trouble." He shivered. "It is all in the room. I feel the pain of it; Anger, Malice. Tell me who is this man you so fight with?"

"My husband's brother. He hate me and make all the trouble he can," the woman said in a tone so even and dull that it was hard to believe she meant what she said. "He must leave this town or die. Yes, it is much better if he is dead." Then she burst out, "Yeah, he should be dead long time ago. Long before he spy upon me, before he tell lies, lies, lies. I should be very happy for his funeral."

"Oh I can feel the great hate around you," Turner said. "It follow you everywhere, but I kill nobody, I send him away if you want so he never come back. I put guards along the road in the spirit world, and these he cannot pass, no. When he go, never will he come back to New Orleans. You see him no more. He will be forgotten and all his works."

"Then I am satisfied, yes," the woman said. "When will you send him off?"

"I ask the spirit, you will know."

She paid him and he sent her off and Turner went to his snake altar and sat in silence for a long time. When he arose, he sent me out to buy nine black chickens, and some Four Thieves Vinegar. He himself went out and got nine small sticks upon which he had me write the troublesome brother-in-law's name—one time on each stick. At ten that night we went out into the small interior court so prevalent in New Orleans and drove nine stakes into the ground. The left leg of a chicken was tied to each stake. Then a fire was built with the nine sticks on which the name had been written. The ground was sprinkled all over with the Four Thieves Vinegar and Turner began his dance. From the fire to the circle of fluttering chickens and back again to the fire. The feathers were picked from the heads of the chickens in the frenzy of the dance and scattered to the four winds. He called the victim's name each time as he whirled three times with the chicken's head-feathers in his hand, then he flung them far.

The terrified chickens flopped and fluttered frantically in the dim firelight. I had been told to keep up the chant of the victim's name in rhythm and to beat the ground with a stick. This I did with fervor and Turner danced on. One by one the chickens were seized and killed by having their heads pulled off. But Turner was in such a condition with his whirling and dancing that he seemed in a hypnotic state. When the last fowl was dead, Turner drank a great draught of wine and sank before the altar. When he arose, we gathered some ashes from the fire and sprinkled the bodies of the dead chickens and I was told to get out the car. We drove out one of the main highways for a mile and threw one of the chickens away. Then another mile and another chicken until the nine dead chickens had been disposed of. The spirits of the dead chickens had been instructed never to let the trouble-maker pass inward to New Orleans again after he had passed them going out.

One day Turner told me that he had taught me all that he could and he was quite satisfied with me. He wanted me to stay and work with him as a partner. He said that soon I would be in possession of the entire business, for the spirit had spoken to him and told him that I was the last doctor that he would make; that one year and seventy-nine days from then he would die. He wanted me to stay with him to the end. It has been a great sorrow to me that I could not say yes.

CAROLINA MARIA DE JESUS
(1913–)

A Brazilian slum dweller who had no more than a second-grade education, Carolina Maria de Jesus single-handedly supported her three children and kept a journal of her difficult life. Through an accidental meeting in 1958, a reporter named Audalio Dantas discovered that Carolina had volumes of writing. His newspaper ran first a story about her, then excerpts from her diary. Published in book form in 1960, the diary became an immediate best seller in Brazil, allowing Carolina to escape the slums and buy herself a clean brick house in the suburbs.

For another account of urban life at its most desperate, compare the selection from Ning Lao T'ai-t'ai, *A Daughter of Han.* For another Brazilian diary, written by a middle-class girl in a diamond-mining town at the end of the nineteenth century and first published in 1942, see *The Diary of "Helena Morley,"* translated and edited by Elizabeth Bishop.

FROM *Beyond All Pity*

December 25   Xmas Day [1958]

João came in saying he had a stomach ache. I knew what it was for he had eaten a rotten melon. Today they threw a truckload of melons near the river.

I don't know why it is that these senseless businessmen come to throw their rotted products here near the favela,* for the children to see and eat.

In my opinion the merchants of São Paulo are playing with the people just like Caesar when he tortured the Christians. But the Caesars of today are worse than the Caesar of the past. The others were punished for their faith. And we, for our hunger!

In that era, those who didn't want to die had to stop loving Christ.

But we cannot stop loving eating.

*Shantytown, slum—ED.

December 26

That woman who lives on Paulino Guimarães Street, number 308, gave a doll to Vera. We were passing when she called Vera and told her to wait. Vera said to me:

"I think I'm going to get a doll."

I replied:

"And I think we are going to get bread."

I sensed her anxiety and curiosity to see what it was going to be. The woman came out of the house with the doll.

Vera said to me:

"Didn't I tell you! I was right!"

She ran to get the doll. She grabbed it and ran back to show me. She thanked the woman and told her that the other girls in the favela would be jealous. And that she would pray every day that the woman should be happy and that she was going to teach the doll how to pray. I'm going to take her to Mass so she can pray for the woman to go to Heaven and not to have any painful illnesses.

December 27

I tired of writing, and slept. I woke up with a voice calling Dona Maria. I remained quiet, because I am not Maria. The voice said:

"She said that she lives in number 9."

I got up, out of sorts, and went to answer. It was Senhor Dorio. A man that I got to know during the elections. I asked Senhor Dorio to come in. But I was ashamed. The chamber pot was full.

Senhor Dorio was shocked with the primitive way I live. He looked at everything surprisedly. But he must learn that a favela is the garbage dump of São Paulo, and that I am just a piece of garbage.

December 28

I lit a fire, put water on to boil, and started to wash the dishes and examine the walls. I found a dead rat. I'd been after him for days, and set a rat trap. But what killed him was a black cat. She belongs to Senhor Antonio Sapateiro.

The cat is a wise one. She doesn't have any deep loves and doesn't let anyone make a slave of her. And when she goes away she never comes back, proving that she has a mind of her own.

If I talk about a cat it is because I am happy that she has killed the rat that was ruining my books.

December 29

I went out with João and Vera and José Carlos. João took the radio to be fixed. When I was on Pedro Vicente Street, the watchman at the junk yard called me and said that I was to go and look for some bags of paper that were near the river.

I thanked him and went to find the sacks. They were bags of rice that had rotted in a warehouse and were thrown away. I was shocked seeing that wasted rice. I stared at the bugs that were there, and the cockroaches and rats that ran from one side to another.

I thought: Why is the white man so perverse? He has money, buys and stores rice away in the warehouse. He keeps playing with the people just like a cat with a rat.

December 30

When I went to wash the clothes I met some women who were discussing the courage of Maria, the "companion" of a *Baiano.* *

They had separated and she went to live with another *Baiano,* that was their neighbor.

A woman's tongue is a candlewick. Always burning.

December 31

I spent the afternoon writing. My boys were bouncing a ball near the shacks. The neighbors started to complain. When their kids play I don't say anything. I don't fight with the children because I don't have glass in the windows and a ball can't hurt a board wall.

José Carlos and João were throwing a ball. The ball fell in Victor's yard, and Victor's wife punched a hole in it. The boys started to curse her. She grabbed a revolver and ran after them.

If the revolver had fired!

I'm not going to sleep. I want to listen to the São Silvestre race.† I went to the house of a gypsy who lives here. It bothers me to see his children sleeping on the ground. I told him to come to my shack at night and I would give him two beds. If he came during the day the women would transmit the news, because everything here in the favela is news.

*A "Baiano" is a person from Bahia, a state on the Atlantic coast of Brazil—Ed.
†São Silvestre race: a traditional footrace through the downtown streets of São Paulo every New Year's Eve.

When the night came, he came. He said he wants to settle here and put his children in school. That he is a widower and likes me very much. And asked me if I want to live with or marry him.

He hugged me and kissed me. I stared into his mouth adorned with gold and silver. We exchanged presents. I gave him some candy and clothes for his children and he gave me pepper and perfume. Our discussion was on art and music.

He told me that if I married him he would take me out of the favela. I told him that I'd never get use to riding in a caravan. He told me that a traveler's life was poetic.

He told me that the love of a gypsy is as deep as the ocean and as hot as the sun.

That was all I needed. When I get old I'm going to become a gypsy. Between this gypsy and me there exists a spiritual attraction. He did not want to leave my shack. And if I could have I would not have let him leave.

I invited him to come over any time and listen to the radio. He asked me if I was alone. I told him that my life was as confusing as a jigsaw puzzle. He likes to read so I gave him some books.

I went to see the appearance of the shack. It was pleasanter after he set up the beds. João came looking for me, saying that I was lingering too long.

The favela is excited. The *favelados* are celebrating because it is the end of a year of life.

Today a *nortista* woman went to the hospital to have a baby and the child was born dead. She is taking transfusions. Her mother is crying because she is the only daughter.

There is a dance in Victor's shack.

January 1, 1959

I got out of bed at 4 A.M. and went to carry water, then went to wash clothes. I didn't make lunch. There is no rice. This afternoon I'm going to cook beans with macaroni. The boys didn't eat anything. I'm going to lie down because I'm sleepy. It was 9 o'clock. João woke me up to open the door. Today I'm sad.

January 4

In the old days I sang. Now I've stopped singing, because the happiness has given way to a sadness that ages the heart. Every day another poor creature shows up here in the favela. Ireno is a poor creature with anemia. He is looking for his wife. His wife doesn't want him. He told me that his mother-in-law provoked his wife against him. Now he is in his brother's house. He spent a few days in his sister's house, but came back. He said they were throwing hints at him because of the food.

Ireno says that he is unhappy with life. Because even with health life is bitter.

January 5

It's raining. I am almost crazy with the dripping on the beds, because the roof is covered with cardboard and the cardboard is rotten. The water is rising and invading the yards of the *favelados*.

January 6

I got out of bed at 4 A.M., turned on the radio, and went for water. What torture it is to walk in water in the morning. And I catch cold so easily! But life is like that. Men are leaving for work. They are carrying their shoes and socks in their hands. Mothers keep the children inside the house. They get restless because they want to go out and play in the water. People with a sense of humor say that the favela is a sailors' city. Others say it is the São Paulo Venice.

I was writing when the son of the gypsy came to tell me that his father was calling me. I went to see what he wanted. He started to complain about the difficulties of living here in São Paulo. He went out to get a job and didn't find one.

He said he was going back to Rio, because there it is easier to live. I told him that here he could earn more money.

"In Rio I earn more," he insisted. "There I bless children and get a lot of money."

I knew that when the gypsy was talking to somebody he could go on for hours and hours, until the person offered money. There is no advantage in being friendly with a gypsy.

I started out and he asked me to stay. I went out and went to the store. I bought rice, coffee, and soap. Then I went to the Bom Jardim Butcher Shop to buy meat. When I got there the clerk looked at me with an unhappy eye.

"Do you have lard?"

"No."

"Meat?"

"No."

A Japanese came in and asked:

"Do you have lard?"

She waited until I had gone out to tell him:

"Yes, we have."

I returned to the favela furious. Then the money of a *favelado* is worthless? I thought: today I'm going to write and am going to complain about that no-good clerk at the Bom Jardim Butcher Shop.

Common!

January 7

Today I fixed rice and beans and fried eggs. What happiness. Reading this you are going to think Brazil doesn't have anything to eat. We have. It's just that the prices are so impossible that we can't buy it. We have dried fish in the shops that wait for years and years for purchasers. The flies make the fish filthy. Then the fish rots and the clerks throw it in the garbage, and throw acid on it so the poor won't pick it up and eat it. My children have never eaten dried fish. They beg me.

"Buy it, Mother!"

But buy it—how? At 180 cruzeiros a kilo? I hope, if God helps me, that before I die I'll be able to buy some dried fish for them.

January 8

I met a driver who had come to dump sawdust here in the favela. He asked me to get into the truck. The blond driver then asked me if here in the favela it was easy to get a woman. And if he could come to my shack. He told me that he was still in form. His helper said he was on a pension.

I said good-by to the driver and went back to the favela. I lit a fire, washed my hands, and started to prepare food for the children.

January 10

Senhor Manuel came over. It was 8 o'clock. He asked me if I still talked to the gypsy. I told him that I did. And that the gypsy had some land in Osasco and that if they tore down the favela and I didn't have any place to go, I could go to his property. That he admired my spirit and if he could, would like to live at my side.

Senhor Manuel became angry and said he wasn't coming back any more. That I could stay with the gypsy.

What I admire in the gypsy is his calmness and understanding. Things that Senhor Manuel doesn't possess. Senhor Manuel told me he wouldn't show up any more. We'll see.

January 11

I am not happy with my spiritual state. I don't like my restless mind. I keep thinking about the gypsy, but I'm going to dominate these feelings. I know that when he sees me he gets happy. Me too. I have the feeling that I am one shoe and just now have found the other.

I've heard many things said about gypsies. But he doesn't have any of the bad qualities that they blab about. It seems that this gypsy wants a place in my heart.

In the beginning I distrusted his friendship. But now if it increases for me, it will be a pleasure. If it diminishes, I'll suffer. If I could only fasten myself to him!

He has two boys. One of them is always with me. If I go to wash clothes, he comes along, and sits at my side. The boys of the favela get jealous when they see me pampering the boy. Pleasing the boy, I get closer to the father.

The name of the gypsy is Raimundo. He was born in the capital of Bahia. He looks like Castro Alves.* His eyebrows meet.

January 12

I made supper and gave it to the children. Rosalina came over. She came looking for a few beans. I gave them.

Senhor Raimundo arrived. He came for his boys. He watched the children eating. I offered him some supper but he didn't want it. He picked out a sardine and asked me if I had any pepper. I don't put pepper in the food because of the children.

I thought: if I was alone I would give him a hug. What feelings I have seeing him at my side. I thought: if someday I was exiled and this man came along to accompany me, it would make the punishment easier.

I asked Rosalina to eat the sardines. I gave her the beans. Raimundo told me that he was going away to his house, and that if one day the favela was destroyed, for me to look for him there. He gave the same invitation to Rosalina. I didn't appreciate it. It wasn't egoism. It was jealousy. He left and I kept thinking. He never parks. He has gypsy

*Castro Alves: Brazilian nineteenth-century abolitionist poet.

blood. I thought: if someday this man was mine I would chain him to my side. I want to introduce him to another world.

January 14

I walked through the streets. I went to Dona Julita. I went to the Blue Cross to get money for the cans. I got home before the rain. Senhor Raimundo sent his son to call me. I changed myself and went to him. He told me he was going to Volta Redonda to work in the steel mill. I know I'm going to miss him. I hurried away saying that I needed to write and it was something that couldn't wait.

January 15

I got out of bed at 4 o'clock and went to carry water. I turned on the radio to hear the tango program.

Senhor Manuel said he was never going to come back. He walked through the water to get to my shack. He caught a cold.

Today I'm happy. I earned some money. I got 300! Today I'm going to buy meat. Nowadays when a poor man eats meat he keeps smiling stupidly.

January 16

I went to the post office to take out the notebooks that returned from the United States. I came back to the favela as sad as if they had cut off one of my arms. *The Readers' Digest* returned my novels. The worst slap for those who write is the return of their works.

To dispel the sadness that was making me blue, I went to talk with the gypsy. I picked up the notebooks and the ink bottle and went there. I told him that I had received the originals back in the mail and now wanted to burn the notebooks.

He started to tell me of his adventures. He said he was going to Volta Redonda, and would stay in the house of a fourteen-year-old girl who was with him. If the girl went out to play he was right after her, watching her carefully. I didn't like the way he was looking at the girl. I thought: what does he want with this youngster?

My sons came into the shack. He was lying on the floor. I asked him if he used a knife.

"No. I prefer a revolver, like this one."

He showed me a .32 revolver. I am not very friendly with revolvers. He gave the gun to João to hold and said:

"You are a man. And a man must learn to handle these things."

João told him he had better not say anything to anyone, that he didn't want the people in the favela to know he had a revolver.

"I showed it to your mother because she likes me. And when a woman likes a man she never denounces him. I bought this revolver when I was a soldier."

"You were a soldier?"

"In Bahia. But I left the corps because I was earning very little."

He showed me a photo taken in uniform. When I got up to go he said: "It's early!"

He ordered coffee to be made. The girl said there wasn't any sugar. I sent João to get some sugar and butter. He sent his son to buy six cruzeiros worth of bread. He said:

"I never eat without meat. I never eat bread without butter. Here in this shack I eat. This shack made me put on weight."

His boy returned with the bread. José Carlos came in and started to fight with the boy. He told them not to fight because they were all brothers.

"I'm not his brother. Oh, no!"

"You are brothers because of Adam and Eve!"

He grabbed José Carlos by the arms, forcing him to lie down beside him on the floor. José Carlos got loose and ran into the street.

I put my eyes to the notebook and started to write. When I raised my head his eyes were on the girl's face. I didn't like the strange look he had.

My mind began to unmask the sordidness of this gypsy. He used his beauty. He knows that women can be fooled with pretty faces. He attracts girls telling them he will marry them, then satisfies his desires and sends them away. Now I understand his eyeing that girl. This is a warning to me. I would never let Vera in the same house with him.

I looked at the gypsy's face. A beautiful face. But I got nauseated. It was the face of an angel with the soul of the devil. I went back to my shack.

JOYCE JOHNSON
(1935–)

Writer and editor Joyce Glassman Johnson grew up in a middle-class household in New York City which she found stifling. By fourteen she was escaping to Greenwich Village and continued to find a refuge there during her years at Barnard College. At twenty-one, on a blind date arranged by Allen Ginsberg, she met Jack Kerouac, and their affair placed her at the hot center of the Beat Generation. Her memoir *Minor Characters* won the National Book Critics' Circle Award for biography and autobiography in 1983. She has also written novels, including the semiautobiographical *In the Night Café* (1989), which portrays artists' lives in lower Manhattan in the 1960s.

This selection describes some of what followed Johnson's self-liberation, including an abortion and the affair with Kerouac. For other accounts by famous-writer consorts, compare Sophia Tolstoy, *Diary*, Caitlin Thomas, *Leftover Life to Kill*, Simone de Beauvoir, *The Prime of Life*, and, parodically, Gertrude Stein, *The Autobiography of Alice B. Toklas*. For another account of New York life by a Jewish intellectual, compare Vivian Gornick, *Fierce Attachments*. For another Beat Generation memoir, inspired by *Minor Characters*, by the woman who married the poet Le Roi Jones, now Imamu Amiri Baraka, see *How I Became Hettie Jones*.

FROM *Minor Characters*

I moved out of 116th Street on Independence Day, 1955—a date I'd chosen not for its symbolism but because it was the first day of a long weekend. I'd taken a tiny maid's room in an apartment on Amsterdam Avenue five blocks away, to which I planned to move all my things, going back and forth with my mother's shopping cart.

I got up early that morning and started putting books into shopping bags. When I thought my parents would be awake, I walked into their room. They were dozing in their twin beds, an oscillating fan whirring between them. I said, "I have something to tell you. I'm moving out today." I felt sick to my stomach, as if I had murdered these two mild people. I could see their blood on the beige summer covers.

Two weeks earlier I'd found the room. With the first paychecks from my new job, I'd bought an unpainted rocking chair, a small desk, two sheets, and a poster of Picasso's *Blue Boy*—the furnishings of my first freedom. I knew children did not own furniture.

All this had been accomplished in secret, like the arrangements for a coup d'état. I wouldn't speak until it was time to leave. There was nothing to discuss. I was terribly afraid of being talked out of it.

"I need to borrow the cart," I said to my mother, "for my clothes and books."

"Don't think—" she said. "Don't think you can just come around here for dinner any time you want."

All day long I dragged the cart back and forth over the hot red brick sidewalks of the Columbia campus. No one shouted. No one stood at the door on 116th Street and tried to bar my way. In the stillness of their house, my parents moved slowly around the rooms as if injured.

I was done by evening. On my way out for the last time, I wrote my address on a piece of paper and left it on the kitchen table. From my new apartment, I called Elise and Sheila, who were sharing a place in Yorkville. "I really did it, I guess," I said.

Everyone knew in the 1950s why a girl from a nice family left home. The meaning of her theft of herself from her parents was clear to all—as well as what she'd be up to in that room of her own.

On 116th Street the superintendent knew it. He'd seen my comings and goings with the cart. He spread the word among the neighbors that the Glassmans' daughter was "bad." His imagination rendered me pregnant. He wrote my parents a note to that effect. My mother called and, weeping over the phone, asked me if this was true.

The crime of sex was like guilt by association—not visible to the eye of the outsider, but an act that could be rather easily conjectured. Consequences would make it manifest.

I, too, knew why I'd left—better than anyone. It was to be with Alex. He was the concrete embodiment of my more abstract desire to be "free." By which I meant—if I'd been pressed to admit it—sexually free. The desire for this kind of freedom subsumed every other. For this I was prepared to make my way in the world at the age of nineteen, incurring all the risks of waifdom on fifty dollars a week. In fact, fifty dollars seemed a lot to me, since I'd never had more than ten dollars in my pocket all at once. I opened a charge account at Lord and Taylor.

I didn't think I'd actually be living in my new room for very long. It was just until Alex and I got married. All I had to do was prove to him how different I was going to be, now I was no longer under my parents' roof. I would demonstrate how independent I was, how little I really expected from him. In my strange scheme of things, independence seemed the chief prerequisite for marriage. But it was for Alex's sake, not mine, that I was going to be independent.

In the room of my own, on the nights I was there—which became more and more frequent—I'd lie on my bed with my eyes wide open, waiting until it was time to go to sleep. I wouldn't feel homesick so much as uninhabited, like a coat Alex had taken off and hung up on a hook.

In the morning I'd inhabit myself again, getting up to go to the office, plunging into the subway rush hour. Emerging into daylight at Fiftieth Street, I'd feel I'd been swept into an enormous secretarial army advancing inexorably upon Madison Avenue. There was comfort in this, a way of leaving the girl on the bed behind me. As part of this army, I typed, read manuscripts, answered the phone, ate egg-salad sandwiches in the downstairs luncheonette (I'd learned very quickly to locate the cheapest item on a menu).

My boss, Naomi Burton, who'd hired me despite my lack of a B.A., took an interest in me. I was talented, she told me. I could become a literary agent myself if I worked for her for a few more years. She persuaded me to show her a story I'd written at Barnard and published in the college literary magazine. "You're a writer," she said. "You should try your hand at a novel." She rang up a friend of hers, an editor named Hiram Haydn who ran a famous novel workshop at the New School for Social Research, and asked him to let me into the course.

It was thrilling but terrifying—as if I were really in danger of fulfilling the destiny my mother had wanted for me, which I had gone to such lengths to avoid. It seemed to be happening to a person outside the person I really was. I'd hidden from my mother's eyes the story Naomi Burton was sending Hiram Haydn—a story I'd written over and over again in various forms ever since my high-school days—about a thirteen-year-old girl whose mother confides in her one day her bitter disappointment with her marriage.

Some time that year *Bonjour Tristesse* was published, causing a great furor in the United States. It was about a young French girl's loss of innocence in an affair with an older man married to a woman who had been very kind to her. The author, Françoise Sagan, was only a year older than I was. Her prose was like an elegant shrug of Gallic detachment and sophisticated regret. Sagan's schoolgirl face, knowing and slightly melancholy beneath her *gamin* haircut, appeared in every magazine and newspaper for a while. Her right thumb hovered just at the corner of her mouth, an indecisive gesture half infantile, half provocative. She seemed, however, to have taken possession of her fame with great aplomb, living it up the way young male writers were supposed to. She had a predilection for very fast driving in expensive sports cars; she dashed from literary parties to weekends at chateaux, alighting occasionally at cafés to be photographed with her thumb in its memorable position. Anyhow, that was my envious vision of her. She was a girl F. Scott Fitzgerald could have invented to torment poor Dick Diver. Americans forgave her amorality because she was French.

Sagan came to America for a few weeks, and Alex read every interview with her he could find. There was something in her speed, her coolness, that seemed to him totally new. He kept saying he wished there was some way he could meet her. Fortunately this wasn't likely. I loved Alex so much myself I was positive Sagan would find him irresistible.

Around April, Alex fell in love with a girl named Bobbie Weintraub, who wasn't anything like Sagan. He took her away from his roommate Anton, a graduate student in physics who'd moved in to share expenses and whom Bobbie visited on trumped-up overnight passes from the Barnard dorms. She was small and earnest and neat as a pin and planned to be a social worker; she'd always tidy up the living room on 112th Street much better than I could. She seemed either struck with wonder by everything Alex said or greatly shocked and offended by it, which he also enjoyed. One night she came over when Anton was at the library, and she and Alex went to bed. For weeks Anton threatened suicide.

I couldn't seem to get past my violent anguish. Each morning it would tear through me when I woke up remembering that Alex now wanted Bobbie Weintraub and not me. I knew that since I could never love anyone else, I was going to be alone for the rest of my life. "I want you as a friend," Alex insisted, but he'd only speak to me on the phone, always sounding curt and hurried and making it plain that if he met me anywhere, he'd have to bring Bobbie along as well.

"Try therapy," he'd urge me. "Promise me you'll try therapy."

In June I didn't get my period. First it was a little late, and then a lot, but I still thought it would come anyway, and I waited, thinking I felt it sometimes. But finally it didn't come. A tangible, unbelievable fact, like sealed doom.

I was going to have a baby. But it was impossible for me to have a baby.

The father wasn't Alex. The father was a child of my own age—a wrecked boy I'd known from Columbia who already had a drinking problem and lived, doing nothing, with his parents in Connecticut. I didn't love this boy. Sometimes you went to bed with people almost by mistake, at the end of late, shapeless nights when you'd stayed up so long it almost didn't matter—the thing was, not to go home. Such nights lacked premeditation, so you couldn't be very careful, you counted on a

stranger's carefulness. The boy promised to pull out before the danger—
but he didn't. And although I could have reminded him of his promise in
time, I didn't do that either, remembering too late it was the middle of
the month in a bedroom on East Ninety-sixth Street that smelled of
smoke and soiled clothing, with leftover voices from that night's party
outside the closed door.

I'd gotten a therapist by then—a $7.50 man, a rejected boyfriend of
the woman whose apartment I was living in. I told him my problem. "I
see," he said, rubbing his large chin, staring out over Central Park West.

There was a box of Kleenex on the small Danish-modern table near
my head. He had pointedly placed boxes of tissues in several locations in
his office. But I never cried.

I explained to this therapist why I didn't see how I could become a
mother. Aside from being twenty years old, I lived on fifty dollars a week
and had cut myself off from my family. I said I would rather die. And
then I asked him what Elise had told me to: "Could you get me a
therapeutic abortion?" (I'd never heard the term before she explained
what it meant.)

"Oh, I wouldn't even try," he said.

I hadn't thought he wouldn't try.

Life was considered sacred. But independence could be punishable by
death. The punishment for sex was, appropriately, sexual.

There were women in those days who kept slips of paper, like talismans to ward off disaster, on which were written the names of doctors
who would perform illegal abortions. Neither Elise nor I knew any of
these women. You had to ask around. You asked friends and they asked
friends, and the ripples of asking people widened until some person
whose face you might never see gave over the secret information that
could save you. This could take time, and you only had two months, they
said, and you'd lost one month anyway, through not being sure.

The therapist called my roommate, got from her the name of the boy
who had made me pregnant. He called the boy and threatened to dis-
close the whole matter to his parents unless the boy came up with the
money for an illegal abortion. The boy called me, drunk and wild with
fear. I hadn't expected anything of this boy except one thing—that
when I had an abortion he'd go there with me; there had to be someone
with you, I felt, that you knew. But as for blaming this boy—I didn't. I
knew I had somehow let this happen to me. There had been a moment
in that bedroom on Ninety-sixth Street, a moment of blank suspension,
of not caring whether I lived or died. It seemed important to continue to
see this moment very clearly. I knew the boy wouldn't come with me
now.

I went to see the therapist one last time to tell him he had done
something terribly wrong.

"Yes," he admitted, looking sheepish. "I've probably made a mistake."

I said, "I'm never coming back. I owe you thirty-seven fifty. Try and
get it."

Someone finally came up with a person who knew a certain doctor in
Canarsie. If you called this person at the advertising agency where he
worked, he wouldn't give you the doctor's name—he'd ask you if you
wanted to have a drink with him in the Rainbow Room, and over martinis he might agree to escort you out to see the doctor. This person
wasn't a great humanitarian; he was a young man who had a weird
hobby—taking girls to get abortions. He'd ask you if you wanted to
recuperate afterward at his house on Fire Island. You were advised to
say no.

Blind dates were a popular social form of the fifties. As I sat in the
cocktail lounge of the Rainbow Room, staring through the glass doors at
crew-cutted young men in seersucker suits who came off the elevator
lacking the red bow tie I'd been told to watch out for, I realized that
despite the moment in the bedroom, I probably didn't want to die, since
I seemed to be going to an enormous amount of effort to remain living.
If it happened that I died after all, it would be an accident.

He turned up a half-hour late in his blue and white stripes. "Why,
you're pretty," he said, pleased. He told me he liked blondes. He made a
phone call after we had our drinks, and came back to the table to say the
doctor would see us that night. "I hope you don't have anything lined
up," he said.

He offered me sticks of Wrigley spearmint chewing gum on the BMT
to Canarsie. People in jokes sometimes came from there, but I'd never
been to that part of Brooklyn in my life.

Canarsie was rows of small brick houses with cement stoops and yards
filled with wash and plaster saints. Boys were playing stickball in the
dusk. You could disappear into Canarsie.

The doctor seemed angry that we had come, but he led us into his
house after we rang the bell, and switched on a light in his waiting room.
He was fat, with a lot of wiry grey hair on his forearms; a white shirt wet
and rumpled with perspiration stretched over his belly. The room looked
like a room in which only the very poor would ever wait. There were
diplomas on the walls, framed behind dusty glass; I tried to read the
Latin. He glared at me and said he wanted me to know he did tonsillectomies. To do "the other"—he didn't say *abortions*—disgusted him. I
made efforts to nod politely.

My escort spoke up and said, "How about next week?"

"All right. Wednesday."

I felt panic at the thought of Wednesday. What if my mother called the office and found out I was sick, and came running over to the apartment? "No," I said, "Friday. It has to be Friday."

"Friday will cost you extra," the doctor said.

That night I called Alex and asked if he'd please go with me on the day of the abortion.

"Only if you and I and Bobbie can have a drink."

I'd managed to borrow the five hundred dollars from a friend in her late twenties, who'd borrowed it from a wealthy married man who was her lover. With the cash in a sealed envelope in my purse, I stood for an hour that Friday morning in front of a cigar store on Fourteenth Street, waiting for the young advertising executive. I got awfully scared that he wouldn't come. Could I find the doctor's house myself in those rows of nearly identical houses?

There was a haze over Fourteenth Street that made even the heat seem grey. I stared across the street at Klein's Department Store, where my mother had taken me shopping for bargains, and imagined myself dying a few hours later with the sign KLEIN's the last thing that flashed through my consciousness.

But finally the young man did materialize out of a cab. "Sorry to have kept you waiting." He'd brought some back issues of *The New Yorker*, and planned to catch up on his reading during the operation.

Upstairs in Canarsie, the doctor who did tonsillectomies had a room where he only did abortions. A freshly painted room where every surface was covered with white towels. He himself put on a mask and a white surgeon's gown. It was as if all that white was the color of his fear.

"Leave on the shoes!" he barked as I climbed up on his table almost fully clothed. Was I expected to make a run for it if the police rang his doorbell in the middle of the operation? He yelled at me to do this and do that, and it sent him into a rage that my legs were shaking, so how could he do what he had to do? But if I didn't want him to do it, that was all right with him. I said I wanted him to do it. I was crying. But he wouldn't take the money until after he'd given me the local anesthetic. He gave me one minute to change my mind before he handed me my purse.

The whole thing took two hours, but it seemed much longer through the pain. I had the impression that this doctor in all his fear was being extremely careful, that I was even lucky to have found him. He gave me pills when it was over, and told me I could call him only if anything went wrong. "But don't ever let me catch you back here again, young lady!"

I staggered down the cement steps of his house with my life. It was noon in Canarsie, an ordinary day in July. My escort was saying he thought it would be hard to find a cab, we should walk in the direction of the subway. On a street full of shops, I leaned against the window of a supermarket until he flagged one down. Color seemed to have come back into the world. Housewives passed in floral nylon dresses; diamonds of sunlight glinted off the windshields of cars.

On the cab ride across the Manhattan Bridge, the young man from the ad agency placed his hand on my shoulder. "I have this house out on Fire Island," he began. "I thought that this weekend—"

"No thanks," I said. "I'll be okay in the city."

He removed his hand, and asked if I'd drop him off at his office— "unless you mind going home alone."

I said I'd get there by myself.

.   .   .

As of 1982, there is the Jack Kerouac Society for Disembodied Poetics, founded in Boulder, Colorado, in 1976. There is *Jack's Book*, as well as *Desolation Angel: Jack Kerouac, the Beat Generation and America* and *Kerouac: A Biography* and—the one I like best—*Kerouac: A Chicken Essay*, by a French-Canadian surrealist poet; as well as proliferating pamphlets, theses, articles, chapters in books. A journal published annually celebrates the Beats and the "Unspeakable Visions of the Individual." It's hagiography in the making. Jack, now delivered into the Void, would be amazed to know there's even a literary fan magazine devoted entirely to him, called *Moody Street Irregulars* (after the street in Lowell where he lived as a child). For a back issue, a graduate student somewhere put together a rather randomly chosen chronology of Jack Kerouac's life. In a column labeled *1957*, there's a cryptic entry: *Meets Joyce Glassman.*

"Hello. I'm Jack. Allen tells me you're very nice. Would you like to come down to Howard Johnson's on Eighth Street? I'll be sitting at the counter. I have black hair and I'll be wearing a red and black checked shirt."

I'm standing in Elise's kitchen, holding the phone Allen has just handed me. It's a Saturday night shortly after New Year's.

"Sure," I say.

I put on a lot of eye shadow and my coat and take the subway down to

Astor Place and begin walking westward, cross-town, passing under the bridge between the two buildings of Wanamaker's Department Store and the eye of the giant illuminated clock. It's a dark, bitter January night with ice all over the pavements, so you have to be careful, but I'm flying along, it's an adventure as opposed to a misadventure—under which category so far I've had to put most of the risky occurrences in my life.

The windows of Howard Johnson's are running with steam so you can't see in. I push open the heavy glass door, and there is, sure enough, a black-haired man at the counter in a flannel lumberjack shirt slightly the worse for wear. He looks up and stares at me hard with blue eyes, amazingly blue. And the skin of his face is so brown. He's the only person in Howard Johnson's in color. I feel a little scared as I walk up to him. "Jack?" I say.

There's an empty stool next to his. I sit down on it and he asks me whether I want anything. "Just coffee." He's awfully quiet. We both lack conversation, but then we don't know each other, so what can we say? He asks after Allen, Lafcadio, that kind of thing. I'd like to tell him I've read his book, if that wouldn't sound gauche, obvious and uncool.

When the coffee arrives, Jack looks glum. He can't pay for it. He has no money, none at all. That morning he'd handed his last ten dollars to a cashier in a grocery store and received change for a five. He's waiting for a check from a publisher, he says angrily.

I say, "Look, that's all right. I have money. Do you want me to buy you something to eat?"

"Yeah," he says. "Frankfurters. I'll pay you back. I always pay people back, you know."

I've never bought a man dinner before. It makes me feel very competent and womanly.

He has frankfurters, home fries, and baked beans with Heinz ketchup on them. I keep stealing looks at him because he's beautiful. You're not supposed to say a man is beautiful, but he is. He catches me at it and grins, then mugs it up, putting on one goofy face after another, a whole succession of old-time ridiculous movie-comedian faces flashes before me until I'm laughing too at the absurdity of this blind date Allen has arranged. (The notion of Allen Ginsberg arranging blind dates will crack people up years later when they ask me how on earth I met Kerouac.)

As for what he saw in me that night, I'm not sure at all. A very young woman in a red coat, round-faced and blonde. "An interesting young person," he wrote in *Desolation Angels*. "A Jewess, elegant middleclass sad and looking for something—she looked Polish as hell . . ." Where am I in all those funny categories?

As our paths converge in Howard Johnson's, we're looking for different things. At thirty-four, Jack's worn down, the energy that had moved him to so many different places gone. He's suddenly waited too long. The check for *The Subterraneans* will never arrive; *On the Road* will never be published. Why not let Allen rescue him? He can't go back to the two Virginias.

I see the blue, bruised eye of Kerouac and construe his melancholy as the look of a man needing love because I'm, among other things, twenty-one years old. I believe in the curative powers of love as the English believe in tea or Catholics believe in the Miracle of Lourdes.

He tells me he's spent sixty-three days on a mountaintop without anyone. He made pea soup and wrote in his journal and sang Sinatra songs to keep himself company.

Some warning to me in all this. "You really liked being alone like that?" I ask.

"I wish I was there now. I should've stayed up there."

He could somehow cancel you out and make you feel sad for him at the same time. But I'm sure any mountaintop would be preferable to where he's staying—the Marlton Hotel on Eighth Street, with the dirty shades over the windows and the winos lounging on the steps.

"And where do you live?" Jack asks. He likes it that it's up near Columbia and the West End Bar where he used to hang out. Was Johnny the bartender still there? Johnny the bartender would remember him from the days he was a football hero at Columbia but he broke his leg in his sophomore year and stayed in his room reading Céline and Shakespeare and never went back to football again—thus losing his scholarship at Columbia, but he's always had affection for the neighborhood. "Why don't you let me stay at your place?" he says.

"If you wish," I say in *Desolation Angels,* deciding fast. And I know how I said it, too. As if it was of no great moment, as if I had no wishes of my own—in keeping with my current philosophy of nothing-to-lose, try anything.

We stood up and put on our coats, we went down into the subway. And there on the IRT, on a signboard I'd never seen before that night, was an ad for an airline with a brand-new slogan: FLY NOW, PAY LATER.

"That's a good title for a novel," I said, and finally told Jack I was writing one, I wasn't just a secretary. He said *Pay Me the Penny After* would be a better title. "You should call your novel that." He asked me who my favorite writer was. I said Henry James, and he made a face, and said he figured I had all the wrong models, but maybe I could be a great writer anyway. He asked me if I rewrote a lot, and said you should never revise, never change anything, not even a word. He regretted all the rewriting he'd done on *The Town and the City.* No one could make him do that again, which was why he always got nowhere with publishers. He was going to look at my work and show me that what you wrote first was always best. I said okay, feeling guilty for all that I'd rewritten, but I still loved Henry James.

All through this literary conversation, Jack stood swaying above me on the subway, hanging on to the strap. Just before we got off, he leaned down. Our foreheads scraped, our eyeballs loomed up on each other—a funny game where I knew you weren't supposed to blink, no matter what.

That was the start of *Meets Joyce Glassman.*

The apartment I lived in at the time was dark and cavernous, on the first floor of a brownstone halfway down the block from the Yorkshire Hotel. Two furnished rooms—the furnishings being the uselessly massive, weak-jointed kind found in the lobbies of antediluvian apartment buildings. A small refrigerator and a two-burner stove stood behind a screen in one corner of the living room, but you had to wash your dishes in the bathroom sink. The windows looked out on a rank back yard where a large tree of heaven battened on bedsprings and broken bottles. I always felt very small in that apartment. One night outside the house a huge grey tomcat with a chewed ear had rubbed against my legs. I'd hauled him inside under the impression I was rescuing him, but he spent his days on the windowsill longing for the street, trying to pry the window open with his paw, or he lurked in the closet vengefully spraying shoes. Jack was the only person I'd brought home so far who saw the beauty of this animal, whom I'd unimaginatively named Smoke. He said he was going to call it Ti Gris, after a cat he once had in Lowell. He seemed to like to rename things. On the walk from the subway I'd become Joycey, which no one had called me since I was little, and he'd put his arm around me, leaning on me playfully and letting his hand dangle down over my breast—that was how men walked with their women in Mexico, he said. "Someday when you go there, you'll see that for yourself."

When we got in the door, he didn't ask to see my manuscript. He pulled me against him and kissed me before I even turned on the light. I kissed him back, and he acted surprised. He said I was even quieter than he was, he had no idea quiet girls liked kissing so much, and he undid the buttons of my coat and put both his hands up my back under my sweater. "The trouble is," Jack said with his voice against my ear, "I don't . . . like . . . blondes."

I remember laughing and saying, "Well, in that case I'll just dye my hair"—wondering all the same if it was true.

In the morning Jack left to get his stuff out of the Marlton. He returned with a sleeping bag and a knapsack in which there were jeans and a few old shirts like the one he was already wearing and some notebooks he'd bought in Mexico City. That was all he owned. Not even a typewriter—he'd been borrowing other people's typewriters, he said. I'd never seen such foreign-looking notebooks, long and narrow with shiny black covers and thin, bluish paper on which Jack's slanted penciled printing sped across page after page, interrupted here and there by little sketches. One notebook was just for dreams. He wrote in it every morning.

There was something heartbreakingly attractive in these few essentials to which Jack had reduced his needs. He reminded me of a sailor— not that I knew any sailors—something too about the way he looked coming out of the shower, gleaming and vigorous and ruddy with a white towel around his neck.

Very quickly it didn't seem strange to have him with me, we were somehow like very old friends—"buddies," Jack said, squeezing me affectionately, making me feel both proud and a little disappointed. Crazy as it was, I sometimes really wished I was dark—like this Virginia I felt jealous of for making him so wild. Or the girl named Esmeralda who lived in Mexico City and whom he'd loved tragically for a long time and written an entire novel about in one of his notebooks, calling her Tristessa. But he'd slept with her only once. She was a whore and a saint, so beautiful and lost—one of his mysterious *fellaheen* women, primeval and of the earth.

I was unprimeval and distinctly of the city. I was everydayness, bacon and eggs in the morning or the middle of the night, which I learned to cook just the way he liked—sunny-side up in the black iron frying pan. I'd buy slab bacon in the grocery store, like he'd always had in Lowell— not the skinny kind in packages—and add canned applesauce (a refinement I'd learned from Bickford's Cafeteria), which Jack had never thought of as anything that might enhance eggs. He took extraordinary pleasure in small things like that.

As a lover he wasn't fierce but oddly brotherly and somewhat reticent. I'd listen in amazement to his stories of Berkeley parties where everyone was naked and men and women engaged in some exotic Japanese practice called *yabyum* (but Jack, fully clothed, had sat apart brooding over his bottle of port, something he didn't tell me). In my memories of Jack in the good times we had together, I'm lying with my head on his chest, his heart pulsing against my ear. His smooth hard powerful arms are around me and I'm burying my face into them because I like them so much, making him laugh, "What are you doing there, Joycey?" And there's always music on the radio. Symphony Sid, whom he taught me to find on the dial, who always comes on at the stroke of midnight, bringing you the sounds of Charlie Parker, Lester Young, Miles Davis, and Stan Getz, and who, according to Jack, is a subterranean himself—you can hear it in his gravel voice smoked down to a rasp by innumerable weird cigarettes. "And now—after a few words about that fan-tastic Mo-gen David wine—the great Lady Day . . ." In the darkness of the room we drift together as Billie Holiday bewails lost loves . . .

But then Jack leaves me. He goes into the small back bedroom where I never sleep because there's no radiator there. He pulls the window all the way up, closes the door, and lies down on the floor in his sleeping bag alone. This is the cure for the cough he brought with him from Mexico City. In the morning he'll do headstands with his feet against the wall, to reverse the flow of blood in his body. He tells me a frightening thing about himself. He's known for eight years that a blood clot could finish him off at any minute.

How can you bear living, I wonder, knowing death could be so close? Little by little I'm letting go of what I learned on the abortionist's table in the white upstairs room in Canarsie.

I'm good for him, Jack tells me. I don't mind anything he does. I don't mind about the sleeping bag, do I?

I didn't really mind, that was the strange part. Everything seemed so odd, so charmed, so transformed. At night when the cold air came with a rush into the little room where Jack was sleeping, and seeped under the edges of the closed door, I could imagine myself in a place without walls, an immense campground where, lying wrapped in blankets, I could feel in my own warmth absolute proof of my existence.

HELEN KELLER
(1880–1967)

Helen Keller was six and had been deaf, blind, and severely speech-impaired since an illness at the age of nineteen months when Anne Sullivan, a recent graduate of Boston's Perkins Institution for the Blind, came to her family's home in Alabama to try to teach her. The story of Keller's initial tormented resistance and triumphal breakthrough to an understanding of language has moved and inspired generations of readers. Everything that she learned was finger-spelled into her hand by her teacher, and in this cumbersome way she acquired French, German, and Latin and was graduated from Radcliffe College. The physical production of texts was hard for her. She typed but had to have what she had written finger-spelled back to her. Perhaps for that reason she evolved an especially elegant prose style. For all her adult life she wrote and lectured on behalf of the deaf and the blind and advised many political figures on issues involving the handicapped. Her autobiography, *The Story of My Life* (1903), was originally published in magazine form while Keller was still an undergraduate. *The Story of My Life* was followed in 1929 by another autobiographical volume, *Midstream: My Later Life.*

For another account of a discovery of language, compare Eva Hoffman, *Lost in Translation.* For another memoir by an early graduate of Radcliffe, compare Gertrude Stein, *The Autobiography of Alice B. Toklas.* Narratives about illness or handicap form an enormous subgenre within the literature of women's lives, along with narratives about a child's handicap or a husband's illness. For a favorite of mine in the latter group, see Molly Haskell, *Love and Other Infectious Diseases.*

FROM *The Story of My Life*

The most important day I remember in all my life is the one on which my teacher, Anne Mansfield Sullivan, came to me. I am filled with wonder when I consider the immeasurable contrasts between the two lives which it connects. It was the third of March, 1887, three months before I was seven years old.

On the afternoon of that eventful day, I stood on the porch, dumb, expectant. I guessed vaguely from my mother's signs and from the hurrying to and fro in the house that something unusual was about to happen, so I went to the door and waited on the steps. The afternoon sun penetrated the mass of honeysuckle that covered the porch, and fell on my upturned face. My fingers lingered almost unconsciously on the familiar leaves and blossoms which had just come forth to greet the sweet southern spring. I did not know what the future held of marvel or surprise for me. Anger and bitterness had preyed upon me continually for weeks and a deep languor had succeeded this passionate struggle.

Have you ever been at sea in a dense fog, when it seemed as if a tangible white darkness shut you in, and the great ship, tense and anxious, groped her way toward the shore with plummet and sounding-line, and you waited with beating heart for something to happen? I was like that ship before my education began, only I was without compass or sounding-line, and had no way of knowing how near the harbour was. "Light! give me light!" was the wordless cry of my soul, and the light of love shone on me in that very hour.

I felt approaching footsteps. I stretched out my hand as I supposed to my mother. Some one took it, and I was caught up and held close in the arms of her who had come to reveal all things to me, and, more than all things else, to love me.

The morning after my teacher came she led me into her room and gave me a doll. The little blind children at the Perkins Institution had sent it and Laura Bridgman* had dressed it; but I did not know this until afterward. When I had played with it a little while, Miss Sullivan slowly spelled into my hand the word "d-o-l-l." I was at once interested in this finger play and tried to imitate it. When I finally succeeded in making the letters correctly I was flushed with childish pleasure and pride. Running downstairs to my mother I held up my hand and made the letters for doll. I did not know that I was spelling a word or even that words existed; I was simply making my fingers go in monkeylike imitation. In the days that followed I learned to spell in this uncomprehending way a great many words, among them *pin, hat, cup* and a few verbs like *sit, stand* and *walk*. But my teacher had been with me several weeks before I understood that everything has a name.

One day, while I was playing with my new doll, Miss Sullivan put my big rag doll into my lap also, spelled, "d-o-l-l" and tried to make me understand that "d-o-l-l" applied to both. Earlier in the day we had had a

---

*Laura Bridgman was a deaf and blind woman who had managed to get an education. Dickens wrote about her case in *American Notes,* and she was an inspiration to Helen Keller's family—Ed.

tussle over the words "m-u-g" and "w-a-t-e-r." Miss Sullivan had tried to impress upon me that "m-u-g" is *mug* and that "w-a-t-e-r" is *water,* but I persisted in confounding the two. In despair she had dropped the subject for the time, only to renew it at the first opportunity. I became impatient at her repeated attempts and, seizing the new doll, I dashed it upon the floor. I was keenly delighted when I felt the fragments of the broken doll at my feet. Neither sorrow nor regret followed my passionate outburst. I had not loved the doll. In the still, dark world in which I lived there was no strong sentiment or tenderness. I felt my teacher sweep the fragments to one side of the hearth and I had a sense of satisfaction that the cause of my discomfort was removed. She brought me my hat, and I knew I was going out into the warm sunshine. This thought, if a wordless sensation may be called a thought, made me hop and skip with pleasure.

We walked down the path to the well-house, attracted by the fragrance of the honeysuckle with which it was covered. Some one was drawing water and my teacher placed my hand under the spout. As the cool stream gushed over one hand she spelled into the other the word *water,* first slowly, then rapidly. I stood still, my whole attention fixed upon the motions of her fingers. Suddenly I felt a misty consciousness as of something forgotten—a thrill of returning thought; and somehow the mystery of language was revealed to me. I knew then that "w-a-t-e-r" meant the wonderful cool something that was flowing over my hand. That living word awakened my soul, gave it light, hope, joy, set it free! There were barriers still, it is true, but barriers that could in time be swept away.

I left the well-house eager to learn. Everything had a name, and each name gave birth to a new thought. As we returned to the house every object which I touched seemed to quiver with life. That was because I saw everything with the strange, new sight that had come to me. On entering the door I remembered the doll I had broken. I felt my way to the hearth and picked up the pieces. I tried vainly to put them together. Then my eyes filled with tears; for I realized what I had done, and for the first time I felt repentance and sorrow.

I learned a great many new words that day. I do not remember what they all were; but I do know that *mother, father, sister, teacher* were among them—words that were to make the world blossom for me, "like Aaron's rod, with flowers." It would have been difficult to find a happier child than I was as I lay in my crib at the close of that eventful day and lived over the joys it had brought me, and for the first time longed for a new day to come.

·   ·   ·

I had now the key to all language, and I was eager to learn to use it. Children who hear acquire language without any particular effort; the words that fall from others' lips they catch on the wing, as it were, delightedly, while the little deaf child must trap them by a slow and often painful process. But whatever the process, the result is wonderful. Gradually from naming an object we advance step by step until we have traversed the vast distance between our first stammered syllable and the sweep of thought in a line of Shakespeare.

At first, when my teacher told me about a new thing I asked very few questions. My ideas were vague, and my vocabulary was inadequate; but as my knowledge of things grew, and I learned more and more words, my field of inquiry broadened, and I would return again and again to the same subject, eager for further information. Sometimes a new word revived an image that some earlier experience had engraved on my brain.

I remember the morning that I first asked the meaning of the word, "love." This was before I knew many words. I had found a few early violets in the garden and brought them to my teacher. She tried to kiss me; but at that time I did not like to have any one kiss me except my mother. Miss Sullivan put her arm gently round me and spelled into my hand, "I love Helen."

"What is love?" I asked.

She drew me closer to her and said, "It is here," pointing to my heart, whose beats I was conscious of for the first time. Her words puzzled me very much because I did not then understand anything unless I touched it.

I smelt the violets in her hand and asked, half in words, half in signs, a question which meant, "Is love the sweetness of flowers?"

"No," said my teacher.

Again I thought. The warm sun was shining on us.

"Is this not love?" I asked, pointing in the direction from which the heat came. "Is this not love?"

It seemed to me that there could be nothing more beautiful than the sun, whose warmth makes all things grow. But Miss Sullivan shook her head, and I was greatly puzzled and disappointed. I thought it strange that my teacher could not show me love.

A day or two afterward I was stringing beads of different sizes in symmetrical groups—two large beads, three small ones, and so on. I had made many mistakes, and Miss Sullivan had pointed them out again and again with gentle patience. Finally I noticed a very obvious error in the sequence and for an instant I concentrated my attention on the lesson and tried to think how I should have arranged the beads. Miss Sullivan touched my forehead and spelled with decided emphasis, "Think."

In a flash I knew that the word was the name of the process that was going on in my head. This was my first conscious perception of an abstract idea.

For a long time I was still—I was not thinking of the beads in my lap, but trying to find a meaning for "love" in the light of this new idea. The sun had been under a cloud all day, and there had been brief showers; but suddenly the sun broke forth in all its southern splendour.

Again I asked my teacher, "Is this not love?"

"Love is something like the clouds that were in the sky before the sun came out," she replied. Then in simpler words than these, which at that time I could not have understood, she explained: "You cannot touch the clouds, you know; but you feel the rain and know how glad the flowers and the thirsty earth are to have it after a hot day. You cannot touch love either; but you feel the sweetness that it pours into everything. Without love you would not be happy or want to play."

The beautiful truth burst upon my mind—I felt that there were invisible lines stretched between my spirit and the spirits of others.

From the beginning of my education Miss Sullivan made it a practice to speak to me as she would speak to any hearing child; the only difference was that she spelled the sentences into my hand instead of speaking them. If I did not know the words and idioms necessary to express my thoughts she supplied them, even suggesting conversation when I was unable to keep up my end of the dialogue.

This process was continued for several years; for the deaf child does not learn in a month, or even in two or three years, the numberless idioms and expressions used in the simplest daily intercourse. The little hearing child learns these from constant repetition and imitation. The conversation he hears in his home stimulates his mind and suggests topics and calls forth the spontaneous expression of his own thoughts. This natural exchange of ideas is denied to the deaf child. My teacher, realizing this, determined to supply the kinds of stimulus I lacked. This she did by repeating to me as far as possible, verbatim, what she heard, and by showing me how I could take part in the conversation. But it was a long time before I ventured to take the initiative, and still longer before I could find something appropriate to say at the right time.

The deaf and the blind find it very difficult to acquire the amenities of conversation. How much more this difficulty must be augmented in the case of those who are both deaf and blind! They cannot distinguish the tone of the voice or, without assistance, go up and down the gamut of tones that give significance to words; nor can they watch the expression of the speaker's face, and a look is often the very soul of what one says.

．　　．　　．

It was in the spring of 1890 that I learned to speak. The impulse to utter audible sounds had always been strong within me. I used to make noises, keeping one hand on my throat while the other hand felt the movements of my lips. I was pleased with anything that made a noise and liked to feel the cat purr and the dog bark. I also liked to keep my hand on a singer's throat, or on a piano when it was being played. Before I lost my sight and hearing, I was fast learning to talk, but after my illness it was found that I had ceased to speak because I could not hear. I used to sit in my mother's lap all day long and keep my hands on her face because it amused me to feel the motions of her lips; and I moved my lips, too, although I had forgotten what talking was. My friends say that I laughed and cried naturally, and for awhile I made many sounds and word-elements, not because they were a means of communication, but because the need of exercising my vocal organs was imperative. There was, however, one word the meaning of which I still remembered, *water*. I pronounced it, "wa-wa." Even this became less and less intelligible until the time when Miss Sullivan began to teach me. I stopped using it only after I had learned to spell the word on my fingers.

I had known for a long time that the people about me used a method of communication different from mine; and even before I knew that a deaf child could be taught to speak, I was conscious of dissatisfaction with the means of communication I already possessed. One who is entirely dependent upon the manual alphabet has always a sense of restraint, of narrowness. This feeling began to agitate me with a vexing, forward-reaching sense of a lack that should be filled. My thoughts would often rise and beat up like birds against the wind; and I persisted in using my lips and voice. Friends tried to discourage this tendency, fearing lest it would lead to disappointment. But I persisted, and an accident soon occurred which resulted in the breaking down of this great barrier—I heard the story of Ragnhild Kaata.

In 1890 Mrs. Lamson, who had been one of Laura Bridgman's teachers, and who had just returned from a visit to Norway and Sweden, came to see me, and told me of Ragnhild Kaata, a deaf and blind girl in Norway who had actually been taught to speak. Mrs. Lamson had scarcely finished telling me about this girl's success before I was on fire with eagerness. I resolved that I, too, would learn to speak. I would not rest satisfied until my teacher took me, for advice and assistance, to Miss Sarah Fuller, principal of the Horace Mann School. This lovely, sweet-natured lady offered to teach me herself, and we began the twenty-sixth of March, 1890.

Miss Fuller's method was this: she passed my hand lightly over her face, and let me feel the position of her tongue and lips when she made a sound. I was eager to imitate every motion and in an hour had learned six elements of speech: M, P, A, S, T, I. Miss Fuller gave me eleven lessons in all. I shall never forget the surprise and delight I felt when I uttered my first connected sentence, "It is warm." True, they were broken and stammering syllables; but they were human speech. My soul, conscious of new strength, came out of bondage, and was reaching through those broken symbols of speech to all knowledge and all faith.

No deaf child who has earnestly tried to speak the words which he has never heard—to come out of the prison of silence, where no tone of love, no song of bird, no strain of music ever pierces the stillness—can forget the thrill of surprise, the joy of discovery which came over him when he uttered his first word. Only such a one can appreciate the eagerness with which I talked to my toys, to stones, trees, birds and dumb animals, or the delight I felt when at my call Mildred ran to me or my dogs obeyed my commands. It is an unspeakable boon to me to be able to speak in winged words that need no interpretation. As I talked, happy thoughts fluttered up out of my words that might perhaps have struggled in vain to escape my fingers.

But it must not be supposed that I could really talk in this short time. I had learned only the elements of speech. Miss Fuller and Miss Sullivan could understand me, but most people would not have understood one word in a hundred. Nor is it true that, after I had learned these elements, I did the rest of the work myself. But for Miss Sullivan's genius, untiring perseverance and devotion, I could not have progressed as far as I have toward natural speech. In the first place, I laboured night and day before I could be understood even by my most intimate friends; in the second place, I needed Miss Sullivan's assistance constantly in my efforts to articulate each sound clearly and to combine all sounds in a thousand ways. Even now she calls my attention every day to mispronounced words.

All teachers of the deaf know what this means, and only they can at all appreciate the peculiar difficulties with which I had to contend. I had to use the sense of touch in catching the vibrations of the throat, the movements of the mouth and the expression of the face; and often this sense was at fault. In such cases I was forced to repeat the words or sentences, sometimes for hours, until I felt the proper ring in my own voice. My work was practice, practice, practice. Discouragement and weariness cast me down frequently; but the next moment the thought that I should soon be at home and show my loved ones what I had accomplished, spurred me on, and I eagerly looked forward to their pleasure in my achievement.

"My little sister will understand me now," was a thought stronger than all obstacles. I used to repeat ecstatically, "I am not dumb now." I could not be despondent while I anticipated the delight of talking to my mother and reading her responses from her lips. It astonished me to find how much easier it is to talk than to spell with the fingers, and I discarded the manual alphabet as a medium of communication on my part; but Miss Sullivan and a few friends still use it in speaking to me, for it is more convenient and more rapid than lip-reading.

Just here, perhaps, I had better explain our use of the manual alphabet, which seems to puzzle people who do not know us. One who reads or talks to me spells with his hand, using the single-hand manual alphabet generally employed by the deaf. I place my hand on the hand of the speaker so lightly as not to impede its movements. The position of the hand is as easy to feel as it is to see. I do not feel each letter any more than you see each letter separately when you read. Constant practice makes the fingers very flexible, and some of my friends spell rapidly— about as fast as an expert writes on a typewriter. The mere spelling is, of course, no more a conscious act than it is in writing.

When I had made speech my own, I could not wait to go home. At last the happiest of happy moments arrived. I had made my homeward journey, talking constantly to Miss Sullivan, not for the sake of talking, but determined to improve to the last minute. Almost before I knew it, the train stopped at the Tuscumbia station, and there on the platform stood the whole family. My eyes fill with tears now as I think how my mother pressed me close to her, speechless and trembling with delight, taking in every syllable that I spoke, while little Mildred seized my free hand and kissed it and danced, and my father expressed his pride and affection in a big silence. It was as if Isaiah's prophecy had been fulfilled in me. "The mountains and the hills shall break forth before you into singing, and all the trees of the field shall clap their hands!"

MAXINE HONG KINGSTON
(1941–)

Maxine Hong Kingston was born in the United States, the eldest of six children of Chinese immigrant parents. She was educated at the University of California, Berkeley and there met Earll Kingston, who became her husband. They lived for seventeen years in Honolulu, where she taught English and creative writing at a private school. *The Woman Warrior: Memoirs of a Girlhood among Ghosts* was her first book (1976), followed by *China Men* (1980) and *Tripmaster Monkey* (1988).

For other versions of American girlhoods, compare Annie Dillard, *An American Childhood*, Maya Angelou, *I Know Why the Caged Bird Sings*, Eleanor Munro, *Memoir of a Modernist's Daughter*, and Audre Lorde, *Zami*. For an earlier practitioner of the Chinese talk-story, compare Ning Lao T'ai-t'ai, *A Daughter of Han*. For another woman warrior, compare Le Ly Hayslip, *When Heaven and Earth Changed Places*.

from *The Woman Warrior*

A SONG FOR A BARBARIAN REED PIPE

We were working at the laundry when a delivery boy came from the Rexall drugstore around the corner. He had a pale blue box of pills, but nobody was sick. Reading the label we saw that it belonged to another Chinese family, Crazy Mary's family. "Not ours," said my father. He pointed out the name to the Delivery Ghost, who took the pills back. My mother muttered for an hour, and then her anger boiled over. "That ghost! That dead ghost! How dare he come to the wrong house?" She could not concentrate on her marking and pressing. "A mistake! Huh!" I was getting angry myself. She fumed. She made her press crash and hiss. "Revenge. We've got to avenge this wrong on our future, on our health, and on our lives. Nobody's going to sicken my children and get away with it." We brothers and sisters did not look at one another. She would do something awful, something embarrassing. She'd already been hinting that during the next eclipse we slam pot lids together to scare the frog from swallowing the moon. (The word for "eclipse" is *frog-swallow-ing-the-moon.*) When we had not banged lids at the last eclipse and the shadow kept receding anyway, she'd said, "The villagers must be bang-ing and clanging very loudly back home in China."

("On the other side of the world, they aren't having an eclipse, Mama. That's just a shadow the earth makes when it comes between the moon and the sun."

"You're always believing what those Ghost Teachers tell you. Look at the size of the jaws!")

"Aha!" she yelled. "You! The biggest." She was pointing at me. "You go to the drugstore."

"What do you want me to buy, Mother?" I said.

"Buy nothing. Don't bring one cent. Go and make them stop the curse."

"I don't want to go. I don't know how to do that. There are no such things as curses. They'll think I'm crazy."

"If you don't go, I'm holding you responsible for bringing a plague on this family."

"What am I supposed to do when I get there?" I said, sullen, trapped. "Do I say, 'Your delivery boy made a wrong delivery'?"

"They know he made a wrong delivery. I want you to make them rectify their crime."

I felt sick already. She'd make me swing stinky censers around the counter, at the druggist, at the customers. Throw dog blood on the druggist. I couldn't stand her plans.

"You get reparation candy," she said. "You say, 'You have tainted my house with sick medicine and must remove the curse with sweetness.' He'll understand."

"He didn't do it on purpose. And no, he won't, Mother. They don't understand stuff like that. I won't be able to say it right. He'll call us beggars."

"You just translate." She searched me to make sure I wasn't hiding any money. I was sneaky and bad enough to buy the candy and come back pretending it was a free gift.

"Mymotherseztagimmesomecandy," I said to the druggist. Be cute and small. No one hurts the cute and small.

"What? Speak up. Speak English," he said, big in his white druggist coat.

"Tatatagimme somecandy."

The druggist leaned way over the counter and frowned. "Some free candy," I said. "Sample candy."

"We don't give sample candy, young lady," he said.

"My mother said you have to give us candy. She said that is the way the Chinese do it."

"What?"

"That is the way the Chinese do it."

"Do what?"

"Do things." I felt the weight and immensity of things impossible to explain to the druggist.

"Can I give you some money?" he asked.

"No, we want candy."

He reached into a jar and gave me a handful of lollipops. He gave us candy all year round, year after year, every time we went into the drugstore. When different druggists or clerks waited on us, they also gave us candy. They had talked us over. They gave us Halloween candy in December, Christmas candy around Valentine's day, candy hearts at Easter, and Easter eggs at Halloween. "See?" said our mother. "They understand. You kids just aren't very brave." But I knew they did not understand. They thought we were beggars without a home who lived in back of the laundry. They felt sorry for us. I did not eat their candy. I did not go inside the drugstore or walk past it unless my parents forced me to. Whenever we had a prescription filled, the druggist put candy in the medicine bag. This is what Chinese druggists normally do, except they give raisins. My mother thought she taught the Druggist Ghosts a lesson in good manners (which is the same word as "traditions").

.   .   .

We have so many secrets to hold in. Our sixth grade teacher, who liked to explain things to children, let us read our files. My record shows that I flunked kindergarten and in first grade had no IQ—a zero IQ. I did remember the first grade teacher calling out during a test, while students marked X's on a girl or a boy or a dog, which I covered with black. First grade was when I discovered eye control; with my seeing I could shrink the teacher down to a height of one inch, gesticulating and mouthing on the horizon. I lost this power in sixth grade for lack of practice, the teacher a generous man. "Look at your family's old addresses and think about how you've moved," he said. I looked at my parents' aliases and their birthdays, which variants I knew. But when I saw Father's occupations I exclaimed, "Hey, he wasn't a farmer, he was a . . ." He had been a gambler. My throat cut off the word—silence in front of the most understanding teacher. There were secrets never to be said in front of the ghosts, immigration secrets whose telling could get us sent back to China.

Sometimes I hated the ghosts for not letting us talk; sometimes I hated the secrecy of the Chinese. "Don't tell," said my parents, though we couldn't tell if we wanted to because we didn't know. Are there really secret trials with our own judges and penalties? Are there really flags in Chinatown signaling what stowaways have arrived in San Francisco Bay, their names, and which ships they came on? "Mother, I heard some kids say there are flags like that. Are there? What colors are they? Which buildings do they fly from?"

"No. No, there aren't any flags like that. They're just talking-story. You're always believing talk-story."

"I won't tell anybody, Mother. I promise. Which buildings are the flags on? Who flies them? The benevolent associations?"

"I don't know. Maybe the San Francisco villagers do that; our villagers don't do that."

"What do our villagers do?"

They would not tell us children because we had been born among ghosts, were taught by ghosts, and were ourselves ghost-like. They called us a kind of ghost. Ghosts are noisy and full of air; they talk during meals. They talk about anything.

"Do we send up signal kites? That would be a good idea, huh? We could fly them from the school balcony." Instead of cheaply stringing dragonflies by the tail, we could fly expensive kites, the sky splendid in Chinese colors, distracting ghost eyes while the new people sneak in. Don't tell. "Never tell."

Occasionally the rumor went about that the United States immigration authorities had set up headquarters in the San Francisco or Sacramento Chinatown to urge wetbacks and stowaways, anybody here on fake papers, to come to the city and get their files straightened out. The immigrants discussed whether or not to turn themselves in. "We might as well," somebody would say. "Then we'd have our citizenship for real."

"Don't be a fool," somebody else would say. "It's a trap. You go in there saying you want to straighten out your papers, they'll deport you."

"No, they won't. They're promising that nobody is going to go to jail or get deported. They'll give you citizenship as a reward for turning yourself in, for your honesty."

"Don't you believe it. So-and-so trusted them, and he was deported. They deported his children too."

"Where can they send us now? Hong Kong? Taiwan? I've never been to Hong Kong or Taiwan. The Big Six? Where?" We don't belong anywhere since the Revolution. The old China has disappeared while we've been away.

"Don't tell," advised my parents. "Don't go to San Francisco until they leave."

Lie to Americans. Tell them you were born during the San Francisco earthquake. Tell them your birth certificate and your parents were burned up in the fire. Don't report crimes; tell them we have no crimes and no poverty. Give a new name every time you get arrested; the ghosts won't recognize you. Pay the new immigrants twenty-five cents an hour and say we have no unemployment. And, of course, tell them we're against Communism. Ghosts have no memory anyway and poor eyesight. And the Han people won't be pinned down.

Even the good things are unspeakable, so how could I ask about deformities? From the configurations of food my mother set out, we kids had to infer the holidays. She did not whip us up with holiday anticipation or explain. You only remembered that perhaps a year ago you had eaten monk's food, or that there was meat, and it was a meat holiday; or you had eaten moon cakes or long noodles for long life (which is a pun). In front of the whole chicken with its slit throat toward the ceiling, she'd lay out just so many pairs of chopsticks alternating with wine cups, which were not for us because there were a different number from the number in our family, and they were set too close together for us to sit at. To sit at one of those place settings a being would have to be about two inches wide, a tall wisp of an invisibility. Mother would pour Seagram's 7 into the cups and, after a while, pour it back into the bottle. Never explaining. How can Chinese keep any traditions at all? They don't even make you pay attention, slipping in a ceremony and clearing the table before the children notice specialness. The adults get mad, evasive, and shut you up if you ask. You get no warning that you shouldn't wear a white ribbon in your hair until they hit you and give you the sideways glare for the rest of the day. They hit you if you wave brooms around or drop chopsticks or drum them. They hit you if you wash your hair on certain days, or tap somebody with a ruler, or step over a brother whether it's during your menses or not. You figure out what you got hit for and don't do it again if you figured correctly. But I think that if you don't figure it out, it's all right. Then you can grow up bothered by "neither ghosts nor deities." "Gods you avoid won't hurt you." I don't see how they kept up a continuous culture for five thousand years. Maybe they didn't; maybe everyone makes it up as they go along. If we had to depend on being told, we'd have no religion, no babies, no menstruation (sex, of course, unspeakable), no death.

.   .   .

I thought every house had to have its crazy woman or crazy girl, every village its idiot. Who would be It at our house? Probably me. My sister did not start talking among nonfamily until a year after I started, but she was neat while I was messy, my hair tangled and dusty. My dirty hands broke things. Also I had had the mysterious illness.* And there were adventurous people inside my head to whom I talked. With them I was frivolous and violent, orphaned. I was white and had red hair, and I rode a white horse. Once when I realized how often I went away to see these free movies, I asked my sister, just checking to see if hearing voices in motors and seeing cowboy movies on blank walls was normal, I asked, "Uh," trying to be casual, "do you talk to people that aren't real inside your mind?"

"Do I *what?*" she said.

"Never mind," I said fast. "Never mind. Nothing."

My sister, my almost-twin, the person most like me in all the world, had said, *"What?"*

I had vampire nightmares; every night the fangs grew longer, and my angel wings turned pointed and black. I hunted humans down in the long woods and shadowed them with my blackness. Tears dripped from my eyes, but blood dripped from my fangs, blood of the people I was supposed to love.

I did not want to be our crazy one. Quite often the big loud women came shouting into the house, "Now when you sell this one, I'd like to buy her to be my maid." Then they laughed. They always said that about my sister, not me because I dropped dishes at them. I picked my nose while I was cooking and serving. My clothes were wrinkled even though we owned a laundry. Indeed I was getting stranger every day. I affected a limp. And, of course, the mysterious disease I had had might have been dormant and contagious.

But if I made myself unsellable here, my parents need only wait until China, and there, where anything happens, they would be able to unload us, even me—sellable, marriageable. So while the adults wept over the letters about the neighbors gone berserk turning Communist ("They do funny dances; they sing weird songs, just syllables. They make us dance; they make us sing"), I was secretly glad. As long as the aunts kept disappearing and the uncles dying after unspeakable tortures, my parents would prolong their Gold Mountain stay. We could start spending our fare money on a car and chairs, a stereo. Nobody wrote to tell us that Mao himself had been matched to an older girl when he was a child and that he was freeing women from prisons, where they had been put for refusing the businessmen their parents had picked as husbands. Nobody told us that the Revolution (the Liberation) was against girl slavery and

*At the start of junior high school, Kingston has told us, she spent eighteen months in bed because of a mysterious illness. She is never more explicit about it—Ed.

girl infanticide (a village-wide party if it's a boy). Girls would no longer have to kill themselves rather than get married. May the Communists light up the house on a girl's birthday.

I watched our parents buy a sofa, then a rug, curtains, chairs to replace the orange and apple crates one by one, now to be used for storage. Good. At the beginning of the second Communist five-year plan, our parents bought a car. But you could see the relatives and the villagers getting more worried about what to do with the girls. We had three girl second cousins, no boys; their great-grandfather and our grandfather were brothers. The great-grandfather was the old man who lived with them, as the river-pirate great-uncle was the old man who lived with us. When my sisters and I ate at their house, there we would be—six girls eating. The old man opened his eyes wide at us and turned in a circle, surrounded. His neck tendons stretched out. "Maggots!" he shouted. "Maggots! Where are my grandsons? I want grandsons! Give me grandsons! Maggots!" He pointed at each one of us, "Maggot! Maggot! Maggot! Maggot! Maggot! Maggot!" Then he dived into his food, eating fast and getting seconds. "Eat, maggots," he said. "Look at the maggots chew."

"He does that at every meal," the girls told us in English.

"Yeah," we said. "Our old man hates us too. What assholes."

Third Grand-Uncle finally did get a boy, though, his only great-grandson. The boy's parents and the old man bought him toys, bought him everything—new diapers, new plastic pants—not homemade diapers, not bread bags. They gave him a full-month party inviting all the emigrant villagers; they deliberately hadn't given the girls parties, so that no one would notice another girl. Their brother got toy trucks that were big enough to climb inside. When he grew older, he got a bicycle and let the girls play with his old tricycle and wagon. My mother bought his sisters a typewriter. "They can be clerk-typists," their father kept saying, but he would not buy them a typewriter.

"What an asshole," I said, muttering the way my father muttered "Dog vomit!" when the customers nagged him about missing socks.

Maybe my mother was afraid that I'd say things like that out loud and so had cut my tongue.* Now again plans were urgently afoot to fix me up, to improve my voice. The wealthiest villager wife came to the laundry one day to have a listen. "You better do something with this one," she told my mother. "She has an ugly voice. She quacks like a pressed duck." Then she looked at me unnecessarily hard; Chinese do not have

---

*Kingston has told us that her mother snipped her frenum when she was a baby, to loosen her tongue and help her master languages. In our selection from *Zami*, Audre Lorde reports having undergone the same procedure.—ED.

to address children directly. "You have what we call a pressed-duck voice," she said. This woman was the giver of American names, a powerful namer, though it was American names; my parents gave the Chinese names. And she was right: if you squeezed the duck hung up to dry in the east window, the sound that was my voice would come out of it. She was a woman of such power that all we immigrants and descendants of immigrants were obliged to her family forever for bringing us here and for finding us jobs, and she had named my voice.

"No," I quacked. "No, I don't."

"Don't talk back," my mother scolded. Maybe this lady was powerful enough to send us back.

I went to the front of the laundry and worked so hard that I impolitely did not take notice of her leaving.

"Improve that voice," she had instructed my mother, "or else you'll never marry her off. Even the fool half ghosts won't have her." So I discovered the next plan to get rid of us: marry us off here without waiting until China. The villagers' peasant minds converged on marriage. Late at night when we walked home from the laundry, they should have been sleeping behind locked doors, not overflowing into the streets in front of the benevolent associations, all alit. We stood on tiptoes and on one another's shoulders, and through the door we saw spotlights open on tall singers afire with sequins. An opera from San Francisco! An opera from Hong Kong! Usually I did not understand the words in opera, whether because of our obscure dialect or theirs I didn't know, but I heard one line sung out into the night air in a woman's voice high and clear as ice. She was standing on a chair, and she sang, "Beat me, then, beat me." The crowd laughed until the tears rolled down their cheeks while the cymbals clashed—the dragon's copper laugh—and the drums banged like firecrackers. "She is playing the part of a new daughter-in-law," my mother explained. "Beat me, then, beat me," she sang again and again. It must have been a refrain; each time she sang it, the audience broke up laughing. Men laughed; women laughed. They were having a great time.

"Chinese smeared bad daughters-in-law with honey and tied them naked on top of ant nests," my father said. "A husband may kill a wife who disobeys him. Confucius said that." Confucius, the rational man.

The singer, I thought, sounded like me talking, yet everyone said, "Oh, beautiful. Beautiful," when she sang high.

Walking home, the noisy women shook their old heads and sang a folk song that made them laugh uproariously:

> Marry a rooster, follow a rooster.
> Marry a dog, follow a dog.

> Married to a cudgel, married to a pestle,
> Be faithful to it. Follow it.

I learned that young men were placing ads in the *Gold Mountain News* to find wives when my mother and father started answering them. Suddenly a series of new workers showed up at the laundry; they each worked for a week before they disappeared. They ate with us. They talked Chinese with my parents. They did not talk to us. We were to call them "Elder Brother," although they were not related to us. They were all funny-looking FOB's, Fresh-off-the-Boat's, as the Chinese-American kids at school called the young immigrants. FOB's wear high-riding gray slacks and white shirts with the sleeves rolled up. Their eyes do not focus correctly—shifty-eyed—and they hold their mouths slack, not tight-jawed masculine. They shave off their sideburns. The girls said *they'd* never date an FOB. My mother took one home from the laundry, and I saw him looking over our photographs. "This one," he said, picking up my sister's picture.

"No. No," said my mother. "This one," my picture. "The oldest first," she said. Good. I was an obstacle. I would protect my sister and myself at the same time. As my parents and the FOB sat talking at the kitchen table, I dropped two dishes. I found my walking stick and limped across the floor. I twisted my mouth and caught my hand in the knots of my hair. I spilled soup on the FOB when I handed him his bowl. "She can sew, though," I heard my mother say, "and sweep." I raised dust swirls sweeping around and under the FOB's chair—very bad luck because spirits live inside the broom. I put on my shoes with the open flaps and flapped about like a Wino Ghost. From then on, I wore those shoes to parties, whenever the mothers gathered to talk about marriages. The FOB and my parents paid me no attention, half ghosts half invisible, but when he left, my mother yelled at me about the dried-duck voice, the bad temper, the laziness, the clumsiness, the stupidity that comes from reading too much. The young men stopped visiting; not one came back. "Couldn't you just stop rubbing your nose?" she scolded. "All the village ladies are talking about your nose. They're afraid to eat our pastries because you might have kneaded the dough." But I couldn't stop at will anymore, and a crease developed across the bridge. My parents would not give up, though. "Though you can't see it," my mother said, "a red string around your ankle ties you to the person you'll marry. He's already been born, and he's on the other end of the string."

At Chinese school* there was a mentally retarded boy who followed

---

*From five to seven-thirty every day, after her regular school day, Kingston attended Chinese School—ED.

me around, probably believing that we were two of a kind. He had an enormous face, and he growled. He laughed from so far within his thick body that his face got confused about what the sounds coming up into his mouth might be, laughs or cries. He barked unhappily. He didn't go to classes but hung around the playgrounds. We suspected he was not a boy but an adult. He wore baggy khaki trousers like a man's. He carried bags of toys for giving to certain children. Whatever you wanted, he'd get it for you—brand-new toys, as many as you could think up in your poverty, all the toys you never had when you were younger. We wrote lists, discussed our lists, compared them. Those kids not in his favor gave lists to those who were. "Where do you get the toys?" I asked. "I . . . own . . . stores," he roared, one word at a time, thick tongued. At recess the day after ordering, we got handed out to us coloring books, paint sets, model kits. But sometimes he chased us—his fat arms out to the side; his fat fingers opening and closing; his legs stiff like Frankenstein's monster, like the mummy dragging its foot; growling; laughing-crying. Then we'd have to run, following the old rule, running away from our house.

But suddenly he knew where we worked. He found us; maybe he had followed us in his wanderings. He started sitting at our laundry. Many of the storekeepers invited sitting in their stores, but we did not have sitting because the laundry was hot and because it was outside Chinatown. He sweated; he panted, the stubble rising and falling on his fat neck and chin. He sat on two large cartons that he brought with him and stacked one on top of the other. He said hello to my mother and father, and then, balancing his heavy head, he lowered himself carefully onto his cartons and sat. My parents allowed this. They did not chase him out or comment about how strange he was. I stopped placing orders for toys. I didn't limp anymore; my parents would only figure that this zombie and I were a match.

I studied hard, got straight A's, but nobody seemed to see that I was smart and had nothing in common with this monster, this birth defect. At school there were dating and dances, but not for good Chinese girls. "You ought to develop yourself socially as well as mentally," the American teachers, who took me aside, said.

I told nobody about the monster. And nobody else was talking either; no mention about the laundry workers who appeared and disappeared; no mention about the sitter. Maybe I was making it all up, and queer marriage notions did not occur to other people. I had better not say a word, then. Don't give them ideas. Keep quiet.

I pressed clothes—baskets of giants' BVD's, long underwear even in summertime, T-shirts, sweat shirts. Laundry work is men's clothes, unmarried-men's clothes. My back felt sick because it was toward the monster who gave away toys. His lumpishness was sending out germs that would lower my IQ. His leechiness was drawing IQ points out of the back of my head. I maneuvered my work shifts so that my brothers would work the afternoons, when he usually came lumbering into the laundry, but he caught on and began coming during the evening, the cool shift. Then I would switch back to the afternoon or to the early mornings on weekends and in summer, dodging him. I kept my sister with me, protecting her without telling her why. If she hadn't noticed, then I mustn't scare her. "Let's clean house this morning," I'd say. Our other sister was a baby, and the brothers were not in danger. But the were-person would stalk down our street; his thick face smiled between the lettering on the laundry window, and when he saw me working, he shouldered inside. At night I thought I heard his feet dragging around the house, scraping gravel. I sat up to listen to our watchdog prowl the yard, pulling her long chain after her, and that worried me too. I had to do something about that chain, the weight of it scraping her neck fur short. And if she was walking about, why wasn't she barking? Maybe somebody was out there taming her with raw meat. I could not ask for help.

Every day the hulk took one drink from the watercooler and went once to the bathroom, stumbling between the presses into the back of the laundry, big shoes clumping. Then my parents would talk about what could be inside his boxes. Were they filled with toys? With money? When the toilet flushed, they stopped talking about it. But one day he either stayed in the bathroom for a long time or went for a walk and left the boxes unguarded. "Let's open them up," said my mother, and she did. I looked over her shoulder. The two cartons were stuffed with pornography—naked magazines, nudie postcards and photographs.

You would think she'd have thrown him out right then, but my mother said, "My goodness, he's not too stupid to want to find out about women." I heard the old women talk about how he was stupid but very rich.

Maybe because I was the one with the tongue cut loose, I had grown inside me a list of over two hundred things that I had to tell my mother so that she would know the true things about me and to stop the pain in my throat. When I first started counting, I had had only thirty-six items: how I had prayed for a white horse of my own—white, the bad, mournful color—and prayer bringing me to the attention of the god of the black-and-white nuns who gave us "holy cards" in the park. How I wanted the horse to start the movies in my mind coming true. How I had picked on a girl and made her cry. How I had stolen from the cash register and bought candy for everybody I knew, not just brothers and sisters, but strangers too and ghost children. How it was me who pulled up the onions in the garden out of anger. How I had jumped head-first off the dresser, not accidentally, but so I could fly. Then there were my fights at Chinese school. And the nuns who kept stopping us in the park, which was across the street from Chinese school, to tell us that if we didn't get baptized we'd go to a hell like one of the nine Taoist hells forever. And the obscene caller that phoned us at home when the adults were at the laundry. And the Mexican and Filipino girls at school who went to "confession," and how I envied them their white dresses and their chance each Saturday to tell even thoughts that were sinful. If only I could let my mother know the list, she—and the world—would become more like me, and I would never be alone again. I would pick a time of day when my mother was alone and tell her one item a day; I'd be finished in less than a year. If the telling got excruciating and her anger too bad, I'd tell five items once a week like the Catholic girls, and I'd still be through in a year, maybe ten months. My mother's most peaceful time was in the evenings when she starched the white shirts. The laundry would be clean, the gray wood floors sprinkled and swept with water and wet sawdust. She would be wringing shirts at the starch tub and not running about. My father and sisters and brothers would be at their own jobs mending, folding, packaging. Steam would be rising from the starch, the air cool at last. Yes, that would be the time and place for the telling.

And I wanted to ask again why the women in our family have a split nail on our left little toe. Whenever we asked our parents about it, they would glance at each other, embarrassed. I think I've heard one of them say, "She didn't get away." I made up that we are descended from an ancestress who stubbed her toe and fell when running from a rapist. I wanted to ask my mother if I had guessed right.

I hunkered down between the wall and the wicker basket of shirts. I had decided to start with the earliest item—when I had smashed a spider against the white side of the house: it was the first thing I killed. I said, clearly, "I killed a spider," and it was nothing; she did not hit me or throw hot starch at me. It sounded like nothing to me too. How strange when I had had such feelings of death shoot through my hand and into my body so that I would surely die. So I had to continue, of course, and let her know how important it had been. "I returned every day to look at its smear on the side of the house," I said. "It was our old house, the one we lived in until I was five. I went to the wall every day to look. I studied the stain." Relieved because she said nothing but only continued squeezing the starch, I went away feeling pretty good. Just two hundred and six more items to go. I moved carefully all the next day so as not to do anything or have anything happen to me that would make me go back to two hundred and seven again. I'd tell a couple of easy ones and work up to how I had pulled the quiet girl's hair and how I had enjoyed the year being sick. If it was going to be this easy, maybe I could blurt out several a day, maybe an easy one and a hard one. I could go chronologically, or I could work from easy to hard or hard to easy, depending on my mood. On the second night I talked about how I had hinted to a ghost girl that I wished I had a doll of my own until she gave me a head and body to glue together—that she hadn't given it to me of her own generosity but because I had hinted. But on the fifth night (I skipped two to reward myself) I decided it was time to do a really hard one and tell her about the white horse. And suddenly the duck voice came out, which I did not use with the family. "What's it called, Mother"—the duck voice coming out talking to my own mother—"when a person whispers to the head of the sages—no, not the sages, more like the buddhas but not real people like the buddhas (they've always lived in the sky and never turned into people like the buddhas)—and you whisper to them, the boss of them, and ask for things? They're like magicians? What do you call it when you talk to the boss magician?"

" 'Talking-to-the-top-magician,' I guess."

"I did that. Yes. That's it. That's what I did. I talked-to-the-top-magician and asked for a white horse." There. Said.

"Mm," she said, squeezing the starch out of the collar and cuffs. But I had talked, and she acted as if she hadn't heard.

Perhaps she hadn't understood. I had to be more explicit. I hated this. "I kneeled on the bed in there, in the laundry bedroom, and put my arms up like I saw in a comic book"—one night I heard monsters coming through the kitchen, and I had promised the god in the movies, the one the Mexicans and Filipinos have, as in "God Bless America," that I would not read comic books anymore if he would save me just this once; I had broken that promise, and I needed to tell all this to my mother too—"and in that ludicrous position asked for a horse."

"Mm," she said, nodded, and kept dipping and squeezing.

On my two nights off, I had sat on the floor too but had not said a word.

"Mother," I whispered and quacked.

"I can't stand this whispering," she said looking right at me, stopping her squeezing. "Senseless gabbings every night. I wish you would stop. Go away and work. Whispering, whispering, making no sense. Madness. I don't feel like hearing your craziness."

So I had to stop, relieved in some ways. I shut my mouth, but I felt something alive tearing at my throat, bite by bite, from the inside. Soon there would be three hundred things, and too late to get them out before my mother grew old and died.

I had probably interrupted her in the middle of her own quiet time when the boiler and presses were off and the cool night flew against the windows in moths and crickets. Very few customers came in. Starching the shirts for the next day's pressing was probably my mother's time to ride off with the people in her own mind. That would explain why she was so far away and did not want to listen to me. "Leave me alone," she said.

The hulk, the hunching sitter, brought a third box now, to rest his feet on. He patted his boxes. He sat in wait, hunching on his pile of dirt. My throat hurt constantly, vocal cords taut to snapping. One night when the laundry was so busy that the whole family was eating dinner there, crowded around the little round table, my throat burst open. I stood up, talking and burbling. I looked directly at my mother and at my father and screamed, "I want you to tell that hulk, that gorilla-ape, to go away and never bother us again. I know what you're up to. You're thinking he's rich, and we're poor. You think we're odd and not pretty and we're not bright. You think you can give us away to freaks. You better not do that, Mother. I don't want to see him or his dirty boxes here tomorrow. If I see him here one more time, I'm going away. I'm going away anyway. I am. Do you hear me? I may be ugly and clumsy, but one thing I'm not, I'm not retarded. There's nothing wrong with my brain. Do you know what the Teacher Ghosts say about me? They tell me I'm smart, and I can win scholarships. I can get into colleges. I've already applied. I'm smart. I can do all kinds of things. I know how to get A's, and they say I could be a scientist or a mathematician if I want. I can make a living and take care of myself. So you don't have to find me a keeper who's too dumb to know a bad bargain. I'm so smart, if they say write ten pages, I can write fifteen. I can do ghost things even better than ghosts can. Not everybody thinks I'm nothing. I am not going to be a slave or a wife. Even if I am stupid and talk funny and get sick, I won't let you turn me into a slave or a wife. I'm getting out of here. I can't stand living here anymore. It's your fault I talk weird. The only reason I flunked kindergarten was because you couldn't teach me English, and you gave me a zero IQ. I've brought my IQ up, though. They say I'm smart now. Things follow in lines at school. They take stories and teach us to turn them into essays. I don't need anybody to pronounce English words for me. I can figure them out by myself. I'm going to get scholarships, and I'm going away. And at college I'll have the people I like for friends. I don't care if their great-great-grandfather died of TB. I don't care if they were our enemies in China four thousand years ago. So get that ape out of here. I'm going to college. And I'm not going to Chinese school anymore. I'm going to run for office at American school, and I'm going to join clubs. I'm going to get enough offices and clubs on my record to get into college. And I can't stand Chinese school anyway; the kids are rowdy and mean, fighting all night. And I don't want to listen to any more of your stories; they have no logic. They scramble me up. You lie with stories. You won't tell me a story and then say, 'This is a true story,' or, 'This is just a story.' I can't tell the difference. I don't even know what your real names are. I can't tell what's real and what you make up. Ha! You can't stop me from talking. You tried to cut off my tongue, but it didn't work." So I told the hardest ten or twelve things on my list all in one outburst.

My mother, who is champion talker, was, of course, shouting at the same time. "I cut it to make you talk more, not less, you dummy. You're still stupid. You can't listen right. I didn't say I was going to marry you off. Did I ever say that? Did I ever mention that? Those newspaper people were for your sister, not you. Who would want you? Who said we could sell you? We can't sell people. Can't you take a joke? You can't even tell a joke from real life. You're not so smart. Can't even tell real from false."

"I'm never getting married, never!"

"Who'd want to marry you anyway? Noisy. Talking like a duck. Disobedient. Messy. And I know about college. What makes you think you're the first one to think about college? I was a doctor. I went to medical school. I don't see why you have to be a mathematician. I don't see why you can't be a doctor like me."

"I can't stand fever and delirium or listening to people coming out of anesthesia. But I didn't say I wanted to be a mathematician either. That's what the ghosts say. I want to be a lumberjack and a newspaper reporter." Might as well tell her some of the other items on my list. "I'm going to chop down trees in the daytime and write about timber at night."

"I don't see why you need to go to college at all to become either one of those things. Everybody else is sending their girls to typing school. 'Learn to type if you want to be an American girl.' Why don't you go to typing school? The cousins and village girls are going to typing school."

"And you leave my sister alone. You try that with the advertising again, and I'll take her with me." My telling list was scrambled out of order. When I said them out loud I saw that some of the items were ten years old already, and I had outgrown them. But they kept pouring out anyway in the voice like Chinese opera. I could hear the drums and the cymbals and the gongs and brass horns.

"You're the one to leave your little sisters alone," my mother was saying. "You're always leading them off somewhere. I've had to call the police twice because of you." She herself was shouting out things I had meant to tell her—that I took my brothers and sisters to explore strange people's houses, ghost children's houses, and haunted houses blackened by fire. We explored a Mexican house and a redheaded family's house, but not the gypsies' house; I had only seen the inside of the gypsies' house in mind-movies. We explored the sloughs, where we found hobo nests. My mother must have followed us.

"You turned out so unusual. I fixed your tongue so you could say charming things. You don't even say hello to the villagers."

"They don't say hello to me."

"They don't have to answer children. When you get old, people will say hello to you."

"When I get to college, it won't matter if I'm not charming. And it doesn't matter if a person is ugly; she can still do schoolwork."

"I didn't say you were ugly."

"You say that all the time."

"That's what we're supposed to say. That's what Chinese say. We like to say the opposite."

It seemed to hurt her to tell me that—another guilt for my list to tell my mother, I thought. And suddenly I got very confused and lonely because I was at that moment telling her my list, and in the telling, it grew. No higher listener. No listener but myself.

"Ho Chi Kuei," she shouted. "Ho Chi Kuei. Leave then. Get out, you Ho Chi Kuei. Get out. I knew you were going to turn out bad. Ho Chi Kuei." My brothers and sisters had left the table, and my father would not look at me anymore, ignoring me.

Be careful what you say. It comes true. It comes true. I had to leave home in order to see the world logically, logic the new way of seeing. I learned to think that mysteries are for explanation. I enjoy the simplicity. Concrete pours out of my mouth to cover the forests with freeways and sidewalks. Give me plastics, periodical tables, t.v. dinners with vegetables no more complex than peas mixed with diced carrots. Shine floodlights into dark corners: no ghosts.

I've been looking up "Ho Chi Kuei," which is what the immigrants call us—Ho Chi Ghosts. "Well, Ho Chi Kuei," they say, "what silliness have you been up to now?" "That's a Ho Chi Kuei for you," they say, no matter what we've done. It was more complicated (and therefore worse) than "dogs," which they say affectionately, mostly to boys. They use "pig" and "stink pig" for girls, and only in an angry voice. The river-pirate great-uncle called even my middle brother Ho Chi Kuei, and he seemed to like him best. The maggot third great-uncle even shouted "Ho Chi Kuei!" at the boy. I don't know any Chinese I can ask without getting myself scolded or teased, so I've been looking in books. So far I have the following translations for *ho* and/or *chi:* "centipede," "grub," "bastard carp," "chirping insect," "jujube tree," "pied wagtail," "grain sieve," "casket sacrifice," "water lily," "good frying," "non-eater," "dustpan-and-broom" (but that's a synonym for "wife"). Or perhaps I've romanized the spelling wrong and it is *Hao* Chi Kuei, which could mean they are calling us "Good Foundation Ghosts." The immigrants could be saying that we were born on Gold Mountain and have advantages. Sometimes they scorn us for having had it so easy, and sometimes they're delighted. They also call us "Chu Sing," or "Bamboo Nodes." Bamboo nodes obstruct water.

I like to look up a troublesome, shameful thing and then say, "Oh, is that all?" The simple explanation makes it less scary to go home after yelling at your mother and father. It drives the fear away and makes it possible someday to visit China, where I know now they don't sell girls or kill each other for no reason.

Now colors are gentler and fewer; smells are antiseptic. Now when I peek in the basement window where the villagers say they see a girl dancing like a bottle imp, I can no longer see a spirit in a skirt made of light, but a voiceless girl dancing when she thought no one was looking. The very next day after I talked out the retarded man, the huncher, he disappeared. I never saw him again or heard what became of him. Perhaps I made him up, and what I once had was not Chinese-sight at all but child-sight that would have disappeared eventually without such struggle. The throat pain always returns, though, unless I tell what I really think, whether or not I lose my job, or spit out gaucheries all over a party. I've stopped checking "bilingual" on job applications. I could not understand any of the dialects the interviewer at China Airlines tried on me, and he didn't understand me either. I'd like to go to New Society Village someday and find out exactly how far I can walk before people stop talking like me. I continue to sort out what's just my childhood, just my imagination, just my family, just the village, just movies, just living.

Soon I want to go to China and find out who's lying—the Communists who say they have food and jobs for everybody or the relatives who write that they have not the money to buy salt. My mother sends money she earns working in the tomato fields to Hong Kong. The relatives there can send it on to the remaining aunts and their children and, after a good harvest, to the children and grandchildren of my grandfather's two minor wives. "Every woman in the tomato row is sending money home," my mother says, "to Chinese villages and Mexican villages and Filipino villages and, now, Vietnamese villages, where they speak Chinese too. The women come to work whether sick or well. 'I can't die,' they say, 'I'm supporting fifty,' or 'I'm supporting a hundred.' "

What I'll inherit someday is a green address book full of names. I'll send the relatives money, and they'll write me stories about their hunger. My mother has been tearing up the letters from the youngest grandson of her father's third wife. He has been asking for fifty dollars to buy a bicycle. He says a bicycle will change his life. He could feed his wife and children if he had a bicycle. "We'd have to go hungry ourselves," my mother says. "They don't understand that we have ourselves to feed too." I've been making money; I guess it's my turn. I'd like to go to China and see those people and find out what's a cheat story and what's not. Did my grandmother really live to be ninety-nine? Or did they string us along all those years to get our money? Do the babies wear a Mao button like a drop of blood on their jumpsuits? When we overseas Chinese send money, do the relatives divide it evenly among the commune? Or do they really pay 2 percent tax and keep the rest? It would be good if the Communists were taking care of themselves; then I could buy a color t.v.

TETSUKO KUROYANAGI
(1931–)

Tetsuko Kuroyanagi has been to Japan what Johnny Carson was to America. For years she has had a daily television interview program called "Tetsuko's Room." Her memoirs, *Totto-Chan: The Little Girl at the Window,* published in Japan in 1981, focus on the years when she was a very young student at a Tokyo progressive school called Tomoe. Its founder and headmaster, Sosaku Kobayashi, had studied avant-garde educational methods in Europe and introduced them to Japan: eurythmics, for example, which encouraged children to move gracefully and expressively in patterns of their own devised in response to music. Tomoe, founded in 1937, was destroyed by air raids in 1945. *Totto-Chan* was an immense best seller in Japan, selling four and a half million copies in one year.

For other accounts of unusual education, compare Bernadette Devlin, *The Price of My Soul*, Santha Rama Rau, *Gifts of Passage*, and Jessica Mitford, *Hons and Rebels*.

FROM *Totto-Chan*

AMATEUR DRAMA

"We're going to put on a play!"

It was the first play in Tomoe's history. The custom of someone giving a talk at lunchtime was still going on, but imagine performing a play on the little stage with the grand piano the headmaster always played for eurythmics and inviting an audience. None of the children had even seen a play, not even Totto-chan. Apart from *Swan Lake,* she had never once been to the theater. Nevertheless, they all discussed what sort of program they should put on for their end-of-year performance.

Totto-chan's class decided to do *Kanjincho* ("The Fund-Raising Charter"). This famous old Kabuki play was not exactly what you would expect to see at Tomoe, but it was in one of their textbooks and Mr. Maruyama would coach them. They decided Aiko Saisho would make a good Benkei, the strong man, since she was big and tall, and Amadera, who could look stern and had a loud voice, should play Togashi, the commander. After talking it over, they all came to the conclusion that Totto-chan should be the noble Yoshitsune, who, in the play, is disguised as a porter. All the others would be strolling monks.

Before they could begin rehearsing, the children had to learn their lines. It was nice for Totto-chan and the monks, for they had nothing to say. All that the monks were required to do was stand silently throughout, while Totto-chan, as Yoshitsune, had to remain kneeling, with her face hidden by a large straw hat. Benkei, in reality Yoshitsune's servant, beats and upbraids his master in a clever attempt to get the party past the Ataka Checkpoint by posing as a band of monks collecting funds to restore a temple. Aiko Saisho, playing Benkei, had a tremendous part. Besides all the verbal thrust and parry with Togashi, the checkpoint commander, there was the exciting bit where Benkei has to pretend to read out the Fund-Raising Charter when ordered by the commander to do so. The scroll he "reads" from is blank, and he brilliantly extemporizes an appeal for funds in pompous ecclesiastical language: "Firstly, for the purpose of the restoration of the temple known as Todaiji . . ."

Aiko Saisho practiced her "Firstly" speech every day.

The role of Togashi, too, had lots of dialogue, as he tries to refute Benkei's arguments, and Amadera struggled to memorize it.

Finally rehearsal time came. Togashi and Benkei faced each other, with the monks lined up behind Benkei, and Totto-chan, as Yoshitsune, kneeling, huddled over, in front. But Totto-chan didn't understand what it was all about. So when Benkei had to knock Yoshitsune over with his staff and strike him, Totto-chan reacted violently. She kicked Aiko Saisho in the legs and scratched her. Aiko cried and the monks giggled.

Yoshitsune was supposed to remain still, looking cowed, no matter how much Benkei beat and hit him. The idea is that while Togashi suspects the truth, he is so impressed by Benkei's ruse and the pain it must cost him to ill-treat his noble master, that he lets them through the checkpoint.

To have Yoshitsune resisting would ruin the whole plot. Mr. Maruyama tried to explain this to Totto-chan. But Totto-chan was adamant. She insisted that if Aiko Saisho hit her she would hit back. So they made no progress.

No matter how many times they tried the scene, Totto-chan always put up a fight.

"I'm terribly sorry," said Mr. Maruyama to Totto-chan finally, "but I think we had better ask Tai-chan to play the part of Yoshitsune."

Totto-chan was relieved. She didn't like being the only one who got knocked about.

"Totto-chan, will you please be a monk?" asked Mr. Maruyama. So Totto-chan stood with the other monks, but right at the back.

Mr. Maruyama and the children thought everything would be fine now, but they were wrong. He shouldn't have let Totto-chan have a monk's long staff. Totto-chan got bored with standing still so she started poking the feet of the monk next to her with the staff, and tickling the monk in front under his armpits. She even pretended to conduct with it, which was not only dangerous for those nearby but also ruined the scene between Benkei and Togashi.

So eventually she was deprived of her role as a monk, too.

Tai-chan as Yoshitsune, gritted his teeth manfully as he was knocked over and beaten, and the audience must surely have felt sorry for him. Rehearsals progressed smoothly without Totto-chan.

Left by herself, Totto-chan went out into the school grounds. She took off her shoes and started to improvise a Totto-chan ballet. It was lovely dancing according to her own fancy. Sometimes she was a swan, sometimes the wind, sometimes a grotesque person, sometimes a tree. All alone in the deserted playground she danced and danced.

Deep in her heart, however, there was a tiny feeling that she would like to be playing Yoshitsune. But had they allowed her to, she would surely have hit and scratched Aiko Saisho.

Thus it was that Totto-chan was not able to take part in the first and last amateur drama at Tomoe.

CHALK

Tomoe children never scrawled on other people's walls or on the road. That was because they had ample opportunity for doing it at school.

During music periods in the Assembly Hall, the headmaster would give each child a piece of white chalk. They could lie or sit anywhere they liked on the floor and wait, chalk in hand. When they were all ready, the headmaster started playing the piano. As he did so, they would write the rhythms, in musical notation, on the floor. It was lovely writing in chalk on the shiny light brown wood. There were only about ten pupils in Totto-chan's class, so when they were spread around the large Assembly Hall, they had plenty of floor on which to write their notes as large as they wanted without encroaching on anyone else's space. They didn't need lines for their notation, since they just wrote down the rhythm. At Tomoe musical notes had special names the children devised themselves after talking it over with the headmaster. Here they are:

was called a skip, because it was a good rhythm to skip and jump to.

♪   was called a flag, because it looked like one.

♫   was called a flag-flag.

♪   was called a double-flag.

♩   was called a black.

♩   was called a white.

♩.   was called a white-with-a-mole, or a white 'n' dot.

○   was called a circle.

This way they learned to know the notes well and it was fun. It was a class they loved.

Writing on the floor with chalk was the headmaster's idea. Paper wasn't big enough and there weren't enough blackboards to go around. He thought the Assembly Hall floor would make a nice big blackboard on which the children could note the rhythm with ease no matter how fast the music was, and writing as large as they liked. Above all, they could enjoy the music. And if there was time afterward, they could draw airplanes and dolls and anything they wanted. Sometimes the children would join up their drawings just for fun and the whole floor would become one enormous picture.

At intervals during the music class, the headmaster would come over and inspect each child's rhythms. He would comment, "That's good," or "It wasn't a flag-flag there, it was a skip."

After he had approved or corrected their notation, he played the music over again so they could check what they had done and familiarize themselves with the rhythms. No matter how busy he was, the headmaster never let anyone else take these classes for him. And as far as the children were concerned, it wouldn't have been any fun at all without Mr. Kobayashi.

Cleaning up after writing rhythms was quite a job. First you had to wipe the floor with a blackboard eraser, and then everyone joined forces to make the floor spick and span again with mops and rags. It was an enormous task.

In this way Tomoe children learned what trouble cleaning off graffiti could be, so they never scribbled anywhere except on the floor of the

Assembly Hall. Moreover, this class took place about twice a week, so the children had their fill of scribbling.

The children at Tomoe became real experts on chalk—which kind was best, how to hold it, how to manipulate it for the best results, how not to break it. Every one of them was a chalk connoisseur.

· · ·

THE TEA PARTY

Ryo-chan, the janitor at Tomoe, whom all the children liked so much, was finally called up. He was a grown-up, but they all called him by his childish nickname. Ryo-chan was a sort of guardian angel who always came to the rescue and helped when anyone was in trouble. Ryo-chan could do anything. He never said much, and only smiled, but he always knew just what to do. When Totto-chan fell into the cesspool, it was Ryo-chan who came to her rescue straight away, and washed her off without so much as a grumble.

"Let's give Ryo-chan a rousing, send-off tea party," said the headmaster.

"A tea party?"

Green tea is drunk many times during the day in Japan, but it is not associated with entertaining—except ceremonial powdered tea, a different beverage altogether. A "tea party" would be something new at Tomoe. But the children liked the idea. They loved doing things they'd never done before. The children didn't know it, but the headmaster had invented a new word, *sawakai* (tea party), instead of the usual *sobetsukai* (farewell party) on purpose. A farewell party sounded too sad, and the older children would understand that it might really be farewell if Ryo-chan got killed and didn't come back. But nobody had ever been to a tea party before, so they were all excited.

After school, Mr. Kobayashi had the children arrange the desks in a circle in the Assembly Hall just as at lunchtime. When they were all sitting in a circle, he gave each one a single thin strip of roasted dried squid to have with their green tea. Even that was a great luxury in those wartime days. Then he sat down next to Ryo-chan and placed a glass before him with a little saké in it. It was a ration obtainable only for those leaving for the front.

"This is the first tea party at Tomoe," said the headmaster. "Let's all have a good time. If there's anything you'd like to say to Ryo-chan, do so. You can say things to each other, too, not just to Ryo-chan. One by one, standing in the middle."

It was not only the first time they had ever eaten dried squid at Tomoe, but the first time Ryo-chan had sat down with them, and the first time they had seen Ryo-chan sipping saké.

One after the other the children stood up, facing Ryo-chan, and spoke to him. The first children just told him to take care of himself and not get sick. Then Migita, who was in Totto-chan's class, said, "Next time I go home to the country I'll bring you all back some funeral dumplings."

Everyone laughed. It was well over a year since Migita first told them about the dumplings he had once had at a funeral and how good they were. Whenever the opportunity arose, he promised to bring them some, but he never did it.

When the headmaster heard Migita mention funeral dumplings, it gave him quite a start. Normally it would have been considered bad luck to mention funeral dumplings at such a time. But Migita said it so innocently, just wanting to share with his friends something that tasted so good, that the headmaster laughed with the others. Ryo-chan laughed heartily, too. After all, Migita had been telling him for ages that he would bring him some.

Then Oe got up and promised Ryo-chan that he was going to become the best horticulturist in Japan. Oe was the son of the proprietor of an enormous nursery garden in Todoroki. Keiko Aoki got up next and said nothing. She just giggled shyly, as usual, and bowed, and went back to her seat. Whereupon Totto-chan rushed forward and said for her, "The chickens at Keiko-chan's can fly! I saw them the other day!"

Then Amadera spoke. "If you find any injured cats or dogs," he said, "bring them to me and I'll fix them up."

Takahashi was so small he crawled under his desk to get to the center of the circle and was there as quick as a wink. He said in a cheerful voice, "Thank you, Ryo-chan. Thank you for everything. For all sorts of things."

Aiko Saisho stood up next. She said, "Ryo-chan, thank you for bandaging me up that time I fell down. I'll never forget." Aiko Saisho's great-uncle was the famous Admiral Togo of the Russo-Japanese War, and Atsuko Saisho, another relative of hers, was a celebrated poetess at Emperor Meiji's court. But Aiko never mentioned them.

Miyo-chan, the headmaster's daughter, knew Ryo-chan the best. Her eyes were full of tears. "Take care of yourself, won't you, Ryo-chan. Let's write to each other."

Totto-chan had so many things she wanted to say she didn't know where to begin. So she just said, "Even though you're gone, Ryo-chan, we'll have a tea party every day."

The headmaster laughed, and so did Ryo-chan. All the children laughed, too, even Totto-chan herself.

But Totto-chan's words came true the very next day. Whenever there was time the children would form a group and play "tea party." Instead of dried squid, they would suck things like tree bark, and they sipped glasses of water instead of tea, sometimes pretending it was saké. Someone would say, "I'll bring you some funeral dumplings," and they'd all laugh. Then they'd talk and tell each other their thoughts. Even though there wasn't anything to eat, the "tea parties" were fun.

The "tea party" was a wonderful farewell gift that Ryo-chan left the children. And although none of them had the faintest idea then, it was in fact the last game they were to play at Tomoe before the children parted and went their separate ways.

Ryo-chan went off on the Toyoko train. His departure coincided with the arrival of the American airplanes. They finally appeared in the skies above Tokyo and began dropping bombs every day.

ANNE MORROW LINDBERGH
(1906–)

Anne Morrow's father was the American ambassador to Mexico when Charles Lindbergh, the hero of aviation, flew into Mexico City for a visit. The young, bookish woman, who had been educated at Smith, and the handsome pilot fell in love and were married in 1929. After the kidnapping for ransom and the murder of their first child, the Lindberghs moved to an island off the coast of Brittany for privacy and safety. When the war forced them back to the States, they settled in Connecticut, where they wrote and brought up their five children.

Her classic *Gift from the Sea* (1955), based on time she spent alone on Captiva Island in Florida to recover from the rigors of family life, is structured as a series of meditations on different shells she found on the beach. This selection, "Channelled Whelk," opens the sequence. Lindbergh has also published two volumes of extracts from her journals and letters, *Bring Me a Unicorn* (1971) and *Hour of Gold, Hour of Lead* (1973).

For another encounter between a natural object and a symbolic mind, compare the selection from Lillian Hellman, *Pentimento,* which is called "Turtle." For meditative temperaments a bit like Lindbergh's, compare Anne Truitt, *Daybook* and Florida Scott-Maxwell, *The Measure of My Days.*

FROM *Gift from the Sea*

CHANNELLED WHELK

The shell in my hand is deserted. It once housed a whelk, a snail-like creature, and then temporarily, after the death of the first occupant, a little hermit crab, who has run away, leaving his tracks behind him like a delicate vine on the sand. He ran away, and left me his shell. It was once a protection to him. I turn the shell in my hand, gazing into the wide open door from which he made his exit. Had it become an encumbrance? Why did he run away? Did he hope to find a better home, a better mode of living? I too have run away, I realize, I have shed the shell of my life, for these few weeks of vacation.

But his shell—it is simple; it is bare, it is beautiful. Small, only the size of my thumb, its architecture is perfect, down to the finest detail. Its shape, swelling like a pear in the center, winds in a gentle spiral to the pointed apex. Its color, dull gold, is whitened by a wash of salt from the sea. Each whorl, each faint knob, each criss-cross vein in its egg-shell texture, is as clearly defined as on the day of creation. My eye follows with delight the outer circumference of that diminutive winding staircase up which this tenant used to travel.

My shell is not like this, I think. How untidy it has become! Blurred with moss, knobby with barnacles, its shape is hardly recognizable any more. Surely, it had a shape once. It has a shape still in my mind. What is the shape of my life?

The shape of my life today starts with a family. I have a husband, five children and a home just beyond the suburbs of New York. I have also a craft, writing, and therefore work I want to pursue. The shape of my life is, of course, determined by many other things; my background and childhood, my mind and its education, my conscience and its pressures, my heart and its desires. I want to give and take from my children and husband, to share with friends and community, to carry out my obligations to man and to the world, as a woman, as an artist, as a citizen.

But I want first of all—in fact, as an end to these other desires—to be at peace with myself. I want a singleness of eye, a purity of intention, a central core to my life that will enable me to carry out these obligations and activities as well as I can. I want, in fact—to borrow from the language of the saints—to live "in grace" as much of the time as possible. I am not using this term in a strictly theological sense. By grace I mean an inner harmony, essentially spiritual, which can be translated into outward harmony. I am seeking perhaps what Socrates asked for in the prayer from the *Phaedrus* when he said, "May the outward and inward man be at one." I would like to achieve a state of inner spiritual grace from which I could function and give as I was meant to in the eye of God.

Vague as this definition may be, I believe most people are aware of periods in their lives when they seem to be "in grace" and other periods when they feel "out of grace," even though they may use different words to describe these states. In the first happy condition, one seems to carry all one's tasks before one lightly, as if borne along on a great tide; and in the opposite state one can hardly tie a shoe-string. It is true that a large part of life consists in learning a technique of tying the shoe-string, whether one is in grace or not. But there are techniques of living too; there are even techniques in the search for grace. And techniques can be cultivated. I have learned by some experience, by many examples, and by the writings of countless others before me, also occupied in the search, that certain environments, certain modes of life, certain rules of conduct are more conducive to inner and outer harmony than others. There are, in fact, certain roads that one may follow. Simplification of life is one of them.

I mean to lead a simple life, to choose a simple shell I can carry easily—like a hermit crab. But I do not. I find that my frame of life does not foster simplicity. My husband and five children must make their way in the world. The life I have chosen as wife and mother entrains a whole caravan of complications. It involves a house in the suburbs and either household drudgery or household help which wavers between scarcity and non-existence for most of us. It involves food and shelter; meals, planning, marketing, bills, and making the ends meet in a thousand ways. It involves not only the butcher, the baker, the candlestickmaker, but countless other experts to keep my modern house with its modern "simplifications" (electricity, plumbing, refrigerator, gas-stove, oil-burner, dish-washer, radios, car, and numerous other labor-saving devices) functioning properly. It involves health; doctors, dentists, appointments, medicine, cod-liver oil, vitamins, trips to the drugstore. It involves education, spiritual, intellectual, physical; schools, school conferences, car-pools, extra trips for basket-ball or orchestra practice; tutoring; camps, camp equipment and transportation. It involves clothes, shopping, laundry, cleaning, mending, letting skirts down and sewing buttons on, or finding someone else to do it. It involves friends, my husband's, my children's, my own, and endless arrangements to get together; letters, invitations, telephone calls and transportation hither and yon.

For life today in America is based on the premise of ever-widening circles of contact and communication. It involves not only family demands, but community demands, national demands, international demands on the good citizen, through social and cultural pressures, through newspapers, magazines, radio programs, political drives, charitable appeals, and so on. My mind reels with it. What a circus act we women perform every day of our lives. It puts the trapeze artist to shame. Look at us. We run a tight rope daily, balancing a pile of books on the head. Baby-carriage, parasol, kitchen chair, still under control. Steady now!

This is not the life of simplicity but the life of multiplicity that the wise men warn us of. . . . Plotinus was preaching the dangers of multiplicity of the world back in the third century. Yet, the problem is particularly and essentially woman's. Distraction is, always has been, and probably always will be, inherent in woman's life.

For to be a woman is to have interests and duties, raying out in all directions from the central mother-core, like spokes from the hub of a wheel. The pattern of our lives is essentially circular. We must be open to all points of the compass; husband, children, friends, home, community; stretched out, exposed, sensitive like a spider's web to each breeze that blows, to each call that comes. How difficult for us, then, to achieve a balance in the midst of these contradictory tensions, and yet how necessary for the proper functioning of our lives. How much we need, and how arduous of attainment is that steadiness preached in all rules for holy living. How desirable and how distant is the ideal of the contemplative, artist, or saint—the inner inviolable core, the single eye.

With a new awareness, both painful and humorous, I begin to understand why the saints were rarely married women. I am convinced it has nothing inherently to do, as I once supposed, with chastity or children. It has to do primarily with distractions. The bearing, rearing, feeding and educating of children; the running of a house with its thousand details; human relationships with their myriad pulls—woman's normal occupations in general run counter to creative life, or contemplative life, or saintly life. The problem is not merely one of *Woman and Career, Woman and the Home, Woman and Independence.* It is more basically: how to remain whole in the midst of the distractions of life; how to remain balanced, no matter what centrifugal forces tend to pull one off center; how to remain strong, no matter what shocks come in at the periphery and tend to crack the hub of the wheel.

What is the answer? There is no easy answer, no complete answer. I have only clues, shells from the sea. The bare beauty of the channelled whelk tells me that one answer, and perhaps a first step, is in simplification of life, in cutting out some of the distractions. But how? Total retirement is not possible. I cannot shed my responsibilities. I cannot permanently inhabit a desert island. I cannot be a nun in the midst of family life. I would not want to be. The solution for me, surely, is neither in total renunciation of the world, nor in total acceptance of it. I must find a balance somewhere, or an alternating rhythm between these two extremes; a swinging of the pendulum between solitude and communion, between retreat and return. In my periods of retreat, perhaps I can learn something to carry back into my worldly life. I can at least practice for these two weeks the simplification of outward life, as a beginning. I can follow this superficial clue, and see where it leads. Here, in beach living, I can try.

One learns first of all in beach living the art of shedding; how little one can get along with, not how much. Physical shedding to begin with, which then mysteriously spreads into other fields. Clothes, first. Of course, one needs less in the sun. But one needs less anyway, one finds suddenly. One does not need a closet-full, only a small suitcase-full. And what a relief it is! Less taking up and down of hems, less mending, and—best of all—less worry about what to wear. One finds one is shedding not only clothes—but vanity.

Next, shelter. One does not need the airtight shelter one has in winter in the North. Here I live in a bare sea-shell of a cottage. No heat, no telephone, no plumbing to speak of, no hot water, a two-burner oil stove, no gadgets to go wrong. No rugs. There were some, but I rolled them up the first day; it is easier to sweep the sand off a bare floor. But I find I don't bustle about with unnecessary sweeping and cleaning here. I am no longer aware of the dust. I have shed my Puritan conscience about absolute tidiness and cleanliness. Is it possible that, too, is a material burden? No curtains. I do not need them for privacy; the pines around my house are enough protection. I want the windows open all the time, and I don't want to worry about rain. I begin to shed my Martha-like anxiety about many things. Washable slipcovers, faded and old—I hardly see them; I don't worry about the impression they make on other people. I am shedding pride. As little furniture as possible; I shall not need much. I shall ask into my shell only those friends with whom I can be completely honest. I find I am shedding hypocrisy in human relationships. What a rest that will be! The most exhausting thing in life, I have discovered, is being insincere. That is why so much of social life is exhausting; one is wearing a mask. I have shed my mask.

I find I live quite happily without those things I think necessary in winter in the North. And as I write these words, I remember, with some shock at the disparity in our lives, a similar statement made by a friend of mine in France who spent three years in a German prison camp. Of course, he said, qualifying his remark, they did not get enough to eat, they were sometimes atrociously treated, they had little physical freedom. And yet, prison life taught him how little one can get along with, and what extraordinary spiritual freedom and peace such simplification can bring. I remember again, ironically, that today more of us in America than anywhere else in the world have the luxury of choice between simplicity and complication of life. And for the most part, we, who could choose simplicity, choose complication. War, prison, survival periods, enforce a form of simplicity on man. The monk and the nun choose it of their own free will. But if one accidentally finds it, as I have for a few days, one finds also the serenity it brings.

Is it not rather ugly, one may ask? One collects material possessions not only for security, comfort or vanity, but for beauty as well. Is your sea-shell house not ugly and bare? No, it is beautiful, my house. It is bare, of course, but the wind, the sun, the smell of the pines blow through its bareness. The unfinished beams in the roof are veiled by cobwebs. They are lovely, I think, gazing up at them with new eyes; they soften the hard lines of the rafters as grey hairs soften the lines on a middle-aged face. I no longer pull out grey hairs or sweep down cobwebs. As for the walls, it is true they looked forbidding at first. I felt cramped and enclosed by their blank faces. I wanted to knock holes in them, to give them another dimension with pictures or windows. So I dragged home from the beach grey arms of driftwood, worn satin-smooth by wind and sand. I gathered trailing green vines with floppy red-tipped leaves. I picked up the whitened skeletons of conchshells, their curious hollowed-out shapes faintly reminiscent of abstract sculpture. With these tacked to walls and propped up in corners, I am satisfied. I have a periscope out to the world. I have a window, a view, a point of flight from my sedentary base.

I am content. I sit down at my desk, a bare kitchen table with a blotter, a bottle of ink, a sand dollar to weight down one corner, a clam shell for a pen tray, the broken tip of a conch, pink-tinged, to finger, and a row of shells to set my thoughts spinning.

I love my sea-shell of a house. I wish I could live in it always. I wish I could transport it home. But I cannot. It will not hold a husband, five children and the necessities and trappings of daily life. I can only carry back my little channelled whelk. It will sit on my desk in Connecticut, to remind me of the ideal of a simplified life, to encourage me in the game I played on the beach. To ask how little, not how much, can I get along with. To say—is it necessary?—when I am tempted to add one more accumulation to my life, when I am pulled toward one more centrifugal activity.

Simplification of outward life is not enough. It is merely the outside. But I am starting with the outside. I am looking at the outside of a shell, the outside of my life—the shell. The complete answer is not to be found on the outside, in an outward mode of living. This is only a technique, a road to grace. The final answer, I know, is always inside. But the outside can give a clue, can help one to find the inside answer. One is free, like the hermit crab, to change one's shell.

Channelled whelk, I put you down again, but you have set my mind on a journey, up an inwardly winding spiral staircase of thought.

ONNIE LEE LOGAN
(c. 1910–)

Oral history, the recording and transcribing of spoken accounts, has made available a much wider range of life stories than ever before. Many people who do not know how to write or do not write fluently are nonetheless bursting to tell their own stories, as was Onnie Lee Logan, a domestic servant and midwife in Mobile, Alabama. "I got so much experience in here that I just want to explode," she said to Katherine Clark, a professor of English at the University of Alabama in Tuscaloosa, who collaborated with her to produce *Motherwit: An Alabama Midwife's Story* (1989).

The fourteenth of sixteen children in a black family in rural Alabama, Logan followed both her mother and her grandmother in becoming a midwife. By 1931, when she started delivering babies, the percentage of American babies delivered by midwives had dropped to 15 as the medical establishment gradually enforced obstetrics and hospital births in an effort to curb infant mortality rates. "Granny" (lay) midwifery lasted longer in the South than elsewhere in the United States but was outlawed in Alabama in 1976. Logan was allowed to keep practicing until 1984, when despite her excellent record, the board of health refused to renew her permit—ironically just when a shortage of obstetricians in Alabama had made infant mortality rates again the highest in the country and one solution under consideration was a nurse midwife program.

For other oral histories, compare *Nisa: The Life and Words of a !Kung Woman* and Ning Lao T'ai-t'ai, *A Daughter of Han*. For other accounts of southern black life, compare Anne Moody, *Coming of Age in Mississippi* and Maya Angelou, *I Know Why the Caged Bird Sings*. For another professional's account of her trade, compare Margaret Mead, *Blackberry Winter*.

FROM *Motherwit*

When I go to deliver a baby I wear white. All white. My white coat. All white. We wears a lil white cap. That's a lil white cap comes around here tied to my head. It's mo' sanitary than havin yo' hair loose. I carry in my bag my scrub brush, my orange stick, a separate brush in a separate bag with my scrub brush in that. I sterile it when I get home and hang it out on the line to dry and don't open it again until I get ready to use it next time, my scrub brush what I scrub up with. The orange stick and the scrub brush is in a lil separate bag inside of the big bag. I have my sterile cord and silver nitrate and whatever to go in there is all sterile and wrapped from the bo'd a health. It's been steriled there and not to be opened until I get ready to use it. My coat that I deliver in, my gown, which has been steriled and pressed and turned on the wrong side. One side of my bag is my equipment such as my gown, my scrub brush, my orange stick. On the other side of my bag is all the equipment and stuff that belongs to the baby. One side is for my personals and the other side is for the baby with silver nitrate, sterile gauze, Q-tips, and all things that goes along with my baby when I deliver it.

I never have done without or been without my orange stick, my scrub brush. Not a single time since I've been workin. Now if those old mid-wives in those rare days didn't have any of that to work with I feel like they was doin the best they could. Got a job well done such as what they knew how to do. We're not supposed to carry any kinda medicine in our bags. We wasn't to do that. And we are not allowed to give any medicine other than prescribed by a doctor.

Now this is the way I did it. There was a beautiful setup with mother and daddy when their baby was conceived. They enjoyed it. When she get in labor—another beautiful setup. I think the husband and wife should be by themselves durin the first stage of labor. That mother and daddy is together quietly by themselves at her beginnin of labor until labor get so severe. Now this just comes from me. Even though some of em get kinda skittish and want me to come right on. I tells em this. "It was you and yo' husband in the beginning and it was fine. It's you and you' husband should be in the beginning a the birth a the baby, quiet and easy, talkin and lovin and happy with one another. You don't need nobody there. Me nor nobody else until a certain length a time." That's the reason I tell my patients, "When you get in labor, you call me when you think you in labor"—especially the ones right here in the city.

"Let's have telephone conversations befo' I come cause that's beauti-ful for you and yo' husband to be together. Then every so often befo' I get there you call me and let me know how you're comin on." And she will call me. Call me back in thirty minutes. Time yo' pains and see how many you've had within the thirty minutes and if it be a good ways apart I says, "Well don't call me no mo' until they start pickin up." We stay in touch with each other through telephone conversations. And when their pains start gettin severe I say, "Well I better come on out so I can start gettin things ready." Once labor gets so severe that's when the two both wanna call somebody in that's experienced that knows what to do. I be prepared myself sittin ready at home so when they call and say they're getting rapid now, I'll be ready to just shoot out.

I look for the first two contractions befo' I move to do anything when I first get there. See how they're percolatin along and then I start to work. Most of em, the general run of em have the bed all fixed because we done already talked about how and discussed it. We done made our pads three and fo' weeks befo'. Sometime two and three months. Pads for the bed to take care of the linens. We make the pads we can just roll all the ways in their clean bed. We made pads that big you know to take care of things like that. We use a plastic cover on the mattress and then there is a sheet on that. Then on top of the sheet we use these pads that we make that has been covered with a sterile old sheet. When we get through with that we just roll it all up. Roll it out from under her. Roll another one under her. And then she's layin there in a nice clean bed. No spots. The ones that hasn't laid the baby's clothes out, I get all a that. A fresh basin for the baby and a fresh basin for the mother so I can bathe her. Not in the same one. One for the baby and one for the mother. I have that all sterile and I go in and I sterile my scissors which I have a lil sterilizer to put on the stove and boilin water. I get all a that lined up. I time the contractions and I see how she's dilated.

You got some time now befo' and I just leave em alone. I get me a book and get in the livin room somewheres in a quiet co'ner and leave em by themselves. I wait awhile till that time comes a lil bit later when pains get so severe that I get up to scrub up my hands because I got to scrub em up two or three different times befo' the baby is born. Because we don't wear gloves. Scrub em up real good with a brush halfway up our arms. I did that through the rules and regulations of the bo'd a health in my trainin. They said that we could scrub our arms much better than trying to wear gloves that we can't sterile. Of co'se we could use those gloves now that you throw away but they didn't have em when I first started workin. We was not allowed to go inside the vagina with our hands like a doctor anyway.

I tell you one thing that's very impo'tant that I do that the doctors don't do and the nurses doesn't do because they doesn't take time to do it. And that is I'm with my patients at all times with a smile and keepin her feelin good with kind words. The very words that she need to hear it comes up and come out. And that means alot. Most of the doctors when they do say somethin to em it's so harsh. They already had contractions, and then with a ugly word to come out not suitable to how they're feelin. Some of em say that if they wasn't strapped down there they would get down and come home. Alot a women are left totally alone. And plenty of em have had their babies right by themselves. Well see I don't leave my patient like that. I'm there givin her all the love and all the care and I be meaning it and they know I mean it. It's from my heart and they can feel me. You see what I mean? There's alot of a certain lil black gal—they can feel that black gal. They can feel the love from her—the care from her. What she's goin through with I'm goin through right along with her.

Now I know how to stay away. In another room. Right. While I'm sitting right in here now, if you need me befo' I walk back here you call me. I be right here. That's what I tell em and that works. And they like it. I'm right there. The most impo'tant thing is that I'm with em givin em love and care the whole time. I'm there from beginnin to end with smile, good words, happy words. Keepin you happy. And that's a very happy experience for you.

That baby works slow as I said. They work slow. When the mother gets severe contractions I tells her how to breathe. Alot a womens knows how because they've had a class. Now that breathin is just like a dose of medicine to the mother these days. It takes care of em so good and so much. It's so helpful. You have to breathe what suits you. It's whatever suit yo' contractions. I he'p em find the way that suit em in their labor. I tell em when to breathe and when not to breathe.

Durin labor I kep' em on their feet where in the hospital they buckle em down. I'd let my mother stay up on her feet until she'd have to lay down. Kep' em on their feet and when they got tired and still in labor I would let her sit down and rest. Relax themselves. Then I know exactly what time to get em up. I know when they get tired they need to rest. That is a whole lot better than her layin there just lyin there hurtin. If she's up on her feet and havin contractions she don't feel nearly as much pain. They don't like bein buckled down to have their baby. They don't likes it when they have the baby, they buckles em down and the nurse and the doctors leaves em. They get so uncomfortable bein there and nobody sayin nothin to em and I'm right there to give em a word of encouragement all the time and tell em the way of life and the way of God. "Now look, honey—this will be over with soon, honey." And this is what God intended to do. This pain is intended to be. I'm tellin you so many of my white girls they don't fear. They reads up on it. They want to do it. They know what they be goin through with. They want to do it. They just set themselves.

I do all my work keepin em from having lacerations and havin to have stitches. That doctor would've took her in there and give her a long laceration to get the baby. I had my own method of workin on those ladies so they could dilate. I didn't get it in class at the bo'd a health neither. It was given to me by God. I put em in a tub of water. Hot water. Hot as they can stand. Then they get on the bed, I get my basin and hot water and a towel. Just boil it on the stove. Make a lil sterile. Greaze mother with lil oil. A lil white Vaseline real good. Then I start these hot towels. Just as hot as they can stand. And they say, "Oh, that feels so good. Oh, that hot compact make me feel so good." Because it's beginnin to get that burnin sensation where the skin has got to stretch. And that hot wash do good on em. Make em feel good. It eases em and it just stretches the skin out. And so I just constantly keep that thing on em. When that done cool off, not cold but just not hot, I'd heat it up again and put it back there. And they dilate so good without me doin any lacerations at all. Beautiful. I do that for everybody. He'p em to really dilate without needin any lacerations.

Alot a people wonder, "How do you keep em from tearin?" So I'm lettin out one a my secrets. I don't want to bury em. There's so much that I don't want to die with. Not sharin it with somebody. That's what give me the idea to do a book because I have so much experience in here that I want to explode. I was not taught to do that. God give that to me.

. . .

Back in the days when my mother was a midwife they didn't do anything about lacerations then. What could they do about it? But I'll tell you why and what the score was with em. They kep' em clean and they stayed on the bed nine days anyhow. That would make em heal back together—the grooves right in there meet the same grooves that it was torn from. If you're gettin up you're making it up either one way or the other. It will heal like that whenever it stick itself and that's not makin the grains stick together. Even if it won't buckle up it will slide by the grains that it's supposed to make connection with. Sometimes when it heals it don't even go back together. That makes her mo' larger than she was. Makes her mo' bigger. A woman she got to stay closed so that man can get the feeling between that. He don't want it so big.

As far as havin a laceration, nature's supposed to take care of that and it does along with me knowin what to do so she won't have a laceration and that's to use my hot towels and my oil. Be sho to let her take her time with her contractions and breathe and not push too hard. That's where the laceration comes from. When it gets to the point where she start dilatin beautiful, then she get to the place that she don't wanna breathe or cain't breathe. She get that urge to push instead of breathin. I tell em to stop if they get the urge to push. You gotta make em hold up off a that because they won't get through then.

I don't let em do it in a hurry. Just enough to give em a lil relief. Because you do mo' harm pushin right now than you do good. You prolong the labor. See that baby would come down and get hung behind this birth canal, the pelvis right there. When you get the head behind that it takes alot a long pains to bring the head up so it can come out. That baby's head got to make its own way. Breathe and let it come on down itself. Contractions will pull it. When it gets there it get that balance. That's when they can push slowly. I know when that point comes. You can only see the head. You see the dilation, alot a times it stretch like that with the head back inside and that's beautiful. When you can look inside and see the head. You know then that baby is not gonna get trapped behind. Because you done dilated her all you need then and a lil bit mo' pressure so it can come out. I tell em how much to give and how much not to give.

When they get in that last stage of labor they sometime get to cryin and start to say what they cain't do. "I just cain't—I done tried. I done all I could. There ain't no mo' I can do." That is the worst feelin for the mother at that stage of labor. Mostly those contractions is the worst. I just tell em to leave the rest to God. "All I want you to do is be calm and easy." Plenty times I say, "All you got to do is hush yo' mouth and you'll see it ain't worth the vibration you're makin, you'll be through." Plenty times I say, "You done had yo' baby. All you gotta do is hush yo' mouth and let me reach in there." They done had all the contractions it takes to bring that baby down comin through the birth canal. All they have to do is be a lil patient. Just a lil patient. You see who gonna handle the rest of it. I say, "Now right here is where God comes in. You say you done all you could. You done beared as much as you could. Leave the rest to God. He'll do it."

In the last stages of labor when the baby is fixin to crown, that's when really, you really get irritable. They don't want to be bothered and they easily gets furious. Just like I had one girl, I says, "Well, honey, you're doin fine." "Mrs. Logan, you don't know what you're talkin about. You ain't never had no babies." Well that wasn't her. That was the stage she was in at the time, see. When they get in that last stage of labor just most anything they say would come up. And all at the same time the baby was crownin, it was comin out. I stay cool and calm. Don't you get irritable like they are. You got to know better than that which I do know better than that. I know better and I just keep my calm. Smile and say somethin to em. Finally they get right along with you. But if you gonna start actin up along with em and gettin disgusted with em—now that's somethin I have never: really got disgusted with a patient.

I ask em not to push at this point. Cause at that time they're right at that stage if I would let em start pushin, that would give em relief. But see I didn't want em to push right there. It just do a lil bit mo' harm than good. When they get to the stage that they rally cain't he'p but push, well I knows when that stage come. And they know it. And I say, "Come on, dear, push just easy, not hard. Don't give it all you got. You understand? Just push easy." And it works simple. So simple. They do, it starts workin right there. And then they get relief from the pressure when they can push. But they're not supposed to push at some of the last stages.

Just breathe. When they get that baby's head crowned, then that's when they're supposed to push. If that shoulder is a lil wider than the head, they got another stage there that they got to put a lil pressure on. And when they get that shoulder through, then the body will just slide on out.

If you push too soon, instead of that head comin like it's supposed to you pushin behind that pelvis right there. Instead of pushin it so it would come out, it's pushing against that. As long as you push against that it's not gonna come. It takes alot a pushin to pull it up so it can come. But if you don't push too soon it'll bounce right up and start out. On its own. I know exactly when to keep em from pushin too hard. Slow em cause some of em will be in such a hurry and want to get through with it. Cause they don't want to hurt. They want to get it behind em.

The contractions can leave awhile completely. That's God's way. That's what I love about it. Give mother time to rest between the contractions. This is a beautiful point about it. They gets so sleepy just befo' that baby is really fixin to crown on us yet, mother gets so sleepy. That's the anesthesia that God give em. I know that's true. They can rest. I don't care what no doctor say or nobody else say. That is the anesthesia that God give mother. He said He wouldn't put no mo' on em than they could bear. And befo' you think you're gonna give or it's gonna kill you, He take it completely away and make you sleepy. You cain't stay awake to save yo' life. That's anesthesia from God. Man had nothin to do with that. It's true. These thirty-eight years that I've been workin it's true. God have deal it with me. I have experienced it. I have looked it over and over and over and God give it to me. That is true.

Some of em say this. "Onnie, if these pains would just hold up so I could sleep just one minute I would feel better." God take it away. I don't care if they don't hold up for that lil length of time—they sleep just that quick. Just befo' it crowns they get those hard severe contractions that they're not gonna be able to do nothing but push. Befo' they get the urge to push that's when they get sleepy for a rest. That's true. Honey, when it get right to the last minute they think, Well, I done gone as far as I can go. But God give me new strength. He will take the contractions away from em and they get so sleepy. He gives em some anesthesia between time. I've told so many people that. They looks at me and say, "Where is it you get that from?" I said, "God gives that to me and tells me to tell you that and it's true."

I had a hernia for years befo' the doctors knew what it was. He'pin that mother with those last contractions. Makin her strain through here with these arms. A hernia come mostly from strain. Strainin in the chest from here using these arms. They would be pullin on me or alot a times I would be pushin em. The mo' pressure they could put on me the better they would get relief. Not only relief but the work that they was doin would act. It would come better. It would dilate better if they had somethin to go against. I was just as tired as they were until I learned better not to bear along with em. Not to let the contraction strike me as it was strikin em. So I found other ways.

I have mothers that enjoyed the last pains so much so in the bathroom sittin on the toilet stool. When the baby could crown at any minute. It he'ps em. They get relief from their contractions to sit up on that toilet stool. That's a good place if you know that water gonna break in there without that baby comin with the water. Alot a times they come together. I said, "Why don't you go on back in there? Get back on the bed. You done dilated too much like that. Now go on back in there." "I just cain't. I got to urinate and I just cain't do it." You know the baby do press against yo' bladder and make you want to urinate. I said, "Yes, you can." "Won't you please just come on and go with me back there just one mo' time?" "I'm not gonna let you have it in the bathroom. . . . Okay, sugar, come on. Let's go."

I always stay with em when they go to the bathroom especially when the pains get pretty close together. The water might break and the baby may come right there. I coach em if the baby is crownin while they're on the toilet. It was understand to em now if you get a contraction that won't turn loose while you are on there, I want you to drop to yo' knees. Couldn't get em back to bed on account of that contraction. And I couldn't tow em back to bed.

I say, "All right. I'm gonna take you to the bathroom and if that baby start comin through the birth canal, you cannot walk back to the bed. That's breakin the baby's neck. You got to do what I say. Do you understand?" "All right, I'll do it, Onnie." She's sittin on the toilet like this. When I see that baby comin I say, "Breathe, honey, breathe. Breathe fast. I want you to drop to you' knees. I want you to come right on down and lean on the tub." I run over to the bed and pull all my paddin I had on the bed. Throw the pads on the flo'. Nice comfortable bed for the baby to come. And I get behind em. Get down right behind her in the bathroom on the flo'. I get the baby's head and get it on down and she is up on her knees like this. I say, "When I tell you to start sittin back you sit back." That's in order not to pull that cord from the placenta and the baby be too tight, you understand. So when she leans back, she go down fur enough that the baby is on the flo' on the pad and the cord had alot a slack in it. I say, "Now relax yo'self, relax." And she relax herself down. Then I run get the scissors and the sterile gauze and I tie the knot and I get the baby leavin her still hangin over the bathtub. Leavin her hanging over the bathtub. I went get the baby from the placenta and I leave the placenta with her. I run in the bedroom with the baby and wrap it good and warm and lay it there and let it stay there. Then I go back and get her. I get the placenta. Get her all washed up still on her knees over the bathtub. I get it down all on the paper. Pull all my paddin. No spots on the flo', no nothin. All right on that paddin I have all ready on the bed for her. And then I get her up and go and pad the bed right quick again cause I have another pad to put on her after the baby anyway. Put that on there and get her back on there, and she is just as happy. See how God works? I wished I had a flower for every time I did that.

There are so many women that want to have babies in that sittin position. It's not unusual. It feels good. Mother gets mo' relief. Now it might not be mo' relief for you but it will be for her. There may be another position that would suit you better. I have delivered babies on purpose on their knees like that with a chair like this here. Because that makes her comfortable. I had mine on my knees. It's whatever makes you comfortable. I will do that for a home delivery cause that's the purpose of a home delivery. That's the privilege of stayin at home. You let em do what they wanna do. You name it and I've done it. The doctors just don't do that. In a hospital you cain't move. You're so tired of layin that way and you get cramps in yo' legs and then you' knees. That's how come women holler so when they're in the hospital. Their whole body hurts. That's miserable, honey. You think it's not but that's miserable to lay up there with both of yo' legs up like this and you're layin down and you cain't move nothin but yo' head.

I let em walk until their baby get ready to come through the birth canal. You walk and sit down and you walk. Try to make mother comfortable from these contractions. Let her do mostly what she want to do. That's the good purpose of stayin at home havin a baby. If you got a good midwife or somebody that knows what she's doin and knows how to watch mother and knows how mother's comin on, she'll let mother do just exactly what she want to do. And say, "Now I'm gonna let you do yo' thing but now when it get to this point, I want you to do what I tell you to do." You tell her that between contractions. You don't tell her that when she's havin a contraction. And she'll pay strict attention. And it'll work out.

As I say, I let em do first one thing and then another. Sometimes they want to be first in the bed, first out the bed, in bed, out bed. Well I know the baby is not fixin to crown and that's good for mother and I just let her do it. Now don't get me wrong. I'm right there with her, watchin her, holding her. Right at her fingertips for her. When I get em up to walk, contractions slow down, and see usually when the contractions start they want to hurry back to bed. I say, "Don't do that. Right where yo' contractions start, a table or anything, just lean awhile until that contractions leaves. It's no use tryin to hurry back tryin to lay down cause yo' baby ain't comin yet."

I have had some of my white girls want me to let em have their baby lyin on their side and I don't like that. That wouldn't work and I just told em in a nice way that wouldn't work. That's not too safe for the baby. I cain't protect the baby's neck on the side as well as I can on yo' back or on yo' knees. If she's on her knees I say, "Now as I talk to you, you do exactly what I say. As that baby's comin through the birth canal like that, squat back until I get the baby just gradually start comin out and then yo' buttocks is close to the flo'." The birth canal is close to the flo' and then when the baby come I lay it down and get the cord out far enough and then she can pull back on her knees. Kinda come back up. It's easy and the baby's perfectly safe layin on the flo' on the pad.

I do whatever is suitable for that minute or that hour or that situation. I do it. I do it. Whether I've seen it in a book or read it or not, I do it. And it works. Alot a mothers says, "I didn't do that with my other baby." I say, "That was that baby, honey. This is this one. They are all different. What I did for you then I might not be able to do for you next time. Honey, everything it changes. And you got to have knowledge and wisdom which comes from God on high enough to change with it. When it says do this you do that and don't think about what you done last time. I gave you that hand to do that then. Now I'm givin you another hand to do this. This baby is different."

I've seen so many and there are so many different ways a baby can come into the world until I'll be lookin for a different every time. This is the beautiful part about it. When the baby comes, its face is down when its head get through the birth canal. A no'mal birth. The face is down like that on the mattress—down that way. But befo' that whole body get out—you would think that neck is breakin but it be done turned and his face is up. It's beautiful. Some babies they don't get to turn all the way over. They turn from down on the side. Their face is on the side when they come. Then you may get a case every so often that the face some-time come all the way out and the baby too befo' it turns over. You don't pull the baby. You just guide the baby's head. It's alot a times when the water and baby comes together right under the mother is maybe a puddle of water. I puts my hand under its lil face and head to keep its lil nose outa that water cause the head's gonna turn anyway. But you got to guide it. It's just a matter of guidin that body. All you got to know is how to handle it. Sometimes I see my baby with a cord around its neck. As long as I could get this hand between that neck and that cord, it's not gonna choke that baby. I've had it wrapped around his neck three times. If it's not too tight as soon as the baby all the way birthin, I can get it out right over its head.

When the baby's delivered you wait so many minutes until that baby is gettin whatcha call a blood transfusion from the placenta to the body. The heart is beatin through that cord that's attached to the baby's navel to the placenta. I usually wait calmly until you cannot feel that heart beatin through that cord. You catch it like this and when you stop feelin it through there you tie it and cut it loose and I usually tell my babies, "Now, darlin, you're on yo' own." You ain't on yo' mother no mo' from that minute on. That's what my sterile scissors are for. That's all I have. That's it. You tie two knots befo' you get the placenta from the mother. You tie one bout an inch from the baby's stomach and then about two inches from that tie up the cord. Then you cut between there to get the baby from the placenta. I don't have to clean the baby up first. I get mother comfortable first because to get the baby comfortable is to get it out loose from the afterbirth and wrap it up so it could get warm cause he'll go back to sleep if he done gotten warm.

Then I get the placenta from the mother. Mother usually give slight contractions, especially the second baby. You want her to have a certain po'tion of afterpains because that he'ps clean the uterus out. Usually mothers don't have afterpains with their first babies. Now and then. And if they do, it's just minor enough to clean the uterus out. The afterpains usually start after the second baby. And then after the third baby, they're a lil bit harder than after the second baby. And the fo'th baby it's a lil bit mo'. I don't know why that is. God aimed for us to know just so much and that's it. Because He's gonna take care of that part anyhow. Now it could be that it takes mo' pains to clean the uterus each time or to make their uterus get back in its place. You see what I mean? Ain't God beautiful? Make me wanna scream on how it all works. There's a purpose for it. There's a call. There's a reason for all that. It's amazin.

Mother get a slight contraction and she kinda press it out slightly and the placenta come on. Alot a times it's not turnin loose from the uterus as yet so we just wait a lil while. I wrap mother up and go back and tend my baby then go back to mother and the placenta's ready then to discard itself. That's the afterbirth. Take it out and open it wide and look to see if any pieces are left. Most of mine I examine real good to see if there are any lost pieces cause it's like poison, you know. If there are any left, you don't have to get em out, you watch for em to pass through the flow. If it doesn't pass then they'd have to go to the doctor or the hospital to get what you call a curettage. I had only one patient to have that happen. If no pieces are left you roll it back up just like it was, then wrap it in paper.

They required me to get rid of the placenta, to burn it. Fact is, we was taught in our class to burn it. But then through wisdom and knowledge I learned better cause it takes you a long time to burn those things. It all depends on how much wood you have. It takes a long time befo' it gets hot enough to start burnin it. It draws up in a knot and get just as tight. Draw up in a knot and get just as tight and it takes alot a fire coal wood. Done burnt down to hard coal to start that placenta to burnin. It makes a big hard ball when it gets hot and it stays in that big hard ball a long time if you don't have wood. You keep it on a good base fire to get it to started to burn.

I never will fo'get, years ago when I delivered out on the south part of town one night, myself and another lady that was workin with me. That was when I first started workin. They wasn't as particular about fire durin that times. So right off the street kinda in the back, we had this big fire out there in the backyard. Must've been about two or three o'clock in the morning. We were burnin all the trash. We use paper now with a cloth on it and we burn all that. So we were burnin all a that and had a big fire out there and the police stopped by. They come and say, "What's happenin? What's the big idea for such a big fire this time a the mornin?" "Just cleanin up after from deliverin a baby. You like to give me a hand?" And they walked on back. "No thank you. You're doin a good job at it." Sho did.

I was so glad when they got to the stage that I didn't have to burn it. If they have a shovel and a backyard, the husband dig a long deep hole and put it in and bury it. Then right in the city where they didn't have no place to even bury it, when they was livin in the projects, they didn't even have places that they could bury it. I wrapped em up in plastic and carried em home. You want to see me count the many that are buried in my backyard? There's a million of em buried in my backyard. A million, million placentas. A million placentas is buried in my backyard. I have peach trees and whatnot trees back there. I buried alot of placentas around that peach tree. I had the biggest peaches you ever did see. Mo' than I could sto' off that one lil tree but Hurricane Frederick messed it up. After that, if I delivers like the morning about daylight or befo', if the garbage man is comin on we put it in the garbage can if he's coming that same time. Or if it was like late in the evenin and the garbage men was comin on tomorrow mornin, we put it in the garbage. But you couldn't keep it there for a couple of days especially in the summertime.

When I first started to work as a midwife, alot a em, especially white patients, didn't want you to do the silver nitrate. We put drops in the baby's eyes, the silver nitrate. The babies would look like somebody give em a black eye the next morning after putting the silver nitrate in. Cause wherever the silver nitrate gets on that white skin it's just as black around his lil eye. My supervisor said, "Well if they don't want you to put it in don't put it in." Then the law took a hold to it. It's a law now that we have to do it. So one morning befo' day I woke up, somethin told me in my sleep. Next time you have yo' white babies, get the blue-sealed Vaseline and rub around their lil eyes real good befo' you put the silver nitrate in. When it hit it doesn't hit the skin. It hit that Vaseline. No mo' black eyes. That's been years ago. I carried that back to the bo'd a health and they all did it from there.

AUDRE LORDE
(1934–1992)

Audre Lorde's parents came to New York City from Grenada in 1924. Their first child was born in the month that the stock market crashed. Audre, their third daughter, felt separate from the older two—not like an only child but "an only planet, or some isolated world in a hostile, or at best, unfriendly, firmament. The fact that I was clothed, sheltered, and fed better than many other children in Harlem in those Depression years was not a fact that impressed itself too often upon my child's consciousness."

A poet and professor of English at Hunter College of the City University of New York who proudly identified herself as a black lesbian feminist, Audre Lorde published, in addition to her many volumes of poetry, *The Cancer Journals* (1980), a volume of essays based on her experience of breast cancer and mastectomy. Her autobiography, *Zami: A New Spelling of My Name* (1982), takes its title from a Caribbean word for women who work together as friends and lovers.

For another memoir about West Indians in New York, see Itabari Njeri, *Every Goodbye Ain't Gone.* For another account of Depression-era Harlem, compare Billie Holiday, *Lady Sings the Blues.* For another account of childhood discomfiture, compare Maxine Hong Kingston, *The Woman Warrior.*

FROM *Zami: A New Spelling of My Name*

After the children came, my father went to real-estate school, and began to manage small rooming-houses in Harlem. When he came home from the office in the evening, he had one quick glass of brandy, standing in the kitchen, after we greeted him and before he took off his coat and hat. Then my mother and he would immediately retire into the bedroom where we would hear them discussing the day's events from behind closed doors, even if my mother had only left their office a few hours before.

If any of us children had transgressed against the rule, this was the time when we truly quaked in our orthopedic shoes, for we knew our fate was being discussed and the terms of punishment sealed behind those doors. When they opened, a mutual and irrefutable judgment would be delivered. If they spoke of anything important when we were around, Mother and Daddy immediately lapsed into patois.

Since my parents shared all making of policy and decision, in my child's eye, my mother must have been *other* than woman. Again, she was certainly not man. (The three of us children would not have tolerated that deprivation of womanliness for long at all; we'd have probably packed up our *kra* and gone back before the eighth day—an option open to all African child-souls who bumble into the wrong milieu.)

My mother was different from other women, and sometimes it gave me a sense of pleasure and specialness that was a positive aspect of feeling set apart. But sometimes it gave me pain and I fancied it the reason for so many of my childhood sorrows. *If my mother were like everybody else's maybe they would like me better.* But most often, her difference was like the season or a cold day or a steamy night in June. It just *was*, with no explanation or evocation necessary.

My mother and her two sisters were large and graceful women whose ample bodies seemed to underline the air of determination with which they moved through their lives in the strange world of Harlem and america. To me, my mother's physical substance and the presence and self-possession with which she carried herself were a large part of what made her *different*. Her public air of in-charge competence was quiet and effective. On the street people deferred to my mother over questions of taste, economy, opinion, quality, not to mention who had the right to the first available seat on the bus. I saw my mother fix her blue-grey-brown eyes upon a man scrambling for a seat on the Lenox Avenue bus, only to have him falter midway, grin abashedly, and, as if in the same movement, offer it to the old woman standing on the other side of him. I became aware, early on, that sometimes people would change their actions because of some opinion my mother never uttered, or even particularly cared about.

My mother was a very private woman, and actually quite shy, but with a very imposing, no-nonsense exterior. Full-bosomed, proud, and of no mean size, she would launch herself down the street like a ship under full sail, usually pulling me stumbling behind her. Not too many hardy souls dared cross her prow too closely.

Total strangers would turn to her in the meat market and ask what she thought about a cut of meat as to its freshness and appeal and suitability for such and such, and the butcher, impatient, would nonetheless wait for her to deliver her opinion, obviously quite a little put out but still deferential. Strangers counted upon my mother and I never knew why, but as a child it made me think she had a great deal more power than in fact she really had. My mother was invested in this image of herself also, and took pains, I realize now, to hide from us as children the many instances of her powerlessness. Being Black and foreign and female in New York City in the twenties and thirties was not simple, particularly when she was quite light enough to pass for white, but her children weren't.

In 1936–1938, 125th Street between Lenox and Eighth Avenues, later to become the shopping mecca of Black Harlem, was still a racially mixed area, with control and patronage largely in the hands of white shopkeepers. There were stores into which Black people were not welcomed, and no Black salespersons worked in the shops at all. Where our money was taken, it was taken with reluctance; and often too much was asked. (It was these conditions which young Adam Clayton Powell, Jr., addressed in his boycott and picketing of Blumstein's and Weissbecker's market in 1939 in an attempt, successful, to bring Black employment to 125th Street.) Tensions on the street were high, as they always are in racially mixed zones of transition. As a very little girl, I remember shrinking from a particular sound, a hoarsely sharp, gutteral rasp, because it often meant a nasty glob of grey spittle upon my coat or shoe an instant later. My mother wiped it off with the little pieces of newspaper she always carried in her purse. Sometimes she fussed about low-class people who had no better sense nor manners than to spit into the wind no matter where they went, impressing upon me that this humiliation was totally random. It never occurred to me to doubt her.

It was not until years later once in conversation I said to her: "Have you noticed people don't spit into the wind so much the way they used to?" And the look on my mother's face told me that I had blundered into one of those secret places of pain that must never be spoken of again. But it was so typical of my mother when I was young that if she couldn't stop white people from spitting on her children because they were Black, she would insist it was something else. It was so often her approach to the world; to change reality. If you can't change reality, change your perceptions of it.

Both of my parents gave us to believe that they had the whole world in the palms of their hands for the most part, and if we three girls acted correctly—meaning working hard and doing as we were told—we could have the whole world in the palms of our hands also. It was a very confusing way to grow up, enhanced by the insularity of our family. Whatever went wrong in our lives was because our parents had decided that was best. Whatever went right was because our parents had decided that was the way it was going to be. Any doubts as to the reality of that situation were rapidly and summarily put down as small but intolerable rebellions against divine authority.

All our storybooks were about people who were very different from us.

They were blond and white and lived in houses with trees around and had dogs named Spot. I didn't know people like that any more than I knew people like Cinderella who lived in castles. Nobody wrote stories about us, but still people always asked my mother for directions in a crowd.

It was this that made me decide as a child we must be rich, even when my mother did not have enough money to buy gloves for her chilblained hands, nor a proper winter coat. She would finish washing clothes and dress me hurriedly for the winter walk to pick up my sisters at school for lunch. By the time we got to St. Mark's School, seven blocks away, her beautiful long hands would be covered with ugly red splotches and welts. Later, I remember my mother rubbing her hands gingerly under cold water, and wringing them in pain. But when I asked, she brushed me off by telling me this was what they did for it at "home," and I still believed her when she said she hated to wear gloves.

At night, my father came home late from the office, or from a political meeting. After dinner, the three of us girls did our homework sitting around the kitchen table. Then my two sisters went off down the hall to their beds. My mother put down the cot for me in the front bedroom, and supervised my getting ready for bed.

She turned off all the electric lights, and I could see her from my bed, two rooms away, sitting at the same kitchen table, reading the *Daily News* by a kerosene lamp, and waiting for my father. She always said it was because the kerosene lamp reminded her of "home." When I was grown I realized she was trying to save a few pennies of electricity before my father came in and turned on the lights with "Lin, why you sitting in the dark so?" Sometimes I'd go to sleep with the soft chunk-a-ta-chink of her foot-pedal-powered Singer Sewing Machine, stitching up sheets and pillow-cases from unbleached muslin gotten on sale "under the bridge."

I only saw my mother crying twice when I was little. Once was when I was three, and sat on the step of her dental chair at the City Dental Clinic on 23rd Street, while a student dentist pulled out all the teeth on one side of her upper jaw. It was in a huge room full of dental chairs with other groaning people in them, and white-jacketed young men bending over open mouths. The sound of the many dental drills and instruments made the place sound like a street-corner excavation site.

Afterwards, my mother sat outside on a long wooden bench. I saw her lean her head against the back, her eyes closed. She did not respond to my pats and tugs at her coat. Climbing up upon the seat, I peered into my mother's face to see why she should be sleeping in the middle of the day. From under her closed eyelids, drops of tears were squeezing out and running down her cheek toward her ear. I touched the little drops of water on her high cheekbone in horror and amazement. The world was turning over. My mother was crying.

The other time I saw my mother cry was a few years later, one night, when I was supposed to be asleep in their bedroom. The door to the parlor was ajar, and I could see through the crack into the next room. I woke to hear my parents' voices in english. My father had just come home, and with liquor on his breath.

"I hoped I'd never live to see the day when you, Bee, stand up in some saloon and it's drink you drinking with some clubhouse woman."

"But Lin, what are you talking? It's not that way a-tall, you know. In politics you must be friendly-friendly so. It doesn't mean a thing."

"And if you were to go before I did, I would never so much as look upon another man, and I would expect you to do the same."

My mother's voice was strangely muffled by her tears.

These were the years leading up to the Second World War, when Depression took such a terrible toll, and of Black people in particular.

Even though we children could be beaten for losing a penny coming home from the store, my mother fancied a piece of her role as lady bountiful, a role she would accuse me bitterly of playing years later in my life whenever I gave something to a friend. But one of my earlier memories of World War II was just before the beginning, with my mother splitting a one-pound tin of coffee between two old family friends who had come on an infrequent visit.

Although she always insisted that she had nothing to do with politics or government affairs, from somewhere my mother had heard the winds of war, and despite our poverty had set about consistently hoarding sugar and coffee in her secret closet under the sink. Long before Pearl Harbor, I recall opening each cloth five-pound sack of sugar which we purchased at the market and pouring a third of it into a scrubbed tin to store away under the sink, secure from mice. The same thing happened with coffee. We would buy Bokar Coffee at the A&P and have it ground and poured into bags, and then divide the bag between the coffee tin on the back of the stove, and the hidden ones under the sink. Not many people came to our house, ever, but no one left without at least a cupful of sugar or coffee during the war, when coffee and sugar were heavily rationed.

Meat and butter could not be hoarded, and throughout the early war, my mother's absolute refusal to accept butter substitutes (only "other people" used margarine, those same "other people" who fed their children peanut butter sandwiches for lunch, used sandwich spread instead of mayonnaise and ate pork chops and watermelon) had us on line in front of supermarkets all over the city on bitterly cold Saturday mornings, waiting for the store to open so we each could get first crack at buying our allotted quarter-pound of unrationed butter. Throughout the war, Mother kept a mental list of all the supermarkets reachable by one bus, frequently taking only me because I could ride free. She also noted which were friendly and which were not, and long after the war ended there were meat markets and stores we never shopped in because someone in them had crossed my mother during the war over some precious scarce commodity, and my mother never forgot and rarely forgave.

When I was five years old and still legally blind, I started school in a sight-conservation class in the local public school on 135th Street and Lenox Avenue. On the corner was a blue wooden booth where white women gave away free milk to Black mothers with children. I used to long for some Hearst Free Milk Fund milk, in those cute little bottles with their red and white tops, but my mother never allowed me to have any, because she said it was charity, which was bad and demeaning, and besides the milk was warm and might make me sick.

The school was right across the avenue from the catholic school where my two older sisters went, and this public school had been used as a threat against them for as long as I could remember. If they didn't behave and get good marks in schoolwork and deportment, they could be "transferred." A "transfer" carried the same dire implications as "deportation" came to imply decades later.

Of course everybody knew that public school kids did nothing but "fight," and you could get "beaten up" every day after school, instead of being marched out of the schoolhouse door in two neat rows like little robots, silent but safe and unattacked, to the corner where the mothers waited.

But the catholic school had no kindergarten, and certainly not one for blind children.

Despite my nearsightedness, or maybe because of it, I learned to read at the same time I learned to talk, which was only about a year or so before I started school. Perhaps *learn* isn't the right word to use for my beginning to talk, because to this day I don't know if I didn't talk earlier because I didn't know how, or if I didn't talk because I had nothing to say that I would be allowed to say without punishment. Self-preservation starts very early in West Indian families.

I learned how to read from Mrs. Augusta Baker, the children's librarian at the old 135th Street branch library, which has just recently been torn down to make way for a new library building to house the Schomburg Collection on African-American History and Culture. If that was the only good deed that lady ever did in her life, may she rest in peace. Because that deed saved my life, if not sooner, then later, when sometimes the only thing I had to hold on to was knowing I could read, and that that could get me through.

My mother was pinching my ear off one bright afternoon, while I lay spreadeagled on the floor of the Children's Room like a furious little brown toad, screaming bloody murder and embarrassing my mother to death. I know it must have been spring or early fall, because without the protection of a heavy coat, I can still feel the stinging soreness in the flesh of my upper arm. There, where my mother's sharp fingers had already tried to pinch me into silence. To escape those inexorable fingers I had hurled myself to the floor, roaring with pain as I could see them advancing toward my ears again. We were waiting to pick up my two older sisters from story hour, held upstairs on another floor of the dry-smelling quiet library. My shrieks pierced the reverential stillness.

Suddenly, I looked up, and there was a library lady standing over me. My mother's hands had dropped to her sides. From the floor where I was lying, Mrs. Baker seemed like yet another mile-high woman about to do me in. She had immense, light, hooded eyes and a very quiet voice that said, not damnation for my noise, but "Would you like to hear a story, little girl?"

Part of my fury was because I had not been allowed to go to that secret feast called story hour since I was too young, and now here was this strange lady offering me my own story.

I didn't dare to look at my mother, half-afraid she might say no, I was too bad for stories. Still bewildered by this sudden change of events, I climbed up upon the stool which Mrs. Baker pulled over for me, and gave her my full attention. This was a new experience for me and I was insatiably curious.

Mrs. Baker read me *Madeline*, and *Horton Hatches the Egg*, both of which rhymed and had huge lovely pictures which I could see from behind my newly acquired eyeglasses, fastened around the back of my rambunctious head by a black elastic band running from earpiece to earpiece. She also read me another storybook about a bear named Herbert who ate up an entire family, one by one, starting with the parents. By the time she had finished that one, I was sold on reading for the rest of my life.

I took the books from Mrs. Baker's hands after she was finished reading, and traced the large black letters with my fingers, while I peered again at the beautiful bright colors of the pictures. Right then I decided I was going to find out how to do that myself. I pointed to the black marks which I could now distinguish as separate letters, different from my sisters' more grown-up books, whose smaller print made the pages only one grey blur for me. I said, quite loudly, for whoever was listening to hear, "I want to read."

My mother's surprised relief outweighed whatever annoyance she was still feeling at what she called my whelpish carryings-on. From the background where she had been hovering while Mrs. Baker read, my mother moved forward quickly, mollified and impressed. I had spoken. She scooped me up from the low stool, and to my surprise, kissed me, right in front of everybody in the library, including Mrs. Baker.

This was an unprecedented and unusual display of affection in public, the cause of which I did not comprehend. But it was a warm and happy feeling. For once, obviously, I had done something right.

My mother set me back upon the stool and turned to Mrs. Baker, smiling.

"Will wonders never cease to perform!" Her excitement startled me back into cautious silence.

Not only had I been sitting still for longer than my mother would have thought possible, and sitting quietly. I had also spoken rather than screamed, something that my mother, after four years and a lot of worry, had despaired that I would ever do. Even one intelligible word was a very rare event for me. And although the doctors at the clinic had clipped the little membrane under my tongue so I was no longer tongue-tied, and had assured my mother that I was not retarded, she still had her terrors and her doubts. She was genuinely happy for any possible alternative to what she was afraid might be a dumb child. The ear-pinching was forgotten. My mother accepted the alphabet and picture books Mrs. Baker gave her for me, and I was on my way.

I sat at the kitchen table with my mother, tracing letters and calling their names. Soon she taught me how to say the alphabet forwards and backwards as it was done in Grenada. Although she had never gone beyond the seventh grade, she had been put in charge of teaching the first grade children their letters during her last year at Mr. Taylor's School in Grenville. She told me stories about his strictness as she taught me how to print my name.

I did not like the tail of the Y hanging down below the line in Audrey, and would always forget to put it on, which used to disturb my mother greatly. I used to love the evenness of AUDRELORDE at four years of age, but I remembered to put on the Y because it pleased my mother, and because, as she always insisted to me, that was the way it had to be because that was the way it was. No deviation was allowed from her interpretations of correct.

So by the time I arrived at the sight-conservation kindergarten, braided, scrubbed, and bespectacled, I was able to read large-print books and write my name with a regular pencil. Then came my first rude awakening about school. Ability had nothing to do with expectation.

There were only seven or eight of us little Black children in a big classroom, all with various serious deficiencies of sight. Some of us were cross-eyed, some of us were nearsighted, and one little girl had a patch over one of her eyes.

We were given special short wide notebooks to write in, with very widely spaced lines on yellow paper. They looked like my sister's music notebooks. We were also given thick black crayons to write with. Now you don't grow up fat, Black, nearly blind, and ambidextrous in a West Indian household, particularly my parents' household, and survive without being or becoming fairly rigid fairly fast. And having been roundly spanked on several occasions for having made that mistake at home, I knew quite well that crayons were not what you wrote with, and music books were definitely not what you wrote in.

I raised my hand. When the teacher asked me what I wanted, I asked for some regular paper to write on and a pencil. That was my undoing. "We don't have any pencils here," I was told.

Our first task was to copy down the first letter of our names in those notebooks with our black crayons. Our teacher went around the room and wrote the required letter into each one of our notebooks. When she came around to me, she printed a large A in the upper left corner of the first page of my notebook, and handed me the crayon.

"I can't," I said, knowing full well that what you do with black crayons is scribble on the wall and get your backass beaten, or color around the edges of pictures, but not write. To write, you needed a pencil. "I can't!" I said, terrified, and started to cry.

"Imagine that, a big girl like you. Such a shame, I'll have to tell your mother that you won't even try. And such a big girl like you!"

And it was true. Although young, I was the biggest child by far in the whole class, a fact that had not escaped the attention of the little boy who sat behind me, and who was already whispering "fatty, fatty!" whenever the teacher's back was turned.

"Now just try, dear. I'm sure you can try to print your A. Mother will be so pleased to see that at least you tried." She patted my stiff braids and turned to the next desk.

Well, of course, she had said the magic words, because I would have walked over rice on my knees to please Mother. I took her nasty old soft smudgy crayon and pretended that it was a nice neat pencil with a fine point, elegantly sharpened that morning outside the bathroom door by my father, with the little penknife that he always carried around in his bathrobe pocket.

I bent my head down close to the desk that smelled like old spittle-and-rubber erasers, and on that ridiculous yellow paper with those laughably wide spaces I printed my best AUDRE. I had never been too good at keeping between straight lines no matter what their width, so it slanted down across the page something like this: A

U

D

R

E

The notebooks were short and there was no more room for anything else on that page. So I turned the page over, and wrote again, earnestly and laboriously, biting my lip, L

O

R

D

E

half-showing off, half-eager to please.

By this time, Miss Teacher had returned to the front of the room.

"Now when you're finished drawing your letter, children," she said, "Just raise your hand high." And her voice smiled a big smile. It is surprising to me that I can still hear her voice but I can't see her face, and I don't know whether she was Black or white. I can remember the way she smelled, but not the color of her hand upon my desk.

Well, when I heard that, my hand flew up in the air, wagging frantically. There was one thing my sisters had warned me about school in great detail: you must never talk in school unless you raised your hand. So I raised my hand, anxious to be recognized. I could imagine what teacher would say to my mother when she came to fetch me home at noon. My mother would know that her warning to me to "be good" had in truth been heeded.

Miss Teacher came down the aisle and stood beside my desk, looking down at my book. All of a sudden the air around her hand beside my notebook grew very still and frightening.

"Well I never!" Her voice was sharp. "I thought I told you to draw this letter? You don't even want to try and do as you are told. Now I want you to turn that page over and draw your letter like everyone . . ." and turning to the next page, she saw my second name sprawled down across the page.

There was a moment of icy silence, and I knew I had done something terribly wrong. But this time, I had no idea what it could be that would get her so angry, certainly not being proud of writing my name.

She broke the silence with a wicked edge to her voice. "I see," she said. "I see we have a young lady who does not want to do as she is told. We will have to tell her mother about that." And the rest of the class snickered, as the teacher tore the page out of my notebook.

"Now I am going to give you one more chance," she said, as she printed another fierce A at the head of the new page. "Now you copy that letter exactly the way it is, and the rest of the class will have to wait for you." She placed the crayon squarely back into my fingers.

By this time I had no idea at all what this lady wanted from me, and so I cried and cried for the rest of the morning until my mother came to fetch me home at noon. I cried on the street while we stopped to pick up my sisters, and for most of the way home, until my mother threatened to box my ears for me if I didn't stop embarrassing her on the street.

That afternoon, after Phyllis and Helen were back in school, and I was helping her dust, I told my mother how they had given me crayons to write with and how the teacher didn't want me to write my name. When my father came home that evening, the two of them went into counsel. It was decided that my mother would speak to the teacher the next morning when she brought me to school, in order to find out what I had done wrong. This decision was passed on to me, ominously, because of course I must have done something wrong to have made Miss Teacher so angry with me.

The next morning at school, the teacher told my mother that she did not think that I was ready yet for kindergarten, because I couldn't follow directions, and I wouldn't do as I was told.

My mother knew very well I could follow directions, because she herself had spent a good deal of effort and arm-power making it very painful for me whenever I did not follow directions. And she also believed that a large part of the function of school was to make me learn how to do what I was told to do. In her private opinion, if this school could not do that, then it was not much of a school and she was going to find a school that could. In other words, my mother had made up her mind that school was where I belonged.

That same morning, she took me off across the street to the catholic school, where she persuaded the nuns to put me into the first grade, since I could read already, and write my name on regular paper with a real pencil. If I sat in the first row I could see the blackboard. My mother also told the nuns that unlike my two sisters, who were models of deportment, I was very unruly, and that they should spank me whenever I needed it. Mother Josepha, the principal, agreed, and I started school.

My first grade teacher was named Sister Mary of Perpetual Help, and she was a disciplinarian of the first order, right after my mother's own heart. A week after I started school she sent a note home to my mother asking her not to dress me in so many layers of clothing because then I couldn't feel the strap on my behind when I was punished.

Sister Mary of Perpetual Help ran the first grade with an iron hand in the shape of a cross. She couldn't have been more than eighteen. She was big, and blond, I think, since we never got to see the nuns' hair in those days. But her eyebrows were blond, and she was supposed to be totally dedicated, like all the other Sisters of the Blessed Sacrament, to caring for the Colored and Indian children of america. Caring for was not always caring about. And it always felt like Sister MPH hated either teaching or little children.

She had divided up the class into two groups, the Fairies and the Brownies. In this day of heightened sensitivity to racism and color usage, I don't have to tell you which were the good students and which were the baddies. I always wound up in the Brownies, because either I talked too much, or I broke my glasses, or I perpetrated some other awful infraction of the endless rules of good behavior.

But for two glorious times that year, I made it into the Fairies for brief periods of time. One was put into the Brownies if one misbehaved, or couldn't learn to read. I had learned to read already, but I couldn't tell my numbers. Whenever Sister MPH would call a few of us up to the front of the room for our reading lesson, she would say, "All right, children, now turn to page six in your readers." or, "Turn to page nineteen, please, and begin at the top of the page."

Well, I didn't know what page to turn to, and I was ashamed of not being able to read my numbers, so when my turn came to read I couldn't, because I didn't have the right place. After the prompting of a few words, she would go on to the next reader, and soon I wound up in the Brownies.

This was around the second month of school, in October. My new seatmate was Alvin, and he was the worst boy in the whole class. His clothes were dirty and he smelled unwashed, and rumor had it he had once called Sister MPH a bad name, but that couldn't have been possible because he would have been suspended permanently from school.

Alvin used to browbeat me into lending him my pencil to draw endless pictures of airplanes dropping huge penile bombs. He would always promise to give me the pictures when he was finished. But of course, whenever he was finished, he would decide that the picture was too good for a girl, so he would have to keep it, and make me another. Yet I never stopped hoping for one of them, because he drew airplanes very well.

He also would scratch his head and shake out the dandruff onto our joint spelling book or reader, and then tell me the flakes of dandruff were dead lice. I believed him in this, also, and was constantly terrified of catching cooties. But Alvin and I worked out our own system together for reading. He couldn't read, but he knew all his numbers, and I could read words, but I couldn't find the right page.

The Brownies were never called up to the front of the room; we had to read in anonymity from our double seats, where we scrunched over at the edges, ordinarily, to leave room in the middle for our two guardian angels to sit. But whenever we had to share a book our guardian angels had to jump around us and sit on the outside edge of our seats. Therefore, Alvin would show me the right pages to turn to when Sister called them out, and I would whisper the right words to him whenever it came his turn to read. Inside of a week after we devised this scheme of things, we had gotten out of the Brownies together. Since we shared a reader, we always went up together to read with the Fairies, so we had a really good thing going there for a while.

But Alvin began to get sick around Thanksgiving, and was absent a lot, and he didn't come back to school at all after Christmas. I used to miss his dive-bomber pictures, but most of all I missed his page numbers. After a few times of being called up by myself and not being able to read, I landed back in the Brownies again.

Years later I found out that Alvin had died of tuberculosis over Christmas, and that was why we all had been X-rayed in the auditorium after Mass on the first day back to school from Christmas vacation.

I spent a few more weeks in the Brownies with my mouth almost shut during reading lesson, unless the day's story fell on page eight, or ten, or twenty, which were the three numbers I knew.

Then, over one weekend, we had our first writing assignment. We were to look in our parents' newspaper and cut out words we knew the meaning of, and make them into simple sentences. We could only use one "the." It felt like an easy task, since I was already reading the comics by this time.

On Sunday morning after church, when I usually did my homework, I noticed an ad for White Rose Salada Tea on the back of the *New York Times Magazine* which my father was reading at the time. It had the most gorgeous white rose on a red background, and I decided I must have that rose for my picture—our sentences were to be illustrated. I searched through the paper until I found an "I," and then a "like," which I dutifully clipped out along with my rose, and the words "White," "Rose," "Salada," and "Tea." I knew the brand-name well because it was my mother's favorite tea.

On Monday morning, we all stood our sentence papers up on the chalk-channels, leaning them against the blackboards. And there among the twenty odd "The boy ran," "it was cold," was "I like White Rose Salada Tea" and my beautiful white rose on a red background.

That was too much coming from a Brownie. Sister Mary of PH frowned.

"This was to be our own work, children," she said. "Who helped you with your sentence, Audre?" I told her I had done it alone.

"Our guardian angels weep when we don't tell the truth, Audre. I want a note from your mother tomorrow telling me that you are sorry for lying to the baby Jesus."

I told the story at home, and the next day I brought a note from my father saying that the sentence had indeed been my own work. Triumphantly, I gathered up my books and moved back over to the Fairies.

The thing that I remember best about being in the first grade was how uncomfortable it was, always having to leave room for my guardian angel on those tiny seats, and moving back and forth across the room from Brownies to Fairies and back again.

This time I stayed in the Fairies for a long time, because I finally started to recognize my numbers. I stayed there until the day I broke my glasses. I had taken them off to clean them in the bathroom and they slipped out of my hand. I was never to do that, and so I was in disgrace. My eyeglasses came from the eye clinic of the medical center, and it took three days to get a new pair made. We could not afford to buy more than one pair at a time, nor did it occur to my parents that such an extravagance might be necessary. I was almost sightless without them, but my punishment for having broken them was that I had to go to school anyway, even though I could see nothing. My sisters delivered me to my classroom with a note from my mother saying I had broken my glasses despite the fact they were tied to me by the strip of elastic.

I was never supposed to take my glasses off except just before getting into bed, but I was endlessly curious about these magical circles of glass that were rapidly becoming a part of me, transforming my universe, and remaining movable. I was always trying to examine them with my naked, nearsighted eyes, usually dropping them in the process.

Since I could not see at all to do any work from the blackboard, Sister Mary of PH made me sit in the back of the room on the window seat with a dunce cap on. She had the rest of the class offer up a prayer for my poor mother who had such a naughty girl who broke her glasses and caused her parents such needless extra expense to replace them. She also had them offer up a special prayer for me to stop being such a wicked-hearted child.

I amused myself by counting the rainbows of color that danced like a halo around the lamp on Sister Mary of PH's desk, watching the starburst patterns of light that the incandescent light bulb became without my glasses. But I missed them, and not being able to see. I never once gave a thought to the days when I believed that bulbs were starburst patterns of color, because that was what all light looked like to me.

It must have been close to summer by this time. As I sat with the dunce cap on, I can remember the sun pouring through the classroom window hot upon my back, as the rest of the class dutifully entoned their Hail Marys for my soul, and I played secret games with the distorted rainbows of light, until Sister noticed and made me stop blinking my eyes so fast.

·   ·   ·

When I was around the age of four or five, I would have given anything I had in the world except my mother, in order to have had a friend or a little sister. She would be someone I could talk to and play with, some-one close enough in age to me that I would not have to be afraid of her, nor she of me. We would share our secrets with each other.

Even though I had two older sisters, I grew up feeling like an only child, since they were quite close to each other in age, and quite far away from me. Actually, I grew up feeling like an only planet, or some isolated world in a hostile, or at best, unfriendly, firmament. The fact that I was clothed, sheltered, and fed better than many other children in Harlem in those Depression years was not a fact that impressed itself too often upon my child's consciousness.

Most of my childhood fantasies revolved around how I might acquire this little female person for my companion. I concentrated upon magical means, having gathered early on that my family had no intention of satisfying this particular need of mine. The Lorde family was not going to expand any more.

The idea of having children was a pretty scary one, anyway, full of secret indiscretions peeked at darkly through the corner of an eye, as my mother and my aunts did whenever they passed a woman on the street who had one of those big, pushed-out-in-front, blouses that always in-trigued me so. I wondered what great wrong these women had done, that this big blouse was a badge of, obvious as the dunce cap I sometimes had to wear in the corner at school.

Adoption was also out of the question. You could get a kitten from the corner grocery store man, but not a sister. Like ocean cruises and board-ing schools and upper berths in trains, it was not for us. Rich people, like Mr. Rochester in the movie *Jane Eyre,* lonely in their great tree-lined estates, adopted children, but not us.

Being the youngest in a West Indian family had many privileges but no rights. And since my mother was determined not to "spoil" me, even those privileges were largely illusory. I knew, therefore, that if my family were to acquire another little person voluntarily, that little person would most probably be a boy, and would most decidedly belong to my mother, and not to me.

I really believed, however, that my magical endeavors, done often enough, in the right way, and in the right places, letter-perfect and with a clean soul, would finally bring me a little sister. And I did mean little. I frequently imagined my little sister and I having fascinating conversations together while she sat cradled in the cupped palm of my hand. There she was, curled up and carefully shielded from the inquisitive eyes of the rest of the world, and my family in particular.

When I was three and a half and had gotten my first eyeglasses, I stopped tripping over my feet. But I still walked with my head down, all the time, counting the lines on the squares in the pavement of every street which I traveled, hanging onto the hand of my mother or one of my sisters. I had decided that if I could step on all the horizontal lines for one day, my little person would appear like a dream made real, waiting for me in my bed by the time I got home. But I always messed up, or skipped one, or someone pulled my arm at a crucial moment. And she never appeared.

Sometimes on Saturdays in winter, my mother made the three of us a little clay out of flour and water and Diamond Crystal Shaker Salt. I always fashioned tiny little figures out of my share of the mixture. I would beg or swipe a little vanilla extract from my mother's shelf in the kitchen, where she kept her wonderful spices and herbs and extracts, and mix that with the clay. Sometimes I dabbed the figures on either side of the head behind the ears as I had seen my mother do with her glycerine and rosewater when she got dressed to go out.

I loved the way the rich, dark brown vanilla scented the flour-clay; it reminded me of my mother's hands when she made peanut brittle and eggnog at holidays. But most of all, I loved the live color it would bring to the pasty-white clay.

I knew for sure that real live people came in many different shades of beige and brown and cream and reddish tan, but nobody alive ever came in that pasty-white shade of flour and salt and water, even if they were called white. So the vanilla was essential if my little person was to be real. But the coloring didn't help either. No matter how many intricate rituals and incantations and spells I performed, no matter how many Hail Marys and Our Fathers I said, no matter what I promised god in return, the vanilla-tinted clay would slowly shrivel up and harden, turn gradually brittle and sour, and then crumble into a grainy flour dust. No matter how hard I prayed or schemed, the figures would never come alive. They never turned around in the cupped palm of my hand, to smile up at me and say "Hi."

I found my first playmate when I was around four years old. It lasted for about ten minutes.

It was a high winter noontime. My mother had bundled me up in my thick one-piece woolen snowsuit and cap and bulky scarf. Once she had inserted me into all this arctic gear, pulled rubber galoshes up over my shoes and wrapped yet another thick scarf around the whole as if to keep the mass intact, she planted me out upon the stoop of the apartment building while she dressed herself hurriedly. Although my mother never liked to have me out of her sight for any period of time, she did this to keep me from catching my death of cold from becoming overheated and then going outdoors.

After many weighty warnings to me not to move from that spot, dire descriptions of what would happen to me if I did, and how I was to yell if any strangers spoke to me, my mother disappeared down the few feet of hallway back to our apartment to get her coat and hat, and to check all the windows of the house to make sure that they were locked.

I loved these few minutes of freedom, and treasured them secretly. They were the only times I ever got to be outside without my mother urging me along on my short stubby little legs that could never run fast enough to keep up with her purposeful strides. I sat quietly where she had put me on the slated top of the stone banisters of the stoop. My arms stuck out a little from my sides over the bulk of my clothing, my feet were heavy and awkward with sturdy shoes and galoshes, and my neck was stiffly encased in the woolen cap and wrapped scarf.

The sun shone with a winter milkiness onto the sidewalks across the street, and onto the few banks of dirty soot-covered snow that lined the sidewalks near the gutter's edge. I could see up to the corner of Lenox Avenue, about three houses away. At the corner near the building line, the Father Divine man ran his Peace Brother Peace shoe repair business from a ramshackled wooden kiosk heated by a small round stove. From the roof of the kiosk, a thin strand of smoke drifted upward. The smoke was the only sign of life and there was nobody on the street that I could see. I wished the street was warm and beautiful and busy, and that we were having cantaloupe for lunch instead of the hot homemade pea soup that was simmering on the back of the stove awaiting our return.

I had almost made a boat of newspaper just before I had to start being dressed to go out, and I wondered if my bits of newspaper would still be on the kitchen table when we got back, or was my mother even now sweeping them away into the garbage bag? Would I be able to rescue them before lunch or would there be nasty wet orange-peelings and coffee grounds all over them?

Suddenly I realized that there was a little creature standing on a step in the entryway of the main doors, looking at me with bright eyes and a big smile. It was a little girl. She was right away the most beautiful little girl I had ever seen alive in my life.

My lifelong dream of a doll-baby come to life had in fact come true. Here she stood before me now, smiling and pretty in an unbelievable wine-red velvet coat with a wide, wide skirt that flared out over dainty little lisle-stockinged legs. Her feet were clad in a pair of totally impractical, black patent-leather mary-jane shoes, whose silver buckles glinted merrily in the drab noon light.

Her reddish-brown hair was not braided in four plaits like mine, but framed her little pointy-chinned face, tight and curly. On her head sat a wine-colored velvet beret that matched her coat, and on the very top of that sat a big white fur pompom.

Even with decades of fashion between us now, and the dulling of time, it was the most beautiful outfit I had ever seen in my not quite five years of clothes-watching.

Her honey-brown skin had a ruddy glow that echoed the tones of her hair, and her eyes seemed to match both in a funny way that reminded me of my mother's eyes, the way, although light in themselves, they flashed alight in the sun.

I had no idea how old she was.

"What's your name? Mine's Toni."

The name called up a picture book I was just finished reading, and the image came out *boy*. But this delectable creature in front of me was most certainly a girl, and I wanted her for my very own—my very own what, I did not know—but for my very own self. I started to image in my head where I could keep her. Maybe I could tuck her up in the folds under my pillow, pet her during the night when everybody else was asleep, and I was fighting off nightmares of the devil riding me. Of course, I'd have to be careful that she didn't get squeezed into the cot in the morning, when my mother folded up my bed, covered it with an old piece of flowered cretonne bedspread and shoved the whole thing tidily into a corner behind the bedroom door. No, that certainly wouldn't work. My mother would most assuredly find her when, in my mother's way, she plumped up my pillows.

While I was trying to image a safe place to keep her by a rapid succession of pictures in my mind's eye, Toni had advanced towards me, and was now standing between my outspread snowsuited legs, her dark-bright fire-lit eyes on a level with my own. With my woolen mittens dangling down from cords which emerged from the cuffs at each of my wrists, I reached out my hands and lightly rubbed the soft velvet shoulders of her frock-coat up and down.

From around her neck hung a fluffy white fur muff that matched the white fur ball on the top of her hat. I touched her muff, too, and then raised my hand up to feel the fur pompom. The soft silky warmth of the fur made my fingers tingle in a way that the cold had not, and I pinched and fingered it until Toni finally shook her head free of my hand.

I began to finger the small shiny gold buttons on the front of her coat. I unbuttoned the first two of them at the top, just so I could button them back up again, pretending I was her mother.

"You cold?" I was looking at her pink and beige ears, now slowly turning rosy from the cold. From each delicate lobe hung a tiny gold loop.

"No," she said, moving even closer between my knees. "Let's play."

I stuck both of my hands into the holes of her furry muff, and she giggled delightedly as my cold fingers closed around her warm ones inside the quilted dark spaces of the fur. She pulled one hand out past mine and opened it in front of my face to reveal two peppermint life-savers, sticky now from the heat of her palm. "Want one?"

I took one hand out of her muff, and never taking my eyes off her face, popped one of the striped candy rings into my mouth. My mouth was dry. I closed it around the candy and sucked, feeling the peppermint juice run down my throat, burning and sweet almost to the point of harshness. For years and years afterward, I always thought of peppermint lifesavers as the candy in Toni's muff.

She was beginning to get impatient. "Play with me, please?" Toni took a step backward, smiling, and I was terrified suddenly that she might disappear or run away, and the sunlight would surely vanish with her from 142nd Street. My mother had warned me not to move from that spot where she had planted me. But there was no question in my mind; I could not bear to lose Toni.

I reached out and pulled her back gently towards me, sitting her down crosswise upon my knees. She felt so light through the padding of my snowsuit that I thought she could blow away and I would not feel the difference between her being there and not being there.

I put my arms around her soft red velvet coat, and clasping my two hands together, I slowly rocked her back and forth the way I did with my sisters' big Coca-Cola doll that had eyes that opened and closed and that came down from the closet shelf every year around Christmas time. Our old cat Minnie the Moocher did not feel much lighter sitting on my lap.

She turned her face around to me with another one of her delighted laughs that sounded like the ice cubes in my father's nightly drink. I could feel the creeping warmth of her, slowly spreading all along the front of my body through the many layers of clothing, and as she turned her head to speak to me the damp warmth of her breath fogged up my spectacles a little in the crisp winter air.

I started to sweat inside my snowsuit as I usually did, despite the cold. I wanted to take off her coat and see what she had on underneath it. I wanted to take off all of her clothes, and touch her live little brown body and make sure she was real. My heart was bursting with a love and happiness for which I had no words. I unbuttoned the top buttons of her coat again.

"No, don't do that! My grandma won't like it. You can rock me some more." She cuddled down again into my arms.

I put my arms back around her shoulders. Was she really a little girl or a doll come alive? There was only one way I knew for sure of telling. I turned her over and put her across my knees. The light seemed to change around us on the stoop. I looked over once at the doorway leading into the hall, half-afraid of who might be standing there.

I raised up the back of Toni's wine-red velvet coat, and the many folds of her full-skirted green eyelet dress underneath. I lifted up the petticoats under that, until I could see her white cotton knickers, each leg of which ended in an embroidered gathering right above the elastic garters that held up her stockings.

Beads of sweat were running down my chest to be caught at my waist by the tight band of my snowsuit. Ordinarily I hated sweating inside my snowsuit because it felt like roaches were crawling down the front of me.

Toni laughed again and said something that I could not hear. She squirmed around comfortably on my knees and turned her head, her sweet face looking sideways up into mine.

"Grandma forgot my leggings at my house."

I reached up under the welter of dress and petticoats and took hold of the waistband of her knickers. Was her bottom going to be real and warm or turn out to be hard rubber, molded into a little crease like the ultimately disappointing Coca-Cola doll?

My hands were shaking with excitement. I hesitated a moment too long. As I was about to pull down Toni's panties I heard the main door open and out of the front hallway hurried my mother, adjusting the brim of her hat as she stepped out onto the stoop.

I felt caught in the middle of an embarrassing and terrible act from which there could be no hiding. Frozen, I sat motionless as Toni, looking up and seeing my mother, slid nonchalantly off my lap, smoothing down her skirts as she did so.

My mother stepped over to the two of us. I flinched, expecting instant retribution at her capable hands. But evidently the enormity of my intentions had escaped my mother's notice. Perhaps she did not care that I was about to usurp that secret prerogative belonging only to mothers about to spank, or to nurses with thermometers.

Taking me by the elbow, my mother pulled me awkwardly to my feet.

I stood for a moment like a wool-encased snow-girl, my arms stuck out a little from my body and my legs spread slightly apart. Ignoring Toni, my mother started down the steps to the street. "Hurry now," she said, "you don't want to be late."

I looked back over my shoulder. The bright-eyed vision in the wine-red coat stood at the top of the stoop, and pulled one hand out of her white rabbit-fur muff.

"You want the other candy?" she called. I shook my head frantically. We were never supposed to take candy from anybody and certainly not strangers.

My mother urged me on down the steps. "Watch where you're stepping, now."

"Can you come out and play tomorrow?" Toni called after me.

Tomorrow. Tomorrow. Tomorrow. My mother was already one step below, and her firm hand on my elbow kept me from falling as I almost missed a step. Maybe tomorrow . . .

Once on the street pavement, my mother resumed hold of my hand and sailed forth determinedly. My short legs in their bulky wrappings and galoshes chugged along, trying to keep up with her. Even when she was not in a hurry, my mother walked with a long and purposeful stride, her toes always pointed slightly outward in a ladylike fashion.

"You can't tarry now," she said. "You know it's almost noon." Tomorrow, tomorrow, tomorrow.

"What a shame, to let such a skinny little thing like that out in this weather with no snowsuit or a stitch of leggings on her legs. That's how among-you children catch your death of cold."

So I hadn't dreamed her. She had seen Toni too. (What kind of name anyway was that for a girl?) Maybe tomorrow . . .

"Can I have a red coat like hers, Mommy?"

My mother looked down at me as we stood waiting for the street light to change.

"How many times I tell you not to call me Mommy on the street?" The light changed, and we hurried forward.

I thought about my question very carefully as I scurried along, wanting to get it exactly right this time. Finally, I had it.

"Will you buy me a red coat, please, Mother?" I kept my eyes on the treacherous ground to avoid tripping over my galoshed feet, and the words must have been muffled or lost in the scarf around my neck. In any case, my mother hurried on in silence, apparently not hearing. Tomorrow tomorrow tomorrow.

We had our split-pea soup, and hurriedly retraced our steps back to my sisters' school. But that day, my mother and I did not return directly home. Crossing over to the other side of Lenox Avenue, we caught the Number 4 bus down to 125th Street, where we went marketing at Weissbecker's for the weekend chicken.

My heart sank into hopelessness as I stood waiting, kicking my feet in the sawdust that covered the market's floor. I should have known. I had wanted too much for her to be real. I had wanted to see her again too much for it to ever happen.

The market was too warm. My sweaty skin itched in places I couldn't possibly scratch. If we were marketing today, that meant tomorrow would turn out to be Saturday. My sisters did not go to school on Saturday, which meant we couldn't go pick them up for lunch, which meant I would spend all day in the house because my mother had to clean and cook and we were never allowed out alone to play on the stoop.

The weekend was an eternity past which I could not see.

The following Monday I waited again on the stoop. I sat by myself, bundled up as usual, and nobody came except my mother.

I don't know how long I looked for Toni every day at noontime, sitting on the stoop. Eventually, her image receded into that place from which all my dreams are made.

BERYL MARKHAM
(1902–1986)

From the age of four Beryl Markham was raised in East Africa by her father, who had built a horse farm out of wilderness. She played as a child with Masai youths. She was completely at home in Africa, not a latecomer like Karen Blixen. After spending many years helping to breed and tame horses, she took up aviation and became a professional pilot, flying mail and supplies around Africa and scouting game from the air. She worked with Karen Blixen's husband, the hunter and safari guide Bror Blixen, and this selection describes her air rescue of Blixen and his client, Winston Guest, when hunting an elephant, they were cut off by floods.

In 1936 Beryl Markham became the first person to do a solo transatlantic flight from east to west, crash-landing in Nova Scotia. That flight provided the title for her memoir, *West with the Night*, written during World War II and published in 1942. Ignored for forty years, the book was republished in 1983 and became a best seller, partly because of its literary merit and Markham's appealingly cool and intrepid persona and partly because of a vogue for European colonial life in Africa which may have been produced and certainly was epitomized by the film version of *Out of Africa*.

For other accounts by pioneers, compare Margaret Mead, *Blackberry Winter* and Emily Hahn, *Times and Places*. For other versions of Africa, compare Isak Dinesen, *Out of Africa*, Emma Mashinini, *Strikes Have Followed Me All My Life*, and *Nisa: The Life and Words of a !Kung Woman*.

FROM *West with the Night*

The trouble is that God forgot to erect any landmarks. From the air every foot of the Yatta Plateau looks like every other foot of it, every mile is like the next mile, and the one after that, and the one after that.

Years of free-lancing, scouting for elephant and flying the mail in Africa, have made me so used to looking for a smudge of smoke that even now I have a particular affinity for chimneys, campfires, and stoves that puff.

But nothing puffed on the morning I looked for Winston and Blix;

nothing stirred. It seemed to me that two intelligent white men with fifteen black porters could have managed a small corkscrew of smoke at least, unless the whole lot of them had been struck dead like the crew of the *Flying Dutchman.*

I knew that the hunting party had taken only enough food for a couple of meals, which, according to my calculations, left them about seven meals short. That might, unless something were done about it, lead to sad, not to say morbid, consequences. What I could not understand was why they had insisted on remaining on top of the plateau when the camp at Ithumba lay just across the Tiva River. I banked and lost altitude and flew low over the Tiva to see if I could find them, perhaps in the act of fording it.

But the river had swallowed itself. It wasn't a river any more; it was a proud and majestic flood, a mile-wide flood, a barrier of swift water defying all things that move on legs to cross it. And yet, beside the Athi, it was a lazy trickle.

The Athi, on the other side of the plateau, had got illusions of grandeur. It was sweeping over the parched country above its banks in what looked like an all-out effort to surpass the Nile. Far up in the Highlands a storm had burst, and while the sky I flew in was clean and blue as a Dutch rooftop, the Yatta was a jungle island in a rain-born sea. The gutters of Mount Kenya and the Aberdares were running deep. Winston and Blix and all their men were caught like kittens on a flooded stump; they were marooned in driest Africa.

In all likelihood the elephant they hunted was marooned as well if he had not already been shot. But in either case, dead or alive, he would have afforded small comfort.

Edible game is scarce on the Yatta, and the swollen rivers would hardly subside within a week. Given time, I knew Blix would be resourceful enough to figure a way out—possibly on rafts built of thorn trees. But, in order to work, men must eat. I nosed the Avian down toward the endless canopy of bush and zigzagged like a homeless bee.

In twenty minutes I saw their smoke. It was a wizened little string of smoke, sad and grey, and looking like the afterglow of a witch's exit.

Blix and Winston stood by a fire, frantically heaping it with weeds and branches. They waved and swung their arms, and signalled me to come down. They were alone, and I saw no porters.

I swung lower and realized that a narrow clearing had been sculptured out of the jungle growth, but a landing seemed impossible. The runway was short and walled with thicket and rough enough to smash the Avian's undercarriage.

If that happened, contact with the camp at Ithumba—and everything beyond Ithumba—would be cleanly broken. And if it didn't happen, how could I take off again? Getting down is one thing, but getting up again is another.

I scribbled a note on the pad strapped to my right thigh, popped the note into a message bag, and aimed the bag at Blix.

"Might get down," I said, "but runway looks too short for take-off. Will return later if you can make it longer."

It seemed a simple message—clear and practical; but, judging from its reception, it must have read like an invitation to arson or like an appeal to warn the countryside by beacon that the fort had been stormed and massacre was imminent.

Blix heaped foliage and wood on his fire until the smoke from it could be smelled in the cockpit as I flew over the clearing, and I think that in the end he cast his terai hat into the blaze, or perhaps it was Winston's. The smoke rose in enormous grey mushrooms, and I could see pink whips of flame snap in the sunlight. Both men leapt up and down and gesticulated with their arms as if, for months past, they had fed alto-gether upon flowers that conferred a kind of inspired lunacy.

Quite plainly I was to have no larger runway, and just as plainly, there was a reason for it. Blix would not ask me to chance a landing in a spot like that unless other possibilities had first been explored.

By now I was pretty sure I could land if I had to, but not at all sure I could get off again in the same space. There was no wind to check a landing nor to aid a take-off. I had to think.

I banked the plane and circled several times, and each time I did it the dark balloons of smoke grew fatter and soared higher and the dance below achieved the tempo of ecstasy. I still could see no porters.

It breaks my heart to land a plane on rough ground; it is like galloping a horse on concrete. I considered side-slipping in, but remembered Tom's* admonition that to do it expertly (to straighten up from the slip and flatten out a few inches from the earth) is impracticable when you have to land on a broken surface. More often than not this is courting a damaged undercarriage or a cracked longeron. "Save your side-slips for a time when the approaches are such that you can't possibly get in any other way," Tom used to say, "or for a day when your motor has quit. But so long as your motor can help you—fly in." So I flew in.

I flew in and the Avian hit the roots and clods and buried stumps with gentle groans and creaks of protest. She churned the loose dust to billows that matched the billows of the fire. She roared to the edge of the thicket as if she meant to leap it, but decided not. Eventually the drag of the tail-skid and manipulation of the rudder pulled her up, and she stopped with a kind of apprehensive shudder.

*Tom Black had taught Markham to fly—Ed.

Blix and Winston stormed her sides like pirates storming a sloop. They were unshaved and dirty. I had never realized before how quickly men deteriorate without razors and clean shirts. They are like potted plants that go to weed unless they are pruned and tended daily. A single day's growth of beard makes a man look careless; two days', derelict; and four days', polluted. Blix and Winston hadn't shaved for three.

"Thank God, you got here!" Winston was smiling, but his normally handsome face was half-mooned in whiskers and his eyes were definitely not gay. Blix, looking like an unkempt bear disturbed in hibernation, gave me his hand and helped me out of the cockpit.

"I hated to ask you to land, but I had to."

"I guessed that. I saw you couldn't get off the plateau. But what I don't understand . . ."

"Wait," said Blix, "everything will be explained—but first, have you brought anything?"

"I'm afraid not—nothing to eat, anyway. Haven't you shot *any-thing*?"

"No. Not even a hare. The place is empty and we haven't eaten for three days. That wouldn't matter so much, but . . ."

"But no word from Doctor Turvy? Well, I'm betraying a trust, but J. C. did send a bottle of gin for Old Man Wicks. I suppose you need it more than he does. What happened to your porters?"

It was the wrong question. Blix and Winston exchanged glances and Blix began to swear rhythmically under his breath. He reached into the locker and got Old Man Wicks's bottle of gin and pulled the cork out. He handed the bottle to Winston and waited. In a minute Winston handed it back and I waited, watching the largesse from Seramai go the way of all good things.

"The porters are on strike," Winston said.

Blix wiped his mouth and returned the bottle to his companion in exile.

"Mutiny. They haven't lifted a hand since they missed their first meal! They've quit."

"That's silly. Porters don't go on strike in Africa. They haven't got a union."

Blix turned away from the plane and looked back across the runway. "They didn't need one. Empty bellies constitute a common cause. Winston and I cleared that runway ourselves. I don't think we could have made it any longer even if you had insisted on it."

I was impressed. Limited as it was, the runway was nevertheless a good hundred yards long and ten yards wide, and the clearing of such a space with nothing but native pangas to use was a herculean job of work. Some of the growth must have been fifteen feet high, and all of it so dense that a man could barely force his body through it. I suppose that more than a thousand small trees, with trunks three to five inches in diameter, had been felled with those ordinary bush knives. Once the trees had fallen, their stumps had to be dug out of the earth and thrown to the side and an effort made to level the cleared ground.

I learned later from Makula—who had diplomatically remained aloof from the labour controversy (as well as from the labour itself)—that for two nights running Blix had slipped out of his blankets when everyone else was presumably asleep and had worked straight into the morning on the clearing. Certainly he deserved his nip of gin.

Every one of Blix's porters, in what still is, to my knowledge, the most wonderful example of nose-slicing to spite the face, had insisted that since they had no food they could do no work. They had lounged around the makeshift camp day after day while Blix and Winston had slaved at the clearing, though it had been explained to the porters very carefully (and no doubt with some heat) that if there were no clearing, they might not see a bowl of posho for weeks to come.

Nevertheless, Blix was worried about his porters. I think that a less just man might have been tempted to say, "Starve, damn you!" But not Blix. His reputation as a White Hunter wasn't entirely built in the cocktail bar at Muthaiga. He said, "Beryl, I know it's asking a lot, but you've got to get Winston out of here first, then come back for me—and then for Makula. Get Farah to give you all the beans and dry food you can carry for the porters, and bring it here after you've dropped Winston. It means two more landings in this hole and three take-offs. But if I didn't think you could manage, I wouldn't ask you to do it."

"I suppose if I ask what happens if I don't manage, you'll tell me how quiet it gets when the goldfish die?"

Blix grinned. "Terribly quiet," he said, "but *so* peaceful."

It was small comfort to know that Winston took the same chance that I did when we attempted the take-off from the runway. I shouldn't think that Winston weighs much less than a hundred and eighty pounds (dismounted and lightly clad), and that much weight made a lot of difference to the Avian under conditions prevailing that day on the Yatta. I insisted on waiting for a breeze, and finally got one strong enough to just bend the column of smoke that still rose from Blix's fire.

Winston got into the front seat, Blix swung the prop, and the Avian moved down the runway—slow, fast, faster. The wall of thicket came nearer and began to look more solid than a wall of thicket ought to look. I saw Winston shake his head and then lower it slightly. He was staring straight before him—a little like a prizefighter in a crouch.

I held the stick forward trying to gather what speed I could before the take-off. I'm afraid I thought of Tom's letter, but a second later I was thinking of Tom's brilliant judgement in suggesting the Avian for African work. No other plane that I knew could have been pulled off the ground, almost literally, the way I pulled her off, without stalling. She responded like a thoroughbred steeplechaser, missing the thicket with inches to spare. Winston abruptly came out of his crouch, swung around in the seat and winked at me—a little like the same prizefighter having won a decision in the fifteenth round. I gained altitude, throttled down, and swung toward the Tiva. It had no recognizable banks. It looked like a lake wandered from home.

It would not be quite true to say that Arab Ruta and Farah were nervous wrecks when we arrived at Ithumba, but they were pretty obviously relieved. Farah, who is a lean, energetic Somali, inclined to talk so fast that you are still coping with his first sentence while he is waiting for an answer to the last, was of the opinion that his Bwana Blixen was touched with immortality. He did not think that anything serious could have happened to Blix, but he was aware that anyone else's misfortune would be, in a way, also Blix's. Farah greeted us with inquiring rather than worried eyes, while Arab Ruta rushed up to the plane and immediately inspected the landing gear, the wings, and the tail-skid. Then, a little tardily, he smiled at me.

"Our plane is unhurt, Memsahib!—and you also?"

I admitted that I was intact, at least, and prepared to take on the food needed for Blix's rebellious porters.

It takes a lot of practice to make perfect, but a little helps. I had no difficulty in picking up Blix or in putting him down again in the camp at Ithumba. And on the third trip, to get Makula, everything went smoothly too, except for Makula himself, who hesitated to go at all.

"Ai-Ai!" he complained in garbled Swahili, "how strange that hunger makes a man shake like a stick in the wind. Hunger does bad things to a man!" He regarded the plane with a disquiet eye. "When one is hungry, it is better, I think, not to move."

"You won't have to move, Makula. You can just sit in front of me until we get to camp."

Makula tugged at his shuka and ran his fingers up and down the sleek surface of his golden bow. He thumbed his rawhide string and made it sing a cautious song. "Each man is a brother to the next, M'sabu, and brothers must lean upon each other. All the porters are alone. Can I leave them?"

The day was shorter than it had been, Blix's fire was dead, and "all the porters" were feeding in happy silence. They had won their strike and they had food enough and time enough, with no cares. What I had brought would last until the floods were down—and there was no work.

But we needed Makula. I remembered an old Swahili phrase, and I said it: "A wise man is not more than a woman—unless he is also brave."

The old tracker regarded me carefully for a long moment—as if I had uttered a truth from a cabala previously known only to himself and the lost ages. Then he nodded solemnly and spat on the ground. He stared at the spittle and then at the failing sun. At last he rubbed his hands on his shuka and climbed into the Avian. I swung the propeller, ran around to the rear cockpit, and got in behind him. His naked neck was rigid and ringed with glinting metal bands. White beads dangled from the bands and glinted too against his black skin. He held his bow in firm fingers and it tapered gracefully up from the cockpit like the magic wand he hoped it was. He waited until the plane moved and then he snatched from somewhere about his waist a thin blanket and bound his head with it, around and around, until he was blind as night and shapeless as fear. And then I took off.

All the way to Ithumba my bundle never moved. Makula had always cultivated the suspicion that he was as deft at witchcraft as at tracking. He carried a little bag of wooden amulets and feathers and odd bones which, because they were rarely seen and never explained, had taken on for his confrères the quality of talismans contrived in hell. I could almost believe that Makula was using them now, calling on their darkly potent powers to suspend sense and consciousness just this once—oh, God or Devil!—for just this little time.

I landed gently and taxied smoothly and stopped, and my bundle stirred. Blix and Winston were on hand, both relieved to see us—and both shaved. At the sound of their voices above the sound of the propeller that still ticked over with lazy ease, Makula began to unwind the blanket that his witchcraft had saved from a shroud's duty. When his head appeared, he did not sigh nor blink his eyes; he stared at the palms of his hands and then at the sky, and nodded at nothing in a gesture of restrained approval. Things had worked out about as he had planned them; he would forgo, for the time, any minor complaints. He climbed out of the plane with a certain grace and arranged his shuka and smiled at everybody.

"Well, Makula," said Blix, "how did you like your first trip through the air?"

I think it was less a question than a pleasant gibe—and there was an audience to hear the answer. Not only Farah and Ruta, but those porters who had stayed with the camp, had joined the circle that honoured old Makula. We thought the glibness of his tongue was being put to test, but he thought it was his dignity. He made himself a little taller and skewered Blix with a glance.

"Baba Yangu (Father of Mine), I have done many things—and so this was no great thing to me. To a Kikuyu, or a Wandorobo, or a Kavirondo, it might be a great thing to fly through the air. But I have seen much of the world."

"As much as you saw today, Makula?"

"Not so much at one time, Baba Yangu. Today, it is true, I saw the great sea down there by Mombasa, and the top of Kilimanjaro, and the place where the Mau Forest ends—but those things I had seen before, by myself."

"You saw all those things today?" Farah's scepticism went undisguised. "You could not have seen those things, Makula. You did not fly so far, and we all know that your head was wrapped in your own blanket! Can men see, then, through darkness?"

Makula let his long fingers caress the little bag of witchery that hung from his waist. He turned to his accuser and smiled with magnificent forgiveness.

"Not *all* men, Farah. Who could expect so much of God?"

You could expect many things of God at night when the campfire burned before the tents. You could look through and beyond the veils of scarlet and see shadows of the world as God first made it and hear the voices of the beasts He put there. It was a world as old as Time, but as new as Creation's hour had left it.

In a sense it was formless. When the low stars shone over it and the moon clothed it in silver fog, it was the way the firmament must have been when the waters had gone and the night of the Fifth Day had fallen on creatures still bewildered by the wonder of their being. It was an empty world because no man had yet joined sticks to make a house or scratched the earth to make a road or embedded the transient symbols of his artifice in the clean horizon. But it was not a sterile world. It held the genesis of life and lay deep and anticipant under the sky.

You were alone when you sat and talked with the others—and they were alone. This is so wherever you are if it is night and a fire burns in free flames rising to a free wind. What you say has no ready ear but your own, and what you think is nothing except to yourself. The world is there, and you are here—and these are the only poles, the only realities.

You talk, but who listens? You listen, but who talks? Is it someone you know? And do the things he says explain the stars or give an answer to the quiet questions of a single sleepless bird? Think of these questions; fold your arms across your knees and stare at the firelight and at the embers waning on its margin. The questions are your questions too.

"Sigilisa!" (Listen!) "Simba is hungry tonight."

So a native boy interprets the first warning of a distant lion stalking in a distant silence. A jackal skirts the red pool of comfort that warms you, a tent flap chatters in the wind.

But Simba is not hungry. He is alone, too, companionless in his courage, friendless in his magnificence—uneasy in the night. He roars, and so he joins our company, and hyenas join it, laughing in the hills. And a leopard joins it, letting us feel his presence, but hear nothing. Rhino—buffalo—where are they? Well, they are here too—somewhere here—just there, perhaps, where that bush thickens or that copse of thorn trees hides the sky. They are here, all are here, unseen and scattered, but sharing with us a single loneliness.

Someone stands up and stirs the fire which needs no stirring, and Arab Ruta brings more logs, though there are logs enough. Another fire burns a little distance from our own where the black porters squat as if they are fitted into niches of the night.

Somebody attempts to break the loneliness. It is Blix, asking a simple question that everybody answers, but nobody has listened to. Winston stares at the tips of his boots like a child who has never before had boots and never wants to lose them. I sit with a notebook on my knee and a pencil in my hand, trying to write a list of what I need, and writing nothing. I must answer Tom, too. He has written to say that he has entered for the International Air Race from Mildenhall to Melbourne. Eleven thousand and three hundred miles—half around the world almost. England to Australia. I should be in England. I ought to fly to England again. I know the route: Khartoum—Wadi Halfa, Luxor, Cairo, Benghazi, Tobruk . . . Tripoli and the Mediterranean . . . France and England. Six thousand miles—only a quarter around the world, and take your time. Well . . . I wonder.

"Want to fly to London, Blix?"

He says yes without even looking up from the rifle he's fiddling with.

"It's funny about that elephant," says Winston.

Winston is still up there on the Yatta. "Not even a spoor!" He shakes his head. "Not a single sign," he says.

Arab Ruta stands just behind me and Farah is next to him. They are there on the pretext of serving, but actually they are there just as we are there—thinking, talking, dreaming.

"In Aden," says Farah to Ruta, "where I was born, there by the Red Sea in Arabia, we used to go out on the water in boats that had each one wing, brown and very high, and the wind pushed this wing and carried us along. Sometimes at night the wind would stop—and then it was like this."

"I have seen the sea at Mombasa," says Arab Ruta, "and at night too. I do not think the sea is like this. It moves. Here, nothing moves."

Farah thinks, Blix whistles a few low notes from a knockabout tune, Winston ponders his phantom elephant, and I scribble by the light of the fire.

"The sea at Mombasa," Farah says, "is not the same sea."

Momentarily the categorical pronouncement confounds Ruta. He bends to pick a log from the ground and toss it into the fire, but he is thoughtful.

"How big would you say that bull was?" Winston looks at Blix and then at me.

Blix shrugs. "The one on the Yatta? Very big."

"Tusks over a hundred?"

"Nearer two," says Blix. "He was very big."

"Well, it's damned funny we never even saw his spoor."

Winston relapses into silence and stares at the night as if his elephant might be there, swinging his huge trunk from side to side in soundless derision. Up on the plateau, the meeting place of Greek and Greek waits with no Greeks at hand.

I return to my list of things needed, but not for long. I wonder if I should have a change—a year in Europe this time—something new, something better, perhaps. A life has to move or it stagnates. Even this life, I think.

It is no good telling yourself that one day you will wish you had never made that change; it is no good anticipating regrets. Every tomorrow ought not to resemble every yesterday.

Still, I look at my yesterdays for months past, and find them as good a lot of yesterdays as anybody might want. I sit there in the firelight and see them all.

The hours that made them were good, and so were the moments that made the hours. I have had responsibilities and work, dangers and pleasure, good friends, and a world without walls to live in. These things I still have, I remind myself—and shall have until I leave them.

I nod stupidly at something Blix says and idly contribute a twig to our fire.

"Are you falling asleep?"

"Asleep? No. No, I am just thinking." And so I am. I spend so much time alone that silence has become a habit.

Often, except for Ruta and Farah, I am alone at safari headquarters day after day, night after night, while the hunters, following a herd that I have found or waiting for me to find one, are camped miles away. At dawn they expect the sound of my Avian, and it always comes.

I awaken long before dawn at such times and always find Ruta ready with my cup of steaming tea, and I drink it, looking at the fading stars that are caught in the triangle of my open tent.

It is always misty when Ruta and I remove the canvas covers from the engine, the propeller, and the cockpit. Each humid, tropic day is still-born, and does not breathe, however lustily pregnant the night that gave it birth. I take off in dead air with the accessories of my singular occupation arranged in their proper places.

There are the message bags stacked in two specially made boxes of teak that stand on either side of me on the floor of the cockpit. The bags are handsome things, in their way. I carry over a dozen of them—tough little brown pouches, leaded, and fitted with long streamers of blue-and-gold silk, for visibility. Blue-and-gold had been my racing colours; they are flying colours now.

There is my note pad fixed on a board and hung with straps to fasten on my thigh, and the quiver of pencils I carry with it. What frantic scribbling that pad and those pencils are a party to!

And there is my vial of morphine. I keep it, like a fetish, in the pocket of my flying jacket because the senior medical officer at Nairobi has told me to keep it, and has mumbled of forced landings in inaccessible wastelands and crackups in the depths of forests that men could hardly reach—in time. He has been insistent about this precaution, making me return the unopened vial at intervals, exchanging it for a fresher one. "You never can tell," he invariably says, "you never can tell!"

And so equipped, I wave kwaheri to Ruta each day in the rheumy morning light, fly until I sight the smoke of the hunters' camp, and dip my wings to greet them. Then I am off over the rolling ocean of bush to find their quarry—and, when I find it, what a thrill it is, what a satisfying moment!

Sometimes I circle a herd for nearly an hour, trying to determine the size of its largest bull. If at last I decide that he carries enough ivory, my work begins. I must figure the course from the herd to the hunters' camp, reverse the course, jot it down on my pad, judge the distance, give details of terrain, warn of other animals in the vicinity, note water holes, and indicate safest approach.

I must find my smoke signal again, keeping an eye on the compass, a hand free for scribbling, and my course and distance calculator ready, should I need it. I feel triumphant when I can drop a note like this which Blix has returned to me and is still folded in my logbook:

> *Very* big bull—tusks quite even—my guess over 180-pounder. In herd of about 500. Two other bulls and many babies in herd—grazing peacefully. Dense growth—high trees—two water holes—one about half-mile from herd NNE. Other about two miles WNW. Fairly open ground between you and herd, with open glade halfway. Many tracks. Large herd buffalo S.W. of elephant. No rhino sighted. Your course 220 degrees. Distance about ten miles. Will be back in one hour. Work hard, trust in God, and keep your bowels open—Oliver Cromwell

Well, Cromwell *did* say it, and it still makes sense.

All of it makes sense—the smoke, the hunt, the fun, the danger. What if I should fly away one morning and not come back? What if the Avian fails me? I fly much too low, of necessity, to pick a landing spot (assuming that there might be a landing spot) in such a case. No, if the engine fails me, if a quick storm drives me into the bush and sansivera— well, that is the chance and that is the job. Anyway, Blix has told Farah and Ruta what to do if I am ever gone for a longer time than my supply of petrol might be expected to last—get to a telegraph by foot or lorry, and wire Nairobi. Maybe somebody like Woody would begin the search.

Meanwhile, haven't I got two quarts of water, a pound of biltong— and the doctor's bottled sleep (should I be hors de combat and the Siafu* hungry that night)? I certainly have, and, moreover, I am not defenceless. I have a Lüger in my locker—a gun that Tom has insisted on my carrying, and which can be used as a short rifle simply by adjusting its emergency stock. What could be better? I am an expedition by myself, complete with rations, a weapon, and a book to read—*Air Navigation,* by Weems.

All this, and discontent too! Otherwise, why am I sitting here dreaming of England? Why am I gazing at this campfire like a lost soul seeking a hope when all that I love is at my wingtips? Because I am curious. Because I am incorrigibly, now, a wanderer.

*Siafu ants eat flesh—ED.

EMMA MASHININI
(1929–)

Emma Mashinini, a black South African, has lived all her life in those areas of Johannesburg reserved for nonwhites. She left junior high school to work, first as a nanny, then in a textile plant, becoming ever more caught up in the trade union movement. She was one of the founders and from 1975 to 1985 the secretary of the Commercial, Catering, and Allied Workers Union, for black workers in the service sector, one of South Africa's largest unions. A national political figure, she suffered police harassment, which included six traumatic months in solitary confinement in Pretoria Central Prison. Since 1985 she has tracked the situation of political prisoners for the Anglican Church of the Province of Southern Africa, working with Bishop Desmond Tutu.

For other accounts of working-class life, compare Carolyn Kay Steedman, *Landscape for a Good Woman* and Kate Simon, *Bronx Primitive.* For another account by a political activist, compare Bernadette Devlin, *The Price of My Soul.* For other accounts of young womanhood in Africa, compare Beryl Markham, *West with the Night* and *Nisa: The Life and Words of a !Kung Woman.*

FROM *Strikes Have Followed Me All My Life*

I left my husband in 1959. In 1956, when I was twenty-six, I had started work in Johannesburg, at a clothing factory called Henochsberg's which provided uniforms for the government forces. It was my first job, apart from working as a nanny to white children when I left school, and I had not begun to develop any political awareness. But I was already angry. The hours my father had been forced to work had contributed to the break-up of my family, and my own need to earn money had put paid to my schooling. And now, when my three children were still young and I could have done with being at home to look after them, I was having to go out to work to earn a tiny wage, which we needed in order to survive.

I found the job through the Garment Workers' Union. Lucy Mvubelo, a woman I admire so much for all she did in those years for her union, was the General Secretary, and she said to me, "Go to number one, Charles Street, they are looking for people there." I went, and within three days they had taken me on as a trainee machinist.

The factory was just opening then. I think it was about the second or third week that it had started running. I started off in a branch factory and then, after about a year, moved on into the central factory, in Commissioner Street. In the branch factory there were no white machinists. It was only when I got to the central factory that there was a mix of black and white on the shop floor.

I remember my first day very clearly. It was November, and when I walked into that building it seemed to me that there were hundreds of people rushing this way and that, and a terrible volume of noise, with a lot of shouting—"Come on, do your job!"—that kind of thing. It was completely bewildering. Immediately I got there, on my first day as a worker, I was started on the machines, working very close to people who had already worked as machinists at other factories, so I was a struggler from the start. I remember most of all how they cursed us when we couldn't keep up. I was in a department headed first by an Afrikaner called Mrs. Smit and then by a German-speaking man, Mr. Becker. He used to shout and scream at us, sometimes for no reason at all, and it wasn't unusual for ten people to be dismissed a day. They were always saying you had to push. They would say, *"Roer jou gat,"* which means, "Push your arse"—"Come on, push your arse and be productive." You would be on the machine sweating, but they would tell you, *"Roer jou, roer jou"*—"Push, push, push," and you would push and push. No one would ever say, "Okay, that's enough. Good." You were working for a target. You'd know there was a target you had to meet, and at the back of your mind you were concerned about the welfare of your children. You would be torn in two, because you were at work and in your mind you were at home. This is the problem of the working mother: you are divided. You are only working because you have to.

Penny was almost three when I moved to the central factory, and she'd started going to a crèche nearby, so I didn't have a baby that I had to carry from one place to another, because even though I stopped work much later than the crèche closed, and after my other two children came home from school, I had a neighbour who wasn't working, and she looked after them. But still at work you were thinking of the children, and at home you were thinking about the job, and then you had this extra person to bother about—a husband.

I'd start factory work at seven-thirty in the morning, after travelling about thirty kilometres to get there. Other workers came from double that distance. People think Soweto is the only township in South Africa, but there are many others, like Tembisa and Alexandra, and all of us would be flocking to the centre of Johannesburg for our jobs. People would be sleeping on the trains. Some would have been travelling for a long time, and even before the train there would be some distance to go for a bus stop, and the bus would already have been travelling and picking up more people. So if you had to be at your machine at seven-thirty you would have to be at your work-place by seven, and you would have to be ready to take the train at five. For some it could be about four.

I would leave my children sleeping, and the night before I would have made my preparations for the coming day, because I had to leave every-thing—bread, uniform, everything—lined up for my neighbour, who would come and wake my children for school. There would be nothing for you at the factory—no tea, no coffee. The tea-break was at a certain time, and if you had brought something from home that would be when you would eat, in that ten-minute tea-break later in the day. And if you had brought nothing, your tea-break would be exhausted while you were walking to the canteen and queuing there. By the time you got your coffee and sat down, five minutes had gone, and you would have to swallow everything and then run to be back on time.

I would get home about seven—and in winter, you know, that was pretty dark. When I got home I'd start making a fire on my coal stove. I used to try to prepare for that the night before, but if not I would have to start chopping wood, getting the coal, getting the ashes out and all that. And there was no one to follow my children when they were getting up, and the basin would be full of dirty water, and I would start emptying that as well, picking up the dirty clothes, and the school clothes they took off when they got home from school, and all that before I actually started cooking.

My husband would not be rushing to come home. What would he rush to come home for? When he got out from his job he would go wherever he wanted to, and because he was a man it had to be so. I couldn't question him, or ask him, and anyway when he got home my time was interfered with because I had to have water to give him to wash his hands—not just ordinary cold water, but warm water. While my fire was still burning I would pump the primus stove quickly to get the warm water for my dear husband to wash his hands, and then with the remain-ing water I would make tea. I would also enjoy that, but standing, be-cause my fire would be burning for me to cook our main meal. My husband would sit and read the newspaper—and sometimes I would wonder if he really understood what he read, or if he just knew that the white boss sits when he comes home, and reads his newspaper.

I never thought to compare. I never thought that while the white boss was doing that, sitting and reading, there was a black man or woman doing everything for them. It was just the order of the day that I had to do everything. And if, after he washed, he emptied the water instead of just leaving it standing, I would be so grateful. I would feel that was so nice of him.

So then I'd cook and give them their food and everything, and if he was tired he would maybe want more water to wash his feet, because he had been standing and maybe he reckoned I'd been sitting at the machine. And then they would go to sleep, and there was the tidying up to do, and the dishes, because that was the only time I had to clean my house, at night, after everyone had gone to bed. I would do the washing as well, at night, and in the morning I would get up and before I left I would hang my washing on the line. We none of us had so many clothes that we could last the week, and so I couldn't do all the washing at the weekend. Then, on alternate days, I would do the ironing, with those heavy irons you put on the stove, and my table would be my ironing board.

My children would do their homework by candle-light. Our only other means of light was a paraffin lamp, which smelled very strong, so to me a candle was an improvement. There was never any time for me to help them—all I could do was make sure they got on with it. I could never open a book to see. My children say they cannot work for longer hours because they must oversee their children's homework. This is all foreign to me. I could never do it with my children, even though I had been educated to a good standard, because there simply was not time.

There was no time to sit and laugh and talk. No time and no energy. Even going to church, trying to cope with catching them, getting them to wash, finding their socks, always shouting. Only on the way there, walking out of that house and holding their hands—I think that was the only loving time I had with my children. Just holding their hands and walking with them to church.

That was the happiest time. They would be sitting there, and going off to Sunday School or whatever, and you could sit down and relax, and listen to someone. Even today I love to go to church, only now my company is my grandchildren instead of my children.

The church was my one pleasure, until we working women got together and had what we called *stokvels*. A *stokvel* is a neighbourhood group that is very supportive, socially and financially. Many black women earn meagre wages and cannot afford to buy the necessary comforts of a home, so we set up these *stokvels*, where we could pool our resources. You have to be a member to enjoy the benefits of a *stokvel*, and they are properly run. The members decide what is the greatest need. It could be a ceiling, a refrigerator, or pots, or anything that you could not pay for yourself. The members collect money in proportion to their wages, and put it into a pool for one person in the group to purchase what has been decided. After that they pass on to the next person, and the group identifies another pressing need, and so it goes until you find that each person in the group has managed to buy some household gadgets without getting into a hire-purchase contract, which has been disastrous to many a housewife.

Another important aspect of *stokvels* is social. Women in the townships are very lonely because their husbands tend to leave them at home when they go to soccer matches, or to the movies, or to taverns to have a drink with the boys. The *stokvel* meetings change from one member's house to another, and you are obliged to serve tea or drinks. After the money has been collected the women start conversing about current affairs, sharing their problems, which leads them to politics. And that is why African women are often much more politically aware than their Coloured and Indian counterparts, who do not have the opportunity of meeting in such a way.

That was the way my neighbourhood was. My house was the second from the corner, and there were no fences dividing the houses from each other. The woman in the first house from the corner worked in a white kindergarten, and she would be able to bring leftovers of sandwiches from rich children, and as she had no young children of her own she would pass those leftovers to me. And so we sustained each other, woman to woman—a woman-to-woman sustaining.

On Sunday afternoons, after church, I would start preparing for the coming week. It would be our first time to have a hot meal, perhaps. And there would be more cleaning. We believed in cleaning those houses. They were our pride. What else did we have to show pride in? Only our little rooms were our pride.

I struggled from the first day I got into the factory. After I had learned the machine better I thought that perhaps the most important thing was to do whatever I had to do perfectly, but because I wanted to do this I couldn't produce the number of garments I was supposed to. It was not possible to chase perfection along with production. They made the choice for you, and they wanted production.

As a result of my attempt to work in this way I was screamed at more than anyone else, but still I couldn't get myself to work as fast as all those other people. Every morning when I walked into that factory I really thought, "Today it will be my turn to be dismissed." But then I was elected a shop steward, and soon after, to my surprise (though looking back it does not seem so unexpected), I was promoted. It was after about three or four years, and I was promoted first to be a set leader and then a supervisor, which was unheard of—a black supervisor in that factory. Instead of dismissing me, they were trying to make me one of them.

We were members of the Garment Workers' Union Number 3.

There were three garment workers' trade unions at that time. The Garment Workers' Union Number 1 was for whites, headed by Johanna Cornelius, and Number 2 was for Coloureds and Indians. Number 3 was for blacks, headed by Lucy Mvubelo, who had sent me to Henochsberg's in the first place. The union for Africans wasn't registered, of course, but the employers accepted it was there. Our subscriptions at that time were deducted from our pay and went to the Number 1 and 2 unions, who would negotiate for working conditions and wages for garment workers. We had an agreement which served for all three branches—whites, Indians and Coloureds, and Africans—and we would benefit from their negotiations in that whatever minimum wage was set we would be paid that amount. The other workers would get over and above that wage, but they would be sure to set a minimum wage for the African workers. In my factory we black women workers made up about 70 per cent of the work force, all earning that basic flat wage. There was no machinery to challenge that wage. It was for the employer to decide to pay over the minimum wage. It was purely voluntary, and that is in fact what it was called, a "voluntary increase." So our union just had to sit and wait for what came out of the negotiations with the Industrial Council. Any action we took over their decision was illegal. For us to strike was illegal.

None the less, on occasion we did strike, or go on a "go slow." I think the strikes that meant the most to me were in the early 1970s, when we fought to earn an extra cent, and also to narrow our hours. When I first started work the day would be from seven-thirty to four-thirty, and we fought, all of us, for the narrowing down of the time, and succeeded in bringing it down to five minutes past four for leaving the factory. We were fighting for a forty-hour week, and in the course of the fight we did go out on strike.

But even more important than the narrowing of hours was that extra cent. By then we were all earning 10 rand 50 cents a week, and only workers earning more than 10 rand 50 cents could contribute to the Unemployment Insurance Fund.

Unemployment insurance was a key issue for me, and I was very glad to have been elected a shop steward and that it was part of my duty to go about and influence people. It's strange, really, that I didn't expect to be elected, but when it came I was more than ready to accept the job. I'd say that has been true of my entire career in that I have never sought to be elected to positions of such responsibility, but when they have been offered to me I have found great fulfilment in the work they entail. You have to work hard, and learn and learn, and work even harder, because you don't have the experience, but despite this, and despite the strain, at the end of the day I can say I have enjoyed my work. Often I can't believe how any particular success or achievement has come about, and I say to myself there is no way I could have managed it, except maybe with God's grace.

On the occasion when we fought for our extra cent, I remember what a struggle we had, and how hostile the employers were. We went on a go slow strike, and they were so angry, being used to dismissing us for the least mistake, for being late or whatever. It took months for us to win— but when we did, we felt joy, great joy.

I had a dual role in the factory, but I was very clear where my first loyalty lay. I was appointed a supervisor, but I was *elected* to be a shop steward by my fellow workers.

As a supervisor I had some access to Mr. Becker, who was held in very high esteem by senior management. He was very much feared by the workers, since he had a way of goading, pushing and bullying them to produce more garments than any of his white colleagues who headed other departments. He was a slave-driver. But as a shop steward I was able to intervene and reduce the numerous dismissals which were taking place.

Circumstances forced me to protect my colleagues. I pointed out to Mr. Becker how counter-productive it was constantly to be dismissing people after I had trained them, and that while it was very easy for him to throw people out, it meant a heavy load of work descended on me, to start training new people all over again. Apart from the inhuman way he dismissed people, I tried to make him see that if he had constantly to train new women to be machinists or table-hands there was no way we could then achieve our work quota.

It was very unusual for a black woman to be a supervisor, and because of the superior attitudes of whites towards blacks I had to be doubly determined to demonstrate that I could do the job very well. I remember that when I first confronted Mr. Becker he was quite taken aback, because he did not expect me to speak out. But with time I saw that he came to respect my views.

Henochsberg's was one of the largest factories in the clothing industry, with almost a thousand workers. We were producing uniforms for the navy, the air force, police and traffic cops. At a later stage we started production of a type of uniform totally unknown to us, which I came to realise was a camouflage uniform. These particular garments I saw on people for the first time in 1976, when on June 16 we had the uprising of the youth in Soweto, and then their massacre. At the onset of the peaceful protest there arrived in Soweto unusual types of army vehicles, from which hundreds of troops flowed out and littered the streets, all dressed in those camouflage uniforms, uniforms used for the slaughter of my people, and which I personally had helped to make. I felt horrified. There was only one non-governmental uniform we made at Henochs-

berg's, and that was for the Zionist Christian Church, the largest independent church, led by Bishop Lekganyane.

Evilly entwined in all the work at our factory was apartheid and all the
disabilities which were imposed on us, the black workers. Job Reservation was one of those punitive decrees. Many jobs—in the cutting room,
and stitching around men's jacket sleeves, for example—were reserved
by statute for whites only. As a supervisor I was only permitted to supervise blacks, and forbidden by law to supervise our "superior" whites,
even though some of the jobs reserved for whites were so simple that we
laughed to ourselves to see how superior they felt in performing them.
The assumptions and arrogance of white South Africans never ceases to
amaze and astound me, even up to this present day.

In the commercial distributive trade even the operating of lifts was
reserved for whites, who were usually elderly retired people, or disabled
people. Can you imagine what this means, that a tired and often retarded white person was considered more valuable and productive than a
young and competent black?

In such a society as this, whites developed into very lazy people, because all the menial and hard tasks were landed on the backs of black
people, and black women in particular gained from this and learned to
develop resourcefulness, and talents and skills, and trained themselves to
become truly competent.

Of course, we had separate facilities. Canteen, toilets, changing
rooms—all these were separated according to sex and according to colour. We had to address the whites as "sir" and "madam," while they
always called us by our first names, or, if we were being shouted at, we
were called *"meid"* and *"Kaffir."* Yet as black women, we were in the
majority—perhaps 70 per cent of the workforce.

The Industrial Conciliation Act of 1956 banned the employers from
deducting union subscriptions from our pay packets, so we shop stewards
would have to collect all the subscriptions ourselves. We would ask to be
first in the queue when we were paid, so that we could then go and stand
at the gate and collect.

It was not easy to act for the workers at that time. A lot of awareness
has been created over the last years, but then they were often frightened
to say aloud that they were not happy with their salaries. Also, they
didn't always tell their plans to me, as shop steward. They would always
be surprising me. They would say to each other, without my knowledge,
"Tomorrow we are not going to start work until a certain demand is
met." I would always be early at work, because I would arrange things
before the workers came in, and when I got there I would see people
were not coming to start work, and I would stand there like a fool. I, a
black person and a worker, would be inside with all these whites standing

around with me and saying, "Why aren't they coming in to work?" And when the whites would address the workers and say, "What is your problem?" perhaps somebody would answer, "We do have a problem." So they would say, "Who are your spokespeople? Let your spokespeople come in and talk to us." And they would say their spokesperson was Emma, meaning me. So the whites would think I had instigated the stoppage, that I was playing a double role, making the workers stand outside and pretending I didn't know.

They could have sacked me if they had wanted. I was a shop steward, but if they wanted to sack you they could still sack you. Instead, they would try and use me to stop the trouble. They would use me like a fire extinguisher, always there to stop trouble. I would have to go to meet with the workers and ask, "Now what is actually going on?" And they would tell me they wanted money, or they wanted that person who had been shouting and yelling at us to behave him or herself. I would listen to all that, and then I would convey it to the employers. They would be adamant, and so the workers would stay outside and not come in. Often the police would arrive with dogs and surround the workers. Many times with the help of the union we would eventually receive assistance, and perhaps the people would achieve a part of what they wanted and go back to work, But during those days, in the factory I worked in, there was one strike after another. And this has followed me all my life. Wherever I am it seems there must always be trouble.

MARY MCCARTHY
(1912–1989)

After Mary McCarthy's parents died in the influenza epidemic of 1918, she and her brothers were sent by their Catholic grandparents to live for five miserable years with a great-aunt and her husband. Rescued from their Dickensian cruelty by her Protestant grandfather and Jewish grandmother, Mary McCarthy moved to Seattle, where she attended a convent school, then public school, then an Episcopal seminary before going east to Vassar College. Originally a critic and an essayist, McCarthy began writing fiction when locked in a room by her second husband, literary critic Edmund Wilson, and urged to do so. Four novels preceded her biggest success, *The Group* (1963), about the evolving fortunes of some Vassar graduates. Much of *Memories of a Catholic Girlhood* (1957) originally appeared in *The New Yorker*, which encouraged memoiristic writing in the 1950s. It was followed thirty years later by another autobiography, *How I Grew*, which covered the same chronological ground as the earlier book but was less artful, more factual. At the time of her death McCarthy was working on yet another autobiography, *Intellectual Memories* (1992), which took up where *How I Grew* left off. Despite its title, the last volume also focused on facts, notably of McCarthy's sexual experience.

For other memories of Catholic girlhoods, see Mary Cantwell, *American Girlhood* and Maureen Howard, *Facts of Life*. For another account of a girl bursting out of her education, compare Gertrude Stein, *The Autobiography of Alice B. Toklas*.

FROM *Memories of a Catholic Girlhood*

C'EST LE PREMIER PAS QUI COÛTE

Like the Jesuits, to whom they stand as nieces, the Ladies of the Sacred Heart are a highly centralized order, versed in clockwork obedience to authority. Their institutions follow a pattern laid down for them in France in the early nineteenth century—clipped and pollarded as a garden and stately as a minuet. All Sacred Heart convent schools are the same—the same blue serge dresses, usually, with white collars and cuffs, the same blue and green and pink moire ribbons awarded for good conduct, the same books given as prizes on Prize Day, the same recitation of "Lepanto" by an English actor in a piped vest, the same *congés,* or holidays, announced by the *Mère Supérieure,* the same game of *cache-cache,* or hide-and-seek, played on these traditional feast days, the same *goûter,* or tea, the same retreats and sermons, the same curtsies dipped in the hall, the same early-morning chapel with processions of girls, like widowed queens, in sad black-net veils, the same *prie-dieu,* the same French hymns (*"Oui, je le crois"*), the same glorious white-net veils and flowers and gold vessels on Easter and Holy Thursday and on feasts peculiar to the order. In the year I came to the Seattle *Mesdames,* at four o'clock on any weekday afternoon in Roscrea, Ireland, or Roehampton, England, or Menlo Park, California, the same tiny old whiskered nun was reading, no doubt, from *Emma* or *A Tale of Two Cities* to a long table of girls stitching French seams or embroidering bureau scarves with wreaths of flowers. "Charles Evrémonde, called Darnay!"—the red-rimmed old black eye leveled and raked us all, summarily, with the grapeshot of the Terror.

I was eleven years old, a seventh-grader, when I was first shown into the big study hall in Forest Ridge Convent and issued my soap dish, my veil, and my napkin ring. The sound of the French words awed me, the luster of the wide moire ribbons cutting, military-wise, across young bosoms, the curtained beds in the dormitories, the soft step of the girls, the curtsies to the floor, the white hands of the music master (a Swedish baron in spats), the cricket played in the playground, the wooden rattle of the *surveillante's* clapper. I could not get used to the idea that here were nuns who did not lose their surnames, as all normal nuns did, becoming Sister Mary Aloysia or Sister Josepha, but were called Madame Barclay or Madame Slattery, or *Ma Mére* or Mother for short. They were not *ordinary* nuns, it was scornfully explained to me, but women of good family, cloistered ladies of the world, just as Sacred Heart girls were not *ordinary* Catholics but daughters of the best families. And my new subjects were not ordinary subjects, like spelling and arithmetic, but rhetoric, French, literature, Christian doctrine, English history. I was fresh from a Minneapolis parochial school, where a crude "citizenship" had been the rule, where we pledged allegiance to the flag every morning, warbled "My Country, 'Tis of Thee," said "grievious" instead of "grievous," competed in paper drives and citywide spelling contests, drew hatchets for Washington's Birthday and log cabins for Lincoln's, gave to foreign missions for our brown and yellow brothers, feared the Ku Klux Klan, sold chances and subscriptions to periodicals, were taken on tours of flour mills and water works; I looked upon my religion as a branch of civics and conformity, and the select Sacred Heart atmosphere took my breath away. The very austerities of our life had a mysterious aristocratic punctilio: the rule of silence so often clapped down on us at mealtimes, the pitcher of water and the bowl for washing at our bedsides, the supervised Saturday-night bath in the cold bath-room, with a red-faced nun sitting on a stool behind a drawn curtain with our bath towel in her lap. I felt as though I stood on the outskirts and observed the ritual of a cult, a cult of fashion and elegance in the sphere of religion.

And, thanks to the standardization of an archaic rule, the past still vibrated in the convent, a high, sweet note. It was the France of the Restoration that was embalmed in the Sacred Heart atmosphere, like a period room in a museum with a silken cord drawn across it. The quarrels of the *philosophes* still echoed in the classrooms; the tumbrils had just ceased to creak, and Voltaire grinned in the background. Orthodoxy had been re-established, Louis XVIII ruled, but there was a hint of Orlean-ism in the air and a whisper of reduced circumstances in the pick-pick of our needles doing fine darning and turning buttonholes. Byron's great star had risen, and, across the sea, America beckoned in the romances of Chateaubriand and Fenimore Cooper and the adventures of the *cou-reurs de bois*. Protestantism did not trouble us; we had made our peace with the Huguenots. What we feared was skepticism, deism, and the dread spirit of atheism—France's Lucifer. Monthly, in the study hall, the Mother Superior, Madame MacIllvra, adjured us, daughters of den-tists and lawyers, grocers and realtors, heiresses of the Chevrolet agency and of Riley & Finn, contractors, against the sin of doubt, that curse of fine intellects. Her blue eyes clouded and her fair white brow ruffled under her snowy coif as she considered, with true feminine sympathy, the awful fate of Shelley, a young man of good family who had con-tracted atheism at Oxford.

These discourses of Madame MacIllvra's fascinated me, peopling the world with new characters and a new sort of hero-villain, alone, noble, bereft; I watched the surge and billow of her bosom, and pulsed with pity and terror. During that first year, I was very unhappy in the convent, or, to be more accurate, I felt like a lorn new soul come to Paradise, elated and charmed by what I saw—by the ranging hierarchies, the thrones and dominions—but unable to get a nod from any of the angels as they brushed by me on errands of bliss. As a revelation of the aristo-cratic principle, the convent overwhelmed me. The beauty and poise of the middling and older girls were like nothing I had seen on earth. If not like angels, they were like the kings' paramours I had read about in history or like Olympian goddesses, tall and swift of tread. Each of these paragons moved in an aureole of mysterious self-sufficiency; each had her pledged admirers among the younger and plainer girls, and disputes about them raged among us as though someone had thrown the apple of discord. In the intensity of the convent light, even a rather ordinary girl could acquire this penumbra of beauty, by gravity and dignity of person; it was a sort of calling, a still hearkening to inward voices, which brought a secret, cool smile to the lips of the one elected.

From the first, of course, I longed to become a member of this exquisite company, if only as a favored satellite or maid-in-waiting. But instead I stepped straight into that fatality that in every school awaits the newcomer who has not learned the first law of social dynamics: be suspicious of tenders of assistance. Around me, from the very first day, as I arranged my books in my desk, circled the rusty rejects of the school system, hungry as crows for friendship, copious with invitations, pointers, and sweets from home to be shared. Every school, every college, every office, every factory has its complement of these miserable creatures, of whom I was soon to be one. No doubt they exist in Heaven, just inside the gate, peering over Saint Peter's shoulder for the advent of a new spirit, whom they can show the ropes; Hell must have them, too, and if I were Dante, for example, knowing what I know today, I would have been a *little* more leery of Vergil and that guided tour. In any case, I fell; I accepted with thanks those offers of aid and companionship. I learned the way to the refectory, how to fold my papers properly, how to stitch on my collars and cuffs, how to pin my veil, and, in return, I found myself the doomed companion of girls with flat, broad faces and huge collections of freckles, girls with dandruff on their uniforms, with spots and gaping seams, wrinkled black stockings, chilblains, owllike glasses, carrot-colored hair—damp, confidential souls with quantities of younger brothers and sisters just like themselves. And I was one of them, too. On Saturday afternoons (we were all five-day boarders, which gave us "a lot in common"), I was the intimate of their mah-jongg parties, eating brick ice cream and frosted cupcakes, curtsying to their mothers, suspiciously hospitable dames with stout golfing legs who were pressing with second helpings, prizes, and "Didn't I know your mother?" On Monday mornings, at recess, Nemesis exacted its price; we wretches all loyally "stuck together," like pieces of melting candy in the linty recesses of a coat pocket. At the time, I thought I was alone in my impulses of savage withdrawal, but now I think that all of us, except those of subnormal mentality, bitterly hated each other and had each other's measure.

I felt the shock of all this the more acutely because nothing had prepared me for it. I had come to the convent anticipating a ready acceptance—or, rather, not even anticipating it, so completely had I taken it for granted. In the parochial school, I had led the class in scholarship and athletics; the fact that I was an orphan and the strange circumstances of my home life, led between rich grandparents and a set of harsh, miserly guardians, had given me a unique social position. Waking up now sometimes in my cubicle at six-thirty in the morning to hear the nuns singing their office, far off in the chapel, I could look back, half unbelieving, to a time when the leading boys and girls in my classroom had positively vied for my favors. I thought of my confirmation, which had been the great event of 6A in St. Stephen's School—what a stir it had made when it was known that Mary McCarthy, who was only ten years old, was going to be confirmed with the seventh- and eighth-graders. I remembered how my friends, full of curiosity and awe, had hung around outside the rectory one afternoon while I went in alone to tackle Father Gaughan, the old parish priest, and persuade him to confirm me, because I was such a prodigy of theological lore. In the dining room, next to the parlor, the priest's housekeeper was rattling the dishes and making angry noises, to indicate that I should go, that the Father's dinner was ready, as I could perfectly well smell for myself. Yet I had lingered, stubbornly, refusing to be put off, reciting passages from the catechism, till finally the old priest had patted my head and said to me, "Perseverance wins the crown," and I had run out into the street, jubilating, to meet my amazed classmates. "Perseverance wins the crown, perseverance wins the crown," I had sung over and over, just under my breath. This maxim and the triumph it capped fortified me now in the convent; I argued that it was only a question of time before I would be noticed by the superior girls with whom I rightfully belonged.

It was the idea of being noticed that consumed all my attention; the rest, it seemed to me, would come of itself. Those goddesses whose society I craved had only to look down, once, to discern among the seventh-graders one who was different from the rest of the speckled crew. The sprinkling of freckles across the bridge of my own turned-up nose I regarded as ornamental; I rather fancied myself as a burning tiger lily among the roses and Easter lilies and Parma violets of the school. But despite my haughty manner, my new jeweled barrettes, my week-end applications of cucumber cream, my studied insolence to my friends, nobody seemed able to distinguish me. Even those very friends, who ought, by this time, to have known better (for I could make them cry whenever I wanted to), treated me comfortably as one of themselves. Only the nuns recognized the difference, and this with a certain sorrow and gentle disapprobation. When I shaved off half my eyebrows, I was given a lecture on vanity, but within the convent no one was permitted to mention my extraordinary appearance. It was thought that I was getting ideas too old for my age, and my library list was examined; following the eyebrow episode, I was given a weekly dose of Fenimore

Cooper as a corrective. When I finally refused this as childish, I was started on *John L. Stoddard's Lectures.*

Though I often stood first in my studies, the coveted pink ribbon for good conduct never came my way. I suppose this was because of my meanness, in particular the spiteful taunts I directed at a supercilious fat girl, the petted daughter of a rich meat packer, with heavy rings on her fingers and a real fur coat, who was my principal rival for honors in the classroom, but at the time I could not understand why the ribbon was denied me. I never broke any of the rules, and was it my fault if she blubbered when I applied, perfectly accurately, a term I had heard mothers whisper—*nouveau riche?* Wasn't it *true,* I argued, when I was rebuked by Madame Barclay, our mistress of studies, and wasn't fat Beryl always boasting of her money and curling her baby lip at girls whose mothers had to work? It wasn't kind of me, replied Madame Barclay, but I did not think it kind of her when she passed me over for Beryl in casting the class play. Everyone could see that I was much the better actress, and the leading role of haughty Lady Spindle was precisely suited to my style. I did not believe Madame Barclay when she explained that in the tryout I sounded too fierce and angry for a comedy; the nuns in the parochial school had never said so. I could see, darkly, that I was being punished, with that inverted favoritism so typical of authority ("Whom the Lord loveth, He chastiseth"), for everyone detested Beryl, even the nuns. Up to the last moment, I could not think they would really do this to me; I knew the part by heart and practiced the lines privately against the time when they would recognize their error and send for me to rescue them. But, incredibly, the play went on without me, and my only satisfaction, as I sat in the audience, was to watch Pork Barrel forget her lines; I supplied them, to my neighbors, in a vindictive whisper, till somebody told me to hush.

Nobody cared, apparently; nobody knew what they had missed; to them, it was just a silly seventh-grade play. My contempt for the seventh grade was stiffened by this experience; I resolved to cut myself off from them. At this time, for reasons of discipline, my desk in study hall was changed, and for the remainder of the term I was put next to an eighth-grader, the vivacious one of a pair of very popular twins; this girl was being punished for chattering with her former deskmate. The gulf between the grades was very wide, and it was reasoned, correctly, that she would have no incentive to repeat her sin with me. Yet the mistress of discipline who put us together must have had a taste for visual punning, for the strange fact was that this girl and I resembled each other far more startlingly than she resembled her studious sister. We had the same brows, the same noses, the same fair skin and dark hair, the same height; the only difference was in the way we parted our hair and in the color of our eyes, hers being hazel and mine green. Louise, unlike me, had a kind disposition but little curiosity, and even the likeness between us, so much remarked on by the nuns, was not enough to focus her merry eye on me for more than a wondering instant. As a twin, doubtless, she had grown indifferent to the oddities of Nature's ways. In any case, she paid me no heed, and the very thing that might have drawn us together underlined the disparity between us. One day, as we sat side by side, bitterness overcame me to see her, my double, exchanging notes with her eighth-grade friends and acting as though I were not there. I took a piece of paper and wrote, "In my other school, I was popular too," and shoved it over onto her desk. She read it and lifted her eyes with a look of quizzical astonishment. "Tell me," she wrote back, and I replied with a dazzling essay on the friends I had had, the contests I had won, the boys who had had crushes on me. As I watched her read, I felt a tremendous satisfaction: I had at last got the facts on record. It had come to me, suddenly, that I was neglected because the convent did not know *who I was*. Once the truth was discovered, I would receive my due, like royalty traveling incognito when it is recognized by someone in the crowd and the whole populace falls on its knees. "It must be very hard," she wrote back, sympathetically. And that, to my amazement, was the end of it. I had only made her vaguely sorry for me, so that she smiled at me from time to time, with looks of encouragement. I was forced to accept the fact that my former self was dead.

But my resolve was not softened. I came back in the fall, as a full-time boarder, with a certain set to my jaw, determined to go it alone. A summer passed in thoughtful isolation, rowing on a mountain lake, diving from a pier, had made me perfectly reckless. I was going to get myself recognized at whatever price. It was in this cold, empty gambler's mood, common to politicians and adolescents, that I surveyed the convent setup. If I could not win fame by goodness, I was ready to do it by badness, and I looked to the past for precedents. Anything that had happened once in a Sacred Heart convent became, so to speak, fossilized in the institutions of the order. Once, long ago, perhaps here or in Bruges or Chicago or nineteenth-century France, a girl had eloped with the music master, so now our piano lessons were chaperoned by a fat sister, one of the domestics, who reclined, snoring gently, in a chair just behind the Baron's. For a few weeks during the fall, the prospect of an elopement held first claim on my thoughts. My twelve-year-old hands trembled with hope whenever, in the stretch of an octave, they grazed the white hands of the professor; he had a few little blond glinting hairs on his plump fingers, which seemed to hint of virility dormant but vibrato, like the sleeping nun. I grew faint when my laced shoe encountered his spatted Oxford on the loud pedal. Examples of child marriages among the feudal nobility crowded through my head, as if to encourage the Baron, but at length I had to bow to the force of American custom and face it: he probably thought I was too young.

The decision to lose my faith followed swiftly on this disappointment. People are always asking me how I came to lose my faith, imagining a period of deep inward struggle. The truth is the whole momentous project simply jumped at me, ready-made, out of one of Madame MacIll-vra's discourses. I had decided to do it before I knew what it was, when it was merely an interweaving of words, lose-your-faith, like the ladder made of sheets on which the daring girl had descended into the arms of her Romeo. "Say you've lost your faith," the devil prompted, assuring me that there was no risk if I chose my moment carefully. Starting Monday morning, we were going to have a retreat, to be preached by a stirring Jesuit. If I lost my faith on, say, Sunday, I could regain it during the three days of retreat, in time for Wednesday confessions. Thus there would be only four days in which my soul would be in danger if I should happen to die suddenly. The only real sacrifice would be forgoing Communion on Sunday. He who hesitates is lost; *qui ne risque rien n'a rien*, observed the devil, lapsing into French, as is his wont. If I did not do it, someone else might—that awful Beryl, for instance. It was a miracle that someone had not thought of it already, the idea seemed so obvious, like a store waiting to be robbed.

Surprised looks were bent on me Sunday morning in the chapel when the line formed for Communion and I knelt unmoving in my pew. I was always an ostentatious communicant. Now girls clambered over me, somebody gave me a poke, but I shook my head sorrowfully, signifying by my expression that I was in a state of mortal sin and dared not approach the table. At lunch, eating little, I was already a center of attention at my table; I maintained a mournful silence, rehearsing what I would say to Madame MacIllvra in her office as soon as the meal was over. Having put in my request for an appointment, I was beginning to be slightly frightened. After lunch, as I stood waiting outside her door, I kept licking my lips. Yet this fear, I argued, was a token of sincerity; naturally you would be frightened if you had just lost your faith.

"*Ma Mère*, I have lost my faith." At her roll-top desk, Madame Mac-Illvra started; one plump white hand fluttered to her heart. She gave me a single searching look. Evidently, my high standing in my studies had prepared her for this catastrophe, for she did not ransack me further as I stood there quaking and bowing and trying to repress a foolish giveaway grin. I had been expecting a long questioning, but she reached, sighing, for the telephone, as though I had appendicitis or the measles.

"Pray, my child," she murmured as she summoned Father Dennis, our chaplain, from the neighboring Jesuit college. "I can't pray," I promptly responded. A classical symptom of unbelief was the inability to pray, as I knew from her own lectures. Madame MacIllvra nodded, turning a shade paler; she glanced at the watch in her bosom. "Go to your room," she said perturbedly. "You are not to speak to anyone. You will be sent for when Father Dennis comes. I will pray for you myself."

Some of her alarm had communicated itself to me. I had not realized that what I had said was so serious. I felt quite frightened now by what I had done and by the prospect of a talk with Father Dennis, who was an old, dry, forbidding man, very different from the handsome missionary father who was going to preach our retreat. The idea of backing down presented itself with more and more attraction, but I did not see how I could do this without being convicted of shallowness. Moreover, I doubted very much that Madame MacIllvra would believe me if I said now that I had got my faith back all at once. She would make me talk to Father Dennis anyway. Once the convent machinery had got into motion, there was no way of stopping it, as I knew from horrendous experience. It was like the mills of the gods.

By the time I reached my cubicle I was thoroughly scared. I saw that I was going to have to go through with this or be exposed before them all as a liar, and for the first time it occurred to me that I would have to have arguments to make my doubts sound real. At the same shaken moment I realized that I knew nothing whatever of atheism. If I were out in the world, I could consult the books that had been written on the subject, but here in the convent, obviously, there could be no access to atheistic literature. From the playground outside floated the voices of the girls, laughing. I went to the window and looked down at them, feeling utterly cut off and imprisoned within my own emptiness. There was no one to turn to but God, yet this was one occasion when prayer would be unavailing. A prayer for atheistic arguments (surely?) would only bring out the stern side of God. What was I going to do?

I sat down on my bed and tried to count my resources. After all, I said to myself suddenly, I did know something about skepticism, thanks to Madame MacIllvra herself. The skeptics' arguments were based on science—false science, said Madame MacIllvra—which reasoned that there was no God because you could not see Him. This was a silly materialistic "proof," to which, unfortunately, I knew the answer. Could you see the wind? And yet its touch was everywhere, like God's invisible grace blowing on our souls. Skeptics denied the life after death and said there was no Heaven, only the blue of space in the celestial vault. Science proved that, they said, and science proved, too, that there was no Hell burning under the earth. We had had the answer to that one, only last week in Christian Doctrine, in Saint Paul's steely words, which we had had to memorize: "That eye hath not seen, nor ear heard, neither hath it entered into the heart of man, what things God hath prepared for them that love Him." I sank into a dull despair. Was I going to have to offer "proofs" that any fool could see through? Any fool knew that man's scientific calipers could not grasp God directly. Hell and Heaven were not contradictory to science but something different altogether, beyond science. But what about miracles?

I sat up suddenly. Miracles were not invisible. They were supposed to happen right here on earth, today. They were attested in the photographs of Lourdes by all the crutches hanging up in token of thankfulness for cures. Nevertheless, I said to myself delightedly, *I* had never seen a miracle, and perhaps all these people were lying or deluded. Christian Science claimed cures, too, and we knew that that was just imagination. Voltaire was an intelligent man and he had laughed at miracles. Why not I?

As I sat there searching my memory, doubts that I had hurriedly stowed away, like contraband in a bureau drawer, came back to me, reassuringly. I found that I had always been a little suspicious of the life after death. Perhaps it was really true that the dead just rotted and I would never rejoin my parents in Heaven? I scratched a spot on my uniform, watching it turn white under my thumbnail. Another memory was tapping at my consciousness: the question of the Resurrection of the Body. At the last trump, all the bodies of men, from Adam onward, were supposed to leap from their graves and rejoin the souls that had left them; this was why the Church forbade cremation. But somewhere, not so long ago, I had heard a priest quote scornfully a materialistic argument against this. The materialist said (yes, that was it!) that people rotted and turned into fertilizer, which went into vegetables, and then other people ate the vegetables, so that when the Resurrection came there would not be enough bodies to go around. The priest answered that for God, anything was possible; if God made man from clay, He could certainly make some extra bodies. But in that case, I thought, pouncing, why did He object to cremation? And in any case they would not be the *same* bodies, which was the whole point. And I could think of an even stronger instance: What about cannibals? If God divided the cannibal into the component bodies he had digested, what would become of the cannibal? God could start with whatever flesh the cannibal had had when he was a baby, before he began eating missionaries, but if his father and mother had been cannibals too, what flesh would he really have that he could call his own?

At that time, I did not know that this problem had been treated by Aquinas, and with a child's pertinacity, I mined away at the foundations of the Fortress Rock. Elation had replaced fear. I could hardly wait now to meet Father Dennis and confront him with these doubts, so remarkable in one of my years. Parallels with the young Jesus, discoursing with the scribes and doctors, bounded through my head: "And all that heard Him were astonished at His Wisdom and His answers." No one now, I felt certain, would dare accuse me of faking. I strolled along proudly with the messenger who had come to fetch me; just as her knock sounded, I had reached the stage of doubting the divinity of Christ. I could see in the wondering looks this Iris was shedding on me that already I was a credit to the milieu.

In the dark parlor, the priest was waiting, still in his cassock—a wrinkled, elderly man with a hairless face and brown, dead curly hair that looked like a wig. He had a weary, abstracted air as he turned away from the window, as though he had spent his life in the confessional box. His voice was hollow; everything about him was colorless and dry. As chaplain to Madame MacIllvra, he must have become a sort of spiritual factotum, like an upper servant in an apron, and there was despondency in his manner, as though his *Nunc Dimittis* would never be pronounced. It was clear that he did not have the resilience of our clever nuns.

"You have doubts, Mother says," he began in a low, listless voice, pointing me to a straight chair opposite him and then seating himself in an armchair, with half-averted face, as priests do in the confessional. I nodded self-importantly. "Yes, Father," I recited. "I doubt the divinity of Christ and the Resurrection of the Body and the real existence of Heaven and Hell." The priest raised his scanty eyebrows, like two little wigs, and sighed. "You have been reading atheistic literature?" I shook my head. "No, Father. The doubts came all by themselves." The priest cupped his chin in his hand. "So," he murmured. "Let us have them then."

I was hurt when he interrupted me right in the middle of the cannibals. "These are scholastic questions," he said curtly. "Beyond the reach of your years. Believe me, the Church has an answer for them." A feeling of disappointment came over me; it seemed to me that I had a right to know the answer to the cannibal question, since I had thought it up all by myself, but my "Why can't I know nows" were brushed aside, just as though I had been asking about how babies were born. "No," said Father Dennis, with finality. My first excitement was punctured and I began to be suspicious of him, in the manner of adolescents. What, I asked myself shrewdly, was the Church trying to hide from me?

"Let us come to more important matters." He leaned forward in his chair, with the first sign of interest he had given. "You doubt the divinity of Our Lord?" I felt a peculiar avidity in his question that made me wish to hold back. A touch of fear returned to me. "I *think* so," I said dubiously, half ready to abandon my ground. *"Think!* Don't you know?" he demanded, raising his voice like a frail thunderbolt. Quailing, I produced my doubt—I was one of those cowards who are afraid not to be brave. Nevertheless, I spoke hurriedly, in gulps, as if swallowing medicine. "We are supposed to know that He was God because He rose from the dead— that was His sign to us that He was more than man. But you can't prove that He rose from the dead. That's only what the Apostles said. How do we know they were telling the truth? They were very ignorant, superstitious men—just fishermen, weren't they? People like that nowadays believe in fairies and spirits." I looked appealingly up at him, half begging recognition for my doubt and half waiting for him to settle it.

The priest passed a hand across his forehead. "You consider Our Lord a liar, then?" he said in a sepulchral tone. "You think He deceived the poor, ignorant Apostles by pretending to be the Son of God. That is what you are saying, my child, though you do not know it yourself. You are calling Our Blessed Saviour a liar and a cheat." "He might have been mistaken," I objected, feeling rather cross. "He might have *thought* He was God." Father Dennis closed his eyes. "You must have faith, my child," he said abruptly, rising from his chair and taking a few quick steps, his cassock bobbing.

I gazed at him in humble perplexity. For the first time, he seemed to me rather holy, as if the word "faith" had elicited something sweet and sanctified from his soul, but by the same token he seemed very remote from me, as if he were feeling something that I was unable to feel. Yet he was not answering my arguments; in fact, he was looking down at me with a grave, troubled expression, as if he, too, were suddenly conscious of a gulf between us, a gulf that could not be bridged by words. The awesome thought struck me that perhaps I *had* lost my faith. Could it have slipped away without my knowing it? "Help me, Father," I implored meekly, aware that this was the right thing to say but meaning it nevertheless.

I seemed to have divided into two people, one slyly watching as the priest sank back into the armchair, the other anxious and aghast at the turn the interview was taking. "The wisdom and goodness of Jesus," Father Dennis said slowly, "as we find it in His life and teachings—do you think mere man was capable of *this?*" I pondered. "Why not?" I queried, soberly. But the priest glanced at me with reproach, as if I were being fresh. "You don't know your history, I see. Among the prophets and the pagans, among the kings and philosophers, among the saints and scholars, was there ever such a One?" A little smile glinted in the corners of his mouth. "No," I admitted. The priest nodded. "There, you see, my child. Such a departure from our ordinary human nature signifies the Divine intervention. If we had only Christ's teaching, we could know that He was God. But in addition we have His miracles, the firm assurance of tradition, and the Living Church, the Rock on which He built and which survived the buffets of the ages, where the false religions foundered and were lost to the mind of man."

He took out his watch and peered at it in the dusk. My pride, again, was offended. "It's not only good things that survive," I said boldly. "There's sin, for instance." "The devil is eternal," said Father Dennis, sighing, with a quick glance at me.

"But then the Church could be the instrument of the devil, couldn't it?" Father Dennis swooped. "Then the teachings of Jesus, which it guards, are of diabolical origin?" I flushed. "Other religions have lasted," I said, retreating. "The Jewish religion and Mohammedanism. Is that because they are diabolic?" I spoke with an air of ingenuousness, but I knew I had him in a corner; there were Jewish girls in the convent. "They have a partial truth," Father Dennis murmured. "Hence they have been preserved." I became impatient with this sparring, which was taking me away from a real point I had glimpsed. "Yes, Father," I said. "But still I don't see that the fact that Christ was an exception proves that He was God." "There are no exceptions in nature," retorted Father Dennis. "Oh, Father!" I cried. "I can think of lots."

I was burning to pursue this subject, for it had come to me, slowly, that Christ really *could* have been a man. The idea of Christ as simply man had something extraordinary and joyous about it that was different, I perceived, from the condescension of God to the flesh. I was glad I had started this discussion, for I was learning something new every second. All fear had left me and all sense of mere willful antagonism. I was intent on showing Father Dennis the new possibilities that opened; my feeling for him was comradely.

But once more he shut me off. "You must accept what I tell you," he said, almost sharply. "You are too young to understand these things. You must have faith." "But you're supposed to give me faith, Father," I protested. "Only God can do that," he answered. "Pray, and He will grant it." "I can't pray," I said automatically. "You know your prayers," he said. "Say them." He rose, and I made my curtsy. "Father!" I cried out suddenly, in desperation at the way he was leaving me. "There's something else!"

He turned back, fatiguedly, but the wild look on my face must have alarmed him. "What is it, my child?" He came a little nearer, peering at me with a concerned, kindly expression. "My child," he said gravely, "do you doubt the existence of God?" "Yes," I breathed, in exultant agony, knowing that it was true.

He sat down with me again and took my hand. Very gently, seeing that this was what I seemed to want of him, he recited for me the five *a posteriori* proofs of God's existence: the argument of the unmoved Mover, the argument of efficient causes, the argument of the Necessary Being implied by contingent beings, the argument of graduated perfections, the argument of the wonderful order and design in the universe. Most of what he said I did not understand, but the gist was clear to me. It was that every effect must have a cause and the cause was, of course, God. The universe could not exist unless some self-sufficient Being had created it and put it in motion. I listened earnestly, trying to test what he said, almost convinced and yet not quite. It was as though the spirit of doubt had wormed its way into the very tissue of my thinking, so that axioms that had seemed simple and clear only an hour or so before now became perplexing and murky. "Why, Father," I asked finally, "does everything *have* to have a cause? Why couldn't the universe just be there, causing itself?"

Father Dennis lit the lamp on the table beside him; the bell rang for *goûter,* a girl poked her head in and hurriedly withdrew. "Because," he said patiently, "I have just explained to you, every effect must have a proportionate cause." I turned this over in my head, reminding myself that I was a child and that he probably thought I did not comprehend him. "Except God," I repeated helpfully. The priest nodded. "But Father," I cried, with a sudden start of discovery, "why can't the universe be self-sufficient if God can? Why can't something in matter be the uncaused cause? Like electricity?"

The priest shook his head sorrowfully. "I cannot tell you, my child." He dropped into a different tone, caustic and reproachful. "I cannot open eyes that blindly refuse to see. Can inert matter give birth to spirit? Did inert matter give you your conscience? Who deny causal necessity make the world a chaos where vice and anarchy reign!" His hollow voice reverberated as if he were addressing a whole dockful of secular philosophers, arraigned in a corner of the room. "Oh, my child," he concluded, rising, "give up reading that atheistic filth. Pray to God for faith and make a good confession." He left the room swiftly, his cassock swelling behind him.

Father Dennis's failure made a great impression on the convent. Wherever I went, eyes regarded me respectfully: there went the girl that a Jesuit had failed to convince. The day girls and five day boarders, returning on Monday, quickly heard the news. Little queens who had never noticed my existence gathered round me at recess and put me whispered questions, for we were not supposed to talk during the retreat. The coincidence of the holy fervor of the retreat with my unsanctified state heightened the sense of the prodigious. It was thought that Father Heeney, the curly-haired, bronzed missionary who had got such results

among the Eskimos, was pitting his oratory against me. In her office, at a
second interview, Madame MacIllvra wiped the corners of her eyes with
her plain cambric handkerchief. She felt that she had betrayed a trust
reposed in her, from Heaven, by my dead mother. Tears came readily
to her, as to most pretty lady principals, especially when she felt that
the *convent* might be open to criticism. By Wednesday, the third time
she saw me, we had come to a serious pass. My deskmate, Louise, had
bet me that I would not get my faith back by Wednesday; as one fiery
sermon followed another and I remained unswayed, a sort of uneasiness
settled down over the convent. It was clear to everyone, including me,
that I would *have* to get my faith back to put an end to this terrible
uncertainty.

I was as much concerned now as Madame MacIllvra herself. I was
trying, with all my power, to feel faith, if only as a public duty, but the
more I tapped and tested myself, the more I was forced to recognize that
there was no belief inside me. My very soul had fled, as far as I could
make out. Curiously enough, for the first time, seeing what I had
wrought, I had a sense of obligation to others and not to my own soul or
to God, which was a proof in itself that I had lost God, for our chief
obligation in life was supposed to be to please Him. God (if there was a
God) would certainly not be pleased if I *pretended* to regain my faith to
satisfy Madame MacIllvra and Madame Barclay and my new friend and
double, Louise, who was mischievous but a good Catholic. Yet this was
the decision I came to after a second unfruitful session in the parlor, this
time with Father Heeney, who could convert me, I felt leadenly, if
anybody could. He had said all the same things that Father Dennis had
said, though calling me by my first name and laughing when I told him
that my father and grandfather were lawyers, as though my serious
doubts were part of what he called the gift of gab. He, too, seemed
convinced that I had been reading atheistic literature and warned me,
jestingly, of the confessional when I denied it. These priests, I thought
bitterly, seemed to imagine that you could do nothing for yourself, that
everything was from inheritance and reading, just as they imagined that
Christ could not have been a "mere man," and just, for that matter, as
they kept saying that you must have "faith," a word that had become
more and more irritating to me during the past few days. "Natural
reason, Mary," expatiated Father Heeney, "will not take you the whole
way today. There's a little gap that we have to fill with faith." I looked up
at him measuringly. So there *was* a gap, then. How was it that they had
never mentioned this interesting fact to us before?

As I left the parlor, I decided to hold Father Heeney personally responsible for the deception he was forcing me into. "I'll see you in the
confessional," he called after me in his full, warm voice, but it was not

me, I promised myself, that he was going to see but a mere pious effigy of myself. By failing to convert me and treating my case so lightly—calling me Thomasina, for instance, in a would-be funny reference to doubting Thomas—he was driving me straight into fraud. Thanks to his incompetence, the only thing left for me to do was to enact a simulated conversion. But I had no intention of giving him the credit. I was going to pretend to be converted in the night, by a dream.

And I did not feel a bit sorry, even on Thursday morning, kneeling in my white veil at the altar railing to receive the Host. Behind me, the nuns, I knew, were rejoicing, as good nuns should, over the reclamation of a soul. Madame MacIllvra's blue eyes were probably misting. Beside me, Pork Barrel was bursting her seams with envy. Louise (I had just informed her in the veiling room) had invited me to spend the night with her during Christmas vacation. My own chief sensation was one of detached surprise at how far I had come from my old mainstays, as once, when learning to swim, I had been doing the dead-man's float and looked back, raising my doused head, to see my water wings drifting, far behind me, on the lake's surface.

MARGARET MEAD
(1901–1978)

Margaret Mead was born in Philadelphia, where her father was a professor at the Wharton School of the University of Pennsylvania. She studied anthropology at Barnard with Franz Boas, the man who earlier had trained Zora Neale Hurston, and with Ruth Benedict, his assistant. Her first field work was carried out in Samoa in 1925, as described in this section of her autobiography, *Blackberry Winter: My Earlier Years* (1972). It resulted in her influential *Coming of Age in Samoa* (1928), which suggested that Americans might learn something from the Polynesians about handling the problems of adolescence. By insisting throughout her long and productive career on making comparisons between America and other cultures, she broadened both the scope and the appeal of anthropology.

At about the time that Mead was studying the Samoans, Karen Blixen was running her coffee farm in Africa and observing her helpers. Compare Isak Dinesen, *Out of Africa*. For other offspring of the professorate, compare Eleanor Munro, *Memoir of a Modernist's Daughter* and Natalia Ginzburg, *Family Sayings,* and see also Mary Catherine Bateson, *With a Daughter's Eye,* a memoir of Mead and Gregory Bateson by their daughter.

FROM *Blackberry Winter*

When I sailed for Samoa, I realized only very vaguely what a commitment to field work and writing about field work meant. My decision to become an anthropologist was based in part on my belief that a scientist, even one who had no great and special gift such as a great artist must have, could make a useful contribution to knowledge. I had responded also to the sense of urgency that had been conveyed to me by Professor Boas and Ruth Benedict. Even in remote parts of the world ways of life about which nothing was known were vanishing before the onslaught of modern civilization. The work of recording these unknown ways of life had to be done now—*now*—or they would be lost forever. Other things could wait, but not this most urgent task. All this came to a head at the

Toronto meetings* in 1924, where I was the youngest participant and everyone else had talked about "my people" and I had no people to talk about. From that time on I was determined to go to the field, not at some leisurely chosen later date, but immediately—as soon as I had completed the necessary preliminary steps.

But I really did not know much about field work. The course on methods that Professor Boas taught was not about field work. It was about theory—how material could be organized to support or to call in question some theoretical point. Ruth Benedict had spent a summer working with a group of quite acculturated Indians in California, where she had taken her mother along for a vacation, and she had worked in Zuñi. I had read Ruth's descriptions of the landscape, of how the Zuñi looked, of the fierceness of the bedbugs and the difficulties of managing food, but I knew little about how she went about her work. Professor Boas always spoke of the Kwakiutl as "my dear friends," but this was not followed by anything that helped me to know what it was like to live among them.

When I agreed to study the adolescent girl and Professor Boas consented to my doing this field work in Samoa, I had a half hour's instruction in which Professor Boas told me that I must be willing to seem to waste time just sitting about and listening, but that I must not waste time doing ethnography, that is, studying the culture as a whole. Fortunately, many people—missionaries, jurists, government officials, and old-fashioned ethnographers—had been to Samoa, and so the temptation to "waste time" on ethnography would be less. During the summer he also wrote me a letter in which he once more cautioned me to be careful of my health and discussed the problem he had set me:

> I am sure you have thought over the question very carefully, but there are one or two points which I have in mind and to which I would like to call your attention, even if you have thought of them before.
>
> One question that interests me very much is how the young girls react to the restraints of custom. We find very often among ourselves during the period of adolescence a strong rebellious spirit that may be expressed in sullenness or in sudden outbursts. In other individuals there is a weak submission which is accompanied, however, by a suppressed rebellion that may make itself felt in peculiar ways, perhaps in a desire for solitude which is really an expression of desire for freedom, or otherwise in forced participation in social affairs in order to drown the mental troubles. I am not at all clear in my mind in how far similar conditions may occur in primitive society and in how far the desire for independence may be simply due to our modern conditions and to a more strongly developed individualism.

*Of the British Association of Science—ED.

Another point in which I am interested is the excessive bashfulness of girls in primitive society. I do not know whether you will find it there. It is characteristic of Indian girls of most tribes, and often not only in their relations to outsiders, but frequently within the narrow circle of the family. They are often afraid to talk and are very retiring before older people.

Another interesting problem is that of crushes among girls. For the older ones you might give special attention to the occurrence of romantic love, which is not by any means absent as far as I have been able to observe, and which, of course, appears most strongly where the parents or society impose marriages which the girls may not want. . . .

. . . Stick to individual and pattern, problems like Ruth Bunzel on art in Pueblos and Haeberlin on Northwest Coast. I believe you have read Malinowski's paper in *Psyche* on the behavior of individuals in the family in New Guinea. I think he is much too influenced by Freudianis, but the problem he had in mind is one of those which I have in mind.

For the rest, there was G. Stanley Hall, who had written a huge book on adolescence in which, equating stages of growth with stages of culture, he had discussed his belief that each growing child recapitulated the history of the human race. There were also the assumptions set forth in textbooks, mainly derived from German theory, about puberty as a period of storm and stress. At that time puberty and adolescence were firmly equated in everyone's thinking. Only much later, students of child development began to say that there was perhaps a "first adolescence" around the age of six and a second crisis at puberty and that adolescence could be prolonged into the twenties and might in some sense reappear in adults in their forties.

My training in psychology had given me ideas about the use of samples, tests, and systematic inventories of behavior. I had also some very slight experience of social case work. My aunt Fanny was working at the Juvenile Protective Association at Hull House, in Chicago, and one summer I had sat on the floor and read their records. This had given me an idea of what the social context of individual behavior was—how one had to look at the household and place the household in the setting of the community.

I knew that I would have to learn the language. But I did not know anyone who was colloquially proficient in the language of the people they studied except missionaries, or the children of missionaries, turned ethnologists. I had read only one essay by Malinowski and did not know how he had used the Trobriand language. I myself had never learned a foreign language; I had only "studied" Latin and French and German in high school. Our training in linguistics had consisted of short demonstrations of extremely exotic languages in the course of which we were confronted, without previous preparation, with phrases like these:

"Adē'," nē'x·lata NEmō'guis lāxis ts'ā'yē Lō'La'watsa; "ꝫoā'LEla sEns
"Friend," he said NEmō'guis to his younger Lō'La'watan; do not us
brother let

hēquä'lē yā'wix·'idag·a x·ins qa yā'yats'ē sEns xunō'kuēx."
go on in let us act us to go on the our son this."
this way sea

In a way this was an excellent method of teaching. It prepared us—as
our classes on forms of kinship and religious belief also did—to expect
almost anything, however strange, unaccountable, and bizarre it might
seem to us. This is, of course, the first lesson the field anthropologist
must learn; that he may well meet up with new, unheard-of, unthought-
of ways of organizing human behavior.

The expectation that we may at any time be confronted by some as
yet unrecorded mode of behavior is the basis on which anthropologists
often clash with psychologists, whose theories have developed out of
their efforts to be "scientific" and out of their skepticism about philosophical constructs. It is also the basis of our clash with economists,
political scientists, and sociologists, to the extent that they use the model
of our own social arrangements in their studies of other societies.

The tough treatment given us by Professor Boas shook us up, prepared
us for the unexpected, and be it said, the extremely difficult. But we did
not learn how to organize work on a strange new language to the point at
which a grammar could be worked out on the basis of which we could
learn to speak the language. Sapir remarked parenthetically on the immorality of learning foreign languages; one was never really honest, he
said, except in one's mother tongue.

There was, in fact, no *how* in our education. What we learned was
what to look for. Years later, Camilla Wedgwood, on her first field trip to
Manam Island, reflected on this point when she wrote in her first letter
back: "How anyone knows who is anybody's mother's brother, only God
and Malinowski know." Lowie, too, illustrated the startling differences
between his field methods and mine when he inquired, "How does anyone know who is whose mother's brother unless somebody tells you?"

Our training equipped us with a sense of respect for the people we
would study. They were full human beings with a way of life that could
be compared with our own and with the culture of any other people. No
one spoke of the Kwakiutl or the Zuñi—or any other people—as savages
or barbarians. They were, it was true, primitive; that is, their culture had
developed without script and was maintained without the use of script.
That was all the term "primitive" meant to us. We were carefully taught
that there was no regular progression from simple "primitive" languages
to complex "civilized" languages; that, in fact, many primitive languages
were far more complex than some written ones. We were taught also

that whereas some art styles had been elaborated from simple designs, other art styles were reduced to simpler forms from originally more elaborate ones.

We had, of course, had lectures on evolution. We knew that it had taken millions of years for the first human-like creatures to develop language, to make tools, to work out forms of social organization that could be taught to the next generation, for all these things, once acquired, had to be taught and learned. But we went to the field not to look for earlier forms of human life, but for forms that were different from those known to us—different because particular groups of primitive people had lived in isolation from the mainstreams of the great civilizations. We did not make the mistake of thinking, as Freud, for example, was misled into thinking, that the primitive peoples living on remote atolls, in desert places, in the depths of jungles, or in the Arctic north were equivalent to our ancestors. True, we might learn from them how long it took to chop down a tree with a stone axe or even how much of the food supply women may have contributed in societies based on male hunting. But these isolated peoples were not in the line of our ancestors. Obviously our ancestors had been located at various crossroads where peoples met and exchanged ideas and traded goods. They had crossed mountains, they had sailed the seas and returned. They had borrowed and copied. They had stimulated and had been stimulated by the discoveries and inventions of other peoples to an extent that was not possible among peoples who lived in much greater isolation.

We knew that in our field work we could expect to find differences—differences far greater than those we would expect to find among the related cultures of the Western world or in the lives of people at different periods in our own history. The record of what we found out about the way of life of each primitive people we studied was to be our principal contribution to the accumulating store of exact knowledge about the world.

As far as anthropology was concerned, this was my intellectual equipment. I had, of course, acquired some knowledge of the techniques in use for categorizing, for example, the uses a people made of their natural resources or the forms of social organizations they had developed. And I had some practice in analyzing the observations that had been made by other fieldworkers.

But nobody really asked what were the young fieldworker's skills and aptitudes—whether he had, for instance, the ability to observe and record accurately or the intellectual discipline to keep at the job, day after day, when there was no one to supervise, no one to compare notes with, to confess delinquencies to, or even to boast to on an especially successful day. Sapir's letters to Ruth Benedict and Malinowski's private diary are filled with self-flagellating confessions of idleness written at a time when, as we also know, they were doing prodigious work. No one considered whether we could stand loneliness. No one inquired how we would get along with the colonial or military or Indian Service officials through whom we would have to work: and no one offered us any advice.

The style, set early in the century, of giving a student a good theoretical orientation and then sending him off to live among a primitive people with the expectation that he would work everything out for himself survives to this day. In 1933, when I gave a girl student who was setting out for Africa some basic instructions on how to cope with the drinking habits of British officials, anthropologists in London sneered. And in 1952, when I arranged for Theodore Schwartz to spend a year learning the new technologies—running a generator, making tape recordings, and working with cameras—that we intended to use in the field, his professors at the University of Pennsylvania thought this was ridiculous. Men who are now professors teach their students as their professors taught them, and if young fieldworkers do not give up in despair, go mad, ruin their health, or die, they do, after a fashion, become anthropologists.

But it is a wasteful system, a system I have no time for. I try to work against it by giving students a chance to work over my own field preparations and notes, by encouraging them to work at photography, and by creating field situations for my class, in which they have to work out a real problem and face up to the difficulties of an actual situation in which there are unknown elements. For only in this way can they find out what kind of recording they do well—or very badly—or how they react when they discover they have missed a clue or have forgotten to take the lens cap off the camera for a critical picture.

But I am also constantly defeated. A year's training in how to protect every object so that it will withstand humidity or being dropped in the river or the sea does not keep a young fieldworker from turning up with a unique copy of a manuscript wrapped in brown paper, or with her passport and money in a flimsy handbag, or without an airtight container for a valuable and essential camera. Yet students in other disciplines do learn; chemists learn laboratory procedure and psychologists learn to use a stopwatch and to write protocols.

The fact that anthropologists insist on learning everything over again for themselves, often including all the theory they have been taught, is, I think, an occupational disease that may well be inseparable from field work itself. For field work is a very difficult thing to do. To do it well, one has to sweep one's mind clear of every presupposition, even those about other cultures in the same part of the world in which one is working. Ideally, even the appearance of a house should come to one as a new, fresh impression. In a sense it should come to one as a surprise that there are houses and that they are square or round or oval, that they do or do not have walls, that they let in the sun or keep out the wind or rain, that people do or do not cook or eat in a dwelling house. In the field one can take nothing for granted. For as soon as one does, one cannot see what is before one's eyes as fresh and distinctive, and when one treats what is new merely as a variant of something already known, this may lead one far astray. Seeing a house as bigger or smaller, grander or meaner, more or less watertight than some other kind of house one already knows about cuts one off from discovering what *this* house is in the minds of those who live in it. Later, when one has come to know the new culture, everything has to be reassimilated into what is already known about other peoples living in that area, into our knowledge about primitive peoples, and into our knowledge about all human beings, *so far.* But the point of going to the field at all is to extend further what is already known, and so there is little value merely in identifying new versions of the familiar when we might, instead, find something wholly new. But to clear one's mind of presuppositions is a very hard thing to do and, without years of practice, all but impossible when one is working in one's own culture or in another that is very close to it.

On one's first field trip one doesn't know all this. All one knows is that there is a tremendous job ahead—that it will be a struggle to learn the language well enough to hear and speak it, to find out who everyone is, to understand a myriad of acts, words, glances, and silences as they are integrated into a pattern one has no way of working out as yet, and, finally, to "get" the structure of the whole culture.

Before I started out for Samoa I was warned that the terms in which others had written about the culture were anything but fresh and uncontaminated. The recorded grammar was contaminated by the ideas of Indo-European grammar and the descriptions of local chiefs by European notions about rank and status. I knew I would have to thread my way through this maze of partial understandings and partial distortions. In addition, I had been given the task of studying a new problem, one on which no work had been done and for which I had no guidelines.

But in essence this is true of every worthwhile field trip. Today students sometimes are sent into the field to work on a small problem that does not involve much more than making the observations necessary to fill out a prearranged questionnaire or giving a few specific tests. Where the questions are unsuitable or the tests are wholly uncongenial to the unwilling subjects, these may not be the easiest things to do. But if the culture has already been properly studied, this kind of work may do as little harm as it does good. But it is not the same thing as being charged with getting the whole configuration of the culture down correctly.

But at the same time one has always to remember that the pattern one discerns is only one of many that might be worked out through different approaches to the same human situation. The grammar you work out is not *the* grammar but *a* grammar of the language. But as it may be the only grammar anyone will ever make, it is crucial that you listen and record as minutely and as carefully as you can and, as far as possible, without reference to the grammar you are tentatively putting into shape.

All this is important, but it gives no sense of what the day-to-day tasks will be. For there is no way of knowing in advance what the people will be like or even what they will look like. There may be photographs of them, but by the time one arrives they may look different. The summer I worked among the Omaha Indians, the girls were getting their first permanent waves—something I could not have foreseen. One doesn't know what the particular officials, the planters, the police, the missionaries, or the traders will be like. One doesn't know where one will live or what there will be to eat or whether it will turn out to be a good thing to have rubber boots, mosquito boots, sandals that keep one's feet cool, or woolen socks to absorb the sweat. So there is a great tendency—and when fieldworkers were poor there was a greater tendency—to take along as little as possible and to make very few plans.

When I set out for Samoa I had half a dozen cotton dresses (including two very pretty ones) for I had been told that silk rotted in the tropics. But when I arrived, I found that the Navy wives dressed in silk. I had a small strongbox in which to keep my money and papers, a small Kodak, and a portable typewriter. Although I had been married for two years, I had never stayed alone in a hotel and I had made only short journeys by train as far as the Middle West. Living in cities and small towns and in the Pennsylvania countryside, I had known a good many different kinds of Americans, but I had no idea of the kind of men who enlisted in the United States Navy in peacetime, nor did I know anything about the etiquette of naval life on an outstation. I had never been to sea.

At a party in Berkeley, where I stopped briefly on my way out, Professor Kroeber came and sat next to me on the floor and asked in a firmly sympathetic voice, "Have you got a good lamp?" I did not have any lamp at all. I had six large fat notebooks, some typing and carbon paper, and a flashlight. But no lamp.

When I arrived in Honolulu I was met by May Dillingham Freer, a Wellesley friend of my mother's. She and her husband and daughter were living in their house up in the mountains, where it was cooler, but she said I could live in Arcadia, their beautiful big house in the town. The fact that my mother had known May Dillingham and her sister-in-law Constance Freer at Wellesley made all the difference in my comings and goings in Honolulu for many years. May Dillingham was the daughter of one of the original missionary families, and her husband Walter Freer had been governor of the Hawaiian Islands. She herself was strangely out of place in her great, extensive, wealthy family; she was full of delicate sentimentalities and was childlike in her approach to life. But she was able to command any resources she needed and her influence, which extended even to Samoa, smoothed my path in a hundred ways. Under her guidance everything was arranged. The Bishop Museum made me an honorary member of the staff; Montague Cook, a member of another old Honolulu family, drove me to the Museum every day; and E. Craighill Handy gave up a week of his vacation to give me daily lessons in Marquesan, a language related to Samoan. A friend of "Mother May"—as I immediately named her—gave me a hundred little squares of torn old muslin "to wipe the children's noses," and she herself gave me a silk boudoir pillow in response to one of the few bits of practical advice I was given, in this case by a biologist who said, "Always take a little pillow and you can lie on anything." Someone else took me to visit two part-Samoan children in school; this meant that their family would be on hand to help me in Samoa.

It was all extremely pleasant. Basking in the Freer and Dillingham prestige, I could not have had a more felicitous beginning to my field trip. But this I only vaguely realized, for I did not know how to sort out the effects of influence and the courtesies that were entirely routine. But many a young fieldworker has known heartbreak in those first weeks. He has been made to feel so miserable, so unwelcomed, and so maligned— perhaps in terms of another anthropologist who got everyone's back up—that his whole field trip has been ruined before he has really got under way. These are the incalculable risks from which one can only try to protect one's students. But the factor of accident is great. Mrs. Freer might have been away from Honolulu when I arrived. Just that.

After two weeks I left, weighed down with flower leis, which in those days we threw from the ship's deck into the sea. Nowadays the Samoans give shell leis, because the admission of flowers and fruits into other ports is forbidden, and they bring a plastic bag in which to carry the leis home. But in those other days the ship's wake was bright with floating flowers.

And so I arrived in Samoa. Remembering Stevenson's rhapsodies, I was up at dawn to see with my own eyes how this, my first South Sea island, swam up over the horizon and came into view.

In Pago Pago there was no one to meet me. I had a letter of introduction from the Surgeon General of the Navy, who had been a fellow student of Luther's father* at medical school. But that day everyone was too busy to pay attention to me. I found a room at the ramshackle hotel

*Luther Cressman was Margaret Mead's husband at the time she went to Samoa—Ed.

and hurried back to the square to watch the dances that had been arranged for the visitors from the ship. Everywhere there were black umbrellas. Most of the Samoans wore cotton clothes—the men were dressed in standard style and the women in heavy, unbecoming overblouses. Only the dancers wore Samoan dress. The chaplain, thinking I was a tourist with whom he could take liberties, turned over my Phi Beta Kappa key to look for my name. I said, "It isn't mine." And this confused things for many months afterward.

Then came the period that young fieldworkers find so trying, even today, no matter how hard we try to prepare them for it. I was in Samoa. I had a room in the hotel—the hotel that had been the scene of Somerset Maugham's story and play, *Rain,* which I had seen performed in New York. I had letters of introduction. But I still had to establish some kind of base for my work. I called on the governor, an elderly and disgruntled man who had failed to attain the rank of admiral. When he told me that he had not learned the language and that I would not learn it either, I incautiously said that it was harder to learn languages after one was twenty-seven. That did not help.

Without the letter from the Surgeon General I do not know whether I would have been able to work as I wished. But that letter opened the doors of the Medical Department. The chief nurse, Miss Hodgeson, assigned a young Samoan nurse, G. F. Pepe, who had been in the United States and spoke excellent English, to work with me an hour a day.

I then had to design a way of working the rest of the time. I was very conscious of being my own and yet of being responsible to the Fellowship Committee whose members had objected to giving me three months' stipend in advance. As there was no other way of measuring how hard I was working, I decided that I must at least work for eight hours a day. For one hour I was tutored by Pepe. The other seven I spent memorizing vocabulary and so, by accident, hit on the best way to learn a language, which is to learn as much of it as fast as possible so that each piece of learning reinforces each other piece.

I sat in the old hotel and ate the dreadful meals prepared by Fa'alavelave—whose name meant Misfortune—which were supposed to accustom me to Samoan food. Occasionally I was asked up to the hospital or to the home of one of the medical staff. The National Research Council had insisted on mailing my checks to me, and the next boat overcarried the mail. This meant that for six weeks I had no money and could not plan to leave until I had paid my hotel bill. Every day I walked about the port town and tried out Samoan phrases on the children, but it was not an atmosphere in which I could do field work.

Finally the boat arrived again. And now, with the help of the mother of the half-Samoan children I had met in Honolulu, I was able to move to a village. She arranged for me to spend ten days in Vaitogi and to live in the household of a chief who enjoyed entertaining visitors. It was there I had all my essential training in how to manage Samoan etiquette. His daughter Fa'amotu was my constant companion. We slept together on a pile of mats at the end of the sleeping house. We were given privacy from the rest of the family by a tapa curtain, but of course the house was open to the eyes of the whole village. When I bathed I had to learn to wear a sarong-like garment which I could slip off under the village shower as I slipped a dry one on in full view of the staring crowds of children and passing adults.

I learned to eat and to enjoy Samoan food and to feel unabashed when, as a guest, I was served first and the whole family sat about sedately waiting for me to finish so that they, in turn, could eat. I learned the complex courtesy phrases and how to pass kava—something I never did as it is only appropriate for an unmarried woman to do so. However, in Vaitogi I did not tell them that I was married; I knew too little about what the consequences might be in the roles that would be assigned to me. Day after day I grew easier in the language, sat more correctly, and suffered less pain in my legs. In the evenings there was dancing and I had my first dancing lessons.

It was a beautiful village with its swept plaza and tall, round, thatched guesthouses against the pillars of which the chiefs sat on formal occasions. I learned to recognize the leaves and plants used for weaving mats and making tapa. I learned how to relate to other people in terms of their rank and how to reply in terms of the rank they accorded me.

There was only one difficult moment when a visiting talking-chief from British Samoa started a conversation based on his experience with the freer sex world in the port of Apia. Still struggling with the new language, I explained that marriage would not be fitting owing to our respective ranks. He accepted the phrasing, but added regretfully, "White women have such nice fat legs."

At the end of the ten days, which were as delightful and satisfying as the previous six weeks had been laborious and frustrating, I returned to Pago Pago to prepare to go to the island of Tau in the Manu'a group. Everyone agreed that the Manu'an islands were much more old-fashioned and were, therefore, much better for my purposes. There was a medical post on Tau, and Ruth Holt, the wife of Chief Pharmacist's Mate Edward R. Holt, who was in charge of the post, was in Pago Pago having a baby. The chief medical officer arranged that I would live on the post, and I crossed over with Mrs. Holt and the new baby on a minesweeper that had temporarily replaced the station ship. In the dangerous landing through the reef a whaleboat carrying schoolchildren upset, and Mr. Holt was relieved to get his new baby, named Moana, safely ashore.

My living quarters were set up on the back veranda of the dispensary. A lattice separated my bed from the dispensary porch and I looked out across a small yard into the village. There was a Samoan-type house in front of the dispensary where I was to work with my adolescents. A Samoan pastor in the next village presented me with a girl who was to be my constant companion, as it would have been unsuitable for me ever to be alone. I set about working out living arrangements with the Holts, who also had a little boy, Arthur, who was not quite two years old and spoke both Samoan and English.

I soon found that having my base in the dispensary household was very useful, for had I lived in a Samoan household I could have had nothing to do with children. I was too important for that. People knew that when the fleet came in to Pago Pago I had dined on the admiral's flagship; that had established my rank. Reciprocally, I insisted that the Samoans call Mrs. Holt *faletua*,* so that there would be no questions about where and with whom I ate.

Living in the dispensary, I could do things that otherwise would have been wholly inappropriate. The adolescent girls, and later the smaller girls whom I found I had also to study, came and filled my screen room day after day and night after night. Later I borrowed a schoolhouse to give "examinations," and under that heading I was able to give a few simple tests and interview each girl alone. Away from the dispensary I could wander freely about the village or go on fishing trips or stop at a house where a woman was weaving. Gradually I built up a census of the whole village and worked out the background of each of the girls I was studying. Incidentally, of course, I learned a great deal of ethnology, but I never had any political participation in village life.

My field work was terribly complicated by a severe hurricane that knocked the front veranda off the dispensary, knocked down the house I was to have had as a workroom, and destroyed every house in the village and ruined the crops. Village ceremonies were almost completely halted while the village was being rebuilt and, after I had painfully learned to eat Samoan food, everyone had to live on rice and salmon sent over by the Red Cross. The Navy chaplain who was sent over to supervise the food distribution added to the crowding of our small house. In addition, his presence was deeply resented by Mr. Holt, who was only a chief pharmacist's mate because he had refused to go to college; now he smarted under every display of rank.

*The courtesy term for a chief's wife—ED.

In all those months I had almost nothing to read, but it did not matter very much because I worked as many hours a day as I could stay awake. My only relief was writing letters. My accounts of life in family bulletins were fairly evenly balanced between pain and pleasure, but in my letters to friends I laid such heavy stress on points of difficulty that Ruth concluded I was having a hard and disappointing time. The truth was that I had no idea whether I was using the right methods. What were the right methods? There were no precedents to fall back on. I wrote to Professor Boas just before I left Pago Pago, outlining my plans. His reassuring answer arrived after I had finished my work on Tau and was ready to leave!

Still, it is letters that bring back to life that distant scene, and in one I wrote:

> The pleasantest time of day here is at sunset. Then accompanied by some fifteen girls and little children I walk through the village to the end of Siufaga, where we stand on an iron bound point and watch the waves splash us in the face, while the sun goes down, over the sea and at the same time behind the cocoanut covered hills. Most of the adult population is going into the sea to bathe, clad in lavalavas with buckets for water borne along on shoulder poles. All the heads of families are seated in the *faletele* (village guesthouse) making kava. At one point a group of women are filling a small canoe with a solution of native starch (arrowroot). And perhaps, just as we reach the store, the curfew-angelus will stop us, a wooden bell will clang mellowly through the village: The children must all scurry to cover, if we're near the store, it's the store steps, and sit tight until the bell sounds again. Prayer is over. Sometimes we are all back safely in my room when the bell sounds, and then the Lord's Prayer must be said in English, while flowers are all taken out of their hair and the siva song stopped in the middle. But once the bell sounds again, solemnity, never of a very reliable depth, is sloughed off, the flowers replaced in the girls' hair, the siva song replaces the hymn, and they begin to dance, by no means in a puritan fashion. Their supper comes about eight and sometimes I have a breathing spell, but usually the supper hours don't jibe well enough for that. They dance for me a great deal; they love it and it is an excellent index to temperament, as the dance is so individualistic, and the audience thinks it is its business to keep up incessant comment. Between dances they look at my pictures, I am going to have to put Dr. Boas much higher on the wall, his picture fascinates them. . . .

The times I remember with most pleasure are the expeditions we made to other villages, to the other Manu'an islands, and to the other village on Tau, Fitiuta, where I lived like a visiting young village princess. I could summon informants to teach me anything I wanted to know; as a return courtesy, I danced every night. These expeditions came at the end of my field work, after I felt I had completed my project and so could "waste time" on ethnology by bringing up to date all the detail on ways in which Manu'a differed from the other islands.

On all my later field trips when I was working on cultures about which nothing was known, I had the more satisfactory task of learning the culture first and only afterward working on a special problem. In Samoa this was not necessary, and this is one reason why I was able to carry out my work on the life of the adolescent girl in nine months.

KATE MILLETT
(1934–)

Kate Millett was educated at the University of Minnesota, Oxford University, and Columbia University, from which she got her Ph.D. in English in 1970. A version of her doctoral thesis, published in 1970 as *Sexual Politics,* was one of the landmark books of the women's movement in America. Throughout the seventies Millett continued to be active as a writer and as an artist although she was hospitalized for manic depression, against her will, in 1973. After the hospitalization she continued on a regimen of lithium, despite its many unpleasant side effects, including hand tremor.

She dreamed of creating an art colony for women, located on and financed by a Christmas tree farm she bought in rural New York, and in the 1970s her dream seemed to be coming true. She and her lover, Sophie, were transforming the farm buildings into pleasant living spaces. Every summer young women came as apprentices to help them with the work of the farm. The studios functioned. But when Millett decided to take herself off lithium, she felt her friends turn against her.

This selection from *The Loony-Bin Trip* (1990) describes events in the summer of 1980. Later Millett went to Ireland, was institutionalized there, and, after her release, suffered a major depression. But eventually she succeeded in getting herself off lithium and wrote this memoir between 1982 and 1985. Millett has an earlier memoir called *Flying* (1974).

For other accounts of mental illness, compare Janet Frame, *An Angel at My Table,* and see Sarah Ferguson, *A Guard Within.*

FROM *The Loony-Bin Trip*

I am in the coop. Night now, an empty darkness around me—not the resonance of evening sun through the bamboo blinds as the last time here, only a few days but centuries ago. It was bright early evening when the apprentices came to bring us to dinner. Sophie and I on the bed and the pack of them after us, laughing. Coming in sight of the feast, where they were standing to toast like musketeers, I'd said to Sophie that this was the best summer of my life. The revels now are over. Around me the farm goes on, but I am no longer in authority, its author. There was the war at dinner last night, another tonight; though not violent, merely conspiratorial, dour. . . . Things approach a crisis. And now the council proceeds over and around the washing of dishes. I am not invited to join, even excluded. Sophie comes and goes between me and the kitchen, handing me medicines, her voice sharp and reluctant.

"Here, take this. Come on, I haven't got all day." The voice mean, directed toward a wayward adolescent or a thing. I have not been talked to this way for years; one of the blessings of adulthood is that one is no longer addressed as a thing. This is the voice used toward the truant, the ungovernable, the mind in decay. When respect is no longer necessary. But later, the kindness of a nurse in a sickroom, or a lover to a convalescent—"Here, darling, have some orange juice." They used to put Thorazine in orange juice, and for an instant I am overcome with the memory. But no, it is nothing but kindness.

Truly it is night now and feels late, but the talk, the conference or the meeting or whatever is going on in the farmhouse, pulls her away again. "I'll be out in a little while and we'll sleep," she says. Here in her coop? Rather than in the big painting studio in the barn, where we usually sleep, where I love to wake up to see our favorite willow tree and the water of the pond in the freshness of morning? For one night then, the coop. A novelty. To please her. Though it feels so small and dark, so lonely the moment she is gone. No New Orleans whorehouse tonight, a corncrib, a little holding cell, the room where they stash you till you hear the verdict.

The offense of going too far. In fact, did we all go too far? The colony itself, utopia? So that there is a general drawing back now, a nervous return to convention, a reflexive withdrawal from freedom when suppression has been so long the rule. I have often observed this. It may not last forever but it can disrupt, undermine, destroy. Waiting it out in the coop. Anxiety in the dark. The hours going by, seeming forever, waiting for Sophie to return. Her displeasure, the curt dismissive phrases. I am in her view no longer valid. Invalid. Incompetent. Canceled by what I have become to her, a crazy. It is there in her scolding "Take this," "Take that"; little pills, pink, yellow. "What is it?" "Lithium, of course. That's the pink one." "What's the yellow one?" "Sandy thinks it would be good for you, calm you down." "Fine, what is it?" "Why not just take it?" "Why not just tell me what the hell it is?" "It's Valium." "So we give away Valium here now? Sandy isn't even a nurse—she helped out at some feminist health clinic. Did you read that piece in the *Voice* about Valium? It's awful stuff. When you're addicted—" "One little Valium isn't going to hurt you and it might help you sleep." "And if I don't want it?" "That's your own affair. We are only trying to help."

And still I wait in the coop, in the dark and the uncertainty, staying because she will come back and I am in love with her, trust her beyond anyone else, even now when I begin not to trust her yet still must. I wait while at the farmhouse they are deciding my case, arranging my life perhaps. And then the cold chill—they could be calling the cops, the ambulance, the state, and force could be brought into this absurd domestic misunderstanding, this impressionistic bumbling around the issue of my sanity or supposed insanity, which could at any moment become the very real issue of my freedom. In actuality, in locks and bars and keys— and it could be months or years before the mess was sorted out, and I could emerge a broken and condemned being if I emerged at all. Patients with my opinions on psychiatry are treated as hard cases. People with my attitude toward electroshock could easily get it as punishment; disbelief makes those in charge hostile; the battery of doctors and nurses, the very nice person who'd like to hear your history—all those authoritarian elements, whose tone and fabric contract when defied, grow rigid, and the jail reveals itself. Then it's no visitors, no telephone, no exit. And force, the tying up, the stretcher they bound me to going from Highlands into Herrick in California, pinioned facedown.

But that was years ago. You must trust these people, your friends, Sophie, after all. Having glimpsed it herself; she will understand. Unless it has made her afraid way inside. Like anyone who has been a prisoner, you must, after you are free, decide whether you will risk another brush with that or whether you will capitulate. In quietly going back to your life you can usually avoid the danger, and they are through with you; usually you are not likely to strike their eye again. But if you do, then it is time all over again to decide where your allegiance will fall.

Sophie is least likely to call the cops on me, but there are other solid citizens at that farmhouse who'd probably love to do it, for the thrill, for the self-importance, for the tragic dramatic possibilities. That is my house and my phone you are betraying me with, I think, furious even at the thought. But it's always like that; last time I even had to pay the long distance and a number of the airline tickets for those who conspired against my freedom. Tonight, as always, everyone is merely trying to "help," because they were so "worried" about me.

How I loathe that word. How worried it makes me, now hearing Sophie take it up; the harshness of its use in these situations; how it comes to be blame without coherent accusation, a reproach without point or reason. It is the refrain of her visits back and forth to me here at the coop. She arrives to announce this worry, the word aimed at me like a weapon, settling in like a fait accompli, a sentence without either evidence or trial, the same worry hurrying her away again to the others, leaving me on tenterhooks, waiting; one who waits, who is parked and waits. While the others decide her fate. One is not even permitted to hear the discussion.

I maintain that they are in over their heads, that the issue is my own freedom: to take lithium or not to as I choose. It's a voluntary program I was in. Even my shrink doesn't capture people and put them away; he has given me his word on this a number of times. I am free to go off lithium, then, if I so choose, though the results of doing so are in his opinion dire. And the experience of my friend Martha Ravich dire too: she ended up holding a sit-down strike at Rutherford's, one of those huge photography stores full of security guards, because they wouldn't take her check. One understands her chagrin, an old customer and a professional photographer—but they had her busted. Into Rikers Island. No mere loony bin but the jug itself. Took her a week to swing a transfer into Payne Whitney.* And months of recuperation. She was manic as a monkey, they say. I'd like to know what she says. But I know she's back on lithium. Humiliation, capitulation, cure? That was her attempt to throw the drug; the shaky hands (lithium's side effect), which she hated just as I do, needing steady hands for the camera as I do for the brush. The fear in the trembling hands that hold a 16mm movie camera. I always thought her hands were unsteady because they had scared her, broken her confidence. Thereafter you are afraid, unsound; they have said so, proved it with incarceration with the parole of medication, the continual and eternal doses of lithium—without which you will always be crazy, will lapse into it again in weeks. Look at me—it is six weeks, and I do not feel crazy even though now they say I am. Because I stopped lithium? Or because I told them I did? If I had never told, would they know? Is it even possible that the fear in Martha's hands was not only lithium's tremor but also a fear put there? When she stopped being scared, she got angry; at Rutherford's she told a rude clerk she wouldn't leave until her check was honored. A peaceful little protest— we spent the sixties sitting down about this or that—and the son of a bitch called the police.

Martha, let me try the experiment, see if I can pull it off. Of course I could show up at the farmhouse, but the moment I enter the room the council ends, as when a child intrudes upon adults. Because that's it, I am no longer an adult—one of the more irritating aspects of this situation. And now a solicitude I cannot but regard as hypocritical takes over. Sheila inquires about my health in a most cloying manner. Kim and Libby will do the same a few moments later but with the smirking condescension of young persons addressing the professor in dotage: part titter, part a fraudulent high seriousness whose vacuity they cannot hear

*A psychiatric hospital in New York City—ED.

in their righteousness. I think I have had enough of all that for the evening, but the part I cannot see—the mystery, the calls to psychiatry, the invocation of authority, the final quick mean signal to the troopers or Hudson River Psychiatric—that is what I want to know about. Not that knowing can help me. There is nowhere to run; even a car gets you nowhere against this system. My only hope is "good behavior." So I take the lithium, even the Valium, who knows what. Swallowing as I am watched: two tablets—600 mg of lithium never hurt anyone. Even one Valium won't do much against a healthy body and a sound mind. Nor can it make me sleepy. I am in too much danger and far too afraid to sleep. Without the conspiracy I might have been asleep hours ago.

Odd how they manage to keep me awake. Each time I reach calm and have collected my thoughts, Sophie intrudes again. The bitchy denunciation in her tone—how it infuriates me to be addressed this way after two years of living together, loving each other, our voices invariably kind. No one in the world deserves this scorn, no one. Over and over I swallow my rage at that sound and try to answer sweetly, to replace what has come to be—her transformation—with our old way. How dare you, I want to shout, how dare you use that tone to me—to anyone? Who the hell do you imagine you are? Sometimes I even do say it as the last resort. But it makes no impression. When it comes to that, she moves to attack: Who do you think *you* are, ruining this entire summer, ruining the time these women have had here, wrecking everything with your crazy behavior, your irresponsible theories, lording it around here? I fall for it completely: When have I lorded it, over whom? I am sure that I am in the clear. "You were rude to Sandy at dinner." "I would appreciate it if she'd stop leaving her junk all over the living room." "You could have asked her nicely." "I thought I did." "You did not, you hurt her feelings— she's a very sensitive person." I burn to observe that we are all sensitive persons but I desist and go on for an hour grieving over Sandy. Will she leave now?

Sophie has begun to threaten me again with apprentices leaving, a mass defection or one by one. They are all "sick to death" of me, she says; the colony will be lost. All because of my own foolishness, my headstrong behavior. I have caused this disaster, the general failure of confidence. Because I am mad.

Mystical state, madness, how it frightens people. How utterly crazy *they* become, remote, rude, peculiar, cruel, taunting, farouche as wild beasts who have smelled danger, the unthinkable. One must maintain one's reason now in this, yet how difficult not to give way to rage. And after hours of patience I blow up, full Irish steam, a stream of words, abuse matching theirs. Mine counts against me, theirs does not. I know this. Better be cool, then; you have a lot to lose, may even have lost it—for all you know, they're on the phone right now getting the dogs on you. If that happens you haven't a chance. But if you are cool, calm, the soul of reason—you have to be—you could make it through. Till the accusation passes. How crazy craziness makes everyone, how irrationally afraid. The madness hidden in each of us, called to, identified, aroused like a lust. And against that the jaw sets. The more I fear my own insanity the more I must punish yours: the madman at the crossroad, the senile old woman, the wild-eyed girl, the agitated man talking to himself on the subway. But they are at a distance; we are close. If I am mad the farm itself is suspect, the colony, even the barns and studios become somehow insubstantial, the Christmas trees in their rows are suspicious, a con game or pointless. The whole utopian scheme is folderol, an illusion; they have been deceived. That is how they must see it.

And as for my work, the books that brought them here, the drawings, the silk screens, the mind behind the place and the plan—all ashes now, vanished. Figure their disappointment. Sophie's too; figure that into her nasty manner, her arrogance, her insufferable contempt and impatience with even my slightest expression of opinion or preference. Be patient, then, and don't get operatic about your ego or bellow your importance. Ah, but I don't. Right up to the fiftieth put-down I can still swallow my anger. I admire how grandly Sophie has become the lady of the manor even as I am furious at being bossed around and relegated to a bundle. That I can do without, but the sight of her queening it is still lovely.

When we were first lovers—that first time we slept together at the farm, July two years ago, when the Fourth of July guests had gone back down to town and we were alone—I watched them leaving, knowing we would be alone here then. . . .

That night we became lovers, but the next day at evening she came and knelt by me and said that I could cancel it all if I pleased, if it was awkward for me, if I had thought it all over and regarded what had happened as a mistake. Part of me admired this as sublime; how generous to offer one an outlet it had never occurred to me to take. But for a second, part of me also thought it too much meekness. That side of her has vanished now forever. Very well, I had always thought Sophie coddled me too much, spoiled me. "How she adores you," a friend congratulated me back in town. "That is the charming part." The words gave me a start. No one should be adored, it's fundamentally immoral. And the other part of it is that no one is adored for very long. I wanted to be loved, and for a very long time. . . .

The promise of it creeping over me these two years until this summer I felt the full force of marriage, even wanted to celebrate it with a will, the sort of thing she snorts at now. After all I'm a very shaky number now, unstable, unbalanced; being endowed with this farm is the last thing she'd think of, she'd be lucky if she can keep me from ruining the place in the next few weeks. And she's by no means sure she wants to stay that long. Several times a day references to the future become provisional. She'd like to run. To continue with me is to take on an invalid, a monster no longer my former self whom she loved. I can see the dead lover in her eyes. But not quite dead, only mangled and disfigured beyond hope. And then there is hope: medicine, shrinks, friends, the collective support to see her through the disaster, the comfort of all those goddamned long-distance phone calls in which my disease is spread and my reputation canceled from New York to California, eager conversants ready to report the news: Kate Millett's flipped again. Solicitude, the wagging of heads. What a pity. It happened once before; they kept it pretty quiet. Then she was okay for years. "She's up at her farm now and Sophie doesn't know what to do." "Has she got a doctor?" "Dakota's friend Marcy has a brother who is finishing an internship in psychiatry." "Really, you better give him a call, try anything, good grief." All the outside helping and the apprentices too, whom Sophie must frequently see as schoolgirls far less able than herself, capable of hysterics and intrigue with which she hardly needs to complicate things further; but then at times they must overpower her with their physical presence, their youth and energy, their blooming health, their humor and good looks, even their sensuality. Libby's succulent bosom to lean on, to weep on, for there is weeping late at night. Away from me, the culprit.

But the tragedy of my madness is not played out with me—in my company, there is simply annoyance at the headstrong sinner. The real tragedy, where the love and the home Sophie had have now perished, the woman she loved transformed into a lunatic, all that is played out with visitors and apprentices, with the voices at the other end of long distance who commiserate and reiterate how awful it is, what should be done. Finally, comforters admit they don't know what to advise; she must keep in touch. I have overheard bits of this, conversations ending when I appear: "There are moments, even days, when she's okay and then all of a sudden she flips again and all she does is talk and talk like a maniac." A pause. "Well, it's mania, what else can I tell you?" There is almost laughter at this, a little relaxation in the voice and then the tenseness as Sophie understands all over again that she has to cope with it all, she alone. And the responsibility, either of leaving me at liberty or locking me up—the responsibility is overwhelming. She knows how I would hate it; she must remember some of how she hated it. There is also the issue of how she would be judged if she did it. Most assure her she is in the right, even that she has no alternative. But she holds off; if it gets worse, if it doesn't get better, if it goes on longer, if it won't go away.

JESSICA MITFORD
(1917–)

The muckraking journalist who exposed the shady practices of the American funeral industry (*The American Way of Death*, 1963) was born into the British aristocracy, the daughter of Lord and Lady Redesdale, entitled to be addressed as "the Honorable Jessica Mitford." She was one of six sisters known for their beauty and brains, including Nancy Mitford, the novelist, and Deborah ("Debo"), who became the duchess of Devonshire. Their eccentric upbringing produced a wide range of political opinion, from socialism in Jessica's case to fascism in Unity's. Her sister Diana's husband, Oswald Mosley, was the leading British fascist and an enthusiastic supporter of Hitler. After her first marriage had ended in divorce, Jessica Mitford married an American and moved to California. Her autobiography, *Hons and Rebels*, was published in 1960.

For other accounts of sisters, compare Santha Rama Rau, *Gifts of Passage* and Sara Suleri, *Meatless Days*. For family amusements, including politics and religion, compare Natalia Ginzburg, *Family Sayings*, Eleanor Munro, *Memoir of a Modernist's Daughter*, and the second selection from Maya Angelou, *I Know Why the Caged Bird Sings*.

FROM *Hons and Rebels*

The Cotswold country, old and quaint, ridden with ghosts and legends, is today very much on the tourist route. After "doing" Oxford, it seems a shame not to travel on another twenty miles or so to see some of the historic villages with the picturesque names—Stow-on-the-Wold, Chipping Norton, Minster Lovell, Burford. The villages themselves have responded prettily to all this attention. Burford has, indeed, become a sort of minor Stratford-on-Avon, its ancient inns carefully made up to combine modern comfort with a Tudor air. You can even get Coca-Cola there, though it may be served at room temperature, and the little shops are full of Souvenirs of Historic Burford, bearing the unobtrusive legend *Made in Japan*.

For some reason Swinbrook, only three miles away, seems to have escaped the tourist trade, and has remained as I remember it more than thirty years ago. In the tiny village post office the same four kinds of sweets—toffee, acid drops, Edinburgh Rock and butterscotch—are still displayed in the same four large cut-glass jars ranged in the window. Hanging in the back of the shop, as they have hung for two generations, are bright framed prints of contrasting Victorian beauties, one a golden-haired, delicate young lady with luminous blue eyes, her soft white shoulders draped in a pre-Raphaelite something, the other a roguishly pretty gypsy maiden whose incredibly thick black hair falls in great round curls. As a child, I always thought them amazingly like Nancy and Diana, my older sisters. Next to these, the unnaturally pink and white faces of King George V and Queen Mary still gaze benignly at the world.

The only other public buildings are a one-room schoolhouse and the church. Around these a dozen gray stone cottages lie huddled like Cotswold sheep, quiet and timeless. Inside the church, the rows of varnished oak pews—contributed by my father after the first World War, out of the proceeds of a successful bet on the Grand National—still seem to strike a too modern note in contrast to the medieval flagstones, buttresses, pillars and arches. The Redesdale coat of arms, bearing its blandly self-assured motto, "God Careth For Us," which hangs above the family pews, still looks a little too shiny and contemporary beside the crumbling gray stone memorials to an earlier Swinbrook family, whose statues have lain stiffly in place for four hundred years.

Two miles up the hill from Swinbrook village stands a large rectangular gray structure of three stories. Its style is neither "modern" nor "traditional" nor simulated antique; it bears rather the utilitarian look of frankly institutional architecture. It could be a small barracks, a girls' boarding school, a private lunatic asylum, or, in America, a country club. There has been more than a suspicion of all of these functions in its short history. It is actually Swinbrook House, built by my father to satisfy the needs, as then seen, of a family with seven children. We moved there in 1926, when I was nine years old.

Swinbrook had many aspects of a fortress or citadel of medieval times. From the point of view of the inmates it was self-contained in the sense that it was neither necessary, nor generally possible, to leave the premises for any of the normal human pursuits. Schoolroom with governess for education, riding stables and tennis court for exercise, seven of us children for mutual human companionship, the village church for spiritual consolation, our bedrooms for hospital wards even when operations were necessary—all were provided, either in the house itself or within easy walking distance. From the point of view of outsiders entry, in the rather unlikely event that they might seek it, was an impossibility. According to my father, outsiders included not only Huns, Frogs, Americans, blacks and all other foreigners, but also other people's children, the majority of my older sisters' acquaintances, almost all young men—in fact, the whole teeming population of the earth's surface, except for some, though not all, of our relations and a very few tweeded, red-faced country neighbors to whom my father had for some reason taken a liking.

In a way, he was not "prejudiced" in the modern sense. Since the thirties, this term has come to mean the focussing of passionate hatred against a selected race or creed, Negro, Oriental, or Jew; the word "discrimination" has even become almost synonymous with prejudice. My father did not "discriminate"; in fact, he was in general unaware of distinctions between different kinds of foreigners. When one of our cousins married an Argentinian of pure Spanish descent, he commented, "I hear that Robin's married a black."

Unceasing tug-of-war was waged with Farve by Nancy, Pam and Diana, the three grown-up daughters, to be allowed to have their friends to stay. Since my mother rather enjoyed having visitors she was often an ally, and these battles were frequently won. My brother Tom's friends— portly, blond young men known by Nancy as "the Fat Fairs"—were an exception; they were always allowed.

For the three younger children, Unity, Debo and me, the company of one another was thought to be amply sufficient. Except for very rare visits from cousins, the three of us were brought up in complete isolation from our contemporaries. My mother thought the company of other children unnecessary and overstimulating. Nevertheless, there had been a time when we had been taken on rare occasions to birthday parties or Easter egg hunts at the homes of neighboring county families.

Even this limited social life came to an abrupt halt, never to be renewed, when I was nine—and I inadvertently caused its cessation. I was enrolled in a dancing class which met weekly, rotating among various neighbors' houses. Little girls in organdy dresses and cashmere shawls, accompanied by starched nannies, were delivered by their chauffeurs at the appointed place to await the teacher, who came out from Oxford by bus. One fateful afternoon the teacher was an hour late, and I took the opportunity to lead the other children up to the roof, there to impart some delightful information that had just come my way concerning the conception and birth of babies. "And—even the King and Queen do it!" I added impressively. The telling was a great success, particularly as I couldn't help making up a few embellishments as I went along. They begged to hear more, and swore solemnly on the Bible never to repeat a word to a living soul. Several weeks later my mother sent for me. Her face was like thunder; one look, and I knew what must have happened. In the dreadful scolding that followed, I learned that one of the little girls had wakened night after night with screaming nightmares. She had grown pale and thin, and seemed on the verge of a mental crisis. Finally, her governess had pried the truth out of her, and had found out about the horrifying session on the roof. (Luckily for me, she did not reveal that I had brought the King and Queen into it.) Just retribution quickly followed. My participation in the dancing class was abruptly terminated; it was clear to everyone, even to me, that I couldn't be considered fit company for nice children after that. The enormity of my ill-advised act, the scope and enduring quality of its impact, was such that years later, when I was a debutante of seventeen, I learned from an older cousin that two young men of the neighborhood were still forbidden to associate with me.

Unity, Debo and I were thrown much on our own resources. As a lost tribe, separated from its fellow men, gradually develops distinctive characteristics of language, behavior, outlook, so we developed idiosyncracies that would no doubt have made us seem a little eccentric to other children our age. Even for England, in those far-off days of the middle twenties, ours was not exactly a conventional upbringing. Our accomplishments, hobbies and amusements took distinctly unusual forms. Thus, at an age when other children would be occupied with dolls, group sports, piano lessons or ballet, Debo spent silent hours in the chicken house learning to do an exact imitation of the look of pained concentration that comes over a hen's face when it is laying an egg, and each morning she methodically checked over and listed in a notebook the stillbirths reported in the vital statistics columns of the *Times*. I amused myself by giving my father daily Palsy Practice, which consisted of gently shaking his hand while he was drinking his tea: "In a few years, when you're really old, you'll probably have palsy. I must give you a little practice now, before you actually get it, so that you won't be dropping things all the time."

Unity and I made up a complete language called Boudledidge, unintelligible to any but ourselves, into which we translated various dirty songs (for safe singing in front of the Grownups) and large chunks of the *Oxford Book of English Verse*. Debo and I organized the Society of Hons, of which she and I were the officers and only members. Proceedings were conducted in Honnish, the official language of the society, a sort of mixture of North of England and American accents. Contrary to a recent historian's account of the origin of the Hons the name derived, not from the fact that Debo and I were Honorables, but from the Hens which played so large a part in our lives. These hens were in fact the mainspring of our personal economy. We kept dozens of them, my mother supplying their food and in turn buying the eggs from us—a sort of benevolent variation of the share-cropping system. (The H of Hon, of course, is pronounced, as in Hen.)

The main activity of the Hons was to plan the outwitting and defeat of the Horrible Counter-Hons, of which Tom was the chief representative. "Death to the Horrible Counter-Hons!" was our slogan as we chased him all over the house with homemade spears. We developed and played endlessly a Honnish game called "Hure, Hare, Hure, Commencement" (of unbearable pain), a contest to see who could best stand being pinched really hard. "Hure, Hare, Hure" was a refinement on an earlier sport known as "slowly working away." Slowly working consisted of unobtrusively taking the hand of an elder, usually Tom, when he was reading a book. Very gently at first, and with infinite patience, one would scratch away at one spot. The goal was to draw blood before the victim noticed what was happening. "Hure, Hare, Hure," on the other hand, required the active co-operation of two players. The first player pinched the arm of the second, increasing the pressure while slowly and rhythmically chanting "Hure, Hare, Hure, Commencement" four times. The player who could endure in silence till the fourth time was the winner. We thought it a marvelous game, and were constantly begging Tom, who was reading law, to look into the possibilities of copyrighting it so that we could exploit it commercially—a royalty to be paid to the Hons' Treasury each time it was played.

Tom, our only brother, occupied a rather special place in family life. We called him Tuddemy, partly because it was the Boudledidge translation of Tom, partly because we thought it rhymed with adultery. "Only one brother and six sisters! How you must love him. How spoilt he must be," strangers would say. "Love him! You mean *loathe* him," was the standard Honnish answer. Debo, asked by a census taker what her family consisted of, replied furiously, "Three Giants, three Dwarfs and one Brute." The Giants were Nancy, Diana and Unity, all exceptionally tall; the Dwarfs Pam, Debo and me; the Brute, poor Tuddemy. My mother has to this day a cardboard badge on which is carefully lettered: "League against Tom. Head: Nancy."

In fact, the anti-Tuddemy campaign, which raged throughout childhood, was merely the curious Honnish mirror-world expression of our devotion to him. For years, he was the only member of the family to be "on speakers" with all the others.

In spite of frequent alliances of brief duration for Boudledidge or Honnish pursuits, or for the purpose of defeating some common enemy—generally a governess—relations between Unity, Debo and me were uneasy, tinged with mutual resentment. We were like ill-assorted animals tied to a common tethering post.

Occasionally Unity and I united in the forbidden sport of "teasing Debo." The teasing had to be done well out of earshot of my father, as

Debo was his prime favorite, and fearful consequences could follow if we made her cry. She was an extraordinarily softhearted child, and it was easy to make her huge blue eyes brim with tears—known as "welling" in family circles.

Unity invented a tragic story involving a Pekingese puppy. "The telephone bell rang," it went. "Grandpa got up from his seat and went to answer it. 'Lill ill!' he cried . . ." Lill was on her deathbed, a victim of consumption. Her dying request was that Grandpa should care for her poor little Pekingese. However, in all the excitement of the funeral, the peke was forgotten, and was found several days later beside his mistress's grave, dead of starvation and a broken heart.

This story never failed to send Debo into paroxysms of grief, no matter how often it was retold. Naturally, we were severely punished for telling it. Months of allowance would be confiscated, and often we were sent to bed as well. A more borderline case would be merely to say, in tones fraught with tragedy, "THE TELEPHONE BELL RANG," in which case Debo howled as loudly as if we had told the story to its bitter end.

Odd pursuits, indeed, and little wonder that my mother's continual refrain was, "You're very silly children."

My mother personally arranged and supervised our education, and taught us our lessons herself until we reached the age of eight or nine. Thereafter we entered the schoolroom, presided over by a fast-moving series of governesses. No doubt, educators all over the world were at that time debating the theories of John Dewey versus those of the traditionalists; no doubt thousands were somewhere flocking to lectures on the new "Child Psychology." If the fight for equal education for women raged somewhere as a part of the twentieth century struggle for equal rights, no hint of these controversies reached us at Swinbrook. Tom, of course, had been sent away to school at the age of eight, and thence to Eton; but my mother felt that school for girls was unnecessary, probably harmful, and certainly too expensive. She prided herself that she was able to finance our entire education out of the proceeds of her chicken farm, which, after paying all expenses, including the wages of the chicken man, whose name was appropriately "Lay," netted something like one hundred and twenty pounds a year, about the right amount for a governess's annual wage in those days.

Lessons with Muv in the drawing room still stand out for me far more clearly than anything I learned later from the governesses. (The name Muv, set down in black and white, may convey the image of a petite, cozier-than-Mummy mother surrounded by children whom she refers to as "my brood." The name Farve may likewise conjure up the picture of a pallier-than-Daddy father. Not to me. In my earliest memory of them

Muv and Farve were actually as tall as the sky and as large as the Marble Arch, and were somewhat more powerful than King and Parliament rolled into one.)

Muv taught English history from a large illustrated book called *Our Island Story,* with a beautiful picture of Queen Victoria as its frontis-piece. "See, England and all our Empire possessions are a lovely pink on the map," she explained. "Germany is a hideous mud-colored brown." The illustrations, the text, and Muv's interpretative comments created a series of vivid scenes: Queen Boadicea, fearlessly riding at the head of her army . . . the poor little Princes in the Tower . . . Charlemagne, claimed by Grandfather as our ancestor . . . hateful, drab Cromwell . . . Charles I, Martyred King . . . the heroic Empire Builders, bravely quell-ing the black hordes of Africa for the glory of England . . . the wicked Indians of the Black Hole of Calcutta . . . the Americans, who had been expelled from the Empire for causing trouble, and who no longer had the right to be a pretty pink on the map . . . the Filthy Huns, who killed Uncle Clem in the war . . . the Russian Bolshies, who shot down the Czar's dogs in cold blood (and, as a matter of fact, the little Czarevitch and Czarevnas, only their fate didn't seem quite so sad as that of the poor innocent dogs) . . . the good so good, and the bad so bad; history as taught by Muv was on the whole very clear to me.

Muv had invented a method of teaching which obviated the necessity for examinations. We simply read the passage to be mastered, then closed the book and related whatever portion of the text we happened to retain. "I always think a child only needs to remember the part that seems important to her," she would explain vaguely. Sometimes it didn't work very well. "Now, Little D.,* I've read you a whole chapter. Tell me what you remember of it." "I'm afraid I don't remember anything." "Come now, Little D., can't you remember a single word?" "Very well then—THE." Fatal sentence! For years after I could be reduced to tears by sisters and cousins teasing in chorus, "Very well, then—THE."

I graduated to the schoolroom when I was nine. Our schoolroom at Swinbrook, big and airy, with bay windows, a small coal fireplace and chintz-covered furniture, was on the second floor, next to the governess's bedroom. It was separated from the visitors' rooms and my parents' rooms by a green baize door. Here we spent most of our time. We had lunch, and sometimes dinner, downstairs with the grownups except when there were visitors, in which case meals were sent up and we ate in the unenthralling company of the governess, fretfully wondering what delicious things they were having downstairs.

*Jessica was called Decca or Little D.—ED.

Unity—Bobo to the rest of the family but Boud to me—was the only other schoolroom-age child; Debo was only six, still having lessons with Muv, and otherwise in the nursery under the jurisdiction of Nanny. Nancy and Pam were long since grown up, Tom had gone to live abroad for a bit, and Diana was in Paris, restlessly poised between schoolroom and first London season.

Boud was a huge, outsize child of twelve. She reminded me of the expression "great girl" in Victorian children's books. "Oh dear, poor Boud, she is rather enormous," Muv complained when the semi-annual boxes of children's clothes arrived on approval from Daniel Neal's in London, to be tried on and invariably, in Boud's case, sent back for a larger size. Nancy gave her the blunt nickname of Hideous, but Boud wasn't really hideous. Her immense, baleful blue eyes, large, clumsy limbs, dead straight tow-colored hair, sometimes in neat pigtails but more often flowing loose, gave her the appearance of a shaggy Viking or Little John. She was the bane of governesses, few of whom could stand up for long to her relentless misbehavior, and as a result we never had the same one for any length of time. They came and left in bewildering succession, and each replacement brought with her a new slant on the sum total of human knowledge.

Miss Whitey taught us to repeat, "A-squared-minus-B-squared-equals-A-squared-minus-2-AB-plus-B-squared," but she did not stay long enough to explain why that should be. Boud found out that she had a deadly fear of snakes, and left Enid, her pet grass snake, neatly wrapped around the W.C. chain one morning. We breathlessly awaited the result, which was not long in coming. Miss Whitey locked herself in, there was shortly an earsplitting shriek followed by a thud. The unconscious woman was ultimately released with the aid of crowbars, and Boud was duly scolded and told to keep Enid in her box thereafter. Miss Whitey was succeeded by Miss Broadmoor, who taught us to say *mensa, mensa, mensam* all the way through. Nancy, even in those early days preoccupied with U and non-U usage, made up a poem illustrative of the main "refainments" of Miss Broadmoor's speech: "Ay huff a löft, and öft, as ay lay on may ayderdown so söft (tossing from sade to sade with may nasty cöff) ay ayther think of the loft, or of the w-h-h-h-h-eat in the tröff of the löft." We couldn't resist reciting it each morning as lesson time drew near. Latin lessons came to an end after Miss Broadmoor left. Miss McMurray grew beans on bits of wet flannel and taught the names of different parts of these growing beans—plumule, radical, embryo.

She was soon followed by Miss Bunting, whose main contribution to our education was to teach a little mild shoplifting. Miss Bunting was a dear little round giggly woman, shaped like a Toby Jug, with a carefree and unorthodox approach to life that we found most attractive. Boud towered over her, and sometimes scooped her up and put her, squealing, on the schoolroom piano.

We made occasional trips to Oxford. "Like to try a little jiggery-pokery, children?" Miss Bunting suggested. There were two main methods: the shopping bag method, in which an accomplice was needed, was used for the larger items. The accomplice undertook to distract the shop lady while the lifter, or Jiggery-Poker in Miss Bunting's idiom, stuffed her bag with books, underclothes or boxes of chocolates, depending on the wares of the particular store. The dropped hanky method was suitable for lipsticks or small pieces of jewelry. Miss Bunting in her governessy beige coat and gloves, Boud and I in matching panama straw hats, would strut haughtily past the deferential salespeople to seek the safety of Fuller's Tea Room, where we would gleefully take stock of the day's haul over cups of steaming hot chocolate.

Miss Bunting was very relaxed about lessons. Only when we heard my mother's distinctive tread approaching the schoolroom did she signal us to buckle down to work. She knew nothing and cared less about algebra, Latin or the parts of the bean, and needless to say we liked her much better than any of her predecessors. We did all we could to make life tolerably attractive for her, with the result that she stayed on for some years.

Participation in public life at Swinbrook revolved around the church, the Conservative Party and the House of Lords. My parents took a benevolent if erratic interest in all three, and they tried from time to time to involve us children in such civic responsibilities as might be suitable to our age.

My mother was a staunch supporter of Conservative Party activities. Although she was never particularly enthusiastic about our local Member of Parliament ("such a *dull* little creature," she would say sadly), Muv campaigned faithfully at each election. Crowds of placid villagers were assembled on the lawn at Swinbrook House to be harangued by our uncles on the merits of the Conservative Party, and later to be fed thick meat sandwiches, pound cake and cups of nice strong tea. Our family always had its booth at the annual Oxfordshire Conservative Fete, where we sold eggs, vegetables from the kitchen garden, and quantities of cut flowers. Debo and I, dressed in our expensive Wendy frocks, were allowed to parade around selling bouquets. Debo hated these occasions because the grownups always cooed over her: "Oh, doesn't Debo look *sweet!*" "Well, Decca's sweet too," was her furious rejoinder.

At election time, sporting blue rosettes, symbol of the Party, we often accompanied Muv to do canvassing. Our car was decorated with Tory blue ribbons, and if we should pass a car flaunting the red badge of Socialism, we were allowed to lean out of the window and shout at the occupants: "Down with the horrible Counter-Honnish Labor Party!"

The canvassing consisted of visiting the villagers in Swinbrook and neighboring communities, and, after exacting a promise from each one to vote Conservative, arranging to have them driven to the polls by our chauffeur. Labor Party supporters were virtually unknown in Swinbrook. Only once was a red rosette seen in the village. It was worn by our gamekeeper's son—to the bitter shame and humiliation of his family, who banished him from their house for this act of disloyalty. It was rumored that he went to work in a factory in Glasgow, and there became mixed up with the trade unions.

The General Strike of 1926 provided enormous excitement. There was a thrilling feeling of crisis in the air. The grownups, unnaturally grave, pored over the daily national bulletin that replaced the newspapers. I managed to smuggle my pet lamb, Miranda, into my bedroom at night to prevent her from being shot down by the Bolshies. Everyone was pressed into service for the emergency. Nancy and Pam, then in their early twenties, established a canteen in an old barn on the highway, about two miles from our house, in which they took alternate shifts serving tea, hot soup and sandwiches to the scabbing lorry drivers. After lessons, Boud and I with our governess, and Debo with Nanny would toil up the hill to help, Miranda strictly at heel in case a Bolshie should jump out of the hedges.

Since lorries keep going all night (a fact none of us had realized before), it was necessary to start the first shift very early in the morning, before sunrise. Pam was detailed for this first shift; she was easily the best at running the canteen, as she was interested in home economics and knew how to make the tea and sandwiches and how to wash the cups. Nancy was known to be hopeless at this sort of thing, and moaned sadly when called on for anything more than handing round the sandwiches: "Oh darling, you know I don't know how to take things out of ovens, one's poor hands . . . besides, I do so hate getting up early."

One morning, about five o'clock, Pam was alone at the canteen as usual when a filthy tramp lurched in from the eerie pre-dawn darkness. Dressed in a ragged suit and worker's cap, his face grimy and hideously scarred, he was a terrifying sight. "Can I 'ave a cup o' tea, miss?" he leered at Pam, thrusting his dreadful face close to hers, winking with his horribly bright green eyes. Pam nervously started to pour the tea, but he nimbly stepped round the counter. "Can I 'ave a kiss, Miss?" and he put his arm round her waist. Pam, thoroughly terrified, let out a fearful shriek, and in her mad haste to get away from him fell and sprained her ankle. The tramp turned out to be Nancy in disguise. All in all, we were rather sad when the General Strike came to an end and life returned to dull normalcy.

Rather to my mother's disappointment, Farve's interest in politics was much more sporadic than her own. On very rare occasions he lumbered into his London clothes and with much heavy breathing prepared for the trip—always considered a tremendously arduous journey, although it was actually only eighty miles—to sit in the House of Lords. But he only went if the matter being debated presented really burning issues, such as whether peeresses in their own right should be granted permission to sit as equals with Their Lordships. On this occasion Farve roused himself to go and vote against their being admitted; Nancy maintained that the real reason for his opposition to seating the peeresses was that there is only one W.C. in the House of Lords, and he was afraid they might get in the habit of using it.

Farve's deepest ire, however, was reserved for a proposal to reform the House of Lords by limiting its powers. The Lords who sponsored this measure did so out of a fear that unless such a course was taken, a future Labor Government might abolish the House altogether. Farve angrily opposed this tricky political maneuver. His speech was widely quoted in the press: "May I remind your Lordships that denial of the hereditary principle is a direct blow at the Crown? Such a denial is, indeed, a blow at the very foundation of the Christian faith." To Farve's annoyance, even the Conservative press poked fun at this concept, and the Labor press had a field day with it. "What *did* you mean to say?" we asked, and he patiently explained that just as Jesus became God because he was the Son of God, so the oldest son of a Lord should inherit his father's title and prerogatives. Nancy pretended to be surprised at this explanation: "Oh, I thought you meant it would be a blow at the Christian faith because the Lord's son would lose the right to choose the clergyman."

The right to hire and fire the clergy was one which my father would have been loath to relinquish. He had the "living" at Swinbrook, which meant that if the incumbent vicar died or left the parish it became Farve's responsibility to interview and choose among prospective replacements. Shortly after we moved to Swinbrook such choice was made necessary by the death of the Reverend Foster, the parish clergyman. Debo and I managed to eavesdrop on at least one of the interviews that followed. A pallid young man in regulation dog collar was admitted by the parlormaid. "Would you come this way, sir? His Lordship's in the Closing Room," she explained. My father's study had once been known by the more usual terms for such rooms—library, business room, smoking room—but I pointed out to Farve that since he spent virtually his entire life within its walls, one day, inevitably, his old eyes would close there, never to open again. Thus it came to be called the Closing Room, even by the servants. The Closing Room was a pleasant enough place to spend time in if one was not there under duress; it was lined from floor to ceiling with thousands of books amassed by Grandfather, and there was a lot of comfortable leather-covered furniture and a huge gramophone— but the idea of being summoned for an interview with Farve filled us with vicarious terror.

"Oh, poor thing! There he goes. He's for it," Debo whispered from our hiding place under the stairs. We heard Farve explaining that he would personally choose the hymns to be sung at Sunday service. "None of those damn complicated foreign tunes. I'll give you a list of what's wanted: 'Holy, Holy, Holy,' 'Rock of Ages,' 'All Things Bright and Beautiful,' and the like." He went on to say that the sermon must never take longer than ten minutes. There was little danger of running over-time, as Farve made a practice of setting his stop watch and signaling two minutes before the allotted time was up.

"Do you go in for smells and lace?" he suddenly roared at the aston-ished applicant. "Er?" Questioning sounds could be heard through the walls of the Closing Room. "Incense, choir robes and all that Popish nonsense! You know what I'm driving at!" Debo and I squirmed in sympathy.

The poor vicar who was finally selected must often have wished for a softer berth. For one thing, church attendance was an inflexible rule for the whole Mitford family. Every Sunday morning, rain or shine, we stumped off down the hill with Nanny, governess, Boud's goat, her pet snake Enid, Miranda, several dogs, and my pet dove. Some of the graves in Swinbrook churchyard were conveniently surrounded by high railings for better preservation and privacy. These made good cages for the assorted animals, whose loud yelps, cooing and baaing blended nicely with the lusty voices of the village choir and effectively drowned out most of the ten-minute sermon. If Tom was at home, Debo, Boud and I amused ourselves during the service by trying to "make him blither"—a Honnish expression for an unwilling or suppressed giggle. The best mo-ment for this occurred during the reading of the Ten Commandments. Ranged in the family pew, prayerbooks open, we'd wait for the signal: "Thou shalt not commit adultery," then nudge all down the row to where poor Tom was sitting, desperately trying to suffocate the giggles. We were sure he led a glamorous life of sin abroad and in his London flat, and needed emphasis on this particular Commandment.

My mother was hard to pin down in theological discussions. "Do you believe in Heaven and Hell?" I asked. "Well, one always hopes there'll be some sort of afterlife. I'd like to see Uncle Clem again one day, and

Cicely, she was such a good friend of mine . . ." She seemed to envisage the afterlife as a pleasant afternoon gathering where anyone might drop in. "But if you don't believe in the miracles and things, what's the point of having to go to church every Sunday?" "Well, Little D., after all it *is* the Church of England, we have to support it, don't you see."

The support took various forms. When Muv remembered she invited the Vicar and his wife for Sunday luncheon: "Poor things, they always look so hungry, I rather wonder if they get *quite* enough to eat." Her vagueness about church procedure must have caused the Vicar some uneasy moments. Once he came to the house to ask her if she would contribute some money to help purchase the bier. "Certainly, how much is needed?" Muv asked. The vicar opined that five pounds would do nicely. "Five pounds? But who on earth is going to drink all that beer?"

Muv often took me with her to visit the village women in Swinbrook with small gifts of charity. Their poverty worried me and filled me with uneasiness. They lived in ancient, tiny cottages, pathetically decorated with pictures of the Royal Family and little china ornaments. The smell of centuries of overcooked cabbage and strong tea lurked in the very walls. The women were old, and usually toothless, at thirty. Many had goiters, wens, crooked backs and other deformities associated with generations of poverty. Could these poor creatures be people, like us? What did they think about, what sort of jokes did they think funny, what did they talk about at meals? How did they fill their days? Why were they so poor?

On the long walk home after one such visit, a brilliant thought suddenly occurred to me.

"I say, wouldn't it be a good idea if all the money in England could be divided up equally among everybody? Then there wouldn't be any really poor people."

"Well, that's what the Socialists want to do," Muv explained. I was abashed to learn that the counter-Honnish Socialists had already thought of my good idea, but pursued the subject nevertheless.

"Why couldn't it be done?"

"Because it wouldn't be fair, darling. You wouldn't like it if you saved up all your pocket money and Debo spent hers, and I made you give up half your savings to Debo, would you?" I immediately saw the point. My idea was pretty hopeless after all.

Shortly after this I was taken to a Conservative Party campaign meeting in the village. Uncle Geoff made the speech. "The trouble with the Labor Party is that they want everyone to be *poor*," he said, "but we want everyone to be *rich*." I had never heard this ancient cliché before, and it struck me as a penetratingly original thought of enduring significance. It was several years before I gave any more thought to Socialist ideas.

Growing up in the English countryside seemed an interminable process. Freezing winter gave way to frosty spring, which in turn merged into chilly summer—but nothing ever, ever happened. The lyrical, soft beauty of changing seasons in the Cotswolds literally left us cold. "Oh, to be in England, Now that April's there," or, "Fair daffodils, we weep to see you haste away so soon . . ." The words were evocative enough, but I was not much of an April noticer or daffodil fancier. It never occurred to me to be happy with my lot. Knowing few children of my age with whom to compare notes, I envied the children of literature to whom interesting things were always happening: "Oliver Twist was so *lucky* to live in a fascinating orphanage!"

Nevertheless, there were occasional diversions. Sometimes we went up to London to stay at our mews in Rutland Gate for Christmas shopping (or shoplifting, depending on whether we were accompanied by Nanny or by Miss Bunting), and sometimes, when Swinbrook was let for a few months, a full-scale migration, Nanny, governess, maids, dogs, Enid, Miranda, dove and all of us, went to my mother's house on the outskirts of High Wycombe. But these small excursions only served to emphasize the dullness of life at Swinbrook.

We were as though caught in a timeproofed corner of the world, foster children, if not exactly of silence, at least of slow time. The very landscape, cluttered up with history, was disconcertingly filled with evidence of the changelessness of things. The main road to Oxford, built by Julius Caesar two thousand years ago, had been altered only by modern surfacing for the convenience of motorists; Roman coins, thrown up by the plow as though carelessly dropped only yesterday, were to be had for the gathering. As part of our lessons we kept Century Notebooks, a page for each century, in which we listed by date the main battles, reigns of kings and queens, scientific inventions. Human history seemed so depressingly short as one turned the pages. The French Revolution only two pages back, and flip! here we are at the twenty-first century, all of us dead and buried—but what will there be to show for it? "Precious little, if we're going to be stuck at Swinbrook for the rest of our lives," I mused sadly.

The great golden goal of every childhood—being a Grownup—seemed impossibly far away. There were for us no intermediate goals to fill the great, dull gap; no graduation from one stage of education to the next; no adolescent "first parties" to look forward to. You were a child, living within all the bounds and restrictions of childhood, from birth until you reached the age of seventeen or eighteen, depending on where your birthday fell in relation to the London season. Life broke down to an endless series of unconnected details, the days punctuated by lessons, meals and walks, the weeks by occasional visits from relations or the older children's friends, the months and years by the unexpected and unplanned for.

．　　　．　　　．

I longed passionately to go to school. The warm, bright vision of living away from home with girls my own age, learning all sorts of fascinating things, dominated my thoughts for years. But no arguments I could advance would move my mother on this point. Besides, she had heard them all before; the older children, with the exception of Pam, had all in turn begged to go. Pam was the only one of the older four who had consistently loved living at home in the country. As a child she had wanted to be a horse, and spent long hours practicing to be one, realistically pawing the ground, tossing her head and neighing.

"I want to go to a university when I grow up," I insisted.

"Well, darling, when you grow up you can do whatever you like."

"But you can't go to the university unless you've passed the exams, and how can I possibly learn enough to pass with a stupid old governess?"

"That's a very rude way to talk. If you went to school you'd probably hate it. The fact is children always want to do something different from what they are doing. Childhood is a very unhappy time of life; I know I was always miserable as a child. You'll be all right when you're eighteen."

This, then, was life: a Gustave Doré mountain, steep, dark and arduous on the way up, thorny, toe-stubbing—but the other side, after reaching the sunlit peak of eighteen, would be easy traveling, pleasure-filled . . . it sounded right, but would one ever reach the peak?

ANNE MOODY
(1940–)

Anne Moody grew up in Centreville, Mississippi, during a period of escalating violence against blacks, about which she was largely kept ignorant by her mother, who didn't want her to get in trouble or offend white employers. She was in high school when, in another Mississippi town, fourteen-year-old Emmett Till was killed by white men for whistling at a white woman. Later she attended two-year Natchez College on a basketball scholarship and finished at Tougaloo College on an academic scholarship, supporting herself with money made waiting on tables in the summer at a restaurant in New Orleans. She became a civil rights activist and participated in some of the historic sit-ins of the early 1960s, the subject of the second of these selections from her autobiography, *Coming of Age in Mississippi* (1968).

For another account of growing up black in the South, compare Maya Angelou, *I Know Why the Caged Bird Sings.* For another civil rights activist's autobiography, compare Bernadette Devlin, *The Price of My Soul.* For a memoir by a young black woman of her education at an exclusive and largely white eastern prep school, see Lorene Cary, *Black Ice,* and see Charlayne Hunter-Gault, *In My Place* for a memoir by the woman who broke the color bar at the University of Georgia in 1961.

FROM *Coming of Age in Mississippi*

HIGH SCHOOL

I was fifteen years old when I began to hate people. I hated the white men who murdered Emmett Till and I hated all the other whites who were responsible for the countless murders Mrs. Rice* had told me about and those I vaguely remembered from childhood. But I also hated Negroes. I hated them for not standing up and doing something about the murders. In fact, I think I had a stronger resentment toward Negroes

*Mrs. Rice was the author's homeroom teacher in high school—ED.

for letting the whites kill them than toward the whites. Anyway, it was at this stage in my life that I began to look upon Negro men as cowards. I could not respect them for smiling in a white man's face, addressing him as Mr. So-and-So, saying yessuh and nossuh when after they were home behind closed doors that same white man was a son of a bitch, a bastard, or any other name more suitable than mister.

Emmett Till's murder provoked a lot of anger and excitement among whites in Centreville. Now just about every evening when I got to work, Mrs. Burke* had to attend a guild meeting. She had more women coming over now than ever. She and her friends had organized canvassing teams and a telephone campaign, to solicit for new members. Within a couple of months most of the whites in Centreville were taking part in the Guild. The meetings were initially held in the various houses. There were lawn parties and church gatherings. Then when it began to get cold, they were held in the high school auditorium.

After the Guild had organized about two-thirds of the whites in Centreville, all kinds of happenings were unveiled. The talk was on. White housewives began firing their maids and scolding their husbands and the Negro communities were full of whispered gossip.

The most talked-about subject was a love affair Mr. Fox, the deputy sheriff, and one of my classmates were carrying on. Bess was one of the oldest girls in my class. She was a shapely, high brown girl of about seventeen. She did general housekeeping and nursing for Fox and his wife.

It was general policy that most young white couples in Centreville hired only older Negro women as helpers. However, when there were two or more children in the family, it was more advantageous to hire a young Negro girl. That way, they always had someone to baby-sit when there was a need for a baby-sitter. My job with Linda Jean had been this kind. I kept Donna and Johnny on Sundays and baby-sat at night when they needed me.

Even though the teen-age Negro girls were more desirable for such jobs, very few if any were trusted in the homes of the young couples. The young white housewife didn't dare leave one alone in the house with her loyal and obedient husband. She was afraid that the Negro girl would seduce him, never the contrary.

There had been whispering in the Negro communities about Bess and Fox for some time. Just about every young white man in Centreville had a Negro lover. Therefore Fox, even though he was the deputy sheriff, wasn't doing anything worse than the rest of the men. At least that's the

*Mrs. Burke was the unpleasant white woman for whom the author did domestic work. Her Guild was a kind of white supremacist women's auxiliary—ED.

way the Negroes looked at the situation. Fox wasn't anyone special to them. But the whites didn't see it that way. The sheriff and all of his deputies were, in the eyes of their white compatriots, honorable men. And these honorable men were not put into office because they loved Negroes. So when the white community caught on about Fox and Bess, naturally they were out to expose the affair. Such exposure would discourage other officers from similar misbehavior.

Mrs. Fox was completely devoted to her husband. She too thought he was an honest man and she was willing to do anything that would prove him innocent. Soon a scheme was under way. Mrs. Fox was to leave home every so often. It had been reported that every time she was out and Bess was left there alone, Fox found his way home for one reason or another. Mrs. Fox left home purposely a couple of times while the neighbors kept watch. They confirmed the report that Fox would always return home. So one day Mrs. Fox decided to take the children and visit her mother—but she only went as far as the house next door. Bess was to come and give the house a thorough cleaning on the same day.

Mrs. Fox waited almost an hour at her neighbors' and nothing happened. It was said she was ready to go home and apologize to Bess and call her husband and do likewise. But just as she was about to do so, Fox drove up and went inside. She waited about thirty minutes more, then went home.

When she walked into her bedroom there they were, her husband and Bess, lying in her bed all curled up together. Poor Bess was so frightened that she ran out of the house clothed only in her slip with her panties in her hands. She never set foot in Mrs. Fox's house again. Neither did she return to school afterward. She took a job in the quarters where we lived, in a Negro café. It was said that she didn't need the job, though. Because after her embarrassing episode with Fox, her reputation was beyond repair, and he felt obligated to take care of her. Last I heard of Bess, she was still in Centreville, wearing fine clothes and carrying on as usual. Fox is no longer deputy, I understand, but he and his wife are still together.

It appeared after a while that the much talked about maid raids were only a means of diverting attention from what was really taking place in those guild meetings. In the midst of all the talk about what white man was screwing which Negro woman, new gossip emerged—about what Negro man was screwing which white woman. This gossip created so much tension, every Negro man in Centreville became afraid to walk the streets. They knew too well that they would not get off as easily as the white man who was caught screwing a Negro woman. They had only to look at a white woman and be hanged for it. Emmett Till's murder had proved it was a crime, punishable by death, for a Negro man to even whistle at a white woman in Mississippi.

I had never heard of a single affair in Centreville between a Negro man and a white woman. It was almost impossible for such an affair to take place. Negro men did not have access to white women. Whereas almost every white man in town had a Negro woman in his kitchen or nursing his babies.

The tension lasted for about a month before anything happened. Then one day, a rumor was spread throughout town that a Negro had been making telephone calls to a white operator and threatening to molest her. It was also said that the calls had been traced to a certain phone that was now under watch.

Next thing we heard in the Negro community was that they had caught and nearly beaten to death a boy who, they said, had made the calls to the white operator. All the Negroes went around saying, "Y'all know that boy didn't do that." "That boy" was my classmate Jerry. A few months later I got a chance to talk to him and he told me what happened.

He said he had used the telephone at Billups and Fillups service station and was on his way home when Sheriff Ed Cassidy came along in his pickup truck.

"Hey, buddy," Cassidy called, "you on your way home?"

"Yes," Jerry answered.

"Jump in, I'm goin' your way, I'll give you a lift."

Then Jerry told me that when they got out there by the scales where the big trucks weigh at the old camp intersection, Cassidy let him out, telling him that he had forgotten something in town and had to go back and pick it up. At that point, Jerry told me, he didn't suspect anything. He just got out of the truck and told Cassidy thanks. But as soon as the sheriff pulled away, a car came along and stopped. There were four men in it. A deep voice ordered Jerry to get into the car. When he saw that two of the men were Jim Dixon and Nat Withers, whom he had often seen hanging around town with Cassidy, he started to run. But the two in the back jumped out and grabbed him. They forced him into the car and drove out into the camp area. When they got about five miles out, they turned down a little dark dirt road, heavily shaded with trees. They pushed Jerry out of the car onto the ground. He got up and dashed into the woods but they caught up with him and dragged him farther into the woods. Then they tied him to a tree and beat him with a big thick leather strap and a piece of hose pipe.

I asked him if they told him why they were beating him.

"No, not at first," Jerry said, "but when I started screamin' and cryin' and askin' them why they were beatin' me Dixon told me I was tryin' to be smart and they just kept on beatin' me. Then one of the men I didn't know asked me, 'Did you make that phone call, boy?' I said no. I think he kinda believed me 'cause he stopped beatin' me but the others didn't. The rest of them beat me until I passed out. When I came out of it I was lying on the ground, untied, naked and bleeding. I tried to get up but I was hurtin' all over and it was hard to move. Finally I got my clothes on that them sonofabitches had tore offa me and I made it out to the main highway, but I fainted again. When I woke up I was home in bed.

"Daddy them was scared to take me to the hospital in Centreville. I didn't even see a doctor 'cause they were scared to take me to them white doctors. Wasn't any bones or anything broken. I was swollen all over, though. And you can see I still have bruises and cuts from the strap, but otherwise I guess I'm O.K."

When I asked him whether they were going to do anything about it, he said that his daddy had gotten a white lawyer from Baton Rouge. But after the lawyer pried around in Centreville for a few days, he suddenly disappeared.

Jerry's beating shook up all the Negroes in town. But the most shocking and unjust crime of all occurred a few months later, about two weeks before school ended.

One night, about one o'clock, I was awakened by what I thought was a terrible nightmare. It was an empty dream that consisted only of hollering and screaming voices. It seemed as though I was in an empty valley screaming. And the sounds of my voice were reflected in a million echoes that were so loud I was being lifted in mid-air by the sound waves. I found myself standing trembling in the middle of the floor reaching for the light string. Then I saw Mama running to the kitchen, in her nightgown.

"Mama! Mama! What's all them voices? Where're all those people? What's happening?"

"I don't know," she said, coming to my bedroom door.

"Listen! Listen!" I said, almost screaming.

"Stop all that loud talking fo' you wake up the rest of them chaps. It must be a house on fire or somethin' 'cause of all the screamin'. Somebody must be hurt in it or somethin' too. Ray* is getting the car, we gonna go see what it is," she said and headed for the back door.

"You going in your gown?" I asked her.

"We ain't gonna git out of the car. Come on, you can go," she said. "But don't slam the door and wake them chaps up."

I followed her out of the back door in my pajamas. Raymond was just backing the car out of the driveway.

*Raymond was the author's stepfather—ED.

When we turned the corner leaving the quarters, Raymond drove slowly alongside hundreds of people running down the road. They were all headed in the direction of the blaze that reddened the sky.

The crowd of people began to swell until driving was utterly impossible. Finally the long line of cars stopped. We were about two blocks away from the burning house now. The air was so hot that water was running down the faces of the people who ran past the car. The burning house was on the rock road, leading to the school, adjacent to the street we stopped on. So we couldn't tell which house it was. From where we sat, it seemed as though it could have been two or three of them burning. I knew every Negro living in the houses that lined that rock road. I passed them every day on my way to and from school.

I sat there in my pajamas, wishing I had thrown on a dress or something so I could get out of the car.

"Ray, ask somebody who house it is," Mama said to Raymond.

"Hi! Excuse me." Raymond leaned out of the car and spoke to a Negro man. "Do you know who house is on fire?"

"I heard it was the Taplin family. They say the whole family is still in the house. Look like they are done for, so they say."

Didn't any one of us say anything after that. We just sat in the car silently. I couldn't believe what the man had just said. "A whole family burned to death—impossible!" I thought.

"What you think happened, Ray?" Mama finally said to Raymond.

"I don't know. You never kin tell," Raymond said. "It seems mighty strange, though."

Soon people started walking back down the road. The screams and hollering had stopped. People were almost whispering now. They were all Negroes, although I was almost sure I had seen some whites pass before. "I guess not," I thought, sitting there sick inside. Some of the ladies passing the car had tears running down their faces, as they whispered to each other.

"Didn't you smell that gasoline?" I heard a lady who lived in the quarters say.

"That house didn't just catch on fire. And just think them bastards burned up a whole family," another lady said. Then they were quiet again.

Soon their husbands neared the car.

"Heh, Jones," Raymond said to one of the men. "How many was killed?"

"About eight or nine of them, Ray. They say the old lady and one of the children got out. I didn't see her nowhere, though."

"You think the house was set on fire?" Raymond asked.

"It sho' looks like it, Ray. It burned down like nothing. When I got there that house was burning on every side. If it had started on the inside of the house at some one place then it wouldn't burn down like it did. All the walls fell in together. Too many strange things are happening round here these days."

Now most of the people and cars were gone, Raymond drove up to the little rock road and parked. I almost vomited when I caught a whiff of the odor of burned bodies mixed with the gasoline. The wooden frame house had been burned to ashes. All that was left were some iron bedposts and springs, a blackened refrigerator, a stove, and some kitchen equipment.

We sat in the car for about an hour, silently looking at this debris and the ashes that covered the nine charcoal-burned bodies. A hundred or more also stood around—Negroes from the neighborhood in their pajamas, nightgowns, and housecoats and even a few whites, with their eyes fixed on that dreadful scene. I shall never forget the expressions on the faces of the Negroes. There was almost unanimous hopelessness in them. The still, sad faces watched the smoke rising from the remains until the smoke died down to practically nothing. There was something strange about that smoke. It was the thickest and blackest smoke I had ever seen.

Raymond finally drove away, but it was impossible for him to take me away from that nightmare. Those screams, those faces, that smoke, would never leave me.

The next day I took the long, roundabout way to school. I didn't want to go by the scene that was so fixed in my mind. I tried to convince myself that nothing had happened in the night. And I wanted so much to believe that, to believe anything but the dream itself. However, at school, everybody was talking about it. All during each class there was whispering from student to student. Hadn't many of my classmates witnessed the burning last night. I wished they had. If so, they wouldn't be talking so much, I thought. Because I had seen it, and *I* couldn't talk about it. I just couldn't.

I was so glad when the bell sounded for the lunch hour. I picked up my books and headed home. I couldn't endure another minute of that torture. I was in such a hurry to get away from the talk at school I forgot to take the roundabout way home. Before I realized it, I was standing there where the Taplins' house had been. It looked quite different by day than it had at night. The ashes and junk had been scattered as if someone had looked for the remains of the bodies. The heavy black smoke had disappeared completely. But I stood there looking at the spot where I had seen it rising and I saw it again, slowly drifting away, disappearing before my eyes. I tore myself away and ran almost all the way home.

When I walked in the house Mama didn't even ask me why I came home. She just looked at me. And for the first time I realized she understood what was going on within me, or was trying to anyway. I took two aspirins and went to bed. I stayed there all afternoon. When it was time for me to go to work after school, Mama didn't come in. She must have known I wasn't in the mood for Mrs. Burke that evening. I wasn't in the mood for anything. I was just there inside of myself, inflicting pain with every thought that ran through my mind.

That night Centreville was like a ghost town. It was so quiet and still. The quietness almost drove me crazy. It was too quiet for sleeping that night, yet it was too restless for dreams and too dry for weeping.

A few days later, it was reported that the fire had started from the kerosene lamp used by Mrs. Taplin as a light for the new baby. Nobody bought that story. At least none of those who witnessed that fire and smelled all that gasoline. They were sure that more than a lampful of kerosene caused that house to burn that fast.

There was so much doubt and dissension about the Taplin burning that finally FBI agents arrived on the scene and quietly conducted an investigation. But as usual in this sort of case, the investigation was dropped as soon as public interest died down.

Months later the story behind the burning was whispered throughout the Negro community. Some of the Taplins' neighbors who had been questioned put their scraps of information together and came up with an answer that made sense:

Living next door to the Taplin family was a Mr. Banks, a high yellow mulatto man of much wealth. He was a bachelor with land and cattle galore. He had for some time discreetly taken care of a white woman, the mother of three whose husband had deserted her, leaving her to care for the children the best way she knew how. She lived in a bottom where a few other poor whites lived. The Guild during one of its investigations discovered the children at home alone one night—and many other nights after that. Naturally, they wondered where the mother was spending her nights. A few days' observation of the bottom proved she was leaving home, after putting the children to bed, and being picked up by Mr. Banks in inconspicuous places.

When the Taplin family was burned, Mr. Banks escaped his punishment. Very soon afterward he locked his house and disappeared. And so did the white lady from the bottom.

I could barely wait until school was out. I was so sick of Centreville. I made up my mind to tell Mama I had to get away, if only for the summer. I had thought of going to Baton Rouge to live with my Uncle Ed who was now married and living there with his family.

A few days before school ended I sat in the midst of about six of my classmates who insisted on discussing the Taplin family. By the time I got home, my nerves were in shreds from thinking of some of the things they had said. I put my books down, took two aspirins, and got into bed. I didn't think I could go to work that evening because I was too nervous to be around Mrs. Burke. I had not been myself at work since the Emmett Till murder, especially after the way Mrs. Burke had talked to me about the Taplin family. But she had become more observant of my reactions.

"What's wrong with you? Is you sick?" Mama asked me.

I didn't answer her.

"Take your shoes off that spread. You better git up and go to work. Mrs. Burke gonna fire you."

"I got a headache and I don't feel like going," I said.

"What's wrong with you, getting so many headaches around here?"

I decided not to wait any longer to tell Mama my plan.

"Mama, I am gonna write Ed and see can I stay with him this summer and get a job in Baton Rouge. I am just tired of working for Mrs. Burke for a dollar a day. I can make five dollars a day in Baton Rouge and I make only six dollars a week here."

"Ed them ain't got enough room for you to live with them. Take your shoes off," Mama said, and left me lying in bed.

As soon as she left, I got up and wrote my letter. About five days later I received an answer from Ed. He said I was welcome, so I started packing to leave the next day. Mama looked at me as if she didn't want me to go. But she knew better than to ask me.

I was fifteen years old and leaving home for the first time. I wasn't even sure I could get a job at that age. But I had to go anyway, if only to breathe a slightly different atmosphere. I was choking to death in Centreville. I couldn't go on working for Mrs. Burke pretending I was dumb and innocent, pretending I didn't know what was going on in all her guild meetings, or about Jerry's beating, or about the Taplin burning, and everything else that was going on. I was sick of pretending, sick of selling my feelings for a dollar a day.

.   .   .

THE MOVEMENT

I had counted on graduating in the spring of 1963, but as it turned out, I couldn't because some of my credits still had to be cleared with Natchez College. A year before, this would have seemed like a terrible disaster, but now I hardly even felt disappointed. I had a good excuse to stay on campus for the summer and work with the Movement, and this was what I really wanted to do. I couldn't go home again anyway, and I couldn't go to New Orleans—I didn't have money enough for bus fare.

During my senior year at Tougaloo, my family hadn't sent me one penny. I had only the small amount of money I had earned at Maple Hill.* I couldn't afford to eat at school or live in the dorms, so I had gotten permission to move off campus. I had to prove that I could finish school, even if I had to go hungry every day. I knew Raymond and Miss Pearl† were just waiting to see me drop out. But something happened to me as I got more and more involved in the Movement. It no longer seemed important to prove anything. I had found something outside myself that gave meaning to my life.

I had become very friendly with my social science professor, John Salter, who was in charge of NAACP activities on campus. All during the year, while the NAACP conducted a boycott of the downtown stores in Jackson, I had been one of Salter's most faithful canvassers and church speakers. During the last week of school, he told me that sit-in demonstrations were about to start in Jackson and that he wanted me to be the spokesman for a team that would sit-in at Woolworth's lunch counter. The two other demonstrators would be classmates of mine, Memphis and Pearlena. Pearlena was a dedicated NAACP worker, but Memphis had not been very involved in the Movement on campus. It seemed that the organization had had a rough time finding students who were in a position to go to jail. I had nothing to lose one way or the other. Around ten o'clock the morning of the demonstrations, NAACP headquarters alerted the news services. As a result, the police department was also informed, but neither the policemen nor the newsmen knew exactly where or when the demonstrations would start. They stationed themselves along Capitol Street and waited.

To divert attention from the sit-in at Woolworth's, the picketing started at J. C. Penney's a good fifteen minutes before. The pickets were allowed to walk up and down in front of the store three or four times before they were arrested. At exactly 11 A.M., Pearlena, Memphis, and I entered Woolworth's from the rear entrance. We separated as soon as we stepped into the store, and made small purchases from various counters. Pearlena had given Memphis her watch. He was to let us know when it was 11:14. At 11:14 we were to join him near the lunch counter and at exactly 11:15 we were to take seats at it.

*The restaurant in New Orleans where Moody had worked—ED.
†The author did not get on well with her stepfather, Raymond, and his mother, Miss Pearl—ED.

Seconds before 11:15 we were occupying three seats at the previously segregated Woolworth's lunch counter. In the beginning the waitresses seemed to ignore us, as if they really didn't know what was going on. Our waitress walked past us a couple of times before she noticed we had started to write our own orders down and realized we wanted service. She asked us what we wanted. We began to read to her from our order slips. She told us that we would be served at the back counter, which was for Negroes.

"We would like to be served here," I said.

The waitress started to repeat what she had said, then stopped in the middle of the sentence. She turned the lights out behind the counter, and she and the other waitresses almost ran to the back of the store, deserting all their white customers. I guess they thought that violence would start immediately after the whites at the counter realized what was going on. There were five or six other people at the counter. A couple of them just got up and walked away. A girl sitting next to me finished her banana split before leaving. A middle-aged white woman who had not yet been served rose from her seat and came over to us. "I'd like to stay here with you," she said, "but my husband is waiting."

The newsmen came in just as she was leaving. They must have discovered what was going on shortly after some of the people began to leave the store. One of the newsmen ran behind the woman who spoke to us and asked her to identify herself. She refused to give her name, but said she was a native of Vicksburg and a former resident of California. When asked why she had said what she had said to us, she replied, "I am in sympathy with the Negro movement." By this time a crowd of cameramen and reporters had gathered around us taking pictures and asking questions, such as Where were we from? Why did we sit-in? What organization sponsored it? Were we students? From what school? How were we classified?

I told them that we were all students at Tougaloo College, that we were represented by no particular organization, and that we planned to stay there even after the store closed. "All we want is service," was my reply to one of them. After they had finished probing for about twenty minutes, they were almost ready to leave.

At noon, students from a nearby white high school started pouring in to Woolworth's. When they first saw us they were sort of surprised. They didn't know how to react. A few started to heckle and the newsmen became interested again. Then the white students started chanting all kinds of anti-Negro slogans. We were called a little bit of everything. The rest of the seats except the three we were occupying had been roped off to prevent others from sitting down. A couple of the boys took one end of the rope and made it into a hangman's noose. Several attempts were made to put it around our necks. The crowds grew as more students and adults came in for lunch.

We kept our eyes straight forward and did not look at the crowd except for occasional glances to see what was going on. . . . Memphis suggested that we pray. We bowed our heads, and all hell broke loose. A man rushed forward, threw Memphis from his seat, and slapped my face. Then another man who worked in the store threw me against an adjoining counter.

Down on my knees on the floor, I saw Memphis lying near the lunch counter with blood running out of the corners of his mouth. As he tried to protect his face, the man who'd thrown him down kept kicking him against the head. If he had worn hard-soled shoes instead of sneakers, the first kick probably would have killed Memphis. Finally a man dressed in plain clothes identified himself as a police officer and arrested Memphis and his attacker.

Pearlena had been thrown to the floor. She and I got back on our stools after Memphis was arrested. There were some white Tougaloo teachers in the crowd. They asked Pearlena and me if we wanted to leave. They said that things were getting too rough. We didn't know what to do. While we were trying to make up our minds, we were joined by Joan Trumpauer. Now there were three of us and we were integrated. The crowd began to chant, "Communists, Communists, Communists." Some old man in the crowd ordered the students to take us off the stools.

"Which one should I get first?" a big husky boy said.

"That white nigger," the old man said.

The boy lifted Joan from the counter by her waist and carried her out of the store. Simultaneously, I was snatched from my stool by two high school students. I was dragged about thirty feet toward the door by my hair when someone made them turn me loose. As I was getting up off the floor, I saw Joan coming back inside. We started back to the center of the counter to join Pearlena. Lois Chaffee, a white Tougaloo faculty member, was now sitting next to her. So Joan and I just climbed across the rope at the front end of the counter and sat down. There were now four of us, two whites and two Negroes, all women. The mob started smearing us with ketchup, mustard, sugar, pies, and everything on the counter. Soon Joan and I were joined by John Salter, but the moment he sat down he was hit on the jaw with what appeared to be brass knuckles. Blood gushed from his face and someone threw salt into the open wound. Ed King, Tougaloo's chaplain, rushed to him.

At the other end of the counter, Lois and Pearlena were joined by George Raymond, a CORE field worker and a student from Jackson State College. Then a Negro high school boy sat down next to me. The mob took spray paint from the counter and sprayed it on the new demonstrators. The high school student had on a white shirt; the word "nigger" was written on his back with red spray paint.

We sat there for three hours taking a beating when the manager decided to close the store because the mob had begun to go wild with stuff from other counters. He begged and begged everyone to leave. But even after fifteen minutes of begging, no one budged. They would not leave until we did. Then Dr. Beittel, the president of Tougaloo College, came running in. He said he had just heard what was happening.

About ninety policemen were standing outside the store; they had been watching the whole thing through the windows, but had not come in to stop the mob or do anything. President Beittel went outside and asked Captain Ray to come and escort us out. The captain refused, stating the manager had to invite him in before he could enter the premises, so Dr. Beittel himself brought us out. He had told the police that they had better protect us after we were outside the store. When we got outside, the policemen formed a single line that blocked the mob from us. However, they were allowed to throw at us everything they had collected. Within ten minutes, we were picked up by Reverend King in his station wagon and taken to the NAACP headquarters on Lynch Street.

After the sit-in, all I could think of was how sick Mississippi whites were. They believed so much in the segregated Southern way of life, they would kill to preserve it. I sat there in the NAACP office and thought of how many times they had killed when this way of life was threatened. I knew that the killing had just begun. "Many more will die before it is over with," I thought. Before the sit-in, I had always hated the whites in Mississippi. Now I knew it was impossible for me to hate sickness. The whites had a disease, an incurable disease in its final stage. What were our chances against such a disease? I thought of the students, the young Negroes who had just begun to protest, as young interns. When these young interns got older, I thought, they would be the best doctors in the world for social problems.

Before we were taken back to campus, I wanted to get my hair washed. It was stiff with dried mustard, ketchup and sugar. I stopped in at a beauty shop across the street from the NAACP office. I didn't have on any shoes because I had lost them when I was dragged across the floor at Woolworth's. My stockings were sticking to my legs from the mustard that had dried on them. The hairdresser took one look at me and said, "My land, you were in the sit-in, huh?"

"Yes," I answered. "Do you have time to wash my hair and style it?"

"Right away," she said, and she meant right away. There were three other ladies already waiting, but they seemed glad to let me go ahead of them. The hairdresser was real nice. She even took my stockings off and washed my legs while my hair was drying.

There was a mass rally that night at the Pearl Street Church in Jackson, and the place was packed. People were standing two abreast in the aisles. Before the speakers began, all the sit-inners walked out on the stage and were introduced by Medgar Evers. People stood and applauded for what seemed like thirty minutes or more. Medgar told the audience that this was just the beginning of such demonstrations. He asked them to pledge themselves to unite in a massive offensive against segregation in Jackson, and throughout the state. The rally ended with "We Shall Overcome" and sent home hundreds of determined people. It seemed as though Mississippi Negroes were about to get together at last.

Before I demonstrated, I had written Mama. She wrote me back a letter, begging me not to take part in the sit-in. She even sent ten dollars for bus fare to New Orleans. I didn't have one penny, so I kept the money. Mama's letter made me mad. I had to live my life as I saw fit. I had made that decision when I left home. But it hurt to have my family prove to me how scared they were. It hurt me more than anything else—I knew the whites had already started the threats and intimidations. I was the first Negro from my hometown who had openly demonstrated, worked with the NAACP, or anything. When Negroes threatened to do anything in Centreville, they were either shot like Samuel O'Quinn or run out of town, like Reverend Dupree.

I didn't answer Mama's letter. Even if I had written one, she wouldn't have received it before she saw the news on TV or heard it on the radio. I waited to hear from her again. And I waited to hear in the news that someone in Centreville had been murdered. If so, I knew it would be a member of my family.

ELEANOR MUNRO
(1928–)

Eleanor Munro's father was an influential museum curator who helped Alfred Barnes amass his notable collection of art and who introduced both African and modernist art to American audiences. Munro, raised in the Midwest, moved to New York and became an art historian and critic herself. She is the author of *Originals: American Women Artists* (1979) and *On Glory Roads: A Pilgrim's Book about Pilgrimage* (1987).

This selection describes life within the Munros' cultivated and somewhat bohemian household in the suburbs of Cleveland, at first harmonious and then, as the author reaches adolescence and rebels against her father, tumultuous. For other accounts of forceful fathers and cultivated families, compare Jessica Mitford, *Hons and Rebels* and Natalia Ginzburg, *Family Sayings*. For another memoir by a daughter of her remarkable father, see Susan Cheever, *Home Before Dark*.

FROM *Memoir of a Modernist's Daughter*

The September of the year that we moved, 1939, the year my sister Elisabeth was born and I became fertile, was also the year in which Hitler invaded Poland and Britain and France declared war. The next spring, Paris fell. My high school years would be lived against the distant background of war, only somewhat more fantastic to me than the inner city that lay just below my line of vision, only somewhat more inaccessible to me than the theories about the universality of form my father was shaping. And the spring I graduated, the atom bomb would be dropped. Thus my first maturing, like the rest of my generation's, kept pace with a far-off Armageddon and a widening cultural unknown. These circumstances added apocalyptic resonance and a depth of deeper mystery to my own small conflagrations. For my father, to this point the optimistic liberal, showed the first signs of temperamental change which he would, laboringly, year after year, attribute to the erosion of global social order, but which I, in my youthful narcissism, took to be his response to my deviation from his Way.

The Twenties had seen the springtime of his hopes, and my early childhood witnessed their rooting in the soil of an institution with a democratic mandate. If the Thirties were for many Americans a time of embattled suffering—strikes at automotive plants not a dozen miles from the museum, bank failures and breadlines—for my father they were still a time of productive growth. Salaried and underwritten in his pioneer art programs for the public schools, he had no cause to oppose the American political process. The International Congress of the Communist Party in 1935, responded to by so many Western liberals and intellectuals, left him unaffected. On the contrary, he saw hope in the New Deal, in the WPA, in regional and socially responsive painting and sculpture. And he was absorbed in illuminating exchanges with behaviorist psychologists, anthropologists and other progressive educators.

So while some of his old friends moved to the political Left during these years, he didn't, though his voting Democratic made him a maverick to the museum trustees. In fact, we were all a little cocky about our politics in those days. I flashed my Roosevelt button at school in the face of buttons for Landon, later Willkie, Dewey and Taft, and felt proud the day I watched from a window of the new house as our Negro postman slowed his pace to unfold and read our issue of *P.M.* No one else I knew subscribed to it.

But the 1930s also, of course, brought war step by step closer. Having traveled much in Europe, my father felt foreboding over Germany's move into the Rhineland and the Italian invasion of Ethiopia. Those were the first unusual geographical names I'd heard and matched for oddness the faint, shrieking and crackling voice coming from a radio set installed on our school stage that was identified as "Hitler." When the Sudetenland was taken, my father turned from our radio at home and said in a voice I'd never heard him use, "I see no reason why they shouldn't roll right across Europe." The 1939 mass evacuation of women and children out of London, talked about only in ominous half-sentences before us children, was surely one of the things that made our Christmas Eve walk in the snow that year so strange to me, as if we were part of some vast and frightening universal turmoil.

In our small domestic sphere there were also darkening changes. In the economic boom of the war, my father's scholarly salary shrank in buying power compared to the profits made by Cleveland's industrialists. Beyond that, of course, there was a turning away nationwide from the liberal consensus of before. The Moscow trials of 1939 cut through the American intellectual community. My father would have said, "I told you so," but his sense of distance from the Left increased. By 1943, the WPA had collapsed in factional argument, and Left and Right would further polarize as the war drew on.

Yet for a while, it was as if the new house were another Eden, shaggier, with more corners and possibilities, but heaven still. There was a towering elm in the front lawn and another as tall in the back overlooking an English garden, a romantic geometry of curved beds around a birdbath before a pair of flowering quince. Here my mother would come into her own, nurturing, with the same driving energy she applied to her piano and kitchen, a garden like an Anglo-Chinese dream. She loved the night-blooming flowers, nicotiana and verbena, which filled the summer air with perfume, and she loved a wild-seeming tangle of stock and peonies, columbine and asters, and roses—the same hues of rosy pink and blue, lavender and sour green she now adopted for her summer dresses in accord with my father's esthetic dictum: "No black! With all the colors of the rainbow, why black?" And these colors turned up again in her platters of food, Della Robbia roundels of meats and legumes composed as much for their dappled tonalities as their flavors, corn yellow and tomato red, burgundy beef and curries, and all the various greens.

Outside and in, my father's taste also found expression here. He would have been at home in Georgian England and happily dined at Brighton Pavilion between the porcelain Buddhas and Chinoiserie peacocks. In his own small collection, beside the African sculptures on the bookcases, were a fresco from a Tang Dynasty tomb, a bronze Osiris and a bust of Homer, a bronze Art Deco dancing girl with rippled hair and a marvelous Tanagra Europa being carried off by the bull. There was a Bauhaus candlestick—a single up-shooting silver rod set in a silver disk—and bits of Chinese, Turkish, Venetian, Coptic and African textiles. In the bookshelf was an early edition of Joyce's *Ulysses,* bought in Paris. Also, having limited funds but great reverence for the Modernist masters Cézanne, Renoir, Matisse, Picasso and Kandinsky, my father hung, as his mother had, framed reproductions on the walls without embarrassment. Every object in the house was interesting, nothing coarse or ugly. Among them I grew into an acquisitive creature, desirous of holding beautiful things in my hands, turning them over, exploring their undersides and backs, laying my invisible mark on them. A perilous taste for a daughter of the provincial intelligentsia in a century of economic distress and war!

If my father was proud of his collection, he was as proud of the artists and intellectuals he invited to speak at the museum and then visit our house. I suppose they entered our little midwestern oasis with surprise, to be greeted, then politely served and listened to by us children dressed in Japanese, Hawaiian or Mexican costumes our parents had brought back from trips. Gertrude Stein had been one of his first guests, back in 1935 when she made her famous lecture tour. Later, many of his worldwide network of colleagues came: Tugwell and Margaret Mead, Lewis Mumford and Susanne Langer, George Boas, Rudolf Arnheim, and Hilla Rebay, Chinese and Indian musicians, and an Indonesian dancer of voluptuous charm who, after her performance, sat in our living room in a circle of museum trustees gesturing with delicate fingers as she recounted the love plots she had enacted. And as she fixed her shining triangular eyes on this, now that midwestern male face, I saw each take on the glow of candle wax about to melt.

Then, and for years to come, since my brother and I had grown too old for stories and our little sisters had other entertainments, family evenings would be spent listening to records from our father's encyclopedic collection. It might be African circumcision ceremonies recorded by anthropological outfits, or Chinese flutes and drums, but it was as often the romantic French music we all loved. And Bach. Save the Masses. And Beethoven. Save the Ninth.

Moreover, when they became available but long before they were popular, he brought home recordings of plays and poetry, Shakespeare, Marvell, Milton, Whitman, the Old Testament and so on. And other evenings were filled, in a pilgrimage that would go on for forty years, with Mother's reading aloud from the world's great myths, epics, histories, novels—always the classics, never books of passing fashion, political or otherwise.

And there was appreciation expressed for our school papers and such, so that each child who shone in some art or event had the feeling of contributing to the general good of the family as someday we would contribute to the world, though in what way was unclear.

There was also an extension of our family life reenacted yearly long after our Cleveland lives would come apart. My father had an epicurean detestation for Cleveland winters and, the proper pragmatist, scheduled his academic holiday from January through March, moving us all, with his books and typewriter, Mother's spaghetti pots and our own school workbooks, out of our normal routines to a cottage on stilts in an undeveloped fishing village on the bay side of Florida. The beach there was so easy a slope we swam and roamed the sandbars looking for shells without supervision, while Dad applied himself to his work, then took long walks, swinging his cane and conversing in his most lighthearted philosophical way. And in the evenings, we sat on the porch in the dark, hearing the palms scrape the roof and the waves splash just beyond our feet, and we'd gravitate soon enough to the kind of thoughts he liked to stir in his children: what is beyond the stars and what is the mind; how should one live, and what is life, after all.

He was, as I've suggested, though the Modernist, also a shy and lonely man in ways, as I suppose a philosopher is likely to be, and undoubtedly took as much comfort from our presence around him there as we did from his. For whatever else we drifted to, there was always, as I think of it now, one unvoiceable question in the air those evenings: How can we survive the breaking of this circle, as we will have to one day?

For all these many reasons, in these first years in the new house, my sense of our difference from my friends' families sharpened. Our father's work and taste set us apart, we knew. But with our mother, the difference lay in the way she *was*. Or was not. Which was it? I didn't know, having never seen another female nonconformist. Was it her driving concentration at the piano, in the garden, the kitchen and the authoritarian way she sometimes marshaled us to do the same? Was it her frequent lamentation that she was so tired she was "dead"? Or that I was hanging on her, being a pest, whining for attention? Or was it her occasional voluptuary self-indulgence, unlike the straightforward plainness of other mothers I knew? She had brought along to the new house the little green perfume bottles, though now nearly empty, and when she dressed to go out, she went through the old pantomime of searching out a bit of scent. By now, her jewelry collection, made by my father, was elaborate and curious, consisting of ethnic or antique necklaces, brooches, bracelets. Her clothes, too, were quietly theatrical, richly textured, in colors to point up her hair. Unusually, when she was carrying Elisabeth, she sometimes wore black, an evening dress of net spangled with tiny metallic stars. Amply pregnant, wrapped in that drifting galaxy, she was the most heavenly thing I had ever seen. And added to her appearance was the sense she always communicated that she was on the point of going away forever, or breathless from just having arrived—that her real place was somewhere else.

Therefore her medium, music, retained its unfathomably painful hold on me. As we would sit in the semi-darkness of a summer or winter evening listening to records, slowly, as if the whole house became a diving bell, we sank together through the surface of things. Often it was only the three of us there, my parents and me, for my brother early went off to boarding school and my sisters had early bedtimes. Then the defections of the day—mine—were as if forgiven, and a sense of near-anguishing hunger for her would possess me together with guilt for my recent bad behavior, of whatever kind it had been. Then I would lie on the couch, or Mother would, and she would rub, or I would rub, her back, my back, while the music played and, in his chair, my father sat at the center of his universe, protected from the bad news beyond by the deepening black in our windows. Once—if only I could remember the circumstances—Mother burst out in the middle of some music, "I could die and be buried to that piece . . . ," and I swore never to forget what it was. And of course I have, for I have no musical memory at all.

All the same, in spite of so much good cultural experience, as our father saw it, the temperature of trouble within the house as without went on rising. When did vague disagreement turn into rebellious discontent? As ever, one can choose a day. It was that first spring of my fertility when both parents told me to "wait," and I howled with impatience.

The next school year, a trio of us girls began to leave our neighborhood daily for a long trolley-car ride out into the farther suburbs where our new private school was located. Before long, I began to see Cedar Hill for what it was, an enclave of decades-old homes now too close to the inner city to be entirely fashionable, kept up in the face of possible "falling real estate values," while the newer money—our classmates'— was streaming farther east into still undeveloped reaches of Shaker Heights.

In our new school, my old friends and I went on mouthing conventions of the time but began to strain at our lines. "Would you rather be rich or poor?" was an article of our middle-class catechism we often rehearsed, jostling eastward on the trolley car toward school.

"Neither. Just in the middle."

"Me too."

"Me too."

"Me too."

But then seated on the same wicker seats, returning west in fading late-afternoon light, it went differently.

"I'll never compromise, will you?"

"Not I, no never."

"No, never."

"Not me either. Never."

To compromise would be to live without love. Our notion of romantic love was our heritage from unknown evangelical great-grandparents who waited, breathless and overheated, in little country churches for the spirit fever to catch. So it would come to us each and set the mold for the rest of our lives.

    ·   ·   ·

So my friends and I moved in the first summer of our heat, moths caught in the lamp of our years.

For a while, good manners held us to form. "Sir," the boys called my father as they shoved and tripped into our living room, staring sideways at the African sculptures with their jutting phalluses, their needle-tipped breasts. "Sir," they repeated, leaping to their feet and bowing when he left or reentered the room. The term, like filed teeth or cicatrices among the Africans, signified both hierarchy and bond, a recognition of the transfer of dominance to take place by custom in time.

Good girls, by contrast, deferred to one and all, curtsied to elders, leapt up from table to clear and dry dishes. Girls, after a sleepover, made the bed with fresh sheets. We girls, in frocks of taffeta or velveteen, in patent pumps with slippery soles, by our fathers were driven, in elated clusters as if gale-blown, to Friday dancing school. This high hour in each week's unfurling took place in a hotel ballroom washed in golden light, to the trills of a single piano. There, shy by fits or ecstatic, forward, hopeful or heartbroken, we all went together (turn-side-close, turn-side-close, backward-side-close, turn-side-close), learning the ways, we were told, of the great world beyond.

But the real forays into the unknown were made in other circumstances, like our side porch on summer evenings, when the peonies glowed from the garden beyond, and the elm cast a shadow intricate as a web over the lawn, the hedges, the flower beds.

Lampenfieber, the Germans call stage fright. We spent those summers of the war in a transport of lamp fever, pushing one another forward, shrinking back, pushing again toward the proscenium that framed the luminous world beyond the porch. At first, of an evening, sitting on the porch in the pall of the yellow light bulb, we played games of secret choices, making lists of favorite boys, favorite girls, favorite *Hit Parade* songs. Then we ran out into the garden to play, as if for the last time forever, games like hide-and-seek, dashing back and forth across the black bars of moonshadow on the grass, pretending our innocence of that solemn season in our lives, as Ondine said to her fisherman, "before you will have kissed me."

Another summer, we paired off with experimental mates. First kisses led on to a hand on a blouse; the next night, the hand within; then trembling lips would be pressed for the first time to a nipple. By the summer's end we were lying for hours in each other's arms, but chastely, for this was still the early 1940s. In a spirit of inquiry, therefore, I lay one summer night on the swinging bench on our porch while my boyfriend of the season took a handkerchief out of his pocket and laid it over the erection he had produced out of his trousers. "So you won't have to touch it," he said. In the shadows, with one finger, gingerly I explored its length, then circled it with my hand. The next day in a swimming pool with my girlfriends, I spied an iron water spout. I swam to it and spanned it with my thumb and fingers. It was the same! Thereafter all afternoon in joy and curiosity I eyed it and from time to time swam casually over to confirm the fitting with my hand.

In time, the threshold of our ethics shifted, and we applied ourselves to deeper anatomy, still holding back from final pleasure, building toward an orgasm that—as convention conspired for many females of my time—would take years to complete. For relief we went to little bars where there would be a jukebox, rum in thick glasses, and heaped ash-trays, and there we jitterbugged for hours, tossing our Veronica Lake hairdos in which we'd pinned fresh carnations. And self-consciousness was humming in our ears all the time, saying, Remember these times, this dancing at the end of a snake-arm, twirling out when he sends me, twirling back when he pulls, catching the beat, not wanting it to end. . . .

The fever rose. I lay on my bed looking out through my window, still sealed against winter, while the spring storm broke over our roof.

Wind entered the top branches of the elm tree setting them lunging while it drove black funnels of rain clouds over the rooftops. When a low roll of thunder made my bed shake, I ran downstairs and pushed the porch door against the wind to stand in the open while lightning flashed over the house and spat along the iron frames of the awnings. Twice, bolts split our elms to the base, leaving splintered limbs to be reset later by tree surgeons. And later the earth would be like a marsh underfoot, sucking at my feet, making me want to sink my hands in its rank muck, running off to the gutters, overflowing as I was myself to be out and gone from the child I had been.

Nymph, nympholet, my own nympha unfolding, I suffocated for the metamorphosis that would release me into my new self. This flushing of my body with the hormones of change lifted me daily, hourly, out of myself. And inevitably, the balance in our house was wrecked by the clash of wills between my father and me.

He was baffled, disappointed and fearful. He thought his program for my development had been so enlightened. All he wanted was for me to be liberated, free of what was apparently driving me crazy: the deplor-able female need, as he put it repeatedly, "to marry the first one who comes along." He couldn't see the contradiction: that having encour-aged me to develop "clear spontaneous feelings" and even the primitive beginnings of a "fresh untrammeled personal vision," he now expected me to cut my behavior to patterns of his own anxious choosing. I suppose he turned the problem over in his mind at first and meant to act with restraint. Anger would come in time, perhaps against his better judg-ment at first, but once he saw how effective an outburst was in making me shape up, he used it as an instrument in my training.

"Your child seems to be having a difficult adolescence," one of mother's friends said to her, and she reported to me in a fatigued voice, after yet another explosion in our house had nearly shattered the windows.

Well, what of that? I could have gone my way, would have had I been born two decades later, and come back a wiser being ready to go on with my life. But my will was read as treachery and my hunger to *live,* as I saw it, a sign of psychological imbalance. And so began the mutual confusion, pain and guilt that would keep me in my father's thrall, and possibly him in mine, long after the years would have taken both of us elsewhere.

In fact, his anxieties were laid upon me one by one, sequentially over time to come, as if in a narrative order. And there would be a novelistic theme concealed there, which I would understand in full only later on. The first imperative was Obedience. It was the law of the tribe, Hiawatha-Painted-feather's first rule of thumb. But now I questioned the law. At the top of my lungs, I questioned by what authority and to whom I owed obedience? It seemed to me a parody of reason to exact it from a helpless individual who had not agreed to be so.

My father would approach me from behind or the side, impelled on a flare of his own sudden decision, and shout into my ear, causing me to start, my heart to pound, adrenaline to pour through my body. "What's this about last night? What about tonight?

"Go upstairs and get my glasses," he would direct as if to to restore a balance of power. "Get out of that chair. Get my glasses."

"Get them yourself," I once shrieked, criminal daughter lost to civilization. His rage came in a recoil quickly brought under control. In measured words, he described my failings. "You are disobedient. Obstreperous. Why do you raise your voice? Everyone in the neighborhood is listening.

"You will never be happy. You will have an unhappy life. You are selfish. What makes you selfish?

"Learn to control yourself or you'll ruin your life.

"Ah!" he would reply to my anguished protest, for his predictions always struck me with terror. "You want freedom. Who doesn't? But you have to earn it. Your wild behavior fills me with foreboding. Change. Let me see you have changed. Then I may have confidence in you."

In a way, he succeeded with his science of behaviorism, though he did it by laying on me a trial I believe he would have wanted to spare me. For with every hammer blow of negative conditioning he let fall on the child I had been, my will, the will of the woman I would be, belled out in the opposite direction impelled by my sense of desperate self-respect: if he called me selfish, *I would one day, by all the gods, be caring of others.* If he called me ungovernable, *I would one day subject myself to controls of my own election.* Or on the other side, if he called me disobedient, I would be a slave for years to the mystery of why he had become what he was, and why I had.

And through that long slavery to a hard question, I would in fact learn many things. For having loved him unquestioningly before, I would be driven to a further end than just rebellion: that is, to understand. And to understand in slowly widening perspectives not centered any more on Eden but on the Adamic figure he became in my mind, who had begun as one man, then become another. . . .

For the time being, back there in Cleveland, I was all inarticulate confusion. "But I feel . . . ," I would stammer. "But I want . . ."

"Ridiculous. Inappropriate. Some children have total freedom. Come and go as they please. Nobody cares. I care. I'm severe because I care. Would you rather grow up without guidance . . . ?"

By then I would be weeping uncontrollably, feeling the rightness of his appeal, the genuineness of his concern, the justice of his view that there was some wild girl or alien person in me who needed tempering before I was fit to face the world.

And yet through my sobs I would record the fact, too, that he was now watching me. He saw that he had reached me. His technique had worked. I was his again.

ANAÏS NIN
(1903–1977)

Anaïs Nin's greatest accomplishment was her diary, which she wrote daily for well over fifty years. When the first volume was published in the mid-1960s, it was a revelation to many women. Never had a female sensibility revealed itself so fully. Her following in her late years was enormous, overshadowing any reputation she had achieved with her guarded experimental novels. Influenced by D. H. Lawrence, the subject of her first book, she wanted to write about the deepest levels of emotion, those close to the unconscious. Her diary ignores most of daily reality and explores the interior—especially the erotic—life. As a young woman she pursued sexual experience relentlessly. At the time of these passages, she was living outside Paris in Louveciennes, married to Hugo Guiler, a banker. She was also involved with the writer Henry Miller, his wife, June, and her cousin Eduardo, convinced that all this activity was keeping her marriage sound, as perhaps it was. Her sexual adventures are fully covered in her diary, whose unexpurgated version could not begin to be published until 1990, after she, her husband, Miller, and June all had died. The original handwritten journals, thirty-five thousand pages of them, of which the published portion is small, are at UCLA. Child of an American mother and Spanish father, reared in Europe, she wrote in French until 1920, then English.

For another writer's diary, compare Virginia Woolf's. For another account of sexual experience, compare *Nisa: The Life and Words of a !Kung Woman.*

FROM *Diary*

January 1932

We met, June and I, at American Express. I knew she would be late, and I did not mind. I was there before the hour, almost ill with tenseness. I would see her, in full daylight, advance out of the crowd. Could it be possible? I was afraid that I would stand there exactly as I had stood in other places, watching a crowd and knowing no June would ever appear because June was a product of my imagination. I could hardly believe she would arrive by those streets, cross such a boulevard, emerge out of a handful of dark, faceless people, walk into that place. What a joy to watch that crowd scurrying and then to see her striding, resplendent, incredible, towards me. I hold her warm hand. She is going for mail. Doesn't the man at American Express see the wonder of her? Nobody like her ever called for mail. Did any woman ever wear shabby shoes, a shabby black dress, a shabby dark blue cape, and an old violet hat as she wears them?

I cannot eat in her presence. But I am calm outwardly, with that Oriental placidity of bearing that is so deceptive. She drinks and smokes. She is quite mad, in a sense, subject to fears and manias. Her talk, mostly unconscious, would be revealing to an analyst, but I cannot analyze it. It is mostly lies. The contents of her imagination are realities to her. But what is she building so carefully? An aggrandizement of her personality, a fortifying and glorifying of it. In the obvious and enveloping warmth of my admiration she expands. She seems at once destructive and helpless. I want to protect her. What a joke! I, protect her whose power is infinite. Her power is so strong that I actually believe it when she tells me her destructiveness is unintentional. Has she tried to destroy me? No, she walked into my house and I was willing to endure any pain from her hands. If there is any calculation in her, it comes only afterwards, when she becomes aware of her power and wonders how she should use it. I do not think her evil potency is directed. Even she is baffled by it.

I have her in myself now as one to be pitied and protected. She is involved in perversities and tragedies she cannot live up to. I have at last caught her weakness. Her life is full of fantasies. I want to force her into reality. I want to do violence to her. I, who am sunk in dreams, in half-lived acts, see myself possessed by a furious intention: I want to grasp June's evasive hands, oh, with what strength, take her to a hotel room and realize her dream and mine, a dream she has evaded facing all her life.

I went to see Eduardo, tense and shattered by my three hours with June. He saw the weakness in her and urged me to act out my strength.

I could hardly think clearly because in the taxi she had pressed my hand. I was not ashamed of my adoration, my humility. Her gesture was not sincere. I do not believe she could love.

She says she wants to keep the rose dress I wore the first night she saw me. When I tell her I want to give her a going-away present, she says she wants some of that perfume she smelled in my house, to evoke memories. And she needs shoes, stockings, gloves, underwear. Sentimentality? Romanticism? If she *really* means it . . . Why do I doubt her? Perhaps she is just very sensitive, and hypersensitive people are false when others doubt them; they waver. And one thinks them insincere. Yet I want to believe her. At the same time it does not seem so very important that she should love me. It is not her role. I am so filled with my love of her. And at the same time I feel that I am dying. Our love would be death. The embrace of imaginings.

When I tell Hugo the stories June has told me, he says they are simply very cheap. I don't know.

Then Eduardo spends two days here, the demoniac analyst, making me realize the crisis I am passing through. I want to see June. I want to see June's body. I have not dared to look at her body. I know it is beautiful.

Eduardo's questions madden me. Relentlessly, he observes how I have humbled myself. I have not dwelt on the successes which could glorify me. He makes me remember that my father beat me, that my first remembrance of him is a humiliation. He had said I was ugly after having typhoid fever. I had lost weight and my curls.

What has made me ill now? June. June and her sinister appeal. She has taken drugs; she loved a woman; she talks the cops' language when she tells stories. And yet she has kept that incredible, out-of-date, uncallous sentimentalism: "Give me the perfume I smelled in your house. Walking up the hill to your house, in the dark, I was in ecstasy."

I ask Eduardo, "Do you really think I am a lesbian? Do you take this seriously? Or is it just a reaction against my experience with Drake?" He is not sure.

Hugo takes a definite stand and says he considers everything outside of our love extraneous—phases, passionate curiosities. He wants a security to live by. I rejoice in his finding it. I tell him he is right.

Finally Eduardo says I am not a lesbian, because I do not hate men—on the contrary. In my dream last night I desired Eduardo, not June. The night before, when I dreamed of June, I was at the top of a skyscraper and expected to walk down the façade of it on a very narrow fire ladder. I was terrified. I could not do it.

She came to Louveciennes Monday. I asked her cruelly, just as Henry had, "Are you a lesbian? Have you faced your impulses in your own mind?"

She answered me so quietly. "Jean* was too masculine. I have faced my feelings, I am fully aware of them, but I have never found anyone I wanted to live them out with, so far." And she turned the conversation evasively. "What a lovely way you have of dressing. This dress—its rose

*A woman June had lived with in New York—Ed.

color, its old-fashioned fullness at the bottom, the little black velvet jacket, the lace collar, the lacing over the breasts—how perfect, absolutely perfect. I like the way you cover yourself, too. There is very little nudity, just your neck, really. I love your turquoise ring, and the coral."

Her hands were shaking; she was trembling. I was ashamed of my brutality. I was intensely nervous. She told me how at the restaurant she had wanted to see my feet and how she could not bring herself to stare. I told her how I was afraid to look at her body. We talked brokenly. She looked at my feet, in sandals, and thought them lovely.

I said, "Do you like these sandals?" She answered that she had always loved sandals and worn them until she had become too poor to have them. I said, "Come up to my room and try the other pair I have."

She tried them on, sitting on my bed. They were too small for her. I saw she wore cotton stockings, and it hurt me to see June in cotton stockings. I showed her my black cape, which she thought beautiful. I made her try it on, and then I saw the beauty of her body, its fullness and heaviness, and it overwhelmed me.

I could not understand why she was so ill-at-ease, so timid, so frightened. I told her I would make her a cape like mine. Once I touched her arm. She moved it away. Had I frightened her? Could there be someone more sensitive and more afraid than I? I couldn't believe it. I was not afraid at that moment. I wanted desperately to touch her.

When she sat on the couch downstairs, the opening of her dress showed the beginning of her breasts, and I wanted to kiss her there. I was acutely upset and trembling. I was becoming aware of her sensitiveness and fear of her own feelings. She talked, but now I knew she talked to evade a deeper inner talk—the things we could not say.

We met the next day at American Express. She came in her tailored suit because I had said I liked it.

She had said she wanted nothing from me but the perfume I wore and my wine-colored handkerchief. But I insisted that she had promised to let me buy her sandals.

First I made her go to the ladies' room. I opened my bag and pulled out a pair of sheer stockings. "Put them on," I pleaded. She obeyed. Meanwhile I opened a bottle of perfume. "Put some on." The attendant was there, staring, waiting for her tip. I did not care about her. June had a hole in her sleeve.

I was terribly happy. June was exultant. We talked simultaneously. "I wanted to call you last night. I wanted to send you a telegram," June said. She had wanted to tell me she was very unhappy on the train, regretting her awkwardness, her nervousness, her pointless talk. There had been so much, so much she wanted to say.

Our fears of displeasing each other, of disappointing each other were the same. She had gone to the café in the evening as if drugged, full of thoughts of me. People's voices reached her from afar. She was elated. She could not sleep. What had I done to her? She had always been poised, she could always talk well, people never overwhelmed her.

When I realized what she was revealing to me, I almost went mad with joy. She loved me, then? June! She sat beside me in the restaurant, small, timid, unworldly, panic-stricken. She would say something and then beg forgiveness for its stupidity. I could not bear it. I told her, "We have both lost ourselves, but sometimes we reveal the most when we are least like ourselves. I am not trying to think any more. I can't think when I am with you. You are like me, wishing for a perfect moment, but nothing too long imagined can be perfect in a worldly way. Neither one of us can say just the right thing. We are overwhelmed. Let us be overwhelmed. It is so lovely, so lovely. I love you, June."

And not knowing what else to say I spread on the bench between us the wine-colored handkerchief she wanted, my coral earrings, my turquoise ring, which Hugo had given me and which it hurt me to give, but it was blood I wanted to lay before June's beauty and before June's incredible humility.

We went to the sandal shop. In the shop the ugly woman who waited on us hated us and our visible happiness. I held June's hand firmly. I commandeered the shop. I was the man. I was firm, hard, willful with the shopkeepers. When they mentioned the broadness of June's feet, I scolded them. June could not understand their French, but she could see they were nasty. I said to her, "When people are nasty to you I feel like getting down on my knees before you."

We chose the sandals. She refused anything else, anything that was not symbolical or representative of me. Everything I wore she would wear, although she had never wanted to imitate anyone else before.

When we walked together through the streets, bodies close together, arm in arm, hands locked, I could not talk. We were walking over the world, over reality, into ecstasy. When she smelled my handkerchief, she inhaled me. When I clothed her beauty, I possessed her.

She said, "There are so many things I would love to do with you. With you I would take opium." June, who does not accept a gift which has no symbolical significance; June, who washes laundry to buy herself a bit of perfume; June, who is not afraid of poverty and drabness and who is untouched by it, untouched by the drunkenness of her friends; June, who judges, selects, discards people with severity, who knows, when she is telling her endless anecdotes, that they are ways of escape, keeping herself all the more secret behind that profuse talk. Secretly mine.

Hugo begins to understand. Reality exists only between him and me, in our love. All the rest, dreams. Our love is solved. I can be faithful. I was terrifyingly happy during the night.

But I must kiss her, I must kiss her.

If she had wanted to, yesterday I would have sat on the floor, with my head against her knees. But she would not have it. Yet at the station while we wait for the train she begs for my hand. I call out her name. We stand pressed together, faces almost touching. I smile at her while the train leaves. I turn away.

The stationmaster wants to sell me some charity tickets. I buy them and give them to him, wishing him luck at the lottery. He gets the benefit of my wanting to give to June, to whom one cannot give anything.

What a secret language we talk, undertones, overtones, nuances, abstractions, symbols. Then we return to Hugo and to Henry, filled with an incandescence which frightens them both. Henry is uneasy. Hugo is sad. What is this powerful magical thing we give ourselves to, June and I, when we are together? Wonder! Wonder! It comes with her.

Last night, after June, filled with June, I could not bear Hugo reading the newspapers and talking about trusts and a successful day. He understood—he does understand—but he couldn't share, he could not grasp the incandescent. He teased me. He was humorous. He was immensely lovable and warm. But I could not come back.

So I lay on the couch, smoking, and thinking of June. At the station, I had fainted.

The intensity is shattering us both. She is glad to be leaving. She is less yielding than I am. She really wants to escape from that which is giving her life. She does not like my power, whereas I take joy in submitting to her.

When we met for half an hour today to discuss Henry's future, she asked me to take care of him, and then she gave me her silver bracelet with a cat's-eye stone, when she has so few possessions. I refused at first, and then the joy of wearing her bracelet, a part of her, filled me. I carry it like a symbol. It is precious to me.

Hugo noticed it and hated it. He wanted to take it from me, to tease me. I clung to it with all my strength while he crushed my hands, letting him hurt me.

June was afraid that Henry would turn me against her. What does she fear? I said to her, "There is a fantastic secret between us. I only know about you through my own knowledge. Faith. What is Henry's knowledge to me?"

Then I met Henry accidentally at the bank. I saw that he hated me, and I was startled. June had said that he was uneasy and restless, because he is more jealous of women than of men. June, inevitably, sows madness. Henry, who thought me a "rare" person, now hates me. Hugo, who rarely hates, hates her.

Today she said that when she talked to Henry about me she tried to be very natural and direct so as not to imply anything unusual. She told him, "Anaïs was just bored with her life, so she took us up." That seemed crude to me. It was the only ugly thing I have heard her say.

Hugo and I yield entirely to each other. We cannot be without each other, we cannot endure discord, war, estrangement, we cannot take walks alone, we do not like to travel without each other. We have yielded in spite of our individualism, our hatred of intimacy. We have absorbed our egocentric selves into our love. Our love *is* our ego.

I do not think June and Henry have achieved that, because both their individualities are too strong. So they are at war; love is a conflict; they must lie to each other, mistrust each other.

June wants to go back to New York and do something well, be lovely for me, satisfy me. She is afraid of disappointing me.

We had lunch together in a softly lighted place which surrounded us with velvety closeness. We took off our hats. We drank champagne. June refused all sweet or tasteless food. She could live on grapefruit, oysters, and champagne.

We talked in half-spoken abstractions, clear to us alone. She made me realize how she eluded all of Henry's attempts to grasp her logically, to reach a knowledge of her.

She sat there filled with champagne. She talked about hashish and its effects. I said, "I have known such states without hashish. I do not need drugs. I carry all that in myself." At this she was a little angry. She did not realize that I achieved those states without destroying my mind. My mind must not die, because I am a writer. I am the poet who must see. I am not just the poet who can get drunk on June's beauty.

It was her fault that I began to notice discrepancies in her stories, childish lies. Her lack of coordination and logic left loopholes, and when I put the pieces together, I formed a judgment, a judgment which she fears always, which she wants to run away from. She lives without logic. As soon as one tries to coordinate June, June is lost. She must have seen it happen many times. She is like a man who is drunk and gives himself away.

We were talking about perfumes, their substance, their mixtures, their meaning. She said casually, "Saturday, when I left you, I bought some perfume for Ray." (Ray is a girl she has told me about.) At the moment I did not think. I retained the name of the perfume, which was very expensive.

We went on talking. She is as affected by my eyes as I am by her face. I told her how her bracelet clutched my wrist like her very fingers, holding me in barbaric slavery. She wants my cape around her body.

After lunch we walked. She had to buy her ticket for New York. First we went in a taxi to her hotel. She brought out a marionette, Count Bruga, made by Jean. He had violet hair and violet eyelids, a prostitute's eyes, a Pulcinella nose, a loose, depraved mouth, consumptive cheeks, a mean, aggressive chin, murderer's hands, wooden legs, a Spanish sombrero, a black velvet jacket. He had been on the stage.

June sat him on the floor of the taxi, in front of us. I laughed at him.

We walked into several steamship agencies. June did not have enough money for even a third-class passage and she was trying to get a reduction. I saw her lean over the counter, her face in her hands, appealing, so that the men behind the counter devoured her with their eyes, boldly. And she so soft, persuasive, alluring, smiling up in a secret way at them. I was watching her begging. Count Bruga leered at me. I was only conscious of my jealousy of those men, not of her humiliation.

We walked out. I told June I would give her the money she needed, which was more than I could afford to give, much more.

We went into another steamship agency, with June barely finishing some mad fairy tale before she stated her errand. I saw the man at the counter taken out of himself, transfixed by her face and her soft, yielding way of talking to him, of paying and signing. I stood by and watched him ask her, "Will you have a cocktail with me tomorrow?" June was shaking hands with him. "Three o'clock?" "No. At six." She smiled at him as she does at me. Then as we left she explained herself hurriedly. "He was very useful to me, very helpful. He is going to do a lot for me. I couldn't say no. I don't intend to go, but I couldn't say no."

"You must go, now that you said yes," I said angrily, and then the literalness and stupidity of this statement nauseated me. I took June's arm and said almost in a sob, "I can't bear it. I can't bear it." I was angry at some undefinable thing. I thought of the prostitute, honest because in exchange for money she gives her body. June would never give her body. But she would beg as I would never beg, promise as I would not promise unless I were to give.

June! There was such a tear in my dream. She knew it. So she took my hand against her warm breast and we walked, I feeling her breast. She was always naked under her dress. She did it perhaps unconsciously, as if to soothe an angry child. And she talked about things that were not to the point. "Would you rather I had said no, brutally, to the man? I am sometimes brutal, you know, but I couldn't be in front of you. I didn't want to hurt his feelings. He had been very helpful." And as I did not know what angered me, I said nothing. It was not a question of accepting or refusing a cocktail. One had to go back to the root of why she should need the help of that man. A statement of hers came back to me: "However bad things are for me I always find someone who will buy me champagne." Of course. She was a woman accumulating huge debts which she never intended to pay, for afterwards she boasted of her sexual inviolability. A gold digger. Pride in the possession of her own body but not too proud to humiliate herself with prostitute eyes over the counter of a steamship company.

She was telling me that she and Henry had quarreled over buying butter. They had no money and . . . "No money?" I said. "But Saturday I gave you 400 francs, for you and Henry to eat with. And today is Monday."

"We had things to pay up that we owed. . . ."

I thought she meant the hotel room. Then suddenly I remembered the perfume, which cost 200 francs. Why didn't she say to me, "I bought perfume and gloves and stockings Saturday." She did not look at me when she intimated they had the rent to pay. Then I remembered another thing she had said. "People say to me that if I had a fortune, I could spend it in a day, and no one would ever know how. I can never account for the way I spend money."

This was the other face of June's fantasy. We walked the streets, and all the softness of her breast could not lull the pain.

I went home and was very heavy in Hugo's arms. I said to him, "I have come back." And he was very happy.

But yesterday at four, when I was waiting for her at American Express, the doorman said to me, "Your friend was here this morning and she said good-bye to me as if she were not coming back." "But we had agreed to meet here." If I were never again to see June walking towards me— impossible. It was like dying. What did it matter, all I thought the day before. She was unethical, irresponsible—it was her nature. I would not tamper with her nature. My pride about money matters was aristocratic. I was too scrupulous and proud. I would not change anything in June which was basic and at the root of her fantastic being. She alone was without fetters. I was a fettered, ethical being, in spite of my amoral intellect. I could not have let Henry go hungry. I accepted her entirely. I would not fight her. If only she would come and meet me for that last hour.

I had dressed ritually for her, in the very costume which created a void between me and other people, a costume which was a symbol of my individualism and which she alone would understand. Black turban, old rose dress with black lace bodice and collar, old rose coat with Medici collar. I had created a stir as I walked, and I was lonelier than ever because the reaction was partly hostile, mocking.

Then June came, all in black velvet, black cape and plumed hat, paler and more incandescent than ever, and carrying Count Bruga, as I had asked her to do. The wonder of her face and smile, her smileless eyes . . .

I took her to a Russian tearoom. The Russians sang as we felt. June wondered if they were really burning, as it seemed from their voices and intense playing. Probably they were not burning as June and I were.

Champagne and caviar with June. It is the only time one knows what champagne is and what caviar is. They are June, Russian voices and June.

Ugly, unimaginative, dead people surround us. We are blind to them. I look at June, in black velvet. June rushing towards death. Henry cannot rush on with her because he fights for life. But June and I together do not hold back. I follow her. And it is an acute joy to go along, giving in to the dissolution of the imagination, to her knowledge of strange experiences, to our games with Count Bruga, who bows to the world with the weeping willowness of his purple hair.

It is all over. In the street, June says regretfully, "I had wanted to hold you and caress you." I put her in a taxi. She sits there about to leave me and I stand by in torment. "I want to kiss you," I say. "I want to kiss you," says June, and she offers her mouth, which I kiss for a long time.

When she left, I just wanted to sleep for many days, but I still had something to face, my relationship with Henry. We asked him to come to Louveciennes. I wanted to offer him peace and a soothing house, but of course I knew we would talk about June.

We walked off our restlessness, and we talked. There is in both of us an obsession to grasp June. He has no jealousy of me, because he said I brought out wonderful things in June, that it was the first time June had ever attached herself to a woman of value. He seemed to expect I would have power over her life.

When he saw that I understood June and was ready to be truthful with him, we talked freely. Yet once I paused, hesitant, wondering at my faithlessness to June. Then Henry observed that although truth, in June's case, had to be disregarded, it could be the only basis of any exchange between us.

We both felt the need of allying our two minds, our two different logics, in understanding the problem of June. Henry loves her and always her. He also wants to possess June the character, the powerful, fictionlike personage. In his love for her he has had to endure so many torments that the lover has taken refuge in the writer. He has written a ferocious and resplendent book about June and Jean.

He was questioning the lesbianism. When he heard me say certain things he had heard June say, he was startled, because he believes me. I said, "After all, if there is an explanation of the mystery it is this: The love between women is a refuge and an escape into harmony. In the love between man and woman there is resistance and conflict. Two women do not judge each other, brutalize each other, or find anything to ridicule. They surrender to sentimentality, mutual understanding, romanticism. Such love is death, I'll admit."

Last night I sat up until one o'clock reading Henry's novel, *Moloch*, while he read mine. His was overwhelming, the work of a giant. I was at a loss to tell him how it affected me. And this giant sat there quietly and read my slight book with such comprehension, such enthusiasm, talking about the deftness of it, the subtlety, the voluptuousness, shouting at certain passages, criticizing, too. What a force he is!

I gave him the one thing June cannot give him: honesty. I am so ready to admit what a supremely developed ego would not admit: that June is a terrifying and inspiring character who makes every other woman insipid, that I would live her life except for my compassion and my conscience, that she may destroy Henry the man, but Henry the writer is more enriched by ordeals than by peace. I, on the other hand, cannot destroy Hugo, because he has nothing else. But like June, I have a capacity for delicate perversions. The love of only one man or one woman is an enclosure.

My conflict is going to be greater than June's, because she has no mind watching her life. Others do it for her, and she denies all they say or write. I have a mind which is bigger than all the rest of me, an inexorable conscience.

Eduardo says, "Go and be psychoanalyzed." But that seems too simple. I want to make my own discoveries.

I do not need drugs, artificial stimulation. Yet I want to experience those very things with June, to penetrate the evil which attracts me. I seek life, and the experiences I want are denied me because I carry in me a force which neutralizes them. I meet June, the near-prostitute, and she becomes pure. A purity which maddens Henry, a purity of face and being which is awesome, just as I saw her one afternoon in the corner of the divan, transparent, supernatural.

Henry speaks to me of her extreme vulgarity. I know her lack of pride. Vulgarity gives the joy of desecrating. But June is not a demon. Life is the demon, possessing her, and their coition is violent because her voraciousness for life is enormous, a tasting of its bitterest flavors. . . .

I have an acute struggle to keep Henry, whom I don't want to give up, and to keep the relationship between June and me a precious secret.

Yesterday at the café he tore bits of our story from me. It hurt and maddened me. I came home and wrote him a long, feverish letter. If he showed this letter to June, I would lose her. Henry cannot make me love her less, but he can torment me by making her appear more unreal, more self-less, by proving that there is no June, only an image, invented by us, by Henry's mind, and my poetry. He talked about influences on her. The influence of Jean, the woman in New York. This was torture to me.

And then he said, "You mystify me." And I said nothing. Is he going to hate me? When we first met he was so warm and so responsive to my presence. His whole body was aware of me. We leaned over eagerly to look at the book I had brought him. We were both exultant. He forgot to drink his coffee.

I am trapped, between the beauty of June and the genius of Henry. In a different way, I am devoted to both, a part of me goes out to each of them. But I love June madly, unreasoningly. Henry gives me life, June gives me death. I must choose, and I cannot. For me to give Henry all the feelings I have had about June is exactly like giving my body and soul to him.

.   .   .

I meet Henry in the dim, cavernous Viking. He has not received my note. He has brought me another love letter. He almost cries out, "You are veiled now. Be real! Your words, your writing, the other day. You were real." I deny it. Then he says humbly, "Oh, I knew it, I knew I was too presumptuous to aspire to you. I'm a peasant, Anaïs. Only whores can appreciate me." That brings out the words he wants to hear. Feebly, we argue. We recall the beginning: we began with the mind. "Did we, but did we?" says Henry, trembling. And suddenly he leans over and engulfs me in an endless kiss. I do not want the kiss to end. He says, "Come to my room."

How stifling the veil about me, which Henry struggles to tear, my fear of reality. We are walking to his room, and I do not feel the ground, but I feel his body against mine. He says, "Look at the carpet on the stairs, it is worn," and I do not see, I only feel the ascension. My note is in his hands. "Read it," I say, at the bottom of the stairs, "and I'll leave you." But I follow him. His room, I do not see. When he takes me in his arms, my body melts. The tenderness of his hands, the unexpected penetration, to the core of me but without violence. What strange, gentle power.

He, too, cries out, "It is all so unreal, so swift."

And I see another Henry, or perhaps the same Henry who walked that day into my house. We talk as I wished we would talk, so easily, so truly. I lie on his bed covered by his coat. He watches me.

"You expected—more brutality?"

His mountains of words, of notes, of quotations are sundered. I am surprised. I did not know this man. We were not in love with each other's writing. But what are we in love with now? I cannot bear the picture of June's face on the mantelpiece. Even in the photograph, it is uncanny, she possesses us both.

I write crazy notes to Henry. We cannot meet today. The day is empty. I am caught. And he? What does he feel? I am invaded, I lose everything, my mind vacillates, I am only aware of sensations.

There are moments in the day when I do not believe in Henry's love, when I feel June dominating both of us, when I say to myself, "This morning he will awake and realize he loves no one but June." Moments when I believe, madly, that we are going to live something new, Henry and I, outside of June's world.

How has he imposed truth on me? I was about to take flight from the prison of my imaginings, but he takes me to his room and there we live a dream, not a reality. He places me where he wants to place me. Incense. Worship. Illusion. And all the rest of his life is effaced. He comes with a new soul to this hour. It is the sleeping potion of fairy tales. I lie with a burning womb and he scarcely notices it. Our gestures are human, but there is a curse on the room. It is June's face. I remember, with great pain, one of his notes: "life's wildest moment—June, kneeling on the street." Is it June or Henry I am jealous of?

He asks to see me again. When I wait in the armchair in his room, and he kneels to kiss me, he is stranger than all my thoughts. With his experience he dominates me. He dominates with his mind, too, and I am silenced. He whispers to me what my body must do. I obey, and new instincts rise in me. He has seized me. A man so human; and I, suddenly brazenly natural. I am amazed at my lying there in his iron bed, with my black underwear vanquished and trampled. And the tight secrecy of me broken for a moment, by a man who calls himself "the last man on earth."

Writing is not, for us, an art, but breathing. After our first encounter I breathed some notes, accents of recognition, human admissions. Henry was still stunned, and I was breathing off the unbearable, willing joy. But the second time, there were no words. My joy was impalpable and terrifying. It swelled within me as I walked the streets.

It transpires, it blazes. I cannot conceal it. I am woman. A man has made me submit. Oh, the joy when a woman finds a man she can submit to, the joy of her femaleness expanding in strong arms.

Hugo looks at me as we sit by the fire. I am talking drunkenly, brilliantly. He says, "I've never seen you look so beautiful. I have never felt your power so strongly. What is the new confidence in you?"

He desires me, just as he did that other time, after John's visit. My conscience dies at that moment. Hugo bears down on me, and I instinctively obey Henry's whispered words. I close my legs about Hugo, and he exclaims in ecstasy, "Darling, darling, what are you doing? You're driving me wild. I've never felt such joy before!"

I cheat him, I deceive him, yet the world does not sink in sulphur-colored mists. Madness conquers. I can no longer put my mosaics together. I just cry and laugh.

After a concert, Hugo and I left together, like lovers, he said. That was the day after Henry and I acknowledged certain feelings at the Viking. Hugo was so attentive, so tender. It was a holiday for him. We were having dinner in a restaurant in Montparnasse. I had invented a pretext to call at a friend's for Henry's first love letter. It was in my pocketbook. I was thinking of it while Hugo asked me, "Do you want oysters? Take oysters tonight. It's a special night. Every time I go out with you I feel as if I were taking my mistress out. You are my mistress. I love you more than ever."

I want to read Henry's letter. I excuse myself. I go to the washroom. I read the letter there. It is not very eloquent, and I am touched by the fact. I don't know what else I feel. I return to the table, dizzy. This was where we met Henry when he returned from Dijon and where I realized I was happy he had returned.

On another occasion Hugo and I go to the theatre. I am thinking of Henry. Hugo knows, and he shows the same old tender uneasiness, the desire to believe, and I reassure him. He himself had given me a message that I should call Henry at eight-thirty.

So before the play we go to a café, and Hugo helps me to find the number of Henry's office. I joke about what he is going to hear. Henry and I do not say very much: "Did you get my letter?" "Yes." "Did you get my note?" "No."

I have a bad night after the play. Hugo gets up in the early morning to bring me medicine, a sleeping pill. "What is the matter?" he asks. "What do you feel?" He offers the refuge of his arms.

The first time I come back from Henry's room, stunned, I find difficulty in talking in my usual lively way.

Hugo sits down, takes up his diary book and writes wildly about me and "art" and how everything I do is right. While he reads this to me, I bleed to death. Before the end he begins to sob. He doesn't know why. I get on my knees before him. "What is it, darling, what is it?" And I say this terrible thing: "Do you have an intuition?"—which, because of his faith and his slow senses, he cannot understand. He believes Henry only stimulates me imaginatively, as a writer. And it is because he believes this that he sits down to write also, to woo me with writing.

I want to cry out, "That is so young of you; it's like the faith of a child." God, I'm old, I'm the last *woman* on earth. I am aware of a monstrous paradox; By giving myself I learn to love Hugo more. By living as I do I am preserving our love from bitterness and death.

The truth is that this is the only way I can live: in two directions. I need two lives. I am two beings. When I return to Hugo in the evening, to the peace and warmth of the house, I return with a deep contentment, as if this were the only condition for me. I bring home to Hugo a whole woman, freed of all "possessed" fevers, cured of the poison of restlessness and curiosity which used to threaten our marriage, cured through action. Our love lives, because I live. I sustain and feed it. I am loyal to it, in my own way, which cannot be his way. If he ever reads these lines, he must believe me. I am writing calmly, lucidly while waiting for him to come home, as one waits for the chosen lover, the eternal one.

NING LAO T'AI-T'AI
(1867–?)

Ida Pruitt, an American woman living in Peking before the Second World War, wanted to learn more about the old customs of Chinese families and was put in touch with the mother of a man who worked for her husband. The old woman came at breakfast three days a week for two years and talked to Pruitt, telling tales to illustrate various Chinese customs, using her own life as an example, until, as Pruitt said, "the story of her life lay before me." Enjoying each other's company, they continued to meet until 1938, when Pruitt returned to the States and Ning disappeared in the Japanese-occupied city. Pruitt could never get word of Ning Lao T'ai-t'ai again. (*Lao T'ai-t'ai* is a respectful title meaning "revered old lady" which is applied to a family name, so Ning Lao T'ai-t'ai is something like "Revered Old Lady Ning.")

She was the second daughter in a family whose fortunes had declined, and she fell even further after her marriage to a man addicted to opium. His inability to keep a job forced her to "come out" of her house onto the streets and to beg, as described in this selection. The city Ning lived in at the time of these events was Penglai, in Shandong Province to the east of the Yellow River, on the peninsula jutting into the Yellow Sea.

Ida Pruitt wrote *A Daughter of Han: The Autobiography of a Chinese Working Woman* based on the stories Ning Lao T'ai-t'ai had told her, and the book was published in 1945.

For other oral autobiographies, compare *Nisa: The Life and Words of a !Kung Woman* and Onnie Lee Logan's *Motherwit*. For other accounts of women struggling to support their children, without a husband's help, compare Carolina Maria de Jesus, *Beyond All Pity* and Emma Mashinini, *Strikes Have Followed Me All My Life*.

FROM *A Daughter of Han*

1889

When we had finished what they gave us we begged as before. One day as I was walking along a man called to me.

"Is not your name Ning?" I hurried along. I tucked the stick* further up my sleeve. I was now in the part of the city where my people had lived. I had moved back into the home nest, but would not shame them by being known as a beggar.

"Is there not a man named Ning, called so and so?" asked the stranger. I said that I knew nothing about what he was saying. Then the man said, "I have heard of such a man bargaining to sell a child."

I was young then and had no experience. I thought, "Could he really think to sell our child?"

When I got home I asked him. He laughed and said, "They must have heard me joking one day."

I believed him. I was young and simple then. I was only twenty-two.

In the winter the rich of the city built mat sheds under which they gave out gruel to the poor. We went every day for one meal of hot gruel. We met there, for he begged in one part of the city, carrying Chinya, and I begged in another, leading Mantze.

One day when my husband handed the baby over to me as usual, saying, "Nurse her," one of the men in charge of the gruel station saw him do it.

"Is that your man?" said the man from the gruel station. I answered that he was.

"He is trying to sell the child. He tells people that her mother died last Seventh Month."

"Oh, that is the talk that he uses for begging," I said. But in my heart I wondered if it was true that he was trying to sell our child and to keep the knowledge from me.

One day, when the ground was wet with melting snow, I found that even with the three pairs of shoes my feet were not covered. The bare flesh showed through.

"You stay at home," he said, "and I will beg." He took the child in his arms as usual. "You wait at home," he said. "I will bring you food."

We waited, Mantze and I. The day passed; it got dark; and still he did not come. It was cold. I opened my clothes and took Mantze inside my garments to give her warmth, and still he did not come. We lay in the dark. We had no lights that winter; we had no money for oil. I heard the watchman beating the third watch and I knew the night was half over. Still he did not come.

Then I heard him push open the door and stumble as he crossed the threshold. He was opium sodden and uncertain in his movements. I waited for him to say as usual, "Here, take the child and nurse her." But there was no word. I heard him throwing something heavily on the bed.

---

*Beggars were known by the sticks they carried to beat off dogs—Ed.

"Now you have knocked the breath out of the child. Give her to me."
Still he said nothing.

"What is the matter? Give me the child." And he only grunted.

"Light the lamp and I will tell you," he said.

"It is not the custom to light lamps in this house. Do you not know me or do I not know you that we must have a light to talk by to each other? Tell me." Then he struck a match and I saw that there was no child, only a bundle, a bundle of sweet potatoes.

"I have sold her."

I jumped out of bed. I had no thought left for Mantze. I seized him by the queue. I wrapped it three times around my arm. I fought him for my child. We rolled fighting on the ground.

The neighbors came and talked to pacify us.

"If the child has not left the city and we can keep hold of this one, we will find her," they said.

So we searched. The night through we searched. We went to the south city through the Drum Tower and back to the examination halls. We walked a great circle inside the city, and always I walked with my hands on his queue. He could not get away.

We found a house. The father of the child knocked. Some men came to the door. It was the house of dealers who buy up girls and sell them to brothels in other cities. Their trade is illegal, and if they are caught they are put in prison and punished. They dared not let me make a noise. I had but to call aloud and the neighbors would be there. So the dealer in little girls said soft words. My neighbors said, "What he says, he will do. Now that we have him we will find the child." But the child was not in that house.

"Take me to my child," I demanded. The man promised. So again we started out in the night, walking and stumbling through the streets. Then one of my neighbors who had more power to plan than the others said, "Why do you still hold on to him? He is now useless." I still had my arm twisted in my husband's queue. "Hold on to that one so he does not run away. He it is that knows where the child is."

So I let go of my husband's queue and in one jump was beside the man and had seized him by the slack of his coat. "Why do you seize me?" he said.

"So that you will not run away and I lose my child again." My husband was gone into the night, and still we walked. We came to the entrance of a narrow street.

"You stay here," said the man, "I will go in and call them."

"No," said I. "Where you go, I go. What kind of a place is this that I cannot go with you?"

And when he said that it was a residence, I said, "A residence! If you, a man, can go, surely I, a woman can do so. If it was a bachelor's lair I still would go in to find my child." I held onto him by the slack of his coat as we went down the narrow street to a gate. He knocked and still I held to him.

The man who opened it held the two parts of the gate together with his hands to prevent anyone going in. But I ducked under his arm before he could stop me and ran into the passage. I went through the courts, calling, "Chinya, Chinya." The child heard my voice and knew me and answered, and so I found her. The woman of the house tried to hide the child behind her wide sleeves, but I pushed her aside and took the child into my arms. The man barred the door and said that I could not leave.

"Then," I said, "I will stay here. My child is in my bosom. Mother and child, we will die here together." I sat on the floor with my child in my arms.

The neighbors gathered and talked. A child, they said, could not be sold without the mother's consent. He had, they said, got another five hundred cash from them by saying that I had not at first consented. They had first paid him three thousand. He had sold my child for a mere three thousand and five hundred cash.

They tried to frighten me. They said they would sell us both to get their money back. I was young then, and salable. But I said, "No. I have another child at home. I must go to that child also." The neighbors all began to talk and said that I had another child and that I must go home to her, and the dealers talked of their money that they must have back.

"You stay here until we go and get the money back," they said. But at last we all started out together. I was carrying the child and they came along to get their money. They lighted a lantern and let it shine under my feet.

Then a neighbor who thought more quickly than others said, "It is cold tonight and the way is long. We have walked far. Let me carry the child."

I said that I was well and strong and could carry her myself.

But again she said, "My coat is bigger than yours. I can carry the child inside and protect her from the cold." So I gave the child to her. She walked ahead, and gradually as they lighted the way for me she disappeared into the night. When we got home she was there with the child, but my old opium sot was gone. She knew that he would have spent all the money and would have been unable to pay, and that when they had found this out they would have taken him out and beaten him. So she had gone ahead and warned him and he had slipped away into the night. And she also had the child safely at home.

So that passed over.

He promised not to sell her again and I believed him.

The old people tell us that her husband is more important to a woman than her parents. A woman is with her parents only part of her life, they say, but she is with her husband forever. He also feels that he is the most important. If a wife is not good to her husband, there is retribution in heaven.

My husband would sit on the k'ang* with his legs drawn up under his chin and his head hanging. He would raise his head suddenly and peer at me from under his lids.

"Ha! Why don't you make a plan? Why don't you think of a way for us to eat?"

I would answer, "What can I do? My family have no money. I know no one."

Then, at last, he would get up and go out to beg. People urged me to leave him and follow another man, to become a thief or a prostitute. But my parents had left me a good name, though they had left me nothing else. I could not spoil that for them.

In those years it was not as it is now. There was no freedom then for women. I stayed with him.

For another year we lived, begging and eating gruel from the public kitchen.

The father of my children was good for a while, and I thought he had learned his lesson. He promised never to sell the child again and I believed him. Then one day he sold her again and I could not get her back that time.

My little daughter was four when her father sold her the second time. When he came home without her I knew what he had done. I said that I would hang myself and that I would hang Mantze, and that we, mother and child, should die together. I rolled on the ground in my agony, in my anger, and my pain. He was frightened and said that there was no need to hang myself. He took me to the family to whom he had sold her.

It was the family of an official who had two wives. The first wife had many children but the second had none. She had been a prostitute but she was a good woman. It was she who had bought my child. She came out into the court to see me and she said many words. She said, "How can you, by begging, support two children? Your man is no good, you know that. I will not treat your child as a slave girl. I will treat her as my child. Is she not better off with me than with you? If you take her back will he not sell her again? Also you may come to see her when you like."

I knew that her words were true so I went away.

He sold her for three thousand five hundred cash the first time. I do not know for how much he sold her this second time.

---

*The mud-brick bed—ED.

Many times I went to see my little daughter and I saw that they treated her well.

They left Penglai when she was seven and I did not hear from them again until my granddaughter was half grown. Then I heard that they had done well by her. They had brought her up as a daughter, and taught her to do fine embroidery and married her to a young fruit merchant. She was well treated in the family but I never saw her again.

But because he sold her, I left my husband. I took Mantze and went away. I told him that he could live his life and that I would live mine. He lived in the house I had leased but I did not go home. When the lease was up I let it go. I let him live where he would. He lived from one opium den to another. I taught my daughter Mantze to run at the sight of him and to hide. What if he sold her also? I would not live with him.

The life of the beggar is not the hardest one. There is freedom. Today perhaps there is not enough to eat, but tomorrow there will be more. There is no face to keep up. Each day is eaten what has been begged that day. The sights of the city are free for the beggars. The temple fairs with their merrymaking crowds, the candy sticks with fluttering pennants, the whirligigs spreading noise and the colors of the rainbow in the air, women dressed in gay colors, the incense burning before the shrines and piling up in the iron pots, the flames leaping high, are harvest time for the beggars. There is drama on the open-air stage. No lady can get as close to the stage as a beggar. The ladies have their dignity to maintain and must sit in a closed cart or on the edge of the throng in tea booths. No woman but a beggar woman could see the magistrate in his embroidered ceremonial robes ride to the temples to offer sacrifice at the altars of the city in the times of festival.

At noon the beggars come to the gruel kitchen where all the other beggars have gathered, and find human companionship. There is warm food, pleasantry, and the close feel of people around. There is no future but there is no worry. An old proverb says, "Two years of begging and one will not change places with the district magistrate." All this if a beggar is not sick.

But I was through with begging. For a year I had begged for my food but had lived in my own home. Now I could not live in my home and must "come out," even though women of my family had never "come out" before.

NISA
(c. 1921–?)

Nisa was about fifty when Marjorie Shostak, an American anthropologist, interviewed her in 1971. A member of one of the last-remaining tribes of pre-agricultural hunters and gatherers, she lived in a remote section of the Kalahari Desert in southern Africa. In their sessions together Shostak elicited from Nisa a remarkably detailed and vivid account of life lived close to subsistence level. The !Kung are nomads who own only what they can carry with them, yet their lives are rich with talk, jokes, music, sociability, family ties, and sexual escapades.

Shostak learned the !Kung language and interviewed nine !Kung women for hundreds of hours before fastening on Nisa as her ideal informant. For various reasons, none of the other women was capable of collaborating to produce her life story. Some were too preoccupied with what was happening in their lives to put much effort into the work of recollection. Some spoke too complicated a language for Shostak to understand. Some were too inexperienced, and some had too abstract and general a way of describing their experience.

Not only was Nisa articulate, but she also had extraordinary recall of very early events in her life, such as her weaning, described in the first of these selections from *Nisa: The Life and Words of a !Kung Woman* (1981). She was paid by Shostak for her work, but she seems independently of that to have enjoyed the chance to explain herself and to offer her own experience as a guide for the younger American woman. Nisa had outlived all her own children, so there was special poignancy in her connection with Shostak.

For another oral autobiography of an African woman gathered by an anthropologist, see *Baba of Karo: A Woman of the Muslim Hausa* by Mary F. Smith. Other oral autobiographies in this collection include Ning Lao T'ai-t'ai, *A Daughter of Han* and Billie Holiday, *Lady Sings the Blues.* For another account of eating, compare M. F. K. Fisher, "I Was Really Very Hungry," from *As They Were;* for other accounts of sex in marriage, compare Colette, *My Apprenticeships,* Anaïs Nin, *Diary,* and V. Sackville-West, *Confession;* and for another account of childbirth, compare Onnie Lee Logan, *Motherwit.*

FROM *Nisa: The Life and Words of a !Kung Woman*

EARLIEST MEMORIES

Fix my voice on the machine so that my words come out clear. I am an old person who has experienced many things and I have much to talk about. I will tell my talk, of the things I have done and the things that my parents and others have done. But don't let the people I live with hear what I say.

Our father's name was Gau and our mother's was Chuko. Of course, when my father married my mother, I wasn't there. But soon after, they gave birth to a son whom they called Dau. Then they gave birth to me, Nisa, and then my younger brother was born, their youngest child who survived, and they named him Kumsa.

I remember when my mother was pregnant with Kumsa. I was still small and I asked, "Mommy, that baby inside you . . . when that baby is born, will it come out from your belly button? Will the baby grow and grow until Daddy breaks open your stomach with a knife and takes my little sibling out?" She said, "No, it won't come out that way. When you give birth, a baby comes from here," and she pointed to her genitals. Then she said, "And after he is born, you can carry your little sibling around." I said, "Yes, I'll carry him!"

Later, I asked, "Won't you help me and let me nurse?" She said, "You can't nurse any longer. If you do, you'll die." I left her and went and played by myself for a while. When I came back, I asked to nurse again but she still wouldn't let me. She took some paste made from the dch'a root and rubbed it on her nipple. When I tasted it, I told her it was bitter.

When mother was pregnant with Kumsa, I was always crying. I *wanted* to nurse! Once, when we were living in the bush and away from other people, I was especially full of tears. I cried all the time. That was when my father said he was going to beat me to death; I was too full of tears and too full of crying. He had a big branch in his hand when he grabbed me, but he didn't hit me; he was only trying to frighten me. I cried out, "Mommy, come help me! Mommy! Come! Help me!" When my mother came, she said, "No, Gau, you are a man. If you hit Nisa you will put sickness into her and she will become very sick. Now, leave her alone. I'll hit her if it's necessary. My arm doesn't have the power to make her sick; your arm, a man's arm, does."

When I finally stopped crying, my throat was full of pain. All the tears had hurt my throat.

Another time, my father took me and left me alone in the bush. We had left one village and were moving to another and had stopped along the way to sleep. As soon as night sat, I started to cry. I cried and cried and cried. My father hit me, but I kept crying. I probably would have cried the whole night, but finally, he got up and said, "I'm taking you and leaving you out in the bush for the hyenas to kill. What kind of child are you? If you nurse your sibling's milk, you'll die!" He picked me up, carried me away from camp and set me down in the bush. He shouted, "Hyenas! There's meat over here . . . Hyenas! Come and take this meat!" Then he turned and started to walk back to the village.

After he left, I was so afraid! I started to run and, crying, I ran past him. Still crying, I ran back to my mother and lay down beside her. I was afraid of the night and of the hyenas, so I lay there quietly. When my father came back, he said, "Today, I'm really going to make you shit! You can see your mother's stomach is huge, yet you still want to nurse." I started to cry again and cried and cried; then I was quiet again and lay down. My father said, "Good, lie there quietly. Tomorrow, I'll kill a guinea fowl for you to eat."

The next day, he went hunting and killed a guinea fowl. When he came back, he cooked it for me and I ate and ate and ate. But when I was finished, I said I wanted to take my mother's nipple again. My father grabbed a strap and started to hit me, "Nisa, have you no sense? Can't you understand? Leave your mother's chest alone!" And I began to cry again.

Another time, when we were walking together in the bush, I said, "Mommy . . . carry me!" She said yes, but my father told her not to. He said I was big enough to walk along by myself. Also, my mother was pregnant. He wanted to hit me, but my older brother Dau stopped him, "You've hit her so much, she's skinny! She's so thin, she's only bones. Stop treating her this way!" Then Dau picked me up and carried me on his shoulders.

When mother was pregnant with Kumsa, I was always crying, wasn't I? I would cry for a while, then be quiet and sit around, eating regular food: sweet nin berries and starchy chon and klaru bulbs, foods of the rainy season. One day, after I had eaten and was full, I said, "Mommy, won't you let me have just a little milk? Please, let me nurse." She cried, "Mother! My breasts are things of shit! Shit! Yes, the milk is like vomit and smells terrible. You can't drink it. If you do, you'll go, 'Whaagh . . . Whaagh . . .' and throw up." I said, "No, I won't throw up, I'll just nurse." But she refused and said, "Tomorrow, Daddy will trap a spring-hare, just for you to eat." When I heard that, my heart was happy again.

The next day, my father killed a springhare. When I saw him coming home with it, I shouted, "Ho, ho, Daddy! Ho, ho, Daddy's come! Daddy killed a springhare; Daddy's bringing home meat! Now I will eat and won't give any to *her.*" My father cooked the meat and when it was done, I ate and ate and ate. I told her, "You stinged your milk, so I'll stinge this meat. You think your breasts are such wonderful things? They're not, they're terrible things." She said, "Nisa, please listen to me—my milk is not good for you anymore." I said, "Grandmother! I don't want it anymore! I'll eat meat instead. I'll never have anything to do with your breasts again. I'll just eat the meat Daddy and Dau kill for me."

Mother's stomach grew very large. The first labor pains came at night and stayed with her until dawn. That morning, everyone went gathering. Mother and I stayed behind. We sat together for a while, then I went and played with the other children. Later, I came back and ate the nuts she had cracked for me. She got up and started to get ready. I said, "Mommy, let's go to the water well, I'm thirsty." She said, "Uhn, uhn, I'm going to gather some mongongo nuts." I told the children that I was going and we left; there were no other adults around.

We walked a short way, then she sat down by the base of a large nehn tree, leaned back against it, and little Kumsa was born. At first, I just stood there; then I sat down and watched. I thought, "Is that the way it's done? You just sit like that and that's where the baby comes out? Am I also like that?" Did I have any understanding of things?

After he was born, he lay there, crying. I greeted him, "Ho, ho, my baby brother! Ho, ho, I have a little brother! Some day we'll play to-gether." But my mother said, "What do you think this thing is? Why are you talking to it like that? Now, get up and go back to the village and bring me my digging stick." I said, "What are you going to dig?" She said, "A hole. I'm going to dig a hole so I can bury the baby. Then you, Nisa, will be able to nurse again." I refused. "My baby brother? My little brother? Mommy, he's my *brother!* Pick him up and carry him back to the village. I don't want to nurse!" Then I said, "I'll tell Daddy when he comes home!" She said, "You won't tell him. Now, run back and bring me my digging stick. I'll bury him so you can nurse again. You're much too thin." I didn't want to go and started to cry. I sat there, my tears falling, crying and crying. But she told me to go, saying she wanted my bones to be strong. So, I left and went back to the village, crying as I walked.

I was still crying when I arrived. I went to the hut and got her digging stick. My mother's younger sister had just arrived home from the nut groves. She put the mongongo nuts she had gathered into a pile near her hut and sat down. Then she began roasting them. When she saw me, she said, "Nisa, what's wrong? Where's your mother?" I said, "By the nehn tree way out there. That's where we went together and where she just now gave birth to a baby. She told me to come back and get her digging stick so she could . . . bury him! This is terrible!" and I started to cry again. Then I added, "When I greeted him and called him 'my little brother' she told me not to. What she wants to do is bad . . . that's why I'm crying. Now I have to bring this digging stick to her!"

My mother's sister said, "Oooo . . . people! This Chuko, she's certainly a bad one to be talking like that. And she's out there alone with the baby! No matter what it is—a boy or a girl—she should keep it." I said, "Yes, he's a little boy with a little penis just resting there at the bottom of his stomach." She said, "Mother! Let's go! Let's go and talk to her. When I get there I'll cut his umbilical cord and carry him back."

I left the digging stick behind and we ran to where my mother was still sitting, waiting for me. Perhaps she had already changed her mind, because, when we got there, she said, "Nisa, because you were crying like that, I'll keep the baby and carry him back with me." My aunt went over to Kumsa lying beside my mother and said, "Chuko, were you trying to split your face into pieces? You can see what a big boy you gave birth to, yet you wanted Nisa to bring back your digging stick? You wanted to bury this great big baby? Your own father worked to feed you and keep you alive. This child's father would surely have killed you if you had buried his little boy. You must have no sense, wanting to kill such a nice big baby."

My aunt cut his umbilical cord, wiped him off, put him into her kaross, and carried him back to the village. Mother soon got up and followed, shamed by her sister's talk. Finally, she said, "Can't you understand? Nisa is still a little child. My heart's not happy that she hasn't any milk to drink. Her body is weak. I want her bones to grow strong." But my aunt said, "When Gau hears about this, he'll beat you. A grown woman with one child following after another so nicely, doesn't behave like this." When we arrived back in the village, my mother took the baby and lay down.

Everyone was now coming back from the mongongo groves. After they put down their gatherings, they came to look at Kumsa. The women all said, "Oooh . . . this woman has no sense! She gave birth to such a big baby, yet she was going to kill it!" My mother said, "I wanted his older sister to nurse, that's why I would have done it, and if I had been alone, I would have! I did the wrong thing by not taking my digging stick with me, but others did the wrong thing by taking him away from me. That's why I'm here with him at all." The women did not agree. They told my aunt, "You did very well. You were right to take the baby from Chuko and save him for his father. Wouldn't Chuko have had to answer to him if she had killed his baby?"

When the sun was low in the sky, my father came home from hunting. I greeted him, "Ho, ho, Daddy! Ho, ho, Daddy's home! There's Daddy!" He came and sat down beside the hut. He asked my mother, "What's wrong? Why are you lying down? Is something hurting you?" She said, "No, I'm just lying down." Then he said, "Eh-hey . . . my wife gave birth? Chuko, it's a boy?" She said, "Yes, a little boy." Then her sister said, "And a very large baby, too! But Chuko said she was going to . . ." I interrupted, *"Kill* him!" I rushed on, "She told me to come back and get her digging stick so she could kill my baby brother. I started to cry and came back to the village. But Aunt Koka went back with me and took the baby away from her." My aunt said, "Yes, I pulled the baby from his grave and carried him back." Then I said, "There he is lying over there. Mommy wanted to kill him."

My father said, "Chuko, why did you want to kill my son? If you had, I would have killed you. I would have struck you with my spear and killed you. Do you think I wouldn't do that? I surely would. What was making you feel so much pain that you would have killed such a large baby? You'll keep both children, now. Nisa will continue to grow up eating regular food."

After Kumsa was born, I sometimes just played by myself. I'd take the big kaross and lie down in it. I'd think, "Oh, I'm a child playing all alone. Where could I possibly go by myself?" Then I'd sit up and say, "Mommy, take my little brother from your kaross and let me play with him." But whenever she did, I hit him and made him cry. Even though he was still a little baby, I hit him. Then my mother would say, "You still want to nurse, but I won't let you. When Kumsa wants to, I'll let him. But whenever you want to, I'll cover my breasts with my hand and you'll feel ashamed."

I wanted the milk she had in her breasts, and when she nursed him, my eyes watched as the milk spilled out. I'd cry all night, cry and cry until dawn broke. Some mornings I just stayed around and my tears fell and I cried and refused all food. That was because I saw him nursing. I saw with my eyes the milk spilling out, the milk *I* wanted. I thought it was mine.

One day, my older brother came back from hunting carrying a duiker he had killed. I was sitting, playing by myself when I saw him, "Mommy! Mommy! Look! Big brother killed a duiker! Look over there, he's killed a duiker." My mother said, "Eh, didn't I tell you this morning that you should stop crying and wait for your older brother to come home? Now, see what he's brought back for you!"

When my brother started to skin it, I watched. "Oooo, a *male* duiker. Mommy . . . look, it's a male." I pointed, "There are its testicles and there's its penis." My older brother said, "Yes, those are its testicles and there's its penis."

After he skinned it, he gave me the feet. I put them in the coals to roast. Then he gave me some meat from the calf and I put that in the coals, too. When it was ready, I ate and ate and ate. Mother told me to give her some, but I refused, "Didn't you stinge your breasts? Didn't I say I wanted to nurse? I'm the only one who's going to eat this meat. I won't give any of it to you!" She said, "The milk you want belongs to your brother. What's making you still want to nurse?" I said, "My big brother killed this duiker. You won't have any of it. Not *you*. He'll cut the rest into strips and hang it to dry for me to eat. You refused to let me nurse so your son could. Now you say I should give you meat?"

Another day, my mother was lying down asleep with Kumsa, and I quietly sneaked up on them. I took Kumsa away from her, put him down on the other side of the hut, and came back and lay down beside her. While she slept, I took her nipple, put it in my mouth and began to nurse. I nursed and nursed and nursed. Maybe she thought it was my little brother. But he was still lying where I left him, while I stole his milk. I had already begun to feel wonderfully full when she woke up. She saw me and cried, "Where . . . tell me . . . what did you do with Kumsa? Where is he?" At that moment, he started to cry. I said, "He's over there."

She grabbed me and pushed me, hard, away from her. I lay there and cried. She went to Kumsa, picked him up, and laid him down beside her. She insulted me, cursing my genitals, "Have you gone crazy? Nisa-Big-Genitals, what's the matter with you? What craziness grabbed you that you took Kumsa, put him somewhere else, then lay down and nursed? Nisa-Big-Genitals! You must be crazy! I thought it was Kumsa nursing!" I lay there, crying. Then I said, "I've already nursed. I'm full. Let your baby nurse now. Go, feed him. I'm going to play." I got up and went and played. Later, I came back and stayed with my mother and her son. We stayed around together the rest of the day.

Later, when my father came back from the bush, she said, "Do you see what kind of mind your daughter has? Go, hit her! Hit her after you hear what she's done. Your daughter almost killed Kumsa! This tiny little baby, this tiny little thing, she took from beside me and dropped somewhere else. I was lying down, holding him, and fell asleep. That's when she took him from me and left him by himself. She came back, lay down, and started to nurse. Now, hit your daughter!"

I lied, "What? She's lying! Me . . . Daddy, I didn't nurse. I didn't take Kumsa and leave him by himself. Truly, I didn't. She's tricking you. She's lying. I didn't nurse. I don't even want her milk anymore." My father said, "If I ever hear of this again, I'll beat you! Don't ever do something like that again!" I said, "Yes, he's my little brother, isn't he? My brother, my little baby brother, and I *love* him. I won't do that again. He can nurse all by himself. Daddy, even if you're not here, I won't steal mommy's breasts. They belong to my brother." He said, "Yes, daughter. But if you ever try to nurse your mother's breasts again, I'll hit you so that it *really* hurts." I said, "Eh, from now on, I'm going to go wherever you go. When you go to the bush, I'll go with you. The two of us will kill springhare together and you'll trap guinea fowl and you'll give them all to me."

My father slept beside me that night. When dawn broke, he and my older brother left to go hunting. I watched as they walked off. I thought, "If I stay here, mother won't let me nurse," so I got up and ran after them. But when my brother saw me, he pushed me back toward the village, "Go back and stay in the village. When the sun is hot like this, it could kill you. Why do you want to come with us, anyway?"

This was also when I used to steal food, although it only happened once in a while. Some days I wouldn't steal anything and would just stay around playing, without doing any mischief. But other times, when they left me in the village, I'd steal and ruin their things. That's what they said when they yelled at me and hit me. They said I had no sense.

It happened over all types of food: sweet nin berries or klaru bulbs, other times it was mongongo nuts. I'd think, "Uhn, uhn, they won't give me any of that. But if I steal it, they'll hit me." Sometimes, before my mother went gathering, she'd leave food inside a leather pouch and hang it high on one of the branches inside the hut. If it was klaru, she'd peel off the skins before putting them inside.

But as soon as she left, I'd steal whatever was left in the bag. I'd find the biggest bulbs and take them. I'd hang the bag back on the branch and go sit somewhere to eat. When my mother came back, she'd say, "Oh! Nisa was in here and stole all the bulbs!" She'd hit me and yell, "Don't steal! What's the matter with you that inside you there is so much stealing? Stop taking things! Why are you so full of something like that?"

One day, right after they left, I climbed the tree where she had hung the pouch, took out some bulbs, put the pouch back, and mashed them with water in a mortar. I put the paste in a pot and cooked it. When it was ready, I ate and finished everything I had stolen.

Another time, I took some klaru and kept the bulbs beside me, eating them very slowly. That's when mother came back and caught me. She grabbed me and hit me, "Nisa, stop stealing! Are you the only one who wants to eat klaru? Now, let me take what's left and cook them for all of us to eat. Did you really think you were the only one who was going to eat them all?" I didn't answer and started to cry. She roasted the rest of the klaru and the whole family ate. I sat there, crying. She said, "Oh, this one has no sense, finishing all those klaru like that. Those are the ones I had peeled and had left in the pouch. Has she no sense at all?" I cried, "Mommy, don't talk like that." She wanted to hit me, but my father wouldn't let her.

Another time, I was out gathering with my mother, my father, and my older brother. After a while, I said, "Mommy, give me some klaru." She said, "I still have to peel these. As soon as I do, we'll go back to the village and eat them." I had also been digging klaru to take back to the village, but I ate all I could dig. My mother said, "Are you going to eat all your klaru right now? What will you eat when you get back to the village?" I started to cry. My father told me the same, "Don't eat all your klaru here. Leave them in your pouch and soon your pouch will be full." But I didn't want that, "If I put all my klaru in my pouch, which ones am I going to eat now?"

Later, I sat down in the shade of a tree while they gathered nearby. As soon as they had moved far enough away, I climbed the tree where they had left a pouch hanging, full of klaru, and stole the bulbs. I had my little pouch, the one my father had made me, and as I took the bulbs, I put them in it. I took out more and more and put them all in together. Then I climbed down and sat, waiting for them to return.

They came back, "Nisa, you ate the klaru! What do you have to say for yourself?" I said, "Uhn, uhn, I didn't take them." My mother said, "So, you're afraid of your skin hurting, afraid of being hit?" I said, "Uhn, uhn, I didn't eat those klaru." She said, "You ate them. You certainly did. Now, don't do that again! What's making you keep on stealing?"

My older brother said, "Mother, don't punish her today. You've already hit her too many times. Just leave her alone. We can see. She says she didn't steal the klaru. Well then, what did eat them? Who else was here?"

I started to cry. Mother broke off a branch and hit me, "Don't steal! Can't you understand! I tell you, but you don't listen. Don't your ears hear when I talk to you?" I said, "Uhn, uhn. Mommy's been making me feel bad for too long now. I'm going to go stay with Grandma. Mommy keeps saying I steal things and hits me so that my skin hurts. I'm going to go stay with Grandma. I'll go where she goes and sleep beside her wherever she sleeps. And when she goes out digging klaru, I'll eat what she brings back."

But when I went to my grandmother, she said, "No, I can't take care of you this time. If you stay with me, you'll be hungry. I'm old and only go gathering one day in many. Most mornings I just stay around. We'll sit together and hunger will kill you. Now, go back and sit beside your mother and father." I said, "No, Daddy will hit me. Mommy will hit me. My skin hurts from being hit. I want to stay with you."

I lived with her for a while. But I was still full of tears. I just cried and cried and cried. I sat with her and no matter if the sun was setting or was high in the sky, I just cried. One month, when the nearly full moon rose just after sunset, I went back to my mother's hut. I said, "Mommy, you hate me. You always hit me. I'm going to stay on with Grandma. You hate me and hit me ..til I can't stand it any more. I'm tired."

Another time when I went to my grandmother, we lived in another village, nearby. While I was there, my father said to my mother, "Go, go bring Nisa back. Get her so she can be with me. What did she do that you chased her away from here?" When I was told they wanted me to come back I said, "No, I won't go back. I'm not going to do what he said. I don't want to live with Mother. I want to stay with Grandma; my skin still hurts. Today, yes, this very day here, I'm going to just continue to sleep beside Grandma."

So, I stayed with her. Then, one day she said, "I'm going to take you back to your mother and father." She took me to them, saying, "Today, I'm giving Nisa back to you. But isn't there someone here who will take good care of her? You don't just hit and hit a child like this one. She likes food and likes to eat. All of you are lazy. You've just left her so she hasn't grown well. If there were still plenty of food around, I'd continue to take care of her. She'd just continue to grow up beside me. Only after she had grown up, would she leave. Because all of you have killed this child with hunger. With your own fingers you've beaten her, beaten her as though she weren't a Zhun/twa.* She was always crying. Look at her now, how small she still is." But my mother said, "No, listen to me. Your little granddaughter . . . whenever she saw food with her eyes, she'd just start crying."

Oh, but my heart was happy! Grandmother was scolding Mother! I held so much happiness in my heart that I laughed and laughed. But when Grandmother went home and left me there I cried and cried. My father yelled at me, but he didn't hit me. His anger usually came out only from his mouth. "You're so senseless! Don't you realize that after you left, everything felt less important? We wanted you to be with us. Yes, even your mother wanted you and missed you. Today, everything will be all right when you stay with us. Your mother will take you where she

*This group's name for itself—ED.

goes; the two of you will do things together and go gathering together. Why do you refuse to leave your grandmother now?"

But I cried and cried. I didn't want to leave her. "Mommy, let me go back and stay with Grandma, let me follow after her." But my father said, "That's enough. No more talk like that. There's nothing here that will hit you. Now, be quiet." And I was quiet. After that, when my father dug klaru bulbs, I ate them, and when he dug chon bulbs, I ate them. I ate everything they gave me, and I wasn't yelled at any more.

. . .

MARRIAGE

That Zhun/twa, that Tashay, he really caused me pain.

Soon after we were married, he took me from my parents' village to live at his parents' village. At first my family came and lived with us, but then one day they left, left me with Tashay and his parents. That's when I started to cry. Tashay said, "Before your mother left, you weren't crying. Why didn't you tell me you wanted to go with them? We could have followed along." I said, "I was afraid of you. That's why I didn't tell you."

But I still wanted to be with my mother, so later that day, I ran away. I ran as fast as I could until I finally caught up with them. When my mother saw me she said, "Someday a hyena is going to kill this child in the bush. She's followed us. Here she is!" I walked with them back to their village and lived with them a while.

A long time passed. One day Tashay left and came to us. When I saw him, I started to cry. He said, "Get up. We're going back." I said, "Why does this person keep following me? Do I own him that he follows me everywhere?" My father said, "You're crazy. A woman follows her husband when he comes for her. What are you just sitting here for?"

Tashay took me with him and I didn't really refuse. We continued to live at his village and then we all went and lived at another water hole. By then, I knew that I was no longer living with my mother. I had left my family to follow my husband. . . .

After Tashay and I had been living together for a long time, we started to like each other with our hearts and began living nicely together. It was really only after we had lived together for a long time that he touched my genitals. By then, my breasts were already big.

We were staying in my parents' village the night he first had sex with me and I didn't really refuse. I agreed, just a little, and he lay with me.

But the next morning, I was sore. I took some leaves and wound them around my waist, but I continued to feel pain. I thought, "Ooo . . . what has he done to my insides that they feel this way?"

I went over to my mother and said, "That person, last night . . . I'm only a child, but last night he had sex with me. Move over and let me eat with you. We'll eat and then we'll move away. Mother . . . mother . . ."

My mother turned to my father and said, "Get up, get a switch and hit this child. She's ruining us. Get up and find something to hit her with." I thought, "What? Did I say something wrong?"

My father went to find a switch. I got up and ran to my aunt's hut. I sat there and thought, "What was so bad? How come I talked about something yet . . . is that something so terrible?"

My father said to my aunt, "Tell Nisa to come back here so I can beat her. The things this young girl talks about could crack open the insides of her ears."

My mother said, "This child, her talk is terrible. As I am now, I would stick myself with a poison arrow; but my skin itself fears and that's why I won't do it. But if she continues to talk like that, I will!"

They wanted me to like my husband and not to refuse him. My mother told me that when a man sleeps with his wife, she doesn't tell; it's a private thing.

I got up and walked away from them. I was trembling, "Ehn . . . nn . . . nn . . ." I looked at my genitals and thought, "Oh, this person . . . yesterday he took me and now my genitals are ruined!" I took some water and washed my genitals, washed and washed.

Because, when my genitals first started to develop, I was afraid. I'd look at them and cry and think something was wrong with them. But people told me, "Nothing's wrong. That's what you yourself are like."

I also thought that an older person, an adult like my husband, would tear me apart, that his penis would be so big that he would hurt me. Because I hadn't known older men. I had only played sex play with little boys. Then, when Tashay did sleep with me and it hurt, that's when I refused. That's also when I told. But people didn't yell at him, they only yelled at me, and I was ashamed.

That evening, we lay down again. But this time, before he came in, I took a leather strap, held my leather apron tightly against my legs, tied the strap around my genitals, and then tied it to the hut's frame. I was afraid he'd tear me open and I didn't want him to take me again.

The two of us lay there and after a long time, he touched me. When he touched my stomach, he felt the leather strap. He felt around to see what it was. He said, "What is this woman doing? Last night she lay with me so nicely when I came to her. Why has she tied her genitals up this way? What is she refusing to give me?"

He sat me up and said, "Nisa . . . Nisa . . . what happened? Why are you doing this?" I didn't answer. He said, "What are you so afraid of that you had to tie up your genitals?" I said, "Uhn, uhn. I'm not afraid of anything." He said, "No, now tell me. In the name of what you did, I'm asking you."

Then he said, "What do you think you're doing when you do something like this? When you lie down with me, a Zhun/twa like yourself, it's as though you were lying with another, a stranger. We are both Zhun/twasi, yet you tied yourself up!"

I said, "I refuse to lie down with anyone who wants to take my genitals. Last night you had sex with me and today my insides hurt. That's why I've tied myself up and that's why you won't take me again."

He said, "Untie the strap. Do you see me as someone who kills people? Am I going to eat you? No, I'm not going to kill you, but I have married you and want to make love to you. Do you think I married you thinking I wouldn't make love to you? Did you think we would just live beside each other? Do you know any man who has married a woman and who just lives beside her without having sex with her?"

I said, "I don't care. I don't want sex. Today my insides hurt and I refuse." He said, "Mm, today you will just lie there, but tomorrow, I will take you. If you refuse, I'll pry your legs open and take you by force."

He untied the strap and said, "If this is what use you put this to, I'm going to destroy it." He took his knife and cut it into small pieces. Then he put me down beside him. He didn't touch me; he knew I was afraid. Then we went to sleep.

The next day we got up, did things and ate things. When we returned to our hut that night, we lay down again. That's when he forced himself on me. He held my legs and I struggled against him. But I knew he would have sex with me and I thought, "This isn't helping me at all. This man, if he takes me by force, he'll really hurt me. So I'll just lie here, lie still and let him look for the food he wants. But I still don't know what kind of food I have because even if he eats he won't be full."

So I stopped fighting and just lay there. He did his work and that time it didn't hurt so much. Then he lay down and slept.

After that, we just lived. I began to like him and he didn't bother me again, he didn't try to have sex with me. Many months passed—those of the rainy season, those of the winter season, and those of the hot season. He just left me alone and I grew up and started to understand about things. Because before that, I hadn't really known about men.

But I started to learn. People told me, "A man is someone who has sex with you. He doesn't marry you and just keep you there, like a string of beads. No, a man marries you and makes love to you." They told me more, "A man, when he marries you, he doesn't marry you for your face, he doesn't marry you for your beauty, he marries you so he can have sex with you."

And more. My mother told me, "When a woman marries a man, he doesn't just touch her body, he touches her genitals and has sex with her." And my aunt, "A man marries you and has sex with you. Why are you holding that back from him? What's the matter with your genitals, the ones right there?" And even Tashay talked about it. I used to watch other couples who were together and he'd say, "The old people told you that people make love to one another, didn't they? That's what people do, they make love."

I listened to what everyone said and then I understood, my thoughts finally understood.

We were living in his parents' village again when my breasts began to swell. They grew bigger and bigger and then they were huge. I thought, "Why are my breasts hurting me?" Because they were tender and painful.

Some days, I would tell Tashay that I wanted to go gathering with the other women. But often, he refused, "We two, just the two of us will go about together." He'd refuse to let me go. He was jealous; he said that when I followed along with the women, a man might come and make love to me.

He didn't want me to leave him, and we were always together: when he went to gather food, it was the two of us that went; when we went to get water, it was the two of us that went. Even to collect firewood, that's the way we went—together.

One day, my breasts felt especially sore and painful. Earlier that morning, the women had said, "Tashay, won't you lend Nisa to us so we can take her gathering? You take the springhare hook and go with your younger brother Twi to look for springhare. Nisa will go with us to gather things and to collect dcha fruits; we'll go to the well before we return."

Tashay refused, "Nisa's not going to do that. She's going to go with Twi and me. I'll take them both with me. If you find food that Nisa would have gathered, collect it for yourself. Nisa will go kill springhare with us and help carry back the meat."

I was unhappy. I wanted to go with the women, but I followed along instead with the two men. There wasn't another woman, only the two of them and myself. We walked for a long time and then came to a springhare burrow. They trapped the animal and killed it. They gave it to me and I carried it in my kaross. We walked and walked and walked. They were a little ahead of me. I was walking behind and stopped to urinate. I saw something red. I thought, "Is it the urine that's red or am I menstruating?" I took something and wiped my genitals. I looked at it, "Oh, I'm menstruating! I have followed along with the men and now I'm menstruating, way out here! What am I going to do?"

Because when you first menstruate, you don't tell anyone. A child who begins to menstruate isn't supposed to talk. I was stunned. I started to shake; I was trembling. I took my digging stick and threw it aside, because whatever a young girl was supposed to do, that's what I did. I took off my kaross and lay down on a part of it and covered myself with the rest.

My heart was miserable. I thought how I was still a child and how I didn't want to menstruate yet. I don't know why I was so afraid. Perhaps, of the days of hunger during the menstrual ceremony; I really don't know.

Tashay and his brother had walked on ahead and had reached the next group of trees. Tashay called to me, "Nisa . . . he—ey! Nisa . . . he—ey!" But I didn't call back. I was silent.

Tashay said to his brother, "Twi, Nisa's breasts are very big. Maybe she has begun to menstruate. Or, maybe she just ran away, following those other people whose tracks we passed. Go look for her. Call out to her and see if you can find her tracks. If she ran away with those other people, just leave her. But if she started to menstruate, come back to me."

Twi followed back along their tracks, calling out to me as he went. I lay still. When he came near to where I was lying, he saw the digging stick. He acted respectfully, as custom dictates, because a man isn't supposed to be there when a woman first menstruates. He stood there, then took the digging stick back to Tashay.

He said, "Here's your wife's digging stick. Just this morning Mother said, 'Your wife's a child. Now leave her and let the women take her with them.' But you refused to let her go. Now, she has begun the moon. I found her lying down at the base of a tree."

Tashay walked and walked, following the tracks, until he saw me lying there. He thought, "Oh, there's my wife. She has started to menstruate, but there are no other women around!" He stayed with me while Twi went to bring back the others. He told them, "Tashay and I went with Nisa today and while she was way out in the bush, she started to menstruate. We two men didn't know what to do."

All the women came to me. They took their beads and ornaments and tied them in my hair; they rubbed oil on my skin. Then Tashay's younger sister, my friend, picked me up and carried me back to the village. They made a place for me to lie down, then made the hut. After they put grass on it, they laid me down inside and started to dance and sing. I lay there and listened. They sang like this:

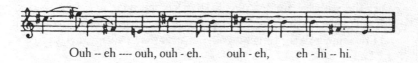

Ouh -- eh ---- ouh, ouh - eh.　　ouh - eh,　　eh - hi -- hi.

They sang and talked and danced and danced. I thought, "Mm . . . I don't see my mother . . . I'm living with Tashay's people . . ." Then I thought, "When am I going to be like the others again. I'm feeling terrible. When are they going to give me food to eat?"

Because they didn't give me much food to eat or water to drink. I just got up in the morning and stayed there, resting in the hut. I hardly ate or drank. I just lay there. I started getting thin, thin to death. The third day, my husband said, "What is this? My wife is only a child. It was days ago that she started to menstruate but she has hardly eaten food or drunk water. Why is that?"

He got up and went out to get some food. He dug for sha roots and cooked a springhare. He roasted and peeled the roots and gave them to his younger sister and said, "Go, give this to my wife. A child doesn't live for days with hunger." She came and gave it to me and I ate, but only very little. Wouldn't my stomach have hurt otherwise? I ate just a little and gave the rest to the others. His sister also gave me water to drink.

They danced every day until it was finished. Then they washed me, and we continued to live.

One day, soon after that, Tashay asked, "Do you want to go to your mother's?" I said yes, so we traveled the long distance to my mother's village. I was, of course, very beautiful then, young and beautiful. Not drawn and lined like a horse's face, as I am now.

When we finally arrived at my mother's village, my mother saw me. She asked, "What young woman has just arrived and is sitting over there? Whose daughter is that?" My father said, "It's Nisa and her husband." My mother cried out, "My daughter . . . little Nisa . . . my daughter . . . my little Nisa!"

I sat at a distance from her hut, by another hut, out of respect and due to custom. My husband got up and went and sat with them. Then my mother and my aunt came and brought me back to their hut. My mother asked, "The way you are sitting . . . the way you are acting . . . because you were sitting over there by that hut, does that mean you started to menstruate?" I said, "Mm." She cried, "Oh, my daughter! Is it right for a little girl like yourself to have menstruated for the first time in someone else's village, without your relatives? Could they possibly have taken care of you well?"

I stayed with her for a while. Tashay left me there and I just stayed with my mother. I thought, "Today, I'm happy. I've come to my mother and I'm happy. All the time I was living at Tashay's village, I wasn't. But now I am."

Tashay left me to spend time with my mother for a while. Then he came back and brought me again to his village. We lived on and then I menstruated again. Both of my ceremonial months occurred in Tashay's village and not in my mother's. The women danced for me again during the days of the flow, and then it was over. I left the hut and the women washed me.

We continued to live and it was as if I was already an adult. Because, beginning to menstruate makes you think about things. Only then did I bring myself to understand, only then did I begin to be a woman.

When Tashay wanted to lie with me, I no longer refused. We just had sex together, one day and then another. In the morning, I'd get up and sit beside our hut and I wouldn't tell. I'd think, "My husband is indeed my husband now. What people told me, that my husband is mine, is true."

We lived and lived, the two of us, together, and after a while I started to really like him and then, to love him. I had finally grown up and had learned how to love. I thought, "A man has sex with you. Yes, that's what a man does. I had thought that perhaps he didn't."

We lived on and I loved him and he loved me. I loved him the way a young adult knows how to love; I just *loved* him. Whenever he went away and I stayed behind, I'd miss him. I'd think, "Oh, when is my husband ever coming home? How come he's been gone so long?" I'd miss him and want him. When he'd come back my heart would be happy, "Eh, hey! My husband left and once again has come back."

We lived and when he wanted me, I didn't refuse; he just lay with me. I thought, "Why had I been so concerned about my genitals? They aren't that important, after all. So why was I refusing them?"

I thought that and gave myself to him, gave and gave. We lay with each other and my breasts were very large. I was becoming a woman.

·   ·   ·

First Birth

My stomach grew larger and I became angry. I yelled at Tashay and bit him. I said, "Let's go to my mother so she can help me give birth to my child." But he refused to let me go or to bring me to her; he said I should give birth in his mother's village. Because after we married, we went and stayed with Tashay and his relatives. Mother was far away. I had left her and was living where Tashay's people lived. That was where Tashay took me. That was also where I got pregnant and where I gave birth.

While I was pregnant, I'd think, "Here I am, just a child. The old people tell me that childbirth is something that hurts and that after I have lived with being pregnant, the child will start to move. It will change position and I will cry." But I thought, "No, I won't cry. If I do, people will laugh at me and say I was afraid. I won't cry." Then I thought, "Uhn, uhn. I'll surely cry. Everyone says that childbirth is painful. I know what I'll do! When I'm near the end of my pregnancy, I'll go to the white people and give myself to them. They'll open the mouth of my stomach and take the baby out. That way it won't hurt." Then I thought, "No, even if the pain feels as though I will surely die, I'll just sit there and feel it. Then my child will be born."

A few days before I gave birth, we went to live in a bush camp so the men could hunt. There were very few of us: Tashay, myself, his grandmother, and his grandfather.

One day Tashay and I were walking in the bush together, playing around and grabbing each other. I felt the first pains; they came in my lower back. I thought, "What's making my back and stomach hurt like this?" I told Tashay to stop grabbing me and we walked on. After a while we sat down again and he started to play with me again—pushing my clothes from my stomach and saying, "My wife! How come you're naked today?" I said, "What are you talking about? Something's hurting me!"

We spent the rest of the day digging sha roots and walking about. My stomach was huge and stood far out. The pains in my lower back came again. I thought, "Am I going to give birth today? I'm only a child. How am I going to give birth? Will I be afraid?"

We slept that night and morning broke. We slept another night and another morning broke. The baby was still with me; its time was ready but it didn't want to leave. I started to worry that it might make me sick.

The next night we slept where we had camped the previous few nights. Tashay brought some firewood and made a fire. I sat there. I started to feel the baby again and the hurt. I thought, "Is this what the older people told me about? Is this what they meant when they said a baby hurts?" Because, Mother! Even though I had seen others, when I gave birth for the first time, I didn't really know what a baby did or how much it hurt or how it actually got born. The only pain I myself had known before that was the pain of being sick.

I sat there and started to cry. I thought, "No, I won't cry. Me, I'm not going to cry." So I just sat there, thinking my thoughts. When the pains came again, they hurt for a while and then were quiet. They came and they went. I thought, "This really hurts! Hey . . . hey . . . everyone . . . how come my stomach hurts so much?" But I didn't say anything.

Later that night, the pains came again. I thought, "Why should this hurt so much? If only I were with my mother, then I would be able to cry. But I'm living with other people and I won't cry. If I do, they'll laugh at me and say, 'How come you're already a young woman, yet, when you feel the labor, you start to cry?' Later they'll laugh and say I cried during childbirth."

I tried to stay away from them, just so I wouldn't cry.

We all lay down to sleep that night, but when dawn was just breaking—the time when the rooster first crows—I woke up. It was hurting again. I thought, "Is it sickness that's hurting me or is it the baby?" Because I didn't really understand. I was in pain and wasn't sure what I was supposed to do. I thought, "People told me that a baby hurts your insides like when you're sick."

I lay there and felt the pains as they came, over and over again. Then I felt something wet, the beginning of the childbirth. I thought, "Eh hey, maybe it is the child." I got up, took a blanket and covered Tashay with it; he was still sleeping. Then I took another blanket and my smaller duiker skin covering and I left. Was I not the only one? The only other woman was Tashay's grandmother, and she was asleep in her hut. So, just as I was, I left.

I walked a short distance from the village and sat down beside a tree. I sat there and waited; she wasn't ready to be born. I lay down, but she still didn't come out. I sat up again. I leaned against the tree and began to feel the labor. The pains came over and over, again and again. It felt as though the baby was trying to jump right out! Then the pains stopped. I said, "Why doesn't it hurry up and come out? Why doesn't it come out so I can rest? What does it want inside me that it just stays in there? Won't God help me to have it come out quickly?"

As I said that, the baby started to be born. I thought, "I won't cry out. I'll just sit here. Look, it's already being born and I'll be fine." But it really hurt! I cried out, but only to myself. I thought, "Oh, I almost cried out in my in-laws' village." Then I thought, "Has my child already been born?" Because I wasn't really sure; I thought I might only have been sick. That's why I hadn't told anyone when I left the village.

After she was born, I sat there; I didn't know what to do. I had no sense. She lay there, moving her arms about, trying to suck on her fingers. She started to cry. I just sat there, looking at her. I thought, "Is this my child? Who gave birth to this child?" Then I thought, "A big thing like that? How could it possibly have come out from my genitals?" I sat there and looked at her, looked and looked and looked.

The cold started to grab me. I covered her with my duiker skin that had been covering my stomach and pulled the larger kaross over myself. Soon, the afterbirth came down and I buried it. I started to shiver. I just sat there, trembling with the cold. I still hadn't tied the umbilical cord. I looked at her and thought, "She's no longer crying. I'll leave her here and go to the village to bring back some coals for a fire."

I left her, covered with leather skins. (What did I know about how to do things?) I took a small skin covering, tied it around my stomach, and went back to the village. While I was on the way, she started to cry, then she stopped. I was rushing and was out of breath. Wasn't my genital area hurting? I told myself to run, but my judgment was gone; my senses had left me.

My heart was pounding and throbbing when I arrived. I sat down by the fire outside my hut to rest and to warm myself. Tashay woke up. He saw me with my little stomach, and he saw the blood on my legs. He asked how I was. I told him everything was all right. He asked, "Where is that which I thought I heard crying?" I told him the baby was lying covered where I had given birth. He asked if it was a boy. I said she was a girl. He said, "Oh! Does a little girl like you give birth to a baby all alone? There wasn't even another woman to help!"

He called to his grandmother, still asleep, and yelled, "What happened to you that you, a woman, stayed here while a little girl went out by herself to give birth? What if the childbirth had killed her? Would you have just left her there for her mother to help, her mother who isn't even here? You don't know that the pain of childbirth is fire and that a child's birth is like an anger so great that it sometimes kills? Yet, you didn't help! She's just a little girl. She could have been so afraid that the childbirth might have killed her or the child. You, an adult, what were you asking of her?"

Just then, the baby started to cry. I was afraid that maybe a jackal had come and hurt her. I grabbed some burning wood and ran back to her. I made a fire and sat. Tashay continued to yell, "Find her. Go over there and cut the baby's umbilical cord. What happened to you that you let my wife give birth by herself?"

His grandmother got up and followed Tashay to where I was sitting with the baby. She arrived and called out softly to me, "My daughter-in-law . . . my daughter-in-law . . ." She talked to the infant and greeted her with lovely names. She cut her umbilical cord, picked her up, and carried her as we all walked back to the village. Then they laid me down inside the hut.

That day, my husband went gathering and came back with sha roots and mongongo nuts, which he cracked for me to eat. But my insides were still sore and I was in pain. He went out again and killed a spring-hare. When he came back, he cooked it and I drank the gravy. That was supposed to help the milk come into my breasts, but my milk didn't come down.

We lived in the bush and there was no one else to help feed her. She just lay there and didn't eat for three nights. Then milk started to fill one breast, and the same night the other one filled. I spilled out the colostrum, the bad thing, and when my chest filled with good milk, she nursed and nursed and nursed. When she was full, she went to sleep.

CYNTHIA OZICK
(1928–)

Cynthia Ozick is the author of three collections of short fiction *The Pagan Rabbi, Bloodshed,* and *Levitation*—as well as novels, including *The Cannibal Galaxy* and *The Messiah of Stockholm,* and powerful essays, some of which were collected in *Art & Ardor* (1983) and others in *Metaphor & Memory* (1989). She grew up in the Pelham Bay section of the Bronx, as described in this autobiographical essay, "A Drugstore in Winter," which is also a meditation on loss and the birth of a writer.

For another novelist's account of her start, see Eudora Welty, *One Writer's Beginnings,* and compare Janet Frame, *An Angel at My Table.* For other Bronx childhoods, compare Kate Simon, *Bronx Primitive* and Vivian Gornick, *Fierce Attachments,* and see Laura Cunningham, *Sleeping Arrangements.*

FROM *Art & Ardor*

A DRUGSTORE IN WINTER

This is about reading; a drugstore in winter; the gold leaf on the dome of the Boston State House; also loss, panic, and dread.

First, the gold leaf. (This part is a little like a turn-of-the-century pulp tale, though only a little. The ending is a surprise, but there is no plot.) Thirty years ago I burrowed in the Boston Public Library one whole afternoon, to find out—not out of curiosity—how the State House got its gold roof. The answer, like the answer to most Bostonian questions, was Paul Revere. So I put Paul Revere's gold dome into an "article," and took it (though I was just as scared by recklessness then as I am now) to the *Boston Globe,* on Washington Street. The Features Editor had a bare severe head, a closed parenthesis mouth, and silver Dickensian spectacles. He made me wait, standing, at the side of his desk while he read; there was no bone in me that did not rattle. Then he opened a drawer and handed me fifteen dollars. Ah, joy of Homer, joy of Milton! Grub Street bliss!

The very next Sunday, Paul Revere's gold dome saw print. Appetite for more led me to a top-floor chamber in Filene's department store: Window Dressing. But no one was in the least bit dressed—it was a dumbstruck nudist colony up there, a mob of naked frozen enigmatic manikins, tall enameled skinny ladies with bald breasts and skulls, and legs and wrists and necks that horribly unscrewed. Paul Revere's dome paled beside this gold mine! A sight—mute numb Walpurgisnacht— easily worth another fifteen dollars. I had a Master's degree (thesis topic: "Parable in the Later Novels of Henry James") and a job as an advertising copywriter (9 A.M. to 6 P.M. six days a week, forty dollars per week; if you were male and had no degree at all, sixty dollars). Filene's Sale Days—Crib Bolsters! Lulla-Buys! Jonnie-Mops! Maternity Skirts with Expanding Invisible Trick Waist! And a company show; gold watches to mark the retirement of elderly Irish salesladies; for me the chance to write song lyrics (to the tune of "On Top of Old Smoky") honoring our Store. But "Mute Numb Walpurgisnacht in Secret Downtown Chamber" never reached the *Globe*. Melancholy and meaning business, the Advertising Director forbade it. Grub Street was bad form, and I had to promise never again to sink to another article. Thus ended my life in journalism.

Next: reading, and certain drugstore winter dusks. These come together. It is an aeon before Filene's, years and years before the Later Novels of Henry James. I am scrunched on my knees at a round glass table near a plate glass door on which is inscribed, in gold leaf Paul Revere never put there, letters that must be read backward: PARK VIEW PHARMACY There is an evening smell of late coffee from the fountain, and all the librarians are lined up in a row on the tall stools, sipping and chattering. They have just stepped in from the cold of the Traveling Library, and so have I. The Traveling Library is a big green truck that stops, once every two weeks, on the corner of Continental Avenue, just a little way in from Westchester Avenue, not far from a house that keeps a pig. Other houses fly pigeons from their roofs, other yards have chickens, and down on Mayflower there is even a goat. This is Pelham Bay, the Bronx, in the middle of the Depression, all cattails and weeds, such a lovely place and tender hour! Even though my mother takes me on the subway far, far downtown to buy my winter coat in the frenzy of Klein's on Fourteenth Street, and even though I can recognize the heavy power of a quarter, I don't know it's the Depression. On the trolley on the way to Westchester Square I see the children who live in the boxcar strangely set down in an empty lot some distance from Spy Oak (where a Revolutionary traitor was hanged—served him right for siding with redcoats); the lucky boxcar children dangle their stick-legs from their train-house maw and wave; how I envy them! I envy the orphans of the Gould Foundation, who have their own private swings and seesaws. Sometimes I imagine I am an orphan, and my father is an impostor pretending to be my father.

My father writes in his prescription book: *#59330 Dr. O'Flaherty Pow .60/ #59331 Dr. Mulligan Gtt .65/ #59332 Dr. Thron Tab .90.* Ninety cents! A terrifically expensive medicine; someone is really sick. When I deliver a prescription around the corner or down the block, I am offered a nickel tip. I always refuse, out of conscience; I am, after all, the Park View Pharmacy's own daughter, and it wouldn't be seemly. My father grinds and mixes powders, weighs them out in tiny snowy heaps on an apothecary scale, folds them into delicate translucent papers or meticulously drops them into gelatin capsules.

In the big front window of the Park View Pharmacy there is a startling display—goldfish bowls, balanced one on the other in amazing pyramids. A German lady enters, one of my father's cronies—his cronies are both women and men. My quiet father's eyes are water-color blue, he wears his small skeptical quiet smile and receives the neighborhood's life-secrets. My father is discreet and inscrutable. The German lady pokes a punchboard with a pin, pushes up a bit of rolled paper, and cries out—she has just won a goldfish bowl, with two swimming goldfish in it! Mr. Jaffe, the salesman from McKesson & Robbins, arrives, trailing two mists: winter steaminess and the animal fog of his cigar,* which melts into the coffee smell, the tarpaper smell, the eerie honeyed tangled drugstore smell. Mr. Jaffe and my mother and father are intimates by now, but because it is the 1930s, so long ago, and the old manners still survive, they address one another gravely as Mr. Jaffe, Mrs. Ozick, Mr. Ozick. My mother calls my father Mr. O, even at home, as in a Victorian novel. In the street my father tips his hat to ladies. In the winter his hat is a regular fedora; in the summer it is a straw boater with a black ribbon and a jot of blue feather.

What am I doing at this round glass table, both listening and not listening to my mother and father tell Mr. Jaffe about their struggle with "Tessie," the lion-eyed landlady who has just raised, threefold, in the middle of that Depression I have never heard of, the Park View Pharmacy's devouring rent? My mother, not yet forty, wears bandages on her ankles, covering oozing varicose veins; back and forth she strides, dashes, runs, climbing cellar stairs or ladders; she unpacks cartons, she toils behind drug counters and fountain counters. Like my father, she is on her feet until one in the morning, the Park View's closing hour. My

---

*Mr. Matthew Bruccoli, another Bronx drugstore child, has written to say that he remembers with certainty that Mr. Jaffe did not smoke. In my memory the cigar is somehow there, so I leave it.

mother and father are in trouble, and I don't know it. I am too happy. I feel the secret center of eternity, nothing will ever alter, no one will ever die. Through the window, past the lit goldfish, the gray oval sky deepens over our neighborhood wood, where all the dirt paths lead down to seagull-specked water. I am familiar with every frog-haunted monument: Pelham Bay Park is thronged with WPA art—statuary, fountains, immense rococo staircases cascading down a hillside, Bacchus-faced stelae—stone Roman glories afterward mysteriously razed by an avenging Robert Moses. One year—how distant it seems now, as if even the climate is past returning—the bay froze so hard that whole families, mine among them, crossed back and forth to City Island, strangers saluting and calling out in the ecstasy of the bright trudge over such a sudden wilderness of ice.

In the Park View Pharmacy, in the winter dusk, the heart in my body is revolving like the goldfish fleet-finned in their clear bowls. The librarians are still warming up over their coffee. They do not recognize me, though only half an hour ago I was scrabbling in the mud around the two heavy boxes from the Traveling Library—oafish crates tossed with a thump to the ground. One box contains magazines—*Boy's Life, The American Girl, Popular Mechanix*. But the other, the other! The other transforms me. It is tumbled with storybooks, with clandestine intimations and transfigurations. In school I am a luckless goosegirl, friendless and forlorn. In P.S. 71 I carry, weighty as a cloak, the ineradicable knowledge of my scandal—I am cross-eyed, dumb, an imbecile at arithmetic; in P.S. 71 I am publicly shamed in Assembly because I am caught not singing Christmas carols; in P.S. 71 I am repeatedly accused of deicide. But in the Park View Pharmacy, in the winter dusk, branches blackening in the park across the road, I am driving in rapture through the Violet Fairy Book and the Yellow Fairy Book, insubstantial chariots snatched from the box in the mud. I have never been *inside* the Traveling Library; only grownups are allowed. The boxes are for the children. No more than two books may be borrowed, so I have picked the fattest ones, to last. All the same, the Violet and the Yellow are melting away. Their pages dwindle. I sit at the round glass table, dreaming, dreaming. Mr. Jaffe is murmuring advice. He tells a joke about Wrong-Way Corrigan. The librarians are buttoning up their coats. A princess, captive of an ogre, receives a letter from her swain and hides it in her bosom. I can visualize her bosom exactly—she clutches it against her chest. It is a tall and shapely vase, with a hand-painted flower on it, like the vase on the secondhand piano at home.

I am incognito. No one knows who I truly am. The teachers in P.S. 71 don't know. Rabbi Meskin, my *cheder* teacher, doesn't know. Tessie the lion-eyed landlady doesn't know. Even Hymie the fountain clerk can't know—though he understands other things better than anyone: how to tighten roller skates with a skatekey, for instance, and how to ride a horse. On Friday afternoons, when the new issue is out, Hymie and my brother fight hard over who gets to see *Life* magazine first. My brother is older than I am, and doesn't like me; he builds radios in his bedroom, he is already W2LOM, and operates his transmitter (*da-di-da-dit, da-da-di-da*) so penetratingly on Sunday mornings that Mrs. Eva Brady, across the way, complains. Mrs. Eva Brady has a subscription to *The Writer;* I fill a closet with her old copies. How to Find a Plot. Narrative and Character, the Writer's Tools. Because my brother has his ham license, I say, "I have a license too." "What kind of license?" my brother asks, falling into the trap. "Poetic license," I reply; my brother hates me, but anyhow his birthday presents are transporting: one year *Alice in Wonderland, Pinocchio* the next, then *Tom Sawyer.* I go after Mark Twain, and find *Joan of Arc* and my first satire, *Christian Science.* My mother surprises me with *Pollyanna,* the admiration of her Lower East Side childhood, along with *The Lady of the Lake.* Mrs. Eva Brady's daughter Jeannie has outgrown her Nancy Drew and Judy Boltons, so on rainy afternoons I cross the street and borrow them, trying not to march away with too many—the child of immigrants, I worry that the Bradys, true and virtuous Americans, will judge me greedy or careless. I wrap the Nancy Drews in paper covers to protect them. Old Mrs. Brady, Jeannie's grandmother, invites me back for more. I am so timid I can hardly speak a word, but I love her dark parlor; I love its black bookcases. Old Mrs. Brady sees me off, embracing books under an umbrella; perhaps she divines who I truly am. My brother doesn't care. My father doesn't notice. I think my mother knows. My mother reads the *Saturday Evening Post* and the *Woman's Home Companion;* sometimes the *Ladies' Home Journal,* but never *Good Housekeeping.* I read all my mother's magazines. My father reads *Drug Topics* and *Der Tog,* the Yiddish daily. In Louie Davidowitz's house (waiting our turn for the rabbi's lesson, he teaches me chess in *cheder*) there is a piece of furniture I am in awe of: a shining circular table that is also a revolving bookshelf holding a complete set of Charles Dickens. I borrow *Oliver Twist.* My cousins turn up with *Gulliver's Travels, Just So Stories, Don Quixote,* Oscar Wilde's *Fairy Tales,* uncannily different from the usual kind. Blindfolded, I reach into a Thanksgiving grabbag and pull out *Mrs. Leicester's School,* Mary Lamb's desolate stories of rejected children. Books spill out of rumor, exchange, miracle. In the Park View Pharmacy's lending library I discover, among the nurse romances, a browning, brittle miracle: *Jane Eyre.* Uncle Morris comes to visit (*his* drugstore is on the other side of the Bronx) and leaves behind, just like that, a three-volume Shakespeare. Peggy and Betty Provan, Scottish sisters around the corner, lend me their *Swiss Family Robinson.* Norma Foti, a whole year older, transmits a rumor about Louisa May Alcott; afterward I read *Little Women* a thousand times. Ten thousand! I am no longer incognito, not even to myself. I am Jo in her "vortex"; not Jo exactly, but some Jo-of-the-future. I am under an enchantment: who I truly am must be deferred, waited for and waited for. My father, silently filling capsules, is grieving over his mother in Moscow. I write letters in Yiddish to my Moscow grandmother, whom I will never know. I will never know my Russian aunts, uncles, cousins. In Moscow there is suffering, deprivation, poverty. My mother, threadbare, goes without a new winter coat so that packages can be sent to Moscow. Her fiery justice-eyes are semaphores I cannot decipher.

Some day, when I am free of P.S. 71, I will write stories; meanwhile, in winter dusk, in the Park View, in the secret bliss of the Violet Fairy Book, I both see and do not see how these grains of life will stay forever, papa and mama will live forever, Hymie will always turn my skatekey.

Hymie, after Italy, after the Battle of the Bulge, comes back from the war with a present: *From Here to Eternity.* Then he dies, young. Mama reads *Pride and Prejudice* and every single word of Willa Cather. Papa reads, in Yiddish, all of Sholem Aleichem and Peretz. He reads Malamud's *The Assistant* when I ask him to.

Papa and mama, in Staten Island, are under the ground. Some other family sits transfixed in the sun parlor where I read *Jane Eyre* and *Little Women* and, long afterward, *Middlemarch.* The Park View Pharmacy is dismantled, turned into a Hallmark card shop. It doesn't matter! I close my eyes, or else only stare, and everything is in its place again, and everyone.

A writer is dreamed and transfigured into being by spells, wishes, goldfish, silhouettes of trees, boxes of fairy tales dropped in the mud, uncles' and cousins' books, tablets and capsules and powders, papa's Moscow ache, his drugstore jacket with his special fountain pen in the pocket, his beautiful Hebrew paragraphs, his Talmudist's rationalism, his Russian-Gymnasium Latin and German, mama's furnace-heart, her masses of memoirs, her paintings of autumn walks down to the sunny water, her braveries, her reveries, her old, old school hurts.

A writer is buffeted into being by school hurts—Orwell, Forster, Mann!—but after a while other ambushes begin: sorrows, deaths, disappointments, subtle diseases, delays, guilts, the spite of the private haters of the poetry side of life, the snubs of the glamorous, the bitterness of those for whom resentment is a daily gruel, and so on and so on; and then one day you find yourself leaning here, writing at that selfsame round glass table salvaged from the Park View Pharmacy—writing this, an impossibility, a summary of how you came to be where you are now, and where, God knows, is that? Your hair is whitening, you are a well of tears, what you meant to do (beauty and justice) you have not done, papa and mama are under the earth, you live in panic and dread, the future shrinks and darkens, stories are only vapor, your inmost craving is for nothing but an old scarred pen, and what, God knows, is that?

SYLVIA PLATH
(1932–1963)

Sylvia Plath and Virginia Woolf, two writers of enormous intensity who ended as suicides, might seem to have a lot in common, but their diaries display great differences. Plath uses hers to plan strategies, including how to make the most of life and how to succeed as a poet. Through tremendous mood swings, she takes her own pulse and offers herself prescriptions for action. The fact that she can accept no flaws in herself leads to self-doubt and self-loathing. Her combination of personal perfectionism, 1950s existentialism, and suburban careerism makes Woolf seem easygoing and pleasure-loving by contrast.

Following her graduation from Smith College in 1955, Plath spent two years in England on a Fulbright fellowship. She married the British poet Ted Hughes in June 1956. With Hughes, she returned to America and spent 1957–1958 as an instructor in English at her alma mater, the period from which this diary excerpt is drawn.

For another diary by a creative woman, in addition to Virginia Woolf's, compare Anne Truitt, *Daybook*.

FROM *Diary*

Tuesday, October 1, [1957]

Letter to a demon:

Last night I felt the sensation I have been reading about to no avail in James:* the sick, soul-annihilating flux of fear in my blood switching its current to defiant fight. I could not sleep, although tired, and lay feeling my nerves shaved to pain & the groaning inner voice: oh, you can't teach, can't do anything. Can't write, can't think. And I lay under the negative icy flood of denial, thinking that voice was all my own, a part of me, and it must somehow conquer me and leave me with my worst visions: having had the chance to battle it & win day by day, and having failed.

*Henry James—Ed.

I cannot ignore this murderous self: it is there. I smell it and feel it, but I will not give it my name. I shall shame it. When it says: you shall not sleep, you cannot teach, I shall go on anyway, knocking its nose in. Its biggest weapon is and has been the image of myself as a perfect success: in writing, teaching, and living. As soon as I sniff nonsuccess in the form of rejections, puzzled faces in class when I'm blurring a point, or a cold horror in personal relationships, I accuse myself of being a hypocrite, posing as better than I am, and being, at bottom, lousy.

I am middling good. And I can live being middling good. I do not have advanced degrees, I do not have books published, I do not have teaching experience. I have a job teaching. I cannot rightly ask myself to be a better teacher than any of those teaching around me with degrees, books published and experience. I can only, from day to day, fight to be a better teacher than I was the day before. If, at the end of a year of hard work, partial failure, partial dogged communication of a poem or a story, I can say I am easier, more confident & a better teacher than I was the first day, I have done enough. I must face this image of myself as good for myself, and not freeze myself into a quivering jelly because I am not Mr. Fisher or Miss Dunn or any of the others.

I have a good self, that loves skies, hills, ideas, tasty meals, bright colors. My demon would murder this self by demanding that it be a paragon, and saying it should run away if it is anything less. I shall doggedly do my best and know it for that, no matter what other people say. I can learn to be a better teacher. But only by painful trial and error. Life is painful trial and error. I instinctively gave myself this job because I knew I needed the confidence it would give me as I needed food: it would be my first active facing of life & responsibility: something thousands of people face every day, with groans, maybe, or with dogged determination, or with joy. But they face it. I have this demon who wants me to run away screaming if I am going to be flawed, fallible. It wants me to think I'm so good I must be perfect. Or nothing. I am, on the contrary, something: a being who gets tired, has shyness to fight, has more trouble than most facing people easily. If I get through this year, kicking my demon down when it comes up, realizing I'll be tired after a day's work, and tired after correcting papers, and it's natural tiredness, not something to be ranted about in horror, I'll be able, piece by piece, to face the field of life, instead of running from it the minute it hurts.

The demon would humiliate me: throw me on my knees before the college president, my department chairman, everyone, crying: look at me, miserable, I can't do it. Talking about my fears to others feeds it. I shall show a calm front & fight it in the precincts of my own self, but never give it the social dignity of a public appearance, me running from it, and giving in to it. I'll work in my office roughly from 9 to 5 until I find myself doing better in class. In any case, I'll do something relaxing, different reading, etc., in the evenings. I'll keep myself intact, outside this job, this work. They can't ask more of me than my best, & only I know really where the limits on my best are. I have a choice: to flee from life and ruin myself forever because I can't be perfect right away, without pain & failure, and to face life on my own terms & "make the best of the job."

Each day I shall record a dogged step ahead or a marking time in place. The material of reading is something I love. I must learn, slowly, how to best present it, managing class discussion: I must reject the groveling image of the fearful beast in myself, which is an elaborate escape image, and face, force, days into line. I have an inner fight that won't be conquered by a motto or one night's resolution. My demon of negation will tempt me day by day, and I'll fight it, as something other than my essential self, which I am fighting to save: each day will have something to recommend it: whether the honest delight at watching the quick furred body of a squirrel, or sensing, deeply, the weather and color, or reading and thinking of something in a different light: a good explanation or 5 minutes in class to redeem a bad 45. Minute by minute to fight upward. Out from under that black cloud which would annihilate my whole being with its demand for perfection and measure, not of what I am, but of what I am not. I am what I am, and have written, lived and traveled: I have been worth what I have won, but must work to be worth more. I shall not be more by wishful thinking.

So: a stoic face. A position of irony, of double vision. My job is serious, important, but nothing is more important than my life and my life in its fullest realized potential: jealousy, envy, desperate wishes to be someone else, someone already successful at teaching, are naïve: Mr. Fisher, for all his student-love, has been left by his wife & children; Miss F., for all her experience and knowledge, is irrevocably dull. Every one of these people . . . has some flaw, some crack, and to be one of them would be to be flawed & cracked in another fashion. I'll shoulder my own crack, work on my James today, Hawthorne for next week & take life with gradual ease, dogged at first, but with more & more joy. My first victory was accepting this job, the second, coming up & plunging into it before my demon could say no, I wasn't good enough, the third, going to class after a night of no sleep & desperation, the fourth, facing my demon last night with Ted & spitting in its eye. I'll work hard on my planning, but work just as hard to build up a rich home life: to get writing again, to get my mind fertilized outside my job. . . .

No more knuckling under, groaning, moaning: one gets used to pain. This hurts. Not being perfect hurts. Having to bother about work in order to eat & have a house hurts. So what. It's about time. This is the month which ends a quarter of a century for me, lived under the shadow of fear: fear that I would fall short of some abstract perfection: I have often fought, fought & won, not perfection, but an acceptance of myself as having a right to live on my own human, fallible terms.

Attitude is everything. No whining or fainting will get me out of this job & I'd not like to think what would happen to my integral self if it did. I've accepted my first check: I've signed on, and no little girl tactics are going to get me off, nor should they.

To the library. Finish James book, memorize my topics, maybe the squirrel story. Have fun. If I have fun, the class will have fun.

Come home tonight: read Lawrence, or write, if possible. That will come too.

Vive le roi; le roi est mort, vive le roi.

Tuesday night, November 5.

Brief note: to self. Time to take myself in hand. I have been staggering about lugubrious, black, bleak, sick. Now to build into myself, to give myself backbone, however much I fail. If I get through this year, no matter how badly, it will be the biggest victory I've ever done. All my spoiled little girl selves cry to escape before my bad teaching, ignorant somnolence is made drearily public among my old teachers and my new students. If I fainted, or paralyzed myself, or pleaded gibberingly to Mr. Hill that I couldn't carry on, I'd probably escape all right: but how to face myself, to live after that? To write or be intelligent as a woman? It would be a worse trauma than this, although escape looks very sweet & plausible. This way, I can build up a dull, angry resentment & feel I'm going through with it & will deserve my freedom in June, for sacrificing a year of my life. 7 more months.

First of all? Keep quiet with Ted about worries. With him around, I am disastrously tempted to complain, to share fears and miseries. Misery loves company. But my fears are only magnified when reflected by him. So Mr. Fisher called tonight & is coming to sit in on my class Friday. Instead of complaining to Ted, feeling my tension grow, echoed in him, I am keeping quiet about it. I will make my test of self-control this week being quiet about it till it's over. Ted's knowing can't help me in my responsibility. I've got to face it & prepare for it myself. My first day of Lawrence. Wednesday & Thursday to prepare for it. Keep rested. That's the main thing. Make up a couple of little lectures. Get class prepared.

The main thing is to get on top of this preparation. To figure how to start teaching them about style. For the first lesson, make up general lectures about form of papers, organization, read from papers. Don't get exasperated. A calm front: start at *home.* Even with Ted I must learn to be very calm & happy: to let him have his time & not be selfish & spoil it. Maturity begins here, however bad I am. I must prepare lectures, however poor.

. . .

January 22, Wednesday.

Absolutely blind fuming sick. Anger, envy and humiliation. A green seethe of malice through the veins. To faculty meeting, rushing through a gray mizzle, past the Alumnae House, no place to park, around behind the college, bumping, rumping through sleety frozen ruts. Alone, going alone, among strangers. Month by month, colder shoulders. No eyes met mine. I picked up a cup of coffee in the crowded room among faces more strange than in September. Alone. Loneliness burned. Feeling like a naughty presumptuous student. Marlies in a white jumper and red dark patterned blouse. Sweet, deft: simply can't come. Wendell and I are doing a textbook. Haven't you heard? Eyes, dark, lifted to Wendell's round simper. A roomful of smoke and orange-seated black painted chairs. Sat beside a vaguely familiar woman in the very front, no one between me and the president. Foisted forward. Stared intently at gilt leaved trees, orange-gilt columns, a bronze frieze of stags, stags and an archer, bow bent. Intolerable, unintelligible bickering about plusses and minuses, graduate grades. On the back cloth a Greek with white-silver feet fluted to a maid, coyly kicking one white leg out of her Greek robe. Pink and orange and gilded maidens. And a story, a lousy sentimental novel chapter 30 pages long and utterly worthless at my back: on this I lavish my hours, this be my defense, my sign of genius against those people who know somehow miraculously how to be together, au courant, at one. Haven't you heard? Mr. Hill has twins. So life spins on outside my nets. I spotted Alison, ran for her after meeting—she turned, dark, a stranger. "Alison," Wendell took her over, "are you driving down?" She knew. He knew. I am deaf, dumb. Strode into slush, blind. Into snow and gray mizzle. All the faces of my student shining days turned the other way. Shall I give, unwitting, dinners? to invite them to entertain us? Ted sits opposite: make his problems mine. Shut up in public. Those bloody private wounds. Salvation in work. What if my work is lousy? I want to rush into print any old tripe. Words, words, to stop the deluge through the thumbhole in the dike. This be my secret place. All my life have I not been outside? Ranged against well-meaning foes? Desperate, intense: why do I find groups impossible? Do I even want them? Is it because I cannot match them, tongue-shy, brain-small, that I delude my dreams into grand novels and poems to astound? I must bridge the gap between adolescent glitter and mature glow. Oh, steady. Steady on. I have my one man. To help him I will.

.   .   .

Thursday morning, February 20.

I want *all* my time, time for a year, the first year since I was four years old, to work and read *on my own*. And away from Smith. Away from my past, away from this glass-fronted, girl-studded and collegiate town. Anonymity. Boston. Here the only people to see are the twenty people on the faculty whom I just don't want to see another year. Will I write a word? Yes. By the time I write in here again this ghastly day will be over, I having walked out my dreamy drugged state and given three classes, botched and unsure. The next three weeks, however, I shall prepare violently and fully a week ahead if it's the last thing I do. Oh, resolves. The three red apples, yellow speckled, thumb-dinted brown, mock me. I myself am the vessel of tragic experience. I muse not enough on the mysteries of Oedipus—I, weary, resolving the best and bringing, out of my sloth, envy and weakness, my own ruins. What do the gods ask? I must dress, rise, and send my body out. . . .

A day in a life—such gray grit, and I feel apart from myself, split, a shadow, and yet when I think of what I have taught and what I will teach, the titles have still a radiant glow and the excitement and not the dead weary plod of today. I have gotten back the life-vision, whatever that is, which enables people to live out their lives and not go mad. I am married to a man whom I miraculously love as much as life and I have an excellent job and profession (this one year), so the cocoon of childhood and adolescence is broken—I have two university degrees and now will turn to my own profession and devote a year to steady apprenticeship, and to the symbolic counterpart, our children. Sometimes I shiver in a preview of the pain and the terror of childbirth, but it will come and I live through it.

.   .   .

Saturday night, March 8.

One of those nights when I wonder if I am alive, or have been ever. The noise of the cars on the pike is like a bad fever: Ted sickish, flagging in discontent: "I want to get clear of this life: trapped." I think: Will we be less trapped in Boston? I dislike apartments, suburbs. I want to walk directly out my front door onto earth and into air free from exhaust. And I: what am I but a glorified automaton hearing myself, through a vast space of weariness, speak from the shell speaking-trumpet that is my mouth the dead words about life, suffering, and deep knowledge and ritual sacrifice. What is it that teaching kills? The juice, the sap—the substance of revelation: by making even the insoluble questions and multiple possible answers take on the granite assured stance of dogma. It does not kill this quick of life in students who come, each year, fresh, quick, to be awakened and pass on—but it kills the quick in me by forcing to formula the great visions, the great collocations and cadences of words and meanings. The good teacher, the proper teacher, must be ever-living in faith and ever-renewed in creative energy to keep the sap packed in herself, himself, as well as the work. I do not have the energy, or will to use the energy I have, and it would take all, to keep this flame alive. I am living and teaching on rereadings, on notes of other people, sour as heartburn, between two unachieved shapes: between the original teacher and the original writer: neither. And America wears me, wearies me. I am sick of the Cape, sick of Wellesley: all America seems one line of cars, moving, with people jammed in them, from one gas station to one diner and on. I must periodically refresh myself in this crass, crude, energetic, demanding and competitive new-country bath, but I am, in my deep soul, happiest on the moors—my deepest soul-scape, in the hills by the Spanish Mediterranean, in the old, history-crusted and still gracious, spacious cities: Paris, Rome.

SANTHA RAMA RAU
(1923–)

Born in Madras, Santha Rama Rau spent her early childhood in India, often in the home of her traditionally Hindu grandmother. When she was six, her father, a diplomat, was sent to England, and the family lived there for many years. She has also lived in South Africa and Japan and went to college in the United States. Married to an American writer, Faubion Bowers, whom she met in Japan, Santha Rama Rau has written fiction, travel books, and memoirs, including an account of her reintroduction to India after years abroad called *Home to India.* Many of the pieces that make up her autobiography, *Gifts of Passage* (1961), were originally published in *The New Yorker.*

The first of these selections is about her attendance at a school for English girls, and the second about a time she thought she saw a ghost. For other ghosts, compare Maxine Hong Kingston, *The Woman Warrior.* For another child's sighting of adult romance, compare Kate Simon, *Bronx Primitive.* For other pupils, other schools, compare Tetsuko Kuroyanagi, *Totto-Chan,* Bernadette Devlin, *The Price of My Soul,* and Audre Lorde, *Zami.*

FROM *Gifts of Passage*

BY ANY OTHER NAME

At the Anglo-Indian day school in Zorinabad to which my sister and I were sent when she was eight and I was five and a half, they changed our names. On the first day of school, a hot, windless morning of a north Indian September, we stood in the headmistress's study and she said, "Now you're the *new* girls. What are your names?"

My sister answered for us. "I am Premila, and she"—nodding in my direction—"is Santha."

The headmistress had been in India, I suppose, fifteen years or so, but she still smiled her helpless inability to cope with Indian names. Her rimless half-glasses glittered, and the precarious bun on the top of her head trembled as she shook her head. "Oh, my dears, those are much too hard for me. Suppose we give you pretty English names. Wouldn't that be more jolly? Let's see, now—Pamela for you, I think." She shrugged in a baffled way at my sister. "That's as close as I can get. And for *you,*" she said to me, "how about Cynthia? Isn't that nice?"

My sister was always less easily intimidated than I was, and while she kept a stubborn silence, I said, "Thank you," in a very tiny voice.

We had been sent to that school because my father, among his responsibilities as an officer of the civil service, had a tour of duty to perform in the villages around that steamy little provincial town, where he had his headquarters at that time. He used to make his shorter inspection tours on horseback, and a week before, in the stale heat of a typically postmonsoon day, we had waved good-by to him and a little procession—an assistant, a secretary, two bearers, and the man to look after the bedding rolls and luggage. They rode away through our large garden, still bright green from the rains, and we turned back into the twilight of the house and the sound of fans whispering in every room.

Up to then, my mother had refused to send Premila to school in the British-run establishments of that time, because, she used to say, "you can bury a dog's tail for seven years and it still comes out curly, and you can take a Britisher away from his home for a lifetime and he still remains insular." The examinations and degrees from entirely Indian schools were not, in those days, considered valid. In my case, the question had never come up, and probably never would have come up if Mother's extraordinary good health had not broken down. For the first time in my life, she was not able to continue the lessons she had been giving us every morning. So our Hindi books were put away, the stories of the Lord Krishna as a little boy were left in mid-air, and we were sent to the Anglo-Indian school.

That first day at school is still, when I think of it, a remarkable one. At that age, if one's name is changed, one develops a curious form of dual personality. I remember having a certain detached and disbelieving concern in the actions of "Cynthia," but certainly no responsibility. Accordingly, I followed the thin, erect back of the headmistress down the veranda to my classroom feeling, at most, a passing interest in what was going to happen to me in this strange, new atmosphere of School.

The building was Indian in design, with wide verandas opening onto a central courtyard, but Indian verandas are usually whitewashed, with stone floors. These, in the tradition of British schools, were painted dark brown and had matting on the floors. It gave a feeling of extra intensity to the heat.

I suppose there were about a dozen Indian children in the school— which contained perhaps forty children in all—and four of them were in my class. They were all sitting at the back of the room, and I went to join them. I sat next to a small, solemn girl who didn't smile at me. She had long, glossy-black braids and wore a cotton dress, but she still kept on her Indian jewelry—a gold chain around her neck, thin gold bracelets, and tiny ruby studs in her ears. Like most Indian children, she had a rim of black kohl around her eyes. The cotton dress should have looked strange, but all I could think of was that I should ask my mother if I couldn't wear a dress to school, too, instead of my Indian clothes.

I can't remember too much about the proceedings in class that day, except for the beginning. The teacher pointed to me and asked me to stand up. "Now, dear, tell the class your name."

I said nothing.

"Come along," she said, frowning slightly. "What's your name, dear?"

"I don't know," I said, finally.

The English children in the front of the class—there were about eight or ten of them—giggled and twisted around in their chairs to look at me. I sat down quickly and opened my eyes very wide, hoping in that way to dry them off. The little girl with the braids put out her hand and very lightly touched my arm. She still didn't smile.

Most of that morning I was rather bored. I looked briefly at the children's drawings pinned to the wall, and then concentrated on a lizard clinging to the ledge of the high, barred window behind the teacher's head. Occasionally it would shoot out its long yellow tongue for a fly, and then it would rest, with its eyes closed and its belly palpitating, as though it were swallowing several times quickly. The lessons were mostly concerned with reading and writing and simple numbers—things that my mother had already taught me—and I paid very little attention. The teacher wrote on the easel blackboard words like "bat" and "cat," which seemed babyish to me; only "apple" was new and incomprehensible.

When it was time for the lunch recess, I followed the girl with braids out onto the veranda. There the children from the other classes were assembled. I saw Premila at once and ran over to her, as she had charge of our lunchbox. The children were all opening packages and sitting down to eat sandwiches. Premila and I were the only ones who had Indian food—thin wheat chapatties, some vegetable curry, and a bottle of buttermilk. Premila thrust half of it into my hand and whispered fiercely that I should go and sit with my class, because that was what the others seemed to be doing.

The enormous black eyes of the little Indian girl from my class looked at my food longingly, so I offered her some. But she only shook her head and plowed her way solemnly through her sandwiches.

I was very sleepy after lunch, because at home we always took a siesta.

It was usually a pleasant time of day, with the bedroom darkened against the harsh afternoon sun, the drifting off into sleep with the sound of Mother's voice reading a story in one's mind, and, finally, the shrill, fussy voice of the ayah waking one for tea.

At school, we rested for a short time on low, folding cots on the veranda, and then we were expected to play games. During the hot part of the afternoon we played indoors, and after the shadows had begun to lengthen and the slight breeze of the evening had come up we moved outside to the wide courtyard.

I had never really grasped the system of competitive games. At home, whenever we played tag or guessing games, I was always allowed to "win"—"because," Mother used to tell Premila, "she is the youngest, and we have to allow for that." I had often heard her say it, and it seemed quite reasonable to me, but the result was that I had no clear idea of what "winning" meant.

When we played twos-and-threes that afternoon at school, in accordance with my training, I let one of the small English boys catch me, but was naturally rather puzzled when the other children did not return the courtesy. I ran about for what seemed like hours without ever catching anyone, until it was time for school to close. Much later I learned that my attitude was called "not being a good sport," and I stopped allowing myself to be caught, but it was not for years that I really learned the spirit of the thing.

When I saw our car come up to the school gate, I broke away from my classmates and rushed toward it yelling, "Ayah! Ayah!" It seemed like an eternity since I had seen her that morning—a wizened, affectionate figure in her white cotton sari, giving me dozens of urgent and useless instructions on how to be a good girl at school. Premila followed more sedately, and she told me on the way home never to do that again in front of the other children.

When we got home we went straight to Mother's high, white room to have tea with her, and I immediately climbed onto the bed and bounced gently up and down on the springs. Mother asked how we had liked our first day in school. I was so pleased to be home and to have left that peculiar Cynthia behind that I had nothing whatever to say about school, except to ask what "apple" meant. But Premila told Mother about the classes, and added that in her class they had weekly tests to see if they had learned their lessons well.

I asked, "What's a test?"

Premila said, "You're too small to have them. You won't have them in your class for donkey's years." She had learned the expression that day and was using it for the first time. We all laughed enormously at her wit. She also told Mother, in an aside, that we should take sandwiches to school the next day. Not, she said, that *she* minded. But they would be simpler for me to handle.

That whole lovely evening I didn't think about school at all. I sprinted barefoot across the lawns with my favorite playmate, the cook's son, to the stream at the end of the garden. We quarreled in our usual way, waded in the tepid water under the lime trees, and waited for the night to bring out the smell of the jasmine. I listened with fascination to his stories of ghosts and demons, until I was too frightened to cross the garden alone in the semidarkness. The ayah found me, shouted at the cook's son, scolded me, hurried me in to supper—it was an entirely usual, wonderful evening.

It was a week later, the day of Premila's first test, that our lives changed rather abruptly. I was sitting at the back of my class, in my usual inattentive way, only half listening to the teacher. I had started a rather guarded friendship with the girl with the braids, whose name turned out to be Nalini (Nancy, in school). The three other Indian children were already fast friends. Even at that age it was apparent to all of us that friendship with the English or Anglo-Indian children was out of the question. Occasionally, during the class, my new friend and I would draw pictures and show them to each other secretly.

The door opened sharply and Premila marched in. At first, the teacher smiled at her in a kindly and encouraging way and said, "Now, you're little Cynthia's sister?"

Premila didn't even look at her. She stood with her feet planted firmly apart and her shoulders rigid, and addressed herself directly to me. "Get up," she said. "We're going home."

I didn't know what had happened, but I was aware that it was a crisis of some sort. I rose obediently and started to walk toward my sister.

"Bring your pencils and your notebook," she said.

I went back for them, and together we left the room. The teacher started to say something just as Premila closed the door, but we didn't wait to hear what it was.

In complete silence we left the school grounds and started to walk home. Then I asked Premila what the matter was. All she would say was "We're going home for good."

It was a very tiring walk for a child of five and a half, and I dragged along behind Premila with my pencils growing sticky in my hand. I can still remember looking at the dusty hedges, and the tangles of thorns in the ditches by the side of the road, smelling the faint fragrance from the eucalyptus trees and wondering whether we would ever reach home. Occasionally a horse-drawn tonga passed us, and the women, in their pink or green silks, stared at Premila and me trudging along on the side of the road. A few coolies and a line of women carrying baskets of vegetables on their heads smiled at us. But it was nearing the hottest time of day, and the road was almost deserted. I walked more and more slowly, and shouted to Premila, from time to time, "Wait for me!" with increasing peevishness. She spoke to me only once, and that was to tell me to carry my notebook on my head, because of the sun.

When we got to our house the ayah was just taking a tray of lunch into Mother's room. She immediately started a long, worried questioning about what are you children doing back here at this hour of the day.

Mother looked very startled and very concerned, and asked Premila what had happened.

Premila said, "We had our test today, and She made me and the other Indians sit at the back of the room, with a desk between each one."

Mother said, "Why was that, darling?"

"She said it was because Indians cheat," Premila added. "So I don't think we should go back to that school."

Mother looked very distant, and was silent a long time. At last she said, "Of course not, darling." She sounded displeased.

We all shared the curry she was having for lunch, and afterward I was sent off to the beautifully familiar bedroom for my siesta. I could hear Mother and Premila talking through the open door.

Mother said, "Do you suppose she understood all that?"

Premila said, "I shouldn't think so. She's a baby."

Mother said, "Well, I hope it won't bother her."

Of course, they were both wrong. I understood it perfectly, and I remember it all very clearly. But I put it happily away, because it had all happened to a girl called Cynthia, and I never was really particularly interested in her.

THE GHOST IN THE GARDEN

In India you can always recognize a ghost by his feet, which are attached to his ankles the wrong way around, with the heels in front and the toes pointing backward. The rest of his appearance may be entirely normal, and, of course, since a ghost doesn't wish to be recognized, he usually takes the trouble to hide his feet. Indian clothes are particularly well suited to this purpose. The loose pajamas of a northern Indian man, the southern man's *mundu* (a sort of long sarong), a woman's sari, and the robes of a holy man—a *sanyasi*—are all floor-length, all excellent disguises.

The problem of recognizing a ghost by somehow persuading him to expose his feet occupied a great deal of my time the spring I was ten. My mother, my sister, and I spent some months in my mother's family home, just outside Allahabad, while my father traveled in south India, and I learned a few days after we arrived that the house—or, rather, the garden—was haunted.

It wasn't a particularly big house, but it was full of people. My great-grandmother was alive, at that time, very old, incredibly frail, almost deaf, and quite blind. In the late afternoons, she used to sit cross-legged on a wooden platform out in the courtyard behind the house, her white hair turned luminous and pink by the declining sun, her maid beside her, from time to time wrapping her special concoction of tobacco and lime in betel leaves and handing her the little bright-green packages.

The platform—platforms are the chief items of furniture in Indian homes—was about the size of a low double bed, and was the only thing to sit on in the courtyard. Occasionally, my grandfather would join my great-grandmother on it, but since he was very jolly and loved to talk, he soon became bored with so remote an audience, and would call the children to him. My four cousins, my sister, and I—or as many of us as were in the courtyard—would then collect around him and listen while, accompanied by the gentle bubbling of his hookah, he told us stories of kings and battles, or fragments of his childhood, or bits of family history. One of his favorites, I remember, concerned an ancestor of ours, a man who was deplored by his family and mocked by his acquaintances because he would never work. He would only sit in his garden, watch the brilliant flights of birds, and write poetry. This was in the early eighteenth century, during the days of the Mogul rule of India, and one day, when the court of the Great Mogul announced a poetry competition, our family wastrel decided to travel to the capital and read his poems to the Emperor. When he arrived, the Muslim courtiers laughed at the impudence of a Hindu who thought he could compete with the great Persian tradition of poetry, and declared that he should be the last of the contestants to appear before the Mogul.

"It was well known," my grandfather used to say, "that Hindus could not hear the song that lies within the simplest words of our daily language. But *he* had studied the music of the birds, he had listened to the leaves in his trees, and had heard the fall of the dew. His poetry was far more beautiful than anything the Mogul court could write. The Emperor was so deeply moved that at the end of the reading he exclaimed, 'I cannot simply say that you are the best poet, for you are the king, the shah, of poets!' "

From that time on our ancestor was called Shah. "Your second cousins," my grandfather would invariably conclude, "are still named Shah. Has it never struck you as strange that there should be a *Muslim* name in our family?"

If I hadn't been worried about the ghost, those last couple of hours before sunset would have been a pleasant time of day, with the great violet shadows moving across the courtyard and the old lady sitting, nodding in silence. Back and forth, from the storerooms to the kitchen—a separate building, opening off the courtyard—my grandmother and one or another of my aunts would go, busy about their household duties. On the kitchen doorstep the servants would be squatting with shallow brass pans before them, cleaning the rice and vegetables for the evening meal. My oldest cousin, Radha, would return from her classes at the Allahabad University. Another of my cousins, Mohan, younger than Radha but also at the university, would wheel in later on his bicycle, sweaty from playing tennis with his friends. My grandfather would pause for a second to greet each new arrival, and then continue with his stories.

Most of the time I only half listened to my grandfather, because this was also the time of the day when my anxiety about the ghost began to intensify. Actually, the story of the ghost was a good deal more banal than most of my grandfather's stories. All of us had been forbidden to talk about it—not so much because the family disapproved of superstition as because the story was not considered suitable for young children.

It concerned a gardener who had worked in the family's compound a generation before. He was a widower, but in the last years of his life he decided to marry again. He had saved enough money, he felt, to command the best, and, in fact, he did secure as his wife the prettiest girl in his native village, a few miles the other side of Allahabad, and brought her to live in his house near the compound. I don't suppose he was in love with her—I don't suppose he thought in such terms—but she was undeniably his most cherished possession. She was a beautiful ornament, and even if she wasn't a particularly talented or economical housekeeper, still, he didn't seem to mind although he made quite a point of chiding or disparaging her in public.

She, it later turned out, was resentful of her old and bossy husband, and rather repelled by him, but most of all she felt lonely and homesick, for her husband's friends were old and her own seemed far away. So, when a distant relative of hers, a young man, found a job (through her husband's recommendation) in a neighboring compound, she saw a lot of him, and inevitably they became lovers. For some months they managed their affair with remarkable discretion, but nothing is secret very long in India, and eventually the gardener heard about it. He was angry, of course, at his wife's ingratitude, and jealous of her beauty, and he returned home unexpectedly one afternoon when he was supposed to be working in the orchards, and discovered the lovers together. He hadn't, the story goes, expected to find so great a fury in himself—an old man, past the age for such emotions.

His wife saw his face and ran screaming from the house. He followed her, waving the long stick with a hooked knife on the end that he used in cleaning the springy undergrowth from around the fruit trees. He caught her as she reached the well just outside the courtyard of our house. He tried to hold her—or did he try to push her? Anyway, in the confusion of his anger and her fear, she fell down the well—a huge, old-fashioned well, bricked on the inside, with an old wooden scaffold above it, a rope, and a winding handle—and was drowned.

The gardener went back to his house, bewildered and in despair. He never went to work again but merely sat in his one room staring at the mud walls, the uneven floor, the litter of cooking pans and discarded clothes. The wives of the other servants brought him food every day, and sometimes he ate it and sometimes he didn't. But he needed something more than food to keep him alive, and he never recaptured it. He died a few months later, alone and still bewildered, without having talked to anyone after his wife's death.

As for the lover, he fled, and was never seen again. My cousins and I believed, for some reason, that he had been in a ghastly accident soon afterward, and that, although nobody had ever seen his ghost, it lurked in the branches of the huge neem tree that shaded our courtyard. The wife was a less cautious ghost, and several people had seen her. Mohan, for instance, claimed, with entirely convincing detail, that he had watched her wandering disconsolately under the mango trees beyond the well—searching, he assumed, for her lover. (Her husband, to whom we assigned no guilt, wasn't driven to return by the traditional restlessness of ghosts.) Mohan said he had come home after dark from the house of one of his college friends and was getting off his bicycle just outside the courtyard when he saw her, a faint, fugitive figure in the deep shadows. He assured us that the starlight caught an occasional gleam of silver from her sari or her jewelry—and why, he demanded, would she be wearing her wedding finery except to delight her lover? Certainly she had never worn it for her husband after the day of her ceremonial arrival at his house.

We might have doubted Mohan's unsupported word. He loved to tease us. He would tell us to rush out to the garden and see an airplane— one of our greatest excitements at that time—when there was nothing in the sky but the high, hovering hawks and the mist of dust over the town. Once he made us crouch for a long time staring into the eye of a cobra that had been killed in the garden and watching for a picture of the man who had killed him to form. This, Mohan told us, was how the mate of the cobra would know whom to strike for her revenge. But in the case of the ghost, a couple of the servants corroborated Mohan's story. They, too, had glimpsed the mysterious white figure, and there was much agitated discussion among them of why, after so many years, the ghost had chosen this time to appear. Was it a portent? A warning? Should they, perhaps, be less confident of the fidelity of their wives? And then a friend who came to call on the family after dinner one evening asked casually if it wasn't rather late for one of the girls to be walking alone in the garden. My grandmother quickly and sternly said that it was probably just the sweeper's wife returning home. The friend began to protest that she was too well dressed, but he dropped the matter in the face of my grandmother's obvious annoyance.

My youngest cousin, Gita—Mohan's sister—and I talked endlessly about what we would do if we should happen to meet the ghost. Gita, who was eleven, was both braver and more skeptical than I was, and felt very strongly that it would be silly and rude to assume that any mysterious woman in the garden after dark was a ghost until we had made sure by looking at her feet. Suppose, Gita said, it really *was* the sweeper's wife. She would think we had gone off our heads if we ran away from her without even a word of greeting.

In the slow, hot hours of the afternoon, when the grownups were resting indoors and the house was closed tight against the sun, Gita and I used to walk down to the guava orchard, each carrying a small package of salt. There we would lie in the dusty shade of the trees, eating unripe guavas dipped in the salt and making pleased, sour faces at the taste. Daily we discussed the ghost. We had several ingenious schemes for getting her to show her feet. We thought, for instance, of suggesting that she come with us to a mosque or temple, where she would have to remove her shoes before she entered. That would undoubtedly give us an opportunity to look at her feet. But there were flaws in this plan. A ghost would be sure to refuse to go with us in the first place. Besides, there were no mosques or temples closer than the town itself, and neither of us really had the courage to walk for nearly an hour with a possible ghost.

We thought of trying to find her footprints, too. Most of the garden was too dry and the ground baked too hard, at that time of year, to hold a print, but there was always a muddy patch near the well, where water was spilled or the damp seeped up from below. Conveniently enough, this was the part of the garden where the servants said the ghost liked to walk, but so many other people came to the well in the course of the day that we were sure we would never be able to distinguish her footprints from the hundreds of others, especially since—it occurred to us—they would probably look like natural ones.

We even considered the possibility of using mice. Were ghosts afraid of them? we wondered. If we released one suddenly, would she, without thinking, raise her sari in alarm? We thought she probably would, but we would have the inconvenience of going around every evening of our lives armed with a mouse for the emergency.

It was all very complicated and usually, after some time, we would revert to our other major topic of conversation—whom our cousin Radha would marry when she graduated from college. He would have to be a Brahmin, and preferably a Kashmiri Brahmin, because that was the community to which we all belonged. It was a large, very cliquish minority in the town; all its members were descended from the Brahmins who had fled into voluntary exile when Kashmir was invaded by the Muslims and had settled in Allahabad. Almost all of them were related, in one way or another, so Radha's match had to be carefully planned; the man must be one whose connection with our family was distant enough to be religiously acceptable but who was still within the community.

Radha's should have been an extremely easy marriage to arrange, because she was very beautiful in a way that is much admired by Kashmiris. She was tall and slender, with wavy reddish hair, a white skin, and rather startling gray eyes set with a slight tilt up toward her temples. In every way, she was most eligible, but Radha herself said disdainfully that she had no intention of getting married, that she wanted to get a job, and that people could think what they wished but she wasn't going to discuss the matter further.

None of the family took this announcement seriously. My grandmother didn't believe the part about the job at all, but she was, on the whole, rather pleased that Radha could afford to be so offhand about her marriage. Too great an eagerness for a husband was scarcely becoming in a girl, and, besides, having a marriageable daughter sought after rather than seeking put the family in a strong position.

Gita and I knew that negotiations had already been begun. The parents of various young men had, in the conventional way, sent the horoscopes of their sons for the family priest and astrologer to compare with Radha's horoscope and see if the combination augured well for the young couple. Actually, the main purpose of this practice was to give the girl's family a graceful way of refusing proposals and selecting the most desirable suitor.

Gita and I had already chosen our favorite. We had borrowed the horoscopes from their hiding place in my grandmother's big metal trunk, which contained the household linen, and had decided on the one whose owner would be "a leader of men" whose fame was to spread beyond the province. We interpreted this to mean that he would somehow become a prince, and we were very taken with the idea of a real shah in the family, instead of only the namesakes of the old poet. It was a great relief, in the long afternoons, to forget the ghost for a while and daydream about visiting Radha in her palace after she became a queen.

Mohan, typically, used to tease Radha to a fury about her admirers in college, the students who sat and stared at her during lectures, when they should have been taking notes. "Ridiculous!" Radha would say. "What nonsense you talk!"

But Mohan would go on, in his plaguing singsong, and talk about Radha's "special"—a most unsuitable admirer, wrong in both caste and community, who was so much in love with her that his college work had gone to pot and nobody thought he would pass his final examinations.

Radha, caught between anger and tears, once shouted, "You fool! What do *you* know about anything? It's because of politics. He spends all his time on *politics*!" And she ran weeping from the room. My grandmother scolded Mohan, and afterward Radha was more scornful than ever about the proposals and suggestions for her marriage.

This mention of politics worried my grandmother. At that time the Indian independence movement had caught fire all across the country, and we heard a lot about *Swaraj** and civil disobedience. In the colleges, particularly, groups of fervent nationalists were forming, ready to lead strikes, carry flags bearing anti-British slogans, or go to jail, like Gandhi. My grandmother forbade Radha to meddle in such things, and Radha was sulky and silent, but she defiantly had the borders of her white muslin saris dyed orange and green, and so went to college every day wearing the nationalist colors.

Gita and I were generally on Radha's side, but, talking lazily in the shade of the guava trees, we worried a good deal lest she remain stubborn for so long that her chances might slide away until she had grown too old to be desirable. Eventually, the salt and the sour guavas would make us so thirsty that we'd wander back to the courtyard to get a drink from the big terra-cotta jar that stood in one corner, in the shade. The water in it always tasted of the smell of earth after rain. Soon tea would be served, my great-grandmother would take up her place on the platform, my grandfather would emerge with his hookah, and the evening would begin.

At night the servants carried the family's beds—light wooden frames crisscrossed with a webbing of tape—out into the courtyard, put the thin mattresses and the bedclothes on them, and set mosquito nets over them. The whole family slept outdoors, in a long column of beds, in the tepid darkness. Gita and I usually went to bed only a little while before the grownups. From within our white cubes of netting, we whispered to each other, identifying the members of the family as they passed us— indistinct shapes accompanied by the soft flapping of sandals. After they

*Self-rule—Ed.

had all been accounted for, we often stayed awake a little longer to be sure that no additional figure was moving about the courtyard—that the ghost had in fact stayed safely outside the wall.

We would wake, in the sweet chill of the early morning, to the sound of my grandmother singing hymns in her prayer room, to the smell of the first wood smoke from the kitchen fire, and to the creaking of the winding rope of the well, where two blindfolded oxen with painted foreheads and silver-tipped horns were walking round and round, turning the wheel and raising the day's supply of water. The only reminder of the ghost came when we broke off twigs of the neem tree to brush our teeth with. I used to wonder briefly then about the man that haunted its branches, and decide that I needn't think about it until evening came again.

The night I saw the ghost must have been at the end of April. I remember that the first mangoes had arrived, and that the corroding heat of the last two months before the monsoon had already set in. Those nights we dined later and stayed up later than we had been doing, not wanting to lose the few comfortable hours of the day. On one such evening, when the grownups were deep in uninteresting family talk, when Radha had gone indoors saying she had to study for her examinations, and Mohan and my other cousins were playing a complicated card game, which they told us we were too young for, Gita and I decided to watch the moonrise.

We climbed the courtyard wall and seated ourselves precariously on top of it, looking over the dusty fruit trees beyond the well to the paleness on the horizon where the moon would appear. We had a theory that if we could catch the exact moment when the rim of the moon was level with the rim of the earth, we would see a vivid green flash leap from the horizon. We had never actually managed to prove this, either because we blinked or because something distracted us, but still we hopefully watched the moonrise from time to time. That night, we missed the green flash once more because we both turned at the same instant, aware of some slight stirring under the mango trees. We couldn't see anything there, but by the time we turned back, the edge of the moon was already showing, and it was rising, in the way of the Indian moon, almost visibly.

Again there was a stirring in the shadows, this time more distinct, and when we stared, we could make out a pale figure walking away from us and see the first, slanting glitter of moonlight on the silver at her wrists.

I think I must have made a movement to get down from the wall, for something just then loosened a piece of the old mortar, which fell whispering down the bricks and landed with an alarmingly loud noise on the ground. The ghost must have heard it. At once, she vanished into the deeper darkness. Then Gita and I, still staring, saw that the taller figure of a man was still standing, entirely motionless and all in white, under the trees where we had seen the other.

We scrambled down the inside of the wall and stood breathless in the courtyard. It had not, of course, occurred to either of us to check on the figures' feet. We held on to each other, unable to speak, for what must, I suppose, have been several minutes. It was only after we had got back to the family, still sitting and talking in an ordinary way, to the security of the oil lamp with the big, stupid moths bumping into it, to the quarrels of the cardplayers, that our excitement exploded and we gabbled the story over and over. My cousins dropped their cards, the grownups began to protest. We had made it all up, they said, or we were dreaming.

Radha came out of the house looking flushed and worried.

"We *saw* them! We *saw* them!" Gita shouted. "We were—"

"Shut *up*!" Radha said, her face tense with anger.

"But it's true! We saw the ghosts—*both* of them!"

"Ghosts?" Radha said, and then, with a sudden change of tone, "Oh, ghosts." Almost vaguely she added, "You foolish children, can't you ever think of anything but that boring old ghost? I thought the world was coming to an end the way you were yelling out here." She shook back her bangles, gleaming silver in the lamplight, glanced out into the dark reaches of the courtyard, and went back indoors.

"She's studying too hard," her mother said. "She's nervous."

But my grandmother was looking very thoughtful. Slowly she got to her feet and followed Radha into the house.

MARJORIE KINNAN RAWLINGS
(1896–1953)

The author of the children's classic *The Yearling* left newspaper work and city life to run an orange grove in backwoods Florida. *Cross Creek* (1942) is a memoir of her life there that draws on her affection for the hammock country of north-central Florida and the people around her, as does her fiction. This selection, "A Pig Is Paid For," shows how the community heals itself after a small tear in the social fabric.

For another woman running a farm against the odds, compare Isak Dinesen, *Out of Africa*, and see also Betty MacDonald, *The Egg and I.* For another female anomaly in a small and tight-knit community, compare Caitlin Thomas, *Leftover Life to Kill.*

FROM *Cross Creek*

A Pig Is Paid For

I suppose there is nowhere in the world a more elemental exchange of goods than among ourselves at the Creek. The exchange does not even become barter and trade. We merely return favors. Old Boss uses my truck to haul his vegetable crops to the station and I use his mules for my occasional light plowing. We have never sat down to figure which has the higher rental value, for it does not matter. I have the only pecan trees at the Creek, so each fall two or three families pick the crop for me, by their request, and take for pay only enough pecans to last them through the winter. They refuse the actual cash value of the work. As a matter of fact, they could not have been hired. One fisherman borrows a few dollars of me in lean times, and I have a drawing account for fish, never calculated exactly, but well tipped in my favor. Another man borrows between jobs and appears unsummoned when a freeze comes in and I must fire my young orange grove. Sometimes his two or three nights of the cold and arduous work come to much more than he has borrowed and he waves aside the proffered difference.

"You don't owe me a nickel," he says.

I contracted one debt, however, that involved me in so labyrinthine a maze that I thought I should never find my way out of it. It was my punishment, I suppose, for shooting a pig of Mr. Martin's. I never planned to shoot the pig and I certainly didn't know it belonged to Mr. Martin. As a matter of fact, I didn't care. It could have belonged to the devil himself, and many a morning I was sure of it. I am a patient woman as far as other people's stock is concerned. I know stock. If I were a pig, I should search out the green pastures, as did the pigs of Mr. Martin. If I knew where skimmed milk lay white and frothy in open pans, I should push my way under a stout barbed-wire fence and bury my snout in that milk. But even if I were a pig, I can see no reason for rooting up fluffy-ruffle petunias.

There were eight of the pigs. The first thing I heard every morning at daybreak was the whole outfit crashing under the fence and rushing under the floor of my bedroom for a matutinal rubbing of backs against the crosspiece. The rubbing ended, and the grunts, my room stopped shaking, and the commotion passed. I turned over for a nap. While I was napping, the happy congregation moved on to the trays of biddy-mash, the skimmed milk and the fluffy-ruffle petunias. Fluffy-ruffle petunias are delicate plants. The seed is as expensive as gold dust and as fine. It takes weeks to germinate. The seedlings must be nursed by hand. When transplanted, they are the prey of cutworms, of drought, of the slightest adversity. Once brought months later to maturity, the huge multicolored blooms represent beauty flowered into life by the most desperate of measures. So while I could forgive the heavy supplying to alien porkers of chicken feed and milk, I simply could not forgive the fluffy-ruffle petunias. The intruders dug up altogether four consecutive plantings and on the third uprooting I was a trifle demented. I lay in watch.

I discovered that the litter had a leader. He was as pretty a young barrow as I have ever seen, Titian-haired and light of spirit and rounded into delicious curves by his long diet of biddy-mash, skimmed milk and petunias. It was he who broke his way through and under the fence, he who raced joyously under my bedroom to scratch, he who galloped, butt wobbling, tail curling, to the trays of feed and the petunia bed. His brothers and sisters only followed where he led. Where they came from, where they went when the sun had set, I did not know. I knew only that the bright-red barrow was my enemy. One morning I sat on my veranda. The litter was peaceful, ready to lie quietly and decently in the shade. But not the red-bristled fiend. He pranced to the front yard and gave himself with abandon to my fourth planting of fluffy-ruffle petunias. I arose as one in a trance, picked up my gun, stepped to the petunia bed and shot him dead where he fed.

Psychologists might say, trying me before a jury of my peers, that murder lay ready in my heart. The act was not premeditated, yet the will to kill was waiting. I know only that I pulled the trigger with joy and looked down at my fallen foe with delight and triumph. There would be no more battening of outlaw stock on feed and flowers. I wondered to whom the pigs belonged. They were none of my immediate neighbors'. I looked again at the red menace. He was appallingly fat and succulent. I picked him up by his curly tail, put him in my car and drove to Citra. I arranged to have Mr. Hogan dress him, and Ward the storekeeper to store him in his refrigerator. I sent a wire to my friend Norton in Ocala, "Bring ten or twelve Saturday night for whole roast pig barbecue."

The roast pig was perfection. The meat was as white as the skimmed milk and the petunia roots on which it had been fattened. After, I read aloud Charles Lamb's essay on "Roast Pig." It was a fine evening.

On Sunday, neighbor Tom stopped by and said with a queer look in his eyes, "You been having pig trouble?"

"Yes, but it's all over."

"Could be, it's just begun. You know anything about the man named Martin?"

"Never heard of him."

"Well, he's settled across the Creek. Put out the word he's a man won't be trifled with. Has notches on his gun. I just wondered." He went away.

On Monday morning I heard knuckles pound on the steps at the side porch. A huge man stood there with his broad-brimmed Stetson hat pushed back from his forehead.

"Mornin'. My name's Martin."

"Good morning, Mr. Martin. What can I do for you?"

He shifted his weight.

"Mis' Rawlings, do you remember hit rainin' last Monday?"

"Why, no, Mr. Martin, I don't."

"Well, hit rained. Mis' Rawlings, do you remember loadin' your truck to Dorsey Townsend last Monday?"

"Why, yes. I don't remember that it was Monday, but he borrowed it one day last week."

"Well, hit were Monday. Mis' Rawlings"—he squinted casually at the sky—"do you remember a gun shootin' last Monday? A 12-guage, maybe. Maybe a 16. Could of been a 20."

"Why, yes indeed," I said. "It was I who shot. I shot a pig. With my 20-gauge. I don't know whose pig it was. It led a pack that came through my stock-proof fences. It tormented me to death. Why, Mr. Martin, maybe it was your pig. The mark was a half-moon in one ear and a bit in the other."

He drew a long breath.

"That were my pig," he said.

He stared at me.

"Of course," I said, "I expect to pay for it. In a way, I had a right to shoot it, because it was an outlaw. In another way, the right is on your side, because in a no-fence county you have the right to turn your stock loose. But I'll pay for it very gladly. Oh, Mr. Martin, I did so enjoy shooting that pig."

He stepped back and studied me.

"Them pigs was practically pets," he said.

"They were very tame," I said. "That was the trouble."

"You could of ketched it with your bare hands," he lamented.

"Yes, Mr. Martin," I said, "but then I wouldn't have had the pleasure of shooting it."

Suddenly I remembered the notches on his gun.

"In a way, Mr. Martin," I said, "I'm sorry. But that's the way I am. I go along quietly for a while, and then out of a clear sky I just don't know what I'm doing. I pick up a gun and I shoot whatever makes me angry. This time it was a pig. I'm so afraid some time it may be a person. After it was over, I'd be terribly sorry. But then it would be too late, wouldn't it?"

He wiped his forehead.

"I don't know what to think," he burst out. "From the beginning, I ain't knowed what to think. I went to all your neighbors, and they all said, 'Oh, no, Mis' Rawlings wouldn't do a thing like that.' But all the time something told me, if you got mad enough, you'd do it."

"It's too bad, isn't it?" I condoled with him. "When I'm so sorry afterward."

He grew confidential.

"I heard the shot and I placed it about here, and my pig come up missing. I stopped Dorsey and I got it out of him he'd heard you shoot. I went to Citra and I found out where you'd had it dressed and where you'd had it stored, and they all said, 'Why, yes, Mis' Rawlings come in with a pig she said she'd shot.' I saw the constable and turned out he was a buddy of yours and he just laughed. I studied and I studied and I decided to have the law on you. I aimed to put you in the jailhouse. And if they wouldn't put you in the jailhouse I aimed to settle it my way. I aimed to make all the trouble for you I knew to do. And now—now you talk so honest—why, I just don't know what to do."

"Don't you worry about it another minute," I soothed him. "Now it's all over, and I'm so sorry, I can't bear to have you worried. You just decide on your price, and whatever that pig was worth to you, why, it's worth the same to me. And if you'd rather have another pig of the same size and pedigree, I'll replace it."

"I don't know how to figure the price," he said. "I'd not of dreamed of selling one of them pigs."

He turned away, then back again.

"I could of stood everything," he said, "but then you went and had a drunken party—and *ate* it."

"Oh, Mr. Martin," I said, "the meat was delicious. I wish I'd sent you some. I never had better pork in my life. And why wouldn't it be good? It had fed on biddy-mash and skimmed milk and fluffy-ruffle petunias."

I suppose that Mr. Martin gave it all up then as a matter in the realm of madness. He went away, murmuring that the pig was beyond price and replacement would be practically impossible. I gave no further thought to pig or payment, waiting for the bill to arrive. The pig was worth several dollars, but I decided that I would pay anything up to fifteen without protest. Or I should go to market and buy its valuable duplicate. And then Mr. Higgenbotham entered the picture.

My relations with Mr. Higgenbotham were already involved. We first became friends over the matter of snakes. Adrenna came mincing to my room one morning as though she were announcing the President.

"Mr. Higgenbotham is calling," she said. "Mr. Higgenbotham wishes to show you a snake."

I put on a house-coat and went to the front door. I knew Mr. Higgenbotham to speak to, for his ramshackle open truck passed the house going and coming on his business of frog-hunting and snake-catching. Mr. Higgenbotham is a small ragged man with hair shaggy in his eyes. He had his campaign planned. As I came to the door, he held up one hand in command, unfurled a crocus sack, and with great drama rolled a large king snake onto the grass.

"There! Look at him! Six foot long! I ain't been getting but forty cents for 'em. I just want you to see. Why, a snake like that is worth forty cents in the woods!"

His grievance, it appeared, was over the low market on snakes.

"You know folks in the up-country," he said, "and I want you to see can you get me a better market for my snakes."

His confidence touched me. I could think of no friend at the moment who might be interested in upping the price on king snakes. But I assured him that I would do my best. A king snake six feet long was certainly worth forty cents in the woods. We became immediately fast friends. The king snake was to Mr. Higgenbotham an individual. It was his pet and its name was Oscar. He put it through its tricks. It coiled like a rattlesnake and struck playfully at him. He tapped it on its glistening head.

"That's enough o' that, Oscar. You wouldn't believe how smart he is. I cain't fool him on his rations. I hold a little snake for him, or a mouse, and he takes it as dainty as a lady. Give him a stick or a strip of shoestring and he turns away disgusted. And when I turn him a-loose, he's after the rats in the house like lightning."

Foolishly, idiotically, regretting it in an instant, I said, "That's fine. I have terrible trouble with rats in my attic."

"I'll lend you Oscar," he said. "I want to do something for you, helping me with my business. I'll put Oscar in your attic."

I could have cut out my tongue. Mr. Higgenbotham was gathering up Oscar with enthusiasm, to put him in my attic.

"It's all sealed up," I said. "We couldn't very well get to it."

"We'll cut a hole," he said. "Oscar would have to have a hole, anyway, so he could come down to get water."

I had visions of awakening and staring into the black beady eyes of Oscar, come down for water. The rats seemed pleasant companions.

"It wouldn't be safe," I said, inspired. "My cat is death on snakes."

He put Oscar reluctantly into the crocus sack.

"Well—I'd sure hate to have that happen."

I was so happy to be rid of Oscar that I did my best about the snake market. I wrote to Ditmars and to the Cincinnati Zoo and the Washington Zoo. The replies were courteous and I think amused. The general opinion was that if my friend was getting forty cents for king snakes, he was doing nicely. The big zoos had their own collectors and snakes were a glut on the market. Mr. Higgenbotham was grateful for my efforts, satisfied now with his price. He waved violently whenever his truck passed my house. He usually had a cross-eyed child with him, and I could see him nudge the child, so that it too waved to me. One day Mr. Higgenbotham stopped and came up the path with the unhappy air of a man about to try to borrow money.

"I'm in a tight," he said, "and you're my friend, and I figured you was the one to help me out. The sheriff's been after me and been after me about a license for my truck. 'I cain't let you keep that thing on the highways no longer without no license,' he said to me. He said, 'I hate to be hard on a poor man, but next time I catch you out without no license, I'm obliged to run you in.' "

"How much do you need?"

"Not but six dollars. I'll give you a mortgage on the truck."

I looked at it. There was not six dollars' worth of usable parts of any description.

"Or," he added, "in a pinch, I could work it out."

The idea seemed feasible enough. I gave Mr. Higgenbotham six dollars and he agreed to work it out in pruning on my orange trees. Days passed, and weeks, and Mr. Higgenbotham passed and re-passed on his frog- and snake-hunting expeditions and did not stop to prune. It is one thing to help a friend in distress and it is another thing to be done. I was on the roadside one day picking up pecans and flagged down Mr. Higgenbotham. It took him a hundred yards to stop. He backed up. The cross-eyed child began waving dutifully.

"Don't speak," Mr. Higgenbotham shouted. "Don't say it. I know what you're thinking. You're thinking I got no intentions o' paying back what I borrowed. Mis' Rawlings, I had the confidence in you not to borrow without I meant to pay it back. I got my plans. You just wait now. The moon won't be out this month without I pay back that six dollars."

He drove off with a flourish and the child waved as far as it could see. The next week the truck stopped at my gate. In the back stood trussed a lean gray razor-back sow. Mr. Higgenbotham walked jauntily up the path.

"Want to buy a pig?" he called.

"It's just about the last thing in the world I want to buy," I said with possible bitterness.

"Couldn't use a pig to trade?" he asked and winked at me. "Can't think of nobody now you owe a pig to?"

Understanding struck me.

"I do owe a pig to Mr. Martin," I said, "but how did you know?"

"Oh, everybody knows you owe Mr. Martin a pig. Now what I got figgered out is this. That sow there is worth six dollars if she's worth a cent. I owe you six dollars. If Mr. Martin takes that sow, you've paid him and I've paid you. Now how about it?"

I looked at the rangy creature in the truck.

"What makes you think Mr. Martin will take her?"

"Well, when you figger on a sow, you figger on more than a sow. You buy you a sow, and directly you've got a litter of pigs to boot. You've got the sow and you've got eight-ten pigs and the pigs'll soon make shoats and you carry the shoats to market and you get good money for 'em and you've yet got the sow. Now I'm carrying that sow there to Mr. Martin's boar hog. You know sows?"

"No," I said, "not very well."

"Well, a sow's peculiar. Times, she'll take, and again she'll not take. It all depends on the moon. Now last moon, she'd not of took. This moon, I figger she'll take. And if she takes—mind, if she takes—Mr. Martin'll take her for the debt. 'Course, if she don't take, I'm the one loses. In that case, I got a dollar to pay for the use o' the boar."

It seemed very complicated, between Mr. Martin and Mr. Higgenbotham and the rental stud of boars and the ways of sows and the moon, but I had little to lose.

"Very well. If the sow takes, and Mr. Martin accepts her for my debt to him, then your debt to me is paid. Right?"

"Righter'n rain," and he drove off with the gray sow lurching in the back of the truck and the child waving.

Time passed and I had no bill from Mr. Martin and no call from Mr. Higgenbotham. The situation was a little delicate, for a lady is not supposed to inquire too closely into matters either of debts or of breeding. Then I ran into Mr. Martin in the grocery store on a Saturday night in Citra. He was cordial. He was effusive.

"You do any duck-hunting?" he asked.

"Indeed, yes."

"A quick shot like you," he said, "I figgered you'd enjoy duck-hunting. Now when winter comes and you're ready, you just get me word and I'll carry you out to the best duck stand on Orange Lake."

Surely something must have been settled. The moon must have been right. In the formality of the store I could not inquire of the intimate relation of the gray sow to Mr. Martin's boar. I longed to say, "Did she take? Are we all square, you and Mr. Higgenbotham and I?"

I said, "The pig I owed you for. The one I was to replace—"

He put out a big hand for me to shake.

"Mis' Rawlings," he said, "the pig is paid for."

V. SACKVILLE-WEST
(1892–1962)

Vita Sackville-West, oldest child of one of England's most distinguished families but barred by her sex from inheriting Knole Castle, the family seat, was married in 1913 to diplomat and essayist Harold Nicolson. Time would reveal that both of them were essentially homosexual, but they produced two sons and created an enduring, if unconventional, marriage whose story was told by their younger son, Nigel Nicolson, in *Portrait of a Marriage* (1973). The book provided a fascinating example of open marriage, an idea whose time, in the early 1970s, seemed to have come. Nigel Nicolson included a previously unpublished account his mother had written in 1920 of her childhood, her sexuality, and of a just-ended love affair with another woman, Violet Keppel Trefusis, that had almost destroyed her marriage. Nigel Nicolson referred to this account as an autobiography, but his mother called it a confession. A portion of this confession forms the selection here.

V. Sackville-West's published works were many and popular. She wrote poetry, fiction, and columns of garden advice. She and Harold Nicolson shared a passion for gardening, and the garden they made together at Sissinghurst Castle, their home in Kent, is one of England's finest. Virginia Woolf's lover and friend for many years, she inspired Woolf's fantasy-biography *Orlando*, whose hero/heroine begins as an Elizabethan aristocrat and changes gender over the centuries.

For another account of an unconventional marriage, compare Simone de Beauvoir, *The Prime of Life;* of a conventional marriage, compare Émilie Carles, *A Life of Her Own.* For another account of the British upper class, compare Jessica Mitford, *Hons and Rebels.* For another lesbian (or proto-lesbian) episode, compare the last selection from Audre Lorde, *Zami.*

FROM *Confession*

Sept. 27th, 1920

In April, [1918], when we were back in the country, Violet wrote to ask whether she could come and stay with me for a fortnight. I was bored by the idea, as I wanted to work, and I did not know how to entertain her; but I could scarcely refuse. So she came. We were both bored. My serenity got on her nerves, and her restlessness got on mine. She went up to London for the day as often as she could, but she came back in the evenings because the air-raids frightened her. She had been here [Long Barn] I think about a week when everything changed suddenly— changed far more than I foresaw at the time; changed my life. It was the 18th of April. An absurd circumstance gave rise to the whole thing; I had just got clothes like the women-on-the-land were wearing, and in the unaccustomed freedom of breeches and gaiters I went into wild spirits; I ran, I shouted, I jumped, I climbed, I vaulted over gates, I felt like a schoolboy let out on a holiday; and Violet followed me across fields and woods with a new meekness, saying very little, but never taking her eyes off me, and in the midst of my exuberance I knew that all the old under-current had come back stronger than ever and that my old domination over her had never been diminished. I remember that wild irresponsible day. It was one of the most vibrant days of my life. As it happened, Harold was not coming down that night. Violet and I dined alone together, and then, after dinner, we went into my sitting-room, and for some time made conversation, but that broke down, and from ten o'clock until two in the morning—for four hours, or perhaps more—we talked.

Violet had struck the secret of my duality; she attacked me about it, and I made no attempt to conceal it from her or from myself. I talked myself out, until I could hear my own voice getting hoarse, and the fire went out, and all the servants had long since gone to bed, and there was not a soul in the house except Violet and me, and I talked out the whole of myself with absolute sincerity and pain, and Violet only listened— which was skilful of her. She made no comments and no suggestions until I had finished—until, that is, I had dug into every corner and brought its contents out to the light. I had been vouchsafed insight, as one sometimes is. Then, when I had finished, when I had told her how all the gentleness and all the femininity of me was called out by Harold alone, but how towards everyone else my attitude was completely other-wise—then, still with her infinite skill, she brought me round to my attitude towards herself, as it had always been ever since we were children, and then she told me how she had loved me always, and re-minded me of incidents running through years, which I couldn't pretend to have forgotten. She was far more skilful than I. I might have been a boy of eighteen, and she a woman of thirty-five. She was infinitely clever—she didn't scare me, she didn't rush me, she didn't allow me to see where I was going; it was all conscious on her part, but on mine it was simply the drunkenness of liberation—the liberation of half my personality. She opened up to me a new sphere. And for her, of course, it meant the supreme effort to conquer the love of the person she had always wanted, who had always repulsed her (when things seemed to be going too far), out of a sort of fear, and of whom she was madly jealous—a fact I had not realized so adept was she at concealment, and so obtuse was I at her psychology.

She lay on the sofa, I sat plunged in the armchair; she took my hands, and parted my fingers to count the points as she told me why she loved me. I hadn't dreamt of such an art of love. Such things had been direct for me always; I had known no love possessed of that Latin artistry (whether instinctive or acquired). I was infinitely troubled by the softness of her touch and the murmur of her lovely voice. She appealed to my unawakened senses; she wore, I remember, a dress of red velvet, that was exactly the colour of a red rose, and that made of her, with her white skin and the tawny hair, the most seductive being. She pulled me down until I kissed her—I had not done so for many years. Then she was wise enough to get up and go to bed; but I kissed her again in the dark after I had blown out our solitary lamp. She let herself go entirely limp and passive in my arms. (I shudder to think of the experience that lay behind her abandonment.) I can't think I slept at all that night—not that much of the night was left.

I don't know how to go on; I keep thinking that Harold, if he ever reads this, will suffer so, but I ask him to remember that he is reading about a *different person* from the one he knew. Also I am not writing this for fun, but for several reasons which I will explain. (1) As I started by saying, because I want to tell the *entire* truth. (2) Because I know of no truthful record of such a connection—one that is written, I mean, with no desire to appeal to a vicious taste in any possible readers; and (3) because I hold the conviction that as centuries go on, and the sexes become more nearly merged on account of their increasing resemblances, I hold the conviction that such connections will to a very large extent cease to be regarded as merely unnatural, and will be understood far better, at least in their *intellectual* if not in their physical aspect. (Such is already the case in Russia.) I believe that then the psychology of people like myself will be a matter of interest, and I believe it will be recognized that many more people of my type do exist than under the present-day system of hypocrisy is commonly admitted. I am not saying that such personalities, and the connections which result from them, will not be deplored as they are now; but I do believe that their greater prevalence, and the spirit of candour which one hopes will spread with the progress of the world, will lead to their recognition, if only as an inevitable evil. The first step in the direction of such candour must be taken by the general admission of normal but illicit relations, and the facilitation of divorce, or possibly even the reconstruction of the system of marriage. Such advance must necessarily come from the more educated and liberal classes. Since "unnatural" means "removed from nature," only the most civilized, because the least natural, class of society can be expected to tolerate such a product of civilization.

I advance, therefore, the perfectly accepted theory that cases of dual personality do exist, in which the feminine and the masculine elements alternately preponderate. I advance this in an impersonal and scientific spirit, and claim that I am qualified to speak with the intimacy a professional scientist could acquire only after years of study and indirect information, because I have the object of study always to hand, in my own heart, and can gauge the exact truthfulness of what my own experience tells me. However frank, people would always keep back something. I can't keep back anything from myself.

Sept. 29th [1920]

I think Violet stayed on for about five days after that. All the time I was in fantastic spirits; and, not realizing how different she was from me in many ways, I made her follow me on wild courses all over the country, and, because she knew she had me only lightly hooked, she obeyed without remonstrance. There was very little between us during those days, only an immense excitement and a growing wish to go away somewhere alone together. This wish was carried out, by arranging to go down to Cornwall for the inside of a week; it was the first time I had ever been away from Harold, and he obviously minded my going.

We went. We met again in London, lunched at a restaurant, and filled with a spirit of adventure took the train for Exeter. On the way there we decided to go on to Plymouth. We arrived at Plymouth to find our luggage had of course been put out at Exeter. We had only an assortment of French poetry with us. We didn't care. We went to the nearest hotel, exultant to feel that nobody in the world knew where we were; at the booking office we were told there was only one room. It seemed like fate. We engaged it. We went and had supper—cider and ham—over which we talked fast and tremulously; she was frightened of me by then.

The next day we went on to Cornwall, where we spent five blissful days; I felt like a person translated, or re-born; it was like beginning one's life again in a different capacity. We were very miserable to come away, but we were constantly together during the whole of the summer months following. Once we went down to Cornwall again for a fortnight. It was a lovely summer. She was radiant. But I never thought it would last; I thought of it as an adventure, an escapade. I kept telling myself she was fickle, that I was the latest toy; she used to assure me of the contrary. She did this with such gravity that sometimes I was almost convinced; but now the years have convinced me thoroughly.

She no longer flirted, and got rid of the last person she had been engaged to, when we went to Cornwall. But there was a man out in France, who used to write to her; she hardly knew him, and I wasn't jealous. He was called Denzil [Denys Trefusis]. She described him to me as fiery—hair like gold wire, blue eyes starting out of his head, and winged nostrils. I listened, not very much interested. I now hate him more than I have ever hated anyone in this life, or am likely to; and there is no injury I would not do him with the utmost pleasure.

Well, the whole of that summer she was mine—a mad and irresponsible summer of moonlight nights, and infinite escapades, and passionate letters, and music, and poetry. Things were not tragic for us then, because although we cared passionately we didn't care deeply—not like now, though it was deepening all the time; no, things weren't tragic, they were rapturous and new, and one side of my life was opened to me, and, to hide nothing, I found things out about my own temperament that I had never been sure of before. Of course I wish now that I had never made those discoveries. One doesn't miss what one doesn't know, and now life is made wretched for me by privations. I often long for ignorance and innocence. I think that if anything happened to bring my friendship with Violet to an end, I might have the strength of mind to blot all that entirely out of my life.

At the end of that summer Denys came home on leave, and I met him. He was very tall and slender, and had the winged look that she had described—I could compare him to many things, to a race-horse, to a Crusader, to a greyhound, to an ascetic in search of the Holy Grail. I liked him then (oh irony!), and he liked me. I could afford to like him, because I was accustomed to Violet's amusements. Even now I see his good points, and they are many; but I see them only by translating myself into an impersonal spectator, and I see them, above all, when Violet makes him suffer. I see that he is a rare, sensitive, proud idealist, and I recognize that through me he has undergone months of suffering, and that his profound love for Violet has been thwarted of its fulfillment. And I am sorry enough for him, at moments, just sorry enough to wish vaguely that he could have cared for someone other than Violet. I see his tragedy—for he is a tragic person. But none of this softens my hatred of him, which is certainly the most violent feeling I have ever experienced. I only hope he returns it in full measure; he has a hundred times more cause to hate me than I to hate him.

He was in London for about ten days. It was already arranged that

Violet and I were to go abroad together that winter for a month. There were scenes connected with our going. Violet and I had a row over something; I refused to go abroad; she came round to my house and we made friends again; then I had a dreadful scene with Mother, who was furious at my going; however to make a long story short we left for Paris at the end of November [1918]. I was to be away until Christmas!

Oct. 5th [1920]

Paris . . . We were there for about a week, living in a flat that was lent us in the Palais Royal. Even now the intoxication of some of those hours in Paris makes me see confusedly; other hours were, I admit, wretched, because Denys came (the war being just over), and I wanted Violet to myself. But the evenings were ours. I have never told a soul of what I did. I hesitate to write it here, but I must; shirking the truth here would be like cheating oneself playing patience. I dressed as a boy. It was easy, because I could put a khaki bandage round my head, which in those days was so common that it attracted no attention at all. I browned my face and hands. It must have been successful, because no one looked at me at all curiously or suspiciously—never once, out of the many times I did it. My height of course was my great advantage. I looked like a rather untidy young man, a sort of undergraduate, of about nineteen. It was marvellous fun, all the more so because there was always the risk of being found out. Of course it was easy in the Palais Royal because I could let myself in and out by a latchkey; in hotels it was more difficult. I had done it once already in England; that was one of the boldest things I ever did. I will tell about it: I changed in my own house in London late one evening (the darkened streets made me bold), and drove with Violet in a taxi as far as Hyde Park Corner. There I got out. I never felt so free as when I stepped off the kerb, down Piccadilly, alone, and knowing that if I met my own mother face to face she would take no notice of me. I walked along, smoking a cigarette, buying a newspaper off a little boy who called me "sir," and being accosted now and then by women. In this way I strolled from Hyde Park Corner to Bond Street, where I met Violet and took her in a taxi to Charing Cross. (The extraordinary thing was, how natural it all was for me.) Nobody, even in the glare of the station, glanced at me twice. I had wondered about my voice, but found I could sink it sufficiently. Well, I took Violet as far as Orpington by train, and there we found a lodging house where we could get a room. The landlady was very benevolent and I said Violet was my wife. Next day of course I had to put on the same clothes, although I was a little anxious about the daylight, but again nobody took the slightest notice.

We went to Knole!, which was, I think, brave. Here I slipped into the stables, and emerged as myself.

Well, this discovery was too good to be wasted, and in Paris I practically lived in that role. Violet used to call me Julian. We dined together every evening in cafés and restaurants, and went to all the theatres. I shall never forget the evenings when we walked back slowly to our flat through the streets of Paris. I, personally, had never felt so free in my life. Perhaps we have never been so happy since. When we got back to the flat, the windows all used to be open onto the courtyard of the Palais Royal, and the fountains splashed below. It was all incredible—like a fairy-tale.

It couldn't go on for ever, and at the end of the week we left for Monte Carlo, stopping on the way at St. Raphael. The weather was perfect, Monte Carlo was perfect, Violet was perfect. Again as Julian, I took her to a dance there, and had a success with a French family, who asked me to come and play bridge with them, and, I think, had an eye on me for their daughter, a plain girl whose head I tried to turn with compliments. They said, *"On voit que monsieur est valseur,"* and their son, a French officer, asked me about my *"blessure,"* and we exchanged war reminiscences.

I didn't go back at Christmas. I didn't go back till nearly the end of March, and everybody was very angry with me, and I felt like suicide after those four wild and radiant months. The whole of that time is dreadful, a nightmare. Harold was in Paris, and I was alone with Mother and Dada, who were both very angry, and wanted me to give Violet up. (There had been a lot of scandal, by then.) On the other hand, Denys had been in England a month, and was agitating to announce his engagement to Violet. Violet was like a hunted creature. I could have prevented the engagement by very few words, but I thought that would be too outrageously selfish; there was Violet's mother, a demon of a woman, longing to get her safely married, and having told all London that she was going to marry Denys. She had already so bad a reputation for breaking engagements that this would have been the last straw. Besides, we both thought she would gain more liberty by marrying, and Denys was prepared to marry her on her own terms—that is, of merely brotherly relations.

I was absolutely miserable. I went to Brighton, alone, in a great empty dust-sheeted house, and all night I used to lie awake, and all day I used to wonder whether I wouldn't throw myself over the cliffs. Everyone questioned me as to why I looked so ill. On the fifth day Violet's engagement was announced in the papers; I bought the paper at Brighton station and nearly fainted as I read it, although I had expected to find it there. Not very long after that I went to Paris, to join Harold, who by that time knew the whole truth of the affair. I was terribly unhappy in Paris. When I came back to London, Violet began to declare that nothing would induce her to go through with the thing, and that I must save her from it by taking her away; in fact I believe she used Denys very largely as a lever to get me to do so. Living permanently with me had become an obsession in her mind. I don't absolutely remember the process in detail, but I know that I ended by consenting. After that we were both less unhappy: I could afford to see her ostensibly engaged to Denys when I knew that instead of marrying him she was coming away with me. I really intended to take her; we had every plan made. We were to go the day before her wedding—not sooner, because we thought we should be overtaken and brought back. It was of course only this looking-forward which enabled me to endure the period of her engagement.

Then about five days before her wedding I suddenly got by the same post three miserable letters from Harold, who had scented danger, because, in order to break it to him more or less gently (and also because I was in a dreadful state of mind myself during all that time), I had been writing him letters full of hints. When I read those letters something snapped in my mind. I saw Harold, all sweet and gentle and dependent upon me. Violet was there. She was terrified. I remember saying, "It's no good, I can't take you away." She implored me by everything she could think of, but I was obdurate. We went up to London together, Violet nearly off her head, and me repeating to myself phrases out of Harold's letters to give myself strength. I telegraphed to him to say I was coming to Paris; I had only one idea, to fly as quickly as I could and to put distance between me and temptation. I saw Violet twice more; once in my own house in London; she looked ill and changed; and once in the early morning at her mother's house, where I went to say goodbye to her on my way to the station. There was a dreary slut scrubbing the doorstep, for it was very early, and I stepped in over the soapy pail, and saw Violet in the morning-room. Then I went to Paris, alone. That is one of the worst days I remember. While I was in the train going to Folkestone I still felt I could change my mind and go back if I wanted to, for she had told me she would wait for me up to the very last minute, and would come straightaway if I appeared, or telephoned for her. At Folkestone I felt it becoming more irrevocable, and tried to get off the boat again, but they were moving the gangway and pushed me back. I had Harold's letters with me, and kept reading them until they almost lost all sense. The journey had never seemed so slow; it remains with me simply as a nightmare. I couldn't eat, and tears kept running down my face. Harold met me at the Gare du Nord. I said I wanted to go straight back, but he said, "No, no," and took me out to Versailles in a motor. The next day was Sunday, and he stayed with me all day. By then I had got such a reaction that I was feverishly cheerful, and he might have thought nothing was the matter. I gave him the book I was writing [*Challenge*], because I knew Violet would hate me to do that, as it was all about her. I was awake nearly all that night. Next day was Monday, 16th June [1919]; Harold had to go into Paris, and I sat quite dazed in my room holding my watch in my hand and watching the hands tick past the hour of Violet's wedding. All that time, I knew, she was expecting a prearranged message from me, which I never sent.

I was so stunned by all this at the time that I could not even think; it is only since then that I have realized how every minute has burnt itself into me.

On Tuesday night Violet and Denys came to Paris. On Wednesday I went to see her, at the Ritz. She was wearing clothes I had never seen before, but no wedding ring. I can't describe how terrible it all was—that meeting, and everything. It makes me physically ill to write about it and think about it, and my cheeks are burning. It was dreadful, dreadful. By then I had left Versailles, and was living alone in a small hotel. I took her there, I treated her savagely, I made love to her, I had her, I didn't care, I only wanted to hurt Denys, even though he didn't know of it. I make no excuse, except that I had suffered too much during the past week and was really scarcely responsible. The next day I saw Denys at an awful interview. Violet told him she had meant to run away with me instead of marrying him; she told him she didn't care for him. He got very white, and I thought he was going to faint. I restrained myself from saying much more. I wanted to say, "Don't you know, you stupid fool, that she is mine in every sense of the word?" but I was afraid that he would kill her if I did that. That night I dined at the Ritz, and from the open window of her room Violet watched me, and Denys sobbed in the room behind her. That day seems to have made a great impression upon him, as he constantly referred to it in his letters to her afterwards.

After that they went away to St. Jean de Luz, and I went to Switzerland with Harold, and then back to England alone. After three weeks Violet came back. Things were not quite so bad then. She had a house in Sussex, and Denys only came there for the weekends, and I spent all the rest of the week there. He and I never met, because in Paris he had said to me it must be war or peace. We met once, when he arrived earlier than was expected; I was just leaving, and Violet threw some things into a bag and came with me. I never saw anyone look so angry as he did. He was dead white and his lips were shaking. I tried to make Violet go back, because I thought it was really humiliating the man too much, but she wouldn't. On the whole, however, she was on friendly terms with him, and I am bound to say that he was friendly as an angel to her, and above all he kept the promises he had made, which I think few men would have done. I think on the whole that that was the period when Violet liked him best.

FLORIDA SCOTT-MAXWELL
(1883–1979)

Florida Scott-Maxwell, born in the state for which she was named, abandoned a career as an actress to marry and live with her husband in his native Scotland. She wrote plays and books, raised a family, and, at the age of fifty, undertook a new career as a Jungian analyst. For twenty-five years she maintained a practice in Britain. She wrote *The Measure of My Days* (1968), a combination journal and meditation on old age, when she was eighty-four.

For a series of journals following its author into old age, see May Sarton, *Journal of a Solitude, At Seventy, After the Stroke,* and *Endgame,* and see also Doris Grumbach, *Coming into the End Zone.* For another inner accounting, compare Anne Morrow Lindbergh, *Gift from the Sea.*

FROM *The Measure of My Days*

Another day to be filled, to be lived silently, watching the sky and the lights on the wall. No one will come probably. I have no duties except to myself. That is not true. I have a duty to all who care for me—not to be a problem, not to be a burden. I must carry my age lightly for all our sakes, and thank God I still can. Oh that I may to the end. Each day then, must be filled with my first duty, I must be "all right." But is this assurance not the gift we all give to each other daily, hourly?

I wonder if we need be quite so dutiful. With one friend of my own age we cheerfully exchange the worst symptoms, and our black dreads as well. We frequently talk of death, for we are very alert to the experience of the unknown that may be so near and it is only to those of one's own age that one can speak frankly. Talking of one's health, which one wants to do, is generally full of risks. Ill health is unpleasant to most healthy people as it makes them feel helpless, threatened, and it can feel like an unjustified demand for sympathy. Few believe in the pains of another, and if the person in pain has nothing to show, can forget the pain when interested, then where is the reality of it? In one's self, where it ought to be kept I suppose. Disabilities crowd in on the old; real pain is there, and if we have to be falsely cheerful, it is part of our isolation.

Another secret we carry is that though drab outside—wreckage to the eye, mirrors a mortification—inside we flame with a wild life that is almost incommunicable. In silent, hot rebellion we cry silently—"I have lived my life haven't I? What more is expected of me?" Have we got to pretend out of noblesse oblige that age is nothing, in order to encourage the others? This we do with a certain haughtiness, realising now that we have reached the place beyond resignation, a place I had no idea existed until I had arrived here.

It is a place of fierce energy. Perhaps passion would be a better word than energy, for the sad fact is this vivid life cannot be used. If I try to transpose it into action I am soon spent. It has to be accepted as passionate life, perhaps the life I never lived, never guessed I had it in me to live. It feels other and more than that. It feels like the far side of precept and aim. It is just life, the natural intensity of life, and when old we have it for our reward and undoing. It can—at moments—feel as though we had it for our glory. Some of it must go beyond good and bad, for at times—though this comes rarely, unexpectedly—it is a swelling clarity as though all was resolved. It has no content, it seems to expand us, it does not derive from the body, and then it is gone. It may be a degree of consciousness which lies outside activity, and which when young we are too busy to experience.

I wonder if living alone makes one more alive. No precious energy goes in disagreement or compromise. No need to augment others, there is just yourself, just truth—a morsel—and you. You went through those long years when it was pain to be alone, now you have come out on the good side of that severe discipline. Alone you have your own way all day long, and you become very natural. Perhaps this naturalness extends into heights and depths, going further than we know; as we cannot voice it we must just treasure it as the life that enriches our days.

.   .   .

We old people are short tempered because we suffer so. We are stretched too far, our gamut is painfully wide. Little things have become big; nothing in us works well, our bodies have become unreliable. We have to make an effort to do the simplest things. We urge now this, now that part of our flagging bodies, and when we have spurred them to further functioning we feel clever and carefree. We stretch from such concerns as these into eternity where we keep one eye on death, certain of continuity, then uncertain, then indifferent.

We cannot read the papers with the response of those younger. We watch the playing for place in great issues, we hear war rumble, and we who have lived long still feel the wounds of two wars endured. We remember the cost; the difference in mood at the beginning of a war and at the end of a war. The initial pride that forbids man to accept an affront and later, when the immeasurable has been accepted by all, the dumb sense of wrong done by all to all. So the old are past comment and almost past reaction, still knowing pity, but outside hope; also knowing—Oh here is the thing we cannot face again—that when man is set on a goal, destruction is nothing to him.

When a new disability arrives I look about to see if death has come, and I call quietly, "Death, is that you? Are you there?" So far the disability has answered, "Don't be silly, it's me."

. . .

I admire a contented mind. I revere enjoyment of simple things. I can imagine that contentment has a high degree of truth. But the human tendency is to take good as normal, and one's natural right, and so no cause for satisfaction or pleasure. This is accompanied by the habit of regarding bad as abnormal and a personal outrage.

The woman who has a gift for old age is the woman who delights in comfort. If warmth is known as the blessing it is, if your bed, your bath, your best-liked food and drink are regarded as fresh delights, then you know how to thrive when old. If you get the things you like on the simplest possible terms, serve yourself lightly, efficiently and calmly, all is almost well. If you are truly calm you stand a chance of surviving much, but calmness is intermittent with me. Sensuous pleasure seems necessary to old age as intellectual pleasure palls a little. At times music justifies living, but mere volume of sound can overwhelm, and I find silence exquisite. I have spent my whole life reading, only to find that most of it is lost, so books no longer have their former command. I live by rectitude or reverence, or courtesy, by being ready in case life calls, all lightly peppered with despair. This makes me rest on comfort. I could use the beauty and dignity of a cat but, denied that, I try for her quiet.

. . .

I don't like to write this down, yet it is much in the minds of the old. We wonder how much older we have to become, and what degree of decay we may have to endure. We keep whispering to ourselves, "Is this age yet? How far must I go?." For age can be dreaded more than death. "How many years of vacuity? To what degree of deterioration must I advance?" Some want death now, as release from old age, some say they will accept death willingly, but in a few years. I feel the solemnity of death, and the possibility of some form of continuity. Death feels a friend because it will release us from the deterioration of which we cannot see the end. It is waiting for death that wears us down, and the distaste for what we may become.

These thoughts are with us always, and in our hearts we know ignominy as well as dignity. We are people to whom something important is about to happen. But before then, these endless years before the end, can we summon enough merit to warrant a place for ourselves? We go into the future not knowing the answer to our question.

But we also find that as we age we are more alive than seems likely, convenient, or even bearable. Too often our problem is the fervour of life within us. My dear fellow octogenarians, how are we to carry so much life, and what are we to do with it?

Let no one say it is "unlived life" with any of the simpler psychological certitudes. No one lives all the life of which he was capable. The unlived life in each of us must be the future of humanity. When truly old, too frail to use the vigour that pulses in us, and weary, sometimes even scornful of what can seem the pointless activity of mankind, we may sink down to some deeper level and find a new supply of life that amazes us.

All is uncharted and uncertain, we seem to lead the way into the unknown. It can feel as though all our lives we have been caught in absurdly small personalities and circumstances and beliefs. Our accustomed shell cracks here, cracks there, and that tiresomely rigid person we supposed to be ourselves stretches, expands, and with all inhibitions gone we realize that age is not failure, nor disgrace; though mortifying we did not invent it. Age forces us to deal with idleness, emptiness, not being needed, not able to do, helplessness just ahead perhaps. All this is true, but one has had one's life, one could be full to the brim. Yet it is the end of our procession through time, and our steps are uncertain.

KATE SIMON
(1912–1990)

Born in Poland, Kaila Grobsmith emigrated to the United States with her family in 1917. Her childhood in an immigrant neighborhood where Jewish and Italian families lived side by side is depicted in *Bronx Primitive: Portraits in a Childhood* (1982), her later years in two succeeding volumes of memoirs, *A Wider World* (1986) and *Etchings in an Hourglass* (1990). Known primarily as a travel writer, Simon published her first book, *New York Places and Pleasures*, in 1959. This was followed by books about Italy, Mexico, Paris, and London and works of social history like *Fifth Avenue* and *A Renaissance Tapestry: The Gonzaga of Mantua*. The sophisticated mixture of personal observation and historical information which she developed in her travel books also informs her memoirs. This selection portrays romance, as she learned to expect it from the movies and as she was able to perceive it in her Bronx tenement.

For other accounts of parental love as viewed by children, compare Jill Ker Conway, *The Road from Coorain* and Audre Lorde, *Zami*. For the memoir of a Jewish immigrant on the Lower East Side swept off to Hollywood in the 1920s, see Anzia Yezierska, *Red Ribbon on a White Horse*.

FROM *Bronx Primitive*

THE MOVIES AND OTHER SCHOOLS

Life on Lafontaine offered several schools. School-school, P.S. 59, was sometimes nice, as when I was chosen to be Prosperity in the class play, blond, plump, dressed in a white pillow case banded with yellow and green crepe paper, for the colors of grasses and grain, and waving something like a sheaf of wheat. The cringing days were usually Fridays, when arithmetic flash cards, too fast, too many, blinded me and I couldn't add or subtract the simplest numbers. (For many years, into adulthood, I carried around a sack of churning entrails on Friday mornings.) The library, which made me my own absolutely special and private person with a card that belonged to no one but me, offered hundreds of books,

all mine and no tests on them, a brighter, more generous school than
P.S. 59. The brightest, most informative school was the movies. We
learned how tennis was played and golf, what a swimming pool was and
what to wear if you ever got to drive a car. We learned how tables were
set, "How do you do? Pleased to meet you," how primped and starched
little girls should be, how neat and straight boys should be, even when
they were temporarily ragamuffins. We learned to look up soulfully and
make our lips tremble to warn our mothers of a flood of tears, and though
they didn't fall for it (they laughed), we kept practicing. We learned how
regal mothers were and how stately fathers, and of course we learned
about Love, a very foreign country like maybe China or Connecticut. It
was smooth and slinky, it shone and rustled. It was petals with Lillian
Gish, gay flags with Marion Davies, tiger stripes with Rudolph Valen-
tino, dog's eyes with Charlie Ray. From what I could see, and I searched,
there was no Love on the block, nor even its fairy-tale end, Marriage.
We had only Being Married, and that included the kids, a big crowded
barrel with a family name stamped on it. Of course, there was Being
Married in the movies, but except for the terrible cruel people in rags
and scowls, it was as silky as Love. Fathers kissed their wives and children
when they came home from work and spoke to them quietly and nobly,
like kings, and never shouted or hit if the kids came in late or dirty.
Mothers in crisp dresses stroked their children's heads tenderly as they
presented them with the big ringletted doll and the football Grandma
had sent, adding, "Run off and play, darlings." "Darling," "dear," were
movie words, and we had few grandmothers, most of them dead or in
shadowy conversation pieces reported from At Home, the Old Country.
And "Run off and play" was so superbly refined, silken gauze to the
rough wool of our hard-working mothers whose rules were to feed their
children, see that they were warmly dressed in the wintertime, and run
to the druggist on Third Avenue for advice when they were sick. Beyond
that it was mostly "Get out of my way." Not all the mothers were so
impatient. Miltie's mother helped him with his arithmetic homework;
my mother often found us amusing and laughed with and at us a lot.
From other apartments, on rainy afternoons: Joey—"What'll I do,
Maaa?" His Mother—*"Va te ne! Gherradi!"* (the Italian version of
"Get out of here"); Lily—"What'll I do, Maaa?" Mrs. Stavicz—
"Scratch your ass on a broken bottle." I sometimes wished my mother
would say colorful, tough things like that but I wasn't sure I wouldn't
break into tears if she did, which would make her call me a *"pianovi
chasto"* (as I remember the Polish phrase), a delicate meringue cake that
falls apart easily, which would make me cry more, which would make her
more lightly contemptuous, and so on. Despite my occasional wish to see
her as one of the big-mouth, storming women, I was willing to settle for

her more modest distinction, a lady who won notebooks in her English class at the library and sang many tunes from "Polish operettas" that, with later enlightenment, I realized were *The Student Prince* and *The Merry Widow*.

Being Married had as an important ingredient a nervous father. There must have been other kitchens, not only ours, in which at about seven o'clock, the fathers' coming-home time, children were warned, "Now remember, Papa is coming home soon. He's nervous from working in the factory all day and riding in the crowded El. Sit quiet at the table, don't laugh, don't talk." It was hard not to giggle at the table, when my brother and I, who played with keen concentration a game of mortal enemies at other times, became close conspirators at annoying Them by making faces at each other. The muffled giggles were stopped by a shout of "Respect!" and a long black look, fork poised like a sword in midair while no one breathed. After the silent meal, came the part we disliked most, the after-dinner lecture. There were two. The first was The Hard Life of the Jewish worker, the Jewish father, the deepest funereal sounds unstopped for the cost of electricity (a new and lovely toy but not as pretty as throbbing little mazda lamps) for which he had to pay an immense sum each time we switched it on and off, like the wastrels we were. Did we think butter cost a penny a pound that we slathered it on bread as if it were Coney Island mud pies? Those good expensive shoes he bought us (he was an expert shoe worker, a maker of samples, and tortured us with embarrassment when he displayed his expertise to the salesman, so don't try to fool him), which were old and scuffed and dirty within a week, did we know how much bloody sweat was paid for them? The second lecture was the clever one whose proud, sententious repetitions I listened to with shame for him, wanting to put my head down not to see my handsome father turn into a vaudeville comic whose old monologues strained and fell. This lecture was usually inspired by my brother who, in spite of the "nervous" call, dashed at my father as soon as he heard the key in the lock with "Hello, Pa. Gimme a penny?" That led it off: "You say you want a penny, *only* a penny. I've got dimes and quarters and half-dollars in my pockets, you say, so what's a penny to me? Well, let's see if you went to the El station and gave the man four cents, he wouldn't let you on the train, you'd need another penny. If Mama gave you two cents for a three-cent ice cream cone, would Mrs. Katz in the candy store give it to you? If Mama had only forty-eight cents for a forty-nine-cent chicken, would the butcher give it to her?" And on and on, a carefully rehearsed long slow aria, with dramatic runs of words and significant questioning pauses. Once or twice I heard my mother mutter as she went out of the room, "That Victrola record again," but her usual policy was to say nothing. She was not afraid of my father, nor particularly in awe of him. (I heard him say frequently how fresh she was, but with a smile, not the way he said it to us.)

In none of my assiduous eavesdropping on the street did I ever hear any mention of unhappy marriage or happy marriage. Married was married. Although a Jewish divorce was a singularly easy matter except for the disgrace it carried, the Jewish women were as firmly imbedded in their marriages as the Catholic. A divorce was as unthinkable as adultery or lipstick. No matter what—beatings, infidelity, drunkenness, verbal abuse, outlandish demands—no woman could run the risk of making her children fatherless. Marriage and children were fate, like being skinny, like skeletal Mr. Roberts, or humpbacked, like the leering watchman at the hat factory. *"Es is mir beschert,"* "It is my fate," was a common sighing phrase, the Amen that closed hymns of woe.

My mother didn't accept her fate as a forever thing. She began to work during our school hours after her English classes had taught her as much as they could, and while I was still young, certainly no more than ten, I began to get her lecture on being a woman. It ended with extraordinary statements, shocking in view of the street mores. "Study. Learn. Go to college. Be a schoolteacher," then a respected, privileged breed, "and don't get married until you have a profession. With a profession you can have men friends and even children, if you want. You're free. But don't get married, at least not until you can support yourself and make a careful choice. Or don't get married at all, better still." This never got into "My mother said" conversations with my friends. I sensed it to be too outrageous. My mother was already tagged "The Princess" because she never went into the street unless fully, carefully dressed: no grease-stained housedress, no bent, melted felt slippers. Rarely, except when she was pregnant with my little sister, did she stop for conversations on the street. She was one of the few in the building who had gone to classes, the only mother who went out alone at night to join her mandolin group. She was sufficiently marked, and though I was proud of her difference, I didn't want to report her as altogether eccentric. In the community fabric, as heavy as the soups we ate and the dark, coarse "soldier's bread" we chomped on, as thick as the cotton on which we practiced our cross-stitch embroidery, was the conviction that girls were to marry as early as possible, the earlier the more triumphant. (Long after we moved from the area, my mother, on a visit to Lafontaine to see appealing, inept little Fannie Herman who had for many years been her charge and mine, met Mrs. Roth, who asked about me. When my mother said I was going to Hunter College, Mrs. Roth, looking both pleased and sympathetic, said, *"My* Helen married a man who makes a nice living, a laundry man. Don't worry, your Katie will find a husband soon." She knew that some of the boys of the block wound up in City

College, but a girl in college? From a pretty, polite child, I must have turned into an ugly, bad-tempered shrew whom no one would have. Why else would my marrying years be spent in college?)

I never saw my mother and father kiss or stroke each other as people did in the movies. In company she addressed him, as did most of the Jewish women, by our family name, a mark of respectful distance. They inhabited two separate worlds, he adventuring among anti-Semites to reach a shadowy dungeon called "Factory," where he labored ceaselessly. In the evening he returned to her world for food, bed, children, and fighting. We were accustomed to fighting: the boys and, once in a while, fiery little girls tearing at each other in the street; bigger Italian boys punching and being punched by the Irish gangs that wandered in from Arthur Avenue; females fighting over clotheslines—whose sheets were blocking whose right to the sun—bounced around the courtyard constantly. The Genoese in the houses near 178th Street never spoke to the Sicilians near 179th Street except to complain that somebody's barbaric little southern slob had peed against a northern tree. To my entranced ears and eyes, the Sicilians seemed always to win, hotter, louder, faster with *"Fangu"*—the southern version of *"Fa' in culo"* (up yours)—than the aristocrats who retired before the Sicilians could hit them with *"Mortacci"*—the utterly insupportable insult. My brother and I fought over who grabbed the biggest apple, who hid the skate key, and where he put my baby picture, I lying on a white rug with my bare ass showing, a picture he threatened to pass among his friends and humiliate me beyond recovery. I would have to kill him.

These sorts of fighting were almost literally the spice of daily life, deliciously, lightly menacing, grotesque and entertaining. The fighting between my mother and father was something else entirely, at times so threatening that I still, decades later, cringe in paralyzed stupidity, as if I were being pelted with stones, when I hear a man shouting. The fights often concerned our conduct and my mother's permissiveness. My father had a rich vocabulary which he shaped into theatrical phrases spoken in a voice as black and dangerous as an open sewer. The opening shot was against my brother, who was six or seven when the attacks began. He was becoming a wilderness boy, no sense, no controls, dirty, disobedient, he did badly in school (not true: with a minimum of attention he managed mediocrity). There was no doubt that he would become a bum, then a thief, wind up alone in a prison cell full of rats, given one piece of bread a day and one cup of dirty water. He would come out a gangster and wind up in the electric chair.

When it was my turn, I was disobedient and careless; I didn't do my homework when I should, I didn't practice enough, my head was always in a book, I was always in the street running wild with the Italian and

Polish beasts. I didn't take proper care of my brother, I climbed with boys, I ran with boys, I skated with them on far streets. Mr. Kaplan had seen me and told him. And how would this life, this playing with boys, end? I would surely become a street girl, a prostitute, and wind up being shipped to a filthy, diseased brothel crawling with hairy tropical bugs, in Buenos Aires. My mother's response was sharp and short: we acted like other children and played like other children; it was he who was at fault, asking more of us than he should. And enough about prisons and electric chairs and brothels. He went on shouting, entranced by his gorgeous words and visions, until she left the room to wash the dishes or scrub the kitchen floor. We, of course, had heard everything from our bedroom; the oratory was as much for us as for our mother. When the big rats in the windowless cell came to our ears, my brother began to shake with terror beyond crying. I tried to comfort him, as accustomed a role as trying to maim him. I didn't know what a street girl was, and I certainly didn't know what a brothel was, but I wasn't afraid—I was too angry. If our father hated us so, why didn't he go away? I didn't examine consequences, who would feed us and pay the rent. I just wanted him out, out, dead.

Other fights were about money, and that, too, involved us. How dare she, without consulting him, change from a fifty-cent-a-lesson piano teacher to another—and who knows how good *he* was?—who charged a dollar? What about the embroidered tablecloth and the stone bowl with the pigeons that she bought from the Arab peddler, that crook. Did she realize how hard he had to work to pay for our school supplies each fall? And add to that the nickel for candy to eat at the movies every Saturday, and the ten cents each for the movie and the three cents for ice-cream cones on Friday nights. And God only knew how much money she slipped us for the sweet garbage we chewed on, which would certainly rot our teeth, and where would he get the money for dentists? Maybe she thought she was still in her shop in Warsaw, dancing and singing and spilling money like a fool. And on and on it went. These tirades, too, were answered very briefly. Our lives were meager enough. Did he ever think of buying us even the cheapest toy, like the other fathers did, instead of stashing every spare penny in the bank and taking it out only for his relatives? The ignorant Italians he so despised, they had celebrations for their children. Where were our birthday presents?

Long silences followed these fights and we became messengers. "Tell your mother to take my shoes to the shoemaker." "Aw, Pa, I'm doing my homework. Later." "Tell your mother I have no clean shirts." "Aw, Pa, I'm just sitting down to practice. I'll tell her later." We used the operative words "homework" and "practice" mercilessly while he seethed at our delays. My mother heard all these instructions but it was her role neither to notice nor to obey. Those were great days and we exploited our roles fattily, with enormous vengeful pleasure.

One constant set of squabbles that didn't circle around us concerned her relaxed, almost loose judgments of other people. She showed no sympathy when he complained about the nigger sweeper in the factory who talked back to him, when he complained about the Italian who reeked of garlic and almost suffocated him in the train. Most loudly he complained about her availability, spoiling his sleep, letting his supper get cold, neglecting her own children, to run to any Italian idiot who didn't know to take care of her own baby. Let them take care of their own convulsions or get some Wop neighbor to help. It was disgraceful that she sat on Mrs. Santini's porch in open daylight trying to teach her not to feed her infant from her own mouth. If the fat fool wanted to give it germs, let her. If it died, she'd, next year, have another; they bred like rabbits. Why didn't my mother mind her own business, what the hell did these people, these foreign ignoramuses, mean to her? The answer was short and always the same, *"Es is doch a mench,"* yet these are human beings, the only religious training we ever had, perhaps quite enough.

There were fights with no messengers, no messages, whispered fights when the door to our bedroom was shut tight and we heard nothing but hissing. The slow unfolding of time and sophistications indicated that these were fights about women, women my father saw some of those evenings when he said he was going to a Workmen's Circle meeting. There was no more "Tell your mother," "Tell your father," and except for the crying of our baby, no more evening sounds. No Caruso, no Rosa Ponselle, no mandolin practice, no lectures. My father busied himself with extra piecework, "skiving" it was called, cutting with breathtaking delicacy leaf and daisy designs into the surface of the sample shoes to be shown to buyers. She, during one such period, crocheted a beaded bag, tiny beads, tiny stitches. We watched, struck dumb by their skill, and because it was no time to open our mouths about anything, anything at all. The silence was dreadful, a creeping, dark thing, a night alley before the murderer appears. The furniture was waiting to be destroyed, the windows to be broken, by a terrible storm. We would all be swept away, my brother and I to a jungle where wild animals would eat us, my parents and the baby, separated, to starve and burn alone in a desert. School now offered the comforts of a church, the street its comforting familiarities, unchanging, predictable. We stayed out as long as we could, dashing up for a speedy supper, and down again. On rainy nights we read a lot, we went to bed early, anything to remove us from our private-faced parents, who made us feel unbearably shy.

One spring evening, invited to jump Double Dutch with a few experts, uncertain that I could leap between two ropes whipping in rapid alternation at precisely the exact moment, and continue to stay between them in small fast hops from side to side, I admitted a need, urgent for some time, to go to the toilet. I ran up the stairs to find our door locked, an extraordinary thing. Maybe they had run away. Maybe they had killed each other. Sick with panic, I kept trying the door, it wouldn't give. Then I heard the baby making squirmy, sucking baby noises. No matter what, my mother would never leave the baby, and anyway, maybe they were doing their whispering fighting again. Still uneasy, I knocked on the Hermans' door and asked to use their toilet. When I came out, I asked Fannie Herman if she knew whether my parents were at home. Yes, she said. Her door was wide open and she would have seen or heard them come out, but they hadn't. The Double Dutch on the street was finished when I got down so I joined the race, boys and girls, around the block, running hard, loving my pumping legs and my swinging arms and my open mouth swallowing the breeze. When most of the kids had gone home and it was time for us, too, I couldn't find my brother, who was hiding from me to destroy my power and maybe get me into trouble. I went up alone. The door had been unlocked, and as I walked uneasily through the long hallway of our railroad flat with wary steps, I heard sounds from the kitchen. My mother was sitting on a kitchen chair, her feet in a basin of water. My father was kneeling before her on spread newspaper. Her plump foot rested in his big hand while he cut her toenails, flashing his sharp work knife, dexterous, light, and swift. She was splashing him a little, playing the water with her free foot. They were making jokes, lilting, laughing. Something, another branch in the twisted tree that shaded our lives, was going to keep us safe for a while.

CAROLYN KAY STEEDMAN
(1947–)

Steedman is a British historian of working-class background who tells the story of her mother's life and her own childhood with the purpose of disproving some widespread assumptions about working-class life. For example, Marxist theory allows class consciousness to workers and their families but not much psychological complexity. Steedman's *Landscape for a Good Woman: A Story of Two Lives* (1986) shows that her family was not so focused on survival or class struggle that there wasn't also time for yearning, ambivalence, and guilt. Moreover, envy was a key motivation for her glamour-starved mother, something Steedman never sees discussed in the scholarly literature on the working class. There's an urgency about Steedman's narrative which comes from its being a critique of theories—Marxist, feminist, and psychoanalytic—which she thinks have bypassed or betrayed her particular experience.

For another story of mother and daughter, compare Vivian Gornick's *Fierce Attachments*. For another example of the fine line between personal narrative and scholarship, see Zora Neale Hurston, *Mules and Men*.

FROM *Landscape for a Good Woman*

THE WEAVER'S DAUGHTER

The War was so palpable a presence in the first five years of my life that I still find it hard to believe that I didn't live through it. There were bomb-sites everywhere, prefabs on waste land, most things still on points, my mother tearing up the ration book when meat came off points, over my sister's pram, outside the library in the High Street in the summer of 1951, a gesture that still fills me with the desire to do something so defiant and final; and then looking across the street at a woman wearing a full-skirted dress, and then down at the forties straight-skirted navy blue suit she was still wearing, and longing, irritatedly, for the New Look; and then at us, the two living barriers to twenty yards of cloth. Back home, she said she'd be able to get it at the side door of the mill; but not here; not with you two.

•   •   •

From a cotton town, my mother had a heightened awareness of fabric and weave, and I can date events by the clothes I wore as a child, and the material they were made of. Post-War children had few clothes, because of rationing, but not only scarcity, rather names like barathea, worsted, gaberdine, twill, jersey, lawn . . . fix them in my mind. . . .

Sometime during 1950, I think before the summer, . . . I was taken north to Burnley and into the sheds, where one afternoon my mother visited someone she used to know as a child, now working there. The woman smiled and nodded at me, through the noise that made a surrounding silence. Afterwards, my mother told me that they had to lip-read: they couldn't hear each other speak for the noise of the looms. But I didn't notice the noise. The woman wore high platform-soled black shoes that I still believe I heard click on the bright polished floor as she walked between her looms. Whenever I hear the word "tending" I always think of that confident attentiveness to the needs of the machines, the control over work that was unceasing, with half a mind and hands engaged, but the looms always demanding attention. When I worked as a primary-school teacher I sometimes retrieved that feeling with a particular clarity, walking between the tables on the hard floor, all the little looms working, but needing my constant adjustment.

The woman wore a dress that seemed very short when I recalled the picture through the next few years: broad shoulders, a straight skirt patterned with black and red flowers that hung the way it did—I know now—because it had some rayon in it. The post-War years were full of women longing for a full skirt and unable to make it. I wanted to walk like that, a short skirt, high heels, bright red lipstick, in charge of all that machinery. . . .

As a teenage worker my mother had broken with a recently established tradition and on leaving school in 1927 didn't go into the sheds. She lied to me though when, at about the age of eight, I asked her what she'd done, and she said she'd worked in an office, done clerical work. Ten years later, on my third and last visit to Burnley and practising the accomplishments of the oral historian, I talked to my grandmother and she, puzzled, told me that Edna had never worked in any office, had in fact been apprenticed to a dry-cleaning firm that did tailoring and mending. On that same visit, the first since I was four, I found a reference written by the local doctor for my mother who, about 1930, applied for a job as a ward-maid at the local asylum, confirming that she was clean, strong, honest and intelligent. I wept over that, of course, for a world where some people might doubt her—my—cleanliness. I didn't care much about the honesty, and I knew I was strong; but there are people everywhere waiting for you to slip up, to show signs of dirtiness and stupidity, so that they can send you back where you belong.

She didn't finish her apprenticeship—I deduce that, rather than know it—sometime, it must have been 1934, came South, worked in Woolworth's on the Edgware Road, spent the War years in Roehampton, a ward-maid again, in the hospital where they mended fighter pilots' ruined faces. Now I can feel the deliberate vagueness in her accounts of those years: "When did you meet daddy?"—"Oh, at a dance, at home." There were no photographs. Who came to London first? I wish now that I'd asked that question. He worked on the buses when he arrived, showed me a canopy in front of a hotel once, that he'd pulled down on his first solo drive. He was too old to be called up (a lost generation of men who were too young for the first War, too old for the second). There's a photograph of him standing in front of the cabbages he'd grown for victory, wearing his Home Guard uniform. But what did he *do* after his time on the buses, and during the War years? Too late now to find out.

During the post-War housing shortage my father got an office job with a property company, and the flat to go with it. I was born in March 1947, at the peak of the Bulge, more babies born that month than ever before or after, and carried through the terrible winter of 1946–7. We moved to Streatham Hill in June 1951, to an estate owned by the same company (later to be taken over by Lambeth Council), and a few years after the move my father got what he wanted, which was to be in charge of the company's boiler maintenance. On his death certificate it says "heating engineer."

In the 1950s my mother took in lodgers. Streatham Hill Theatre (now a bingo hall) was on the pre-West End circuit, and we had chorus girls staying with us for weeks at a time. I was woken up in the night sometimes, the spare bed in my room being made up for someone they'd met down the Club, the other lodger's room already occupied. I like the idea of being the daughter of a theatrical landlady, but that enterprise, in fact, provides me with my most startling and problematic memories. The girl from Aberdeen really did say "Och, no, not on the table!" as my father flattened a bluebottle with his hand, but did he *really* put down a newspaper at the same table to eat his breakfast? I remember it happening, but it's so much like the books that I feel a fraud, a bit-part player in a soft and southern version of *The Road to Wigan Pier.* *

I remember incidents like these, I think, because I was about seven, the age at which children start to notice social detail and social distinc-

*George Orwell's account of working-class life in the north of England—Ed.

tion, but also more particularly because the long lesson in hatred for my father had begun, and the early stages were in the traditional mode, to be found in the opening chapters of *Sons and Lovers* and Lawrence's description of the inculcated dislike of Mr. Morrell, of female loathing for coarse male habits. The newspaper on the table is problematic for me because it was problematic for my mother, a symbol of all she'd hoped to escape and all she'd landed herself in. (It was at this time, I think, that she told me that her own mother, means-tested in the late 1920s, had won the sympathy of the Relieving Officer, who ignored the presence of the saleable piano because she kept a clean house, with a cloth on the table.)

Now, thirty years later, I feel a great regret for the father of my first four years, who took me out and who probably loved me, irresponsibly ("It's alright for him; he doesn't have to look after you"), and I wish I could tell him now, even though he really was a sod, that I'm sorry for the years of rejection and dislike. But we were forced to choose, early on, which side we belonged to, and children have to come down on the side that brings the food home and gets it on the table. By 1955 I was beginning to hate him—because *he* was to blame, for the lack of money, for my mother's terrible dissatisfaction at the way things were working out.

Changes in the market place, the growth of real income and the proliferation of consumer goods that marked the mid-1950s, were used by my mother to measure out her discontent: there existed a newly expanding and richly endowed material world in which she was denied a place. The new consumer goods came into the house slowly, and we were taught to understand that our material deprivations were due entirely to my father's meanness. We had the first fridge in our section of the street (which he'd got cheap, off the back of a lorry, contacts in the trade) but were very late to acquire a television. I liked the new vacuum cleaner at first, because it meant no longer having to do the stairs with a stiff brush. But in fact it added to my Saturday work because I was expected to clean more with the new machine. Now I enjoy shocking people by telling them how goods were introduced into households under the guise of gifts for children: the fridge in the house of the children we played with over the road was given to the youngest as a birthday present—the last thing an eight-year-old wants. My mother laughed at this, scornfully: the clothes and shoes she gave us as birthday presents were conventional gifts for all post-War children, but the record player also came into the house in this way, as my eleventh birthday present. I wasn't allowed to take it with me when I left, though: it really wasn't mine at all.

What happened at school was my own business, no questions ever asked, no encouragement nor discouragement ever given. It became just the thing I did, like my mother's going out to work. Later, the material conditions for educational success were provided: a table in my room, a pattern of domestic work that allowed homework to be done. From the earliest time I was expected to be competent: to iron a blouse, scrub a floor, learn to read, pass an exam; and I was. (There was, though, as my sister was to discover later, all hell to pay if you failed.) Indifference to what happened at school was useful: learning is the one untouched area of my life. So in reconstructing the pattern of this neglect, I am surprised to find myself walking up the hill with my mother from school one afternoon. She was smiling a pleased smile, and working things out, I think it must have been 1956, the day she was told that I'd be going into the eleven-plus class and so (because everyone in the class passed the exam) would be going to grammar school. I remember the afternoon because I asked her what class we were; or rather, I asked her if we were middle class, and she was evasive. I answered my own question, said I thought we must be middle class, and reflected very precisely in that moment on my mother's black, waisted coat with the astrakhan collar, and her high-heeled black suede shoes, her lipstick. She looked so much better than the fat, spreading, South London mothers around us, that I thought we had to be middle class.

The coat and the lipstick came from her own work. "If you want something, you have to go out and work for it. Nobody gives you anything; nothing comes free in this world." About 1956 or 1957 she got an evening job in one of the espresso bars opening along the High Road, making sandwiches and frying eggs. She saved up enough money to take a manicuring course and in 1958 got her diploma, thus achieving a certified skill for the first time in her forty-five years. When I registered her death I was surprised to find myself giving "manicurist" as her trade, for the possibility of a trade was something she seemed to have left behind in the North. She always worked in good places, in the West End; the hands she did were in *Vogue* once. She came home with stories and imitations of her "ladies." She told me how she "flung" a sixpenny piece back at a titled woman who'd given it her as a tip: "If you can't afford any more than that Madam, I suggest you keep it." Wonderful!— like tearing up the ration books.

She knew where we stood in relation to this world of privilege and possession, had shown me the place long before, in the bare front bedroom where the health visitor spoke haughtily to her. . . . What we learned now, in the early 1960s, through the magazines and anecdotes she brought home, was how the goods of that world of privilege might be appropriated, with the cut and fall of a skirt, a good winter coat, with leather shoes, a certain voice; but above all with clothes, the best boundary between you and a cold world.

It was at this time that her voice changed, and her Lancashire accent began to disappear. Earlier, years before, she'd entertained us in the kitchen by talking really broad, not her natural dialect but a stagey variety that always preceded a rapid shift to music-hall cockney for a rendering of "She Was Only a Bird in a Gilded Cage":

> It's the same the whole world over
> Ain't it a bleeding shame
> It's the rich what gets the pleasure,
> It's the poor what gets the blame.

We weren't, I now realize by doing the sums, badly off. My father paid the rent, all the bills, gave us our pocket money, and a fixed sum of seven pounds a week housekeeping money, quite a lot in the late 1950s, went on being handed over every Friday until his death, even when estrangement was obvious, and he was living most of the time with somebody else. My mother must have made quite big money in tips, for the records of her savings, no longer a secret, show quite fabulous sums being stored away in the early 1960s. When she died there was over £40,000 in building-society accounts. Poverty hovered as a belief. It existed in stories of the thirties, in a family history. Even now when a bank statement comes in that shows I'm overdrawn or when the gas bill for the central heating seems enormous, my mind turns to quite inappropriate strategies, like boiling down the ends of soap, and lighting fires with candle ends and spills of screwed up newspaper to save buying wood. I think about these things because they were domestic economies that we practised in the 1950s. We believed we were badly off because we children were expensive items, and all these arrangements had been made for us. "If it wasn't for you two," my mother told us, "I could be off somewhere else." After going out manicuring she started spending Sunday afternoons in bed, and we couldn't stay in the house or play on the doorstep for fear of disturbing her. The house was full of her terrible tiredness and her terrible resentment; and I knew it was all my fault.

Later, in 1977, after my father's death, we found out that they were never married, that we were illegitimate. In 1934 my father left his wife and two-year-old daughter in the North, and came to London. He and my mother had been together for at least ten years when I was born, and we think now that I was her hostage to fortune, the factor that might persuade him to get a divorce and marry her. But the ploy failed.

·   ·   ·

In 1954 the *Pirates of Penzance* was playing at the Streatham Hill Theatre, and we had one of the baritones as a lodger instead of the usual girls. He was different from them, didn't eat in the kitchen with us, but had my mother bake him potatoes and grate carrots which he ate in the isolation of the dining-room. He converted my mother to Food Reform, and when she made a salad of grated vegetables for Christmas dinner in 1955, my father walked out and I wished he'd taken us with him.

I've talked to other people whose mothers came to naturopathy in the 1950s, and it's been explained as a way of eating posh for those who didn't know about continental food. I think it did have a lot to do with the status that being different conferred, for in spite of the austerity of our childhood, we believed that we were better than other people, the food we ate being a mark of this, because our mother told us so—so successfully that even now I have to work hard at actually seeing the deprivations. But much more than difference, our diet had to do with the need, wrenched from restricted circumstances, to be in charge of the body. Food Reform promised an end to sickness if certain procedures were followed, a promise that was not, of course, fulfilled. I spent a childhood afraid to fall ill, because being ill would mean that my mother would have to stay off work and lose money.

But more fundamental than this, I think, a precise costing of our childhood lay behind our eating habits. Brussel sprouts, baked potatoes, grated cheese, the variation of vegetables in the summer, a tin of vegetarian steak pudding on Sundays and a piece of fruit afterwards is a monotonous but healthy diet, and I can't think of many cheaper ways to feed two children and feel you're doing your best for them at the same time. We can't ever have cost very much. She looked at us sometimes, after we'd finished eating. "Good, Kay, eh?" What I see on her face now is a kind of muted satisfaction; she'd done her best, though her best was limited: not her fault. Children she'd grown up with had died in the 1930s: "They hadn't enough to eat."

She brought the food home at night, buying each day's supply when she got off the bus from work. My sister's job was to meet her at the bus-stop with the wheel basket so she didn't have to carry the food up the road. We ate a day's supply at a time, so there was never much in the house overnight except bread for breakfast and the staples that were bought on Saturday. When I started to think about these things I was in a position to interpret this way of living and eating as a variation of the spending patterns of poverty described in Booth's and Rowntree's great surveys at the turn of the century; but now I am sure that it was the cheapness of it that propelled the practice. We were a finely balanced investment, threatening constantly to topple over into the realm of demand and expenditure. I don't think, though, that until we left home we ever cost more to feed and clothe than that seven pounds handed over each week.

Now I see the pattern of our nourishment laid down, like our usefulness, by an old set of rules. At six I was old enough to go on errands, at seven to go further to pay the rent and the rates, go on the long dreary walk to the Co-op for the divi. By eight I was old enough to clean the house and do the weekend shopping. At eleven it was understood that I washed the breakfast things, lit the fire in the winter and scrubbed the kitchen floor before I started my homework. At fifteen, when I could legally go out to work, I got a Saturday job which paid for my clothes (except my school uniform, which was part of the deal, somehow). I think that until I drop I will clean wherever I happen to be on Saturday morning. I take a furtive and secret pride in the fact that I can do all these things, that I am physically strong, can lift and carry things that defeat other women, wonder with some scorn what it must be like to learn to clean a house when adult, and not to have the ability laid down as part of the growing self. Like going to sleep by contrasting a bed with a pavement, I sometimes find myself thinking that if the worst comes to the worst, I can always earn a living by my hands; I can scrub, clean, cook and sew: all you have in the end is your labour.

I was a better deal than my sister, because I passed the eleven plus, went to grammar school, would get a good job, marry a man who would in her words "buy me a house and you a house. There's no virtue in poverty." In the mid-1960s the Sunday colour supplements were full of pictures of student life, and she came to see a university as offering the same arena of advantage as the good job had earlier done. The dreary curtailment of our childhood was, we discovered after my mother's death, the result of the most fantastic saving: for a house, the house that was never bought. . . .

It seems now to have been a joyless childhood. There were neighbours who fed us meat and sweets, sorry for us, tea parties we went to that we were never allowed to return. I recall the awful depression of Sunday afternoons, my mother with a migraine in the front bedroom, the house an absolute stillness. But I don't *remember* the oddness; it's a reconstruction. What I remember is what I read, and playing Annie Oakley by myself all summer long in the recreation ground, running up and down the hill in my brown gingham dress, wearing a cowboy hat and carrying a rifle. Saturday-morning pictures confirmed it all: women worked hard, earned their own living; carried guns into the bargain.

The essence of being a good child is taking on the perspective of those who are more powerful than you, and I was good in this way as my sister never was. A house up the road, Sunday afternoon 1958, plates of roast lamb offered. My sister ate, but I refused; not out of sacrifice, nor because I was resisting temptation (I firmly believed that meat would make me ill, as my mother said) but because I understood (though this is the adult's formulation rather than the ten-year-old's) that the price of the meal was condemnation of my mother's oddness, and I wasn't having that. I was a very upright child.

At eight I had my first migraine (I could not please her; I might as well join her; they stopped soon after I left home) and I started to get rapidly and relentlessly short-sighted. I literally stopped seeing for a very long time. It is through the development of symptoms like these, some of them neurotic, that I can site the disasters of our childhood, and read it from an outsider's point of view. I think I passed those years believing that we were unnoticed, *unseen;* but of course we were seen, and the evidence of witnesses was retrievable by memory much later on. In 1956 when the first migraine opened a tunnel of pain one June morning, my little sister developed acute psoriasis. My teacher was worried at my failing sight, I couldn't see the board by the spring of 1957 and read a book under my desk during arithmetic lessons. Did he send a note to my mother? Surely he must have done; what else could have shaken her conviction that glasses would be bad for me? He said to me the morning after he'd seen her, "Your mother says you're doing exercises for your eyes; make sure you do them properly." I thought he was being kind, and he was; but I preserved the voice that I might later hear the disapproval in it. I think they must have used the eleven-plus and the amount of blackboard work it involved as a lever, because I got a pair of glasses before the exam.

That afternoon she walked up the road with me, what had they told her? The next year, standing by my new teacher's desk, now in the eleven-plus class, he showed my book to what must have been a student on teaching practice. "This one," he said, "has an inferiority complex." I didn't understand, had no dictionary in which to look up the words, but preserved them by my own invented syllabary, rehearsing them, to bring out for much later scrutiny. I must in fact have known that people were watching, being witnesses, for some years later I started to play a game of inviting their comment and disapproval and then withdrawing the spectacle I had placed before their eyes, making them feel ashamed of the pity they had felt. By the time I was fifteen we'd all three of us given up, huddled with tiredness and irritation in the house where my father was only now an intermittent presence. The house was a tip; none of us did any housework any more; broken china wasn't replaced; at meal times my mother, my sister and I shared the last knife between us. Responsible now for my own washing, I scarcely did any, spent the winter changing about the layers of five petticoats I wore to keep warm, top to bottom through the cold months. One morning, asked by the games mistress why I wasn't wearing my school blouse, I said I hadn't been able to find it in the place I'd put it down the night before (not true; I hadn't a clean one), presenting thus a scene of baroque household disorganization, daring her to disapprove, hoping she would.

Ten years before this, school had taught me to read, and I found out for myself how to do it fast. By the time I was six I read all the time, rapidly and voraciously. You couldn't join the library until you were seven, and before that I read my Hans Christian Andersen from back to front when I'd read it from start to finish. Kay was my name at home, and I knew that Kay, the boy in "The Snow Queen," was me, who had a lump of ice in her heart. I knew that one day I might be asked to walk on the edge of knives, like the Little Mermaid, and was afraid that I might not be able to bear the pain. Foxe's *Book of Martyrs* was in the old library, a one-volume edition with coloured illustrations for Victorian children, the text pruned to a litany of death by flame. My imagination was furnished with the passionate martyrdom of the Protestant North ". . . Every blank cries shame; Finish what you have begun, In the Saviour's name."

I see now the relentless laying down of guilt, and I feel a faint surprise that I must interpret it that way. My sister, younger than me, with children of her own and perhaps thereby with a clearer measure of what we lacked, tells me to recall a mother who never played with us, whose eruptions from irritation into violence were the most terrifying of experiences; and she is there, the figure of nightmares, though I do find it difficult to think about in this way. Such reworking of past time is new, infinitely surprising; and against it I must balance what it felt like then, and the implications of the history given me in small doses; that not being hungry and having a warm bed to lie in at night, I had a good childhood, was better than other people; was a *lucky* little girl.

My mother had wanted to marry a king. That was the best of my father's stories, told in the pub in the 1960s, of how difficult it had been to live with her in 1937, during the Abdication months. Mrs. Simpson was no prettier than her, no more clever than her, no better than her. It wasn't fair that a king should give up his throne for her, and not for the weaver's daughter. From a traditional Labour background, my mother rejected the politics of solidarity and communality, always voted Conservative, for the left could not embody her desire for things to be *really* fair, for a full skirt that took twenty yards of cloth, for a half-timbered cottage in the country, for the prince who did not come. For my mother, the time of my childhood was the place where the fairy-tales failed.

GERTRUDE STEIN
(1874–1946)

Born in California, Gertrude Stein was educated at Radcliffe College, where she studied with philosopher and psychologist William James, and then attended the Johns Hopkins Medical School, before establishing herself in Paris in 1903. She wrote fiction, including *The Making of Americans* and *Three Lives* and, with her brother, collected avant-garde painting, that of Matisse and Picasso especially. *The Autobiography of Alice B. Toklas* (1933) was her first popular success. It is not an autobiography by Alice Toklas, Stein's companion from 1907 to her death, but a funny, innovative memoir which pays unusual attention to the "wives of geniuses" as well as the "geniuses" themselves. It focuses on the Paris years, mythologizing the Stein-Toklas household and presenting Stein as the writing member of an international art movement that starred Picasso. A lot of what we remember about Paris in the 1920s comes from *The Autobiography of Alice B. Toklas*. Along the way Stein tells some stories about her past which are, according to her biographer James Mellow, streamlined versions of the truth. She did rather worse at medical school and tried rather harder to graduate than she allows in the following account of her education.

For another piece of writing by a great modernist which skirts the boundary between fiction and autobiography, compare Colette, *My Apprenticeships.*

FROM *The Autobiography of Alice B. Toklas*

And so Gertrude Stein having been in Baltimore for a winter and having become more humanised and less adolescent and less lonesome went to Radcliffe. There she had a very good time.

She was one of a group of Harvard men and Radcliffe women and they all lived very closely and very interestingly together. One of them, a young philosopher and mathematician who was doing research work in psychology left a definite mark on her life. She and he together worked out a series of experiments in automatic writing under the direction of Münsterberg. The result of her own experiments, which Gertrude Stein wrote down and which was printed in the Harvard Psychological Review was the first writing of hers ever to be printed. It is very interesting to read because the method of writing to be afterwards developed in Three Lives and Making of Americans already shows itself.

The important person in Gertrude Stein's Radcliffe life was William James. She enjoyed her life and herself. She was the secretary of the philosophical club and amused herself with all sorts of people. She liked making sport of question asking and she liked equally answering them. She liked it all. But the really lasting impression of her Radcliffe life came through William James.

It is rather strange that she was not then at all interested in the work of Henry James for whom she now has a very great admiration and whom she considers quite definitely as her forerunner, he being the only nineteenth century writer who being an american felt the method of the twentieth century. Gertrude Stein always speaks of America as being now the oldest country in the world because by the methods of the civil war and the commercial conceptions that followed it America created the twentieth century, and since all the other countries are now either living or commencing to be living a twentieth century of life, America having begun the creation of the twentieth century in the sixties of the nineteenth century is now the oldest country in the world.

In the same way she contends that Henry James was the first person in literature to find the way to the literary methods of the twentieth century. But oddly enough in all of her formative period she did not read him and was not interested in him. But as she often says one is always naturally antagonistic to one's parents and sympathetic to one's grandparents. The parents are too close, they hamper you, one must be alone. So perhaps that is the reason why only very lately Gertrude Stein reads Henry James.

William James delighted her. His personality and his teaching and his way of amusing himself with himself and his students all pleased her. Keep your mind open, he used to say, and when some one objected, but Professor James, this that I say, is true. Yes, said James, it is abjectly true.

Gertrude Stein never had subconscious reactions, nor was she a successful subject for automatic writing. One of the students in the psychological seminar of which Gertrude Stein, although an undergraduate, was at William James' particular request a member, was carrying on a series of experiments on suggestions to the subconscious. When he read his paper upon the result of his experiments, he began by explaining that one of the subjects gave absolutely no results and as this much lowered the average and made the conclusion of his experiments false he wished to be allowed to cut this record out. Whose record is it, said James. Miss Stein's, said the student. Ah, said James, if Miss Stein gave no response I should say that it was as normal not to give a response as to give one and decidedly the result must not be cut out.

It was a very lovely spring day, Gertrude Stein had been going to the opera every night and going also to the opera in the afternoon and had been otherwise engrossed and it was the period of the final examinations, and there was the examination in William James' course. She sat down with the examination paper before her and she just could not. Dear Professor James, she wrote at the top of her paper. I am so sorry but really I do not feel a bit like an examination paper in philosophy to-day, and left.

The next day she had a postal card from William James saying, Dear Miss Stein, I understand perfectly how you feel I often feel like that myself. And underneath it he gave her work the highest mark in his course.

When Gertrude Stein was finishing her last year at Radcliffe, William James one day asked her what she was going to do. She said she had no idea. Well, he said, it should be either philosophy or psychology. Now for philosophy you have to have higher mathematics and I don't gather that that has ever interested you. Now for psychology you must have a medical education, a medical education opens all doors, as Oliver Wendell Holmes told me and as I tell you. Gertrude Stein had been interested in both biology and chemistry and so medical school presented no difficulties.

There were no difficulties except that Gertrude Stein had never passed more than half of her entrance examinations for Radcliffe, having never intended to take a degree. However with considerable struggle and enough tutoring that was accomplished and Gertrude Stein entered Johns Hopkins Medical School.

Some years after when Gertrude Stein and her brother were just beginning knowing Matisse and Picasso, William James came to Paris and they met. She went to see him at his hotel. He was enormously interested in what she was doing, interested in her writing and in the pictures she told him about. He went with her to her house to see them. He looked and gasped, I told you, he said, I always told you that you should keep your mind open.

Only about two years ago a very strange thing happened. Gertrude Stein received a letter from a man in Boston. It was evident from the letter head that he was one of a firm of lawyers. He said in his letter that he had not long ago in reading in the Harvard library found that the library of William James had been given as a gift to the Harvard library. Among these books was the copy of Three Lives that Gertrude Stein had dedicated and sent to James. Also on the margins of the book were notes that William James had evidently made when reading the book. The man then went on to say that very likely Gertrude Stein would be very interested in these notes and he proposed, if she wished, to copy them out for her as he had appropriated the book, in other words taken it and considered it as his. We were very puzzled what to do about it. Finally a note was written saying that Gertrude Stein would like to have a copy of William James' notes. In answer came a manuscript the man himself had written and of which he wished Gertrude Stein to give him an opinion. Not knowing what to do about it all, Gertrude Stein did nothing.

After having passed her entrance examinations she settled down in Baltimore and went to the medical school. She had a servant named Lena and it is her story that Gertrude Stein afterwards wrote as the first story of the Three Lives.

The first two years of the medical school were alright. They were purely laboratory work and Gertrude Stein under Llewelys Barker immediately betook herself to research work. She began a study of all the brain tracts, the beginning of a comparative study. All this was later embodied in Llewelys Barker's book. She delighted in Doctor Mall, professor of anatomy, who directed her work. She always quotes his answer to any student excusing him or herself for anything. He would look reflective and say, yes that is just like our cook. There is always a reason. She never brings the food to the table hot. In summer of course she can't because it is too hot, in winter of course she can't because it is too cold, yes there is always a reason. Doctor Mall believed in everybody developing their own technique. He also remarked, nobody teaches anybody anything, at first every student's scalpel is dull and then later every student's scalpel is sharp, and nobody has taught anybody anything.

These first two years at the medical school Gertrude Stein liked well enough. She always liked knowing a lot of people and being mixed up in a lot of stories and she was not awfully interested but she was not too bored with what she was doing and besides she had quantities of pleasant relatives in Baltimore and she liked it. The last two years at the medical school she was bored, frankly openly bored. There was a good deal of intrigue and struggle among the students, that she liked, but the practice and theory of medicine did not interest her at all. It was fairly well known among all her teachers that she was bored, but as her first two years of scientific work had given her a reputation, everybody gave her the necessary credits and the end of her last year was approaching. It was then that she had to take her turn in the delivering of babies and it was at that time she noticed the negroes and the places that she afterwards used in the second of the Three Lives stories, Melanctha Herbert, the story that was the beginning of her revolutionary work.

As she always says of herself, she has a great deal of inertia and once started keeps going until she starts somewhere else.

As the graduation examinations drew near some of her professors were getting angry. The big men like Halstead, Osler etcetera knowing her reputation for original scientific work made the medical examinations merely a matter of form and passed her. But there were others who were not so amiable. Gertrude Stein always laughed, and this was difficult. They would ask her questions although as she said to her friends, it was foolish of them to ask her, when there were so many eager and anxious to answer. However they did question her from time to time and as she said, what could she do, she did not know the answers and they did not believe that she did not know them, they thought that she did not answer because she did not consider the professors worth answering. It was a difficult situation, as she said, it was impossible to apologise and explain to them that she was so bored she could not remember the things that of course the dullest medical student could not forget. One of the professors said that although all the big men were ready to pass her he intended that she should be given a lesson and he refused to give her a pass mark and so she was not able to take her degree. There was great excitement in the medical school. Her very close friend Marion Walker pleaded with her, she said, but Gertrude Gertrude remember the cause of women, and Gertrude Stein said, you don't know what it is to be bored.

The professor who had flunked her asked her to come to see him. She did. He said, of course Miss Stein all you have to do is to take a summer course here and in the fall naturally you will take your degree. But not at all, said Gertrude Stein, you have no idea how grateful I am to you. I have so much inertia and so little initiative that very possibly if you had not kept me from taking my degree I would have, well, not taken to the practice of medicine, but at any rate to pathological psychology and you don't know how little I like pathological psychology, and how all medicine bores me. The professor was completely taken aback and that was the end of the medical education of Gertrude Stein.

SARA SULERI
(1953–)

Sara Suleri was born in Karachi, her father a well-known Pakistani journalist and her mother a Welsh-born teacher. Raised in Pakistan, Suleri has also lived in England and now lives in New Haven, Connecticut, where she is professor of English at Yale University. Her memoir, *Meatless Days* (1989), displays the complicated layering of a truly cosmopolitan mind, simultaneously at home and estranged in various cultures.

For another sophisticated memoir of expatriation, compare Eva Hoffman, *Lost in Translation*. For a memoir from the same part of the world a generation earlier, compare Santha Rama Rau, *Gifts of Passage*.

FROM *Meatless Days*

MEATLESS DAYS

I had strongly hoped that they would say sweetbreads instead of testicles, but I was wrong. The only reason it had become a question in my mind was Tillat's fault, of course: she had come visiting from Kuwait one summer, arriving in New Haven with her three children, all of them designed to constitute a large surprise. As a surprise it worked wonderfully, leaving me reeling with the shock of generation that attends on infants and all the detail they manage to accrue. But the end of the day would come at last, and when the rhythm of their sleep sat like heavy peace upon a room, then Tillat and I could talk. Our conversations were meals, delectable, but fraught with a sense of prior copyright, because each of us was obliged to talk too much about what the other did not already know. Speaking over and across the separation of our lives, we discovered that there was an internal revenue involved in so much talking, so much listening. One evening my sister suddenly remembered to give me a piece of information that she had been storing up, like a squirrel, through the long desert months of the previous year. Tillat at twenty-seven had arrived at womanhood with comparatively little fuss—or so her aspect says—and her astonishing recall of my mother's face has always seemed to owe more to faithfulness than to the accident of physiognomy. "Sara," said Tillat, her voice deep with the promise of surprise, "do you know what *kapura* are?" I was cooking and a little cross. "Of course I do," I answered with some affront. "They're sweetbreads, and they're cooked with kidneys, and they're very good." Natives should always be natives, exactly what they are, and I felt irked to be so probed around the issue of my own nativity. But Tillat's face was kindly with superior knowledge. "Not sweetbread," she gently said. "They're testicles, that's what *kapura* really are." Of course I refused to believe her, went on cooking, and that was the end of that.

The babies left, and I with a sudden spasm of free time watched that organic issue resurface in my head—something that had once sat quite simply inside its own definition was declaring independence from its name and nature, claiming a perplexity that I did not like. And, too, I needed different ways to be still thinking about Tillat, who had gone as completely as she had arrived, and deserved to be reproached for being such an unreliable informant. So, the next time I was in the taut companionship of Pakistanis in New York, I made a point of inquiring into the exact status of *kapura* and the physiological location of its secret, first in the animal and then in the meal. Expatriates are adamant, entirely passionate about such matters as the eating habits of the motherland. Accordingly, even though I was made to feel that it was wrong to strip a food of its sauce and put it back into its bodily belonging, I certainly received an unequivocal response: *kapura,* as naked meat, equals a testicle. Better, it is tantamount to a testicle neatly sliced into halves, just as we make no bones about asking the butcher to split chicken breasts in two. "But," and here I rummaged for the sweet realm of nomenclature, "couldn't *kapura* on a lazy occasion also accommodate something like sweetbreads, which is just a nice way of saying that pancreas is not a pleasant word to eat?" No one, however, was interested in this finesse. "Balls, darling, balls," someone drawled, and I knew I had to let go of the subject.

Yet I was shocked. It was my mother, after all, who had told me that sweetbreads are sweetbreads, and if she were wrong on that score, then how many other simple equations had I now to doubt? The second possibility that occurred to me was even more unsettling: maybe my mother knew that sweetbreads are testicles but had cunningly devised a ruse to make me consume as many parts of the world as she could before she set me loose in it. The thought appalled me. It was almost as bad as attempting to imagine what the slippage was that took me from nipple to bottle and away from the great letdown that signifies lactation. What a falling off! How much I must have suffered when so handed over to the shoddy metaphors of Ostermilk and Babyflo. Gosh, I thought, to think that my mother could do that to me. For of course she must have known, in her Welsh way, that sweetbreads could never be simply sweetbreads in Pakistan. It made me stop and hold my head over that curious possibility: what else have I eaten on her behalf?

I mulled over that question for days, since it wantonly refused to disappear after it had been posed: instead, it settled in my head and insisted on being reformulated, with all the tenacity of a query that actually expects to be met with a reply. My only recourse was to make lists, cramped and strictly alphabetical catalogs of all the gastronomic wrongs I could blame on my mother; but somehow by the time I reached *T* and "tripe," I was always interrupted and had to begin again. Finally it began to strike me as a rather unseemly activity for one who had always enjoyed a measure of daughterly propriety, and I decided that the game was not to be played again but discarded like table scraps. For a brief span of time I felt free, until some trivial occasion—a dinner, where chicken had been cleverly cooked to resemble veal—caused me to re-mind my friends of that obsolete little phrase, "mutton dressed up as lamb," which had been such a favorite of my mother's. Another was "neither flesh nor fowl," and as I chatted about the curiousness of those phrases, I suddenly realized that my friends had fallen away and my only audience was the question itself, heaving up its head again and examin-ing me with reproach and some scorn. I sensed that it would be unwise to offer another list to this triumphant interlocutor, so I bowed my head and knew what I had to do. In order to submit even the most imperfect answer, I had to go back to where I belonged and—past a thousand different mealtimes—try to reconstruct the parable of the *kapura*.

Tillat was not around to hear me sigh and wonder where I should possibly begin. The breast would be too flagrant and would make me too tongue-tied, so I decided instead to approach the *kapura* in a mildly devious way, by getting at it through its mate. To the best of my knowl-edge I had never seen *kapura* cooked outside the company of kidney, and so for Tillat's edification alone I tried to begin with the story of the kidney, which I should have remembered long ago, not twenty-five years after its occurrence. We were living in Lahore, in the 9-T Gulberg house, and in those days our cook was Qayuum. He had a son and two daughters with whom we were occasionally allowed to play: his little girl Munni I specially remember because I liked the way her hair curled and because of all the times that she was such a perfect recipient of fake *pan*. *Pan*, an adult delicacy of betel leaf and nut, can be quite convincingly replicated by a mango leaf stuffed with stones: Ifat, my older sister, would fold such beautifully simulated *pan* triangles that Munni would thrust them into her mouth each time—and then burst into tears. I find it odd today to imagine how that game of guile and trust could have survived even a single repetition, but I recollect it distinctly as a weekly ritual, with us waiting in fascination for Munni to get streetwise, which she never did. Instead, she cried with her mouth wide open and would run off to her mother with little pebbles falling out of her mouth, like someone in a fairy tale.

Those stones get linked to kidneys in my head, as part of the chain through which Munni got the better of me and anticipated the story I really intend to tell. It was an evil day that led her father Qayuum to buy two water buffalo, tethering them at the far end of the garden and making my mother beam at the prospect of such fresh milk. My older brother Shahid liked pets and convinced me that we should beam too, until he and I were handed our first overpowering glasses of buffalo milk. Of milks it is certainly the most oceanic, with archipelagoes and gulf streams of cream emitting a pungent, grassy odor. Trebly strong is that smell at milking-time, which my mother beamingly suggested we attend. She kept away herself, of course, so she never saw the big black cows, with their ominous glassy eyes, as they shifted from foot to foot. Qayuum pulled and pulled at their white udders and, in a festive mood, called up the children one by one to squirt a steaming jet of milk into their mouths. When my turn came, my mother, not being there, did not see me run as fast as I could away from the cows and the cook, past the vegetable garden and the goldfish pond, down to the farthermost wall, where I lay down in the grass and tried to faint, but couldn't.

I knew the spot from prior humiliations, I admit. It was where I had hidden twice in the week when I was caught eating cauliflower and was made to eat kidney. The cauliflower came first—it emerged as a fragrant little head in the vegetable garden, a bumpy vegetable brain that looked innocent and edible enough to make me a perfect victim when it called. In that era my greatest illicit joy was hastily chewing off the top of each new cauliflower when no one else was looking. The early morning was my favorite time, because then those flowers felt firm and crisp with dew. I would go to the vegetable patch and squat over the cauliflowers as they came out one by one, hold them between my knees, and chew as many craters as I could into their jaunty tightness. Qayuum was crushed. "There is an animal, Begum Sahib," he mourned to my mother, "like a savage in my garden. *Maro! Maro!*" To hear him made me nervous, so the following morning I tried to deflect attention from the cauliflowers by quickly pulling out all the little radishes while they were still pencil-thin: they lay on the soil like a pathetic accumulation of red herrings. That was when Munni caught me. *"Abba Ji!"* she screamed for her father like a train engine. Everybody came running, and for a while my squat felt frozen to the ground as I looked up at an overabundance of astonished adult faces. "What are you doing, Sara *Bibi?*" the driver finally and gently asked. "Smelling the radishes," I said in a baby and desperate defiance, "so that the animal can't find the cauliflower." "Which one?" "The new cauliflower." "Which animal, *bibi ji,* you naughty girl?" "The one that likes to eat the cauliflower that I like to smell." And when they laughed at me, I did not know where to put my face for shame.

They caught me out that week, two times over, because after I had been exposed as the cauliflower despoiler and had to enter a new phase of penitence, Qayuum the cook insisted on making me eat kidney. *"Kirrnee,"* he would call it with a glint in his eye, *"kirrnee."* My mother quite agreed that I should learn such discipline, and the complicated ritual of endurance they imposed did make me teach myself to take a kidney taste without dwelling too long on the peculiarities of kidney texture. I tried to be unsurprised by the mushroom pleats that constitute a kidney's underbelly and by the knot of membrane that holds those kidney folds in place. One day Qayuum insisted that only kidneys could sit on my plate, mimicking legumes and ignoring their thin and bloody juices. Wicked Ifat came into the room and waited till I had started eating; then she intervened. "Sara," said Ifat, her eyes brimming over with wonderful malice, "do you know what kidneys do?" I aged, and my meal regressed, back to its vital belonging in the world of function. "Kidneys make pee, Sara," Ifat told me, "That's what they do, they make pee." And she looked so pleased to be able to tell me that; it made her feel so full of information. Betrayed by food, I let her go, and wept some watery tears into the kidney juice, which was designed anyway to evade cohesion, being thin and in its nature inexact. Then I ran out to the farthermost corner of the garden, where I would later go to hide my shame of milking-time in a retch that refused to materialize.

Born the following year, Tillat would not know that cautionary tale. Nor would she know what Ifat did when my father called from Lady Willingdon Hospital in Lahore to repeat that old phrase, "It is a girl." "It's a girl!" Ifat shouted, as though simply clinching for the world the overwhelming triumph of her will. Shahid, a year my senior, was found half an hour later sobbing next to the goldfish pond near the vegetable garden, for he had been banking on the diluting arrival of a brother. He must have been upset, because when we were taken to visit my mother, he left his penguin—a favorite toy—among the old trees of the hospital garden, where we had been sent to play. I was still uncertain about my relation to the status of this new baby: my sister was glad that it was a girl, and my brother was sad that it wasn't a boy, but we all stood together when penguiny was lost.

It is to my discredit that I forgot this story, both of what the kidney said and what it could have told to my still germinating sister. Had I borne something of those lessons in mind, it would have been less of a shock to have to reconceive the *kapura* parable; perhaps I'd have been prepared for more skepticism about the connection between kidneys and sweetbreads—after all, they fall into no logical category of togetherness. The culinary humor of kidneys and testicles stewing in one another's juices is, on the other hand, very fine: I wish I had had the imagination to intuit all the unwonted jokes people tell when they start cooking food. I should have remembered all those nervously comic edges, and the pangs, that constitute most poignancies of nourishment. And so, as an older mind, I fault myself for not having the wits to recognize what I already knew. I must have always known exactly what *kapura* are, because the conversation they provoked came accompanied with shocks of familiarity that typically attend a trade of solid information. What I had really wanted to reply, first to Tillat and then to my Pakistani friends, was: yes, of course, who do you think I am, what else could they *possibly be*? Anyone with discrimination could immediately discern the connection between *kapura* and their namesake: the shape is right, given that we are now talking about goats; the texture involves a bit of a bounce, which works; and the taste is altogether too exactly what it is. So I should have kept in mind that, alas, we know the flavor of each part of the anatomy: that much imagination belongs to everyone's palate. Once, when my sisters and I were sitting in a sunny winter garden, Tillat began examining some ants that were tumbling about the blades of grass next to her chair. She looked acute and then suddenly said, "How very sour those little ants must be." Ifat declared that she had always thought the same herself, and though I never found out how they arrived at this discovery, I was impressed by it, their ability to take the world on their tongues.

So poor Irfani, how much his infant taste buds must have colored his perception of the grimness of each day. Irfan was born in London, finally another boy, but long after Shahid had ceased looking for playmates in the home. It now strikes me as peculiar that my parents should choose to move back to Pakistan when Farni was barely a year old, and to decide on June, that most pitiless month, in which to return to Lahore. The heat shriveled the baby, giving his face an expression of slow and bewildered shock, which was compounded by the fact that for the next year there was very little that the child could eat. Water boiled ten times over would still retain virulence enough to send his body into derangements, and goat's milk, cow's milk, everything liquid seemed to convey malevolence to his minuscule gut. We used to scour the city for aging jars of imported baby-food; these, at least, he would eat, though with a look of profound mistrust—but even so, he spent most of the next year with his body in violent rebellion against the idea of food. It gave his eyes a gravity they have never lost.

Youngster he was, learning lessons from an infant's intuition to fear food, and to some degree all of us were equally watchful for hidden trickeries in the scheme of nourishment, for the way in which things would always be missing or out of place in Pakistan's erratic emotional market. Items of security—such as flour or butter or cigarettes or tea—were always vanishing, or returning in such dubiously shiny attire that we could barely stand to look at them. We lived in the expectation of threatening surprise: a crow had drowned in the water tank on the roof, so for a week we had been drinking dead-crow water and couldn't understand why we felt so ill; the milkman had accidentally diluted our supply of milk with paraffin instead of water; and those were not pistachios, at all, in a tub of Hico's green ice cream. Our days and our newspapers were equally full of disquieting tales about adulterated foods and the preternaturally keen eye that the nation kept on such promiscuous blendings. I can understand it, the fear that food will not stay discrete but will instead defy our categories of expectation in what can only be described as a manner of extreme belligerence. I like order to a plate, and know the great sense of failure that attends a moment when what is potato to the fork is turnip to the mouth. It's hard, when such things happen.

So, long before the *kapura* made its comeback in my life, we in Pakistan were bedmates with betrayal and learned how to take grim satisfaction from assessing the water table of our outrage. There were both lean times and meaty times, however; occasionally, body and food would sit happily at the same side of the conference table. Take, for example, Ramzan, the Muslim month of fasting, often recollected as the season of perfect meals. Ramzan, a lunar thing, never arrives at the same point of time each year, coming instead with an aura of slight and pleasing dislocation. Somehow it always took us by surprise: new moons are startling to see, even by accident, and Ramzan's moon betokened a month of exquisite precision about the way we were to parcel out our time. On the appointed evenings we would rake the twilight for that possible sliver, and it made the city and body both shudder with expectation to spot that little slip of a moon that signified Ramzan and made the sky historical. How busy Lahore would get! Its minarets hummed, its municipalities pulled out their old air-raid sirens to make the city noisily cognizant: the moon had been sighted, and the fast begun.

I liked it, the waking up an hour before dawn to eat the prefast meal and chat in whispers. For three wintry seasons I would wake up with Dadi, my grandmother, and Ifat and Shahid: we sat around for hours making jokes in the dark, generating a discourse of unholy comradeship. The food itself, designed to keep the penitent sustained from dawn till dusk, was insistent in its richness and intensity, with bread dripping clarified butter, and curried brains, and cumin eggs, and a peculiarly potent vermicelli, soaked overnight in sugar and fatted milk. And if I liked the getting up at dawn, then Dadi completely adored the eating of it all. I think she fasted only because she so enjoyed the *sehri* meal and that mammoth infusion of food at such an extraordinary hour. At three in the morning the rest of us felt squeamish about linking the deep sleep dreams we had just conducted and so much grease—we asked instead for porridge—but Dadi's eating was a sight to behold and admire. She hooted when the city's sirens sounded to tell us that we should stop eating and that the fast had now begun: she enjoyed a more direct relation with God than did petty municipal authorities and was fond of declaiming what Muhammad himself had said in her defense. He apparently told one of his contemporaries that *sehri* did not end until a white thread of light described the horizon and separated the landscape from the sky. In Dadi's book that thread could open into quite an active loom of dawning: the world made waking sounds, the birds and milkmen all resumed their proper functions, but Dadi's regal mastication—on the last brain now—declared it still was night.

I stopped that early rising years before Tillat and Irfan were old enough to join us, before Ifat ran away to get married, and before my father returned to ritual and overtook his son Shahid's absent place. So my memories of it are scant, the fast of the faithful. But I never lost my affection for the twilight meal, the dusky *iftar* that ended the fast after the mosques had lustily rung with the call for the *maghrib* prayer. We'd start eating dates, of course, in order to mimic Muhammad, but then with what glad eyes we'd welcome the grilled liver and the tang of pepper in the orange juice. We were happy to see the spinach leaves and their fantastical shapes, deftly fried in the lightest chick-pea batter, along with the tenderness of fresh fruit, most touching to the palate. There was a curious invitation about the occasion, converting what began as an act of penance into a godly and obligatory cocktail hour that provided a fine excuse for company and affability. When we lived in Pakistan, that little swerve from severity into celebration happened often. It certainly was true of meatless days.

The country was made in 1947, and shortly thereafter the government decided that two days out of each week would be designated as meatless days, in order to conserve the national supply of goats and cattle. Every Tuesday and Wednesday the butchers' shops would stay firmly closed, without a single carcass dangling from the huge metal hooks that lined the canopies under which the butchers squatted, selling meat, and without the open drains at the side of their narrow street ever running with a trace of blood. On days of normal trade, blood would briskly flow, carrying with it flotillas of chicken feathers, and little bits of sinew and entrail, or a bladder full and yellow that a butcher had just bounced deftly into the drain. On meatless days that world emptied into a skeletal remain: the hot sun came to scorch away all the odors and liquids of slaughter and shriveled on the chopping blocks the last curlicues of anything organic, making them look both vacant and precise.

As a principle of hygiene I suppose it was a good idea although it really had very little to do with conservation: the people who could afford to buy meat, after all, were those who could afford refrigeration, so the only thing the government accomplished was to make some people's Mondays very busy indeed. The Begums had to remember to give the cooks thrice as much money; the butchers had to produce thrice as much meat; the cooks had to buy enough flesh and fowl and other sundry organs to keep an averagely carnivorous household eating for three days. A favorite meatless day breakfast, for example, consisted of goat's head and feet cooked with spices into a rich and ungual sauce—remarkable, the things that people eat. And so, instead of creating an atmosphere of abstention in the city, the institution of meatless days rapidly came to signify the imperative behind the acquisition of all things fleshly. We thought about beef, which is called "big meat," and we thought about mutton, "little meat," and then we collectively thought about chicken, the most coveted of them all.

But here I must forget my American sojourn, which has taught me to look on chicken as a notably undignified bird, with pimply skin and pockets of fat tucked into peculiar places and unnecessarily meaty breasts. Those meatless day fowls, on the other hand, were a thing apart. Small, not much bigger than the average quail, they had a skin that cooked to the texture of rice paper, breaking even over the most fragrant limbs and wings. Naturally we cherished them and lavished much care on trying to obtain the freshest of the crop. Once I was in Karachi with my sister Nuz when the thought that she had to engage in the social ferocity of buying chickens was making her quite depressed. We went anyway, with Nuz assuming an alacrity that had nothing to do with efficiency and everything to do with desperation. Nuz stood small and dark in the chicken-monger's shop, ordered her birds, paid for them, and then suddenly remembered her housewifely duty. "Are they fresh?" she squawked, clutching at them, "Can you promise me they're fresh?" The chicken-monger looked at her with some perplexity. "But Begum Sahib," he said gently, "they're alive."

"Oh," said Nuz, "so they are," and calmed down immediately. I have always admired her capacity to be reassured by the world and take without a jot of embarrassment any comfort it is prepared to offer. So I thought she had forgotten about the issue of freshness as we drove home (with the dejected chickens tied up in a rope basket on the back seat) and the Karachi traffic grew lunchtime crazed. But "Oh," she said again, half an hour later, "so a fresh chicken is a dead chicken." "Not too dead," I replied. It made us think of meatless days as some vast funeral game, where Monday's frenetic creation of fresh things beckoned in the burial meals of Tuesday and Wednesday. "Food," Nuz said with disgust—"It's what you bury in your body." To make her feel less alone, we stopped at Shezan's on the way home, to get her an adequate supply of marzipan; for she eats nothing but sweet things. Food she'll cook—wonderful *Sindi* tastes, exotic to my palate—but sugar is the only thing Nuz actually wants to taste.

.   .   .

When I left Pakistan, I had to lean how to cook—or, better—how to conceive of a kitchen as a place where I actually could be private. Now I like to cook, although I remain fascinated by my deep-seated inability to boil an egg exactly to the point that I would like to see it boiled, which seems like such an easy accomplishment of the efficient. I have finally come to the realization that I must feel slightly peculiar about eggs, because I am uneasy until they have been opened up and the flagrant separation between yolk and egg can be whisked into some yellow harmony. When I simply try to boil an egg, I've noticed, I am sure to give it an unconsciously advertent crack, so that the humming water suddenly swirls with something viscous, and then I have to eat my eggs with gills and frills. Not that I very frequently boil an egg: once in five years, perhaps. I can distinctly remember the last occasion: it was when I was about to be visited by the tallest man in my acquaintance, in the days when I still used to tolerate such things.

He was a curious chap, whose bodily discomfort with the world was most frequently expressed in two refrains: one was "Not enough food!" and the second, "Too much food!" During the era of our association, I rapidly learned that the one intimacy we had to eschew above all others was the act of making meals and eating them alone. We could eat in restaurants and public places, surrounded by the buffer of other tables and strangers' voices, but for the two of us to be making and taking a meal on our own was such a fearful thought that the physical largess at my side would break into a myriad of tiny quakes. It was revelatory for me, who had never before watched someone for whom a dining table was so markedly more of a loaded domestic space than was a bed, but I was not totally averse to this new logic. It exercised my imagination to devise oblique methods of introducing food into my house, free-floating and aimless items that could find their way into anyone's mouth with such studied carelessness that they could do no damage to the integrity of a flea. I felt as though I were still in Sussex, putting out a saucer of milk and goodwill for the hedgehogs in the garden and then discreetly vanishing before they froze into prickles of shyness and self-dismay. "What is it, after all, between food and the body?" I asked one day in an exasperation of pain, and never got an answer in reply.

Tom and Tillat tried to behave like friends; they cooked together in a way I liked—but with me the man was so large that he could conceive of himself only in bits, always conscious of how segments of his body could go wandering off, tarsals and metatarsals heedlessly autonomous. Such dissipation made him single-minded. He never worried about the top of his head, because he had put it behind him. His mother chose his glasses for him. His desires made him merely material: he looked at himself just as a woman looks when her infant takes its first tremulous step into the upright world, melting her into a modesty of consternation and pride. And his left hand could never see what his right hand was doing, for they were too far apart, occupying as they did remote hemispheres of control. Perhaps I should have been able to bring those bits together, but such a narrative was not available to me, not after what I knew of storytelling. Instead, we watched the twist through which food became our staple metaphor, suggesting that something of the entire event had—against our will—to do with hunger. "You do not have the backbone of a shrimp," I mourned, gazing up at the spread-sheet of that man mountain. "You have a head the size of a bowl of porridge and a brain the size of a pea." This was in a restaurant. I was surprised beyond measure when that big head bent back and wept, a quick summer shower of tears. By the time he left, all surfaces were absolutely dry.

In any event, rain in America has never felt to me like a condition of glad necessity, and Tom and I will never know the conversations that we might have had on something like the twelfth of August in Lahore, for nothing can approximate what the monsoons make available in happy possibility. I think it was the smell that so intoxicated us after those dreary months of nostril-scorching heat, the smell of dust hissing at the touch of rain and then settling down, damply placid on the ground. People could think of eating again: after the first rains, in July, they gave themselves over to a study of mangoes, savoring in high seriousness the hundred varieties of that fruit. When it rained in the afternoons, children were allowed to eat their mangoes in the garden, stripped naked and dancing about, first getting sticky with mango juice and then getting slippery with rain. In our time such games drove Ifat and Shahid and me quite manic in our merriment, while Mamma sat reading on a nearby monsoon veranda to censor us if we transgressed too far. Years later, Tillat and I served a similar function when Ifat left her children with us—we sat on the veranda, letting them play in the rain. Ifat would have rushed off to shop or to do something equally important, while her children would long for Irfan, whom they loved boisterously, to come back from school. Mamma, on such afternoons, would not be there. It returns as a poignancy to me, that I have forgotten where Mamma could possibly be on such an occasion.

She was not there on the afternoon when, after the rains had whetted our appetites, I went out with my old friends Nuzhat Ahmad and Ayla, as the three of us often did, in a comradeship of girlhood. We went driving to Bagh-e-Jinnah, formerly known as Lawrence Gardens, located opposite the Governor's House along the Mall in Lahore. We were trying to locate the best *gol guppa* vendor in town and stopped by to test the new stand in Lawrence Gardens. *Gol guppas* are a strange food: I have never located an equivalent to them or their culinary situation. They are an outdoor food, a passing whim, and no one would dream of recreating their frivolity inside her own kitchen. A *gol guppa* is a small hollow oval of the lightest pastry that is dipped into a fiery liquid sauce made of tamarind and cayenne and lemon and cold water. It is evidently a food invented as a joke, in a moment of good humor. We stopped the car next to some tall jaman trees (which many years before Shahid and I loved to climb) and enjoyed ourselves a great deal, until a friendly elbow knocked the bowl of *gol guppa* sauce all over my lap. It gave me a new respect for foodstuffs, for never has desire brought me to quite such an instantaneous effect. My groin's surprise called attention to passageways that as a rule I am only theoretically aware of owning, all of which folded up like a concertina in protest against such an explosive aeration. For days after, my pupils stayed dilated, while my interiors felt gaunt and hollow-eyed.

I retold this ten-year-old episode to Tillat when she came visiting, shortly after she had hit me over the head with her testicles-equal-*kapura* tale. I was trying to cheer her up and distract her from the rather obvious fact that, once again, her children were refusing to eat. "Do you know how much happier my life would be if my children would eat?" Tillat wailed, and there was little I could say to deny it. "It's your fault, Tatty," I said consolingly, "your body manufactured chocolate milk." Certainly those children had a powerful impulse toward chocolate: it was deranging, to pull out the Cadbury's for breakfast. It gave Tillat a rather peculiar relation to food: it made her a good cook but a somewhat stern one, as though she were always waiting for her meals to undergo a certain neurotic collapse. One day she turned quite tragic, cooking for some visitors of mine, when the *shami kebabs* she was frying obstinately refused to cohere into their traditional shape. I did not expect Tillat's moonface to look so wracked, as though the secret of all things lay in that which made the *shami* cling to the *kebab*. "Never mind, Tillat. We'll just call them Kuwaiti *kebabs* and then no one will know they look peculiar." Of course I was right, and the meal was most satisfactory.

CAITLIN THOMAS
(1913–)

Caitlin Macnamara met Dylan Thomas, the Welsh poet, in a London pub in 1936. They were married a year later, when she was twenty-four and he was twenty-three. Their tumultuous, passionate marriage produced three children: Llewellyn in 1939, Aeronwy in 1943, and Colm in 1949. Four years after Colm's birth Dylan died of alcohol poisoning while on tour in America. Caitlin's grief took some untraditional forms. In Laugherne, Dylan's hometown, she scandalized the townspeople with behavior considered unsuitable in a widow. "I stole their sons and husbands," she wrote, "violating purposefully my most precious holy vows to Dylan." After a suicide attempt and time in a mental hospital, Caitlin put her two older children in the care of relatives and went with little Colm to the island of Elba, where she and Dylan had once spent time and where she hoped she could live anonymously. From her previous visit to Elba, she knew Giovanni, the hotel owner portrayed here, whom she expected to be able to lean on and so nicknamed The Church. But The Church proved to be a jealous protector, constantly reprimanding her for unladylike behavior. He was especially outraged when Caitlin took an eighteen-year-old lover.

Caitlin's memoir of her six months on Elba, avoiding the role of grieving widow but grieving nonetheless, was published in 1957 as *Leftover Life to Kill.* She continued to live in Italy, where she met an actor who nursed her through alcoholism and suicide attempts and with whom, at the age of forty-nine, she had a son.

For another account of the anguish caused to a wife by a great writer, in this case while he was alive, compare Sophia Tolstoy, *Diary.* For another assertion of sexual freedom, compare Anaïs Nin, *Diary.*

FROM *Leftover Life to Kill*

The place, and position, are an Italian dream: high up above a beautiful bay, where I bathe, and have entirely to myself; not counting the sneakers and peepers, who squat in the bushes above to get an eyeful of stray breast or bum. But I have decided to ignore them, and allow these illicit glimpses, as long as they keep far enough away, or all my pleasure would be gone. After all, it is not so much to give and harms nobody. I only start shouting when one gets too near; but it makes me selfconscious all the same, and spoils my laborious peace. I think, when afterwards sitting on my terrace, trellised with vines, and looking down through the superbly leaden, or is it more gunmetal, olive trees, definitely my favourite trees; more terraces of vines; past the solitary overhanging pine tree, that makes a child-drawn circle of shade in the middle of my bay; and into the wide open, blue-eyed, staring back at me sea: anybody but me would be content with this. The bottle of red wine in front of me, and the long bread, the hard parmesan cheese; the mortadella, pomodori, and finocchi. There have been moments, when all the elements combined to create pure contentment; but how rare; there was nothing wrong with the elements very often, but the unyielding acid in me.

One day, for no special reason that I can remember, I suddenly felt whole again; and God, what a change. I was a new person, somebody I had forgotten a long time ago; I wanted to sing, and jump, and hug everybody, and kiss them. But it only lasted a day, then the wind came again and sent me shivering back where I had come from.

All this time Colm had been going to his asylum (*asilo*, as they not very encouragingly call the infant convent school), and I had taken one further perilous step, by leaving him there to lunch, which meant just soup; except that Italian soup is not quite the same as Windsor Brown; with extras supplemented by the mother. On the first day I went to great pains to get him the correct little cardboard case, tin plate, cup and spoon; and put in all the bits and pieces he liked best, including his special bananas; only to find, when I went to collect him later, he had been given the wrong case, full of cheeses and stuff he would not eat; and nearly broke his heart, watching the other boy eating his bananas. I nearly broke mine too; the baffling bewilderments of children, when they are transplanted from one familiar environment, to a frightening strange one, without knowing why; or worse still, the callous initiation into boarding school, which, to me, was the cruellest suffering; have the same quality of poignant unbearableness, as blinding cicadas to make them sing, clipping the wings of birds, tying cans to dogs' tails, leading cats on strings, tripping up cripples, tying goats' legs together, emptying nests of eggs, strewing the fledglings, caging any wild thing. And Colm, with his fair curls, novitiate's round white collar, and buttoned-tight-down-the-back black check tunic; with his stumpy trousered and booted legs coming out below, looked such a story-book angel of innocence, among the sloe-eyed, crafty by comparison, already mature natives. But this did not prevent me afterwards from half-killing him for some act of unmitigated fiendery, far more imaginative than anything the naïve darkies could have dreamed of perpetrating.

At nights we clung together, like the white haired, shipwrecked, ancient mariner and son; and this scrap of Dylan contact was both comforting and disturbing to me. With all Colm's demands and disturbances, I did thank thankless God, because there was nobody else to thank, he was there. He kept me on the move, tied me to certain times; and most of all, gave me a chance to meet the people, whom otherwise I would have had no excuse to talk to. Without him I am sure I would have walked straight over the nearest mountain, into an impenetrable mist, like Oates in the Antarctic, and never been seen again.

One of his near grown-up, but in the Italian sense of the word, completely grown-up friends, was Joseph; although he was only eighteen, three years older than my eldest son. He was a beautiful boy, and I liked him at once; a different type from the pretty boys who spent all their waking time, except for the sacred ritual of eating: (the leading question was always, "Have you eaten yet?" if they had not, they could not take a drink, because it would hurt the stomach; and if they had, they said, with a pained *moue,* that they had already eaten); *passegiaring:* the only word for this full time Italian occupation, along with window-gazing, up and down the main street. Joseph did plenty of that too, when he had the chance, but in the week he had to work very hard: from six in the morning to four in the afternoon; in the iron mines, where most of the men worked, for very little money. This early necessity to earn his living, combined with the "toughness" of the work, had given him an attractive grave hardness, sitting awkwardly on his extreme youthfulness, which, in spite of himself, would burst irrepressibly through on off-moments.

I asked him to look after Colm, while I went to my Italian lesson, with the Englishman's wife; which he did very well, and willingly. And, may I be struck down dead this instant, if this is a word of a lie; I never had an inkling of foreboding, that he might appear in the fantastic rôle of a lover. For one thing my vanity balked at such an absurdity, and I did not fancy myself as a haggard, rabid, avid randy dowager combing the Riviera for young blood. I had plenty of babies of my own, and had no inclination to snatch any more. My dignity was sorely troubled, but then, he was very, very sweet; and it seemed equally absurd to refuse to go about with Colm's friend. Fair play, it never occurred to me, that by making friends with Colm, these charming boys may have had, at the back of their calculating minds, the possible future savoury bite of me. And this manoeuvring, if it were so, was not even flattering to me; since all the other seductible women were firmly locked up in their houses; and I was the only bit of procurable shoddy goods, on the market.

With Joseph I never felt that, and I am sure it was not true, though I am great at blind faith: he was so serious-minded and studious. His chief interest was to improve his English, and I could not make him talk

Italian to me enough: it sounded with him, more mellifluous, more sonorous, more captivating, than anybody else's . . . which I might have guessed were certain ominous signs.

So we went walking together, the three of us; in the boat, where he looked wonderful, lazily rowing, with contained power, over the bouncing waves; to the beaches, where his comical terror at wetting his feet, damped momentarily the glowing picture of him; to the mountains, and the goats, and the herbs; and the beds of dry straw. And so, it involuntarily happened. Between the stalactite separateness of two people, and the first tentative gesture of intimacy, stretches a boundless plain of thorny distance, that appears insurmountable; but the instant that the two bloods meet, there is no stopping the heady, rushing upwards course together; and all the agonized constraints are swept away in the warm flooding; and laughed at, as ridiculous trifles, childish nonsense.

This state of affairs was far from pleasing to me; the last thing I wanted was a repetition of growing pains, from centuries ago, but still horribly clear. It brought back sensations I hoped never to suffer again: going weak at the knees, the stomach turning over, and dropping down, the heart thumping in the throat, a dizzy spinning of sickness, and an incurable impulse to bolt, at the sight of him. Was it fair he should subject me to this lowly pantomime, after the rigours I had undergone? Not even know he was doing it, that was my sole shred of comfort. All the time hammering into my head were those pathetically insufficient eighteen years, making a silly farce of the situation. Love can bear anything better than ridicule. But I could see the crude workings of nature behind it; she was sick to death of this persecuted, on-the-defensive, barbed world, I had entrenched myself into; and was making a strong counter-offensive against it: by offering me, so disarmingly, all the good happy things, I had thought lost to me for ever. But nature, being her jolly haphazard self, had attached a few insuperable snags, to her bountiful gifts; and I had got to the crook in my stony road, where I viewed with the gravest suspicion, anything pleasant that might inadvertently happen to me. I experienced an inexplicable guilt at taking something that did not belong to me: waiting, snail-shelled, for the gleeful foot to trample me; and it never failed in its ultimate trampling.

In this phenomenally childish affair, because, in this respect, I am ashamed to say, I am extremely childish too; which did harm to nobody, and good to both of us; there were fresh complications, disapprovals, and taboos from outside; making me feel as wicked a sinner as in Wales. Mostly from The Church, who was undoubtedly going mad. I had already been made to realize sorrowfully that my first estimation of him was lavishly "too good to be true"; such idealistic saints, as I had painted him, do not run hotels, sit in a big office of the municipio all morning, and, more sinisterly, but equally in keeping, become Fascist heads in wartime. But with all his pompous pretensions to correct behaviour, viced respectability, and phantasy class; he still remained more like "Juno's Paycock" than the stuffed-shirt turkeycock he aspired to be. And, mercifully, could not, with all his determination to rise above his clod-hopping plodding brothers, rub out, at all successfully, his inborn lovableness. But, since I was his accepted friend in front of the town, it became my duty, of necessity, to redound to his credit; which meant, in his language, that I should behave as he saw fit, according to his tight-laced rules. And since his rules allowed me to speak to no one but himself, his family, the Englishman and his; it left me, had I followed them implicitly, a genteelly thin social time.

When I complained about the lack of company to him, he collected a bunch of the more well-to-do female gentility, and brought them along to meet me. A more constrained meeting, with less to say to each other, and no means of saying it, with polite unwillingness on both sides; could scarcely have been cooked up more daintily. While he, the broad, tolerant benefactor of mankind, sat beaming at the end of the table, not saying a word; but thoroughly convinced, that at last he had got me into my correct milieu; and all was well with the prosperous world. But it was not so well as all that: it was a bit late in the day to launch me into a society, that I had spent my life avoiding; so, though I politely acquiesced to his wishes, I also quietly went my own way; and I was not prepared, yet, to relinquish Joseph. The boy who said he would accept nothing, and was afraid of nothing: I seem to remember saying that myself, once.

One night, after supper, when Colm was in bed *and* sleeping, I went out, for the first time, walking alone with Joseph; not on the main road, but into the country. When I got back, after about an hour, I was met by warning shouts. Carabinieri, who have no resemblance to policemen, patrolling the streets, and The Church tearing up and down, on his motor bike, like King Lear riding his madness. So clutching my briary coat about me, I put on my best Queen Mary act, and head high, on stilts, attained the hotel: where my troubles were by no means over. The first thing I saw was Colm, wrapped in a blanket, being nursed by The Church's wife; and I knew, for a positive fact, that they had forcibly hauled him out of bed to dramatize my disgrace. Then when I got to our room, the man followed me in, and cursed and reviled me, as no sewer-swimming strumpet had ever been cursed and reviled before. In fluent Italian oaths, pointing with deranged persistence at my clothes: at tiny clinging burrs and brambles; and, though I did not know the meaning of the words they made themselves very disgracefully felt. There was one in particular that kept recurring: "Vergogna, Vergogna!" which sounded the whoriest Babylonian slut; but which I discovered afterwards in the famous dictionary was comparatively harmless, no more than: "shame, shame." Perhaps the Italian shame is greater than ours.

However, the "filthy" significance of "Vergogna" was made amply clear to me later on by the whole family: I was made to eat my shame, and grovel. If I went to the kitchen to ask for anything, I was met by downcast eyes; and The Church strutted, stuck his belly out, and would not talk to me at all, assuming an expression of exaggerated, sneering disgust; if I barely touched his sleeve, and said, "Please . . ." he shook himself, as though bitten by an adder. The limit of his pained utterance, for over a week was: *"Signora, prego."* To think I expected civilized relaxation; I began to hanker for Laugharne as an exotic Istanbul. However hard I tried to laugh this golden halter off, told myself it was not serious, that nothing could touch me now; yet so potent is the malignancy of public opinion; will I ever stop fighting it? that once again I felt like a fox on the run. What is more, The Church, with all his ties, pulls, strings, and telephone services, had me just where he wanted me: useless for me to say what right had he over me; at his protective mercy. Whatever I did, I was playing straight into his hands; so he openly and ruthlessly blackmailed me. Not only was he Paycock and Lear, but now had taken on the sinister guise of Count Fosca; he led me to the head of the Postal department and poured out, very fast, at the top of his voice, all his denunciations of me, and my lack of deportment, sparing no details. He used this unfortunate man, with a smattering of French; who was obviously utterly nonplussed, giving me despairing winks, passing on tidbits of the discourse, and trying vainly to smooth him down; as interpreter. There was no reason why it should ever have ended had not the constant exasperated screams of Colm eventually intervened. My position was made no stronger by the crude fact that I was living on money borrowed from The Church; and I owed him for the hotel. Thus it had been all through my life with Dylan: never able to pay the necessary amount, at the necessary time; and I did hate the ignominy of it.

One afternoon, as I was on my own in the house, pretending to write: looking back at what had gone before, and asking myself, not only, is the writing utter trash? but, am I an utterly cheap person?—when along strolled Pietro. He was one of the professional glamour boys, deliciously pretty, famed as a Don Juan; making me feel like the proverbial lasting-for-ever leather of hide-bound England. And, though I was brimming with admiration for his seductive arts; making love at that hour in the afternoon, in the crotchety mood I was in, was too incongruous to contemplate. No two people, from opposite ends of the globe, can have been further apart. So, after arguing with him, and trying to persuade him to go, without being too nasty as he was so soft and tender, I left him in the house and went outside, making a show of working at the table there; and hoping this would make him give up, and tiptoe delicately away.

At this moment, there was an impatient rattling at the outer gate, which I had locked, to keep people out; and I hardly had time to whisper agitatedly to Pietro that people were coming, when in strode The Church, having got through the same hole in the hedge, with a look of furious suspicion on his face. He ordered me to unlock the gate at once as he had brought along the aforesaid quartet of Rio society to pay a social call, and have tea with me. In a dithering trance of fear, I obeyed and let them in, muttering vague mixed greetings. In the meantime, I could hear The Church going through the house: there were only three rooms; like an enraged bull, opening and slamming doors. I waited, pent up, in the most distressing frame of mind, for the bellow of the "find." But he reappeared looking perplexed, carrying chairs; and all the time I had no idea where Pietro was, and, of course, dared not look. We settled nervously round the table; and I am sure the crafty women detected something suspiciously wrong in my distracted answers and spasmodic actions. They produced parcels of food and drink for the "Merenda," Italian tea; and, even in my alarmed state of mental squitters, I was amazed at the quantity and variety of it; and dreaded to think how long it would take to polish it off. The only minute glimmer of salvation, through that racking, tittle-tattling ordeal: no condemned man, waiting for the knife to drop, to sever his head from his body, suffered acuter pangs; was the need to fetch Colm from school at four o'clock. But as the time drew gaspingly on, and the merenda was still in touch-and-go swing, one of the smart provincial ladies suggested that it would not matter being half an hour late: that the Sisters would look after him; and I dared not protest for fear of seeming in too much of a hurry. By sipping and nibbling degrees they ate the last olive, started to smoke, dregged the Aleatico, sweet red wine of the country. Confusedly I jumbled the things together, threw chairs into the house, made a senseless clatter; and breathlessly locked the door.

I couldn't believe I was on my own two feet again, tearing down the mountain, to meet Colm: the joy of release was delirious, but I still had the plump "skeleton in the cupboard," to contend with. So I hurried back as fast as I could with Colm, to see, was he there, or was he not. When I got back to that house of terror and unlocked the door again: *there* he was; as cool and collected as a glasshouse of cucumbers, lounging in the one and only deck chair, listening to the radio. My indignation evaporated, and I started to laugh feebly with relief. "But where were you?" He told me he had lain for three quarters of an hour under the bed, on the stone floor, listening to us talk and eat; and when The

Church scoured the room, and bent to pick up his fallen pen, he admitted his heart had gone "pit, pat, pit, pat," which was a revelation of a heart for him.

This musical-comedy, bedroom farce episode, was not at all pleasing to my life of monastic retirement and as I intended, divine contemplation. It gave me a serious turn, fatally endangering my relations with The Church, and having some dirty repercussions later on, where Joseph was concerned. It took a ramification of acting daft bafflement for me to wriggle myself out of those. When Joseph was proud and reproving, there was nothing to touch him; he was more fearful than The Church, because I cared more for him; and I thought, this time I have gone too far, and, through my stupidity, lost him for good.

Later on, in the town, I saw Pietro and Joseph together, furiously talking; as they talk furiously in Italy, over trifles which in England would at most cause a grunt, it did not necessarily mean the floundering of my cockleshell boat; but the prospect before me looked hazardous. Pietro, in his inimitable manner, faded out; and I was left to tackle the rock Joseph; who finally told me that Pietro had spun a very creditable yarn, based on that suggestive boudoir scene heretofore related; but embroidered with some choice additions of his own. That he had brought me a bottle of cognac: there *was* a bottle of cognac from which I had offered Joseph a glass; and after drinking five each: it was a clever touch saying the number; he had made love to me, and I don't know what flagrancies of taste. It was one of those near-truth, could-have-happened, cunningly fabricated tales, that made anything I might say in defence, merely a confirmation of my faithlessness. Joseph listened to my vain ungrammatical protestations, only half understanding; then looking at me, with youthful contempt, said haltingly: "I no love liars."

I was having a tossed-about rough passage between these two rigidly upright men—The Church, who had painstakingly looked up the word "disillusion," to show what he thought of me; he was always looking up words to show the extent of my "fall from grace"; and Joseph, who, knowing nothing, was sure of everything, most of all himself, and the absolute rightness of his ideas, implanted since birth. I think he was mostly right too; but it never occurs to these "right" people, that knowing right, they could wilfully do wrong; just as, having established, for instance, that drink is bad for the stomach at certain times, they would no more think of taking it than flying without wings. That is what I am doing all the time: launching out brazenly, an unbalanced mechanism, with no idea where it will land. And not caring terribly either.

If I seem to have given too much importance to my piddling, mock, frivolous affairs, it is not that I think they are important, but that, to live at all, it is necessary to have the illusion of something going on. They

were but fly spots in the dense mesh of the day; but at night it is important for me to dream that I am looking forward to meeting somebody
tomorrow. I am really not awfully good at being the serene hermit,
which has become my wished-on-me rôle; and I am not awfully good
at meeting people either, unless pumped up with drink. I do everything
to excess, as though for the first and last time; and nothing teaches me
to modulate, to moderate: that there is a morning; always a ghastly
awakening.

Then the wind came, and the burning passions of the hunt were
blown clean away. It was not an ordinary wind, but a searing, demented
thing, with a biting will of its own that penetrated to the cringing mar-
row of the nethermost embedded bone. There is nothing love likes less
than the cold; and this wind was a slaying anathema to it; shrivelling to
its tender roots, the hothouse bloom. For the next few days it was killing
to be out of bed; shivering miserably in that whistling, rattling cave: the
hotel bedroom. Sitting, stiffened with resistance, at my washstand desk,
in my only two pairs of bedsocks, and two sweaters, with a ridiculous
flowery dirndl skirt in between. And not a blessed nook, cranny, or hole,
with a fire, to sit by. For the first time I thought seriously of going home,
for the sole reason of keeping warm; and telegrams flew through my
head. But being always slow to act, though headstrong in action; I waited
superstitiously for a sign, a symbol, a portent in the sky, to tell me what
to do: without which, of course, it was impossible to move. None forthcoming, I hung frigidly on.

In the meantime Colm folded up with sickness and exhaustion, and
simply perishing with the unrelieved cold. I started to get very angry and
indignant at the lack of alleviating amenities; I had still not had a waft of
a hot bath; in fact, there was no such basic article; and bathing in the sea
was now too blistering even for me. All my family furies were awakened
at the threat to Colm, and I stormed impotently at The Church; but it
got me nowhere. There was nothing for it but for us both to go to bed
and stay there, which we did. After two days of stench, stupefying wine,
and stagnation, flat on my back, I felt like an overstuffed, drunken taxi-
dermist's bird. But thank God: since the Pietro escape I believed implicitly in Him: (I was, by nature, a great believer, but could never make up
my mind to discard one God in favour of another, as they all seemed to
me so highly probable: I could see the stern fingers of innumerable Gods,
chastising me, but not one would beckon to me); the weather eased up,
and I was never so pleased to see a downpour of rain. I felt like a fish,
thrown back in the water, after gasping on dry land: in my natural
element again.

I got Colm back to school, improved after his rest, and keen, no
wonder, to get out. While I rushed into the "Campagna" as though it

was the first day of Creation; I was in such a hurry to get away from our congealed mummification. It looked just made, with the earth steaming hotly, after the rain, the grasses stretching, the leaves tingling, and the new air breathing and pulsing through stalk and stem. But when I got to the house my spirits fizzled out, at the sight of yesterweek's leavings; and the prospect of blank hours in front of me, frozen at the table; till it was time to fetch Colm again.

My brain worked better and was clearer among noise and jumble; it wilted and shrank at vistas of space yawning ahead. The small outside things that were happening to me here seemed to have precious little to do with me: seeking, searching, and not all that time left to seek or to search in; for, I did not know what. So, when The Church got so wild over my slight detractions from his holy conventional code; which nevertheless, did not stop him from betraying his sacred wife, whenever the opportunity offered; it was the old, old story, not of right and wrong, but of what is seen, and what is not seen; I felt straightforward envy that he could feel so strongly about, and take so seriously my breaches of his etiquette. As though it mattered all that copulating much who lay with whom: with the black hole grinning up at the comical bodies. People have a blessed natural gift for ignoring that unappetizing, but equally undeniable truth. But I never do, and nor did Dylan; and, since he has proved it, I forget it less than ever.

The Church's latest aberration had been to call round at the house, when Colm, Joseph and I, were locked in, shivering over a squalid cup of tea made in a tin jug. To creep stealthily round the blustering wind-shaken terrace, without letting us know he was there, and pile up against the door, chairs, tables, boxes, anything heavy, to stop us getting out. It was a queer feeling, later, in the half dark, battling through the ghostly barrage. Another day he banged, and barged in, looking disappointed not to find us incriminatingly disarrayed; but, undaunted, turned on poor, awkward, harmless Joseph, and called him, in a passion of rage, all the flowery rogues and scoundrels, so much worse in Italian, he could, most effectively, lay his lascivious tongue to; reserving for me his favourite insult: Strumpet! More meanly still, than any abuse he hurled at random; he forbade me, unconditionally, to have *anybody* in the house, or he would take it straight away from me; which cornered me very prettily. He went so far as to tackle the Englishman, explaining the disgraceful situation to him, and asking for his moral support: to talk to me, as a fellow countryman, and make me see the unseemliness of my ways, and the seemliness of his, The Church's dictates. The truth of the matter was, he had never been crossed in his life before, and I was a maddening constellation of red rags flapping and waving, just out of his reach. The Englishman, though a type such classy miles away from me, had never been so close, as on this occasion: his reaction was wry amusement and, probing for the cause of so exaggerated a wrath over so small an incident, a dry reference to "The green eyes of the little yellow God" . . . that cause such havoc to the stablest, ordinarily pillars-of-rectitude, doubly falling, people.

I felt bad about the Englishman, having typed him as that unapproachable breed: the pugnacious Public School man, *and* Scotch, than which no other is more limited, dogmatic, or, as a rule, further from the point. Greatly against my romantic will, which gave the Italians graceful preference over my own crabbed kind, I had to admit he was the only person I could have anything approaching a conversation with; and though his jokes were of a very prehistoric, juvenile smut order, at least he made a noble attempt at fun. The Italians were not only abysmally deficient in it; but they had never heard of the absurdity, and gazed, with pitying incomprehension, should anyone *not* say precisely what they meant. In my old world of excess of verbal fun-making, I used to scoff at it, and did not appreciate how much it mattered as an underlying ingredient.

When the Englishman announced one night with jubilant elation, that he was off to England in a few days and was staying over Christmas, and perhaps longer: "Was I going back the same time, and could we travel together?" I felt a lurching twist of longing in my guts, to be rid of this artificial show I was amateurishly producing, with me, as the bolstered-up Dame, clowning all the scenes; to wallow in baths, hot water bottles, and anonymous nannies. The thought of losing the last "crust" of rugged turf was devastating to me; as departing people do, we developed a sudden panic affection for each other.

Then came the real show-down with The Church; my drooping flags of independence taunting him, he was marching to a foregone victory. His next move was drastic, after a thunderous Sunday. There was a farewell lunch, with me acting hostess, a job I was hopeless at, to the Englishman and the retired Colonel, with his wife and three children. Not sparkling company; they sat, tensed, silent, spellbound, listening uncomprehendingly, to the Englishman, and my mumbled, rumbled comments; swooping vulture swift over their plates, which to my horror I saw were insufficiently filled: a bit of spite on the part of The Church as I was out of favour. I recalled the lunch they had given me in their house: which was just the one room with the beds, and their all in it, lace-clothed for the occasion, with the kitchen, a stable at the bottom of the path, from which a six course meal was carted up and down: Antipasto, pasta, pesce, carne, frutta, formaggio; all cooked by the Colonel. Then, as the last damnably unpopular touch, to our heavygoing mute unorganized lunch, Joseph joined us at the table.

I asked for a glass for him, which The Church put as far away as possible; and poured with consummate loathing, averting his dignified head, a trickle of wine into. The wretched boy had gone and dolled himself up in his Sunday best, and, for the first time, looked raw and unprepossessing; I could not believe such a grotesque transformation had taken place: stiff cardboard, brand new, jerkin, zipped uncompromisingly up to the chin, zips on pockets to match, glaring almost orange trousers, black patent-leather pointed shoes. Where was my beautiful Joseph with his eternal sweater of navy blue stars, his earth-dulled working trousers, his soft boots; used by everybody on the shelving stones of this country, including me, when all my other shoes had gone to shavings. But *he* was not at all cast down by his spivvy appearance; on the contrary, he was cockily delighted with himself, thought he looked lovely, which was an added offence to me. I despaired: can love be snuffed out so quickly, at the mere change of outer raiment? After a few too many drinks for his unaccustomed constitution, he normally drank nothing, he asked me to come out walking with him; and like a mesmerized sheep I went. That was the turning point in The Church's patience, and caused his drastic move.

As I was returning in the evening; there he was; and if ever the gates of salvation were closed on me, they were padlocked now; his whole enormous frame, with bowed legs set square, and featureless physiognomy, was padlocked. He asked me, with clipped formality, for the keys of my house, said the proprietor would come to see me tonight, and would I get ready to leave for London tomorrow. He did not want me in his Albergo, giving it a bad name, any more. It was no use me pretending I was not shaken, and in terror-struck doubt that this time I would not be able to break down the immense cliff of his towering righteousness. I said nothing then, just ran past him, head hanging, up the stairs. But I could see now that cat-cunning tactics on my part, were very necessary; stumbling words were useless at this dramatic stage if I was to accomplish anything to my profit. The only two effective props at my ignominious disposal were: the dubious advantage that I was a woman, which I was apt to forget myself at times, but which I must lay on thick as cheese spread, with a battleship shovel; using all the ancient weapons of tears, hysterias, destitution in a foreign land, weak, abandoned, no one in the world but him; and, hardest of all for me, pleading brokenly on my bended knees. The other weapon, which I was even more reluctant to use, since it was closer and more true to me, was my cossetted sorrow. But it had got to be done to explain my indifference to what I did, or what happened to me; the to him unnatural lust to do damage to myself; though he was incapable of understanding such a fatalistic attitude.

So, after supper; which for the first time we did not go to the kitchen to choose, but had it slammed down rudely in front of us; when I had put Colm to bed, he came to the room, and told me the proprietor was waiting outside. Not, I swear, the proprietor at all, but a relative; they are all related, as usual, in these small towns; living in a house on the opposite mountain, higher than, and looking straight down into mine. So that he could plainly see, and what he could not see he could make up, all the comings and goings. He had, as plainly to me, been rustled up by The Church, to give authenticity to his threat.

By then I was in a fair state of nerves myself, having been steeling myself, with nips of *caffè corretto* courage, for the interview. I swept in, in my grand manner: the distinguished foreign visitor that moment stepped off the boat, with no idea in the world what all the fuss was about. The stooge proprietor looked even more abject at being put in such an embarrassing corner than I dared to hope; but, with a conspiratorial nod of encouragement from The Church, he started to gabble incoherently about the streams of young men he had observed one after the other visiting the house. It was strange I had not observed them on my long lonely vigils; it must have been as good as the pictures, pinned to his window day and night, like a punctured moth. What was he complaining about? and didn't he have any work to do? Then, with a truly loathsome gesture, he put his tongue out, a good six wet inches, toothless as well; and tapped the tip knowingly, with his greasy finger, to indicate that people were talking. I refrained from saying people always talk, and how lucky for them to have something to talk about: my "house of ill fame" was as good a topic as any. I was beginning to believe in it myself, but I did deserve a rake-off from all the fun and games.

My indignation was gently rising, as between the two of them, all in my own interests of course, they poisonously manufactured this scapegoat of myself. Suddenly, without adequate words to defend myself, they came: the tears that I was afraid would not materialize, they not only came, but I could not stop them. Frustrated beyond all endurance I refused to pick up, or clink glasses with these two mischief-making men, some achievement for me; made a bolt for the bedroom, and slammed the door. Childish, I agree, but gratifyingly effective. I sat trembling on the bed, with the recollective spasms I thought I had lost, getting a galvanized grip on me again; listening with the detached ear, for the *sotto voce* continuation in the next room. I could hear muffled shuffling, urgent whispering, click of lights out; and an instant later The Church was with me; bringing my wine, in chastened servitude, with an almost human look on his face. He said at once that he would not take the key as long as I promised to stick to his conditions, and gave up speaking to, or having anything to do with Joseph, or any of the *giovani;* and, for propriety's face, nobody must go to the house excepting him. He would be pleased to keep me in his hotel, do everything he could for me, so long as I behaved with more decorum, as a decent woman should. He had evidently given the brush-off to the stage proprietor at very short notice.

I had heard all this pontificating, many in-one-ear-and-out-the-others before; but when he brought out my letters, treasured by him; and showed how much they, and I, meant to him; I was moved to compassion at my capricious treatment of him. If it truly was love; but I had stopped believing in that old thing; all his flights of violence were dearly pardonable. Was he not right, come to that? I had no choice in any case, so I promised.

Life in Rio, without The Church's approbation, was as prohibitive as a death sentence; there would have been no alternative but to leave, and I did not want to leave yet, not because I was having a good time, the diametrical reverse, but because, when I got terrible pangs of yearning for my own, somebody to tell things to, to hold on to; somebody who understood my awfulnesses; I had to tell myself scathingly that I had nothing, and nobody, and would I kindly shut up. I know I had the other two children, and I loved them, and wanted very badly to see them; but children are children for all that, and come under a separately aloof heading. They should never be used as washing lines on which to hang out the clinging smalls of affection. Greater love hath no mother than to leave them alone. And, since recapitulating The Church's impetuous actions, in the light of his hotly-denied love for me; they became immediately, vastly more sympathetic, and I set a perceptibly higher value on him: so much for the whipped cream of flattery.

All the same, this new régime he imposed on me, of reinforced exclusiveness, did not leave me a wide range of distractions; since the cafés, and public drinking were out of bounds. A bottle in the house, yes; or a glass in the hotel: meaning no other than that cheerful hotel bedroom, where I had spent so many gnawing, digging deep into the pit of reminiscence hours; trying to summon the courage of will to move, to get out, and to face those strangers' appraising, animal stares. Since the Englishman and his wife had packed up on me, and the classy ladies now kept a safe distance from me, it left me solely the retired Colonel: a very old, very small man, submerged to his bushy eyebrows in his beard, who never spoke to me, but rapped out sharp orders into military vacancy. As for The Church himself, the most I ever got out of him was a snatched coffee or tea; not that he was mean, but he did not drink at the *wrong* hours: I could never discover the right ones. I scarcely saw him at all, except when he brought our breakfast early in the morning; and might or might not, I used to pray *not,* roll me on the bed, in a matter of seconds. Then off to his Municipal office, where in a posh vault of a room: with an almost invisible dark secretary in one corner; he put on his most important face, and tapped, and dictated, and referred back to, on secret official business, till two o'clock. But I did not see him again till I returned, from my frigid gestations, in the evening; nevertheless, if I happened to be wandering up and down the streets, killing time till we could eat, and stopped to talk to someone; he was always just behind me, ready to usher me on. He allowed me one black coffee—surreptitiously laced with cognac by friendly Massimo, the bar boy—after dinner. To make clear his devilish intentions to me, he nodded, winked, heaved his enormous shoulders, and stealthily disappeared; five minutes later, with long-suffering forbearance, I joined him, lingered as long as possible, over the indispensable dictionary, hoping he would leave me to my own devices; but he never failed to see me safely up the stairs first.

But I could not forget there was Joseph to be considered, who knew nothing about these new stringent measures, and who had regained all his weekday charm, with his early rising hacking work, and familiar old, loving clothes. How was I going to tell him? In the end I composed a letter in, as near as I could get to baby English; though I was never good at expressing myself simply; trying to explain to him my difficult position. But to take the sting out of: "I must not see him any more," I added that I loved him still, and perhaps later . . . So reluctant is love to part with any part of itself. Or should I say so tenacious is a bitch of her carrion meat.

Joseph, far from being disheartened by my letter, was bouncier than he'd been for a long time, and I had a tough job persuading him that it was serious. He refused to understand a word that I was saying: and I did feel a daft cow, a free woman of my age, with three children, explaining that I was not allowed even to speak to him in the street, by a mad landlord, who acted, with no right in the world over me, more proprietarily than a jealous husband, Joseph just laughed at me, and wanted to know why I listened to Mussolini, as he called The Church; why didn't I leave the hotel, go somewhere else, do what I wanted, and take no notice of The Church, and his determination to lock me in a box. Life is only as simple as that to the very young; and I wondered why I didn't; if nothing else there was always the unpaid bill to be considered: one of the unpleasant mundanities that took precedence over my waxing and waning romances. But I could not expect Joseph to understand that; or that it was in the realms of possibility to like, while rebelling against, and getting indignant with, the bully who wielded such an unjust, exterminating rod. I was, in truth, torn between disgust at his gross presumption and touched at the sweetness of him bothering at all with me, especially so rageously. Nothing was worse, I discovered, than being cast off altogether, and being given the awful impersonal over-effusive; as everything was over-effusive with him, politeness; of a total, hard, uncaring stranger.

SOPHIA TOLSTOY
(1844–1919)

Sophia Behrs married Count Leo Tolstoy when she was eighteen and he was thirty-four; she gave birth to sixteen children, of whom thirteen lived. She was completely involved in his writing career as copyist, critic, and editor. When, after a late-life religious crisis and conversion to a kind of Christian asceticism, Tolstoy renounced property, including the copyright on future works, Sophia had to take on the management of their estate, Yasnaya Polyana, and the squeezing of an income from Tolstoy's earlier works, of which she kept producing new editions.

She had written a diary as a girl and revived the practice after her marriage, partly at Tolstoy's insistence. He read her diary and she read his as a way of knowing each other's minds. From early in the marriage her diaries registered complaints about her husband, and sometimes, after reading them, he wrote apologies in the margin. But the diaries became increasingly bitter, especially from 1891 on. In 1895 Sophia was shattered by the death at the age of seven of her youngest son.

She found it harder and harder to endure Tolstoy's many followers and disciples, of whom a nearby gentleman named Chertkov was especially ardent. Chertkov's successful campaign to gain possession of Tolstoy's recent diaries was an enormous blow to Sophia, for whom the diaries played an essential part in her marriage. Her jealousy of Chertkov skirted ever closer to madness. She contemplated suicide often and made several attempts.

As the rivalry between his wife and his friend came to a head, Tolstoy, who had been threatening to leave Sophia, left her, saying he wanted to "live out his old age in peace." He was eighty-two. Less than two weeks after leaving Yasnaya Polyana, he died of pneumonia.

In these diary excerpts, which focus on Sophia's perhaps paranoid struggle to defeat Chertkov and to keep her husband and his works for herself, Tolstoy is referred to as Lev Nikolaevich, Lev Nik., L.N., or, affectionately, Lyovochka.

For a more recent "married to genius" diary, compare Eleanor Coppola, *Notes.* For another account of going off the deep end, compare Kate Millett, *The Loony-Bin Trip.* For complaints about a famous husband, played in a comic mode, see the letters of Jane Welsh Carlyle.

FROM *Diary*

July 7, [1910], morning

Rain, wind and damp. I have proof-read *The Fruits of Enlightenment* and finished sewing Maria Aleksandrovna's skirt. I took the proofs of *Resurrection* from Lev Nik.'s divan, before Chertkov sniffed them out and took them away. Lev Nik. went to see his idol today, despite the weather. I realised today that although his last diaries are very interesting, they have all been *composed* for Chertkov and those to whom it pleases Mr. Chertkov to show them! And now Lev Nikol. never *dares* to write a word of love for me in them, for they all go straight to Chertkov and he would not like this. What made them valuable in my hands was their sincerity, their power of thought and feeling. . . .

It is pouring with rain, but despite this Lev Nikol. rode over to Chertkov's, and I waited for him in despair on the porch, worrying and cursing our proximity to Chertkov.

Evening

No, Lev Nik. hasn't been taken from me yet, thank God! The sheer force of my suffering and my passionate love for him has broken the ice which has recently separated us. Nothing can resist the power of this emotional bond—we are joined by our long life together and our great love for one another. I went into his room as he was going to bed and said: "Promise me you won't ever leave me on the sly, without telling me." And he replied: "I wouldn't ever do such a thing—I promise I shall never leave you. I love you," and his voice trembled. I burst into tears and embraced him, saying how afraid I was of losing him, that I loved him so much, and that despite some innocent and foolish passions in the past I had never stopped loving him for a moment, and still in my old age loved him more than anyone else in the world. Lev Nik. said that he felt exactly the same, that I had nothing to fear, that the bond between us was far too strong for anyone to destroy, and I realised that this was true, and I felt so happy. I went into my room, but returned a moment later and thanked him for taking this great weight off my heart.

I said goodnight to him then, and went off to my room, but after a little while the door opened and Lev Nik. came in.

"Don't say anything," he said. "I just want to tell you that our conversation this evening made me so happy too, so very happy . . ." And he burst into tears again, embraced me and kissed me . . . "Mine! Mine!" I said in my heart. I shall be much calmer now, I shall come to my senses, I shall be kinder to everyone, I shall try to get on better with Chertkov.

He wrote me a letter trying to justify his behavior to me. I invited him here today for a reconciliation, and told him that as a decent man he must at least apologise to me for those two appalling things he had said: 1) "If I really wanted to I could *drag you and your children through the mud.* I have enough connections to do so. The only thing that has stopped me is my affection for Lev Nikol—ch." And 2) "If I had such a wife as you, I would have shot myself or run off to America long ago." But he wouldn't apologise for anything, and said that I had misinterpreted his words, and so on.

But what could be clearer? He is a proud, spiteful and very stupid man! Where are these supposedly Christian principles of love, humility and nonresistance? It's all nothing but hypocrisy and lies. He simply has no breeding.

But when he was going downstairs he said he thought he probably should not have made that second remark, and that if his letter did not satisfy me, then he was prepared to express his *regret,* in order to remain on good terms with me. The letter was nothing but cunning and hypocrisy.

But I don't mind any more. Lev Nikolaevich has shown me his heart, shown me that he loves me, and that has given me strength and I am happy. I despise everything else now, for I am invulnerable.

The cocks are crowing, dawn is breaking. Night . . . The trains rumble and the wind rustles the leaves on the trees.

July 8

My husband's kind words soothed me, and this is the first day I have spent in a normal state of mind. I went for a walk, picked a large bunch of wild flowers for Lev Nikolaevich and copied out my old letters to my husband, which I found amongst his papers.

The same people here as usual—Chertkov, Goldenweiser, Nikolaev and Sutkovoi. It has been cool, windy and raining. The fallow field is being double-sowed and the roofs are being painted. Sasha* is in low spirits, has a bad cold and is sulking at me. Lev Nikol. read us a lovely

*Their daughter—ED.

French short story by a new writer called Mille. He enjoyed a story by him yesterday too, called *"La Biche écrasée."*

He would be quite healthy if it weren't for his constipation.

July 9

Lord! When will these vile episodes and intrigues end! My daughter-in-law Olga arrived, and there was yet another conversation about my relations with Chertkov. He was rude to me again and I didn't say one impolite word to him—and they all go into corners and pick over my bones, gossip about me and accuse me of I know not what. I simply cannot get used to the fact that some people simply *lie*—I find it quite astonishing. Sometimes one is horrified and tries naïvely to establish the truth, to remind them or explain . . . But all such attempts are quite unnecessary; people often *simply do not want the truth,* for it is neither necessary nor to their advantage. This has been the case in this Chertkov business. But I shall say no more about it, I have quite enough worries as it is. Today Lev Nikol. and Lyova* went for a ride through the woods. There was a large black rain-cloud ahead, but they rode straight into it; they had not taken anything with them, and Lev Nikol. had nothing but a thin white shirt on, while Lyova was wearing just a jacket. I always beg Lev Nik. to tell me which route he is taking, so that I can send on warm clothes or a carriage for him, but he will never hear of it. Eventually the storm burst, it poured with rain, and for 1½ hours I was running around the terrace in a terrible state of anxiety. My heart contracted painfully, the blood rushed to my head, my mouth was dry and my heart was filled with despair.

They arrived home soaked to the skin. I wanted to rub Lev Nikola-evich's back, chest, arms and legs with spirit of camphor, but he angrily rejected my help and in the end he only grudgingly agreed to let his valet Ilya Vasilevich give him a massage.

Olga got angry for some reason and took her children away without staying for dinner.

My head was aching for the rest of the day and I felt quite ill. I had a slight temperature (37.5) and could not do a thing, although I had a lot of work to do, especially on the new edition, which has now come to a complete stop. I was feeling quite debilitated this afternoon, and went to my room, where I fell asleep and unfortunately slept on and off all evening. . . .

12 degs., damp and unpleasant. Sasha has a harsh, rasping cough, and this is also very worrying.

*Their son—Ed.

And then something is drawing to an *end*. Is it my life, or that of someone in my family, I wonder? . . .

Lev Nikolaevich naturally did not *dare* write in his diary how he came into my room late at night, wept, embraced me and said how happy he was that we had reached some understanding and closeness together. Instead he writes: "I must restrain myself" everywhere. What does this mean? No one could possibly love or care for him as I do, no one could desire his happiness as I do. Yet he gives his diaries to Chertkov, who will publish them and repeat to the whole world what he said to me—that a wife like me would make one want to shoot oneself or run off to America.

L.N. rode with Chertkov into the forest today, where they had some sort of discussion. They gave Bulgakov a horse too, but they made sure he kept his distance, as they did not want him to disturb their privacy. It is *I* who have to "restrain myself" every day at the sight of that odious figure.

In the forest they dismounted twice for some reason, and in the gulley Chertkov pointed his camera at Lev Nik. and took his photograph. As they were riding back, Chertkov noticed that he had lost his watch, and he deliberately got as far as the balcony before telling Lev Nik. where he thought he had lost it. And L.N., looking so pathetic and submissive, promised to go to the gulley after dinner *to look for Mr. Chertkov's watch.* . . .

I thought Lev Nik. would be embarrassed to drag a lot of respectable people off to the gulley in search of Mr. Chertkov's watch. But he lives in such fear of him that even the thought of being made to look foolish—*ridicule*—did not deter him from taking a crowd of 8 people out to the forest. We all stamped around in the wet hay, but did not find the watch—heaven knows where that absent-minded idiot lost it! Why did he have to take a photograph in the soft wet hay anyway? Then for the first time this summer Lev Nik. asked me out for a walk with him, and I was overjoyed, and waited anxiously to get away from the gulley and the watch. But I was wrong, of course. The following morning Lev Nik. got up early, went to the village, summoned some peasant lads, went off to the gulley again and found the watch.

This evening Mr. Salomon read us a boring French allegory about the prodigal son, then we read a light-hearted story by Mille, and another also by him.

. . . I told Lev Nik. how annoyed and embarrassed I had felt when instead of taking everyone out for a walk he had taken them to the gulley to look for Chertkov's watch; he grew angry, of course, there was another quarrel, and I saw the same cruelty and coldness in him, the same desire to shield Chertkov. I felt quite ill and was thrown into another sudden fit of despair. I lay down on the bare boards of the balcony and remembered how it was on that same balcony, 48 years ago, when I was still a girl, that I first became aware of my love for Lev Nikolaevich. It was a cold night and I liked the idea that I should find my death where I had found his love. But I had evidently not earned this yet.

Lev Nikolaevich heard a rustle, came out on to the balcony and stood there shouting at me to go away, as I was preventing him from sleeping. I then went into the garden, and lay on the damp ground for two hours in a thin dress. I was chilled through, but I longed to die—and I still do.

They raised the alarm, and Dushan Petrovich,* N.N. Guét and Lyova came and shouted at me and helped me up off the ground. I was shaking all over from cold and nerves.

If only those foreigners could have seen to what state Lev Tolstoy had reduced his wife, lying on the wet ground at two or three in the morning, numbed and in the throes of despair, how astonished those good people would have been! When I thought this I did not want to leave the wet earth, the grass, the dew and the moon, appearing and vanishing in the sky. I did not want to leave until my husband came out and took me home, because it was he who had driven me out. He did come out eventually—only after my son Lyova shouted at him and demanded that he do so—and he and Lyova took me home. It was now three in the morning, and neither he nor I could sleep. We could not come to any agreement, and I was unable to extract a drop of love or pity from him.

Well, what now! What is to be done! I cannot live without his love and tenderness, and he cannot give it to me. 4 in the morning. . . .

It was already light now, and we were still sitting opposite one another in my bedroom, not knowing what to say. When has that happened before?! I longed to go back to the garden and lie down under the oak; it would have been so much easier there than in my room. Eventually I took Lev Nik. by the arm, begged him to go to bed and we both went into his bedroom. I returned to my room, but then I longed to see him and went back to his room. He looked so old and sad, lying with his face to the wall, wrapped up in the blanket with the Greek design that I had knitted for him, and a desperate feeling of pity and tenderness awoke within me; I kissed the dear, familiar palm of his hand, begging him to forgive me, and the ice melted. We both wept again, and I finally felt his love for me again.

*A servant—Ed.
†A visitor—Ed.

I prayed to God to help us live the last years of our life in peace and happiness, as before.

July 11

I slept only from 4 to 7.30 A.M. Lev Nik. also slept very little. I am ill and exhausted, but my soul is happy. Relations with Lev Nik. are friendly and straightforward again, just as they used to be. I love him so intensely, and so foolishly. And so clumsily! He needs me to make concessions and heroic sacrifices, but I am incapable of doing this, especially now at my age. . . .

We all went to bed early. L.N. himself asked Chertkov not to come this evening. Thank God! Just to breathe freely for one day is such a rest for one's soul.

.   .   .

July 13

After sending Chertkov away yesterday for my sake while he was out riding, Lev Nik. spent the whole evening waiting for him to come so he could explain the reason. Chertkov did not come for a long time. Sensitive to my husband's moods, I saw him anxiously looking about him, waiting like a lover, becoming more and more agitated, and sitting out on the balcony downstairs staring at the road. Eventually he wrote a letter, which I begged him to show me. Sasha brought it, and soon I had it in my hands. It was "dear friend," of course, and endless endearments . . . and I am once again in a frenzy of despair. None the less he gave this letter to Chertkov when he arrived. I took it under the pretext of reading it, and then burnt it. He never writes me tender letters, I am becoming more wicked and unhappy, and even closer to my end. But I am a *coward.* I did not want to go swimming yesterday, because I was afraid of *drowning.* I need only *one moment* of determination, and I have been incapable of even that.

I spent a long time posing for Lyova. Lev Nik. went for a ride with Goldenweiser and the Sukhotins, and I looked for Lev Nik.'s last diary but could not find it. He realised that I had found a way of reading it, and hid it in another place. But I shall find out where he has hidden it, unless it's with Chertkov, Sasha or the doctor.

We are like two silent enemies, constantly suspecting, spying and sneaking up on one another! We hide, or rather Lev Nik. hides everything he can from me, by giving it to that "spiteful pharisee," as one close friend—N.N. Gué, the son—called him. Maybe he gave his last diary to Chertkov yesterday.

Lord take pity on me, people are so evil, they won't spare me . . . Take pity on me and save me from sin . . .!

Night of July 13–14

Let us assume that I have gone mad, and my "fixation" is that Lev Nik. should get his diaries back and not allow Chertkov to keep them. Two families have been thrown into confusion, there have been painful arguments—not to mention the fact that I have suffered to the very limits of my endurance. (I have not eaten a thing all day.) Everyone is depressed, and my tormented appearance annoys everyone like a bothersome fly.

What can be done to make everyone happy again, and put an end to my sufferings?

Get the diaries back from Chertkov, all those little black oilcloth notebooks, and put them back on the desk, letting him have them, one at a time, to make excerpts. That's all!

If I do eventually manage to overcome my cowardice and summon up the courage to kill myself, everyone will see, on looking back, how easy it would have been to grant my wish; they will realise that it really was not worth cruelly and stubbornly refusing my request and tormenting me to death.

When they explain my death to the world they won't give the real reason. They'll say it was hysteria, nerves and my wicked nature—and when they look at my dead body, killed by my husband, no one will *dare* say that the *only* thing which could have *saved* me was the one simple expedient of returning those four or five oilcloth notebooks to my husband's desk. . . .

Where is their Christianity? Where is their love? Where is their "nonresistance"? Nothing but lies, deception and cruelty.

Those two stubborn men, Chertkov and my husband, have joined forces and are crushing me, destroying me. And I am so afraid of them; their iron hands crush my heart, and I long to tear myself from their grip and escape. But I am still so afraid . . .

We speak of a person's "right" to do something, and of course it is Lev Nik.'s "right" to torment me by refusing to take *his* diaries from Chertkov. But does he have the "right" to do this to his wife, with whom he has lived for half a century? And is it also his "right" when it is a matter of life and death, of maintaining the peace and good relations with people, of love and happiness, people's health and tranquillity— and finally the "nonresistance" L.N. is so enamoured of? What about that? . . .

I am telling them how to *save* me—get back the diaries. And if they don't want to they can strike a bargain: Chertkov can have the "rights" to the diaries, and I shall have the "right" to life and death.

The thought of suicide is growing stronger all the time. Thank God my sufferings will soon be over! . . .

July 14

I have not slept all night and was within a hair's-breadth of suicide. These expressions of my suffering, however extreme, could not possibly do them justice. Lev Nikol. came in, and I told him in a terrible state of agitation that everything lay in the balance: it was either the diaries or my life, he could choose. And he did choose, I am thankful to say, and he got the diaries back from Chertkov. In my nervousness I have made a bad job of pasting into this diary the letter he gave me this morning; I am very sorry about this, but there are several copies, including the one I made for the collection of Lev Nikolaevich's letters to me, and the one that our daughter Tanya has.

Sasha drove over to Chertkov's to fetch the diaries and give him a letter from Lev Nikolaevich. But my soul is still grieving, and the thought of suicide, clear and firm, will always be with me the moment they open the wounds in my heart again.

So this is the end of my long and once happy marriage . . . ! But it is not quite the end yet; Lev Nik.'s letter to me today is a scrap of the old happiness, although such a small and shabby scrap!

My daughter Tanya has sealed up the diaries, and tomorrow she and her husband will take them to the bank in Tula. They will fill out a receipt for them in the name of Lev Nik. and his heirs, and will give this receipt to L.N. I hope to God they do not deceive me, and that Jesuit Chertkov doesn't wheedle the diaries out of Lev Nik. on the sly!

Not a thing has passed my lips for three days now, and this has worried everyone terribly for some reason. But this is the least of it . . . It's all a matter of passion and the force of grief.

I bitterly regret that I have made my children Lyova and Tanya suffer, especially Tanya; she is being so sweet, kind and compassionate to me again! I love her so much. Chertkov must be allowed to come here, although this is very, very difficult and unpleasant for me. If I do not let them meet, there will be page upon page of secret, tender letters, and that would be much worse.

July 15

I did not sleep all night; I kept thinking that if it was so easy for Lev Nik. in his letter to break his promise not to leave me, then it would be equally easy for him to break all his promises, and where would all his "true and honest" words be then? I have good reason to worry! First he promised me in front of Chertkov that he would give *me* his diaries, then he deceived me by putting them in the bank. How can one keep calm and well when one lives under the constant threat of "I'll leave, I'll leave!"

I have such a strange headache—at the back of my head. Could it be a nervous attack, I wonder? That would be good—as long as it is fatal. My soul is sick, for my husband is trying to kill me. This morning, after a sleepless night, I asked Lev Nik. to give me the receipt for the diaries which are being taken to the bank tomorrow, so as to set my mind at rest that he will not break his word again and give them to Chertkov, as he did so easily once before (break his word, I mean).

This made him terribly angry. "No, absolutely not, not for anything!" he said, and ran out of the room. I had another frightful nervous attack and longed to drink opium but again lacked the courage to do so, and instead told Lev Nik. a wicked lie and said that I had taken it. I confessed immediately, and wept and sobbed, but I made a great effort and managed to regain my self-control. How ashamed and wretched I feel, but . . . no, I shall say no more: I am sick and exhausted. . . .

Today Lev N.'s diaries were sealed up, all 7 notebooks of them, and tomorrow Tanya and I are taking them to the bank for safekeeping. At the moment they are in Tula with Doctor Grushetskii, which worries me. We were going to take them to the bank today, but everything in Tula was closed as they were holding a public service for the cholera epidemic, so we shall have to collect them from Grushetskii and deposit them at the bank tomorrow. This is a new and unpleasant trait in Lev Nik. Why in the bank? Why not keep them at home or leave them at the Historical Museum, where all his other diaries are? And why am I not allowed to read *these* diaries? Everyone will be able to read them after Lev Nik.'s death, but God forbid his *wife* should read them *now*! It never used to be like this! It hurts my soul so! And this is all Chertkov's influence. . . .

I am so tired of problems, plots, secrets, cruelty—and my husband's acknowledged "growing indifference" to me! Why should I be perpetually in a *fever*, loving him to distraction? My heart too can change and cool towards a man who does all he can to let me know of his indifference. If one has to live, and not kill oneself, one has to find some comfort and happiness in life. "I cannot live like this," I shall say. "You give me your cold heart, and Chertkov your passion."

Now that they have discovered I am keeping a diary every day, they have all started scribbling *their* diaries. They are all out to attack me, condemn me and bring all sorts of malicious evidence against me for daring to defend my conjugal rights and asking for a little more love and trust from my husband, and for the diaries to be taken away from Chertkov.

God be with them all: I need my husband, while I am still not completely frozen by his coldness; I need justice and a clear conscience, not the judgments of others.

I went to Tula with Tanya and we deposited Lev Nikolaevich's seven notebooks in the State Bank. This is a half-measure, i.e. a partial concession to me. They have been removed from Chertkov, thank God, but now I shall never be able to see or read them in Lev Nik.'s lifetime. This is my husband's revenge on me. When they were brought back from Chertkov's I took them frantically and leafed through them to see what he had written (even though I had already read most of them before), and I felt exactly as though my beloved lost child had just been returned to me and was about to be taken away again. I can imagine how furious Chertkov must be with me! This evening he visited us again. I am still tormented by hatred and jealousy of him. A mother whose child is lured away by the gipsies, and then returned to her, must feel exactly what I felt today.

The diaries were deposited in Lev Nik.'s name alone, . . . so they can be taken out only by him, or by power of attorney.

.   .   .

I keep discovering more and more vile things that Chertkov has done. He has now persuaded Lev N. to give instructions that the copyright should not go to his children after his death, but should be made common property, as are his last works. And when L.N. said he would talk to his family about it, Chertkov was *hurt*, and would not let him! Scoundrel and despot! He has taken this poor old man in his dirty hands and forced him into these despicable deeds. But if I live, I shall have my revenge, and he won't be able to do any such thing. He has stolen my husband's heart from me and stolen the bread from my children's and grand-children's mouths, while his son has millions of stray rubles in an English bank, quite apart from the fact that those rubles were partly earned by me, because of all the help I gave L.N. Today I told Lev Nikol. that I knew about these instructions of his, and he looked sad and guilty but said nothing. I said it was a mean trick, that he was plotting strife and discord and that his children would not give up their rights without a struggle. It makes me very sad to think that over the grave of this dear man there will be such a lot of anger, reproaches and painful scenes! Yes, an evil spirit has guided this Chertkov's hand—it is no coincidence that his name derives from the word "devil," and that Lev Nik. wrote in his diary:

"Chertkov has drawn me into a struggle. And this struggle is painful and hateful to me."

I have also discovered just how much Lev Nikol. dislikes me at present. He has forgotten everything—forgotten the time when he wrote in his diary: "If she refuses me, I shall shoot myself." Whereas of course not only did I not refuse him, I lived with him for 48 years and never for one moment stopped loving him.

I am in a hurry to publish the new edition before Lev Nik. does something desperate, since he is capable of anything in his present grim mood. He rode out to meet Sasha but she was late and he missed her. He went to sleep when he came back, and had dinner on his own at 7 o'clock.

He is writing to Tanya. He loves his daughters but does not care for his sons—some of them he actually hates. They are not vile, like Chertkov.

This evening I showed Lev Nik. his diary which I had copied out for 1862, when he fell in love with me and proposed to me. He seemed astonished, then said, "How painful!"

But I now have one consolation, and that is my past! He of course finds this painful. He has replaced a life that was pure, honest and happy for one that is false, secretive, impure, evil—and weak. He suffers terribly, loads everything on to me, and just as I predicted, he casts me in the role of Xantippe,* which is very easy for him thanks to his popularity. But how will he answer to God, his conscience, his children and his grandchildren? We all have to die, and my enemy too will breathe his last, but what will we experience in our last moments? Shall I too be able to forgive my enemy?

---

*Socrates' shrewish wife—ED.

I cannot regard myself as guilty, for I feel with all my being that by keeping Lev Nikolaevich away from Chertkov I am saving him from the enemy—the devil. I pray to God that the heavenly kingdom may enter our house once more. "May *Thy* kingdom come"—not that of the enemy.

.   .   .

October 16

I woke up early and could not get back to sleep for worrying about how to get Lev Nik.'s diaries out of the Tula State Bank. I got up feeling calm but not at all well, went down to breakfast, and Lev Nik. suddenly announced that he was off to see Chertkov. . . .

I cannot express what I felt! It was as though all my insides were falling out! This was the threat I had been living under all this time! But I merely said quietly, "This is only the second day in which I've started to get a little better," and went off to my room. I got dressed and went outside, then came back in, took my husband aside and said to him quietly and tenderly, almost in a whisper, "Please wait a bit before going to see Chertkov if you can, Lyovochka. It's so terribly hard for me!"

At first he did not lose his temper, merely said that he would not promise anything and wanted only to do what was best. But when I repeated my entreaty, beside myself with anguish by now, he repeated in a rage that he had promised nothing. Then I ran out to the woods and clambered into some gulleys where it would have been extremely hard to find me had I been taken ill. Then I came out into the field, and from there I raced to Telyatinki* (carrying the binoculars, so as to be able to see everything from a long way off). When I got to Telyatinki I lay in the ditch near the gates leading to the Chertkov's house and waited for Lev N. to arrive. I don't know what I would have done if he had—I kept imagining that I would lie down on the bridge across the ditch and let his horse trample over my body.

Fortunately, though, he did not come. . . .

At five o'clock I wandered off again. I entered our grounds as it was growing dark, went to the lower pond and lay down for a long time on the bench under the large fir tree there. I was going through such agony at the thought of Lev Nikolaevich's exclusive love for Chertkov, and a resumption of their relations. I could just imagine them locked away together with their endless *secrets*, and these frightful

---

*The nearby estate belonging to Sasha—Ed.

imaginings turned my thoughts to the pond, in whose icy water I could that very moment have found total oblivion and eternal deliverance from my tormenting jealousy and despair! But again I was too much of a coward to kill myself. Eventually I wandered back to the house, although I don't remember which path I took. I did not go in, though, as I was too afraid, and sat down on the bench under the fir tree. Then I lay down on the ground and dozed off.

When it was completely dark and I could see Lev N.'s light through the windows (which meant he had woken up), they came out in search of me with lanterns. Aleksei the yardkeeper found me. . . . I was beside myself with cold, exhaustion and my recent harrowing experiences.

I arrived home numb with cold and utterly insensible; I sat down on the bed without undressing and stayed there like a mummy, without having any dinner or taking off my hat, jacket, or galoshes. This is how you kill people—without weapons but with perfect aim!

It transpired that Lev Nik., having tortured me and promised me nothing, had gone not to Chertkov's . . . and had sent Dushan Petrovich to tell me this. But Dushan Petrovich could not find me, as I had already left for Telyatinki.

When I asked L.N. this evening why he had made me so unhappy, and whether he would be going to see Chertkov later, he would not tell me, then started shouting in a rage: "I want my freedom, I won't submit to your whims and fancies, I'm 82 years old, not a little boy, I won't be tied to my wife's apron strings . . ." and many more harsh and hurtful things besides, which made me suffer terribly. Then I said to him: "But that's not the point, that's not what you're always saying. According to you, man's loftiest achievement is to sacrifice his own happiness to deliver the person closest to him from suffering." He did not like that at all, and merely shouted: "I take back all my promises, I promise nothing, I shall do whatever I want . . ." and so on.

He cannot live without seeing Chertkov, of course, and this is why he gets so angry with me: because I simply *cannot* force myself to endure a resumption of relations with that scoundrel. . . .

October 17

I am so physically and emotionally exhausted that my mind is blank and I don't feel like writing. I would desperately like to know what my husband is writing in his diary. His present diaries are like works of literature, from which people will extract the ideas and draw their own conclusions. Mine are a genuine cry from the heart, and a true description of everything that happens to us. Sasha too is writing a diary. What with her hatred of me and her bad temper I can well imagine how she will go out of her way to attack me and give her own interpretation of my words and feelings! But God knows! At times I feel such tenderness and pity for her. But at the moment she is being her usual coarse, sharp, intolerant self, and I long to get away from her. She serves her father diligently enough, and threatens me with her diaries. God be with her!

I have decided not to go anywhere, neither to Moscow nor to concerts. I now treasure every moment of my life with Lev Nik. I love him as intensely, as though it was all starting anew, like the last flame of a dying fire, and I could not possibly leave him. Maybe if I am gentle with him he will grow more fond of me too, and will not want to leave me. God knows! He has very much changed for the worse, and is now more prone to anger than to spontaneous kindness. Despite my jealousy of Chertkov, I surround him with love, care and tenderness, and anyone else would appreciate this. But he has been spoilt by the rest of the world, which judges him by his books (and his words), rather than his life and deeds. Just as well!

ANNE TRUITT
(1921–)

Anne Truitt is a minimalist sculptor whose work has been widely exhibited, her first one-person show taking place in 1963. Typically her work takes the form of basic shapes, painted in subtly layered color. She was born in Baltimore and grew up on Maryland's Eastern Shore. As an undergraduate at Bryn Mawr she studied psychology, but she began to study art at the Institute for Contemporary Art in Washington, D.C., in 1949. *Daybook: The Journal of an Artist* (1982) mixes reminiscence with discussion of daily concerns, both of art and family. This section was written at Yaddo, the artists' colony in Saratoga Springs, New York, in 1974. Earlier that year Truitt had had a retrospective exhibit at the Corcoran Gallery of Art in Washington, and the organizational work involved as well as the public attention had exhausted her, making the time at Yaddo all the more welcome.

For other journals of creative women, compare the diaries of Virginia Woolf, Anaïs Nin, and Sylvia Plath. For another vacation from family responsibilities, compare Anne Morrow Lindbergh, *Gift from the Sea*.

FROM *Daybook*

1 July [1974]

This household at Yaddo, of which I am now a part, is organized the way my mother organized the household of my childhood. I feel the orderly rolling of routine around me: repetitive, familiar, restorative. Dinner last night was nostalgic, in the perfect balance of nursery food: candied sweet potatoes, a touch of pineapple, peas, cranberry sauce, cottage cheese, a delightful salad, ice cream, and a large glass of milk. The simple joy of childhood rose in me, a joy elicited by food and by welcome into a household of objective routine.

I have the comfortable feeling of being an inconsequential member of a litter, like a puppy or a kitten. I have a place but am not outstanding in any way. This is a feeling I have always enjoyed enormously. It heals me in some subtle way.

My childhood household was too formal to convey the lighthearted feeling of being in a litter. It was not until 1934, when my younger twin sisters and I visited my mother's sister, Aunt Nancy, on her farm outside of Charlottesville, Virginia, that I first encountered the relaxation of being one of many children. At that time, as now, I was overstrained by too much responsibility, too much earnestness, and too much sadness. It is a joy to be here, set free, anonymous within a shelter.

2 July

My studio here is peacefully widening out. The green shades are furled, the windows are open onto a sweet-smelling meadow with purple martin houses stalking among fruit trees. A grapevine flourishes against the gray stones of the south wall—the studio is called Stone South—and meanders in tendrils over my screens. A wide vegetable garden lies beyond a stout privet hedge to the east. Two triangular skylights allow the northern light to flood in, and me to see the changing clouds. My drawing table stands free to itself. In another area there is room for two sawhorses to support an 8' × 4' piece of ¾" plywood on which I can paint, and other surfaces on which I can spread finished work.

My bedroom is small and white and has a turret and a narrow green-tiled adjoining bathroom. I do not have a telephone by my bed, alert for emergency, and I can leave my glasses on my bureau, yards away, when I sleep. Pine-scented wind sings gently within my shell. I am alone, acknowledged in a silent community.

A community as yet mysterious to me. Guests come and go as quixotically as the White Rabbit. Yet we are all drawn together into a kind of tacit intimacy by being artists, which we handle in different ways. We are gently curious about one another, as if we all had the same disease, could compare symptoms and treatments.

My hand is back in. The tourniquet that strain had been twisting around it for the past few months has loosened, and its connection with the part of me that knows how to make work in art is once again vital.

I do not understand why I seem able to make what people call art. For many long years I struggled to learn how to do it, and I don't even know why I struggled. Then, in 1961, at the age of forty, it became clear to me that I was doing work I respected within my own strictest standards. Furthermore, I found this work respected by those whose understanding of art I valued. My first, instinctive reaction to this new situation was, if I'm an artist, being an artist isn't so fancy because it's just me. But now, thirteen years later, there seems to be more to it than that. It isn't "just me." A simplistic attitude toward the course of my life no longer serves.

The "just me" reaction was, I think, an instinctive disavowal of the social role of the artist. A life-saving disavowal. I refused, and still refuse, the inflated definition of artists as special people with special prerogatives and special excuses. If artists embrace this view of themselves, they necessarily have to attend to its perpetuation. They have to live it out. Their time and energy are consumed for social purposes. Artists then make decisions in terms of a role defined by others, falling into their power and serving to illustrate their theories. The Renaissance focused this social attention on the artist's individuality, and the focus persists today in a curious form that on the one hand inflates artists' egoistic concept of themselves and on the other places them at the mercy of the social forces on which they become dependent. Artists can suffer terribly in this dilemma. It is taxing to think out and then maintain a view of one's self that is realistic. The pressure to earn a living confronts a fickle public taste. Artists have to please whim to live on their art. They stand in fearful danger of looking to this taste to define their working decisions. Sometime during the course of their development, they have to forge a character subtle enough to nourish and protect and foster the growth of the part of themselves that makes art, and at the same time practical enough to deal with the world pragmatically. They have to maintain a position between care of themselves and care of their work in the world, just as they have to sustain the delicate tension between intuition and sensory information.

This leads to the uncomfortable conclusion that artists *are,* in this sense, special because they are intrinsically involved in a difficult balance not so blatantly precarious in other professions. The lawyer and the doctor *practice* their callings. The plumber and the carpenter *know* what they will be called upon to do. They do not have to spin their work out of themselves, discover its laws, and then present themselves turned inside out to the public gaze.

4 July

Yesterday's effort—a long day of demanding work in the studio—seems to have triggered a familiar state. I woke up in the middle of last night hot, flustered, nauseated, and dried out. I had counted prematurely on reserve energy. And now, as in Parcheesi, I am back at Home Start again. I am thankful to be here at Yaddo, where I can stay in bed without disturbing anyone, or anyone's even knowing.

What worries me is that I try so hard to be sensitive to the variations in my energy level, and fail so often. It frightens me that my children's security is dependent on my unsturdy, unstable body. Also, the pre-emptive images that present themselves to me in my conception of my work are on a scale way out of proportion to my capacity to bring them into being. My hand is securely in. My working program was brought into order yesterday. All my projects are on schedule, with the delightful prospect of open time at the end for painting on canvas. But today I am jerked back by the reins of my own physical weakness.

Perhaps the human lesson is always submission. We have a choice: to rebel or to recognize our powerlessness while maintaining our faith. In my own case, the first choice is denied me. I simply haven't the energy. What rebellion is possible for me emerges as febrile depression. My preconception of how events should go has tricked me once more; I must try to open myself to the flow of cause and effect (of which I am such a small part) with a clean, trusting simplicity.

So I will try to behave intelligently. A day of solitude in bed with *The Golden Bowl* will probably restore me to work. And I hope I will be here long enough to soak up reserve strength.

5 July

The separation of mind and body seems to appear most distinctly after an illness ends. My mind, now clear, is back in the studio, leans over my drawing board, and turns to consider the progress of the sculptures. If it were on its own, I would intently walk over there and intently work. My body walks to the desk and back to bed, glad to return.

6 July

Balancing intuition against sensory information, and sensitivity to one's self against pragmatic knowledge of the world, is not a stance unique to artists. The specialness of artists is the degree to which these precarious balances are crucial backups for their real endeavor. Their essential effort is to catapult themselves wholly, without holding back one bit, into a course of action without having any idea where they will end up. They are like riders who gallop into the night, eagerly leaning on their horse's neck, peering into a blinding rain. And they have to do it over and over again. When they find that they have ridden and ridden— maybe for years, full tilt—in what is for them a mistaken direction, they must unearth within themselves some readiness to turn direction and to gallop off again. They may spend a little time scraping off the mud, resting the horse, having a hot bath, laughing and sitting in candlelight with friends. But in the back of their minds they never forget that the dark, driving run is theirs to make again. They need their balances in order to support their risks. The more they develop an understanding of all their experience—the more it is at their command—the more they carry with them into the whistling wind.

There seems to be a law that the more conscious knowledge you develop, the more you can expand your consciousness. The artist takes advantage of this law. Wise artists like Titian and Rembrandt and Matisse became greater as they became older. Piero della Francesca died blind at the age of ninety-odd. I think often of what he must have kept on seeing, his own space and color perfectly balanced and alive behind his fixed eyes.

8 July

The central fact of the dark run is its high emotion, and this is in no way avoidable in actually making a work of art, even when—as happened to me early this morning—the *look* of what you are trying to make is clear in your mind's eye. A certain train of thought that absorbed me ten years ago resurfaced about 5 A.M. in the form of a series of drawings and paintings so plain in their essence that I wonder they evaded me for so long.

This work, which I will begin to make today, is a shear turn of my own earth. When Walter Hopps and I worked on my retrospective last winter, his dogged insistence that I search out every extant piece of work I ever put my hand on plowed, cross-plowed, and replowed this field. The process was unbelievably painful, but I had to watch it happen. Are you sure there weren't some drawings in 1958 after Mary was born? What happened to the Tokyo work of spring 1967? Where is it? Is it in the basement? Is it on that shelf in the basement? What's up there, that package? What's in that box? What's behind that box? He even forced me to remember three little sculptures I had totally forgotten doing in 1963, because he *felt* I had made them: three I had forgotten for reasons so close to my psychological bone that I had to stop talking for a moment to collect myself before saying, yes, I had made them, they are here and there, of these dimensions and colors and so forth. He was merciless. He never relented for a second in his intent to see *everything*.

He exposed year after year of labor. We saw together the character of my effort, as lucid as the annular rings of a tree's growth. He was like the Hound of Heaven. I felt it that way. I fled. He followed—and followed and followed. His intuitive leap to the certainty of a gap in the work's natural development prodded my reluctant memory over and over again.

Until finally there came an end. "Now you can stockpile again," he said, and departed from my studio, leaving me as tenderly clean as a wind-washed shell.

The core of my reluctance was, of course, cowardice. I had recorded in order to forget. I had hustled my pain, my despair, my delight, my bafflement onto paper and into clay and wood and stone, and fixed them there as if in magic enchantment. I had thought to hold them, beyond reexamination, reexperience. Sprung from my deliberately wrought tombs, my most secret feelings arose alive, bleeding and dazzling, to overwhelm me once more. I simply could not believe what was happening. And all the while I was in the full midstream of events, decisions to be made, children to be cared for, meals to be cooked, the house to be cleaned, friends to be cherished.

Paradoxically, it was this very pressure that saved me. My past meshed into my present. It had to be taken in, considered, woven. I found, to my surprise, that the experience of my twenties, thirties, and forties had room in my fifties. The warp and woof of my self was looser and stronger than I had known. Thinking I would not survive, I found myself enriched by myself.

9 July

My work is coming steadily along. My pace in the studio is practiced. I move from one task to another with the ease of Tarzan swinging on lianas through the jungle. I am at once totally in jeopardy and totally at home.

13 July

On the edge of awakening this morning, I slid into the happy consciousness that my life here is just right. I thrive in the repetitive routine. Innocent pleasures suit me. I continue to feel as safe as a younger child in a large family.

My mother's cool handling of childhood crises was one of my first lessons in how to live. Once I was bitten by a black snake. Blackberry bushes grew close to the dirt road at Lee Haven, a house near Easton, Maryland, in which we spent a summer when I was about seven. Moving through deceptively soft-looking wild grasses that prickled my legs, and picking and eating as I went, I was pushing farther and farther into the thicket when suddenly I felt a blunt, muscular hit on my leg, a sharp pain, and in that second saw the snake's black body whip out of sight. I remember a moment of paralysis as my seven-year-old mind organized the facts. Then I ran, crying and calling for my mother, to the dark-shingled, frightening house (overshadowed by tall pines, never sunlit), up the white steps onto the wooden porch, in through the wide front door and into the central hall. My mother, in her light cotton dress and white sneakers, was by that time running down the staircase to meet me.

With no loss of time whatsoever and with equally no hurry, she looked at the mark, asked a couple of clear questions about the snake's body, made me lie down on the black, horsehair sofa in the dining room, told the nurse to put some wet soda cloths on my leg, and called the doctor. I can see her now, dignified and reserved as always, with the telephone receiver shaped like a black tulip held to her ear.

My father was always more anxious about me than my mother. He returned home later that afternoon and rounded the corner into the dining room at a fast trot, flushed with concern and love. Comfortable by that time, I was complacently changing my own wet soda cloths.

I cannot remember ever not knowing that my father loved me more than anyone in the world. I abided in that love, loved and honored it as he loved and honored me. But I never truly understood this central stove of warmth and light in my life until long after my father was dead, until I reached the age he had been in my childhood. Because I was born when he was forty-two, it is only in the last few years that I have wholly loved him. When I was younger, his love seemed excessive, embarrassing because of a proportion I could meet only decorously, never realistically.

It was my mother's cooler hand that guided, apparently effortlessly and rather unemotionally, my efforts to learn how to live.

14 July

Three sculptures are finished, small ones: *Parva* I, II, and III. And I have now started a series of drawings I am calling *Stone South.* These are pencil and white paint, very spare: attempts to catch the threshold of consciousness, the point at which the abstract nature of events becomes perceptible. This comes down to the placement of interval: lines meeting and not meeting as close as the force of their lengths will allow; a metaphor for the virtually imperceptible ways in which our lives turn, critical turns of change determined by interval.

I have settled into the most comfortable routine I have ever known in my working life. I wake very early and, after a quiet period, have my breakfast in my room: cereal, fruit, nuts, the remainder of my luncheon Thermos of milk, and coffee. Then I write in my notebook in bed. By this time, the sun is well up and the pine trees waft delicious smells into my room. My whole body sings with the knowledge that nothing is expected of me except what I expect of myself. I dress, do my few room chores, walk to the mansion to pick up my lunch box (a sandwich, double fruit, double salad—often a whole head of new lettuce) and Thermos of milk, and walk down the winding road to my Stone South studio.

At noon, I stop working, walk up through the meadow to West House, have a reading lunch at my desk, and nap. By 2:30 or so I am back in the studio. Late in the afternoon, I return to my room, have a hot bath and dress for dinner. It is heavenly to work until I am tired, knowing that the evening will be effortless. Dinner is a peaceful pleasure. Afterward I usually return to my solitude, happy to have been in good company, happy to leave it. I read, or write letters, have another hot bath in the semidarkness of my room, and sink quietly to sleep.

22 July

One of my mother's bequests to me was the idea of making things run smoothly. It was engrained in me very, very early that I was not only to make as little fuss as possible myself but also to soothe anyone else who was fussing, and furthermore to watch intently for the first sign of situations giving rise to fussing in order to forestall them. This concern was partly temperamental—my mother was delicately calibrated emotionally—and partly traditional. This curve of control matched, convex to concave, her independence of spirit. Her life was lived on its spine, and mine followed. We paid for our independence inside by doing things well outside.

One step further lurked the pit of hypocrisy: thinking one way and acting another. We avoided this, more or less successfully, in two ways. The first was by taking care all the time to rationalize events into what could be handled smoothly. I can remember watching my mother doing this, both in the drawing room and in the nursery. She chose which aspects of a disagreeable situation she would address herself to, and isolated them as artfully as if life were a game of jackstraws. By this kind of manipulation, we tried to define the course of our lives in accordance with our ideas of what we could handle. We kept our actions honest by the complicated effort of constantly defining what we thought about them.

The second guardrail against the pit was a principle much stronger than that of not making a fuss. In the interest of this principle—that intellectual honesty was the bedrock of a life bestowed by God—making a fuss was sometimes crucial. This life, a gift of grace for an unknown reason, must be lived purely, because at death we return with its accruements to our source. Life is entrusted to us, does not belong to us, and has to be restored in honorable condition. We are responsible for this trust, and must live with this fact in mind.

Wherever we stood, my mother and I, we placed ourselves as upright as possible with God above us and the earth under our feet, trying to forget neither.

It has taken me many years to recognize the mistake intrinsic to my mother's approach to shouldering this responsibility: She never developed a faith in natural process strong enough to allow herself to trust it, and herself to it. She permitted the circumstances of her life to wear her out while she gracefully maintained a self-defined position in a self-limited world.

I was, I think, more fortunate. In the fullness of my middle years, at the age of forty-three, just when I stood most in danger of stiffening into my mother's pattern, my husband's career led us to Japan, where I was unable to play the jackstraws game. None of the straws, neither personal nor environmental, could be sufficiently detached for me to control them.

I felt this defeat adumbrated from the air as our plane banked sharply to land in March 1964, and I saw beneath me a wrinkled-prune land, purple in an apricot-violet mist of evening light. A shock of astonishment flashed through every cell of my body: an instinctive realization that nothing in my experience would help me now, but everything in my experience must be in readiness to learn. In that second, something in me went numb. It was as if the jackstraws game had enabled me to meet the demands of ordinary life and to maintain a kind of structural fence within which I could endure the emotional intensity of my work. Without this security, I became frightened. Though I continued to live from day to day as intelligently as I could, the vital force from which my work had been steadily emerging since 1961 simply stopped. Deprived of this natural flow, as well as of my emotional courage, I was driven to make my work with my mind and its quality so dropped that when I was preparing for the retrospectives last winter I destroyed all the sculpture I had made in Japan. It was simply intelligent work, lifeless.

Looking back, I am astonished that I continued to work at all. Something stubborn and dumb in myself had taken over. I worked harder than I had ever worked in my life, had to work harder because so often the sculpture, varied in a neo-constructivist manner out of a desperate intellectual preoccupation with the laws of visual experience, had to be stripped of color several times before I could even get near to what I thought—thought, not felt—I wanted. A complicating element was the light in Japan, entirely different from that of the United States. When I brought sculptures from Japan to New York for exhibition in 1965, I was horrified to see that the color looked wrong. And I was so out of touch with myself that I used aluminum instead of my customary wood for my structures.

The emotional telepathy of the Japanese penetrated my spirit. I had all my life been accustomed to feeling alien. In Japan, I *was* alien. And made to feel it. Most particularly by an old woman who lived a few doors up the alley from my studio. My studios have always meant home to me in a special way, so I was painfully vulnerable to her unrelenting hostility, which felt to me like murder. In all the four years we spent as neighbors, she never once returned my greeting, nor even raised her eyes to mine— except on a single occasion and then only to give me a piercing wound. Her entire waking life was spent, apparently, on her front doorstep. All day long she sat there surrounded by piles and piles of old magazines and papers over which she pored endlessly. Around her spread a pool of dark feeling as palpable as smoke. It was difficult for me to take in the facts of her existence. In snow and rain, in heat, from early to late, she never moved except for the shift of an arm, and that I saw only once or twice as a scarcely identifiable movement of her heavy black garments. There was simply nothing to be done about her existence; I could neither help her in her obviously dire poverty nor alter the fact that her attitude toward me wiped out my own existence.

So, unlike my mother, whose ramparts were never breached, I suffered a frightening rout of my habitual defenses. My fortress was indeed so inundated that I was forced to abandon it. I lost forever a whole methodology of living, including my faith in forming such a methodology. Very slowly and painfully, the thrust of my effort to live my life responsibly moved from the habitual formation of constructions to a simple observation that opened my eyes to the natural flow of events. I was forced to grant grace to natural process, myself naked in it, and my life began to present itself in its own rhythm. At first tentatively and then with more confidence, I began to find delight in acquiescence, and finally even a kind of joy in acceptance.

24 July

From 1948, when I decided to enter the Institute of Contemporary Art in Washington as a student in sculpture, to 1961, when my work suddenly took an autonomous turn, the forces of instinct and the forces of intuition fought for control of my work. Yesterday intuition fell back briefly before instinct. My hand wanted to *draw,* to run free. Colors overran, lines tilted, and with about the same degree of effectiveness as Don Quixote going at the windmills. For one whole day I entertained the notion, which had been creeping up on me, of turning my back on the live nerve of myself and *having fun.*

This morning I am sober. I would be a fool to sacrifice joy to fun.

MARIE VASSILTCHIKOV
(1917–1978)

Prince and Princess Vassiltchikov took two-year-old Marie out of Russia with their other children in 1919. She grew up as a refugee in Germany, France, and Lithuania, where her family owned land. In the 1930s, with economic depression widespread, it was hard for Russian émigrés to find employment except in Nazi Germany. Marie (called Missie) and her sister Tatiana (later married to Prince Paul Metternich) found themselves in Germany at the start of the war and, because of their excellent language skills, managed to get jobs as secretaries in the German Foreign Office, where there was a surprising amount of anti-Nazi feeling. Many of their friends, including members of some of the most distinguished families in Germany, like Gottfried Bismarck and Adam von Trott zu Solz, participated in the anti-Nazi resistance. These men, who considered themselves patriots and Hitler an aberrant madman, took part in the Twentieth of July plot to kill the Führer in 1944. Many of them were executed after the assassination attempt had failed.

Missie recorded daily the effects of the war on Berlin and on her friends. She was such an assiduous diary keeper that her boss would tease her, "Come on, Missie. Set aside your diary and let's get a little work done." She kept the diary in English, in which she was fluent, and when the Twentieth of July plot started, she switched to shorthand. But she held on to the dangerous material, hiding it first at her office, then at friends' homes. Few parts were lost. After the war she transcribed the shorthand, retyped the whole thing, and put it aside for twenty-five years, until, just before her death, she prepared it for publication. Her diary provides a rare firsthand account of the anti-Hitler resistance in Germany, although Christabel Bielenberg, an English woman married to an English-educated, anti-Nazi German lawyer who was imprisoned at Ravensbruck, discussed some of the same events in her memoir, *The Past Is Myself.*

For an account of a childhood in Nazi Germany as recalled during a later return journey, see German novelist Christa Wolf's *Patterns of Childhood.* For a Russian émigrée who took a different path from Vassiltchikov's, see Nina Berberova's treatment of her Paris years in *The Italics Are Mine.* For an account by a Soviet citizen who stayed in the Soviet Union, compare Eugenia Ginzburg, *Journey into the Whirlwind.* For other accounts of World War II, compare Anne Frank, *Diary* and Marguerite Duras, *The War.*

FROM *Berlin Diaries*

Berlin, Thursday, 29 June 1944

Lunched at the Gersdorffs', after which Tony Saurma drove Tatiana, Loremarie Schönburg and me around town to see the damage caused by yesterday's raid. This time the whole district around the Friedrichstrasse Bahnhof is completely gutted, including the Hotels Central and Continental. I had stayed with Loremarie in the Central for two days the last time I was in Berlin.

I had to leave a message at the Adlon and in the hall ran into Giorgio Cini. He has come all the way to Berlin to try and bribe the S.S. into setting his father, old Count Cini, free. When Italy changed sides last year, the latter (a one-time Minister of Finances of Mussolini) was arrested in Venice and has been in Dachau concentration camp, in an underground cell, for the past eight months. He suffers from angina pectoris and is in very bad shape. The Cinis have millions and Giorgio is willing to pay anything to get him out. He himself has changed a lot since I last saw him just before the war. He evidently is desperately worried. He adores his father and for many months did not know his whereabouts, nor whether he still lived. Now he was waiting for some big Gestapo man. Who knows? With that amount of determination and willpower—and money—he may succeed. He wants them to agree to transfer his father to an S.S. hospital and from there to Italy. His family has stayed on in Rome under the Allies, but he seems to be in touch with them.

Friedrichsruh, Saturday, 1 July

As I had to give up my hotel room in Potsdam, I have moved back into town and am now at the Adlon. Otto Bismarck has asked Paul Metternich, Tatiana and me to Friedrichsruh, the family's famous estate near Hamburg, for the weekend. We have never been there and may never have a chance again, so we have accepted. Spent the morning at the office and then rushed over to the station, where the others were waiting. When we arrived, the Bismarcks were very surprised, as our telegram of acceptance had never reached them. Otto, in pyjamas, was taking an afternoon nap; Ann Mari and Giorgio Cini were in the garden. The latter, looking devastating in a pale blue shirt, reminded me of Venice that last summer of peace five years ago.

Sunday, 2 July

Otto Bismarck had arranged a little shooting party—for boar—but nobody hit anything. The only boar we saw, as big as a young calf, stalked straight past Paul Metternich's stand. When Paul, deep in conversation with Ann Mari Bismarck, heard our exclamations, he fired wildly but naturally it got away. Otto was visibly put off, as he had given Paul the best stand.

After dinner we had a long discussion with a famous zoologist about the best way to get rid of Adolf. He said that in India natives use tigers' whiskers chopped very fine and mixed with food. The victim dies a few days later and nobody can detect the cause. But where do we find a tiger's whiskers?

Friedrichsruh is beautifully kept.

Berlin, Monday, 3 July

Got up at 4 A.M. to get back to Berlin on time. Unfortunately, while leaving off my luggage at the Adlon I bumped into Schleier, our nasty new chief of personnel, who could thus see that I had been out of town (private travel is officially discouraged).

Krummhübel, Tuesday, 4 July

Returned to Krummhübel to find that Mamma (whom I had invited to visit me there) had already arrived. For the moment she lives with us, but she cannot stay long, as we are not allowed to have guests. Count Schulenburg is still away and Loremarie Schönburg is back in Berlin, this time for good. She has even been allowed to take sick leave there. Everybody is surprised that Schleier has been so decent to her.

Wednesday, 5 July

Go for long walks with Mamma, who finds the country beautiful and takes photographs tirelessly. I fear she will not see as much of me as she had hoped, as I spend a lot of time at the office and must be back in Berlin next week.

Madonna Blum gave a little dinner party for her, after which we played duos on our accordions. Count Schulenburg's assistant, Sch., has not returned from a trip to Switzerland. He gave the excuse of a broken leg when skiing, but this does not seem to be the real reason and I fear Schulenburg may have trouble on his account.

Berlin, Monday, 10 July

I am back in Berlin, staying at the Adlon. Giorgio Cini is still here.

Adam Trott and I dined there together. We spoke English to the head waiter, who was delighted to show how well he still remembers it. Our neighbors began to stare. Adam then took me for a drive, during which, without going into particulars, we discussed the coming events which, he told me, are now imminent. We don't see eye to eye on this because I continue to find that too much time is being lost perfecting the details, whereas to me only one thing is really important now—the physical elimination of the man. What happens to Germany once he is dead can be seen to later. Perhaps because I am not German myself, it may all seem simpler to me, whereas for Adam it is essential that some kind of Germany be given a chance to survive. This evening we had a bitter quarrel about this and both of us got very emotional. So sad, at this, of all moments . . .

By "imminent events" Adam Trott meant a first attempt to kill Hitler which was planned for the following day and which was postponed at the very last minute because Goering and Himmler (who were to be killed at the same time) were not at Hitler's side.

Tuesday, 11 July

Consulted Professor Gehrbrandt, Maria Gersdorff's doctor. Something evidently is wrong with my health, as I am terribly thin. He puts it down to the thyroid and will recommend a long leave of absence.

Krummhübel, Wednesday, 12 July

Count Schulenburg is back from Salzburg, where he had been summoned by Ribbentrop. He has been ordered to report to Hitler's H.Q. in East Prussia. At long last they seem to want his expert advice. It seems a little late in the game, but it is rumoured that they are cooking up some separate deal in the East.

He had lent me the former Rumanian Foreign Minister Gafencu's book *Préliminaires de la Guerre à l'Est.* It is very interesting and mentions him often, as both Gafencu and he were ambassadors in Moscow before the war together. Sometimes, apparently, Gafencu is mistaken, but when Schulenburg approached him in Geneva he was decent enough to accept all the latter's corrections. This must wait until after the war, however, for these corrections are so damning to the Führer that they would cause a scandal now.

Here, everything is disintegrating and I will be glad to leave Krumm-hübel myself, presumably for good, next week.

Thursday, 13 July

After lunching with us, Count Schulenburg departed.

A letter from Adam Trott, straightening out our last misunderstanding. I answered immediately. He has left for Sweden.

The Russians are suddenly advancing very fast.

Saturday, 15 July

It's pouring with rain. Went to the cinema with Mamma and Madonna Blum.

A new decree forbidding the use of trains by civilians. Mamma will have to leave immediately, as this decree comes into force in two days.

Tuesday, 18 July

Mamma left this morning. Last night, we dined with Madonna Blum and, on our way home, went over to speak with the Russian Cossacks who are here with their horses and, seeing that there are no more cars, are used for the transportation of senior officials. Mamma gave them cigarettes and they danced and sang and were so happy to speak Russian again. The poor fellows are stranded between two chairs, having opted against Communism and never having been really absorbed into the German army.

At the office, the pre-arranged telegram from Adam: I am expected in Berlin tomorrow.

Berlin, Wednesday, 19 July

Today I left Krummhübel—I suspect for good. I had packed everything and have taken with me as little as possible. The rest will stay with Madonna Blum until I know what is to happen to me.

We reached Berlin at eleven, but owing to recent air-raids all stations are in a state of chaos. Ran into old Prinz August Wilhelm, the late Kaiser's fourth son, who kindly helped carry my luggage. We finally boarded a bus. The town is enveloped in smoke; there is rubble everywhere. Eventually, I was deposited at the Gersdorffs'.

Now that it is summer, they take their meals in the upstairs sitting-room, although it still has no windows. I found the usual group of people, plus Adam Trott.

Later, I had a long talk with Adam. He looks very pale and strained, but seems glad to see me. He is appalled that Loremarie Schönburg should be back in town and is very unhappy about her unceasing efforts to bring together people whom she suspects of being sympathetic to what I call *die Konspiration* [the plot] and many of whom are already deeply involved and are having a hard enough time as it is staying above suspicion. Somehow she has found out also about Adam's involvement and now keeps pestering him and his entourage, where she has acquired the nickname "Lottchen" (after Marat's assassin, Charlotte Corday). To many she is a real security risk. He told me that she had even complained about my being unwilling to take an active part in the preparations.

The truth is that there is a fundamental difference in outlook between all of *them* and me: not being German, I am concerned only with the elimination of the Devil. I have never attached much importance to what happens afterwards. Being patriots, *they* want to save their country from complete destruction by setting up some interim government. I have never believed that even such an interim government would be acceptable to the Allies, who refuse to distinguish between "good" Germans and "bad." This, of course, is a fatal mistake on their part and we will probably all pay a heavy price for it.

We agreed not to meet again until Friday. After he had gone, Maria Gersdorff remarked: "I find he looks so pale and so tired; sometimes I think he is not going to live long."

Aga Fürstenberg joined us for supper. She has now moved to the actor Willy Fritsch's house in Grunewald, a charming little cottage he left in a hurry after having a nervous breakdown during one of the recent raids. Apparently, he lay sobbing on his bed all day until his wife came back to Berlin and took him out to the country. Aga shares the house with Georgie Pappenheim, a charming fellow who has been a diplomat for years and who has just been called back from Madrid, probably on account of his name (the Pappenheims are among the oldest families in Germany). He plays the piano beautifully.

I have been granted four weeks' sick leave but may only take two at a time and must first train an assistant to take care of things in my absence.

Thursday, 20 July

This afternoon Loremarie Schönburg and I sat chatting on the office stairs when Gottfried Bismarck burst in, bright red spots on his cheeks. I had never seen him in such a state of feverish excitement. He first drew Loremarie aside, then asked me what my plans were. I told him they were uncertain but that I would really like to get out of the A.A.* as soon as possible. He told me I should not worry, that in a few days everything would be settled and we would all know what was going to happen to us. Then, after asking me to come out to Potsdam with Loremarie as soon as possible, he jumped into his car and was gone.

I went back into my office and dialled Percy Frey at the Swiss Legation to cancel my dinner date with him, as I preferred to go out to Potsdam. While I waited, I turned to Loremarie, who was standing at the window, and asked her why Gottfried was in such a state. Could it be the *Konspiration?* (all that with the receiver in my hand!). She whispered: "Yes! That's it! It's done. This morning!" Just then Percy replied. Still holding the receiver, I asked: "Dead?" She answered: "Yes, dead!" I hung up, seized her by the shoulders and we went waltzing around the room. Then grabbing hold of some papers, I thrust them into the first drawer and shouting to the porter that we were *"dienstlich unterwegs"* ["off on official business"], we tore off to the Zoo station. On the way out to Potsdam she whispered to me the details and though the compartment was full, we did not even try to hide our excitement and joy:

Count Claus Schenck von Stauffenberg, a colonel on the General Staff, had put a bomb at Hitler's feet during a conference at Supreme H.Q. at Rastenburg in East Prussia. It had gone off and Adolf was dead. Stauffenberg had waited outside until the explosion and then, seeing Hitler being carried out on a stretcher covered with blood, he had run to his car, which had stood hidden somewhere, and with his A.D.C.,† Werner von Haeften, had driven to the local airfield and flown back to Berlin. In the general commotion nobody had noticed his escape.

On reaching Berlin, he had gone straight to the O.K.H. [Army Com-

*Auswärtiges Amt, or Foreign Office—ED.
†Aide-de-camp—ED.

mand H.Q.] in the Bendlerstrasse, which had meanwhile been taken over by the plotters and where Gottfried Bismarck, Helldorf and many others were now gathered. (The O.K.H. lies on the other side of the canal from our Woyrschstrasse.) This evening at six an announcement would be made over the radio that Adolf was dead and that a new government had been formed. The new Reichskanzler [Chancellor of the Reich] would be Gördeler, a former mayor of Leipzig. With a socialist background, he is considered a brilliant economist. Our Count Schulenburg or Ambassador von Hassell is to be Foreign Minister. My immediate feeling was that it was perhaps a mistake to put the best brains at the head of what could only be an interim government.

By the time we had reached the Regierung in Potsdam, it was past six o'clock. I went to wash up. Loremarie hurried upstairs. Only minutes had passed when I heard dragging footsteps outside and she came in: "There has just been an announcement on the radio: 'A Count Stauffenberg has attempted to murder the Führer, but Providence saved him . . .' "

I took her by the arm and we raced back upstairs. We found the Bismarcks in the drawing room, Melanie with a stricken expression, Gottfried pacing up and down, up and down. I was afraid to look at him. He had just got back from the Bendlerstrasse and kept repeating: "It's just not possible! It's a trick! Stauffenberg *saw* him dead." "They" were staging a comedy and getting Hitler's double to go on with it. He went into his study to telephone Helldorf. Loremarie followed him and I was left alone with Melanie.

She started to moan: Loremarie had driven Gottfried to this; she had been working on him for years; if he were to die now, she, Melanie, was the one who would be left with three little children; maybe Loremarie could afford that luxury, but who would be left fatherless? Other children, not hers . . . It was really dreadful, and there was nothing I could say.

Gottfried came back into the room. He had not been able to get through to Helldorf, but he had further news: the main radio station had been lost; the insurgents had seized it but had been unable to make it work, and now it was back in S.S. hands. However, the officers' schools in the suburbs had taken up arms and were now marching on Berlin. And, surely enough, an hour later we heard the panzers of the Krampnitz tank training school rolling through Potsdam on their way to the capital. We hung out of the windows watching them go by and prayed. Nobody in the streets, which were practically empty, seemed to know what was going on. Gottfried kept insisting that he could not believe Hitler was unhurt, that "they" were hiding something . . .

A little later the radio announced that the Führer would address the

German people at midnight. We realised that only then would we know for certain whether all this was a hoax or not. And yet Gottfried refused to give up hope. According to him, even if Hitler *was* alive, his Supreme Headquarters in East Prussia was so far away that if things went well elsewhere, the regime could still be overthrown before he could regain control in Germany itself. But the rest of us were getting very uneasy.

Helldorf rang up several times. Also the Gauleiter of Brandenburg, asking the Potsdam Regierungspräsident Graf Bismarck what the devil he proposed to do, as he, the Gauleiter, understood that disorders and perhaps even a mutiny had broken out in the capital. Gottfried had the impudence to tell him that the orders from Supreme Headquarters were that the Führer wished all higher officials to stay put and await further instructions. In fact, he hoped that the insurgent troops would soon come and arrest the Gauleiter.

As night came, rumours began to circulate that the uprising was not succeeding as well as had been hoped. Somebody rang up from the airfield: "Die Luftwaffe macht nicht mit" ["the air force isn't going along"]; they wanted personal orders from Goering or from the Führer himself. Gottfried now began to sound sceptical—for the first time. He said such a thing had to be done fast; every minute lost was irretrievable. It was now long past midnight and still Hitler had not spoken. It all became so discouraging that I saw no purpose in sitting up any longer and went to bed. Loremarie soon followed.

At two in the morning, Gottfried looked in and in a dead voice said: "It was him all right!"

At dawn, we heard the tanks from Krampnitz rolling past again; they were returning to their barracks without having achieved anything.

Friday, 21 July

At breakfast we learnt that Gottfried and Melanie Bismarck had gone to Berlin by car (probably to see Helldorf). Loremarie Schönburg looked like death. I myself returned to Berlin alone, leaving her in bed. We still did not quite realise the scope of the disaster and the dreadful danger they were all in.

On my way into town, I stopped off at Aga Fürstenberg's in Grunewald and left my night things with her. As Potsdam is so far away and the bombs have made life at the Gersdorffs' intolerable, I will try that for a change. Aga was nonplussed by the events but was obviously in the dark as to who was involved. It will be difficult, but from now on one must pretend to know nothing and talk about it all, even to friends, with complete incredulity.

After only a short time at the office, I went to Maria Gersdorff. She was in despair. Count Stauffenberg, she told me, was shot yesterday evening at Army Command H.Q. in the Bendlerstrasse, together with his A.D.C., young Werner von Haeften. General Beck, whom they had planned to make Chief of State, had committed suicide. General Olbricht, another key conspirator, who had replaced the wavering General Fromm as head of the Ersatzheer, had been shot with the rest.

VIRGINIA WOOLF
(1882–1941)

Virginia Woolf was known in her lifetime for her novels and her literary criticism, but she was a passionate diary keeper, and her diary may well be seen as an achievement in itself of the same stature as her novels. Her husband, Leonard Woolf, a magazine editor and, with her, cofounder and copublisher of the Hogarth Press, a hobby that grew into a major business, first presented selections from her diary under the title *A Writer's Diary* in 1953. His selections form a coherent volume, focusing on her creative work, but leave out much of the texture of daily life that makes the diary so delightful. In her daily entries Virginia Woolf gossiped about her friends, complained about the servants, bemoaned interruptions, savored distractions, rhapsodized about the pleasures of the city or the country. Above all, she was true to her moods as they passed and to the particularity of her interest in life.

This selection, an edited version of her entries for the year 1924, finds Woolf, at the age of forty-two, about to take a major step: buying a place in London, after years of living in the suburb of Richmond. (The Woolfs also had a country place in Sussex, where they spent the summer and some weekends.) She loved the city's density and variety, its possibilities for amusement down to its "adorable omnibuses." At the same time as this major household change was being effected, Woolf was writing her novel *Mrs. Dalloway,* called, in its early stages "The Hours."

She usually refers to her husband Leonard as L. and her sister, Vanessa Bell, as Nessa.

For another diary by a member of Woolf's circle, compare V. Sackville-West's account of her affair with Violet Trefusis. For another diary by a creative woman on the same scale as Woolf's, compare Anaïs Nin's.

FROM *Diary*

Hogarth House, Richmond

Thursday 3 January [1924]

This year is almost certainly bound to be the most eventful in the whole of our (recorded) career. Tomorrow I go up to London to look for houses; on Saturday I deliver sentence of death upon Nelly and Lottie;* at Easter we leave Hogarth; in June Dadie† comes to live with us; and our domestic establishment is entirely controlled by one woman, a vacuum cleaner, and electric stoves. Now how much of this is dream, and how much reality? I should like, very much, to turn to the last page of this virgin volume and there find my dreams true. It rests with me to substantiate them between now and then.

Wednesday 9 January

At this very moment, or fifteen minutes ago to be precise, I bought the ten years' lease of 52 Tavistock Square, London WC1. Subject of course to the lease, and to Providence, the house is ours; and the basement, and the billiard room, with the rock garden on top, and the view of the Square in front and the desolated buildings behind, and Southampton Row, and the whole of London—London thou art a jewel of jewels, and jasper of jocunditie—music, talk, friendship, city views, books, publishing, all this is now within my reach, as it hasn't been since August 1913, when we left Clifford's Inn for a series of catastrophes which very nearly ended my life, and would, I'm vain enough to think, have ruined Leonard's. So I ought to be grateful to Richmond and Hogarth, and indeed, I am grateful. Nowhere else could we have started the Hogarth Press, whose very awkward beginning had rise in this very room. Here that strange offspring grew and throve; it ousted us from the dining room, which is now a dusty coffin; and crept all over the house. And people have been here, thousands of them it seems to me. I've sat

---

*Nelly and Lottie were Woolf's servants, from whom she longed to be freed by new household appliances and a more streamlined domestic setup—ED.

†Dadie was G. W. Rylands, the Woolfs' assistant at their small publishing firm, the Hogarth Press—ED.

over this fire many an evening talking, and save for one fit of the glooms last summer, have never complained of Richmond, till I shed it, like a loose skin. I've had some very curious visions in this room too, lying in bed, mad, and seeing the sunlight quivering like gold water on the wall. I've heard the voices of the dead here. And felt, through it all, exquisitely happy.

Saturday 12 January

Nelly has agreed to stay on alone as a general; and I am to find Lottie a place in Gordon Square.* I see difficulty upon difficulty ahead. None of this would much matter if L. were happy; but with him despondent or grim, the wind is taken out of my sails, and I say, what's it all for? Its odd how entirely this house question absorbs one. It is a radical change, though. It means a revision of four lives. Yet for people of our age, which is in full summer, to dread risk and responsibility seems pusillanimous. We have no children to consider. My health is as good as it will be in this world, and a great deal better than it ever has been. The next ten years must see the press into fame or bankruptcy; to loiter on here is a handicap. But I've gone through all these matters time and time again, and wish I could think of something else. I've so much work on hand. Its odd how unimportant my work seems, suddenly, when a practical matter like this blocks the way.

Sunday 20 January

No final news of Tavistock Square yet. Here we are, going through a time of waiting. I shall be happy so soon as my claws are into the move. At present, I feel Oh God another journey? Must I go up by train? Where am I to change before dinner tomorrow, and so on.

Wednesday 23 January

And on Monday if I'd written here I should have had to say "we have lost Tavistock Square." It was a very unpleasant shock, and for my part I don't think we could easily have got over it. But my house finding genius was outraged; what's the good of me, it asked, if you let these sharpers trick you? And I warn you, 52 is your house. So, practically not only

*Virginia's sister, the artist Vanessa Bell, lived in Gordon Square, Bloomsbury—ED.

spiritually speaking it now is. I visited the office with cheque and signature before one today; and then spent a shilling on a plate of beef. Ah well! Now I can sigh contented over my fire, in spite of the rain, and the [rail] strike, and Lady Colefax and Ethel Sands, and all cares and sorrows and perplexities.

I have seen Roger;* seen his pictures, which with the irrepressible vanity of the artist, he makes even the blind like me report on, by electric light, in a hurry. But enough of that; in every other way he abounds; cut him wherever you like, and the juice wells up. Lytton† has bought his house. But now I am going to write till we move—six weeks straight ahead. A letter from Morgan** today saying "To whom first but you and Virginia should I tell the fact that I've put the last words to my novel [*A Passage to India*]?" He is moved, as I am always on these occasions.

Sunday 3 February

I didn't write however, because L. started the 'flu, the very next day, and gave me an unpleasant day; but there's an odd pleasure too, purely feminine I suppose, in "looking after," being wanted; giving up my pen, and sitting with an invalid. But he was up in four days or less; and here we are, on the rails again, a very lovely spring day, which, by Heaven's grace, we have spent alone. No servants at the moment; no callers. The sun laid gold leaf over the trees and chimneys today. The willows on the bank were soft, yellow, plumy, like a cloud; like an infinitely fine spray. I reflect that I shan't be walking here again next spring. I am not sentimental about it: Tavistock Square with the pale tower is more beautiful I think, let alone the adorable omnibuses.

Owing to the influenza, I don't think I have seen more than a handful; went to Ethel Sands's; talked to Arnold Bennett, a loveable sea lion, with chocolate eyes, drooping lids, and a protruding tusk. He has an odd accent; a queer manner; is provincial; very much a character. I suspect he minds things, even my pinpricks. He is slow, kind, affectionate, hauls himself along a sofa.

Nelly went to the flat with me, and next day wrote out a time table, to show that by 3 P.M. she would still have to wash up luncheon and do Leonard's boots. Very well, I said, find a place with Lottie. But the end of a week's consideration is, apparently, that Nelly clings to us. The money is paid over, and the house presumably ours tomorrow. So I shall have a room of my own to sit down in, after almost ten years, in London.

*Roger Fry, art critic and artist—ED.
†Lytton Strachey, author of *Eminent Victorians*—ED.
**E. M. Forster, the novelist—ED.

Saturday 9 February

We have been measuring the flat. Now the question arises Is it noisy? No need to go into my broodings over that point. Fitzroy Square* rubbed a nerve bare which will never sleep again while an omnibus is in the neighbourhood. My feeling about this move is that we're doing the courageous thing.

Morgan was here last night; *A Passage to India* done; and he is much excited, on the boil with it, consulting L. about terms; has been offered £750. So *he's* all right. Marjorie† has put earrings in her ears and left Joad. Poor chit! At twenty-four. I was at Fitzroy then, and devilish unhappy too. I'm working at *The Hours,* and think it a very interesting attempt. (And its just as noisy here, if one listens, as it can possibly be in Tavistock Square. One gets into a habit of not listening. Remember this sage advice.) . . .

Saturday 23 February

Really I've a thousand things to do. I've just said to L. I'm so busy I can't begin, which unfortunately is too true of me. Then I bethink me that with life in its present rush, I may never again write a word of this book at Hogarth House, and so should take a few minutes to lay the sod, or whatever the expression is. Its very cold, barbarous weather. Twice we have meant to go to Rodmell and failed. Warmth is the one need I have. May's will move us on March 13th for fifteen pounds. I am going to force L. into the outrageous extravagance of spending twenty-five pounds on painted panels, by Bell and Grant.** We are trying to hook together all the resources of civilisation—telephone, gas, electric light, and, at this distance, naturally find it arduous. The electric light man doesn't turn up. Lottie is going to Karin‡—I fancy I have forgotten that item. All could not have fallen out better, so far, I say, being by no means ready to bait the deity, who can always show his claws. That reminds me of the celebrated Mr. [Bertrand] Russell the other night at Karin's. (She gives her weekly party in the great gay drawing room at [50 Gordon Square] which is nevertheless a little echoing and lofty and very very chill.) He said "Just as I saw a chance of happiness, the doctors said I had got cancer. My first thought was that was one up to God. When I was

---

*Virginia Woolf had lived in Fitzroy Square when she was younger. Apparently it was noisy—Ed.

†Marjorie Thompson was an assistant at the Hogarth Press—Ed.

**Vanessa Bell and Duncan Grant—Ed.

‡Karin Stephen was married to Virginia's brother, Adrian—Ed.

getting better—I had very nearly died—the thing I liked was the sun: I thought how nice to feel the sun and the rain still. People came a long way after that. The old poets were right. They made people think of death as going where they could not see the sun. I have become an optimist. I realise now that I like life—I want to live. Before that illness, I thought life was bad." So to Charlie Sanger, who is good all through; and then on to [G. E.] Moore: "When he first came up to Cambridge, he was the most wonderful creature in the whole world. His smile was the most beautiful thing I have ever seen. I said to him once, Moore, have you ever told a lie? 'Yes' he said—which was the only lie he ever told." I asked him, as I ask everyone, to write his life for the press. "But my mind is absolutely relevant. I can't ramble. I stick to facts." "Facts are what we want. Now the colour of your mother's hair?" "She died when I was two—there you are, relevant facts. I remember my grand-father's death, and crying, and then thinking it was over. I saw my brother drive up in the afternoon. Hooray! I cried. They told me I must not say hooray at all that day." He had no one to play with. One does not like him. Yet he is brilliant of course; perfectly outspoken; familiar; talks of his bowels; likes people; and yet and yet—He disapproves of me perhaps? This luminous vigorous mind seems attached to a flimsy little car, like that on a large glinting balloon. And he has no chin, and he is dapper. Nevertheless, I should like the run of his headpiece. We parted at the corner of the Square; no attempt to meet again.

Wednesday 12 March

And I'm now going to write the very last pages ever to be written at Hogarth House. My head is stuffy and heavy. Last night we dined at [Edmund] Blunden's farewell party, thirty-five covers laid, six or seven speeches made. My little drama was provided by Murry,* who, as people were going, came and sat beside me. "We're enemies." "Not enemies. We're in different camps. But I've never said a word against you, Vir-ginia." We came into a swift confused wrangle about "writing well," but here L. came up; said we must go. But I shan't meet Murry for ten years, and I want to finish the argument—"Shall I come to the *Adelphi*?" "Do" he said, yet so oleaginously, with a rolling, lustful, or somehow leering, eye, so that I kept thinking how he'd come down in the world, spiritually, what tenth-rate shillyshallying humbugs he must live among. And we said goodbye for ten years. . . . So home that long cold exhaust-ing journey for the last time. Some odds and ends of ideas came to me at

*John Middleton Murry, the critic, who had been Katherine Mansfield's husband—Ed.

the dinner. For one thing, how pungent people's writing is compared with people's flesh. We were all toothless insignificant amiable nonentities—we distinguished writers; Blunden despairing, drooping, crow-like, rather than Keats-like. And did we really all believe in Blunden's "genius"? Had we read his poems? How much sincerity was there in the whole thing? The truth is these collective gatherings must be floated by some conventional song, in which all can join, like He's a jolly good fellow. . . . Subtler impressions did occur to me, but I can't place them at the moment. Nor at the moment can I think of any farewell for this beautiful and lovable house, which has done us such a good turn for almost precisely nine years, so that, as I lay in bed last night, I nearly humanised it, and offered it my thanks.

52 Tavistock Square, WC1

Saturday 5 April

Well, I will make a brief beginning—after three weeks' silence. But it has not been silence at all. The noise of bus and taxi has worried me, and the noise of the human tongue has disturbed me, pleasantly and otherwise, and now I'm half asleep. Leonard working as usual. But can I collect any first impressions? My first night in the basement I saw the moon, with drifting clouds, and it was a terrifying and new London moon; dreadful and exciting, as if the Richmond moon had been veiled. Oh the convenience of this place! and the loveliness too. We walk home from theatres, through the entrails of London. Why do I love it so much? . . . for it is stony hearted, and callous. The tradespeople don't know one—but these disparaging remarks were interrupted and it is now

Tuesday 15 April

—and L. and I have been having one of those melancholy middle aged summings up of a situation which occur from time to time, but are seldom recorded. Indeed most of life escapes, now I come to think of it; the texture of the ordinary day. L. was desperately gloomy. Not a stroke of work done he says, since we came to London. This is largely imagination, I think, though its true fish keep drifting into the net. Gerald Brenan back; Roger rampant to paint us; Morgan, elflike, mocking, aloof; Nessa and Duncan. Then there was Angelica's* accident which, for the psychology of it I should have described. Here was Nessa painting, and I answering the telephone. Louie [nurse] and Angelica have been knocked down by a motor and are in the Middlesex Hospital. I had to repeat it to Nessa: to destroy all that simmering everyday comfort, with the smell of paint in the room, and Tom† just coming upstairs to tea. She ran out and away from the telephone instinctively, ran round in an aimless way for a second. Then off they dashed and I after them, and so to the hospital, holding hands in the cab; and then sheer agony, for there was Louie, with her foot bandaged, and no Angelica; only an evasive nurse, parrying enquiries and taking us behind a screen where Angelica lay in bed, still, her face turned away. At last she moved. "She's not dead" Duncan said. They both thought her dead. Then the young doctor came, and seemed silently and considerately but firmly to wish the mother to know that the case was hopeless: very grave; run over across the stomach. Yes there may have to be an operation. The surgeon had been sent for. So Nessa went back to sit there, and I saw again that extraordinary look of anguish, dumb, not complaining, which I saw in Greece, I think, when she was ill. The feelings of the people who don't talk express themselves thus. My feeling was "a pane of glass shelters me. I'm only allowed to look on at this." Its a queer thing to come so close to agony as this, and just to be saved oneself. What I felt was that death and tragedy had once more put down his paw, after letting us run a few paces. People never get over their early impressions of death I think. I always feel pursued. But there's an end of this. Nothing was wrong with Angelica—it was only a joke this time.

It takes a long time to form a habit—the habit of living at 52 Tavistock Square is not quite formed, but doing well. Already I have spent a week without being bothered by noise. One ceases to hear or to see. Dadie has been—a sensitive vain youth, with considerable grit in him, I judge. Sometimes the future appears perilous; problematical rather, the press that is, but always fruitful and interesting.

Monday 5 May

This is the twenty-ninth anniversary of mother's death. I think it happened on a Sunday morning, and I looked out of the nursery window and saw old Dr. Seton walking away with his hands behind his back, as if to say It is finished, and then the doves descending, to peck in the road, I

*Angelica Bell was Vanessa's daughter by Duncan Grant—ED.
†T. S. Eliot—ED.

suppose, with a fall and descent of infinite peace. I was thirteen, and could fill a whole page and more with my impressions of that day, many of them ill received by me, and hidden from the grown ups, but very memorable on that account: how I laughed, for instance, behind the hand which was meant to hide my tears; and through the fingers saw the nurses sobbing.

But enough of death—its life that matters. London is enchanting. I step out upon a tawny coloured magic carpet, it seems, and get carried into beauty without raising a finger. And people pop in and out, lightly, divertingly, like rabbits; and I look down Southampton Row, wet as a seal's back or red and yellow with sunshine, and watch the omnibuses going and coming, and hear the old crazy organ. One of these days I will write about London. I have left the whole of society unrecorded. Tidmarsh, Cambridge, and now Rodmell. We had a queer little party here the other day—when the sinister and pedagogic Tom cut a queer figure. I cannot wholly free myself from suspicions about him—at the worst they only amount to calling him an American schoolmaster, a very vain man.

Saturday 21 June

I am oh so sleepy; in fact just woken from a hot drowse. If I weren't so sleepy, I would write about the soul. I think its time to cancel that vow against soul description. What was I going to say? Something about the violent moods of my soul. I think I grow more and more poetic. Perhaps I restrained it, and now, like a plant in a pot it begins to crack the earthenware. Often I feel the different aspects of life bursting my mind asunder. Morgan is too restrained in his new book perhaps. I mean, what's the use of facts at our time of life? Why build these careful cocoons?

I look forward with a little alarm to Dadie coming, chiefly I think that it commits us more seriously. But that will wear off soon. It seems to me the beginning of ten years of very hard work. I don't see how Marjorie will fit in, altogether, and rather anticipate some rearrangement. So far, no gossip and no soul. Yet I've seen—Bob, Desmond, Lytton, Sebastian [Sprott], Dorothy Bussy, Mrs. Eliot—this last making me almost vomit, so scented, so powdered, so egotistic, so morbid, so weakly.

I am writing, writing, and see my way clear to the end now, and so shall gallop to it, somehow or other.

Saturday 5 July

Just back, not from the 1917 Club, but from Knole,* where indeed I was invited to lunch alone with his Lordship. His Lordship lives in the kernel of a vast nut. You perambulate miles of galleries; skip endless treasures—chairs that Shakespeare might have sat on—tapestries, pictures, floors made of the halves of oaks; and penetrate at length to a round shiny table with a cover laid for one. A dozen glasses form a circle each with a red rose in it. One solitary peer sits lunching by himself, with his napkin folded into the shape of a lotus flower. Knole is a conglomeration of buildings half as big as Cambridge I daresay. . . . But the extremities and indeed the inward parts are gone dead. Ropes fence off half the rooms; the chairs and the pictures look preserved; life has left them. Not for a hundred years have the retainers sat down to dinner in the great hall. Then there is Mary Stuart's altar, where she prayed before execution. "An ancestor of ours took her the death warrant" said Vita. All these ancestors and centuries, and silver and gold, have bred a perfect body. She is stag like, or race horse like, save for the face, which pouts, and has no very sharp brain. But as a body hers is perfection. So many rare and curious objects hit one's brain like pellets which perhaps may unfold later. But its the breeding of Vita's that I took away with me as an impression, carrying her and Knole in my eye as I travelled up with the lower middle classes, through slums. There is Knole, capable of housing all the desperate poor of Judd Street, and with only that one solitary earl in the kernel.

Monks House, Rodmell†

Saturday 2 August

Here we are at Rodmell, and I with twenty minutes to fill in before dinner. A feeling of depression is on me, as if we were old and near the end of all things. It must be the change from London and incessant occupation. Then, being at a low ebb with my book, I begin to count myself a failure. Now the point of the Press is that it entirely prevents

*Knole was the family seat of the Sackvilles in Kent. Virginia lunched there with V. Sackville-West's father—ED.
†Monks House, the Woolfs' country house, was in the Sussex village of Rodmell, near Lewes—ED.

brooding, and gives me something solid to fall back on. The country is like a convent. The soul swims to the top.

Julian* has just been and gone, a tall young man who, inveterately believing myself to be young as I do, seems to me like a younger brother; anyhow we sit and chatter, as easily as can be. Its all so much the same—his school continues Thoby's† school. He tells me about boys and masters as Thoby used to. It interests me just in the same way. He's a sensitive, very quick witted, rather combative boy; full of Wells, and discoveries, and the future of the world. And, being of my own blood, easily understood—going to be very tall, and go to the Bar, I daresay.

Sunday 3 August

L. has been telling me about Germany, and reparations, how money is paid. Lord what a weak brain I have—like an unused muscle. He talks; and the facts come in, and I can't deal with them. But by dint of very painful brain exercises, perhaps I understand a little more than Nelly does of the International situation. And L. understands it all—picks up all these points of the daily paper absolutely instantly, has them connected, ready to produce. Sometimes I think my brain and his are of different orders. Were it not for my flash of imagination, and this turn for books, I should be a very ordinary woman.

Friday 15 August

By the way, why is poetry wholly an elderly taste? When I was twenty I could not for the life of me read Shakespeare for pleasure; now it lights me as I walk to think I have two acts of *King John* tonight, and shall next read *Richard the Second*. It is poetry that I want now—long poems. I want the concentration and the romance, and the words all glued together, fused, glowing: have no time to waste any more on prose. When I was twenty I liked Eighteenth Century prose; now its poetry I want, so I repeat like a tipsy sailor in front of a public house.

I don't often trouble now to describe cornfields and groups of harvesting women in loose blues and reds and little staring yellow frocked girls. But that's not my eyes' fault; coming back the other evening from Charleston,** again all my nerves stood upright, flushed, electrified

---

*Julian Bell was Vanessa's son by Clive Bell—ED.
†Thoby Stephen, Virginia's brother, had died young—ED.
**Vanessa Bell's country house—ED.

(what's the word?) with the sheer beauty—beauty abounding and superabounding, so that one almost resents it, not being capable of catching it all, and holding it all at the moment.

Sunday 7 September

In my last lap of *Mrs Dalloway.* There I am now—at last at the party, which is to begin in the kitchen, and climb slowly upstairs. It is to be a most complicated spirited solid piece, knitting together everything and ending on three notes, at different stages of the staircase, each saying something to sum up Clarissa.

We had Dadie twice to stay; Clive and Mary yesterday; I slept a night at Charleston; L. went to Yorkshire; rather an odd disjointed wet summer, with people dropping in, Nelly rather moping, but loyal. The garden here flourishes.

Monday 15 September

Vita was here for Sunday, gliding down the village in her large new blue Austin car, which she manages consummately. She was dressed in ringed yellow jersey, and large hat, and had a dressing case all full of silver and night gowns wrapped in tissue. Nelly said "If only she weren't an honourable!"* and couldn't take her hot water. But I like her being honourable, and she is it; a perfect lady, with all the dash and courage of the aristocracy, and less of its childishness than I expected. She is like an over ripe grape in features, moustached, pouting, will be a little heavy; meanwhile, she strides on fine legs, in a well cut skirt, and though embarrassing at breakfast, has a manly good sense and simplicity about her which both L. and I find satisfactory. Oh yes, I like her; could tack her on to my equipage for all time; and suppose if life allowed, this might be a friendship of a sort. [She] took us to Charleston—and how one's world spins round—it looked all very grey and shabby and loosely cut in the light of her presence. As for Monks House, it became a ruined barn, and we picnicking in the rubbish heap.

---

*Nelly was intimidated by Vita's rank. As an earl's daughter, she was entitled to be called the Honorable Mrs. Nicholson—ED.

Monday 29 September

A fortnight later: writing partly to test my new penkala (professing fountain-pen qualities), partly to exorcise my demon. Only Karin and Ann [aged eight]: only a hole blown in my last chapter. There I was swimming in the highest ether known to me, and thinking I'd finish by Thursday; Lottie suggests to Karin we'd like to have Ann: Karin interprets my polite refusal to her own advantage and comes down herself on Saturday, blowing everything to smithereens. More and more am I solitary; the pain of these upheavals is incalculable; and I can't explain it either. *She* saw nothing. "Disturbing the flow of inspiration?" she said this morning, having shouted outside the door till I had to fetch cotton wool. And its down in ruins my house; my wings broken; and I left on the bare ground. But what cares Karin! She slightly chortles to plant us with some of her burdens and makes off well pleased at having got her way. Here am I with my wrecked week—for how serene and lovely like a Lapland night was our last week together—feeling that I ought to go in and be a good aunt—which I'm not by nature. These wails must now have ending, partly because I cannot see.

And of course children are wonderful and charming creatures. I've had Ann in talking about the white seal, and wanting me to read to her. There's a quality in their minds to me very adorable: to be alone with them, and see them day to day would be an extraordinary experience. They have what no grown up has—that directness—chatter, chatter, chatter, on Ann goes, in a world of her own, with its seals and dogs; happy because she's going to have cocoa tonight, and go blackberrying tomorrow; the walls of her mind all hung round with such bright vivid things, and she doesn't see what we see.

52 Tavistock Square, WC1

Friday 17 October

It is disgraceful. I did run upstairs thinking I'd make time to enter that astounding fact—the last words of the last page of *Mrs Dalloway;* but was interrupted. Anyhow I did them a week ago yesterday. "For there she was." But in some ways this book is a feat; finished without break from illness, which is an exception; and written really in one year. The only difficulty is to hold myself back from writing others. I see already

The Old Man.* But enough, enough—yet of what should I write here except my writing. Odd how conventional morality always encroaches. One must not talk of oneself, &c; one must not be vain &c. Even in complete privacy these ghosts slip between me and the page.

The thought of Katherine Mansfield comes to me—as usual rather reprehensibly—thinking yes, if she'd lived, she'd have written on, and people would have seen that I was the more gifted. I think of her in this way off and on—that strange ghost, with the eyes far apart, and the drawn mouth, dragging herself across the room. Katherine and I had our relationship; and never again shall I have one like it.

Lytton dined here the other night—a successful evening. Oh I was right to be in love with him twelve or fifteen years ago. It is an exquisite symphony his nature when all the violins get playing as they did the other night; so deep, so fantastic. We rambled easily. We talked of his writing, and I think now he will write another book; of mine: of the School of Proust, he said; then of Maynard:† one side of him detestable. . . .

Tuesday 18 November

We were, I was rather, at Mary's party last night, and suffer today. The upper classes pretended to be clever. Duff Cooper, Lady Diana and all that set, as they say; and my chief amusement came from seeing them as a set. That is the only merit of these parties, that individuals compose differently from what they do in private.

Dadie came back yesterday and we had a jolly afternoon—oh infinitely better than a party at River House! lie though I did to Mary on the telephone—I in two jackets, for it is freezing, and hair down; he in shirtsleeves. Thus one gets to know people; not poised on the edge of a chair on the slippery floor, trying to laugh, and being spurred by wine and sugar cakes. Clive** of course changes into an upper class man, very loud, familiar, and dashing, at once. Lytton sits in his own green shade, only emerging when the gentle youths come in. I was impressed by Nessa, who went to this party for which we were all titivating and dressing up, in her old red brown dress which I think she made herself.

---

*Probably an allusion to the portrait of her father, which would be the genesis of *To the Lighthouse*—ED.
†John Maynard Keynes, the economist, was a close friend of the Woolfs—ED.
**Clive Bell, the art critic. Although married, he and Vanessa were separated. Virginia considered him too much the man of the world—ED.

Saturday 13 December

This diary may die, not of London, but of the Press. For fourteen days we have been in the thick of a long press revolution—Dadie going, Marjorie going, Marjorie staying, Angus Davidson coming. That is the final result, but achieved only at the cost of forty million words. For my own part, I could never see Dadie as a permanent partner, Dadie in his silver grey suits, pink shirts, with his powdered pink and white face, his nerves, his manners, his love of praise. Angus, however, after three days, already seems to me permanent and dependable.

I am now galloping over *Mrs Dalloway,* re-typing it entirely from the start, a good method, I believe, as thus one works with a wet brush over the whole, and joins parts separately composed and gone dry.

Monday 21 December

Really it is a disgrace—the number of blank pages in this book! The effect of London on diaries is decidedly bad. This I fancy is the leanest of them all. Indeed it has been an eventful year, as I prophesied; and the dreamer of January 3rd has dreamt much of her dream true; here we are in London, with Nelly alone, Dadie gone it is true, but Angus to replace him. What emerges is that changing houses is not so cataclysmic as I thought; after all one doesn't change body or brain.

How sharply society brings one out—or rather others out! Roger the other night with Vita for instance. He became the nonconformist undergraduate at once, the obstinate young man (I could see him quite young with his honest uncompromising eyes), who will *not* say what he does not believe to be true. The effect on Vita was disastrous; and pure honesty is a doubtful quality; it means often lack of imagination. It means self assertiveness, being rather better than other people; a queer trait in Roger to unearth after so many years of smooth intercourse. For the most part he is so sympathetic. His Quaker blood protests against Vita's rich winy fluid; and she has the habit of praising and talking indiscriminately about art, which goes down in her set, but not in ours. It was all very thorny until that good fellow Clive came in, and addressed himself to conciliate dear old obtuse, aristocratic, passionate, Grenadier-like Vita.

All our Bloomsbury relationships flourish, grow in lustiness. Suppose our set to survive another twenty years, I tremble to think how thickly knit and grown together it will be. At Christmas I must write and ask Lytton if I may dedicate *The Common Reader* to him. And that's the last of my books to be dedicated, I think. What do we talk about? I wish

I could write conversation. We go over the same things, undoubtedly. The press however is always casting up wreckage. People come most days. I enjoy my printing afternoons, and think it the sanest way of life—for if I were always writing, or merely recouping from writing, I should be like an inbreeding rabbit—my progeny becoming weakly albinos.

ACKNOWLEDGMENTS

Two books were particularly helpful in setting me off on fruitful paths. *Revelations: Diaries of Women* by Mary Jane Moffat and Charlotte Painter (New York: Random House, 1974), a groundbreaking compilation, introduced me to Florida Scott-Maxwell, Carolina Maria de Jesus, and Sophia Tolstoy, among other fascinating woman diarists such as Marie Bashkirtseff; Hannah Senesh, the Zionist heroine; Mary Chesnut, the southern woman who recorded the Civil War; and Emily Carr, the Canadian painter. *The Tradition of Women's Autobiography: From Antiquity to the Present* by Estelle C. Jellinek (Boston: Twayne, 1986), like *Revelations*, contains an excellent list of suggestions for further reading. Another interesting collection is *A Day at a Time: The Diary Literature of American Women from 1764 to the Present*, by Margo Culley (New York: The Feminist Press at the City University of New York, 1985).

I am very grateful to all the people who suggested reading. For this service and others, warmest thanks to Henry Abelove, Jeanine Basinger, Georges Borchardt, Germaine Bree, Anthony Chambers, Annie Dillard, Ann duCille, Enda Duffy, Tony Eprile, Wendy Gimbel, Jacqueline Gourevitch, Ellen Greenblatt, Nathanael Greene, Gertrude Hughes, Indira Karamcheti, Richard Ohmann, Robert G. O'Meally, Nessa Rapoport, Henry Raymont, Joseph W. Reed, Jr., Anne Roiphe, Vera Schwarcz, Nan A. Talese, and Katharine Weber. Many of these people are my colleagues at Wesleyan University; without the range and human richness of that institution, without its tradition of flexibility and interdisciplinary work, and without its Department of English, I could not have produced this book. I'm grateful to my students in English 203 in the fall of 1989 for allowing me to try out some of this material on them and for discussing it with so much intelligence and enthusiasm.

Steven Forman, my editor at Norton, has been wonderful from start to finish. The idea for this book was his. Early on we met to imagine what it might be. We were like gardeners looking at bare earth who see peonies and poppies, and that shared excitement has helped make this project, over the years it took, the pleasure it has been. I'd also like to thank Kristin Prevallet and Bonnie Hall, Steve's assistants, who did some very tedious and arduous work efficiently and uncomplainingly, and Judith Haas, who was my research assistant in the early stages. My mother, Minnie P. Davidoff, really did me a service with her acute comments on all the selections. Sybil Liebhafsky has generously agreed to take on the proofreading, and, as demanding as that task is for a book this size, I know she has trained on sterner stuff and is up to it.

It pleases me that the women who have helped with this book range in age from late teens to mid-eighties.

Finally, thanks to my son, Ted Rose, and Laurent de Brunhoff, my husband, who have made things for me in the years I've worked on this book about as good as they get.

P. R.
December 1992

COPYRIGHT NOTICES

INDEX